COMPARATIVE POLITICAL SYSTEMS

RONALD COHEN received his Ph.D. in anthropology from the University of Wisconsin in 1960. He has taught anthropology at the University of Toronto from 1958 to 1961, at McGill University from 1961 to 1963, and at Northwestern University from 1963 to the present where he is a member of the Program of African Studies and Associate Professor of Anthropology and Political Science. He has carried out field work in Nigeria and in the Mackenzie valley, Northwest Territories, Canada. He is interested in social and political change as well as in problems of method in the social sciences. Professor Cohen has published on the Kanuri of Nigeria, on Athapascan culture change, and on problems of anthropological theory and method.

JOHN MIDDLETON received his D.Phil. from Oxford in 1953. He has taught anthropology at London, Capetown, and Northwestern universities, and is at present head of the Department of Anthropology at New York University. He has done field research in Uganda, Zanzibar, and Nigeria. He has published mainly on the Lugbara of Uganda and the Shirazi of Zanzibar.

American Museum Sourcebooks in Anthropology, under the general editorship of Paul Bohannan, are published for The American Museum of Natural History by the Natural History Press. Directed by a joint editorial board made up of Dr. Bohannan and members of the staff of the Museum and the Natural History Press, this series is an extension of the Museum's scientific and educational activities, making available to the student and general reader inexpensive, up-to-date, and authoritative books in the field of anthropology. The Natural History Press is a division of Doubleday and Company, Inc., and has its editorial offices at The American Museum of Natural History, Central Park West at 79th Street, New York, New York, 10024, and its business offices at 501 Franklin Avenue, Garden City, New York.

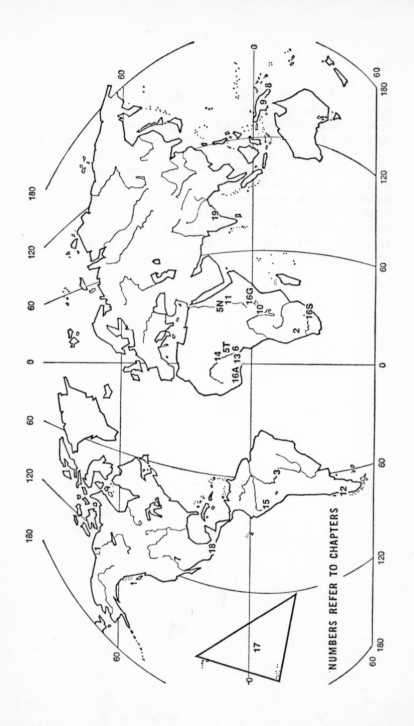

NUMBERS REFER TO CHAPTERS

COMPARATIVE
POLITICAL SYSTEMS

STUDIES IN THE POLITICS
OF PRE-INDUSTRIAL SOCIETIES

EDITED BY RONALD COHEN
AND JOHN MIDDLETON

AMERICAN MUSEUM SOURCEBOOKS IN ANTHROPOLOGY

PUBLISHED FOR

THE AMERICAN MUSEUM OF NATURAL HISTORY

THE NATURAL HISTORY PRESS

1967 · GARDEN CITY, NEW YORK

The illustrations for this book
were prepared by the Graphic Arts Division of
The American Museum of Natural History

CONTENTS

One of the most difficult problems in both anthropology and political science has been to define what is meant by "political." In the history of Western thought the study of politics has been approached in two distinct ways—the normative or ethical, and the empirical. The former stems from a search for the best, the most efficient, or the most ethical means by which a society should be organized so that its people can lead "the good life." In the empirical tradition, research has been directed toward an understanding of how power and authority are distributed in society, how decisions are made and carried out, and what conditions determine the differences between various political systems. Anthropology is firmly grounded in the empirical tradition.

For anthropologists, to define the "political" is a thorny problem, since the variation across the gamut of non-Western political systems is so great that what is considered political in one is often excluded from consideration in another. There are two main ways in which this problem has been tackled: one has been to define the political in terms of political functions and actions, the other has been to do so in terms of political groups. They are, of course, not mutually exclusive.

The former approach is exemplified by Radcliffe-Brown (1940), who suggested that political phenomena are concerned with the territorial rights of a group; with the maintenance of order by means of personal or group action, supernatural sanctions, or processes of adjudication; with the accepted use of violence; and with a set of rules having these functions. The roles that function in this way are political roles and their totality makes up the political system of a society. Other functional approaches have been put forward by Smith (1956) and Easton (1959) among others. For Smith, politics refer to actions by which public affairs are directed and managed, the actions of government. He divides governmental activity into the administrative and the political sectors. The former deals with authoritative structuring of governmental roles, which are hierarchically arranged; the latter deals with the exercise of and competition for power, and are not necessarily hierarchically arranged since anyone may try to influence decisions and policy. Easton, likewise, suggests that the political realm exists in types of action, an act being political when it relates to the formulation and execution of decisions which are binding for a social system. In order to make the political realm deal with politics as conceived in commonsense terms, he limits the applicability of his definition to those political acts that affect the most inclusive groupings in the society.

Another approach is to look at comparative political systems using the structure of political roles in the system as a dependent variable, so that the analysis of diversity and complexity among political systems becomes the task of pointing out the nature of the significant independent variables associated with the different varieties of political systems found. This approach goes back at least to Weber (1947) and his concept of corporate groups, and has been used by, among others, Fortes and Evans-Pritchard (1940), Middleton and Tait (1958), and Smith (1966). It stems out of the classification and description of social structures, a time-honored approach in anthropology. The taxonomy, like all taxonomies, is only a first step, that of identifying a set or series of dependent variables; finding the significant independent variables that explain variation among political systems then becomes a major goal of political anthropology.

The societies dealt with by anthropologists vary in the degree to which their role systems are differentiated, from simple to complex and from universalistic to particularistic. Political systems are closely related to this differentiation, so that the political system increases in complexity along with role differentiation in the society as a whole. This relationship is not, however, a simple one, since factors such as ecology and population mobility produce further variation among the political systems.

In terms of an over-all classification it is convenient to distinguish those societies in which there is a differentiated form of

centralized government having sovereignty over a number of constituent units such as towns, villages, and ethnic groups on the
one hand, from acephalous societies, those societies in which
there is a common sentiment of ethnic identity but no authority
that can be considered a government for the entire society, on the
other hand. This distinction was first made explicit by Fortes and
Evans-Pritchard (1940). It should be remembered, however, that
this distinction, although useful, is only taxonomic and does not
easily cover all variations: there are societies that have elements
of both types.

Among peoples lacking over-all political organization the primary distinction is to be found in their mode of subsistence.
Some obtain their livelihood by foraging, hunting, and gathering;
they live in bands and camps and are continually on the move,
and their political organizations reflect this way of life. Population density is very low; intergroup marriage is the rule, so that
almost all members of a society are related by descent, which
provides a main base for the political organization of the component units. A society includes subgroups, usually called "bands,"
varying from a dozen to a couple of hundred people. If the
food supply is very sparse, wide and shallow descent groups are
common, and an individual may have widely scattered claims
of mutual obligation and help with many living people; where
food resources are more stable and dependable, there is usually
some kind of development of unilineal descent groups (see Forde
1947). In the latter case, too, leadership is more clearly defined.
All bands recognize, though to differing degrees, the authority of
successful men who are better than others in food getting skills
and/or supernatural and religious practices—shamans, prophets,
and similar figures play important political roles, even though
sporadic and non-hereditary.

The other major category of acephalous societies obtain their
livelihood by some form of agriculture and/or livestock rearing.
This usually means that larger groups of people can support
themselves with less effort in a smaller territory. It also means
that groups of people with permanent interests and rights in
plots of land and herds tend to have authority systems and basic
social groupings which reflect these interests. These societies have
problems of organization that result from the increasing population density and need for territorial stability associated with more

efficient food production. The word "tribe" is frequently used to refer to this category of society. Tribes stand in an intermediate position, in terms of political complexity, between band societies and centralized states (see Service 1962). They share in the acephalous political qualities of the hunting and gathering bands, and in the food production base of the states. Although they may all share these rather abstract features, tribes are the most numerous and the most varied of political systems in the range of societies studied by anthropologists. It seems likely that this stage of adaptation is a highly successful one in human social evolution and it has therefore occurred widely around the world, adapting to local conditions where it is found. Out of this level grows the centralized state, and in a few cases re-emergence of hunting and gathering as a dominant subsistence technique (see the essay by Lévi-Strauss in this volume).

Tribal societies vary in the ways they handle recruitment to politically relevant roles and into statuses associated with residence and rights in resources. This can be traced to several factors; the nature of population mobility across the land; the pattern of local settlement growth and development; the degree of ethnic homogeneity and heterogeneity. Basically all varieties of tribal society must handle a problem that is not a pressing one in band societies. This is the adaptation of social life to interests and rights which have continuity beyond the life-span of individuals. Perhaps the simplest (and certainly the most common) solution to this problem is the institution of unilineal descent—the tracing of descent through either men or women only. The notion of unilineal descent may be used as a basis for the recruitment of the corporate groups that make up the formally recognized structure of the political system (see Forde 1947, Fortes 1953). But this is not, of course, universal.

These societies may be classified for heuristic purposes into those whose political systems are based on unilineal descent groups and whose political offices are recruited from members of those groups by virtue of their status within them (perhaps the best known of these are those known as "segmentary lineage systems" —see Middleton and Tait 1958); another category includes those whose political systems are based on non-unilineal descent groups and whose political offices are recruited from members of those groups by virtue of their status within them (see Murdock

1960; Sahlins 1958, 1965; Freeman 1960, 1961; Firth 1957); a third category comprises those societies whose political systems are based upon councils or associations of towns, wards or other territorial groupings; and a fourth comprises those societies in which politically important roles are vested in positions in an age-set system. Corporate descent groups may or may not be present in these last two types, but if they are found they tend not to be of prime political importance; and these groups may also be found in centralized states, again without much political importance.

Tendencies toward centralized political control occur in a number of acephalous societies; and, of course, in all states, by definition. These may be due to internal forces in the society or to external forces, or to a combination of the two. Centralized political authority solves certain problems of organization and adaptation to resources which arise from situations in which local groups have to co-ordinate efforts to control external relations between their polity and the surrounding groups. Some of these problems can be isolated. First, there are the difficulties brought about by increasing cultural heterogeneity within a polity as it absorbs groups from outside it, and the associated or at least similar problem of social stratification with the differentiation of various elements within the society. Second, there are problems arising from the movement of a group into a new territory in which leaders decide to control the local population as subordinates; in this case the leaders may found a dynasty. Third, there are problems facing groups that surround a centralized state and are stimulated to emulate its power and prestige and to defend themselves against it by imitating its political organization. Fourth, there are the consequences of acephalous groups attaching themselves to apparently superior ritual leaders in order to share in the blessings of their supernatural powers. Fifth, there are states that result either from vassal or tributary states becoming independent, or from integral parts of older states breaking away under the leadership of dissident factions, royal usurpers, or rebellious nobles. Discussion of such factors occur in the writings of several authors concerned with pre-industrial states (see Lowie 1927; Nadel 1942; Southall 1956, who coined the term "segmentary state" to refer to a type of incipient state).

Pre-industrial states are characteristically led by monarchs whose persons, while they hold office, are believed to be sacred, or divine, or, at the very least, contain some supernatural attributes. These rulers are rarely despots. Any centralized political structure, whether it is simply a small chieftaincy or a bureaucratic empire, involves a chain of authority from the monarch to a local residential group in which the intermediaries represent those below to those above them, as well as representing those above to those below. This dependence is typically expressed in tribute, either in the form of tax or labor, or in more symbolic objects such as animal skins. On the other hand, there is always some concept of representativeness or accountability by political superiors to those over whom they rule. Thus pressure groups, factionalism, palace intrigues, and political patronage are constant features of pre-industrial states (see Beattie, in this volume; Mair 1962; Gluckman 1965).

This is a brief summary of the type of material that is covered in the field of political anthropology. The generalizations and theoretical formulations adumbrated here are tentative, but serve to order our view of the subject and produce categories so that we may survey the literature and provide examples from ethnography to illustrate the political life of non-Western peoples.

RONALD COHEN

JOHN MIDDLETON

COMPARATIVE POLITICAL SYSTEMS

1 THE STRUCTURE OF
SOCIAL ORGANIZATION
AMONG THE ESKIMO

E. M. Weyer

E. M. Weyer is the author of *An Aleutian Burial* (1929), *Archaeological Material from the Village Site at Hot Springs, Port Moller, Alaska* (1930), *The Eskimos* (1932), *Jungle Quest* (1955), and *Primitive Peoples Today* (1959); he has also been editor of *Natural History Magazine*.

1 ASSOCIATION UNIT

Groups, or Tribes

THE DESIGNATION "tribe" is not exactly applicable to the social organization of the Eskimos. The sparsity of their population and their shifting habits in pursuit of game preclude even an approach toward a unified tribal system. Furthermore, the culture of the Eskimos is so uniform over wide areas that it offers no basis for well-defined tribal divisions. Each group speaks a dialect of the same language, and the transition from one to another is so gradual that lines of demarcation cannot be established (Mauss and Beuchat 1904–5:50 ff).

Literal interpretation of the names applied to separate groups by the Eskimos themselves gives an insight into their own conception of population divisions. In these group names the suffix -*miut* is used generally, meaning simply "people" or "people of."

Representative examples are: Harvaqtôrmiut, "the people where rapids abound," a group of the Caribou Eskimos (Birket-

FROM *The Eskimos: Their Environment and Folkways* (New Haven: Yale University Press, 1932), pp. 203–14, by permission of the author and of the Yale University Press.

Smith 1929:I, 60–61); Arviligjuarmiut, "the people of the land of the great whales," a group related to the Netsilingmiut, or "seal people," of the region of King William Land (Rasmussen 1927:167); Kitdlinermiut (of Queen Maud Gulf, Bathurst Inlet, and southeastern Victoria Island), "the frontier people," with the connotation of "the people farthest north" (Rasmussen 1927: 244–45). In Labrador there are a number of designations, such as Kokso'ákmiut, "the big river people"; Nuvu'gmiut, "people at the point" (Cape Wolstenholme); Su'hi'nimiut, "those who dwell at or in the sun," i.e., the dwellers to the east, the Eskimos on the Atlantic coast and on the Ungava side as far south as Leaf River (Hawkes 1916:22–23).

Such group names refer, for the most part, to rather small divisions. The Eskimos do not think in terms of large population units. Thus, although the Eskimos of Queen Maud Gulf, Bathurst Inlet, and southeastern Victoria Island are called collectively Kitdlinermiut by the natives to the east, among themselves they comprise four subdivisions, the largest of which includes only 116 persons (Rasmussen 1927:244–45).

Discussing the matter of divisions among the Copper Eskimos, Jenness writes that

> "the term 'tribe,' if we use it at all, should be given a very broad interpretation, for the groups into which these natives divide themselves have none of the permanence and stability that we are accustomed to associate with tribes in other parts of the world. It is true that each group has its local name, a name derived from the district it habitually frequents in summer; but the individual members are constantly changing from one group to another, not merely temporarily for some special purpose, such as the acquisition of stone lamps and pots or the obtaining of wood for sleds and tables, but permanently also, whenever the new district offers greater advantages, especially in the matter of game" (Jenness 1922:32).
>
> "The inhabitants of a settlement are all, or nearly all, *nuatkattait*, connected, that is, by blood or marriage. . . . The *nuatkattait* owe special duties to one another. They must provide for each other in sickness, take care of the aged and infirm, the widows and the orphans, and support each other in the blood feud. This gives the community its solidarity. It has a corporate unity, and is called by a tribal name, the suffix *miut* added to the name of the region it inhabits, or to a prominent place in that region, such as a lake or river" (Jenness 1922:86).

Thus the Kogluktomiut is the group that frequents the Kogluktok or Coppermine River.

The Eskimo conception of population groups is based primarily upon locality. The groups are generally comparatively small and far apart. And since there is no rule of exogamy requiring marriage to be between members of separate groups, there is naturally a strong bond of kinship in each settlement. Societal cohesion is restricted to narrow spheres. This fact will be better understood in the light of the extremely rudimentary character of the regulative mores, which will be discussed later.

The Village

The nature of the hunting activities of any group of Eskimos largely determines whether they live in congested settlements comprising many families or in small scattered bands of a few families or even single families. Furthermore, hunting activities change with the succession of the seasons. Therefore, the size of the social unit changes even in a single group. A settlement may be a cluster of snow huts, a group of stable, half-underground, stone, wood, or bone dwellings, or a tented camp.

Favorable hunting opportunities attract families of Eskimos to certain sites, where nodes of population are formed. An Eskimo village of two hundred persons is a fairly large settlement. Indeed, in some areas, notably in the central regions, settlements even of this size do not exist. Rasmussen remarks (Rasmussen 1927:283) that a population of eighty-three natives comprising a settlement near the small island of Ahongahungaoq (Dolphin and Union Strait) is considerable for one village in these regions. Typical of the larger villages of Alaska are Point Barrow, with 250 Eskimos (Rasmussen 1927:304–5), Cape Prince of Wales, with 156 (Weyer), and the village on Little Diomede Island, with 126 (Weyer). Thirty-four villages on Bristol Bay (Alaska) were found to have a total population of 4,340 (Jackson 1886:13)[1], showing an average of 122. Kotzebue Sound (northwestern Alaska), with its camp of about a thousand Eskimos (Rasmussen 1927:355)[2], is an uncommonly large center of population even in Alaska.

[1] For tables giving the Eskimo population of Alaska itemized according to villages, the reader is referred to Petroff (1884).

[2] It is estimated that at one time, however, the village at Point Hope (Alaska) and its immediate neighborhood had a population of something like two thousand, or as many inhabitants as are now found throughout the whole of the Northwest Passage between the Magnetic Pole and

An idea of the size of the Eskimo villages of Labrador may be gained from the following figures giving the populations of some of the settlements in the vicinity of the Moravian Missions (Hawkes 1916:19 ff):

	1840	1890
Nain	298	263
Hopedale	205	331
Okkak	352	350
Rammah	...	59
Zoar	...	89

In West Greenland the average number of inhabitants per settlement (exclusive of Danes) is 76.5. If, however, only the chief settlements of this region are averaged the figure rises to 275 persons, the maximum being represented by Sukkertoppen (335 individuals) and the minimum by Christianshaab (128 individuals). Of the two hundred and seven dwelling places which were to be found on the west coast and in Angmagsalik District in 1921, more than half had under fifty inhabitants, and nearly a fourth only 25 (Birket-Smith 1928:64). Three settlements are tabulated as follows according to their populations in 1884–85 (Holm 1914:26):

Sermilik	132
Angmagsalik	225
Sermiligak	14

The Household

The foregoing statistics indicate that the Eskimo village or camp generally numbers only a few hundred persons or less. Furthermore, the appearance of a settlement is generally dwarfed due to the fact that the natives customarily live in very crowded quarters. The average number of occupants to each dwelling in the region of Norton Sound[3] is twelve, in the region of the

---

Herschel Island. Likewise, evidence from various other regions seems to suggest that formerly the Eskimo population was greater than it is now; but early records are inaccurate and in some cases conflicting. The opposite trend is observed on the west coast of Greenland, where it appears that the population has more than doubled in the course of the last century (Birket-Smith 1928:20).

[3] Averages obtained from Zagoskin's data contained in Petroff's report (1884:37).

Yukon Delta eighteen, and around the Kuskokwim Delta twenty. The average in these three sections combined is seventeen. The emphasis of these figures is strong in view of the fact that the dwellings referred to are generally quite small and contain only one room for sleeping, cooking, and eating. On Diomede Island the author found four or five families comprising sixteen adults and children living in a single dwelling-room about twelve by eighteen feet in size (Weyer). Nelson mentions an instance of twenty-five persons sleeping in a room only fifteen by twenty feet (Nelson 1899:298), and another of sixteen persons sleeping in a small hut ten by twelve feet, where the air was so foul that a candle, upon being lighted, would flare up and immediately become extinguished as though dipped in water! Though from one to three families may occupy the platforms in a single room of the Bering Strait house, each will be quite separate and independent in all of its domestic affairs (Nelson 1899:288). The usual arrangement at Point Barrow is for two families to occupy one house (Murdoch 1892:75).

Copper Eskimo families will sometimes share the same snow hut, or build huts so that they are connected. Convenience is the usual motive, and the association of two particular families usually lasts only until the settlement is moved (Jenness 1922: 65 ff). In summer each family has its own tent, but even so, additional members, visitors, sometimes share their shelter (Jenness 1922:81).

There is no uniformity among the Caribou Eskimos as to the number of families living together. Sometimes two families live in one snow hut, sometimes more; generally they are related (Birket-Smith 1929:I 76). In the Ungava District "several families may dwell under the same shelter . . ." (Turner 1887: 106).

The little pear-shaped stone huts of the Polar Eskimos (Smith Sound), by exception, are regularly built to house only one family (Steensby 1910:311 ff; Rasmussen 1921:19; König 1927: 699). The opposite extreme is observed on the east coast of Greenland, where the people live in large communal winter houses, about sixteen feet in width and twenty-six feet or more in length (Holm 1914:35; Birket-Smith 1928:71). One instance in that section is mentioned of fifty-eight inmates to one dwelling (Rink 1887:25; Holm 1914:57; Hansen 1914a:185; Thalbitzer

1914:356 f). Twenty-two is the average number of persons living in each of thirty-two dwellings comprising the East Greenland settlements in 1923 (Birket-Smith 1928:79). On the west coast, on the other hand, the average to the house is between six and nine (Birket-Smith 1928:78), though in former times large communal winter houses were also used here, at least in the south.

To summarize, the size of the Eskimo household varies widely, but in its typical form consists of two or more families.

Seasonal Changes in the Size of the Association Unit

As intimated earlier in this chapter, the size of the social unit varies sometimes in response to seasonal phases which necessitate different modes of life. According as the game is scattered or localized, the Eskimos disperse or congregate. Naturally, some groups undergo seasonal changes in the size of the social unit more than others.

Almost the entire tribe of Smith Sound Eskimos (the Polar Eskimos), numbering about 271, congregate at one center (Pituarvik) for the period from the middle of February, when the sun reappears, until late May, when the ice begins to break away from the outlying capes and islands. There they live in snow huts and devote themselves to hunting walrus, which are especially plentiful (Kroeber 1899:268–69; Ekblaw 1928).

The East Greenlanders are less scattered in summer than in winter. Their winter houses lie apart from one another; whereas their summer settlements group themselves into three nuclei (Thalbitzer 1914:346).

Among the Copper Eskimos in the dead of winter tribe combines with tribe to wrest a precarious living from the frozen sea by united effort (Jenness 1928:136–37). During the warmer season, on the other hand, they scatter in small bands (Jenness 1922:143–44; Jenness 1928:136–37); so that in midsummer, when fish alone is the reliable food, the tribe no longer exists; the family is the unit (Jenness 1928:136–37). The habitations of the Caribou Eskimos of the Barren Grounds of Canada are most concentrated in autumn, when their camps lie near the crossing places of the caribou, and in winter, when they center chiefly near the lakes for fishing (Birket-Smith 1929:I 71). When they are most widely dispersed the family becomes the social unit, but never, of course, the individual (Birket-Smith 1929:I 98).

It is stated that the Eskimos of Smith Sound ". . . usually travel in groups of three or four families. Greater concentration of num-

bers would be dangerous on account of the scarcity of food"
(Sumner, Keller and Davie 1927:IV 17–18). And the Point Barrow Eskimos during the winter caribou hunting at the rivers "are
scattered in small camps of four or five families, about a day's
journey apart" (Murdoch 1892:267). The Eskimos who winter inland north of Nome at the village of Igloo disperse upon the
advent of summer. Along the Tuksuk River they may be seen in
a series of fishing camps, each composed of one or a few families
(Weyer).

2 RIGHTS AND AUTHORITY

Classes

The social organization of the Eskimos is so simple, as has been
seen, that there are no strictly defined tribal groups. Likewise,
class distinctions are almost nonexistent. Among the Caribou
Eskimos, for instance,

> "there are no chiefs, nobility nor slaves. No clan system and no
> secret society lay bonds upon the initiative of the individual . . .
> (Birket-Smith 1929:I 259). They know no government. Here, for
> once, is a society which is entirely built upon that voluntary agree-
> ment of which Kropotkin dreamt. Subject to personal liability to-
> wards the inherited laws everyone enjoys full individual freedom"
> (Birket-Smith 1929:I 260).

It is stated that among the Central Eskimos sometimes men
who may almost be considered servants are adopted—particularly bachelors without any relatives, cripples who are not able
to provide for themselves, or men who have lost their sledges
and dogs (Boas 1888:581). Similarly, class distinction attending
poverty is implied in a statement concerning the Eskimos of
Hudson Strait. There men who have been too improvident to
provide themselves with the essential property "must live with
the others or dwell by themselves and pass a miserable existence,
scarcely being noticed by their fellows even during a season of
abundance" (Turner 1894:240). Nelson mentions that in the
region of Bering Strait female captives taken in wars, unlike
other captives, were commonly spared from death and taken as
slaves (Nelson 1899:327).

Actual slavery, however, is observed only among the south-
ernmost Eskimos of Alaska. Thus, the natives of Kodiak Island,
who are certainly not typical Eskimos in many respects,

"held slaves, but their number was small, and the wealth of individuals did not depend upon slaves entirely, as among the Thlinkets. The sacrifice of slaves was unknown; they were looked upon only as laborers or servants, and their lot was a happier one than that of their Thlinket neighbors. . . . The principal mode of obtaining slaves was by barter with other tribes; but no slaves have existed in the Kodiak group for at least a generation" (Petroff 1900:228).

These people, the Kaniags, sometimes tortured prisoners of war, sometimes took them as slaves (Petroff 1900:237).

Within the *kaz'-gee,* of the Bering Strait Eskimos, which is their ceremonial chamber and meeting-room, certain social distinctions were observed.

"The sleeping place, near the oil lamp which burns at the back of the room opposite the summer entrance, is the place of honor, where the wise old men sit with the shamans and best hunters. The place near the entrance on the front side of the room is allotted to worthless men who are poor and contribute nothing to the general welfare of the community, also to orphan boys and friendless persons. . . . All guests whom it is desired to honor are given seats on the side of the kashim [*kaz'-gee*] where the old men of the village sit. If that side of the kashim chances to be fully occupied, some of the men make room for their guests" (Nelson 1899:286–87; Hawkes 1913:4 f).

Chieftainship

The Eskimo is unacquainted with the office of chieftain in its ordinary sense. Leadership exists only in a very elementary and restricted form.

The Diomede Islanders assert that they have never had a headman with authority which extended throughout their little village (Weyer). The most influential persons among this clan are the *angutkut* (medicine men), skilful or venerable hunters, and successful traders who have managed to gain some measure of economic prestige. Their authority does not, however, unite the people into a unified body. Whatever unity there is, is the result rather of coöperative mores, the enforcement of which does not require an executive head. The Alaskan Eskimos, so far as Nelson observed, "have no recognized chiefs except such as gain certain influence over their fellow-villagers through superior shrewdness, wisdom, age, wealth, or shamanism. The old men are listened to with respect, and there are usually one or more in each village who by their extended acquaintance with the traditions, customs and rites connected with the festivals, as well as being possessed of an unusual degree of common sense, are deferred to and act as chief advisors of the community.

"On the lower Yukon and beyond to Kuskokwim river such leaders are termed näs-kuk, meaning literally 'the head.' Among the Unalit Eskimos they are called äñ-ai'-yu-kŏk, 'the one to which all listen.'

"These terms are also applied to men who gain leadership by means of their greater shrewdness, whereby they become possessed of more property than their fellows, and by a judicious distribution of food and their superior force of character obtain a higher standing and a certain following among the people.

"The man who has accumulated much property, but is without ability to guide his fellows, is referred to merely as a rich man or tu'-gu.

"All Eskimo villages have a headman, whose influence is obtained through the general belief of his fellow-villagers in his superior ability and good judgment. These men possess no fixed authority, but are respected, and their directions as to the movements and occupations of the villagers are generally heeded. . . . Sometimes they obtain a stronger influence over the people by combining the offices of shaman with those of headman" (Nelson 1899:304–5).

On the Arctic coast of Alaska the captain of a whaleboat has unrestricted authority over his crew and even holds the position of a chieftain in his own community (Stefansson 1914:164; Rasmussen 1927:312). His title, *umialik,* literally means "owner of a boat," but its connotation is wider. The captain of an umiak often strengthens his prestige by accumulating wealth, within limits imposed by public opinion.[4]

"It was not uncommon among the Eskimos, particularly about the shores of Bering Strait and northward, for some man of great courage and superior ability to gather about him a certain following and then rule the people through fear; such men usually confirmed their power by killing anyone who opposed them. In order to keep their followers in a friendly mood, they made particular effort to supply them with an abundance of food in time of scarcity, or to give them presents of clothing at festivals; they also try to secure the good will of white men whenever they think it to their interests to do so" (Nelson 1899:303).

"Sometimes a head man may be succeeded by his son when the latter has the necessary qualities" (Nelson 1899:304).

"During the time that war was carried on between the tribes the best warrior planned the attack, and was known among the Unalik

---

[4] The question of economic prestige is further discussed (Weyer 1932: 196–200).

as mû-gokh'-ch-tă. He, however, had no fixed authority, as each one
fought independently of the others, but all combined in the general
onslaught" (Nelson 1899:306). Neither the Magemiut nor the Yukon men "had any recognized chief, but each fought as he pleased,
with the exception that some of the older men had general supervision and control of the expedition" (Nelson 1899:329).

Among the Alaskan Eskimos the office of chieftain is possibly
developed to a higher degree than in any other group. This is
not strange among the Eskimos of Bering Strait and the adjacent
coast of Alaska, where the natives are outstanding for their
warlike tendencies.

Elsewhere among the Eskimos, even in other parts of Alaska,
there is less centralization of authority.

Even at Point Barrow, for instance, where an *umialik* commands some recognition, the "people have no established form of
government nor any chiefs in the ordinary sense of the word, but
appear to be ruled by a strong public opinion, combined with a
certain amount of respect for the opinions of the elder people, both
men and women . . ." (Murdoch 1892:427). Likewise, the natives
at the headwaters of the Noatak River "have no tribal organization; there is usually one man in a village who is known as the
oomélik, or chief, but he has none of the authority usually implied by the name, and practically has no power over the others.
Shamanism, or the rule of superstition, seems to be the only governing spirit among them" (McLenegan in Healy 1887:75). The
Eskimos in the region of the Yukon Delta "have no chiefs in the
strict sense of the term, although there are individuals among them
who exercise more or less influence through accumulated wealth or
otherwise without necessarily being endowed with the spiritual
powers which the shamans are supposed to possess" (Schwatka in
Petroff 1900:356).

Petroff, who seems to have been the first white man to visit the
Togiagamiut and the Kassianmiut groups in the region of Bristol
Bay, Alaska, reports that there is scarcely any social cohesion beyond the family. He writes: "Among the Eskimo tribes heretofore
described the traveler generally finds someone in each village who
acts as spokesman, though not possessing any real authority, but
the Togiagamutes seem to live in the most perfect state of independence of each other" (Petroff 1900:224).

The Eskimos of the Mackenzie Delta believe through tradition
that long ago there were chiefs who had great powers (Stefansson
1914:168). The natives of Coronation Gulf and Victoria Island
present no exception to the striking absence of chiefs from Eskimo
society. "A man acquires influence by his force of character, his
energy and success in hunting, or his skill in magic. As long as

these last him age but increases his influence, but when they fail
his prestige and authority vanish. Although there were at least
half a dozen shamans in Dolphin and Union strait, and Ikpakhuak
himself professed no shamanistic powers, yet his personal dignity,
his sagacity, and his prowess as a hunter won him the most prominent place among the natives of this region. He had no delegated
powers, no established authority, but his counsels always carried
the greatest weight and his advice was constantly sought in all
matters of importance. . . . The Eskimo is intolerant of anything
like restraint. Every man in his eyes has the same rights and the
same privileges as every other man in the community. One may
be a better hunter, or a more skilful dancer, or have greater control over the spiritual world, but this does not make him more
than one member of a group in which all are free and theoretically
equal" (Jenness 1922:93–94). Rasmussen writes with reference to
the natives of Dolphin and Union Strait, that "the Eskimos of these
regions, like those farther east, have no regular chiefs, but each
settlement has one man who acts as a sort of general advisor and
leader in common undertakings" (Rasmussen 1927:283).

Among the Caribou Eskimos "an elderly, skilful hunter with
great experience always enjoys great esteem as *primus inter pares.*
When a number of families are gathered in a camp, there is often
an elderly *pater familias* who is tacitly looked upon as [ihumatAk],
i.e.: he who thinks, implying: for the others. His advice is often
taken, but voluntarily; he has no legal authority at all and cannot be
called a chief in the ordinary sense. Ordinarily, only the shamans
have stood out from among the mass, but, be it noticed, without
actually enjoying any great respect for that reason. A clever
shaman may possess great power because he is clever and feared,
not actually because he is a shaman. And a poor shaman never
attains the same level as regards respect as an ordinary skilful
hunter" (Birket-Smith 1929:I 259).

Essentially the same condition is observed among the Iglulik
Eskimos: "Within each settlement, which as a rule comprises a few
families, often connected by kinship, there is as a rule an older
man who enjoys the respect of the others and who decides when
a move is to be made to another hunting centre, when a hunt is
to be started, how the spoils are to be divided, when the dogs are
to be fed, etc. He is called isumaitoq, 'he who thinks.' It is not
always the oldest man, but as a rule an elderly man who is a
clever hunter or, as head of a large family, exercises great authority. He cannot be called a chief; there is no obligation to follow
his counsel; but they do so in most cases, partly because they rely
upon his experience, partly because it pays to be on good terms
with this man" (Mathiassen 1930:I 209). "It would seem that among
the Aivilik a man may attain considerable influence, more so than
is the case nowadays in Cumberland Sound. Captain Comer mentions one man, by the name of *Coo-nic Char-ley* (Kunuk ?, Kunuk-

sialuk ?), who was a leader of this tribe. . . . One of his sons, called Albert by the whalers, was also considered a leader of the tribe. When he [Albert] died, his nephew, on account of his ability, became his successor, as a leader of the tribe." This latter person, at his birth, "was blessed by his grandfather with much ceremony, that he might become a great hunter and whaleman. All skins taken by him should be prepared only by the very best workers. His guardian spirit would become angry at the woman who had done work on his skins carelessly, and cause her death" (Boas 1907:115). At the same time we learn that each tribe in Baffin Island has its leader, especially during their wanderings (Rink 1887:27). Hall writes that ". . . in every community, with them as with all the rest of the world, there is some one who, in consideration of his age, shrewdness, or personal prowess is looked up to, and whose opinions are received with more than usual deference; but he has no authority whatever, and an Innuit is subject to no man's control." "Though in olden times there were chiefs among the Innuits, there are none now. There is absolutely no political organization among them" (Hall 1864:316).

It is written that among the Koksoagmiut, of northern Labrador, "there is no such person as a chief; yet there is a recognized leader who is influenced by another, and this last is the conjurer or medicine man. These two persons determine among themselves what shall be done" (Turner 1894:193). The natives of the east coast of Hudson Bay "have no chief, and the authority acknowledged by the community is that of the elders and wealthier individuals, aided at all times, by the decrees of the shaman; the authority of the latter is, however, often set at naught" (Turner 1887:101).

The Labrador Eskimos sometimes have leaders called *angajorkak,* whose authority seems to be confined to localities, each bay or fiord having one of its own. These men must always be first-rate hunters. When one dies, his son has the first claim to be his successor if he possesses the required qualities. If not, another is appointed who probably has already been elected during the father's life (Rink 1887:27). Hawkes, writing on the Labrador Eskimos, states that "the Eskimos have never had any 'chiefs' in the Indian sense of the word. They have had leaders, great hunters or enterprising shamans, who have been accorded position by general appreciation of their worth. But the office has never carried any particular authority with it" (Hawkes 1916:110). Again we read that "the recognized authorities among all the Innuit are the older or wealthier men of the community . . ." (Turner 1887:105); and that the Tahagmiut, of Labrador, "have no chiefs; the decisions and desires of the elders and wealthier men are carried out by the remainder of the people" (Turner 1887:102).

The Polar Eskimos, upon first meeting white men, did not under-

stand the word *nullikab*,[5] which, according to Ross, signifies among
the Eskimos to the south of them a person in authority. They
responded to the word *pisarsuak,* however, used as a title of a
chief, and said that his name was *Tulloowak* (Ross 1819:121).
"They all acknowledged Tuloowah as their king, represented him
as a strong man, as very good, and very much beloved; the name
of his residence was Petowack, which they described to be near
a large island, which could be no other than Wolstenholme island.
He had a large house built of stone, which they described to be
nearly as large as the ship: that there were many houses near it,
and that the mass of the natives lived there; that they paid him a
portion of all they caught or found, and returned to this place
whenever the sun went away, with the fruits of their labours" (Ross
1819:134). Kane writes (Kane 1856:II 118) that among the Smith
Sound Eskimos "the angekok of the tribe . . . directs the policy
and movements of the little state, and though not the titular chief,
is really the power behind the throne." The tenor of the latter two
quotations, it scarcely needs be remarked, is dissonant with what
is now known of the social organization of the Eskimos and must
be considered as being colored by preconceived notions based on
the systems of more advanced peoples. According to Kroeber,[6] the
Smith Sound Eskimos "apply the term 'naligaq' to leaders of Arctic
expeditions; but if used in reference to any of themselves, it means
merely a good hunter. Nalegak is the most skilful hunter, but he
has no authority, states Hayes."

In the Egedesminde District, West Greenland, the old men in a
household were respected and consulted, but a chief with hereditary
powers was unknown (Birket-Smith 1924:153). In East Greenland
the angakok is not the headman. He plays no important part in the
social life. Only the skilful hunters are respected (Holm 1914:58);
". . . each larger household comprising several families has a chief,
as conscientiously venerated and obeyed as heads of communities
or magistrates elsewhere" (Rink 1887:24). The head of the household gives orders when to move into summer habitations, etc.;
". . . the position as chief of the house has no relation to that of
'angakok,' though both dignities may occasionally be united"
(Rink 1887:26).

5 Thalbitzer, in a communication to the author, states, "The form is no
doubt misunderstood instead of 'nallegal' or rather 'nalagkap.'"
6 Hayes (1867:256) quoted in Kroeber (1899:300).

2 !KUNG BUSHMAN BANDS

Lorna Marshall

Mrs. Laurence K. Marshall has been a member of the Marshall expeditions to the Bushmen of Bechuanaland, South West Africa and
Angola. She is the author of several papers on them.

IN THIS PAPER I describe the band organization of the !Kung
Bushmen. The !Kung word *n//a besi*[1] was translated by the
interpreters as 'people who live together'. I use the word *band*
for *n//a besi,* meaning by *band,* in this connexion, the grouping in !Kung social organization which is above the family grouping. It is a grouping precisely of the people who live together.

The study was made of the !Kung in the region of Nyae Nyae
in South West Africa (S.W.A.) and the British Protectorate of
Bechuanaland (B.P.). A sketch-map shows where the region
lies, and the approximate location of the !Kung bands within
it.[2]

The material was gathered for the most part in 1952–53 and
has been brought up to date by additional field trips, the latest
of which was a brief visit in 1959.

I try to show how the !Kung, a nomadic, hunting-gathering
people, live together in bands on the basis of their consanguineous
and affinal ties; how this society, through the organization of

FROM *Africa* 30, No. 4 (1960), 325–54, by permission of the author
and of the International African Institute. The author has very kindly
allowed the paper to be shortened, and for a table showing band populations, a table of genealogies, and photographs, to be omitted.

[1] The four clicks of the !Kung language are symbolized as follows:
/dental; ≠alveolar; !alveolar palatal; //lateral.

[2] This map is based on two maps made for us in the field; one by
Charles Handley, Jr., Assistant Curator, Division of Mammals, the Smithsonian Institution; the other by John Marshall. We wish hereby to express
our thanks to both.

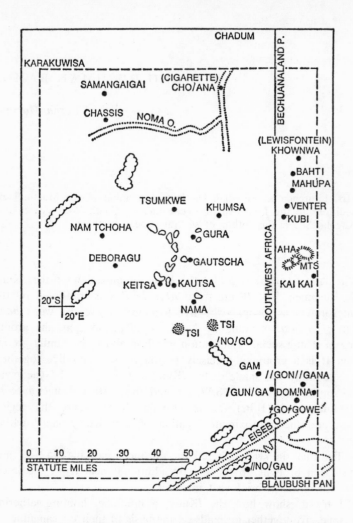

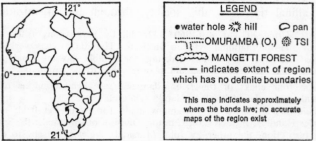

Approximate Location of /Kung Bands in the Region of Nyae Nyae.

bands and headmanship, works out the ownership of water-holes and areas where the wild plants grow from which the *!*Kung, who are entirely without agriculture, gather food. (For convenience we adopt the Afrikaans word *veldkos,* 'field food', for the wild foods. The word applies to all types—nuts, fruits, tubers, roots, leaves, gums, fungi, &c.) I point out how the possibility of choice and change of members from one band to another (within certain limits) allows for adjustment in the size of the band to the relative scarcity of food and water, and mention at the end the ways in which members of different bands interact among themselves.

PART I

The Nyae Nyae region includes some 10,000 square miles. It has several water-holes but no rivers or other surface water, except during the three months of the rains, January through March, usually, and for a few weeks after, when the pans are shallow ponds.

How and when the *!*Kung came into the region no one knows. Although they have many myths, they have no legends or tales which tell of their own particular past or hint where they might have come from. They think they have lived in the Nyae Nyae region since time began. They know almost nothing of the world outside this region. Our informants did not know of the existence of the Atlantic Ocean only slightly more than 400 miles in a bee-line to the west, or of the existence of any ocean. They had heard of the Okavango River.

Knowing them now, one cannot imagine that they took the Nyae Nyae region by force from another people. The region is so dry that it may have been uninhabited when the *!*Kung came to it. They must have just slipped into it, perhaps by simply migrating or by being driven to take refuge in it. In any case, no warrior heroes are sung, no tales of battles of defence or offence are told. As /Ti/kay, the headman of one of the bands, remarked, fighting is very dangerous; 'someone might get killed'.

Population

The *!*Kung population in the Nyae Nyae region we estimate to be about 1,000 souls. They live in 36 or 37 communities. Of

the 36 or 37 communities, 17 or 18 are bands in the interior,
all in S.W.A., 10 are bands on the periphery of the region, some
in S.W.A. and some in the portion of the region which lies
within the western border of B.P. in the territory of the Batawana
tribe of the Chwana nation. The other 9 communities are groups
of /Kung employed by Chwana and Herero on their cattle posts
along the B.P. border. The employed /Kung intermarry and interact with the interior /Kung and still preserve much of the old
/Kung culture but not the band structure.

Our study was made with the interior bands while there were
no inhabitants other than /Kung and when they preserved their
ancient /Kung ways of life.

Infanticide

The /Kung limit their population by infanticide. They generally
space their children at least two and often four or five years
apart. Infant mortality takes another toll and keeps /Kung families small. In a sample taken at random from 16 bands we find
that 68 mothers have 164 living children, an average of 2.41
each. (We have no data on the total number of births.) It so
happens that in this sample there are 82 boys and 82 girls,
showing that there is not marked preference for one sex over
the other. The /Kung say they want as many of one as the
other—as many as possible. A few of the men complained to
us that they did not have as many children as they wanted and
chided their wives for not having kept more.

A woman goes into the veld to give birth either alone or with
her own mother. If she decides not to keep the baby, it probably
never breathes. I did not have the fortitude to learn more. It is
my impression that the /Kung do not feel that they commit a
crime or sin when they practise infanticide, but I believe that it
is very disturbing to them none the less.

These hunting-gathering people are always on the move—
to the mangetti forest for a time, back to their permanent water
with loads of nuts, or to dig for certain roots, or to pick wild
grapes when they are ripe, and always back and forth to water.

A journey of sixty to a hundred miles is not unusual. The
/Kung measure travelling distances by 'sleeps'. Men alone, hunting or travelling without heavy loads, will walk sixty miles or
even more with only one night's sleep. With women and chil-

dren and all their belongings, the band would ordinarily take three sleeps during a sixty-mile walk.

The men carry their various belongings, quivers, loads of meat, nuts, or beans hung in skin bags balanced front and back on carrying sticks on their left shoulders. An assegai over the right shoulder, crossing behind and thrust under the carrying stick in the back, distributes the weight to both shoulders. A man may have, in addition, a loaded carrying net hung from both shoulders across his back. The child of about three to six years—the knee child—rides on one of his father's shoulders or astride both, his legs around his father's neck. Vibrant and at ease at the same time, the children ride with exquisite balance, rarely needing to hold on to their fathers' heads.

On the long treks the mother carries all her worldly goods, including the ten or a dozen ostrich egg shells filled with water, such roots and berries as she may have, and her infant in the pouch of her kaross. The infant does not bounce amidst the ostrich egg shells. He is tied above them in a little leather sling, skin to skin against the mother's left side, where he can reach her breast. On the shorter daily trips into the veld to gather food, the mother usually carries both the infant and knee child as well, most of the way.

Children of about seven and upwards walk their fifteen miles or so per day along with the adults. They do need strong legs.

The Entity and Autonomy of Bands

The band of people who live together is the highest structured social grouping of the !Kung. The bands are autonomous with respect to each other. No !Kung headman has authority over another.

This separateness of the bands, as Schapera called it, does not function, however, as a separating or disruptive force among the people. The population of the region is united by intermarriage (Marshall 1959:335–65). Innumerable kinship bonds entwine the individuals and much interaction and much visiting acquaint everyone with everyone else. It is because these people are so interrelated that we need to refer to the region in which they live as a unit and arbitrarily call it the region of Nyae Nyae.

The entity of a !Kung band, the *n//a besi,* is clearly visible to the eye. When the people are walking in a line, one closely following another, they look to me like an organic thing with many heads, brown and sinuous in the golden grass. When they are encamped, they cluster close together. But, if two or more bands are encamped near the same water-hole, they are always visibly separated. Sometimes their werfs will be only a few yards apart, sometimes a mile or more.

The history of the origin and settlement of the individual bands is lost in the past. The /Kung are a present-oriented people who make no great effort to hold the past in memory or to teach their history to their children. Although the individuals who compose the bands die and others are born, although some move away to live in other bands and others join, and although bands may disband or die out and new bands form, the bands have existed as entities pretty much as they are now for some time. No one remembers a time when things were very different.

PART II

Territories: Food and Water Resources

Each band established itself by some process, probably peaceful, in one of the habitable portions of the Nyae Nyae region, in what we call a territory. The /Kung word for territory or country is *!nore.*

For a unit of land to be a territory inhabitable by a /Kung band it must produce veldkos to sustain that band; there must also be a permanent or semi-permanent water-hole; and, from the point of view of distance, the people must be able to go back and forth from one to the other without perishing—even in the dry season. I am referring to the settling of the /Kung in their territories according to their own traditional concepts. The Government has recently appointed a Bushman Affairs Commissioner for S.W.A. and this appointment will in all probability bring about changes, but up to the present the Government had not affected the internal structure of the /Kung bands in their territorial divisions and in their own concepts of ownership of veldkos and water-holes.

The /Kung band territories take up all of the habitable land in the region. We believe that there are no places yet to be

discovered which offer significant quantities of food and water.
The boundaries of the territories are not precise and are not
marked. To the west and south-west the territories fade off into
waterless uninhabitable country, and I think there are a few
stretches of country between some of the central and northern
territories which are a sort of no-man's-land, but the important areas are known and owned and the aspects of territorial
concepts which are important to them are thoroughly understood and respected. If they define /Ti!kay's territory as 'the
other side of the Gura baobabs', we may think this somewhat
vague but they know what they mean.

Hunting

!Kung hunting customs do not require that hunters confine themselves strictly to their own territory, and the ownership of the
animals which are hunted is not based on territories. The animals
belong to no one until they are shot.

The vastness and emptiness of the country and the nature of
the game combine to allow this lack of strictness of hunting
rights in relation to territory. In thousands of square miles in
the interior there are only the seventeen or eighteen bands, about
450 people. To travel a hundred miles without seeing a living
soul is a common experience.

The game which the /Kung hunt deliberately and purpose-
fully are mainly the several big antelopes which are found in
the region: eland, kudu, gemsbok, wildebeest, hartebeest, spring-
bok. They also hunt the more rarely seen buffalo and occasionally manage to shoot a giraffe. Giraffe are royal game by S.W.A.
law but the /Kung did not know this.

It is these big animals which are worth while. The hunters
would gladly shoot smaller animals which are found, wart hogs,
duikers, other small antelope, spring hare, and ostrich, paouw,
guinea fowl, red-winged partridge, and other birds and occasional
migrating geese, if they happened upon them. The /Kung eagerly
pick up tortoises, lizards, snakes, ostrich eggs, and grasshoppers
when they find them. But they would not devote their pur-
poseful hunting time to the smaller creatures if they could find
fresh enough spoor of the larger animals to follow. Although
there is this considerable variety of kind, there is not a great
abundance of game in the region, compared to some other parts
of Africa which we read or hear about. The herds are small.

The hunts are long and hard, as John Marshall shows in the film which he took while following /Kung hunts—*The Hunters*. The antelope, because they can go without drinking for long periods, do not come regularly to water-holes. They move and drift about anywhere in the vast monotonous veld and are very difficult to find. Hunters often search for days, covering scores of miles, before finding spoor fresh enough to follow, and they may follow it for days before catching up with the animal. Their little arrows kill by poison rather than by piercing deeply, and, when they have shot an animal, if it is big, it may wander for three or four days more until it dies of the poison. Smaller animals succumb in a shorter time. The hunters must track the animal and must find it before the lions, leopards, hyaenas, jackals, and vultures devour it.

A /Kung band gets on an average only about fifteen to eighteen large animals in a usual year, according to our observations. The hunters start out in their own territories and usually hunt in what was interpreted as a 'side'—a direction—which they consider to be more or less theirs. At Gautscha, hunters from one band usually started off toward the east, north-east, or south-east. Hunters from a neighboring band usually went to the west. There was nothing very rigid about this.

However, we heard of a dispute about a hunter starting out to hunt in the territory of another band beyond Kai Kai. Lazy /Qui told Dr. J. O. Brew, who was interrogating him, that once when he was visiting at Kai Kai he had gone hunting toward the east, far from the people he knew. A /Kung hunter from that territory met him and was angry and said, 'Why are you coming to hunt in our area?' He almost started to fight, but an old man named /Kham ran up and stopped him, saying, 'You must not fight for food. We are all looking for food. Nobody is going to fight about food.' When /Qui was asked if he went there again, everyone laughed—knowing him. /Qui said simply, 'I was frightened. I did not go to that side any more.'

Once an arrow has been shot into an animal, that animal belongs to the owner of the arrow. The first arrow which effectively pierces so that it stays in the animal is the one that theoretically counts. The owner of the arrow may or may not be one of the hunters and may be a man or a woman. I shall explain this in more detail later. Regardless of where the animal dies, the meat is taken by the hunters to the band of the arrow-owner. If the animal dies in a territory other than his, the hunters would give a present of meat to the owners of the territory, should they see them, but no tribute is obligatory.

Small creatures like tortoises belong to the person who catches them, birds and animals the size of duikers or smaller to the person who snares or shoots them. The person who owns these may share them with his own nuclear family and dependants alone, and with such others as he wishes to give to.

The large animals, however, are shared with everyone in the band. Visitors also would be given meat. It is the responsibility of the owner of the first arrow to make the first distribution of the meat, in sizeable quantities, according to a system which I shall describe in detail when I describe meat-sharing and gift-giving. Persons who receive meat from the arrow-owner give, in their turn, to their kin, affines, and friends, until everyone present has received some. The gifts are never refused. The person who receives must give in return when he has meat to give.

The custom of sharing meat is so strongly established and so faithfully followed that it has all but extinguished the concept of not sharing meat in the minds of the *!*Kung. It is unthinkable that one family should have much to eat and others nothing when they sit in the werf at night clustered closely together within their wall of firelight. When I brought to their imaginations the image of a hunter hiding meat in the veld for himself and his own family to eat secretly (which would actually be practically impossible because where a *!*Kung goes and what he does all may read in his footprints), the people howled and screeched with laughter. A man would be very bad to do that, they said. He would be like a lion. They would have to treat him like a lion by driving him away or teach him manners by not giving him any meat. They would not give him even a tiny piece. I asked, 'Did they ever know anyone to eat alone like a lion?' They never did, they said.

Veldkos

The *!*Kung depend on veldkos[3] for their daily living. Laurence

---

[3] See Story (1958). In this publication Dr. Story makes the botanical identification and gives a description of eighty-eight kinds of plants which

Marshall estimates that 80 per cent of the food is veldkos. Meat is the longed-for food which they have intermittently.

In the Nyae Nyae region every important source of veldkos on which the people depend is known. /Kung hunters and travellers may find an odd root or truffle or, conceivably, an occasional berry bush they did not know about before and may casually help themselves to them, but that is about the extent of the unknown and the casual. The fertile areas in which the principal wild tubers grow, the groves of mangetti nut trees, clumps of berries, fruit trees, and the rare and coveted patches of *tsi*[4]—all are known. These important sources of food are owned by the bands with strict definition and jealous concern. There is nothing vague or casual about it. We wanted to take moving pictures of one band gathering mangetti nuts. There was evidently a line beyond which they did not have rights to pick the nuts and they refused to go beyond it although we asked them to do so because the light was better.

The territories are shaped in a general way around the fertile areas which the bands own. The areas owned need not all be contiguous. One of the bands owns the Khumsa water-hole and the veldkos relatively near it and also a share in a mangetti forest about fifty miles away, but not all the land in between.

The quantities of veldkos within the various territories vary, but a balance is maintained. If there is only scant veldkos the band remains relatively small; more abundant veldkos attracts more members to the band. In the area as a whole the veldkos sustains the present population, but barely. Though not starved or emaciated, *all* the Nyae Nyae /Kung are thin or slender (except the infants, whose mothers' remarkable lactation frequently rounds them out like butter balls).

The people plan their lives around their veldkos resources, going to them according to the season when it is most advantageous. The gathering of veldkos is the work of women. Usually only the women and children go in groups on the rou-

---

have some edible part. These constitute most of the veldkos gathered by the Bushmen. Our own observations, made independently of Dr. Story, on the methods of gathering, seasonal aspects, relative importance in kind and quantity to the bands we studied, will be given in another paper.

[4] *Bauhinia esculenta* Burch (Story 1958:25). We have heard *tsi* popularly called 'eland beans' or 'eland boontjies.'

tine daily trips to dig tubers or pick berries. However, the men always take the women on the long treks to the mangetti forests or *tsi* patches and help to gather and carry back the heavy loads. When these trips are made in the dry season everyone must carry out as much water as possible and carry back to the water-hole as much food as possible.

Once veldkos is gathered it belongs to the person who gathered it. There is no patterned or required distribution. A woman feeds her own family with her daily gathering. She cooks and pounds and serves the veldkos as a family meal.

Even when some of the band go to gather mangettis and others remain at the water-hole, the mangettis are not distributed, as meat is, in a standardized way. Each gatherer owns what he has gathered and may give it to and share it with whomever he pleases. Visitors are given veldkos by the persons they are visiting or may join a gathering party as a courtesy.

The *!*Kung bands have not encroached or fought each other for veldkos within the memory of living persons, and they know no tales of fights in the past. Encroaching on veldkos would be like stealing, and stealing is a dangerous and exceedingly rare crime among the *!*Kung.

One chilling tale was told of death. There was a theft of honey which was still in the tree. It is the custom, when a man finds honey in a tree or a nest of ostrich eggs, to mark the find with a bunch of grass stuck into a forked stick or a crotch of the tree, to indicate that he has found it and will be back to get it. A man stole such a find of honey and the owner killed him for it.

It is to be remembered that a person's footprints are as well known as his face. This undoubtedly has something to do with the sanctions which so effectively prevent this society from stealing. There is a woeful song which the *!*Kung sing when the mood to lament is upon them. It expresses how they *would* feel *if* they were to go to their *tsi* patch and find footprints there and all the *tsi* picked and gone.

Water

During the three months of the rains, and for a time after the rains, there is water in the several pans and vleys and temporary water-holes of the region. This frees the bands to travel to their

most distant areas of veldkos, and segments of bands may separate if they wish, for a time, to go to different places; it is a
good time for visiting. These rain waters belong to no one in
particular; the people are free to take the water wherever they
find it. It is the permanent or semi-permanent water-holes which
the bands own.

Water is not owned so exclusively or so jealously as veldkos.
Veldkos comes to an end when it is all eaten up or dried up
and will not grow again until the next growing season. The
permanent water-holes, though few and sometimes meagre, do
keep on producing after their fashion. Water seems to belong
more to mankind, as the animals do, and the ownership of
water-holes emphasizes more the managing than the withholding of the water.

The headman's permission should be asked by travellers or
visitors before taking water, 'because he knows how much he
has and knows what can be done', someone said. But one of
the listeners laughed at this and said, 'If you are very thirsty,
you have no time to ask permission.'

We were told that at Gam people no longer know how to
behave properly, as they did in the good old days, and now
take water without asking permission of the headmen. Doubtless the Bushmen feel that their own system is superseded where
the water-holes have been more or less dominated by the Bantu.

PART III

The /Kung organize themselves socially in two groupings and
only two—the family and the band. Both the family and the
band are structured upon consanguineous and affinal bonds. The
band is characterized by the organization of rights to veldkos
areas and water-holes. Individuals have access to these resources
only through their band affiliations. All the /Kung of the Nyae
Nyae region, except those who are in the groups employed by
Chwana or Herero, belong to bands.

In addition to being the grouping through which the resources
are owned and controlled, the band offers the means by which
several families may be organized in residence. The specific
organizational factor by which this is accomplished is the headman. I shall describe this more fully later. First I want to sum-

marize in this connexion some of the facts about bride-service because of its influence on family structure and residence, describe the form of the *!*Kung family in its several phases, and mention in passing some details about the settlement pattern.

Bride-service

*!*Kung society, rigorously and without exception, requires that all men, in first and in subsequent marriages, go to live with the parents of their brides and give them bride-service. Should a bride's parents be dead, the man goes to whatever relatives she lives with and serves them. The service he gives is hunting. The great concern is food. The *!*Kung talk about it constantly and explain bride-service in terms of meat. 'Our daughter's husband must give us meat. We need him to hunt for us. He must feed his bride', they reiterate. They say also, but not with so much emphasis, that they want to see the young man grow to maturity and want to make sure that he is able and responsible and that he will be kind to their daughter.

The *!*Kung are polygynous. First marriages are arranged by the parents. Then a man may take other wives. The number is not limited by rule. However, only one man in nine succeeded in having two wives simultaneously, and none had more than two in the years we have known the region. There is no great excess of women. For a second wife a man must wait until divorce or widowhood makes some woman available. In this society, in which possessions are very much equalized by the fact that everyone carries his own and there is much passing of things around by gift-giving, and where headmen and medicine men have no privilege, by virtue of their office, over other men in obtaining second wives, an agreeable personality and ability to hunt well are to a man's advantage. Bride-service is given for the subsequent wives as for the first.

Wherever he lives a man is responsible for the support of his own and his wife's parents, siblings, and other dependants. Wherever he goes he takes with him those among the above relatives who need or want to accompany him. When he gives bride-service for his second wife he takes with him his first wife, his children by her, and all the relatives who live with him. Thus whole segments of bands join other bands.

The duration of bride-service is indefinite. The people say

it should be long enough for three children to be born. In first marriages, when the young girls have been married for several years before their first menstruation, ten or more years might elapse before three children could be born.

We believe that in second marriages the time requirement is not so strict as in first marriages. Gau has lived for eight years with his second wife's people and Gao Medicine has lived for nine with his. We think that this is not entirely a matter of rule but that preference has entered in. These particular persons all seem to like living together.

If a headman dies, the son who inherits the headmanship may cut short his bride-service with general approval and, with his wife and children, return to his own band to assume the headmanship. Divorce also terminates bride-service.

After his obligations are fulfilled, the man is considered to have the right to return to his own people if he wishes, taking his wife and children and dependants. But he may choose to stay on with his wife's people. A man told me that men prefer on the whole to return to their own bands because it takes a man's whole youth to learn every tree and vley in his country so that he does not get lost when hunting and that one never feels equally secure in the country of another band. Nevertheless, many men find it more advantageous or agreeable to stay on. In some instances their own people were dead, or their bands had disbanded because of insufficient resources. More than once the wives were the cause. They were so unwilling to leave their parents that the men conceded to them.

The Family

The family is the primary and the most cohesive social unit of the /Kung. Its cohesiveness is visible to the eye in the way people sit and move, and is clearly observable when a band disperses temporarily. Whole segments of bands or single families often leave the others and go to different places to gather veldkos or to visit relatives. One can then see the families like insoluble lumps always together.

The family unit is stable from every point of view. As time passes it changes from one phase to another, but in a continuum, repeating the same phases through the generations. There are two principal phases which I call nuclear and extended phases.

The nuclear phase itself may have two or possibly three phases; the extended phase may have two.

In its simplest nuclear phase a *!*Kung family is composed of a man and his wife. It is then augmented by such children as are born to them. The family may have some dependant of the husband or wife living with it, a dependent parent or grandparent, or sibling; an uncle or aunt who has no offspring of his or her own to live with; an orphaned nephew or niece or grandchild.

Since bride-service brings the young husband to live in the bride's family one does not find a young nuclear family in neolocal residence, unless it should happen that the bride's parents were dead. In such circumstances the couple would live beside and somewhat under the authority of some of the bride's people, but this is not a normal family phase.

I include among nuclear families those in which the man has two wives but consider them to be in a later phase than the first, as the first marriage is always arranged with just one wife.

When the daughters marry and the young husbands come to give bride-service, the unit becomes an extended family. In this (earlier) phase the unmarried daughters and sons of the original nuclear family are present. The married sons have left their family to live with their brides' parents.

In the second extended phase the married sons may have returned, with their wives and offspring, from bride-service to be again with their own parents. The married daughters, with their husbands and offspring, may continue to live with their parents or may go to live with their husbands' people.

When the old father of an extended family dies, this extended family breaks up. The nuclear families of the married daughters and sons are independent of each other. Families of siblings may live together in the same band, but one has no authority over another unless one of the siblings happens to be the headman of the band. If they are no longer involved in bride-service themselves, and their offspring are not yet married, these families become again independent nuclear families. When the offspring marry these families become new extended families.

The father is the head of the family. Headship is strongly associated with males among the *!*Kung. Each man is head of his own nuclear family, but when in bride-service he comes under the extended family headship of his father-in-law. I want it to be

clear that I am making a distinction between family headship
and the headmanship of a band, which I shall presently describe
more fully. The /Kung father's authority is not formalized and
is not expressed dictatorially. The young on the whole are respectful and obedient. They seem to fall into this behaviour by imita-
tion and response to group expectation. The behaviour is not
induced by harshness, domineering, specific training, or strict
insistence on obedience in so far as we could observe.

/Kung parents appear to be exceedingly affectionate, permis-
sive, protective, and patient with their young children. Infants
are nursed every time they indicate the slightest desire. Parents
kiss their young children with smacking kisses and seem never to
tire of holding them or letting them climb over them and play
in their midst. The children are seldom fretful, rarely strident or
demanding. They play in very engaging ways. The older children
have toys but the young ones play mostly with the family's
utensils, often imitating what the parents do. Parents are likely
to pause to show three-year-olds how to twirl a drill or dig with
a digging stick or pound berries in the mortar. The children
are never left unattended. Their mothers take them when they
go to the water-hole or into the veld to gather the daily food,
and watch over them constantly to see that they do not stray
away into the tall grass where they might get lost or step on a
snake or meet a leopard. Their fathers and mothers carry them
when the family moves.

I never saw a child punished physically or very harshly repri-
manded. /Ti/kay's idea of the way to discipline a son who tended
to be quarrelsome was to 'keep him right with him, even on
long hunts, till he learned sense'.

The father's family headship and his authority derive, I think,
from the family's habitual dependence on him. He is the strong
male, the hunter, provider, protector, the older more knowledgeable one to whom the wives as well as the children look
for leadership and support. He plans what the family will do and
they, expecting to obey, fall in with his plans. If I were to make
a symbolic painting about a /Kung as a man and father and
head of a family I would show him carrying the whole family
on his shoulders and in his arms as well as the tools for their
living.

Sons-in-law are under the authority of their fathers-in-law while they live in bride-service but not after this has ended. Sons, if I interpret my impressions correctly, continue to feel more or less under the authority of their fathers, if they live with them, at least until their fathers become so decrepit and incapable of leadership that they are really dependent and, though they may still be the titular head of the extended family, they no longer act as heads or leaders.

When the old father of an extended family dies, that particular family headship ends. I believe that headship is so strongly associated with males among the !Kung that a widowed mother is usually regarded as no more than a dependant when the father dies.

The Settlement Pattern

It always amuses me to speak of residence when I visualize the nomadic !Kung settling down for the night, like migrating birds in the bushes, or building their nest-like grass shelters (scherms) for a stay of a few weeks. And it is a delightful insistence on precision to say that ≠Gao, the young headman, before he married in 1959, lived with his elder sister, /U, not with his eldest sister, Di/ai, when they were not more than two arms' lengths apart because the sisters liked to hand things across from one household to the other without getting up. Yet the !Kung do have residence and it does become clear precisely who lives with whom. One way this can be observed is to see whom the woman feeds with her veldkos. It was /U, not Di/ai, who fed ≠Gao.

The fire is the clearest visible symbol of the place of residence. One can see who lives at each. Always, summer and winter, every nuclear family has its fire, which is kept burning all night. The desert sun gives enough warmth on the clear dry winter days to make them comfortable unless a fierce wind is blowing from the Antarctic. The fires are customarily covered with ashes during the day, and the coals are fanned up only when they are wanted for cooking. In the late afternoon men and women go out into the veld to gather dead wood for the night fires. There is plenty of wood for them. Their use is conservative. Even the night fires are not large. You can draw closer together around a small fire and have less smoke in your eyes.

The fire is the nuclear family's home, its place to be. In a

way a fire is a more unchanging home than a house on a spot
on the ground from which a family might depart. A fire-home is
always where the family is.

The family hangs its possessions in the bushes near by, sits
around the fire, cooks at it, sleeps beside it—with two exceptions.
The unmarried boys from about the age of puberty eat and sit
and, in general, live by their family's fire in the day-time but at
night they all sleep at a boys' fire. The unmarried girls of that
age, likewise, sleep away from their parents' fire, at the fire of a
grandmother or some other woman who can chaperon them.

The pattern of settlement of the /Kung has only a few constant
elements. The /Kung settle at some distance from a water-hole,
a mile or so away in any direction. This is not to enable them
to hunt at night from a blind at the water-hole, which is an
extremely rare type of hunting for the /Kung to adopt because
their big game antelopes do not need to drink regularly and
seldom come to the water-holes. The predators do, however. The
Bushmen and our expedition shared a water-hole for three
months with a family of lions. The adult lions minded their own
business, the rambunctious cubs were merely playful when they
destroyed our water pump, but we all slept the better for keeping
our distance.

The Relationships on Which Bands Are Structured

In the second social grouping the band, as distinct from the
family, is based upon the possession of areas of veldkos and a
permanent water-hole, i.e. the band's territory. The band as an
entity is permanently associated with its territory. Membership in
a band carries with it the right to partake of the veldkos and
water of the band. Through their band affiliations persons are
sorted out as to which veldkos and which water-hole they live
upon.

The group of persons who compose the band starts with the
custodian of the territory's veldkos and water-hole. He is the
headman. I previously spoke of the band's ownership of veldkos
and water, but perhaps a more nearly correct interpretation is to
say that the headman is the owner. He does not own the resources
personally or exclusively as property in movables is owned by
the individual. Members of the band share in the ownership by
having rights to the resources, but the headman gives focus and

form and continuity to the ownership in his person. He is the visible symbol and he also administers and controls the consumption of the resources by members of the band, as I shall describe later. Furthermore, the headman is the nucleus of the cluster of persons who are members of the band. These persons live with him and have the right to partake of his veldkos and water resources because their consanguineous or affinal bonds link them with him. His own families of orientation and procreation are linked directly to him; others may be more remotely connected, in a chain-like manner. The relationships which link person with person into bands in *!*Kung society are the three of the nuclear family: the relationship of parent and offspring, the sibling relationship, and the relationship of man and wife.

An extension or continuation of these bonds may bring into residence in a band uncles and aunts with nephews and nieces or cousins with cousins. A grandparent bereft of offspring would live with a grandchild. But the presence together of people in the above relationships comes about because of the original parental or sibling relationships, not because *!*Kung society has established patterns of avuncular or cousin or grandparent residence.

We know of one instance in which the name relationship provided a substitute for kinship as a means of entering a band. A woman whose immediate family had all died went to live with a woman in another band because the two liked living together. This was acceptable because the latter had the same name as the former's deceased daughter.

Stated in another way, parent and offspring, siblings, and man and wife, always have the right to live together in *!*Kung society. Those who have one of these relationships with the owner of the veldkos and water—the headman—have the right to live with him and share his resources. And those who are thus linked to the headman have the right also to bring with them into the band their own parents, offspring, siblings, or spouses, who in turn may bring theirs. Thus a band can be thought of as an aggregation of families.

Membership

Birth accounts for most membership in bands, particularly among lineal descendants of the headman or of close collaterals. Marriage is the second important factor in bringing persons into membership in bands. Choice and circumstance are also factors. Where there is choice, such as married couples have after bride-service is fulfilled, or a widowed mother might have between off-spring, or a sibling between siblings living in different bands, the relative adequacy of the resources would influence the choice. A very small water-hole cannot support a large band. When other choices are possible people will make them. If the resources are about equal, the feeling people have for each other could de-termine the choice. /Qui said he chose to live with his brother, Gao Beard, instead of his father-in-law, for reasons of affection —in his case affection for his brother's mangetti nuts.

Informants gave me the impression that they rarely, if ever, feel a duality of belonging to two bands. Adults seem usually to have made up their minds and feel clearly to which band they belong. The children reflect the sense that a choice has been made with relative permanency and feel that they belong to the band in which their parents settle.

Rights to Veldkos and Water

All members of a band have inherent rights to gather veldkos and take water by being linked to the headman in an accepted kinship pattern. They do not feel that they receive a gift from the bounty of the headman and, though he owns the veldkos and water in the sense we described, he does not have the right to withhold them from rightful members. Neither does the headman have the right to take a larger share than other members. The members have equal rights among themselves, whether they have been born to the band or come into it directly by their own mar-riage or by being a member of the family of an individual who was born to the band or married into it. People who are in the band temporarily for bride-service, who intend not to settle in it permanently, share equally while they are present but do not re-tain rights after they leave.

Permanent members retain their rights throughout their lives. If they move away temporarily, they have the right to return.

New Bands

A new band can be formed at any time that circumstances per-mit and people desire to form one. A man who has inherited rights to adequate resources, the personal qualification of leadership, and enough families who want to follow him may sever from his band, establish another, and become its headman. The brother of a former headman broke off from his band and created another of his own. These bands live in the same territory, are based on the same water-hole, but have taken the habit of usually going in different directions to gather veldkos.

We did not observe the creation of a new band and can only surmise the circumstances in which one might form. Three possibilities occur to me. One would be the death of a headman and the dying out of his line which would result in the re-forming of the band. If resources could be more advantageously used by splitting up a large band, this might be another reason for forming a new band.

Friction in human relations must also, I think, have caused fission of bands from time to time. It is my impression at present that the potential friction between bands is sufficient to keep them from uniting. Gao Beard's jealousy of ≠Toma is such that people say everything goes better when he is away in the west at his mangetti place minding his own business.

The tendency to establish new bands for whatever reason is held in check, however, by the disadvantage of too much fission. One can imagine that the dividing of veldkos resources could cause more rather than less strife. The /Kung dread and fear strife and are practised in avoiding it. They would seek to ally themselves in the way most likely to produce peace. Furthermore, fission is checked because bands which are too small are not advantageous. One nuclear family alone is obviously not enough to sustain the arduous hunting-gathering life of the /Kung. The mutual support and companionship of a larger group is needed. Hunters must help each other. One is needed to guard the kill while another brings the band to the meat, or several hunters are needed to carry the meat to the band.

There is also loneliness. A mood song, called the *Song of the Old Stump*, expresses the feeling of a hunter who got separated from his companions and found himself alone when evening came. In the dusk he saw a man in the distance. He ran to him shouting, glad that there would be two together by the fire that night. When he came near he found only an old stump. The long day of gathering in the veld would be insupportable for a woman alone, and I imagine that even co-wives together could hardly bear the gathering life without other companionship. Living in bands of several families together suits the /Kung.

Much of the time the bands are not seen in their wholeness because the hunters are away or the families have gone to different veldkos areas or to visit their relatives. We were able to observe whole bands together, however, when they went all at one time to gather *tsi,* or at the end of the blazing hot dry seasons when they have to stay near their permanent water, or when we lured them to stay with us for considerable periods with gifts of tobacco and salt. The frequent temporary separation of segments or families from one another may contribute to the band's general stability. Such tensions as exist between them are eased; the people benefit by change and rest from each other.

PART IV

The Words for 'Headman'

We have heard it said by white people who have had long contact with Bushmen in S.W.A. and B.P. that Bushmen have no headmen and both /Kung and /Gikwe Bushmen have been interpreted to us as saying this themselves. We think they must mean they have no personages such as the Bantu tribal chiefs and that the confusion has arisen in the translation. Our word 'headman' is entirely appropriate, I think, to the Bushman head of a band. He has no authority over any other band but he is the head of his own.

There are three words which can be used in /Kung when our English word *headman* is translated. They are *n/iha, gaoxa,*[5] and *kxau.*

N/iha and *gaoxa* were both translated by our interpreters as 'chief'. *Gaoxa* is the more exalted word and shows more respect. Both are applied to the two deities of the /Kung. Both words are applied to earthly chiefs and persons in high authority, for instance to the Native Commissioner of the Okavango Native Territory at Runtu and to the Chwana chiefs. The word *kxau* can be

[5] Bleek (1956) gives *gaoxa* in her northern group II (/Kung) as meaning *chief* and quotes Doke as saying *gao:uxa* means *leader* (p. 45). She gives *xaiha* in her southern group IV and central group II as meaning *old man* (p. 256). This word may have some relation to the /Kung word which I heard as *n/iha.*

used for headman. It means *owner,* and is the commonly used word. Oukwane, the /Gikwe, knew no word for headman other than 'owner'. What the headman owns, in the symbolic way I have mentioned, is the veldkos and water.

Succession in Headmanship

Continuity is given to this ownership by passing the headmanship from father to son.

The rule among the /Kung in the Nyae Nyae region is that the eldest son succeeds to the headmanship at the death of his father. Should the eldest son die or leave the band to live elsewhere, the next eldest son would become headman. Passing from father to son, a headmanship can continue indefinitely.

In all the bands we studied, the headmen were men and had sons to succeed them. We had to pose hypothetical questions to informants to learn what happens in other situations. Several informants concurred in telling us that, if a headman had no son, his headmanship would go to his daughter and then to her son, or, failing a son, again through a daughter to her son. They told us of a woman in a Kai Kai band to whom the headmanship had fallen after her father's death.

We discovered no further verbalized rule for succession. I have a notion that the /Kung do not have practical need to establish a theoretical rule beyond this point and that they seldom actually carry out the succession through daughters as far as DaDaSo. Headmanship, with its patrilineal emphasis, is so strongly associated in the minds of the Nyae Nyae /Kung with males and fatherhood that I believe succession through females beyond DaSo would be unusual. Changes take place. The feeling for the succession might weaken or be extinguished in so much time without the symbol of the father-headman. A band might form itself anew around another headman. Here I think a man's character and abilities would play their part in determining whom the disbanding families would join. If the families remain at the same water-hole it might well be a younger brother of the deceased headman, or a nephew, or a cousin who had rights to the same water, around whom the families would re-form their band. I am interpreting my conjecture as a reorganization of a band. I do not have evidence that there is a systematic rule by which succession shifts to certain collaterals in a formal way.

A man can create a new headmanship by forming a new band around himself as we mentioned previously. To do this he needs only to have the innate initiative, the rights to adequate resources, and a band to follow him. The /Kung have developed no method, however, of electing or appointing a headman to an existing band. When the headman of the Gura people died in about 1951 and his line died out with him, informants told us that the Gura people had remained without a headman, at least until we left in 1953. We do not know how they eventually re-formed their band or bands.

Headmanship Not Especially Desired

We detected no rivalry or connivance to acquire headmanship, and no anxiety about retaining it. It falls by succession upon the proper person. We believe that the kinsmen want continuity through a headman, but do not particularly want the position for themselves. Headmanship is not especially advantageous to the individual. Among the /Kung each person does his own work, carries his own load, and shares meat. Headmen are as thin as the rest. No regalia, special honours, or tributes mark them out. They have considerable responsibility without any specific reward. In common with all /Kung we know, they do not want to stand out or be above others by having more material things than the others, for this draws unfavourable attention to them and arouses envy and jealousy. We often observed the care they take to avoid this. On one occasion even food was refused. ≠Toma, the leader of one band, refused a buck which John Marshall had shot for him as a parting gift. He asked John to give it to someone else, saying he was afraid of the jealousy people would feel if he were more favoured than they. We were told that a headman is likely to feel that he must be more generous than others in gift-giving. This is one of a headman's main problems, one informant said.

Authority and Duties

The authority of a headman derives, I believe, from the concept of the father being the head of the extended family. In the next step the headman is head of the band which may be composed of several families, who expect to subject themselves to his plans as his family expects his leadership.

The authority of a band's headman is limited almost entirely to control of the veldkos and water. It is his responsibility and principal duty to integrate the band's utilization of its resources, to plan to which areas within the territory the band will move, at what time, and in what order they will consume their veldkos.

It is not necessary that the families of the band move all together. Some families may go to one place, some to another. However, their planning is integrated by the headman and it is known to all what the several families will do.

Visitors must conform also to the headman's control and must ask permission before taking veldkos or water.

An informant told us that if members of a band were to quarrel the most probable cause would be disagreement about when to go to this or that veldkos area. Bitter resentment and hostility would arise and it could be a matter of life and death if some members of a band were to take advantage and consume veldkos in excess of their share and unknown to others who were counting on it. The people realize this fully and, in their wisdom about self-preservation and dread of fighting, they do conform to the headman's authority. There is very, very little strife over the consumption of veldkos or the bands' movements. We observed none, but heard of one instance in the past which ended in bitter tragedy. Two men at Gam did quarrel about going to gather veldkos and started to fight. One was Tsamgao, the father of ≠Toma. The young son of the other man, frightened for his father, wanted to protect him. He took a poisoned arrow from his father's quiver and shot and killed ≠Toma's father.

Actually the seasonal patterns of the band's movements follow long-established customs and usually cause little if any controversy. Nature itself dictates most of the seasonal plans by ripening her foods at different times. The pattern is known to all.

Though the /Kung of Nyae Nyae do not have a council of elders, everything is talked over and the actual plan adopted is more likely to be a consensus[6] than the decision of the headman alone. His duties as controller of the veldkos are light.

A headman has few other duties. If a person who was not a member of the band were found stealing veldkos, we were told that it would be the headman's duty to 'chase him away'. How

---

[6] Brownlee's informant (1943:125) said: "It is the wisdom of the old men which causes us to do what they say we should do."

this would be done is left to the imagination. As no one ever steals veldkos, this duty is a very light one.

Informants said that if anyone should attempt to join a band and partake of its veldkos and water who did not have proper kinship affiliations, it would be the duty of the headman to say, 'You are not a relative. You must not come to live in my band.' None of our informants had ever heard of a headman being called upon to do this, so this duty, too, is a light one.

When the band moves, the headman's position is at the head of the line.

He chooses the site for the new werf and has the prerogative of choosing the best spot for his own fire and scherm. The families then choose their sites.

The making of the first fire in a new werf is a ritualistic duty which the headman or an old man performs. If death or misfortune befalls, the band moves at once and makes a new werf and the ritualistic first fire, made with firesticks, is a requisite. Some pieces of veldkos, the best that happen to be at hand, are burned in the fire and a prayer is made for deliverance from misfortune. The members of the band take brands from the first fire and kindle their own family fires. The first fire is then allowed to burn itself out.

Every time a band moves to a new werf, even though no misfortune has occurred, a first fire is supposed to be made. On ordinary moves, the burning of veldkos and the prayer are omitted and sometimes the first fire itself is omitted.

The making of the first fire is not limited exclusively to the headman. An old man may make it and my guess is that it originally involved the old father of the family, not the headman *per se*. The two ritualistic first fires we saw were made by old men. The first fire of an ordinary move of their band was made by Old Gau and ≠Toma, the leader, their two pairs of hands rapidly following one another down the twirling firestick.

A headman has no further administrative duties in his role as headman. As headman he does not necessarily instigate or organize hunting parties, trading trips, the making of artifacts, or giftgiving, nor does he make marriage arrangements. Individuals instigate their own activities.

A headman is not called upon to judge his people or to avenge wrong. A person who is wronged by another may take his own revenge. If the wrong is very great and fierce anger flares, as it may in instances of adultery or stealing, the wronged person may kill the wrong-doer or they may fight and either or both be killed.

Leadership

A headman may or may not be the leader of his band. If he is too young or too old or lacks personal qualities of leadership, the people may turn quite informally to some other man for leadership—go to him for advice, ask his help, and fall in with his plans. A leader has no authority and receives no honours or rewards. We overheard two men talking together about this one day. 'All you get is the blame if things go wrong', they said.

We observed three instances in which the headman was too young and know of one in which he was too old and weak to be a leader. In each of these bands the leadership had fallen to another man in the band who had the personal qualifications for it. ≠Toma, the husband of /U, was one example. We were interested to observe that the leadership of the band had not fallen to the oldest man of the band, Old Gau, though he was much respected and not decrepit. ≠Toma, though much younger, was the more logical choice, probably because his wife was the daughter of the former headman and had been the one of the family to remain consistently at Gautscha, whereas her elder sister and two brothers had been away for years. In addition, ≠Toma is a man of uncommon intelligence and force, skill in hunting, perception in human relations and probity.

PART V

Interrelationship

/Kung society has no wider social structure, such as a tribe with a paramount chief, which organizes the separate bands, with their autonomous headmen, into any sort of political unity. The separate bands, as total units, do not engage together in any organized way in economic, ritualistic, or other activities. Whole bands do come together very frequently, but it is through the interaction of their individual members.

Kinsmen, name-relatives, friends, all visit one another to conduct their affairs. It may be to arrange the marriages of their children, or to carry the news of deaths or births. A woman should visit a namesake at the time of the baby's ceremonial first hair-cutting, and later for the girl's first scarification. People visit to give gifts and to make return gifts. If water and veldkos are low, kin may visit kin who have better resources—within all bounds of propriety, of course. And people also visit simply for the happiness or solace of visiting relatives or friends whom they like to be with. The whole band may go along when individuals visit and all the people come to know each other and thus to interact.

The interaction of the /Kung population as a whole in the Nyae Nyae region is governed by a kinship pattern. This pattern is based on and extends from the numerous actual kinship bonds which exist. Intermarriage, by preference and custom, within the region, for unknown generations, has bound the people together across band demarcations.

Furthermore, /Kung society has taken a form out of the concepts of kinship and cast it upon the relationship of people who have no known consanguineous or affinal ties. It is what we call the name-relationship. The /Kung apply kin terms to persons who have the same names as their consanguineous kin or affines (Marshall 1957:7–8, 13–15, 22–24; 1959:343).

The name-relationship has not developed into a consciously recognized bilateral consanguineous kin group, but is a device which helps very much to consolidate a people who have no political or other structure to unite them.

Name-relationships take in the entire region. /Kung children are named only for certain kin or affines; the names are passed from family to family by intermarriage, down the generations, to such an extent that there are few names in use. Every /Kung in the region has now or has had in the past a kinsman for every one of the names and everyone applies a kin term to everyone else, according to a complex and thoroughly worked out system.

As I explained in the paper on marriage, the primary function of the name-relationship, I believe, is to regulate the extension of the incest tabu and the joking relationship. If persons have the same names they may have had actual lineal ties in the forgotten past. In addition, the /Kung believe that, in having the same name, persons partake of each other's entity in some way. For these reasons they regulate marriage and joking according to the kin terms they apply to each other, which are linked to their names, and feel righteous and secure in behaving properly in this important matter of incest.

Beyond the regulation of marriage, however, the applying of kin terms means to the !Kung that they are not strangers but that they belong together and should accord each other polite, respectful behaviour, as they would to kin or affines, and take care not to give offence. Methods by which the !Kung help to keep peaceful relations amongst individuals within a band, methods such as meat-sharing and gift-giving, which I shall describe later, are employed also with name-relatives and have worked for peace in inter-band relationships. Our informants never heard of a fight between bands in their region even from the old, old people.

3 THE SOCIAL AND PSYCHOLOGICAL ASPECTS OF CHIEFTAINSHIP IN A PRIMITIVE TRIBE: THE NAMBIKUARA OF NORTHWESTERN MATO GROSSO

Claude Lévi-Strauss

Claude Lévi-Strauss is Professor of Social Anthropology at the Col-
lège de France, University of Paris. He is the author of *La vie
familiale et sociale des Indiens Nambikwara* (1948), *Les structures
élémentaires de la parenté* (1949), *Race et histoire* (1952), *Tristes
tropiques* (1955), *Anthropologie structurale* (1958), *Le totémisme
aujourd'hui* (1962), *La pensée sauvage* (1962), and many papers, especially on problems of cosmology and mythology.

FEW ANTHROPOLOGISTS would admit today that human groups displaying an extreme primitiveness either in the field of material culture or that of social organization can teach us something about the early stages of the evolution of mankind. Primitiveness in one field often goes on a par with a great sophistication in another, as shown by the Australian refinements concerning kinship. Since these primitive peoples have their own history, it would be a serious mistake to think that it may be discounted because we know nothing of it. The partial similarities which archaeological remains allow us to infer between primitive societies and those of prehistoric man, while they remain sheer hypotheses, do not preclude the tremendous differences which may have existed in fields outside of the archaeologist's reach. The above considerations, which are only a few among many others, have led most anthropologists in recent years to consider each human group as a particular case which should be studied, analyzed and described from the point of

FROM *Transactions of the New York Academy of Sciences* 7 (1944),
16–32, by permission of the author and the New York Academy of
Sciences.

view of its uniqueness, without any attempt to use the results
for a better understanding of human nature.

However desirable this attitude may have been after the evo-
lutionist orgies, and however fruitful the results obtained, there
are many dangers in it which should raise increasing concern.
Are we condemned, like new Danaids, to fill endlessly the sieve-
like basket of anthropological science; in vain, pouring monographs over monographs without ever being able to collect a
substance with a richer and denser value? Fortunately, primitive societies have not to be considered as illusory stages in the
evolution of mankind to teach us a truth endowed with a general validity. The fact that they are (at least some of them
and all of them in some respect) *simpler* societies than our own
does not need to be taken as a proof of their archaism. They
still throw light, if not on the history of mankind, at least on
some basic forms of activity which are to be found, always
and everywhere, as prerequisites for the existence of human
society.

The simpler organisms may provide a better field for the
study of organic functions than those which exhibit the same
functions, although under a more complex form. Simple human
groups render the anthropologist the same kind of service without any need of surmising that they represent survivals of older
types of organization. Now, to call upon the notion of function
in the field of anthropological sciences is no discovery. This
notion, first introduced by Durkheim in 1894,[1] has been only
too much exploited since then, sometimes in the most abusive
way. There are indeed functions of the social life as well as
functions of the organic life. But neither in one domain nor in
the other does everything correspond to, nor may it be justified
by, its functional value. To state the opposite view could lead
to only two results: either an anthropological come-back to
eighteenth century Providentialism, where culture would play in
relation to man the same utopian tutelary part which was at-

[1] In *Les règles de la méthode sociologique:* "The function is the cor-
respondence between the considered fact and the general needs of the
social organism" (p. 117). This is the translation of the author; the book
itself has been translated by Sarah A. Solovay and John H. Mueller
(Durkheim 1938).

tributed to nature by the author of *Paul et Virginie;*[2] or the reducing of the notion of function to a mere tautology—to say, for instance, that the function of the notched lapel on our coats is to gratify our esthetic feeling would be meaningless, since, here, obviously, the feeling results from the custom, and not the contrary. The custom has a history which explains its existence. It does not, under present circumstances, possess any function.

The preceding may appear to be a very ponderous introduction to an address dedicated by its title to the psychological aspects of chieftainship in a small Brazilian tribe. But I do not believe that the data which I am going to present, if considered only as data on chieftainship among a hitherto little known group, would honestly deserve one hour of attention. Similar facts have been recorded many times, either joined or separately. The particular interest offered by the Nambikuara is that they confront us with one of the simplest conceivable forms of social and political organization. Chiefs and chieftainship exist, among all human groups, under very different forms, but it would be vain to assign a special functional value to each of the modalities down to their smallest details. There is, undoubtedly, a function in chieftainship. This can, however, be reached only through analysis as the underlying principle of the institution. In other words, the differing structure of the digestive organs in man, ox, fish and clam do not point toward different functions of the digestive system. The function is always and everywhere the same, and can be better studied, and more fully understood where it exists under a simple form—for instance, in a mollusc. Similarly, and as Professor Lowie (1920:3) once wrote, if anthropology is to be considered as a scientific study, its subject matter cannot be individual cultures, but culture taken as a whole; the rôle of individual cultures being to offer, according to their own characteristics, special angles from which the basic functions of culture, although universal in application, can be more easily reached.

This will perhaps help us to eliminate preliminary questions which otherwise could have proved very difficult. Anthropologists

[2] In his *Etudes de la Nature* (1784) Bernardin de Saint-Pierre suggested that Nature devised melon ribs to make the fruit easier to divide on the family table, and that it made fleas black so that they could more easily be caught on white skin.

in South America and elsewhere have been eagerly debating
the question of whether these South American tribes—nomadic,
relying mostly on collecting and gathering, with little or no
agriculture, little or no pottery, and, in some cases, with no
dwelling other than crude shelters—should be considered as
truly primitive and as having preserved their exceptionally low
cultural level through tarriance, or whether they did not previously possess a higher type of social and material organization
and have regressed to a pseudo-archaism under unfavorable
circumstances. The Nambikuara are one of those tribes which,
along with the Siriono, on the other side of the Guaporé valley,
the Cayapo, Bororo, Karaja of central Brazil, the so-called *Gé*
of Central and Eastern Brazil, and some others, together form
a kernel of primitiveness surrounded, in the West, by the higher
tribes of the upper Amazon, the Bolivian plain and the Chaco,
and from the Oronoco's to the La Plata's estuaries, by a coastal
strip inhabited mostly by the Arawak, Carib and Tupi-Guarani
linguistic families. An independent linguistic stock divided into
several dialects, the Nambikuara seem to display one of the
more backward cultures in South America. At least, some of
their bands do not build huts and are wholly ignorant of pottery
and, even among the others, these two arts are exceedingly poor.
There is no weaving, except for the narrow arm and leg bands
which are made of cotton; no dress whatsoever, either for the
men or for the women; no sleeping contrivances, such as ham-
mocks or platforms; the natives being used to sleeping on the
bare ground without the protection of blankets, mats or hides.
Gardening exists only during the rainy season and does not
free the Nambikuara from wandering during the seven months
of the dry season, looking for wild roots, fruits and seeds, small
animals such as lizards, snakes, bats, spiders and grasshoppers
and, generally speaking, anything which may prevent them from
starving. As a matter of fact, their geographical surroundings,
which are located in the northwestern part of the state of Mato
Grosso and include the headwaters of the Tapajoz, Rio Roosevelt and Rio Gi-Parana, consist of a desolated savanna with
few vegetal resources and still less game.

Had I approached my subject from a point of view other
than the one outlined above, I could not have avoided a long
discussion in South American cultural history, aimed at clearing

up this apparent primitiveness, on the question as to whether the survival of early conditions of life in South America is genuine or whether we should consider it as a more recent— although undoubtedly pre-columbian—result of culture clashes and processes of acculturation. Whatever the answer may be, it cannot substantially change our problem: whether tarriant or recessive, the Nambikuara society functions, in the present, as one of the simplest forms of human society to be conceived. We shall not seek information from the particular history which kept them in their exceptionally crude organization or brought them back to it. We shall only look at the experiment in social anthropology which they now enact under our very eyes.

This holds especially true in respect to their social and political life. For if we do not know what was the material culture of the Nambikuara forty years ago (they were discovered only in 1907), we do know that their numbers became tremendously reduced after their contact with white civilization. General (then Colonel) Candido Mariano da Silva Rondon, who discovered and studied them, first stated that their number was about 20,000. This was around 1915. I take this figure as greatly exaggerated, but even if reduced by one half, it considerably exceeds the present number which is hardly more than 2,000. Epidemics have taken care of the difference. What does this mean, from the point of view of our study? During the dry season, the Nambikuara live in nomadic bands, each one under the leadership of a chief, who, during the sedentary life of the rainy months, may be either a village chief or a person of position. General Rondon wrote that, at the time he was exploring the country, it was not rare to see bands averaging two or three hundred individuals. Now, sixty or seventy people are seldom met together, the average size of the bands being twenty individuals, women and children included. This demographic collapse cannot possibly have taken place without affecting the structure of the band. But here, too, we do not need to concern ourselves with such questions as the type of political organization in earlier times. It is probably more difficult to understand Nambikuara sociology now than it was thirty years ago. Perhaps, on the contrary, the much reduced Nambikuara band offers, better than in the past, a privileged field for a study in social anthropology. My contention is that, precisely on account of its extreme impoverishment, Nambikuara political structure lays bare some basic functions which may remain hidden in more complex and elaborate systems of government.

Each year, at the end of the rainy season, that is, in April or in early May, the semi-permanent dwellings laid in the vicinity of the gallery-forest where the gardens are cleared and tilled, are abandoned and the population splits into several bands formed on a free choice basis. Each band includes from two to about ten families usually tied by kinship. This may be misleading when a band is met, for one easily gets the impression that it is formed as an extensive family. It does not take long to discover, however, that the kinship tie between two families belonging to separate bands may be as close, and eventually closer, than between two families inside the same band. The Nambikuara have a simple kinship system based on cross-cousin marriage and the subsequent dichotomy between "cross" and "parallel" in every generation. Therefore, all the men in one generation are either "brothers" or "brothers-in-law," and men and women are to one another either siblings (true or classificatory) or spouses (true or classificatory). Similarly, children are, in relation to the adults, either sons and daughters (true or classificatory) or nephews and nieces, which is the same as actual or potential children-in-law (Lévi-Strauss 1943:398–409). As a result, there is no great choice of terms to express kinship, and this explains why kinship inside the band may appear closer than it actually is, and kinship between people belonging to different bands more remote than shown by genealogies. Furthermore, a bilateral cross-cousin marriage system functioning in a relatively small tribe must produce a progressive narrowing, and even a multiplication, of the kinship ties between any two individuals. This is a supplementary reason preventing family relationship from becoming really operative in the constitution of the band. It can be said that, inside the band as well as between the different bands which are the offspring of the same temporary village, everybody is everybody's kin, in pretty much the same fashion.

Why then the splitting-up process? Two different considerations must be brought forth to answer this question. From an economic point of view, the scarcity of wild food resources and the subsequent high square-mileage needed to feed one individual during the nomadic period make the division into small bands almost compulsory. The real question is not why there is a division but rather on what basis it takes place. I have said that this is done by free choice, but this freedom is not arbitrary. There are, in the initial group, several men acknowledged as leaders (who likely acquired this reputation from their behavior during the nomadic life) and who make the relatively stable nuclei around which the different aggregates center. The importance, as well as the permanence of the aggregate through successive years, depend largely upon the ability of each of these leaders to keep his rank and eventually to improve it. Thus, it may be said that leadership does not exist as a result of the band's needs, but, instead, that the band receives its shape, its size, and even its origin, from the potential leader who antedates it.

There is, however, a continuous function of leadership, although not permanently assumed by the same individual. Among the Nambikuara, chieftainship is not hereditary. When a chief grows old, or is taken ill, and when he does not feel able to fulfill his heavy duty any more, he himself designates his successor. "This one—this one will be the chief . . ." he says. It seems likely that this autocratic power to insure one's own succession is more apparent than real. We shall emphasize later on the small amount of authority enjoyed by the chief and, in this case as in many others, the final decision is probably preceded by a careful survey of public opinion, the designated heir being, at the same time, the one with the greater support from the members of the band. The appointment of the new chief is not only limited by the wishes or disapproval of the band; it needs also to correspond to the plans of the individual to be chosen. Not seldom, does the offer of leadership meet with a vehement refusal: "I don't want to be the chief." Then a new choice must be made. As a matter of fact, chieftainship does not seem to be coveted by many people, and the general attitude of the different chiefs I happened to know was less to brag about their importance and authority than to complain of their many duties and heavy responsibilities. What, then, are the privileges of the chief, and what are his obligations?

When, about 1560, the great French moralist of the sixteenth century, Montaigne, met in Rouen with three Brazilian Indians

brought there by some navigator, he asked one of them what
were the privileges of the chief (Montaigne said, "the King") in
his country; and the native, himself a chief, answered: "To
walk ahead on the warpath." Montaigne related this story in a
famous chapter of the *Essays* where he wondered a great deal
about this proud definition;[3] but it was a greater wonder to
me when, almost four centuries later, putting the same question
to my informants I was given the same answer. Civilized countries
are certainly not accustomed to such constancy in the field of
political philosophy! Striking as it may be, this answer is less
significant than the name by which the chief is designated in the
Nambikuara language. *Uilikande,* the native word for chief,
seems to mean "the one who unites" or "the one who joins
together." This etymology suggests that the native mind is fully
conscious of this extremely important phenomenon which I have
pointed out from the beginning, namely, that the leader appears
as the cause of the group's willingness to aggregate rather than
as the result of the need for a central authority felt by a group
already constituted.

Personal prestige and the ability to inspire confidence are thus
the foundations of leadership in Nambikuara society. As a matter of fact, both are necessary in the man who will become the
guide of this adventurous experiment: the nomadic life of the
dry season. For six or seven months, the chief will be entirely
responsible for the management of his band. It is he who orders the start of the wandering period, selects the routes, chooses
the stopping points and the duration of the stay at each of them,
whether a few days or several weeks. He also orders and organizes the hunting, fishing, collecting and gathering expeditions,
and determines the conduct of the band in relation to neighboring groups. When the band's chief is, at the same time, a village
chief (taking the word village with the restricted meaning of
semi-permanent dwelling for the rainy season), his duties do
not stop there. He will determine the moment when, and the
place where, the group will settle; he will also direct the gardening and decide what plants are to be cultivated; and, generally

[3] Montaigne, Michel de, "Des Cannibales," *Essais,* I, xxxi (end of the
chapter). This is the translation of the author; the book itself has been
translated by Donald M. Frame (Montaigne 1958:159).

speaking, he will organize the occupations according to the seasons' needs and possibilities.

These rather versatile duties, it should be pointed out from the start, are not facilitated by any fixed power or recognized authority. Consent is at the origin of leadership, and consent, too, furnishes the only measure of its legitimacy. Disorderly conduct (according to the native standards) and unwillingness to work on the part of one or two discontented individuals may seriously jeopardize the chief's program and the welfare of his small group. In this eventuality, however, the chief has no coercitive power at his disposal. The eviction of the bad people can take place only in so far as the chief is able to make public feeling coincide with his own opinion. Thus, he must continuously display a skill belonging more to the politician trying to keep hold of his fluctuating majority than to an over-powering ruler. Furthermore, he does not only need to keep his group together. Although the band lives practically alone and by itself during the nomadic period, the existence of the other bands is not forgotten. It is not enough to do well; the chief must try— and his people count on him for that—to do better than the others.

No social structure is weaker and more fragile than the Nambikuara band. If the chief's authority appears too exacting, if he keeps too many women for himself (I shall later analyze the special features of the chief's polygamy), or if he does not satisfactorily solve the food problem in times of scarcity, discontent will very likely appear. Then, individuals, or families, will separate from the group and join another band believed to be better managed. For instance, this band may get better fare from the discovery of new hunting or gathering emplacements; or it may have become richer in ornaments or implements, through trade with neighboring groups, or more powerful as a result of a successful war expedition. The day will come when the chief finds himself heading a group too small to face the problems of daily life, and to protect his women from the covetousness of other bands. In such cases, he will have no alternative but to give up his command and to rally, together with his last followers, a happier faction. Therefore, Nambikuara social structure appears continuously on the move. The bands take shape, then disorganize, they increase and they vanish. Within a few months, sometimes, their composition, number and distribution cannot be recognized. Political intrigues within the same band and conflicts between bands impose their rhythm upon these fluctuations, and the ascent or decline of individuals and groups follow each other in a rather surprising manner.

How will the chief be able to overcome these difficulties? The first instrumental force of his power lies in his generosity. Generosity—an all important feature of chieftainship among most primitive peoples, especially in America—plays an outstanding part even on those crude cultural levels where worldly goods are limited to the most primitive weapons and tools, coarse ornaments made of feathers, shells and bones, and raw materials, such as lumps of rosin and wax, hanks of fiber and splinters of bamboo for arrow-making. There cannot be great economic distinctions between families each of which can pack all of its belongings in the baskets carried along by the women during the long travels of the dry season. But, although the chief does not seem to fare better, in this respect, than the others, he must always have at hand surpluses of food, tools, weapons, ornaments which, while being small indeed, acquire great value because of the scarcity which is the prevalent condition. When an individual, a family or the band itself needs or covets something, the chief is called upon to secure the desired article. Generosity is the quality, much speculated on, which is expected of a new chief. Generosity is the string constantly struck which makes the general consent to one's leadership sound clear or out of tune. There is little doubt that, in this respect, the chief's ability to give is exploited to the utmost. Band chiefs used to be my best informants, and, well aware of their difficult position, I liked to reward them liberally; but I seldom saw one of my many gifts remain in their hands for more than a few days. Each time I took leave of a band, after a few weeks or a few months, its members had time to become the happy hoarders of axes, knives, beads, and so on. As a rule, however, the chief was exactly as poor as at my first arrival. Everything he had received from me (and this was considerably more than the average) had already been squeezed out of him. This collective greediness not seldom drives the chief to an almost desperate position; then the refusal to give plays about the same part, in this primitive democracy, as the threat to resign followed by a vote of confidence in a modern parliament. When a chief reaches the point where he must say: "To give away is over! To be generous is over! Let another be generous in my place!", he must, indeed, be sure of his power and prestige, for his rule is undergoing its severest crisis.

Ingenuity is but the intellectual form of generosity. A great deal of skill and initiative are the prerequisites of a good leader. It is he who makes the arrow-poison, although the preparation of *curare* among the Nambikuara is a purely profane activity surrounded by no ceremonial taboos or magic prescriptions. It is he, also, who makes the rubber ball used in the head-ball games which are played occasionally. The chief must be a good singer and dancer, a merrymaker always ready to cheer up the band and to brighten the dullness of daily life. This could easily lead to shamanism; and, in some cases, I have met with chiefs who were at the same time healers and trance addicts. Mystical life, however, is kept in the background among the Nambikuara, and, wherever they exist, magical functions are only secondary attributes of the leader. More often chieftainship and sorcery are divided between two different individuals. In this respect, there is a strong difference between the Nambikuara and their northwestern neighbors the Tupi-Kawahib among whom the chief is, first of all, a shaman, usually a psychotic addicted to dreams, visions, trances and impersonations.

But although they are oriented in a more positive direction, the Nambikuara chief's skill and ingenuity are none the less amazing. He must have a perfect knowledge of the territories haunted by his and other groups, be familiar with the hunting grounds, the location of fruit-bearing trees and the time of their ripening, have some idea of the itineraries followed by other bands, whether hostile or friendly. Therefore, he must travel more, and more quickly, than his people, have a good memory, and sometimes gamble his prestige on hazardous contacts with foreign and dangerous people. He is constantly engaged in some task of reconnoitering and exploring, and seems to flutter around his band rather than lead it.

Except for one or two men without actual power, but eager to cooperate and to receive occasional rewards, the passivity of the band makes a strong contrast with its dynamic leader. It seems as if the band, having relinquished certain advantages to the chief, were in exchange relying entirely upon him for its interests and safety. I received a particularly striking demonstration of this under rather strange circumstances. After several weeks' discussion, I had obtained from a chief the favor of taking me, together with a few companions and some animals loaded with presents, to the semi-permanent dwellings of his band which were uninhabited at that time. This was a chance for me to penetrate more deeply into the unexplored Nambikuara territory and to meet groups too shy to venture forth on the outer fringe. The native band and my own group set out together on a journey supposed to be short; but, because of the animals I had taken, the chief had decided that the usual route through a dense forest could not be used. He led us through the open country, lost his way several times, and we did not reach our destination on the scheduled day. Supplies were exhausted and no game was in sight. The not unfamiliar prospect of a foodless day fell gloomily upon the natives. But, this time, it was the chief's responsibility. The whole project was his own, as well as the attempt to find an easier route. So, instead of trying to discover food, the hungry natives simply lay down in the shadow of the brush and waited for their leader to take them out of this most unpleasant situation. He did not wait or discuss; but, taking the incident as a matter of course, he simply left the camp accompanied by one of his wives. At the camp, the day was spent sleeping, gossiping and complaining. There was no lunch or dinner. But, late at dusk, the chief and his wife reappeared, both heavily laden with baskets filled to the brim. They had hunted grasshoppers the entire day, and, although the expression "to eat grasshoppers" has approximately the same meaning in Nambikuara as the French *manger de la vache enragée*,[4] this food was enthusiastically received, shared and consumed, amidst restored good humor. The following morning, everybody armed himself or herself with a leafless twig and went grasshopper-hunting.

I have several times referred to the chief's wives. Polygamy, which is practically the chief's privilege, brings him a moral and sentimental reward for his heavy duties together with the practical means of fulfilling them. In the Nambikuara band, apart

[4] Closest English equivalent: "to have a rough time of it, to go through the mill."

from rare exceptions, only the chief and the sorcerer (when these functions are divided between two individuals) may have several wives. The chief's polygamy, however, presents special features. It does not constitute a plural marriage but rather a monogamous marriage to which relations of a different nature are added. I have already mentioned the fact that cross-cousin marriage is the usual pattern among the Nambikuara. Another type of marriage also exists, between a man and a woman belonging to the generation following his own, either a wife's "daughter" (true or classificatory) or a sister's niece. Both forms are not uncommon in South America and, together or separately, they have been recorded among many tribes. Now, what do we find in the chief's case? There is first a monogamous marriage of the cross-cousin type, that is, where the wife belongs to the same generation as her husband. This first wife plays the same part as the monogamous wife in ordinary marriages. She follows the sexual pattern of the division of labor, taking care of the children, doing the cooking, and collecting and gathering wild food. To this marriage are added one or several unions, which, technically, are true marriages, but of a different type. Usually, the secondary wives belong to a younger generation. The first wife calls them daughters or nieces. Besides, they do not follow the sexual pattern of the division of labor, but share indifferently in men's or women's activities. At the camp, they disdain domestic tasks and remain idle, either playing with the children to whose generation they belong or flirting with their husband, while the first wife keeps busy with the food and the fire. On the contrary, when the chief leaves on an exploration, a hunt, or some other manly task, they will accompany him and bring him their moral and physical help. These somewhat "tomboy" girls, elected by the chief from among the prettiest and healthiest of the group, are to him rather "girl-friends" than spouses. They live on the basis of an amorous friendship which contrasts strongly with the more conjugal atmosphere of the first marriage.

This system exerts a tremendous influence upon the whole life of the group. The periodical withdrawal by the chief of young women from the regular cycle of marriages creates a permanent unbalance within the group, between the number of boys and girls of marriageable age. Young men are the chief victims of that situation and must either remain bachelors for several years or marry widows or old women discarded by their husbands. Thus, the right to plural marriages represents a concession of considerable importance made by the group to its leader. What does it mean from the latter's point of view? There is little doubt that access to young and pretty girls brings him a much appreciated gratification, not so much from the physical side (as the Nambikuara share in the quiet dispositions of most South American tribes), as from the psychological and sentimental one. But, above all, plural marriage, together with its distinctive features, constitutes the technical means and the functional device placed at the chief's disposal by the group to enable him to carry out his exacting duties. Left by himself, he could hardly do more than the others. His secondary wives, freed by their special status from the customary liabilities of their sex, are his helpers, comforters and assistants. They are, at the same time, leadership's prize and instrument. Can it be said, from the native point of view, that the prize is worth the trouble? To answer that question, I shall now have to consider the problem from a broader angle, namely, what does this elementary social structure, the Nambikuara band, teach us about leadership, its basis and its function?

There is a first point which does not require great elaboration. Nambikuara data contribute, with many others, to destroy the belief originated by early anthropologists, and temporarily revived by psychoanalysis, that the primitive chief could find his prototype in a symbolical father, and that the simpler forms of the State could progressively have grown out of the family. We have found at the root of the crudest forms of chieftainship a decisive step, which introduced something entirely new in respect to biological relations—and this step consists of *consent*. Consent, we have seen, is at the same time the origin and the limit of leadership. Unilateral relations such as right of age, autocratic power, or others, may appear in groups having an already complex structure. In simple forms of social organization, such as the one I have tried to describe, they are inconceivable. Here, on the contrary, the relationship between the chief and the group can be seen as a perpetual process of arbitration where the chief's talents and authority on the one hand and the group's size, cohesion and willingness, on the other, constantly react on and influence each other. If I had the time, and if it were not so far removed from my topic, I would have liked to show what considerable support modern anthropological observations bring, in this respect, to the analysis of the eighteenth century social philosophers. I am well aware of the fact that Rousseau's "social contract," which is the step by which individuals resign their autonomy in favor of the General Will, is entirely different from the nearly contractual relations existing between the chief and his followers. It remains true, however, that Rousseau and his contemporaries displayed a keen sociological feeling when they understood that cultural attitudes and elements such as "contract" and "consent" are not the result of secondary processes, as claimed by their opponents; they are culture's raw materials, and it is impossible to conceive a political or social organization in which they would not already be present. If I understand correctly, the recent analysis, by modern American anthropologists, of the state-growth significance of military societies among the Plains Indians leads to exactly the same conclusion (Lowie 1927:76–107; Llewellyn and Hoebel 1941:99–131).

My second point is but an exemplification of the first: consent is the psychological basis of leadership, but in daily life it expresses itself in, and is measured by, a game of give-and-take played by the chief and his followers, and which brings forth, as a basic attribute of leadership, the notion of reciprocity. The chief has power, but he must be generous. He has duties, but he is entitled to several wives. Between him and the group, there is a perpetual balance of prestations, privileges, services and obligations. The notion of reciprocity, originated by Marcel Mauss, was brilliantly analyzed by Malinowski in his *Crime and Custom in Savage Society*. In respect to leadership, he says: "The claims of chief over commoners, husband over wife, parent over child and vice versa are not exercised arbitrarily and one-sidedly, but according to definite rules, and arranged into well-balanced chains of reciprocal services" (Malinowski 1940:46). This statement needs somewhat to be completed. Malinowski is right when he points out that the chief-commoners' relationship, as every relationship in primitive society, is based on reciprocity. In the first case, however, the reciprocity is not of the same type as in the others. In any human society, whether primitive or civilized, two different cycles of reciprocity are constantly at work: first,

the chain of individual prestations linking the isolated members
of the group; and, next, a relation of reciprocity binding the
group considered as group (not as a collection of individuals)
and its ruler. In the case we have studied, this is well illustrated
by the rules of marriage. Taken in its broadest sense, the incest
prohibition means that everybody in the group is obliged to deliver his sister or daughter to an individual; and, conversely, is
entitled to receive his wife from the latter (whether from the
same man, as in exchange-marriage, or from a different one).
Thus, a continuous chain of reciprocal prestations is directly or
indirectly set up between all the collective or individual members
of the group.[5] This may be called qualitative reciprocity; but incest prohibition also provides the basis for a quantitative reciprocity. We may consider it as a "freezing" measure, which, while
it forbids the appropriation of women who are at one's natural
disposal, prepares the formulation of marriage rules allowing
every man to get a wife. Therefore, a close relationship exists in
a given society between the forbidden degrees and the extent to
which polygamy is allowed. How does the preceding apply to the
Nambikuara? If they had cross-cousin marriage associated exclusively with monogamy, there would be a perfectly simple system of reciprocity (from the individual's point of view) both
qualitative and quantitative. This theoretical formula is, however,
upset by the chief's privilege to polygamy. The withholding of
the simpler rule, in favor of the chief, creates for each individual
an element of insecurity which would otherwise not exist. Let us
state this in other terms: the granting of polygamous privilege to
the chief means that the group has exchanged *individual elements of security* resulting from the monogamous rule for *collective security* provided by leadership. Each man receives a wife
from another man, but the chief receives several wives from the
group. In exchange, he offers to guarantee against need and danger, not to the individuals whose sisters or daughters he marries;
not to those who will be deprived of a spouse by his polygamous
right; but to the group, taken as a whole. For it is the group,
taken as a whole, which has withheld the common law in his
favor. The preceding considerations may have some bearing upon
the theory of plural marriage; but, most of all, they remind us

[5] See the late F. E. Williams' remarkable analysis (1936:167–69).

that the interpretation of the State, conceived as a security system, recently revived by discussions about a national insurance policy (such as the Beveridge plan and others), is not a modern development. It is a return to the basic nature of social and political organization.

So much for the group's point of view on leadership. What about the chief's own attitude in relation to his function? What is his incentive in assuming duties of which I have given a not too favorable account? We saw that the Nambikuara band leader has a tiresome and exacting role; that he must exert himself without pause to maintain his position. What is more, if he does not constantly improve it, he runs the risk of losing what he has taken months or years to achieve. This explains why many men, as I have already said, shun leadership. But why do others accept and even seek it? It is always difficult to appraise psychological motives; and the task is almost impossible when a culture totally alien to our own is considered. I venture to say, however, that the polygamous privilege, highly valued as it may be from the point of view of sexual gratification, sentimental appeal and social prestige, would not suffice to determine a leader's vocation. Plural marriage is but a technical prerequisite of chieftainship; its individual value can only be residual. There must be something more; and, going over the moral and psychological features of the Nambikuara chiefs I knew, and trying to hold on to those fugitive and irreplaceable glimpses at their intimate selves (of which no scientific approach may certify the accuracy, but which gain, from a deep feeling of friendship and human communication, some sort of intuitive value), I feel imperiously led to this answer: there are chiefs because there are, in any human group, men who, unlike most of their companions, enjoy prestige for its own sake, feel a strong appeal to responsibility, and to whom the burden of public affairs brings its own reward. These individual differences are certainly emphasized and "played up" by the different cultures, and to unequal degrees. But their clear-cut existence in a society as little competitive as the Nambikuara strongly suggests to my mind that their origin itself is not cultural. They are rather part of those psychological raw materials out of which any given culture is made. Men are not all alike; and, in primitive societies, believed by early anthropologists to be overwhelmed by the crushing power of custom, these individual differences are as keenly perceived and worked out as in our so-called "individualistic" civilization.

It is remarkable how far the practical experience of colonial administrators has outgrown, in relation to the previous considerations, anthropologists' theoretical studies. During the past twenty years, Lowie's (1920:358) pessimistic appraisal of anthropological work in the field of political institutions has certainly not lost its value. We have much to learn from the scientifically untrained who deal with native institutions. I shall not here record Lyautey's testimony without reservation: "In every society, there is a leading class born for leadership and without which nothing can be accomplished."[6] What may be true for the simpler structures cannot be considered equally valid when considering the complex ones, where the function of leadership does not manifest itself any more in a "pure" state. But let us listen to Eboué who passed away a few months ago. Himself a full-blooded negro, he wrote the following when he was Governor-General of French Equatorial Africa in special relation to those nomadic tribes which, as he put it, "live under a regime of organized anarchy." I quote: "Who is to be chief? I shall not answer, as was the custom in Athens, 'the best.' There is no best chief, there is just a chief"; and further; "the chief is not interchangeable . . . the chief pre-exists" (Eboué 1942). This is precisely what was suggested to us from the start of our analysis of Nambikuara society.

In conclusion, I submit that, when developing the study of political institutions, anthropologists will have to pay more and more attention to the idea of "natural leadership." I am well aware that this expression is almost contradictory. There is no possible form of leadership which does not receive its shape and specification inside of a given cultural context. But this expression can be taken as a borderline case, or as a limit—as say the mathematicians. While the limit can never be reached, simple social structures give us, in the order of their simplicity, an even closer approximation of it. In such studies, we may accordingly foresee a privileged field for close cooperative work between anthropology and individual psychology.

[6] Quoted in Governor-General Félix Eboué's memorandum (1942).

4 SOME ASPECTS OF POLITICAL ORGANIZATION AMONG THE AMERICAN ABORIGINES

Robert H. Lowie

The late R. H. Lowie was Professor of Anthropology at the University of California, Berkeley. He was the author of many books and papers, especially on the Plains Indians; among them are *Primitive Society* (1920), *Primitive Religion* (1924), *The Origin of the State* (1927), *An Introduction to Cultural Anthropology* (1934), *The History of Ethnological Theory* (1937), *Social Organization* (1948), *Indians of the Plains* (1954) and *Robert H. Lowie, Ethnologist: A Personal Record* (1959); *Selected Papers in Anthropology* was edited by Cora DuBois in 1960.

IN A GROSS description of continental areas the American aborigines figure as separatistic and democratic, contrasting in the former respect with the African Negro, in the latter with both African and Polynesian. The illuminating studies on African politics edited by Drs. Fortes and Evans-Pritchard have demonstrated decisively what readers of P. A. Talbot or Henri Labouret had long known, to wit, that the traditional picture of Negro government is over-simplified. To be sure, there have been many powerful monarchies in African history, but east of the Niger, in the Upper Volta region, and in the Anglo-Egyptian Sudan not a few tribes resist integration as much as any people in the world. In 1931 the 69,484 Lobi on French soil in the Upper Volta country were spread over 1,252 mutually independent sham villages (*prétendus villages*); a single one had over 600 residents, while 44 of these hamlets numbered fewer than 100, so that M. Labouret properly speaks of a *particularisme accusé*. Within no unit were there any chiefs, and assemblies convened to adjudicate

FROM the *Journal of the Royal Anthropological Institute* 78, Nos. 1–2 (1948), 11–24, The Huxley Memorial Lecture for 1948, by permission of Mrs. Luella Cole Lowie and of the Council of the Royal Anthropological Institute.

particular issues had no means to execute their decisions. In short, the gamut of possible variations is realized in Negro Africa: we find there vast kingdoms on the pattern of Uganda and Benin, but also minute, headless, "anarchic" groups (Fortes and Evans-Pritchard 1940; Labouret 1931:51, 56, 215, 386).

In the present essay I shall examine the corresponding phenomena in aboriginal America. In a discussion of this sort it is convenient, if not inevitable, to use such terms as "the State," "law," "government," "political," "sovereignty." Conforming to the views of Max Weber, Professor Radcliffe-Brown and Professor Thurnwald as I understand them, I take these words to imply the control of physical force so far as a given society recognizes it as legitimate. Thus, the King of Uganda could rightfully order the execution of a subject, no matter how arbitrary the decree might seem from our point of view; and in West Africa the Mumbo Jumbo organization properly flogged malefactors. On the other hand, similar acts by the Ku Klux Klan are in usurpation of functions monopolized by the State in Western civilization.

However, a genetic view of political structure must reckon with the fact that primeval anarchy could not suddenly blossom forth into a modern State claiming absolute dominance within its territorial limits. It is, indeed, a documented fact that the states of the most advanced modern peoples did not develop contemporary pretensions until relatively recent times, yet their immediate antecedents did have a political organization, in other words, laws and government. A simple society may be differentiated so as to foreshadow government, yet the coercive element may be lacking. The Yurok of north-western California and the Ifugao of Luzon have no chiefs or judges whatsoever, yet a dispute in their midst is settled by unofficial go-betweens approved by public opinion, who offer their services, though without an iota of authority. A logical dichotomy of societies on the rigid definition of Statehood indicated above would rule out such phenomena as quite irrelevant to a study of government, but the common sense of comparative jurists regards them as highly significant. In the following inquiry, then, I shall indeed retain the exercise of force as the criterion of a full-fledged political organization, but I shall also consider what seem evolutionary stages toward that consummation.

The questions I ask concerning American Indians may be

phrased as follows: Within what territorial limits does authority create some measure of solidarity? And what is the nature of the authority encountered? Specifically, where, in America, was a state of modern type realized? What trends can be discerned towards its evolution?

Separatism and Integration

Notwithstanding my initial qualifications, African systems on the whole do differ noticeably from those of the New World. According to Roscoe, the Baganda once numbered three million; by 1911 civil wars and the sleeping sickness had sadly reduced them, but not below the million mark. In 1668 Dapper credited Benin with a regular army of 20,000, which at a pinch could be increased to five times as many; the capital was five or six Dutch miles in circumference and had thirty main streets. In about 1870 Schweinfurth set the Shilluk at over a million; partly because of wars recent estimates are far more modest, yet they fluctuate between 50,000 and 100,000. Shortly before this explorer's visit a million Mangbettu had been under the sway of a single ruler. More recently the king of Ashanti had a quarter of a million subjects (Roscoe 1911:6; Talbot 1926:162 f; Schweinfurth 1873: I 15, II 35).

Except in the few higher civilizations of Mexico, Yucatan, Colombia and Peru, there is nothing to match even the least of these figures, apparent parallels proving deceptive. To be sure, aboriginal Chile is said to have been inhabited by from half a million to a million and a half Araucanians, but "there was no peacetime overall chief, no centralization of authority." There were, indeed, greater and lesser territorial units, but the subordination of the smaller "must have been close to purely nominal." Only during the nineteenth century "the earlier atomistic peacetime political structure assumed somewhat greater unity, cohesion and hierarchization." To take a humbler figure, the 55,000 Navaho now rank as the largest native tribe in the United States. But, in the first place, theirs has been a mushroom growth: in 1868 they did not exceed 15,000—possibly not 9,000. Secondly, it is not clear that even this number were ever under a single government (Cooper 1946:694, 724; Kluckhohn and Leighton 1946:73).

As a matter of fact, a tendency to separatism was general. So advanced a people as the Hopi—some 3,000 in all—live in eleven villages, mislabelled "towns" by grandiloquent ethnographers. Yet even this paltry population neither has nor has had a common head: "between pueblo and pueblo there is an attitude of jealousy, suspicion and subdued hostility" (Titiev 1944:59–68).

Much ado has been made about the Creek Confederacy in the south-eastern United States and the Iroquois League of northern New York State. Unquestionably both prove wider political co-operation than was common in the New World, but their achievements must not be overrated. Authenticated occurrences reduce the cohesion involved in these alliances to a proper scale. It so happened that one of the Creek tribes, the Kasihta, became friendly with the alien Chickasaw. When the latter were at war with the Confederacy in 1793, "the Kasihta refused to take up arms with the other Creeks and their right to act in this independent manner was never questioned." Strictly parallel conduct among the federated Iroquois during the American Revolution was noted by Morgan. Each tribe was permitted to decide upon its course of action: the Oneida and half of the Tuscarora sided with the colonists, the other "leagued" tribes with the English. It was as though in 1914 Bavaria and half of Baden had joined the Allies to fight their fellow-Germans. Apart from this disintegration in a crisis, earlier claims on behalf of the League's influence have been exploded by Fenton's historical researches. The Iroquois did raid far and wide, but it hardly holds true that "their dominion was acknowledged from Ottawa River to the Tennessee and from the Kennebec to Illinois River and Lake Michigan." In any case, at its peak in the seventeenth century the League never embraced over 16,000 or at most 20,000 persons (Swanton 1930:368–76; Hewitt 1907; Fenton 1940; Morgan 1877:2, chap. 5).

Since the one-eyed is king among the blind, the two faltering attempts at consolidation by the Creek and the Iroquois remain noteworthy "climactic" results, as my colleague Professor Kroeber might phrase it. In world perspective, however, they are unimpressive.

If skilful farming populations showed no greater sense of nationalism, little can be expected of the hunters. The Caribou Eskimo lacked permanent political units altogether, each community being in Professor Birket-Smith's judgment "an incoherent conglomerate of families or households, voluntarily connected by a number of generally recognized laws." The largest settlements have a population of about 50, and all of them jointly do not exceed ten times that figure. Earlier reports, to be sure, suggest a recent decline, due largely to famine, but even half a century ago the largest separate tribe of the area was not credited with over 178 souls. To turn toward the southern tip of the New World, the Ona population at its peak is set at between 3,500 and 4,000. Since this embraced 39 wholly independent territorial hordes, the average size of the political unit was about 100 (Birket-Smith 1929:65–75, 260; Gusinde 1946:97).

Extreme as the Eskimo and the Fuegian instances may seem, they are paralleled on varying levels of cultural complexity. The exceptionally favourable food supply of North-west Californians failed to produce solidarity beyond the bounds of kinship and of immediate proximity. Of the seventeen independent Yurok hamlets listed in 1852, the largest had only 165 inhabitants; three others had over 100; five, well under 50.

Up and down the Pacific coast of North America similar conditions prevailed. In north-eastern Washington something less than 1,500 Sanpoil were spread over twenty villages, each of which, except for those conspicuously small, was autonomous. The Quinault, in the south-western part of the same state, probably numbered 800, divided among roughly 20 villages. The Lemhi of Idaho and associated Shoshoneans are set at 1,200 about the beginning of the nineteenth century, and this included more than a single group; Lewis and Clark estimated one group at 100 warriors and 300 women and children; another at 60 warriors. In eastern Brazil the Botocudo stock was split into several distinct tribes, some of them subdivided into bands from 50 to 200. Notwithstanding the existence of tribal chiefs, an authority reports "the constancy of their blood feuds, not only between distinct tribes, but even between bands of the same tribe." The Foot Indians of the Gran Chaco gathered in bands approximating the Botocudo pattern (Kroeber 1925:16; Ray 1932:21–24, 109; Olson 1936:22; Steward 1938:188 f; Nimuendajú 1946a: 97 ff; Métraux 1946a:302; 1946b:536).

No doubt an intermediate order of magnitude occurred. The Cheyenne of the Northern Plains at one time probably numbered not far from 4,000. Of the Ge stock, some members were inconsiderable enough: the recent Canella fluctuated about the 300 mark, but earlier travellers describe the villages of their congeners as rather larger. In 1824, for example, one Apinayé settlement had a population of 1,400; and the more remotely related Sherente display a sense of solidarity beyond the immediate local group. Though a paramount head is wanting, the several village chiefs sometimes jointly depose a grossly deficient colleague and appoint his successor. Characteristically, however, the Sherente have long been at bitter enmity with the Shavante, their closest linguistic and cultural kin (Llewellyn and Hoebel 1941:78; Nimuendajú 1939:7; 1942:9 f).

Similar qualifications apply to the instances from the eastern United States. The League of the Iroquois has already been discussed. The Cherokee and the Choctaw were the two largest south-eastern tribes, being estimated at 22,000 and 15,000 souls, respectively, in 1650. However, once more the *political* unit is incomparably smaller than the linguistic. For the Choctaw, Swanton reasonably suggests some 40 to 50 synchronous communities "constituting small States, each with its chief." An anonymous French writer of *ca.* 1755 does speak of a *grand chef* of the nation, but adds that his authority was negligible. The Cherokee were scattered over at least 80 towns. "These people came under the domain of one tribal chief only in times of great emergency and then most imperfectly." On the whole, it seems likely that the figures set for the Natchez in 1650 and for the Powhatan in 1607—4,500 and 9,000—approach the limits attained within the area by any governmental entity (Gilbert 1943:363; Swanton 1931:90, 95, 243; 1946:114, 123, 161, 175).

At this point it is well to recall the phenomenon luminously illustrated by Durkheim for Australians, by Mauss for the Eskimo, and since demonstrated elsewhere. The seasonal rhythm of life, rooted in economic exigencies, transforms the constitution of a group and, as a corollary, its social life. The consequences we shall consider later. For the present, we merely note that some of the figures quoted would hold only for a relatively brief portion of the year; at other times, the tribe breaks up into minute fragments in order more effectively to exploit the environment (Durkheim 1912; Mauss 1906).

To review the argument, American figures of a population

approximating or exceeding 10,000 rarely, if ever, refer to permanently integrated political units.

How far does this conclusion apply to the four higher civilizations? As for the Aztec, the moot question of whether they totalled three or many more millions need not concern us; we are interested solely in what number belonged to the same state. That the hoary idea of an Aztec empire is untenable, seems certain in the light of modern research. All we find is a belated league of three tribes which remained mutually distrustful: "the Aztecs had no sense of unity," no national spirit. Within the present limits of Mexico City, Tenochtitlan and Tlatelolco long persisted in complete independence of each other. At the time of the Spanish invasion the Texcocans joined the intruders against their former ally, Tenochtitlan. A quarter of a million people, or thereabouts may possibly have had a single government on a strict definition (Vaillant 1941:91, 134, 213f).

Maya ruins are spread from northern Yucatan to Honduras, but they belong to different periods, and it is not easy to estimate the residents of any one state. Possibly in about A.D. 1000, according to legendary history, there was a league of three cities, of which Mayapan gained the ascendancy, establishing a centralized government two or three centuries later. This was followed by disintegration, leaving only petty chieftains for the Spaniards to contend with. In their era the rulers of Mani were "the most powerful in Yucatan." The tribute list for that province demonstrates 13,480 adult males. If we multiply this by six, or even ten, we still get no total population that looks spectacular by an African scale (Tozzer 1941:64; Morley 1915:2–12; Roys 1933:188–95).

The Chibcha numbered possibly a million, but they too, were divided up among several distinct states, of which Zipa, the largest, is credited with 300,000 souls. The untrustworthiness of early estimates is indicated by a fantastic reference to armies of 50,000 whereas no more than 600 Zipa braves attacked the Spanish troops (Kroeber 1946:887–909).

In short, the solitary convincing instance of grandiose expansion in the Western Hemisphere is that of the Incas of Cuzco, Peru. Their realm did extend from Ecuador to northern Chile, embracing possibly 6,000,000 subjects. However, we must recollect that aggrandizement was a very late pre-Columbian achieve-

ment. "In early times neither the *Inca* nor any of their neighbours thought of organizing their conquests as a permanent
domain." Until the reign of Pachakuti (*ca.* A.D. 1438) "towns
very near to Cuzco preserved complete freedom of action and
raided one another's territory whenever there seemed to be
a good opportunity for plunder" (Rowe 1946:184 ff, 201–9,
257 ff).

With a unique exception, then, the American Indians must be
regarded as eminently separatistic.

However, there was certainly no sudden mutation from an
Ona-like to an Inca-like condition. The Creek and the Iroquois
schemes indicate a stage of solidarity, however imperfect, on a
larger than normal scale. Still more illuminating are phenomena
within the historic period. Whereas the two well-known leagues
united mainly communities of like or closely related speech,
Pontiac (1763) and Tecumseh (died 1813) brought together
wholly unconnected tribes. The Ottawa chief rallied not merely
his own people and their Algonkian congeners, but also the
Seneca and the Wyandot of Iroquoian stock and the Siouan Winnebago. The Shawnee leader arrayed Algonkians, Wyandot, and
even Creek Indians against the United States. Though both uprisings proved abortive, though they culminated in negation of
British and American overlordship rather than in the creation of
a close-knit aboriginal state, they do prove that under strong
emotional stimulus exceptional natives could and did visualize
co-operation of major scope. Individuals of comparable organizing skill, however diverse their motivation, must be credited with
the nascent forms of Andean imperialism (Mooney 1896:668 f,
681–91).

Coercive Authority

I now turn to my second theme—the manifestation or adumbra-
tion of coercive authority in aboriginal America. As in Africa,
so here too, the range of observable phenomena is very great. At
one extreme we find the "anarchic" Eskimo, north-west Californians, and Fuegians; at the other, the Incas of Peru. But in
the New World, the latter must be regarded as atypical, and an
intermediate condition represents the norm. By this I mean a
condition with differentiation of one or more individuals as headmen, even though their actual power is circumscribed or even

negligible. For convenience of exposition I shall call these officials "titular chiefs" in contrast to the "strong chiefs" possessing
unquestioned authority. After discussing the functions of these
two types of civil heads, I shall examine the factors that may
have strengthened the titular chief's hands in the American
milieu; and I shall likewise consider what agencies aside from
chiefs of either category have assumed State functions.

Titular Chiefs Titular chiefs vary considerably in actual
status. The Chipewyan individuals who bear the title exercise so
little influence apart from the accident of personality that one
might perhaps just as well put this north Canadian tribe into the
chiefless category with the Eskimo and the Fuegians. Elsewhere
the office is not only honorific, but also fraught with definite public functions. In order to overcome semantic difficulties it will be
best to emphasize what the titular chief is *not,* before trying to
indicate his positive attributes. That he cannot, in many American societies, correspond to an African chief is apparent whenever a single band or tribe has more than one title-bearer. Three
hundred Canella are headed by three "chiefs"; another Ge people, the Pau d'Arco Kayapo, generally had two; the related
Gorotire band, five (in 1940). Until 1880 the Omaha had two
principal chiefs, with a varying number of lesser ones; this
oligarchy was then superseded by a septet of uniform rank.
Among the Arapaho there were four chiefs, and the Cheyenne
with a population never greatly exceeding 4,000 had forty-four!
(Birket-Smith 1930:66; Dorsey 1884:357; Nimuendajú 1943;
Llewellyn and Hoebel 1941:67 ff.) A series of examples from
diverse culture areas will elucidate what American chiefs typically
lacked.

The Ojibwa (round Lake Superior) had a council "with vague
and limited powers." It selected a chief "whose power was even
vaguer than that of the council," and who was "less able to work
his will against an existing custom." Tanner, who lived in this
region from 1789 until 1822, mentions "the unstable power and
influence of the chiefs." In an assembly of 1,400 Assiniboine,
Cree and Ojibwa, he remarks, "not one would acknowledge any
authority superior to his own will." A chief was, indeed, entitled
to some deference, "but this obedience . . . continues no longer
than the will of the chief corresponds entirely with the inclination
of those he leads." About the same time the trader Tabeau

notes that among the Teton Dakota "all authority is as naught
before the opposition of a single individual," and for the related
Assiniboine, Denig—himself the husband of a woman of that
tribe—offers an eyewitness's priceless corroboratory evidence. At
a council attended by him the "leading chief" advocated peace
with the Crow; a tribesman of lesser dignity vigorously and successfully opposed the idea, carrying the assembly with him. The
historian Parkman, on the basis of personal experience in 1846,
declares that very few Oglala Dakota "chiefs could venture without instant jeopardy of their lives to strike or lay hands upon
the meanest of their people" and correctly notes the paradox
that the "soldiers," *i.e.,* police, "have full license to make use of
these and similar acts of coercion." This institution will be discussed later. Among the Shoshoneans of Nevada, "any family
was at liberty to pursue an independent course at any time"; in
Arizona the head of the Maricopa had functions "more admonitory than coercive"; and among the Yuma the tribal leader,
though appealed to in a dispute, was "more significant as an
embodiment of spiritual power than as a lawgiver or executive."
Equivalent testimony comes from Oregon and Washington (Jones
1906:137; Tanner 1940:151; Tabeau 1939:105 f; Denig 1930:
430–56; Parkman 1856:291; Spier 1930:35; 1933:158; Ray
1932:111; Steward 1947:246–60; Goodwin 1942:178 f; Forde
1931:134 f).

Superfically the stratified societies of coastal British Columbia
are different, but only superficially in the questions at issue.
What they emphasize is social eminence, not political power. A
Haisla chief "gives orders only in matters directly concerned with
feasts and potlatches,"—not in cases of quarrels, theft, or murder;
the Tsimshian equivalent was responsible for his followers' safety
in battle and indemnified the mourners if their kindred had been
killed. How different from an African potentate who owns his
subjects' bodies and collects all damages for injuries sustained by
them (Sapir 1915; Olson 1940:182; Boas 1916:429 ff, 499).

South America yields corresponding testimony. In British
Guiana a Barama headman has limited authority. Each of the
three Canella dignitaries works like everyone else; none of them
wears a badge of higher status, or interferes in private affairs,
or issues commands, or imposes penalties. Among the related
Apinayé, the headman does initiate measures against a sorcerer,

but he cannot order an execution without popular assent. To take two more Brazilian examples, Karaya villagers simply desert a chief whose actions they resent; and though a Nambikuara leader enjoys a good deal of influence, he "has no coercitive power at his disposal." In short, the typical American chief may enjoy social standing, but he lacks sovereignty (Gillin 1936:98, 140; Nimuendajú 1939:19f, 131f; 1946b:93, 159–62, 239f; Krause 1911:321; Lévi-Strauss 1944:23).[1]

What, then, are the titular chief's positive attributes and functions? The outstanding one forthwith explains the deficiency I have harped on: he refrains from attempting physical force, because many societies conceive him as primarily a peacemaker. It would be a contradiction in terms for him to mete out punishment when his business is to smooth ruffled tempers, to persuade the recalcitrant, coax and even bribe the justly aggrieved into forgoing vengeance. He is, indeed, a go-between of the Yurok or Ifugao order, but with the essential difference of being the official, recognized, permanent moderator instead of a self-appointed one *ad hoc*. In order to compass his end—maintenance of communal harmony—he might stoop to eating humble-pie and to personal sacrifices. A Sanpoil chief presents each litigant with a blanket; his Cree colleague is expected to give up thoughts of revenge on his own behalf, such as other men freely indulge. A Winnebago went still further: "If necessary, the chief would mortify himself, and with skewers inserted in his back have himself led through the village to the home of the nearest kinspeople of the murdered person." By thus arousing compassion he hoped to avert a feud (Mandelbaum 1940:222; Radin 1923:209).

No wonder that an appeaser *ex officio* was not associated with warfare, was often—in his official capacity—deliberately divorced from violence and discipline. An Iroquois sachem's duties, Morgan reports, "were confined to the affairs of peace. He could not go out to war as a sachem." His position was sharply separated from the military leader's, being hereditary in the clan, whereas a successful captain gained a "chiefly" title of another category by personal bravery. This polarity was widespread. In a Fox Indian (Wisconsin) council, the Quiet and the War Chief were complementary figures, as are the Pueblo Town and War

[1] See Chapter 3 of this reader for Lévi-Strauss.

Chiefs—the former being prescriptively a man of peace who must not even go hunting, the latter a policeman who threatens punishment. The Omaha neither let a chief head a raid nor even allowed him to serve as a subordinate officer of one. Again, "a man who has often been on the warpath," say the Pawnee, "becomes imbued with the desire to take scalps and capture ponies and is no longer fit to be chief." A Winnebago chief always belongs to one clan, a policeman to another (Morgan 1877: pt. II, chaps. II, IV, V; Jones 1939:82; Titiev 1944:59–68; Parsons 1939:154 f; Dorsey 1884:217; Dorsey and Murie 1940: 112 f).

This dichotomy prevails even where a fusion of civil and military pre-eminence seems at first blush easily realized. In several South American tribes the "chief" did lead war parties, but whereas he became a virtual autocrat on a raid he relapsed into his usual impotence on his return. On this point early sources on the Kariri and the Tapuya (eastern Brazil) agree with recent ones on the Taulipang (south of the Roroima) and the Jivaro (Ecuador). One North American phenomenon is instructive in this context. The Iroquois League found it desirable to create two generals "to direct the movements of the united bands," but these officials never aspired to a dictatorship. To quote Morgan, "the essential character of the government was not changed. . . . Among the Iroquois this office never became influential" (Koch-Grünberg 1923:94; Nantes 1706:103; Pompeu Sobrinho 1934:18; Karsten 1923:7 f; Morgan 1877: pt. II, chap. V).

In short, the conceptions of civil and of military leadership were distinct in America. There was sporadic tyranny even in the democratic Northern Plains societies, but it sprang from individual bullying, usually supported by a powerful body of kin or from putative supernatural sanction, not from the *coup d'état* of a captain returning drunk with success and filled with the ambition of a despot.

Besides being a skilful peacemaker, the ideal chief was a paragon of munificence. This may hold more often in North than in South America, but instances are not wanting in the south. Thus, a Nambikuara headman constantly shares with his tribesmen whatever surplus of goods he may have acquired: "Generosity is the quality . . . which is expected of a new chief." In the north, this demand is constant. In Alaska, where the Eskimo were affected by the ideology of their Indian neighbours, the title of "chief" automatically devolved on that Nunivak who entertained most lavishly at village feasts. A chief of the Tanaina Athabaskans (about Cook Inlet) feeds and clothes the destitute, provides for the households of men away on hunting trips, adopts orphans, and even pays for shamanistic services that are beyond a poorer tribesman's means. The coastal tribes of British Columbia, not withstanding their emphasis on hereditary status, insisted that a headman should validate his claims by frequent distribution of property. In the Plains area chieftainship and niggardliness were mutually exclusive. To quote Wissler, "no Blackfoot can aspire to be looked upon as a headman unless he is able to entertain well, often invite others to his board, and make a practice of relieving the wants of his less fortunate band members." The Cheyenne or the Crow had identical standards of behaviour (Lévi-Strauss 1944:24; Lantis 1946: 248; Osgood 1937:132; Sapir 1915; Wissler 1911:23; Llewellyn and Hoebel 1941:79).[2]

A third attribute of civil leadership is the gift of oratory, normally to be exercised on behalf of tribal harmony and the good old traditional ways. Speaking of the Sherente, Nimuendajú reports: "On many evenings . . . I saw the chief assemble the village. Stepping in front of the semi-circle . . . , he would impressively and vividly harangue the crowd for possibly an hour. Usually he began circumstantially explaining the half-forgotten ceremonial of some festival. . . . There followed a lengthy admonition . . . to preserve ancient usage. In conclusion, he would urge all to live in peace and harmony. . . ." The extinct Tupinambá of coastal Brazil regarded a species of falcon as the king of his zoological class: "ils se fondaient sur le fait que cet oiseau se levait de bon matin et haranguait les autres oiseaux, tout comme le chef de la hutte le faisait chaque jour, à l'aube, dans les villages tupinamba." In the Chaco the contemporary Pilaga merely postpone oratory until nightfall: "Ce prurit d'éloquence est commun à tous les caciques et constitue . . . un des principaux attributs de leur dignité. . . . Le thème habituel de ces harangues est la paix, l'harmonie et l'honnêteté,

[2] See Chapter 3 of this reader for Lévi-Strauss.

vertus recommandées à tous les gens de la tribu." In characteristic fashion a Chiriguano explained to Nordenskiöld the existence
of a female head of the tribe: her father had taught her to
speak in public. Thousands of miles to the north, in the Shoshone
vernacular a headman figures as "the talker," which "designates
his most important function." Maricopa and Apache chiefs, too,
were matutinal lecturers; and among the Havasupai (Arizona)
Spier says: "it might be said not that a chief is one who talks,
but that one who talks is a chief" (Métraux 1928:179; 1937:
390; Nordenskiöld 1912:229; Steward 1938:247; Spier 1928:
237 f; 1933:158; Goodwin 1942:165 f, 178).

In my opinion, then, the most typical American chief is not
a lawgiver, executive, or judge, but a pacifier, a benefactor of
the poor, and a prolix Polonius.

Strong Chiefs But not all chiefs were only titular. A relatively
small, but significant number of societies had genuine rulers. It
is best to begin with an unexceptionable example, the Inca state,
the outstanding American sample of Drs. Fortes and Evans-
Pritchard's category A—political systems with a well developed
governmental apparatus.

The Inca emperor, ruling by divine right, undoubtedly did
control means of coercion. Through an elaborate "bureaucracy"
he exacted tribute from his subjects and directed their labours,
even their private lives. He did not scruple to transfer masses
of the population from one province to another in the interests
of the dynasty. What elsewhere in the New World were private
wrongs here became offences against the Crown and called for
summary official penalties.

Emblematic of autocracy were the trappings of royalty otherwise conspicuously rare in America. The ruler wore and carried
impressive regalia, travelled in a litter borne by special attendants, kept a large harem, and surrounded his court with an
elaborate etiquette. His corpse was prepared for preservation in
the palace, and his favourite wives together with a suitable
retinue were strangled to accompany their master to the here-
after (Rowe 1946).

Concerning the Aztec chief the authorities yield contradictory
and confusing evidence, but it seems clear that he did not conform to the Inca pattern. He was apparently not closely identified
with the supreme deity; and, notwithstanding fixed succession

within a lineage, he could be deposed. The hereditary *halach-uinic* of the Maya probably wielded greater power, claiming tribute as well as military service and periodically examining subordinate chiefs in order to weed out pretenders. Significantly, both he and the sacred war leader travelled in a litter, a symbol of exalted rank also attached to a Chibcha monarch, who resembled his Peruvian parallel in other respects. He, too, received tribute, kept a seraglio, hedged himself about with ceremonials, and was buried with several wives and slaves. When he expectorated, an attendant caught the spittle in an extended cloth—a form of flunkeyism hardly conceivable among the Crow or Cheyenne (Roys 1933:192 f; Tozzer 1941:165, 222; Kroeber 1946; Vaillant 1941:113 ff).

It may be natural to find a full-blown political system among the materially advanced populations whose very numerical strength requires some central control if there is to be any solidarity. But, interestingly enough, the outlines of such a system appear also in the tiny states of the south-eastern culture area of North America. This anomaly has been recently stressed by Steward. Indeed, the Natchez sovereign came very close to the Inca conception of royalty. He claimed relationship with the solar deity, his kinsmen ranking as "Little Suns"; held power over life and death; travelled in a litter; and in death was followed by wives and servants, his bones being laid to rest in a temple near those of his predecessors. His subjects were obliged to keep at least four paces away from his person and would hail him "with genuflections and reverences." Elements of this complex, such as the litter, characterize the Timucua of Florida and the Chickasaw of Northern Mississippi; and though the monarchical principle is generally weaker in the south-east as a whole than among the Natchez, it reappears in full force in Virginia. "As halfe a God they esteeme him," Captain John Smith reports in writing of the Powhatan chief. This ruler arbitrarily ordered his subjects to be beaten, tortured and killed, and kept a sizeable bodyguard to execute his will. "What he commandeth they dare not disobey in the least thing." He demanded tribute of skins, beads, corn and game; and numerous concubines waited upon him. Here and there undemocratic usages turn up as far north as New England, where they have been plausibly ascribed to south-eastern influences. However that be, the specific resemblances among Peruvians, Natchez, and Powhatan suggest a common origin for so atypical an American polity (Swanton 1911:100–10, 139 ff; 1946:161, 175, 598 ff, 641–54, 728, 730; Flannery 1939:116 f, 122 f; Steward 1947:97). Of course, this does not imply that the social scheme diffused from the Inca Empire itself, a chronologically impossible assumption, but rather that certain elements of a monarchical system crystallized somewhere between Yucatan and Peru and spread in a period considerably antedating the expansion of Inca sovereignty. If I understand Professor Steward correctly, this agrees with his recent interpretation of the facts.

Given the marked libertarian bias of most American aborigines, how can we conceive the growth of absolutism? What could convert the titular chief who cajoled his tribesmen into preserving the social equilibrium into a veritable king?

Evolutionary Germs   In re-examining the chiefless or virtually chiefless tribes we discover here and there that the Indians willingly subordinate themselves to some individual for a particular enterprise. In a rabbit drive the Washo and neighbouring Shoshoneans of the western Basin temporarily followed a leader noted for his skill as a hunter, though "apart from that special occasion his authority was nil (Lowie 1924:196 f, 284 f, 305).

An exceptionally large gathering may favour the similarly spontaneous acceptance of a director. The Yahgan, who normally move about in very small groups, unite up to the number of eighty when a beached whale provides food for the participants at an initiation ceremony. Without an election some mature man well posted in traditional usage emerges as the master of ceremonies and henceforth plans the daily routine. What is more, he appoints a constable, who in turn chooses a number of deputies. These policemen exercise genuine legal authority: they forcibly drag refractory tyros to the initiation lodge, overpower a troublemaker, bind him, and let him lie for half a day without food or drink. The Yahgan, furthermore, have a men's club: the members as a whole bully their wives into fetching fuel and food for the assemblage, and one man has the duty of keeping women from prying (Gusinde 1937:199–208, 653, 779 ff, 798 ff, 805–961, 1319–76).

Informally established offices are not necessarily ephemeral. The Nambikuara illustrate the rise of a relatively stable chieftaincy, as suggestively described by Lévi-Strauss (1944). A man with inborn gifts of leadership forms the nucleus for a group that voluntarily acclaims him, thereby shifting responsibility to his shoulders. He directs the food quest during the difficult dry season, shares his surplus freely, prepares arrow poison for his adherents, and plans their entertainments. In requital, they concede him certain prerogatives, such as plural marriage, but without their approbation he is powerless. Here, then, there emerges a titular chief with genuine influence, though still not a ruler.

By way of contrast there is a short-lived but absolute authority of the war leader as already noted for several South American groups. For North American parallels we have fuller data. A Crow supposedly organized his raid only when prompted by a supernatural patron, whence the leader's ascendancy over all who joined his expedition: theirs were the menial tasks, his the loot to dispose of as he chose, but also the responsibility for failure and losses. The equalitarian attitudes of everyday life recede, supplanted by a transitory overlordship. Omaha captains even appointed policemen who had the right to beat refractory or lagging warriors. Fleeting dictatorship of this limited range is not irrelevant to our problem. About 1820 the Cheyenne conceived themselves as one huge war party, whose leader thus automatically became supreme, supplanting the tribal council of "chiefs." Yet in consonance with native ideology he retained not a vestige of his special authority when his task was done (Dorsey 1884:321; Llewellyn and Hoebel 1941:163).

Undisputed supremacy for a restricted period was also granted during religious festivals. When a Hopi ceremony is in process, Stephen (1936:728) learned, "the chief of it is chief of the village and all the people." Similarly, the priest who directed a Crow Sun Dance was not merely the master of ceremonies, but the temporary ruler of the tribe, superseding the camp chief.

Non-Chiefly Authority Perhaps the most remarkable instances of authority, full-fledged and not altogether ephemeral, turn up in connection with important, economic undertakings which are to be safeguarded in the common interest.

A pertinent phenomenon from northern Brazil seems to have eluded general notice. The Apinayé chief, if properly qualified, succeeds his maternal uncle in the office, by virtue of which he guards the villagers' interests and orders the execution of evil sorcerers. But at the planting season a pair of men representing the moieties begin to act as independent executives. One of them collects the seeds, invokes the Sun to prosper them, and is the first to plant a plot. Both of these officials watch the crops, chant daily songs to promote growth, and *forcibly prevent or punish premature harvesting.* "Woe to any Indian woman who should dare to remove clandestinely even the most trifling product from her own plots before maturity is officially announced!" If the rule is broken, they "attack the houses of the village or the camp, raging and throwing everything about pell-mell, breaking the vessels and flogging with thorny whips any women who have not fled in good season, or gash them with a special weapon. . . ." Even the chief's wife was once severely chastised for transgressing the law. Apart from the religious feature, the phenomenon reminds an Americanist of the Winnebago or Menomini constables who punished overhasty gatherers of wild rice (Nimuendajú 1939:13, 19, 89, 131 f; Radin 1923:226 f; Skinner 1913:26).

The last-mentioned officers from the Woodlands of North America are obvious variants of the familiar Plains Indian "soldiers" mentioned by Parkman. Their activities developed most spectacularly during a communal hunt, upon whose outcome the very life of the natives would depend. In order to ensure a maximum kill, a police force—either coinciding with a military club, or appointed *ad hoc,* or serving by virtue of clan affiliation—issued orders and restrained the disobedient. In most of the tribes they not only confiscated game clandestinely procured, but whipped the offender, destroyed his property, and, in case of resistance, killed him. The very same organization which in a murder case would merely use moral suasion turned into an inexorable State agency during a buffalo drive. However, Hoebel and Provinse have shown that coercive measures extended considerably beyond the hunt: the soldiers also forcibly restrained braves intent on starting war parties that were deemed inopportune by the chief; directed mass migrations; supervised the crowds at a major festival; and might otherwise maintain law and order (Wissler 1911:22–26; 1912:17, 24; 1922:161, 178; Richardson 1940:9 f; Jenness 1938:11, 41; Mandelbaum

1940:203, 225; Kroeber 1908:147 f; Hoebel 1936:443–48; 1940:82; Provinse 1937:347).

Here, then, we find unequivocal authoritarianism. Theoretically, the police acted, at least in a number of tribes, under the direction of the tribal chief or council. The foundation was thus laid for either an autocracy or an oligarchy. Why did this logical end fail to be consummated?

In the first place, let us revert to the seasonal rhythm of the Plains Indians. During a large part of the year the tribe simply did not exist as such; and the families or minor unions of families that jointly sought a living required no special disciplinary organization. The soldiers were thus a concomitant of numerically strong aggregations, hence functioned intermittently rather than continually.

Secondly, the "constitutional" relationship of chief and police was by no means so simple as might appear. It was definitely not that of the head of a modern state toward his army. Denig, whose observations on the impotence of Assiniboine chiefs have been quoted, ascribes to the police "the whole active power of governing the camp or rather of carrying out the decrees and decisions of the councils." He himself witnessed "two killed and many severely thrashed for their misdemeanours." Were the soldiers, then, strictly subordinate to the *council,* as Denig's phraseology implies? Well, according to the same authority, if councillors threatened to grow violent at a meeting, "two soldiers advanced to the middle of the lodge and laid two swords crosswise on the ground, which signal immediately restored order and quiet." There was thus a dispersal of sovereignty: the titular chief had none, the council was in principle a governing board controlling a police squad that carried out their decisions, but *de facto* the theoretically subordinate police acted with considerable independence (Denig 1930:436, 439, 442, 444 f, 448, 455, 530 ff).

The much fuller data on the Cheyenne collected by Messrs. Llewellyn and Hoebel (1941:67–131) corroborate this interpretation. Here a self-perpetuating council of forty-four "chiefs" with safe tenure during a ten-year term of office was headed by five priest-chiefs, one of whom took precedence as the representative of the mythical culture here, Sweet Medicine. This did not make him the equivalent of a Shilluk king, for he "wielded no consequent special political authority" nor was he above the traditional law. Unlike other Plains peoples, the Cheyenne for ritual reasons conceived homicide as a crime. When Little Wolf, the head chief and man of superb record, killed a tribesman, though under mitigating circumstances, he did not escape the penalty, but went into voluntary exile. A lesser chief is known to have been severely flogged by the soldiers for a similar offence and was likewise banished, though not demoted in rank.

To turn to the council as a whole, it is true that they appointed one of the five existing military clubs to oversee a migration or a communal hunt. But, apart from such matters as directing travel, the "chiefs" were little concerned with secular affairs, sometimes waiving the right to a definitive decision and thus leaving a great deal to the discretion of their appointees. Accordingly, the police became the final authority in a large number of issues either beyond the competence of their electors or deliberately turned over to them by the council for settlement. The soldiers thus could, and repeatedly did, inaugurate legal precedents, nor does it appear that these were ever challenged by the "chiefs."

Llewellyn and Hoebel draw attention to an extraordinary illustration of police autonomy. During a march directed by the Fox society, a councillor named Sleeping Rabbit answered a taunt by shooting the interlocutor, a member of the Dog organization. The arrow could not be extricated. The Foxes severely mauled and kicked the criminal; and when the victim's arm grew worse they decreed that Sleeping Rabbit must amputate it, a novel verdict. Public sentiment, crystallized in the four other societies, favoured exiling the culprit, but he avowed his guilt and, in self-infliction of a fine, presented the Foxes with five good horses. This settled the matter.

As our authorities show, this was emphatically not an example of composition. Damages accrued neither to the victim nor to his kin nor to his society, but to the Foxes. *They* were the State in this case, receiving the indemnity as a Bantu ruler might in corresponding circumstances. Of course, so far as we know, the case is unique and might have remained so throughout Cheyenne history; but the mere possibility of its occurrence is significant.

The relations of the Cheyenne council and soldiers were, of course, determined by the general American conception of chieftaincy. If more than temporary sovereignty were to be attained at all, it would thus more naturally centre in the police. Here we encounter a third factor that militated against autocracy or oligarchy. In this culture area the constabulary force was rarely fixed, being as a rule recruited differently for different seasons or even for specific occasions. In a Pawnee village, for example, the chief's adjutant and three of his deputies acted as police, but for a buffalo hunt a priest chose one of four societies as a nonce police (Dorsey and Murie 1940:113). The Cheyenne, we have noted, had five such organizations; it was not likely that four of them would calmly submit to the oligarchical pretensions of one rival body.

It so happens that in this tribe the Dogs did enjoy an unusual advantage over the other clubs: by an accident of history, a century or more ago, the males of one band collectively joined this society, so that in this solitary instance society and band coincided in adult male membership. The chief of the Dogs was thus *ipso facto* head of his band, and the Dog men remained united during the winter when rival clubs were scattered over various local divisions. Here, then, the germ for hegemony occurred, but it never reached fruition.

A further point must be mentioned. Within any one of the military clubs its chief was supreme, issuing orders like a war captain and sometimes ruling his members with an iron hand. Yet the libertarian impulses of these Indians would not brook servility in an absolute sense; in 1863, characteristically, the Dogs *forbade* their chief to attend a treaty council with American commissioners!

In short, though the Plains Indians indubitably developed coercive agencies, the dispersal of authority and the seasonal disintegration of the tribes precluded a permanent State of modern type. Generalizing for the whole of America, there were sundry gropings towards centralization of power, but counteracting trends made them fall short of permanent results. Yet such results were achieved in Peru and in so relatively simple a setting as that of the Powhatan. What were the circumstances involved in these cases? And is it possible to detect similar factors in the normally libertarian societies?

The Religious Factor When Alexander the Great aspired to imperial grandeur, he was not content with the glory of a successful general, but claimed divinity and, as a mark of its acceptance, prostration. This sacred character, we have seen, supposedly belonged to the Inca ruler and to the Natchez Great Sun; the obeisances and genuflections in their presence are the equivalent of Alexander's demand for *proskúnêsis*. With frankly evolutionary aim I shall assemble some data from the simpler American tribes in order to show that religious beliefs were used to attain political influence there; and I suggest that the awe which surrounded the protégé of supernatural powers formed the psychological basis for more complex political developments. It is possible for a titular chief to add to his standing by combining spiritual blessings with civil eminence, or he may enter an alliance with the religious functionary, thus foreshadowing the familiar spectacle of State and Church joined in the support of the established order.

The latter contingency is classically exemplified in Gayton's (1939) study on the Yokuts, a Central Californian stock of some 18,000 souls divided into over fifty autonomous tribelets, probably never exceeding 800 in population. In each of these units an acceptable member of the Eagle lineage served as chief, representing the mythical Eagle who had ruled the world in dim antiquity. Notwithstanding this lofty role, the chief was not an autocrat, but he did hold more than nominal precedence. Provided with food by his tribesmen, enjoying a monopoly of trade in highly prized products, entitled to a share in doctors' fees, he was the wealthiest man in the community. By way of reciprocity, it was his duty to entertain visitors, to help the poor, and to contribute generously to the cost of festivities. He determined movements from and to the village and alone could authorize the death penalty for a public enemy. In general, he adhered to the part of a peace-preserving headman, rarely making a vital decision without previously consulting other venerable men.

Nevertheless, a chief could *de facto* magnify his power with the aid of a favourite shaman. In lieu of taxation the Yokuts expected the persons attending a festival to defray the expenses. If a wealthy villager evaded this obligation, the chief's medicine-man would smite him with illness and impoverish his victim by exorbitant fees for sham treatment. Since the chief's consent was essential for violent measures against the doctor, he could always dismiss complaints on the subterfuge of insufficient evidence. It is important to note that public opinion as a rule sympathized with the chief and the shaman, for the miser who failed to contribute at festivals thereby imposed extra burdens on his fellows.

Given the native faith, an unscrupulous chief could evidently work his will in collusion with a shamanistic accomplice. Yet in the long run, Dr. Gayton explains, such knavish tricks led to a revulsion of feeling. A chief could not safely give rein to his malevolent inclinations. In the face of continuous suspicion his prestige would wane, in extreme instances he might even be supplanted in office by a less objectionable scion of his line. As for his accessory, the attitude towards doctors being ambivalent here, as in much of North America, a persistently malevolent leech was likely to be killed by the enraged family of his victim. In short, the Yokut system involved a considerable strengthening of chiefly influence without, however, approaching anything like despotic rule. Its instructiveness lies largely in demonstrating religion as a prop of the civil head on the relatively low plane of a simple hunting people.

In a not inconsiderable number of South American societies there is a personal union of temporal and spiritual functions. In Colombia, the Kágaba and the Ijca (the latter linguistic relatives of the Chibcha) do not dissociate the concepts of priest and chief. Among the Yaruro (Venezuela) each moiety recognizes a shaman as its head. In the Matto Grosso the Tupi-Kawahib chief is "first of all, a shaman, usually a psychotic addicted to dreams, visions, trances and impersonations." Another Brazilian group, the Botocudo, had as the leader of a band the "strongest" man, the epithet designating not muscular strength, but spiritual ascendancy. And, suggestively enough, these chiefs played a greater role than their colleagues in neighbouring populations and were in higher measure responsible for their bands, which sometimes took their names from the leaders (Bolinder 1925:111 ff, 126 ff; Preuss 1919–20:364–68; Petrullo 1939:215; Nimuendajú 1946a:97 ff; Lévi-Strauss 1944:25).

But even the Botocudo chief's influence pales before that of the prophets who periodically arose in both Americas (Mooney 1896:662, 672 ff, 676, 686, 700; Spier 1935; Métraux 1931;

Nimuendajú 1914). In my opinion, Nimuendajú, Spier and Métraux have demonstrated that these messiahs did not so much
react against white aggression, which represented merely a special
case of the generic problem of evil, as against the supposed
doom that threatened to engulf the moribund universe. Typically,
the prophets promised salvation to their adherents, whereas un-
believers were to be transformed or destroyed. Given the mental
atmosphere of the aborigines, the more dynamic of the messiahs undoubtedly gained an extraordinary sway over their fellows. One of the early Guarani deliverers affected the pomp of
royalty: refusing to walk, he had himself carried on the shoulders
of his attendants; the common herd were not allowed to approach his person. Such pretensions rested on a claim to supernatural inspiration or to divinity itself. Many of the self-styled
saviours tyrannically imposed their will against common sense
and, what is far more, against previously entrenched beliefs. In
order to dance and chant as required, Obera's Guarani followers
ceased to plant and harvest their crops in 1579. In the nineteenth century, under the spell of successive prophets, the Apapo-
cuva band of this people repeatedly chased the will-o'-the-wisp
of an earthly paradise, undertaking lengthy migrations to escape
the menacing catastrophe. A little over a century ago an Algonkian messiah successfully ordered his people to kill their dogs and
to abandon their hitherto prized sacred bags. For a while, about
1805, Tenskwatawa, the Shawnee prophet, even held the power
over the lives of his tribesmen, having his opponents burnt as
witches.

It is a far cry from the unstable sovereignty of these prophets
to the close-knit Inca state, but the gap is far greater between
the nominal chiefs described by Tanner among the Central
Algonkians and the messiah he met in the very same tribe.
The former were obeyed when the people so chose; at the
latter's behest they humbly killed their dogs, gave up their
strike-a-lights at the expense of "much inconvenience and suf-
fering," and threw away their hitherto holiest possessions. Assume the urge to leadership, as found by Lévi-Strauss in the
Matto Grosso, to be combined with an awe-inspiring supernatural
sanction, and the way is clear to a formative stage on the way
toward a government by divine right. What military prowess

failed to create in aboriginal America is demonstrably possible even in a democratic environment under the hypnosis of religious exaltation and the moral duress that follows in its wake.

Conclusion

It is not part of my plan to squeeze out of the evidence conclusions it will not bear. I cannot trace in detail the sequence of events that led from Ona "anarchy" to the close-knit structure known as the Inca state. I rest content with sketching a probable line of development. The totalitarian concentration of power in Inca Peru is an historic fact; so is the absence of any comparable official authority over most of the New World. If, for the sake of throwing the problem into relief, we assume an otherwise unwarranted teleological point of view, we discover sundry gropings towards the establishment of political authority, which, however, lose themselves in blind alleys. On analogy, what seems simpler than a military despotism under the two Iroquois generals? Yet nothing of the sort arose in the face of an antagonistic cultural tradition. Similarly, the workings of the Cheyenne military societies seem to predestine the tribe to an oligarchical system; but that, too, was precluded by the regnant pattern of social life.

Nevertheless, equalitarianism recedes when confronted with putative supernatural favour. The very same men who flout the pretensions of a fellow-brave grovel before a darling of the gods, render him "implicit obedience and respect." It is probably no mere coincidence that Pontiac was a higher priest in the most sacred organization of his people, that Tecumseh was seconded by his brother, the prophet, and on occasion himself laid claim to supernatural powers. The foundation of a major state, I suggest, was due to men of this type—men who both imagined a unity beyond that of immediate kinship and contiguity and who simultaneously succeeded in investing their mission with the halo of supernaturalism. When not pitted against the terrible odds actually encountered by Pontiac and Tecumseh, natives of their mentality would be able to overcome both the dominant separatism and the dominant libertarianism of their fellows and create the semblance of a modern state.

5 THE SEGMENTARY LINEAGE:
AN ORGANIZATION OF
PREDATORY EXPANSION

Marshall D. Sahlins

Marshall D. Sahlins is Professor of Anthropology at the University of
Michigan. He is the author of *Social Stratification in Polynesia* (1958),
Evolution and Culture (with E. R. Service, 1960), *Moala: Culture
and Nature on a Fijian Island* (1962), and several papers.

I

THERE HAS BEEN a broad inclination in social anthropology
in recent years to apply the designations "segmentary system"
and "segmentary process" to a wide variety of societies. Only
slightly narrower is the application of the concept to lineages or
societies with lineages. While granting certain general similarities
in all the organizations popularly called "segmentary lineage,"
it seems more useful to restrict the term to a very few societies,
most notably the Nuer and the Tiv.

The argument can be made on purely formal grounds: Tiv
and Nuer are in critical respects organized differently from
other societies that have been placed in the category "segmentary
lineage system." Thus, in *Tribes Without Rulers,* Middleton and
Tait were moved to classify Tiv and Nuer—along with Lugbara,
which seems inaccurate—as a *subtype* of segmentary lineage
systems, at one point as the "classical" variety of such systems
(1958:29). But the type can also be considered in an evolutionary perspective: Tiv-Nuer, the segmentary lineage organization properly so-called, is a specific adaptive variety within the
tribal level of society and culture. (The criteria of "tribal level"

FROM *American Anthropologist* 63, No. 2 (1961), 332–45, by permission of the author and of the editor, *American Anthropologist*.

The original draft of this paper was read by Professors D. F. Aberle,
K. G. Aberle, M. Fried, and E. R. Service.

and the meaning of "specific adaptive variety" will be spelled out below.)

This evolutionary perspective is adopted here because it furnishes a practical basis for distinguishing Tiv-Nuer from other "segmentary" societies and, at the same time, it has the power to suggest the circumstances which produce segmentary lineage organization, to "explain" it, at least partly. Conversely—and contrary to the vision of Radcliffe-Brown for a comparative-structural approach—formalism alone has only tended to obscure the salient characteristics of the segmentary lineage organization. Focusing on such general structural and functional resemblances as "segmentation" and "complementary opposition," the formal definition of "segmentary lineage" threatens to become as broad as the formal view of the "lineage" itself. For segmentation and complementary opposition are very widespread—nearly universal—features of human social organization. It is then no wonder that Tiv and Nuer have been lumped with societies that virtually run the evolutionary gamut from simple tribes to protostates, such as the Alur (Southall 1956). Our dissatisfaction with this procedure parallels Fried's discontent with the use of "lineage" in current social anthropology:

> When the analytical framework which is so conducive to functional study is . . . transferred without modification to problems involving comparisons of greater or lesser scope, complications are sure to follow. . . . What happens when societies are classified together merely because they utilize kinship as an articulating principle without determining the nature of their particular kin relations or their quality, may be seen when Fortes links the Hopi with the Nuer, the Beduin, the Yako, the Tallensi, the Gusii, and the Tikopia on the basis of their common possession of unilineal descent groups. While this is correct, it is of little moment since we can also add, *inter alia,* the Northern Tungus and the Chinese, thereby giving a series that ranges from a simple pastoralist and hunting society to a sophisticated world power (Fried 1957:7–8).

The argument for an evolutionary view of Tiv-Nuer segmentary lineage organization—and for the taxonomic distinctions drawn for the purpose of argument—does not rest simply on the existence of differences between Tiv-Nuer and other so-called segmentary lineage systems. The importance of perceiving Tiv-Nuer as a specific tribal form is that this leads to certain empirically testable conclusions about its genesis and incidence. The evolutionary perspective, moreover, does not supersede structural analysis, but complements it and adds to it certain understandings which structural analysis by itself seems incapable of producing. There is hardly need to repeat the oft-made observation that consideration of the relations between parts of a system does not account for the existence of the system (or its parts)—unless one is willing to accept the tautology that the system is what it is because that is the way it is. Yet without wishing to slight the magnificence of Evans-Pritchard's work on the Nuer—the position of *The Nuer* as an ethnographic classic is certainly secure—nonetheless, he does not break out of the circle:

> Physical environment, way of livelihood, mode of distribution, poor communications, simple economy, etc., to some extent explain the incidence of [Nuer] political cleavage, but the tendency towards segmentation seems to be inherent in political structure itself (1940a:284).

Or, perhaps even more explicitly, Evans-Pritchard writes that ecological factors:

> . . . to some extent explain the demographic features of Nuer political segmentation, but the tendency towards segmentation must be defined as a fundamental principle of their social structure (1940b:148).

In brief, Evans-Pritchard seems to reject the adaptive view as of limited value, leaving the impression that the Nuer have a segmentary organization because of the segmentary "principle" of their organization.

The alternative advanced here is that a segmentary lineage system is a social means of intrusion and competition in an already occupied ecological niche. More, it is an organization confined to societies of a certain level of development, the *tribal* level, as distinguished from less-developed *bands* and more advanced *chiefdoms*. Finally, the segmentary lineage is a successful predatory organization in conflicts with other tribes, although perhaps unnecessary against bands and ineffective against chiefdoms and states; it develops specifically in a tribal society which is moving against other tribes, in a *tribal intercultural environment*.

II. The Tribal Level of Cultural Evolution

The evolution of culture can be viewed as a movement in the direction of increasing utilization of the earth's resources, or, alternatively, of increasing transformation of available energy into cultural systems. This broad movement has two aspects. On the one hand, culture tends to diversify into specific cultures through selection and adaptation. This is specific evolution, the ramifying, diversifying, specializing aspect, from homogeneity to heterogeneity. On the other hand, higher cultural forms arise from, and surpass, lower. Culture produces successively higher _levels_ of organization as new forms capable of harnessing increasing amounts of energy emerge. In popular terms, this is culture's movement toward complexity, the general, progressive aspect of evolution.[1]

We are concerned here with the tribal level of general progress, and for comparative purposes with the preceding band level and succeeding chiefdom level. All of these are below the general level of state, or civilization, and are justifiably referred to as "primitive." The discussion focuses primarily on social and political matters, leaving aside other characteristics of general evolution, thus the designation of levels in social terms is particularly apposite.

In the general evolution of society there is movement in the direction of multiplication and specialization of social groups, parts of society, and increasing integration of the whole. In these respects, band societies are clearly least developed. Bands are small autonomous territorial groups of 20 to 50 or so people. They are undifferentiated, consisting of only two kinds of social units: families and the band of related families. They are relatively unintegrated. There is limited social control of the economy, relative economic and political autonomy of families, and for integration and direction there is no leadership beyond the "moral influence" exerted by elders and skilled hunters. Band society was the dominant type of the Paleolithic; it survived until recent times among marginally-situated hunters and gatherers such as the Bushmen, Eskimo, Shoshoni, Semang, and others.

The tribal level may have emerged in a few exceptionally favorable environments in the food-collecting, Paleolithic era. However, it was the Neolithic Revolution that ushered in the

---

[1] A full discussion of the specific-adaptive and general-progressive aspects of evolution may be found in Sahlins and Service (1960), especially chs. 1 and 2. Space does not permit further argumentation here; the reader is asked to consult this book.

dominance of the tribal form, that precipitated great sectors of the cultural world to a new level of general standing. Even in modern times tribes operating on a simple neolithic base have comprised a significant proportion of ethnographically-known cultures. Well-known examples include most North American Indians—excluding bands of Canada and the Great Basin, and chiefdoms of the Southeast and the Northwest Coast—many groups of the South American forest, most Melanesian societies, most Siberian groups, peoples of highland regions of southeast Asia, and a number of African societies.

A band is a simple association of families, but a tribe is an association of kin groups which are themselves composed of families. A tribe is a larger, more segmented society. Without implying this as the specific course of development of tribes, we may nonetheless view a tribe as a coalescence of multifamily groups each of the order of a band. In this, the general evolution of society parallels over-all biological progress: what is at one stage the entire organism (the cell, the band) becomes only the part of the higher organism (simple metazoa, the tribe).

A tribe is a segmental organization. It is composed of a number of equivalent, unspecialized multifamily groups, each the structural duplicate of the other: a tribe is a congeries of equal kin group blocs. The segments are the residential and (usually) proprietary units of the tribe, the people that settle or wander together in a given sector of the tribal domain and that separately exploit a sector of strategic resources. It is sometimes possible to speak of several levels of segmentation. Among Plains Indians, for example, the primary segments, small groups of relatives acknowledging a leader, wandered separately from fellow tribesmen some of the year, combined with like units into larger bands (secondary segments) in other seasons, and the whole tribe gathered briefly for annual ceremonies. "Primary tribal segment" is defined as the smallest multifamily group that collectively exploits an area of tribal resources and forms a residential entity all or most of the year. It is hazardous to speak of absolute numbers in view of the great specific diversity of tribal societies, but in most cases the primary segment seems to fall between 50 and 250 people. The structure of primary and higher (if any) tribal segments likewise varies. The primary segment may be a lineage (e.g., Iroquois), a nonlineal descent group (Malaita, Carrier

Indians), or a loosely organized local kindred (Lapp, Iban, Plains Indians). This is another product of adaptive diversification, specific evolution. It is rather the general characteristics of tribal segments that concern us now.

Small, localized—often primary—tribal segments tend to be economically and politically autonomous. A tribe as a whole is normally *not* a political organization but rather a social-cultural-ethnic entity. It is held together principally by likenesses among its segments (mechanical solidarity) and by pan-tribal institutions, such as a system of intermarrying clans, of age-grades, or military or religious societies, which cross-cut the primary segments. Pan-tribal institutions make a tribe a more integrated social organism (even if weakly so) than a group of intermarrying bands, but tribes as such virtually lack organic solidarity.[2] A tribe may well consider itself one people, often enough *the* people, but a system of order uniting the various kin segments and representing the interests of the whole rather than the several interests of the parts is at best only ephemerally achieved—characteristically it is never achieved.

The simple neolithic mode of production is the key to the fragmented character of tribal polity. In most areas of the world the Neolithic did not immediately bring forth technology requiring intensive division of labor or socialization of the productive process over a wide region. Neolithic economic cooperation is generally localized, usually it is limited to cooperation within primary tribal segments. In addition, such common neolithic techniques as shifting agriculture and simple pastoralism typically disperse a population and confine concentration ("nucleation") at a low level. Tribal unity suffers in consequence.

In many tribes the economic autonomy of primary segments is formally expressed by corporateness: the primary segment is a self-sustaining perpetual body exercising social control over its productive resources. The group manages its own affairs and is highly unified against the outside, acting as a collectivity in de-

[2] In comparison with groupings of intermarrying bands, pan-tribal social institutions are perhaps the most indicative characteristic of tribal society. Such institutions clearly demarcate the borders of a tribe, separating it as a social (and ethnic) entity. Intermarrying bands may carry a vague sense of tribalism—as in Australia—but as dialect shades off into dialect and customs change gradually from band to band, no one can say where one so-called "tribe" ends and another begins. This is a clearly less integrated condition than that of tribalism properly so-called.

fense of its property and persons. But even where it is not expressed by incorporation, the small kin-territorial segments of a tribe tend to be self-sustaining economic and political bodies. Each has an equivalent organization, not one is functionally dependent on another, but each does for itself what the others do for themselves.

Political solidarity is not necessarily completely confined to small tribal segments. Insofar as ecological conditions force segments into contact during certain seasons, a feeling of unity and of necessity to terminate feuds may develop over a wider or narrower range of the tribe. Thus secondary and higher segments may exist as territorially defined tribal sections (subtribal groupings). But this in itself rarely requires organized confederation in the sense that the subtribe has a structure which is more than the sum of its parts. Moreover, the subtribe is not normally the unit of political action.

As a matter of fact, considered as the territorial entity that collectively defends itself against the outside while maintaining the peace internally, the political unit of tribal society is typically variable in extent. The level of political consolidation contracts and expands: primary segments that unite to attack or repel an enemy at one time may fragment into feuding factions at another, quarreling over land or over personal injuries. Moreover, the degree to which political consolidation proceeds typically depends on circumstances *external* to the tribe itself. The existence of a well-organized predatory neighbor, or, conversely, the opportunity to prey upon a nearby society, will give impetus to confederation. Local autonomy breaks down, on a greater or lesser scale, proportionate to the amount of—and during the extent of—concerted action possible against other societies. In an uncontested environment, on the other hand, the primary segments of a tribe will show little inclination toward consolidation. And if, at the same time, internal population growth places a premium on land, pasturage, or other vital resources, the tribe may exist in a virtual state of anarchy, of perpetual feud among small-scale segments.

We take the following then as fundamental facts of tribal political life:

1. Because small, equivalent tribal segments tend to be economically and socially self-sustaining, equal, and autonomous, the normal political state is toward disunity among them. There is no permanent organized confederation of these segments.

2. Small segments of a tribe will, however, consolidate to meet external competition. The specific nature of tribal structure of course permits greater or less consolidation in different cases. But disregarding this for the moment, the level of political consolidation within the tribe is generally proportionate to the requirements of external competition.

3. Yet a tribe will automatically return to the state of disunity —local autonomy—and remain there when competition is in abeyance.

It follows that leadership is weakly developed at the tribal level. Leadership beyond the small—normally, the primary— segment can only be ephemeral because organized action above this level is ephemeral. There is no need, and no field, for permanent tribal leadership. When the competitive objectives that induce confederation have been accomplished, the confederation *de facto* dissolves into its several segments, and leaders that had emerged now fall back into social oblivion, or at best retain only local influence. Once leadership is localized, moreover, it tends to become thereby superfluous. A primary segment is a face-to-face organization of kinsmen; good order here is largely achieved through kinship etiquette with its personal sanctions of ridicule, gossip, and ostracism. The typical leader in a tribal society is only the glorified counterpart of the influential elder in a hunting and gathering society. Like the latter, he achieves status by virtue of his personal characteristics, or to look at it another way, he builds a following on the basis of personally-established ties. He creates loyalties through generosity; fearful acquiescence through magic; inclination to accept his opinions through demonstration of wisdom, oratorical skill, and the like. Leadership here is a charismatic interpersonal relationship. Since it is based on personal ties and qualities, it is not heritable. It is not an *office* within a definite group: it is not *chieftainship*.

An influential man can, of course, "build a name"—this expression is often encountered ethnographically at the tribal level —that is known beyond his local group. And if he has the special qualities selected for in times of confederation, such as skill in fighting, he will direct the confederation. But as soon as the confederacy dissolves, which is as soon as it can, he finds himself with few followers. The man might have little influence even within his primary segment because the very qualities which elevate him in times of confederation, such as fearless belligerence, would alienate him if displayed in the peaceful context of his circle of close kin. He may be without honor in his own camp.

The reader may have already inferred our distinction between tribes and chiefdoms. The latter, unlike the former, witness the development of a permanent political structure and socialization of the economic process over a wide area, embracing different local segments. The several segments of a chiefdom are not separate, equal, and autonomous. Rather, they are ranked relative to each other—and usually also internally ranked—and their leaders, true chiefs, hold offices accordingly in an extensive polity. In the more developed chiefdoms (many Polynesian societies, for example), this political structure becomes coterminous with social and cultural boundaries.

III. Tiv-Nuer Segmentary Lineage Organization

The significance of the preceding discussion lies in this: The Tiv and the Nuer are tribal societies, adaptive varieties of the general type. Their economies are neolithic; the Tiv are small-scale shifting agriculturalists, the Nuer transhumant mixed farmers with a pastoral bias. Both have solidary, autonomous primary segments: the Nuer village and the Tiv "minimal *tar*" (a grouping of related compounds).[3] Like many tribes, neither are permanently organized (integrated) above this level. Yet both are expanding, or rather, intruding into an ecological domain already occupied by other peoples. And success in this intrusive push for "living-space" depends precisely and directly on ability to mobilize above the primary segment level, to deploy the concerted pressure of many local groups on the tribal borders. *The Tiv-Nuer segmentary lineage system is a mechanism for large-scale political consolidation in the absence of any permanent, higher-level tribal organization.* To use the Bohannans' apt phrases, it has the decisive function of unifying "within" for the purpose of standing "against." Evans-Pritchard viewed this, in its manifestation in

[3] It can be argued that the Tiv minimal tar and the Nuer village are secondary segments, that the compound and hamlet are the respective primary segments. While there is some plausibility in this view, the argument has no important bearing on our thesis regarding the segmentary lineage system, and since no great impropriety is done thereby (and the presentation of relevant data is made considerably easier), we shall consider the Tiv minimal tar and the Nuer village as the primary residential-propriety segments.

feud, as a means of preserving equilibrium in Nuer society; yet in the larger and more revealing perspective of the intercultural milieu its significance is precisely that it disturbs equilibrium.

Because of the context in which the segmentary lineage system operates, and because of its singular function as a quasi-political structure, it is a distinctive kind of organization. But before examining the formal elements of the system in detail, it is well to present a brief general description of it.[4]

Nuer is the type site, so to speak, of the segmentary lineage system. But the Tiv are a more perfect example. Among the Tiv, the men of the minimal tar are usually of the *focal* patriline, i.e., the line whose outside connections with other lines is the basis of alliance with other segments. In Nuer villages, only a minority—sometimes, none—need be of the focal line (the "dominant" clans and lineages, in Evans-Pritchard's terms). The Tiv are also a more perfect example because their segmentary system expands through the whole tribe, embracing all Tiv in one patrilineage, whereas the Nuer system cuts off below the level of the Nuer as a people.[5]

It should be stated at once that "lineage" does not describe the basic segment among either the Tiv or the Nuer. The "lineage system" is a set of relations between primary segments; the Tiv minimal tar and the Nuer village are themselves residential composites of different patrilines. Those lines of the local group other than the focal one are related to it cognatically or in other ways, which is the social rationale for their participation in the outside connections of the focal line.

The segmentary lineage system consists of this: the focal lines of primary segments can be placed on a single agnatic genealogy that accounts for much (all, in the Tiv case) of the tribe. The closer the genealogical relation between focal lines, the closer their respective segments are on the ground. Primary (or "minimal") segments whose focal line ancestors are siblings comprise

---

[4] The ethnographic materials on which this description is based are from Laura Bohannan (1958), Laura and Paul Bohannan (1953), Paul Bohannan (1954a; 1954b), and Evans-Pritchard (1940a; 1940b; 1951). Unless quoting directly, we shall not make specific references in this section.

[5] The Nuer system extends through the unit which Evans-Pritchard calls the "tribe," a large subdivision of the Nuer as an ethnic entity. We have been using "tribe" in reference to the latter, hence shall refer to the former (Evans-Pritchard's "tribe") as a subtribe. There is no need to make an issue of terminology; this is done only for consistency.

a territorial entity of higher order, a minor segment, usually named after their common ancestor, the father of the siblings. They comprise an entity, however, only with reference and in opposition to an equivalent lineage segment, one descended from the brother of their common ancestor. In turn, minor segments comprise a higher-level entity, a major lineage, in opposition to the descendants of the brother of their common ancestor. The build-up of inclusive segments can proceed to the level of the tribe itself. Always the level of consolidation has a spatial counterpart; all segments of the same inclusive one form a geographical bloc. "Complementary opposition" and "structural relativity" should also be stressed: no entity above the primary segment exists as such, but it is only called into consciousness or being by reference to its genealogically equivalent segment.

To make this description more concrete, we quote extensively from one of Paul Bohannan's several lucid discussions of the Tiv, also appending one of his diagrams (Fig. 1).

The segmentary lineage system is a *complex* of formal-functional characteristics. Some of the elements of organization can and do appear singly or in various combination in other societies, which is the apparent cause of the popular tendency to apply "segmentary system" quite widely. It is our contention, however, that the full complement occurs only in expanding tribal societies. In other cases the segmentary tendencies remain incomplete, and because they are embedded in different social contexts, they have different "functional values," different roles in society.

We have separated out six salient elements of segmentary lineage organization: lineality, segmentation, local-genealogical segmentation, segmentary sociability, complementary opposition (or the massing effect), and structural relativity.

Lineality Whereas a single segmented lineage extends through much or all of the tribe among the Tiv and the Nuer, lineality actually has comparatively limited functions. The Tiv and Nuer do not have corporate lineages, in the sense we take that term. The corporate groups are local aggregations of different agnatic lines. Lineality thus does not define the primary residential-proprietary segments but rather organizes relations between them according to genealogical ties between their focal lines.

One need not insist on the absence of local corporate lineages as an indicative characteristic of the segmentary lineage system, for it is the presence of a lineage superstructure uniting local

---

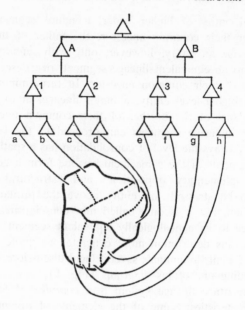

FIG. 1 The lineage whose apical ancestor is some three to six generations removed from living elders and who are associated with the smallest discrete territory (*tar*) I call the minimal segment . . . it can vary in population from 200 people to well over a thousand. . . . The territory of a minimal segment adjoins the territory of its sibling minimal segment. Thus, the lineage comprising two minimal segments also has a discrete territory, and is in turn a segment of a more inclusive lineage, and of its more inclusive territory. In Fig. 1, the whole system can be seen: the father or founder of segment *a* was a brother of the founder of segment *b*. Each is a minimal segment today, and each has its own territory. The two segments taken together are all descended from *1*, and are known by his name—the children of *1*. In the same way, the territory of lineage *1*, made up as it is of the combined minimal territories *a* and *b*, combines with the territory of lineage *2*, made up of the combined minimal territories of *c* and *d*, to form territory *A*, occupied by lineage segment *A*, all descended from a single ancestor "A." This process is extended indefinitely right up to the apex of the genealogy, back in time to the founder who begot the entire people, and outwards in space to the edges of Tivland. The entire 800,000 Tiv form a single "lineage" (*nongo*) and a single land called *Tar Tiv*. The geographical position of territories follows the genealogical division into lineages (P. Bohannan 1954a:3).

groups that is critical.[6] On the other hand, the mere presence of segmented lineages in a society is not sufficient for inclusion in the type. And failure to organize the polity on a unitary lineage model *does disqualify,* no matter how many other "segmentary" elements are present (e.g., the Tallensi, and in *Tribes Without Rulers,* the Dinka, Bwamba, and Konkamba).

Lineality suggests some general ecological preconditions for segmentary lineage development. Lineages and lineality are typically found with a mode of production involving repetitive or periodic use of restricted, localized resources, as in secondary forest or irrigation agriculture and many forms of pastoralism. The rule of descent that makes a lineage is one social aspect of long-term use of the same resources, another aspect being the development of collective proprietary rights in these resources. The rule of descent creates a perpetual social group linked to perpetually valuable strategic property; or, viewed another way, it allocates people with respect to their means of livelihood. Lineages do not form in the absence of long-term exploitation of restricted domains. They are lacking where resources (hence people) vary continuously in temporal and spatial distribution, as among buffalo-hunting Plains tribes or primary forest agriculturalists such as the Iban of Borneo. If ecological conditions preclude lineages (or lineality), they preclude the segmentary lineage system.

Segmentation A *segment* is, generically, "one of an indefinite number of parts comprising a whole in which one part is like another in structure, or composition, and function" (White 1959: 143). A social group or a society as a whole is *segmented* (segmental, segmentary, exhibits segmentation) if composed of subgroups of this character. *Segmentation* also refers to the com-

---

[6] The compositeness of the minimal segment is, however, expectable if our hypothesis about intrusive expansion is correct. Among the Tiv and the Nuer, this compositeness is a manifestation of population mobility evidently due to localized fluctuations in population or per capita productivity of resources. Without open land, this requires some reshuffling of people according to the distribution of economic opportunities within the tribal territory. The composite minimal segment may well be symptomatic of internal population pressure, which is, of course, a complementary—although not absolutely necessary nor sufficient—cause for tribal expansion. In this connection it seems significant that the farms of a given patriline, a "segment within the hut," are not necessarily contiguous within the domain of a Tiv minimal tar but tend to be randomly placed. This negates complementary opposition in matters of land grabbing within the minimal tar, keeping it unified against outside rather than rent by internal strife.

mon process of growth by division into equivalent parts (fission). Tiv-Nuer organization is segmentary in the sense that higher levels of political organization are achieved through integration of equivalent, lower-level parts. It appears also to grow by segmentation.

But all kinds of societies and many varieties of social groups are segmentary in this generic sense. The University of Michigan has minimal, departmental segments (Anthropology, Chemistry, etc.), which are parts of semi-official divisions (Social Science, Natural Science), which are parts of colleges (Literary College, Engineering School, etc.), which together comprise the University—excluding the Administration (an oversight). Obviously, the existence of segmentation alone does not qualify a society as a segmentary lineage system. And even if a unitary lineage system is the organization of political segmentation, it is not a segmentary lineage system unless certain other elements, especially structural relativity (see below), are present.

Local-genealogical segmentation   A political structure is often a system of local segmentation. That is, segments of the same order within the same inclusive political body are contiguous. Among the Tiv and the Nuer, local segmentation is simultaneously lineage segmentation (see Fig. 1). It is not simply that each territorial entity is identified with a lineage segment, but also that contiguous segments of the same inclusive territorial entity are identified with equivalent branches of the same inclusive lineage. Higher political levels are at the same time higher lineage levels. Thus the lineage system can be said to provide the structure for political consolidation—although there is plenty of evidence for the Nuer, at least, that *in origin* the process sometimes works the other way around, that the genealogy is fitted to political realities. (Among the Nuer, also, local-genealogical segmentation is cut off at a high, subtribal level, but as there is rarely confederation beyond this level political alliance consistently remains lineage alliance.)

A society may have local political segments and at the same time segmentary lineages. However, if genealogical segmentation does not consistently correspond to local segmentation, it does not have a segmentary lineage system.

Segmentary sociability (*Love thy neighbor*)   The closer the social position of two groups in a segmentary organization, the more solidary their relations; subgroups of the same inclusive group are more sociable than subgroups of different inclusive segments. This very general (and vague) sociological fact can be applied in many contexts. However, segmentary sociability is particularly marked if segmentation is organized genealogically because kinship itself connotes sociability, and in many societies it more specifically connotes "peace." The closer the kin relation, the greater the sociability and peacefulness; the more distant, or more nearly unrelated, the less.

This is not to say that hostility is absent from close kin or close segmentary relations. It is probably easier to prove—considering interpersonal relations as such—that the closer the social bond, the greater the hostility. However, it is not hostility that is at issue but the necessity to repress it or, conversely, the possibility of enjoining it. The closer the relationship the greater the restraint on belligerence and violence, and the more distant, the less the restraint. Among the Tiv and the Nuer, given the kin quality of segmentation, segmentary sociability is particularly striking; it is virtually institutionalized. Hostility is put down effectively within the Nuer village and the Tiv minimal tar: if factionalism erupts the difficulty is either settled or one party will have to emigrate. These are groups of close kin who must maintain their integrity against the outside, and an unsociable action in this context is sinful. The moral injunction is accompanied by a prohibition on the use of dangerous weapons. But the greater the lineage-segmentary distance, the more dangerous the permitted means of violence—from fists, to clubs, to arrows, poisoned arrows, etc.—and the more difficult it becomes to repair a feud. Correspondingly, violence becomes more honorable in proportion to segmentary distance, reaching the extreme in dealings with foreign tribes. Here violence is an esteemed act, there are practically no holds barred on atrocity, and a state of war may well be the assumed normal relation. The value of segmentary sociability—or the lack thereof—for predatory expansion is obvious: violence is inhibited centripetally, among contiguous, closely related groups, but is directed centrifugally against distant groups and neighboring peoples.

Segmentary sociability of itself is a common political phenomenon. But it is outstanding in segmentary lineage systems because, in the absence of a permanent tribal political structure, it is the salient mechanism of the political process. Operating automatically to determine the level of collective political action, it is the built-in thermostat of a self-regulating political machine. The formal manifestation of segmentary sociability is complementary opposition.

Complementary opposition, or the massing effect Among the Tiv and the Nuer, segmentary sociability materializes in complementary opposition, the massing of equivalent segments in defense or extension of their respective privileges. In any opposition between parties A and B, all those more closely related to A than to B will stand with A against B, and vice versa. Segments are pitted against equivalent segments: any opposition between groups (or members thereof) expands automatically to opposition between the largest equivalent lineages of which the contestants are *respectively* members. The massing effect is self-limiting as well as self-expanding. It cuts off when sibling groups are joined because lineages equivalent to the inclusive one containing opposed sibling groups are equally related (or equally unrelated) to the contestants.

Evans-Pritchard describes complementary opposition among local-lineage segments of the Nuer in this way (Evans-Pritchard's "section" in this passage can be understood in lineage as well as territorial terms):

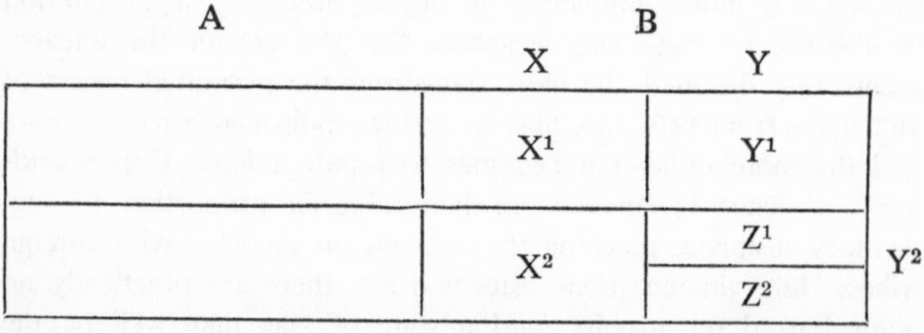

FIG. 2 The principle of segmentation and the opposition between segments is the same in every section of a tribe [our "subtribe"] and extends beyond the tribe to relations between tribes. . . . It can be stated in hypothetical terms by the Nuer themselves and can be represented in this way. In the diagram . . . when Z^1 fights Z^2 no other section is involved. When Z^1 fights Y^1, Z^1 and Z^2 unite as Y^2. When Y^1 fights X^1, Y^1 and Y^2 unite, and so do X^1 and X^2. When X^1 fights A, X^1, X^2, Y^1 and Y^2 all unite as B. When A raids the Dinka A and B may unite. [1940b:143–144. An accurate description of segmentary opposition among the Tiv can be had by substituting letters and figures from Fig. 1 (above) in Evans-Pritchard's passage.]

Among the Tiv and the Nuer, then, conflicts—even those resulting from personal injury—between individuals of equivalent primary segments call forth their respective primary groups en masse; it becomes a fight between segments. By the same logic, the logic of segmentary sociability, minor, major, and larger lineages may be pitted against each other. Thus does the segmentary lineage system operate as a political machine. The less the lineage-spatial distance between groups the more effectively peace is waged, not simply because of moral injunctions and felt obligations to settle, but also because the smaller are the opposed parties. However, the greater the segmental distance the more effectively war is waged because, in addition to use of dangerous weapons and disinclination to settle, the size of contending parties increases proportionately.

Complementary opposition is not peculiar to the Nuer and the Tiv—it occurs to a greater or lesser extent elsewhere. The uniqueness of Tiv-Nuer complementary opposition is that it *is* their political system. Complementary opposition *creates* the structure: without opposition the higher segments do not exist. Masses of people are not organized by social structures so much as organizations are made by massing. This leads us directly to the final and definitive characteristic of the segmentary lineage system, structural relativity. But one cannot refrain from noting beforehand the decisive advantages bequeathed by complementary opposition in intertribal warfare. War is effectively joined by the Nuer or the Tiv against neighboring tribes because, even if it has been initiated by a small lineage segment, it pits "all of us" against "them." More than that, the societies under attack do not form such extensive intratribal alliances, hence it is usually "all of us" against "a few of them."

Structural relativity Tiv-Nuer lineages do not come into existence except through the massing effect, in opposition to equivalent groups. They are not permanent, *absolute* social entities, but *relative* ones. Called into being by external circumstances, the level of organization achieved is in direct proportion to the social order of the opposition, and the lineage segment ceases to function as such when opposition is in abeyance. The lineage segment cannot stand alone but can only stand "against." Correspondingly, no lineage is more than the sum of its parts; it lacks internal structure, a skeleton, such as a system of segmentary chiefs. Lineage segments have only social exoskeletons; they are crystallized at one or another level by outside pressure of greater or less degree.

In a certain sense structural relativity is endemic in any social order that is segmental. At the very least it will be manifest in "relativity of reference," which comes into play to determine the respective status of interacting persons or groups. Thus in Figure 1 (above) a person speaks of himself as a member of group *a* relative to those of group *b*. But the same person is a member of *1* in reference to *c* or *d* (which are *2*) and of *A* in reference to those of *B,* etc. Evans-Pritchard is able to use a very familiar kind of example of such structural relativity, in one stroke thus demonstrating its generality in human societies as well as illustrating his Nuer material:

> If one meets an Englishman in Germany and asks him where his home is, he may reply that it is in England. If one meets the same man in London and asks him the same question he will tell one that his home is in Oxfordshire, whereas if one meets him in that county he will tell one the name of the town or village in which he lives. If questioned in his town or village he will mention his particular street, and if questioned in his street he will indicate his house (1940b:136).

Structural relativity among the Tiv and Nuer is more than a matter of status determination of individuals. Moreover, it is not simply a tendency to define "own group" by opposition in certain contexts; such tendencies exist in other societies with other organization. It is, if we may be permitted, *complete relativity:* the level of political organization that emerges as a collectivity is always relative to the opposition.

A comparison of Tiv-Nuer segmentary lineages with Polynesian ramages may be instructive (cf. Firth 1957; Kaberry 1959; Sahlins 1958). Polynesian ramages have many characteristics of segmentary lineage systems: lineality, segmentation, local-genealogical segmentation (on certain islands), segmentary sociability, and in internal political or jural matters they may show complementary opposition and relativity. But Polynesian ramages are permanent, absolute structures with continuous economic and political functions. Ramage segments are ranked, and the rank of the segment corresponds to its economic and political privileges and obligations. Ramage segments of every order have chiefs who represent and embody their groups and act for them. There is a political order of the whole operating in both internal and external affairs. A higher level of economic and political integration has been irreversibly established here, one that transcends the primary segment sphere. The Polynesian ramage system is an organization of the chiefdom level of general evolution.

But the segmentary lineage system is a tribal institution. It develops in the context of a comparatively restricted economy and polity, in the context of equal, autonomous, small localized kin groups. It may operate in the internal ordering of society (through segmentary sociability), but this is only derivative of the dominant function of consolidating otherwise autonomous primary groups for concerted external action. There are no permanent lineage segments beyond the primary group, but only temporary segments of different size, developing to the level they have to in order to meet opposition.

> We would . . . suggest that Nuer political groups be defined . . . by the relations between their segments and their interrelations as segments of a larger system in an organization of society in certain social situations, and *not as parts of a kind of fixed framework* within which people live (Evans-Pritchard 1940b:149; emphasis ours).

Structural relativity in a segmentary lineage system is paralleled by relativity of leadership. A man may achieve some fame—personal and charismatic—beyond his primary group, enough perhaps to be influential among nearby, related segments. Insofar as these segments combine with his own in opposition to other groups, such a man may act as the spokesman and leader of the whole. But when his own primary segment stands against an equivalent, closely related one in feud or in a land dispute, then he is not heeded by the opposed segment but is only leader of his own. The Bohannans describe relativity of Tiv leadership very well. (See Fig. 3.)

The Tiv and the Nuer, as many other tribal societies, are militantly equalitarian—a corollary of a fragmented kin economy and polity. The Tiv, in fact, have periodic purges of would-be tyrants (P. Bohannan 1958). While the Tiv are capable of mass opposition to other tribes, even here the inherent weakness of their tribal polity shows through. Small clusters of close kin fight parallel to each other; there is no coordinated deployment, no

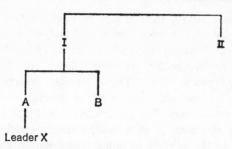

Leader X

FIG. 3 The same segmentary principle which allows very large units
to appear in opposition to equivalent units, makes it impossible for
any unit, from the internal viewpoint, to have unity. Thus in any
affairs between I and II, X appears as the leader of I. In any affairs
solely the concern of I, X appears as the leader of A . . . any account of Tiv leadership must discuss leadership in these two aspects:
"against" and "within," or, if one prefers and will remember that
the lineage level concerned is contextual, "foreign" and "domestic"
affairs. However, the lineage structure itself, by an association of
union with opposition, brings it about that emotively the feeling of
"within" and of unity in any given segment is strongest when "foreign" affairs are concerned, and that the emergence of latent cleavages is most prominent and the achievement of unity most difficult
in "internal" affairs. That is, a leader wields his greatest influence
"within" when he is a leader "against." This principle needs no modification if one remembers that the lineage span is variable. Only if
one attempts to pin leadership to a definite lineage (I), does it break
down unless one specifies that within I, X is the leader of A; within A,
he is the leader of "*i*" and so on literally to the point at which he
is himself "against" his full brother (L. and P. Bohannan 1953:
31–32).

master strategy, no division of military labors; and the scope of
leadership thus remains restricted. As for the Nuer, the most
influential men in the traditional system, the "leopard-skin chiefs,"
characteristically stand *outside* the lineage system. They are usually not agnatic members of the focal lines of their region and
are not segment leaders. Theirs is ritual office, virtually without
secular power, and their function is to compose feuds between
lineage segments rather than to organize feuding factions.

Structural relativity reveals the tribal character of the segmentary lineage system. The one-sided function of the system,
organization for external opposition, also suggests the specific
adaptive circumstance which it meets: intertribal competition.

IV. Predatory Expansion: "We Don't Have a Boundary; We Have an Argument"

The Tiv are centered in the Northern Province of Nigeria, straddling both banks of the Benue River. According to traditions, the Tiv moved into this area from the southeast; their occupation of the plain north of the Benue is comparatively recent and Tiv intrusion in this sector is still progressing. Yet Tiv expansion is not characterized so much by movement in one direction as it is by movement in *all* directions: "when seen from the periphery, and more especially when seen from the viewpoint of surrounding peoples, a centrifugal migration is the most important single factor about the Tiv" (L. and P. Bohannan 1953:54). Only in the south has the Tiv advance been inhibited, and this by boundaries drawn by the British, not for lack of inclination on the Tiv's part to go farther.

Tiv migration has been accomplished specifically at the expense of a number of other peoples, who have either been rolled back by the Tiv wave or else have suffered infiltration of their lands by growing colonies of Tiv, sometimes to the point that these peoples now exist as isolated enclaves within Tivland. This fantastic predatory encroachment is more reminiscent of conquering nomad hordes than of a simple neolithic peasantry:

> To their east they are living intermingled with "Uke": the Hausa-speaking Abakwariga, Jukun, Jukunized Chamba and other peoples; they have even begun to push into Adamawa Province. To their north they are moving into (and leaving behind as enclaves) such groups as the Arago and Ankwe, who are linguistically related to the Idoma. . . . To the west they are exerting pressure on the Idoma and on the other groups called "Akpoto" by the Tiv; Tiv in adjoining areas say they dispossessed the Akpoto of the land on which they now live (P. Bohannan 1953:10).

> Many Tiv have migrated south into the Eastern Provinces and set up their homesteads among the various small tribes of Ogoja Province, known to the Tiv collectively as the Udam . . . (P. Bohannan 1954b:2).

> British administration encountered Tiv migration almost as soon as they encountered the Tiv, in 1912. As a result the "Munshi [i.e., Tiv] Wall" was built between Gaav of Jechira [a large Tiv lineage] and the contiguous peoples of Ogoja, a wall meant to "keep the Munshi in his place—north of the wall" but which "the Munshi merely climbs over" (L. and P. Bohannan 1953:54).

The Tiv evidently intrude themselves wherever they can cultivate and where their opposition is weak. They now number over
800,000 people, by far the largest pagan tribal grouping in Northern Nigeria. The decisive factor in this phenomenal success seems
to be the Tiv segmentary lineage system: the Tiv are able to
exert mass pressure on their borders, while the peoples subjected
to this pressure are incapable of defending their territories on a
commensurate scale. Many of these hapless peoples are small
tribal groups, the "broken tribes" of the north, for example, or the
"congeries of small, semi-Bantu speaking tribes" to the south (L.
Bohannan 1958:33). Speaking of the Tiv's neighbors in general,
L. Bohannan remarks:

> Most of these societies seem to be made up of small descent groups
> —sometimes territorially distinct, sometimes dispersed—crossed and
> integrated by ties of reputed kinship, chiefship and religion. . . .
> In political organization the Tiv are in no way typical of the
> region in which they live (1958:33).

Tiv expansive thrusts germinate at lower levels of the segmentary structure and develop upward through higher levels and outward toward the borders of Tivland. There are no natural or
artificial boundaries between Tiv minimal segments (tar), as distinct from holdings under cultivation: "We don't have a boundary;
we have an argument" (P. Bohannan 1954b:45). Every year
new plots are cleared, as used ones are left fallow, and, as P. Bohannan puts it, every compound headman within the minimal
segment holds a right against the world to sufficient farming land.
The existing fallow between adjacent minimal segments is likely
to be disputed when such rights are exercised, and disputed by
comparatively large groups at that. For the direction of expansion
of cultivation is governed by tactical considerations: one moves
against the bounding segment most distantly related to one's own,
thus bringing the massing effect into maximal play (P. Bohannan
1954a:5).

Now when it is considered that lineage segments are at every
level localized, it follows that an expansive push thus instigated
may reverberate through a great part of the segmentary structure,
inexorably building up intense centrifugal pressure. Minor, major,
and higher order segments are mobilized—through complementary opposition—against their equivalents. Those who are being
pushed from the inside are induced to expand outward, which

movement automatically allies both pushers and pushed, as companion segments, against still higher-order Tiv lineages, and ultimately a large sector of Tiv are pressing foreigners. The Bohannans present an interesting hypothetical model of this process, too long to quote here, in which a man trying to expand holdings against companion segments is reminded at every turn that the segments are brothers and one should take land from the neighboring, higher-level equivalent lineage instead, until it becomes relevant that "'All Tiv are brothers; you should take land from foreigners'" (L. and P. Bohannan 1953:56, cf. P. Bohannan 1954b:59). The segmentary lineage system consistently channels expansion outward, releasing internal pressure in an explosive blast against other peoples.

A border lineage may be forced by internal pressure to move en masse against another tribe; the Bohannans aptly call this "steamroller expansion." A "long and bitter war" will follow (P. Bohannan 1954a:7). The concerted movement of a border village may be entirely against its will: the lineage is simply crowded out as the Tiv side of its land is consumed by the appetites of other Tiv (P. Bohannan 1954a:7). Of course, at the border internal Tiv lineages join their brothers in the good fight. Having advanced the border lineage, the internal lineages then fill in the vacated land, always keeping the same relative positions. Every lineage that does not bound foreigners knows "just which lineages they 'follow' (*chir*), and—though they are likely to push or shove (*kpolom*)—they will assist those in front to take over from foreigners" (P. Bohannan 1954a:9). Steamroller expansion is most characteristic of Tiv expansion in the south where there is intensive competition with neighboring tribes. In the north, "leapfrog" migration is more common: a group from an internal segment catapults over the border and infiltrates a new area. The invading nucleus is eventually joined by people of related segments and all distribute themselves according to genealogical distance, paralleling their original positions.

Across Africa, in the periodically flooded grasslands around the Upper Nile, a similar drama of expansion is played out. The principal protagonists in this arena are the Nuer and their principal victims, the Dinka. The Nuer invasion of Dinkaland—and also of Anuak territory farther east—can be described as a *Drang nach Osten*. This is the main trend, although there is a tendency

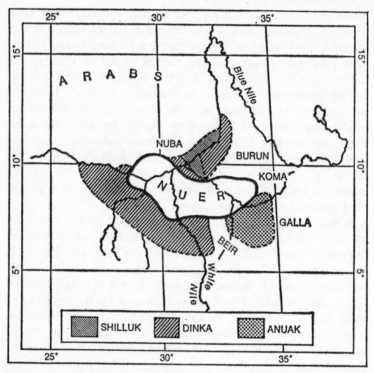

FIG. 4

to expand in other directions, especially against southern and western Dinka. If the tribal map of the area can be used to decipher its history, it appears that the Nuer have simply dis-membered the Dinka, divided them into separate sections south-west and northeast of the Nile (Fig. 4).

The major outlines of Nuer incursions in the Upper Nile are summed up by Evans-Pritchard:

> As far as history and tradition go back, and in the vistas of myth beyond their farthest reach, there has been enmity between the two peoples. Almost always the Nuer have been the aggressors. . . . Every Nuer tribe raided Dinka at least every two or three years, and some part of Dinkaland must have been raided annually. . . . The earliest travellers record that Nuer held both banks of the Nile, but it is probable that the entire Zeraf Island was at one time occupied by Dinka and it is certain that the whole of the country from the Zeraf to the Pibor and, to the north of the Sobat, from the confines of Shillukland to the Ethiopian scarp

was, with the exception of riverain settlements of Anuak, still in their hands as late as the middle of last century, when it was seized by the Nuer. . . . The conquest, which seems to have resulted in absorption and miscegenation rather than extermination, was so rapid and successful that the whole of this vast area is today occupied by Nuer, except for a few pockets of Dinka. . . . Some Dinka tribes took refuge with compatriots to the south, where the Gaawar [Nuer] and Lou [Nuer] continued to raid them. The Western Nuer likewise persistently raided all the Dinka tribes that border them, particularly those to the south and west, obtained a moral ascendancy over them, and compelled them to withdraw farther and farther from their boundaries. . . . Of all the Dinka only the Ngok, to the south of the Sobat, were left in peace, probably on account of their poverty of stock and grazing . . . (Evans-Pritchard 1940b:125–27).

Nuer expansion represents the successful conquest of a particular ecological niche: the true savannah of the Sudan. Nuer relations with neighboring peoples have been directly predicated on the potentialities of their areas for the Nuer mode of production. Thus, not only did the riverain Anuak and Ngok Dinka escape Nuer ravages, but the Nuer have had little to do with the powerful Shilluk kingdom because it is situated in poor pasture land. (Conversely, the Shilluk have probably tolerated the Nuer rather than moved against them because Nuerland is marginal to the Shilluk mode of production.) The Anuak were driven east into tsetse-infested forests; the Nuer wave then spent itself against this ecological barrier (Evans-Pritchard 1940b:68, 133). The Dinka have been the consistent victim of Nuer predation precisely because, "of all neighboring areas Dinkaland alone opposes no serious oecological handicaps to a pastoral people" (1940b:131; cf. 59). [It may be then that the Western Dinka display considerable ingenuity in reconciling their fate, for they contrast themselves to the savannah-dwelling Nuer as primarily "a people of savannah-forest settlement" (Lienhardt 1958:99).]

Nuer expansion is perhaps an outstanding instance of the Law of Cultural Dominance, the principle that the cultural system most effective in a particular environment will spread there at the expense of thermodynamically less effective systems (Kaplan 1960). In any event it is clear that the Nuer have been able to expel the Dinka because of the superior military potential of the Nuer segmentary lineage system. While the Nuer and Dinka are alike in culture, there are differences in social organization.

On the Dinka side these differences amount to the tragic flaw that has condemned them to a history of withdrawal.

The Dinka are, to use Lienhardt's (1958) terms, divided into a number of "tribal groups," each further subdivided into "tribes," "subtribes," and yet smaller segments. However, these are not genealogical segments—they cannot be placed on a single agnatic genealogy—nor are they disposed in local-genealogical segmentation; in fact the "tribes" are not necessarily geographic blocs. Political units among the Dinka are not fixed by complementary opposition. Instead, subtribes, and even smaller segments, display a notable tendency to fragment into *absolute, independent* entities. Subtribes crystallize about two or more unrelated lineages, one a priestly group and another a warrior line, standing for and representing the subtribe, which is itself a camping unit in the wet season and is also concentrated (in one or two sites) in the dry period. The critical thing is that this divisive, segmenting tendency is not matched by fusion with lineage-equivalent segments in higher-order, relative groupings. The Dinka lack the thermostatic mechanism for massing against the outside, a deficiency that has been fatal:

> In the 19th century, when much of Western Dinkaland was pillaged by slavers and adventurers, there was little wide-scale co-operation against the common enemies. It is known that neighbouring tribes of Dinka harried each other in temporary alliances with the invaders until they began to understand the scale of the subjection which they were all inviting. *Even now, however, many Dinka recognize that Nuer are able to unite on a larger scale than are Dinka* (Lienhardt 1958:108; emphasis ours).

This difference between Nuer and Dinka is, we think, related to differences attending their respective occupation of the Sudan. The Dinka appear to have spread without great opposition. *They were first.* They naturally grew by segmentation, and fissioning units could, in the absence of external threat, afford to organize as small, virtually self-contained entities. The Dinka themselves suppose that small settlements inevitably grow and break up into discrete groups, each able to stand by itself. Lienhardt remarks that "such a theory . . . could only develop among a people who know themselves free to move away from each other; *to occupy further tracts of empty or weakly occupied country, and to find new pastures*" (1958:114; emphasis ours). There is no independent confirmatory evidence, according to Lienhardt. However,

the enormous population of the Dinka—about 900,000—coupled
with the weak, fragmented polity, certainly does suggest that they
moved into a large uncontested domain.

The Nuer, by contrast, were invaders. They spread through an
already occupied niche, one held by Dinka, and the very large
Nuer population, over 200,000, is testimony of their success.
The Nuer had different adaptive problems than the Dinka, precisely because *the Dinka were already there.* This selective circumstance placed a premium on the ability to fuse as well as to
segment, on complementary opposition. Nuer segmentary lineage
organization was the adaptive response. The Dinka, whose development in an open environment had favored segmentation but
minimized fusion, then found themselves socially ill-equipped to
cope with Nuer predation.[7]

The well known seasonal movements of the Nuer impose a
particular form of expansion. The outward push seems to origi-
nate from dry season dispersal in search of water and pasturage.
It is significant that lineage segments of relatively low level—
Evans-Pritchard's "tertiary sections" composed of a number of
villages, or else higher-order "secondary sections"—characteristically fan out in different directions in this critical period (although a definite eastward trend in the separate movements appears in some of Evans-Pritchard's maps, e.g., 1940:56).[8] On

[7] The Lugbara also tend to depart from Tiv-Nuer in specific ways that
suggest, among other things, development in an uncontested habitat. We
make special mention of this because the Lugbara are classified as a
"classical" segmentary lineage system in *Tribes Without Rulers.* However,
the Lugbara form discrete, absolute social groupings at a comparatively
low level, that are called "major segments" by Middleton. Neither above
nor below this level is there a consistent tendency for groups to emerge
through complementary opposition—no consistent structural relativity.
Moreover, the major segment tends to be a ranked lineage (or ramage),
the subdivisions of which are graded by genealogical priority. Also, the
major lineage and its segments have "representative elders" whose position depends on genealogical seniority. The Lugbara, 250,000 strong,
clearly entered their sector of the Nile-Congo divide "under a slow process
of migration-drift from the north or the northwest. . . . There is evidence
. . . of a great deal of movement of Lugbara territorial groups relative
to one another. . . . There were no large-scale wars, only small-scale feuds
which might result in territorial expansion" (Middleton 1958:206, 227–28;
cf. Middleton 1954).

[8] The general eastward trend of Nuer invasions may account for the
tendency of their segmentary lineage system to cut off at the subtribal
level. A kind of "leap-frogging" appears to have been the normal mode
of Nuer expansion: a number of groups seem to have successively pulled

the one hand, of course, this minimizes competition for water and pasturage among equivalent segments of larger Nuer lineages. On the other hand, each Nuer segment is thus brought into juxtaposition with outsiders, typically Dinka. The Nuer are too scattered at this point in the cycle to take full advantage of the potential massing effect. But some fighting with foreigners during the dry season dispersal—or at the least something in the nature of a probe or reconnaissance—is indicated (e.g., Evans-Pritchard 1940b:62).

Full-fledged wars and raids prosecuted by large sectors of Nuer (the component sections of a "tribe," in Evans-Pritchard's terms) occurred at the end of the rainy season. The Nuer chronically raided the Dinka for cattle and iron tools, but a raid might transform itself into an actual invasion. The raiders would settle in and systematically extend the sphere of terror until the Dinka were compelled to withdraw (cf. Evans-Pritchard 1940b: 128). The ranks of the invaders might be swelled by additional immigrants from their homeland, and also by Dinka captives and enclaved settlements. These Dinka were integrated into the lineage arrangement of the invading nucleus. (Conquest and absorption of this sort, as opposed to conquest and rule, seems typical of the tribal level, where political and economic means which would make the latter feasible have not yet been achieved.)

As a final note we might consider whether population pressure can be held responsible for Tiv expansion in Nigeria and the comparable Nuer incursions in East Africa. Certain resources, notably dry season water and pasturage, are evidently in short supply among the Nuer, and Evans-Pritchard is prepared to agree that Nuer expansion is due to overpopulation, which is also the Nuer explanation (Evans-Pritchard 1940b:110–11). Among the Tiv, population density is extreme and land has been subjected to dangerously intensive use in some parts of the south, evidently in consequence of modern checks on Tiv migration. But in the sector of rapid recent expansion, the northern frontier, population density falls to levels below one-half of the general Tivland average of 64 per square mile.

---

out of the Nuer homeland west of the Nile and catapulted into Dinka and Anuak territory. These groups are now arranged in a west-east chain of high-level segments, but since the chain has been forged by leap-frogging, local-genealogical segmentation breaks down at this high level.

Perhaps population pressure in critical central locations gives impetus to both Tiv and Nuer predation. Yet it seems to us that a certain relativity is required in assessing land hunger among societies competing for occupation of a specific habitat. Because the success of one contestant is necessarily to the detriment of the other, neither has *enough* land until the other has been eliminated. The need for "living-space" is built in: it becomes a cultural attitude and theory, particularly in that society which has the decisive competitive advantage. Among the invaders a natural increase of population beyond the carrying capacity of present resources will be taken for granted, and at least for them land hunger exists—the idea is adaptively advantageous—even if, by objective standards, there is enough land to support the present population. Thus, in northern and extreme southeastern Tivland, "where no land shortage exists," the search for more land is prominently articulated by Tiv as a cause for migration (L. and P. Bohannan 1953:54). From an adaptive viewpoint this is no paradox.

Conclusions

The segmentary lineage system is an institution appearing at the tribal level of general cultural evolution; it is not characteristic of bands, chiefdoms, or the several forms of civilization. It develops among societies with a simple neolithic mode of production and a correlative tendency to form small, autonomous economic and political groups. The segmentary lineage system is a social means of temporary consolidation of this fragmented tribal polity for concerted external action. It is, in a sense, a substitute for the fixed political structure which a tribal society is incapable of sustaining.

It will not, however, be found among all tribes. Certain social conditions are presupposed—for one thing, the existence of lineality or lineages. In turn, lineality is a product of repetitive, long-term use of restricted resources. If this ecological factor is absent, it seems unlikely that a segmentary lineage system will appear.

A segmentary lineage system develops in a tribe that intrudes into an already occupied habitat rather than a tribe that expands into an uncontested domain. Expansion in an open environment may well be accompanied by segmentation, the normal process of tribal growth and spread. But in the absence of competition small segments tend to become discrete and autonomous, linked together primarily through mechanical solidarity. These circumstances, in other words, favor fission but select against complementary opposition or fusion, and long-term occupation will eventually fix this structure, make it comparatively inflexible. By contrast, growth in the face of opposition selects for complementary opposition as a social means of predation. Thus the *first* tribe in an area is unlikely to develop a segmentary lineage system, but the *second* tribe in that area is more likely to.

That the segmentary lineage system occurs among intrusive tribal societies also suggests that, from a long-term view, it is likely to be ephemeral. Once a society has succeeded in driving competitors from its habitat, the selective force favoring fusion disappears and the fragmenting tendencies of the neolithic economy are free to express themselves. In other words, the segmentary lineage system is self-liquidating. It is advantageous in intertribal competition, but having emerged victorious it has no longer *raison d'être* and the divisive tendencies of tribal polity reassert themselves. This helps to explain why segmentary lineage systems, contrary to the popular view, have a relatively limited ethnographic distribution.

Finally, the segmentary lineage system develops in a specifically *intertribal* environment, in competition between societies of the tribal level. Expansion of a tribe against small, weakly integrated band societies would normally not call for special mechanisms of tribal consolidation. And, on the other side, a segmentary lineage system would be ineffective in competition with chiefdoms and states. To oppose—let alone to prey upon—societies of this order requires large-scale, organic integration of economic and political, especially military, effort. Limited economic coordination, the relativity of leadership and its absence of coercive sanction, the localized, egalitarian character of the polity, the ephemerality of large groupings, all of these would doom a segmentary lineage system if brought into conflict with chiefdoms or states.

The Nuer themselves provide a convincing illustration. When faced with Arab aggression at the turn of this century and with later European intrusion, their segmentary system began to collapse, or rather, it was transformed into something else. The Nuer were rallied against their common and formidable enemies by prophets who transcended the sectional oppositions of lineages, and acted, to use Evans-Pritchard's phrase, as "pivots of federation." A system of hereditary political leadership and extensive political unification began to emerge. If this revolution had not been checked by European dominance—and also if it had been able to muster adequate economic support—the Nuer would not simply have overthrown the segmentary lineage system, but catapulted themselves to the chiefdom level of evolutionary progress (cf. Evans-Pritchard 1940b:184–89).

6 THE GOVERNMENTAL ROLES OF ASSOCIATIONS AMONG THE YAKÖ

Daryll Forde

Daryll Forde is Professor of Anthropology at University College London, University of London. He is the author of *Ethnography of the Yuma Indians* (1931), *Habitat, Economy and Society* (1934), *Marriage and the Family Among the Yakö in Southeastern Nigeria* (1941), *The Native Economies of Nigeria* (1946), *The Ibo and Ibibio Speaking Peoples of Southeastern Nigeria* (with G. I. Jones, 1950), *The Yoruba-speaking Peoples of Southwestern Nigeria* (1951), *The Context of Belief* (1958), and *Yakö Studies* (1964); he is editor or co-editor of *African Systems of Kinship and Marriage* (1950), *African Worlds* (1954), and *Efik Traders of Old Calabar* (1957); and has also written many papers, especially on the Yakö.

IN THE STUDY of indigenous African institutions that exercise control while promoting social cohesion and regulating inter-personal and inter-group competition, much attention has been given to the analysis of the governmental functions of kin groups on the one hand and of ritually sanctioned political chiefship on the other. Institutions of these two types, which correspond to the distinction made by Durkheim between segmental and organic solidarity, were the basis of the well-known classification of *African Political Systems* by Fortes and Evans-Pritchard into two contrasted types labelled lineage or segmentary in one case, and centralized or state-like in the other. In their classification these writers were mainly concerned to distinguish politically centralized chiefdoms from those societies in which the exercise of political authority and social control was confined to recurrent but fluctuating combinations of lineages under their ritual leaders. In this they were led to imply, perhaps as a result of the limited

FROM *Africa* 31, No. 4, 1961:309–23, by permission of the author and of the International African Institute.

range of societies selected for consideration, that apart from
small autonomous bands of kindred, the only alternative to an
acephalous and segmentary lineage system was a centralized
society in which offices and political powers were hierarchically
arranged with definite relations of administrative superiority and
subordination holding between offices and councils at different
levels. 'Administrative machinery' and 'judicial institutions' were
treated as concomitants of centralized authority (1940:5, 6–7,
11–12).

This antithesis, while it served to classify broadly the societies
actually selected for presentation, took no account of important
gaps in its coverage. For it did not consider societies in which
neither of these principles of organization and control could be
held to be dominant, still less exclusive principles of political
organization. That criteria of social obligation other than lineage
membership or chiefly allegiance were prominent in the maintenance of political relations and the exercise of authority in
some African societies has, of course, long been obvious. As
Paula Brown (1951) showed in a comparative analysis of a
number of West African societies some years ago, it was necessary not only to distinguish different kinds of authority (moral,
ritual, and legal in her terminology), but also to recognize that
offices vested in or authoritative over different types of group
(kinship, associational, and territorial) might co-exist in varying
relations and that there could be different allocations of the
various kinds of authority referred to.[1]

But the not uncommon tendency to perpetuate a scheme of
apparently clear-cut categories that has served a useful initial
purpose would seem to have hindered general recognition that
some indigenous forms of government in Africa cannot, even as
a first approximation, be fitted into so simple a dichotomy. Among
these are societies in which self-perpetuating associations exercise
autonomous ritual power and secular authority over part or all
of the population with respect to a major sphere of social life.
In such societies governmental powers—including both political
action and judicial decisions—may be widely distributed among
a number of independent and overlapping agencies. Wider political relations then largely resolve themselves into modes of

[1] A similar criticism has since been made by Middleton and Tait (1958:
1–32). See also Southall (1956).

co-operation with and competition between such associations. The co-ordination of political action in government does not therefore depend directly on the solidarity and co-operation of lineages on the one hand or on the paramount authority of a chief and its delegation to his subordinates on the other. It is achieved to the extent that there is mutual adjustment of their distinct competences by the several associations which may include some form of conciliar organization of their respective leaders. The role of associations among the Yakö is briefly analyzed here as an instance of political organization of this kind.

The Yakö live in five compact politically independent village communities to the east of the Middle Cross River. Each claims exclusive rights over a surrounding tract of territory which is exploited by its component groups for farming and the collection of forest products. These were, according to their traditions, successively established after an initial migration, perhaps rather more than a hundred years ago, of one or more groups from the Oban forest area to the east. These settlements maintained some external trading and other contacts with this eastern area now occupied by Ejagham and other small communities, and appear to have acted as middlemen between it and traders from the Cross River in traffic based on the exchange of camwood, bushmeat, and other forest products for gunpowder and 'trade goods'. At the same time they contributed substantially from at least the beginning of this century to the supply of palm oil and food crops to the Cross River trade. Although they appear to have taken little direct part as traders in the Cross River traffic, the Yakö derived considerable wealth in rods, cloth, and other goods in exchange for their forest and farm products. Their village communities appear to have grown rapidly since at least the beginning of this century. Ranging in population from three to over ten thousand, several of them are as large as were many of the Yoruba or Akan chiefdoms.

Patriclans and Ward Organization

In the nineteen-thirties, the period to which this account relates, Umor, the largest of the Yakö villages with a population of about 11,000, was composed of four wards each occupied by a number of localized patriclans (yepun, sing. kepun) varying in size from 50 to 200 adult men. These in turn comprised a number of lineages of 15 to 30 adult men, within which patri-kinship by birth or through specific adoptions was traced gene-alogically to a depth of three or four generations and constituted the grounds for heritable rights to house sites and tracts of land. Kinship between lineages, and thus for members of a clan as a whole, was postulated as a norm for further rights and obliga-tions, but it was not generally traced genealogically and often recognized as fictive and derived from the incorporation of in-coming lineages and sections of other clans.

Thus little stress was placed on descent within the clan as a whole and there was no ancestral cult. The ritual head of a patriclan (Obot Kepun) was the custodian and priest of a spirit shrine. He presided over gatherings of informally recognized elders of the component lineages, arbitrated disputes among them, and formally represented the patriclan in external relations. His ritual capacity to afford the protection of the clan spirit and expiation of offences within the clan gave him moral authority in the interests of clan solidarity and the observance of custom. But the effectiveness and indeed the content of his judgements depended on the strength of his personality and support within the clan.

The unity and distinctness of a ward (kekpatu, pl. yekpatu) was strictly territorial. Its component patriclans did not claim common descent. It was seen as an aggregation of patriclans formed initially by an early association of a few patriclans among which there had been subsequent fission and to which lineages and sections of patriclans from other wards or villages had attached themselves in the course of the growth of the village (Forde 1950). Over the residential areas and lands claimed by its component clans the authorities of a ward had established rights to organize and control certain collective activ-ities, to defend the rights of its clans against other wards and villages, and to arbitrate disputes among them. Within the ward each patriclan controlled and defended occupation of its own dwelling area and the tracts of land in which its members had established and inherited rights to farm plots, clusters of oil palms, and forest resources.

The wards were accordingly compact aggregates of from five to eleven patriclans each, comprising populations of from 300 to 600 men and their households. There was no dogma of common patrilineal descent of the component clans, nor was there any ranking of clans within the ward. Apart from its more general significance as a neighbourhood within a larger community, it was a ritual unit for initiation of boys and other ceremonies, a higher order of grouping for collective protection of rights to land, both residential and productive, and for internal social control. It was also the unit for the organization of age-sets, to the junior of which periodic tasks were assigned. Thus both the wards and the patriclans of Umor were said to have been formed by processes of fission and accretion associated with growth of population, ruptures of relations between lineages within clans, and coalescence of lineages and migrant men in other units. The effects of these processes in the formation, division, and migrations of patriclans have been analysed elsewhere (Forde 1938). The tradition with regard to the wards was that two settlement areas, Idjiman and ŋkpani, were established when Yakö first settled in Umor. Separate wards were subsequently established by groups separating from Idjiman to form Idjum and Ukpakapi, and two generations ago a new ward, Biko-Biko, was established mainly by migrants from Ukpakapi. Meanwhile early in the history of Umor growing friction between ŋkpani and another ward flared up into serious fighting, which ended by the migration of ŋkpani to found a separate village of that name.

In each ward there was an association of Leaders (Yakamben =Men of the Ward), the Head of which (Ogbolia)—supported by his deputy (Ogometu), the preparer of meat for feasts (Okaladji), and Announcer (Edjukwa)—claimed a general authority in the name of the association over both ritual and secular affairs. The whole body of members assembled only for periodic rituals and at funerals of their members. The membership of this association of Ward Leaders was said in the thirties to have increased considerably in more recent times, when more than one new candidate had been accepted at the mortuary rites of a member. This was attributed to increased wealth, especially among the younger men, from participation in the oil-palm trade.[2] The heads of the several patriclans expected, and were expected, to be members, but they were a minority within it. The successor to a patriclan headship might already be an Okamben, if not he became one only when the payments were offered and accepted and the admission feast was held. Any unresolved dispute within the ward affecting the clan or the man concerned had to be settled to the satisfaction of the Leaders before a new clan head would be admitted. Priests of major village cults resident in the ward were normally admitted on succession to their ritual offices in the same way as patriclan heads. Otherwise succession was of one, or sometimes two, close kinsmen of a deceased member at the latter's death. Such memberships were sometimes spoken of as descending within the lineages in which one of their forebears was an original or early member. But provision of a successor to such former members was also an obligation, and a substantial fine, in lieu of admission payments, would be demanded if no suitable candidate were put forward. In proposing and accepting candidates their personal qualities were considered on both sides. Energetic and ambitious younger men could seek entry and in the thirties were often accepted.

There was in any case no fixed numerical or proportionate membership of the Leaders from the several patriclans and this was often very unequal. Nor was membership restricted to patrilineal succession, for successors to matriclan priesthoods joined the Leaders of the ward in which their shrine was situated. Patrikinsmen had only a right and a duty at the death of a member to present and help pay for the admission of a suitable successor from their lineage or clan. The means of a candidate to provide largely from his own resources for these payments in

[2] Total membership was said to have previously been only about 30 but a count of memberships in associations in one patriclan in 1939 showed that some 30 per cent of adult men claimed to be Yakamben. If this was typical it would give a much higher membership figure. This accounts for a discrepancy in statements about the numbers of Yakamben in an earlier publication (Forde 1950). In the census covering 108 adult men of the major section of one patriclan comprising five lineages of from 13 to 28 men each, 35 per cent claimed membership of the Ward Leaders' association. Their ages covered a wide span. Only a fifth of them were over 50 and more than a third were, according to their age-set memberships, less than 40 years old. In this article Yakamben are referred to as Leaders in place of the ambiguous term Elders used in the earlier publication.

meat and currency was frequently a main consideration in the selection.

Thus the Ward Leaders were not *de jure* an assembly of patriclan heads and elders with an exclusive right to membership representing the clan sections of the ward. On the contrary, the Yakamben constituted and were thought of by the Yakö as a self-recruited and self-perpetuating body of notables, including holders of prominent ritual offices. It controlled succession to its own offices (headship, spirit representation in the ward initiation cult, &c.) by selection from its own members, and most of the power of the association was exercised by its Head in consultation with those concerned in any issue that might arise. Rights to succession to the office of Ogbolia were claimed by three or four patriclans within each of the wards. These were patriclans which professed to date from the founding of the ward in question and sought to nominate one of their members, normally from among those already Leaders, in rotation.[3] It appeared, however, that neither appointment from a particular clan nor strict rotation had been followed, and much depended on inter-clan relations and the prestige of candidates when succession arose. There appeared to be a general tendency for patriclans and indeed patrilineages within them to claim rights of succession to offices in associations. A similar tendency existed in the matrilineages of matriclans with regard to village priesthoods and both were an expression of the solidarity of kin in relation to other groupings and the wider society with reference to questions of status and influence.

The office of Ogbolia could be held concurrently with other offices in other associations. Thus the Ogbolia of Idjum ward in the twenties was said to have been also the Head (Oboi Yakpan) of the village association of Ikpungkara, that of Idjiman was Head (Obot Obunga) of the village corporation of diviners, and accordingly a member of the council of village priests. The Ogbolia of Biko-Biko (Elung Ugopo) in the thirties

---

[3] Thus, in Ukpakapi ward the Egbisum, Usadja, and Lekpangkem patriclans assumed this right and in Idjiman ward, Lebuli, Kebung, Otalosi, and Ugom made similar claims. In Ukpakapi one territorial subdivision of a large patriclan—the Ndai section of Lekpangkem-Ndai—had sought to monopolize the second office (of Ogometu) by demanding a right to nominate the successor when an Ogometu from the Obeten Ogometu lineage of Ndai had died.

was also the priest of the village cult of Obasi Oden and a member of the priests council.[4]

The Ogbolia in the name of the Ward Leaders had moral authority over other men's associations in the ward, i.e. an association of fighters (Eblömbe), of hunters (Kodjo) and a graded ritual, executive, and recreational association known as Ebiabu into which most males were initiated in boyhood. He had to be kept informed of all the important activities and intentions of these organizations. He could demand that they observed customary usages and order them to pay fines to or compensate others for breaches of custom. But these other associations were also self-recruited, with admission dependent on individual capacity and reputation and usually payment of fees. They were autonomous within their own fields of occupational and ritual or recreational activities. Overlapping membership of Ward Leaders in the membership of the Fighters and the senior grade of Ebiabu facilitated the co-ordination of their activities. In particular the Ward Head could, through the latter's senior grade Abu, request the middle grade of Ebiabu to coerce or apprehend recalcitrant offenders or quell intra-ward disturbances.[5]

The Leaders had strong *esprit de corps* with respect to their authority in ward affairs. Their dominance over the component patriclans was also ceremonially and materially emphasized at the death of a member, when they assembled to bid him farewell and dance in his compound. They then demanded from his heirs substantial provisions for holding their own feast in his honour and the nomination of, and admission payments for, a successor.

[4] The overlapping memberships in ward and village associations were further shown in the census of one patriclan section referred to above in which eleven of the men who were Leaders in the ward were also members of various senior village associations. Two, both old men of sixty or more, were members of the inner priesthood of Okengka and one of these was also a priest of Korta. Two others were also members of Korta. Three were members of Ikpungkara and three others were members of Okundom. There were two other members of Okundom who had not joined the Ward Leaders.

[5] The authority and functions of the Ogbolia and the Yakamben as here described were those attributed to them by the Yakö for the period before the Native Court became effective in the twenties. The manner in which the judicial and other secular functions of the Ogbolia came to be superseded by those of Court members ('Warrant Chiefs') selected from the wards has been indicated in Forde (1939).

Within the general body there was also a smaller group consisting of its office holders and a few others who had the privilege of conducting an annual ward rite (Kekpan) at the time of the clearing of farmland. Apart from the office holders there was again obligatory succession by a kinsman which entailed further payments.

Within each ward there was also, however, an association known as ŋkpe that was co-ordinated with and did not accept directions concerning its own affairs from the Leaders. Claiming control of a punitive Leopard Spirit derived from the Ejagham (Ekoi) peoples to the east, it offered supernatural protection to its members, and to others for a fee, against theft of crops and stock and also the seduction and insubordination of wives. ŋkpe had no acknowledged right of physical coercion of its members or others. Its secular power consisted in its right to claim damages for the abuse of its protective emblems when these had been placed on the trees or other property of an applicant. ŋkpe also regarded itself as a means of defence against abuse of power both by the Leaders and the village cult groups. These in turn treated it with suspicion and admitted no leading member of ŋkpe to their ranks. It had become a reluctantly tolerated opposition.

Thus within the ward in Umor secular authority, judicial decisions, and the ritual expression of social cohesion and continuity were in the hands of a number of organizations of an associational character. Participation, office, and influence within them depended on acceptance by their own members. Patriclans and lineages could influence their actions and decisions and also derive prestige only through the membership of their own elders and spokesmen within them. Between the associations themselves there was little explicit hierarchy of political authority. The Leaders had recognized authority over the junior age-sets with regard to customary tasks and a *de facto* means of coercing those who flouted a decision that enjoyed general support through overlapping membership in, and a working arrangement with, the independent association of Ebiabu. At the same time the ability of ŋkpe to establish itself as an independent and generally hostile association was a clear indication of the limitations on the authority of the Leaders.

Village Organization

Needless to say, disputes between individuals, lineages, and other groups from different wards could bring the Leaders and other associations within them into conflict. The outbreak of widespread violence arising from inter-ward disputes was recalled as a serious danger in the past. One such occurrence was particularly remembered, since it ended in the extinction of one of the first two wards early in the history of the village. This ward occupied the area south-east of the market in the angle between Idjiman and Ukpakapi wards. Most of its population was said to have left to found, or perhaps to join, the independent Yakö village of ŋkpani several miles away.

The risk of a resort to force in inter-ward hostilities engendered by such disputes was tempered by the existence of a village cult group to which some Leaders from the several wards belonged. To this ritual fraternity, some fifty strong, known as Okengka, Ward Heads could and should bring disputes they could not otherwise resolve.

Here again, membership in this village cult association was not a formal right of offices vested in either the patriclans or the wards. But since membership carried prestige and a means of influence both for the member and his patrikin, prosperous, energetic, and reliable men who became Ward Leaders usually sought and were supported for membership of Okengka. Only those who were already Leaders in their wards were usually acceptable for membership and each Ward Head (Ogbolia) and his deputy (Ogometu) was expected to join and be admitted on his appointment if he were not already a member. Membership of Okengka was not considered to involve obligatory succession. But, on the other hand, the patrikin of a deceased member would usually request that one of them should be admitted. There were also claims that the Headship of Okengka (Ovar Ekpe) should pass in turn to men of one of three patriclans that were reputed to be the oldest in each of the three long-established wards.

Contravention of a judgement of the Okengka spirit, as made known by the head of the cult group after secret conclave, entailed grave misfortune of an unpredictable character for the offenders and their kin. Ward Heads and Leaders used the sanctions of Okengka to uphold judgements on intractable disputes both within a ward as well as in the settlement of issues between persons and groups of different wards. Thus common participation of their senior members in the Okengka cult both provided means for, and accustomed the Ward Leaders to, co-operation and co-ordinated action in maintaining order.

The Head of Okengka as priest of a village Leopard cult was in turn one of the members of a more restricted body of twenty-four men in which both ritual powers and moral authority in the village as a whole were concentrated. This was a village corporation of priests known simply as the Heads (Yabot). Its nucleus consisted of the ten priests of fertility spirits (ase) with each of which was associated one or more of the twenty-three dispersed matriclans recognized in the village.[6] Each of these priesthoods was vested in a particular matriclan whose elders proposed successors from among its membership. But, as in the case of all the village priesthoods, the recognition and the installation of a fertility priest ultimately rested not with the matriclan, but with the corporation of priests as a body, which had quite often rejected candidates it considered unsuitable. The nomination, on the part of the relevant group, and the acceptance of a candidate by the Yabot was accordingly often the occasion for much rivalry and mobilization of influence among those concerned.

Of the ten fertility spirits, one, known as Odjokobi, was accorded ritual primacy as the oldest and the foremost of the spirits that were brought by a senior matrilineal group at the founding of the village. The powers of Odjokobi were held to be especially concerned with and available for the welfare of the village as a whole and its priest was known as Head of the Village (Obot Lopon). The shrine of this spirit was set apart in a compound at the centre of the village on a site that belonged to no patriclan or ward. Here, in a large compound adjacent to the village market, its priest resided after his installation. The more important village ceremonies began and ended with rites in this compound in which the Yabot also assembled as a council.

But a further and larger number of custodians of other cults

[6] On the character of these spirits and the roles of their priests see Forde (1958:9–12; 1949).

were associated as Yabot with the priests of the fertility shrines. Some of these were priests of particular village spirit shrines. Thus the custodian of the emblems of the Liboku spirit, which was invoked annually in the village First Fruits ritual, was selected and installed by the priests council and incorporated into it. Others were officiants in other organized cult groups. Of these, in addition to Okengka, which has just been mentioned in connexion with the *de facto* ritual and judicial co-ordination of the Leaders of the several wards, there was, for example, the cult of Korta. In the course of a lengthy ritual of renewal of the village held every six years, the spirit of Korta sanctioned the initiation of all boys into the male community of the village. Three priestly offices in Korta, that of its Head (Opalapala), who was custodian of the spirit, his deputy and usual successor (Ogbodum) and the chief drummer (Otomise), were controlled by, and conferred membership in, the Yabot. The Headship was expected to pass in turn to men of one of three long-established patriclans, one in each ward. Successions to other positions in the cult, the Singer (Obenebenekpe) and the Drummers (Yakpapa), were also claimed by other lineages but these did not confer membership of the Yabot.

Further members of the Yabot were priests of certain spirits variously associated with the territory or rivers of the village (e.g. Esandet) or with its foundation site (Elamalama). Two others were responsible for war ritual (Yanun Eko), one with sacred village trumpets (Odele) and another with one of the shrines of the creator god, Obasi Oden. The head of the corporation of diviners, who was also priest of another diviners' cult of Obasi (Iso Obasi) and whose office passed from father to son or other close patrikinsman, was also installed by and became a member of this council.

But the leading public figure in this priestly council was its Speaker (Okpebri). In his custody were certain village drums and the emblems of a spirit on whose safe keeping the unity and continuity of the village was held to depend. The public display and threatened removal of the latter was believed to sanction, under penalty of general disaster, any prolonged disorder in the village. It was the Speaker who, during the successive public rituals at their shrines, actually invoked, on behalf of the village Head and the priests as a body, the beneficence of the fertility spirits during the seasonal rites.

Although there is no documentation from the past and I obtained only sketchy and sometimes variant traditions to confirm it, the formation and composition of this council of village priests in Umor appeared, and was believed by the Yakö, to result from the combination of these diverse cults. And the original nucleus was said to have been the association of the priests of the fertility spirits associated with the various matriclans. However that may be, the leading priests of these various spirit cults, on which a wide range of personal and collective benefits were believed to depend or from which punishment for offences was feared, had come to constitute a corporation of considerable solidarity.

Moreover, in addition to its powers of ritual interdiction and its generally effective moral authority in public affairs, the village priests council had traditionally been a source of judgement with regard not only to ritual offences, such as incest, abortion, and homicide, but also to major and refractory disputes between persons and groups. It was still commonly appealed to despite the establishment of the District Native Court for the area that began to be effective in the twenties. In an issue of the latter kind one party to the dispute could request that it be heard by the council. It was also expected to intervene itself by summoning contestants to state their cases before it if a dispute was dragging on unsettled by the Ward Leaders or by the judgements of one of the village associations. Such judgements were held to have been generally accepted in the past. Expiatory ritual offerings required were made, compensation awarded to injured parties was paid, and fines demanded of those against whom judgements were given were paid to the priests.

The priests council might also take up on its own initiative important public issues that arose in the village. On internal questions it would summon any Ward Leaders and heads of other associations that might be concerned to give information and to receive its views. On occasions it sent messengers bearing complaints or demands to other villages.

These judicial and deliberative capacities of the priests council were supported only by its combined ritual powers and moral authority. But these were not inconsiderable. The beneficence of

matriclan fertility spirits could be withheld from, and the punitive
action of other spirits threatened against, those who flouted their
judgement. In particular, a defiant individual could be ritually
sequestered in his house and his household and kin excom-
municated by the planting of the priests' staves on his veranda.
A judgement of the council also afforded moral authority for
punitive action by other associations whose intervention could be
invoked.

But no secular coercive action was directly available in the
council itself. This limitation on its powers directs attention to
the fact that, in addition to the Okengka cult group already
mentioned, there were in Umor other associations recruited from
the village at large, claiming the custody of other powerful
spirits, which did not participate through their leaders in the
village council of priests, but did claim the right to investigate
offences, give judgement, and enforce penalties by direct action.

One such village association, generally referred to as Okundom or 'The Body of Men', was especially concerned with trespass on farms and the stealing of crops. Against both magical
and material offences of this kind it provided, on receipt or
promise of a payment, the protection of its spirit. When offences
were alleged before it, the Heads of Okundom undertook de-
tection of the culprits, the presentation or support of an ac-
cusation before the Ward Leaders or the village priests council
and the enforcement of any compensation by actual or threatened
destruction of livestock of the offender or his kin. Where the
theft from farm land or trees was explicitly protected by Okundom, as marked by the affixing of its sign on the property concerned, the offender was held to have wronged the association
and the charge was brought against him specifically on those
grounds.

The formation of the Okundom association was traditionally
ascribed to serious thefts early in the history of the village.
This induced the priest of one of the matriclan spirits to sanction
its formation and to recognize as its first head a man from the
patriclan in the dwelling area in which the spirit shrine was
situated. Membership, secured by providing an admission payment and feast, then spread through the village in successive
generations. Nomination of a suitable successor to a deceased
member became both a right and an obligation of that member's

close patrikin. Memorial feasts and admission payments were demanded from them on the occasion of these successions, and the new members shared in the later feasts and the fees provided by those who sought its aid.

Okundom was, however, later overshadowed in prestige by another men's association known as Ikpungkara, the sphere of activity of which had also extended over the village as a whole. Its forty members, who came from all parts of the village, formed a close-knit group, who were on admission pledged by the supernatural sanctions of their spirit cult, both to divulge within the association and to keep secret from outsiders any information on alleged offences and other issues with which the association concerned itself. Ikpungkara was said to have been constituted early in the history of the village, but later than Okundom, by a group of senior men under the leadership of one of the patriclan heads. Apart from the maintenance of its own prestige, its main concern had been with settling land disputes, which had been numerous in the course of the growth of the community, and with detecting and punishing theft of cows which browsed at large in the vicinity of the settlement. As farming and house-building expanded, Ikpungkara investigated on the ground and gave its judgement on several acrimonious disputes between men of different clans and wards over rights to build and to farm certain areas. It has also gained a general influence in all village affairs including external relations, concerning which it might declare and enforce a ban on visits to and trading with neighbouring villages, where bad relations had developed or an unsettled injury had been suffered by members of the village.

Ikpungkara usually announced its findings and judgements to the priests council which, in turn on occasion, suggested investigation by it. It was said to be rare that the council questioned its judgement and the compensation or other action it required. This liaison was facilitated by overlapping membership, since the village Head and several of the other priests of the matriclan fertility spirits were regularly admitted to Ikpungkara on succession on the death of a close kinsman who had been a member. Most of these successions were patrilineal, but a few in addition to those of the matriclan priests were matrilineal. Besides the provision of supplies for a memorial feast to the late member within Ikpungkara, the body of kin concerned were required to assist an acceptable successor in making the large admission payments that were valued in the thirties at some £20.

For its services in investigating offences and settling disputes, Ikpungkara secured payments—fees from those who appealed, and fines from those it found culpable. Like Okundom and the ward associations, it had an ultimate punitive sanction against those that would repudiate its authority or flout its judgement. Livestock in the compounds where the offenders resided were raided and killed or carried off. The offender was then left to settle as best he could with his kin and neighbours, who, in fear of a repetition so long as the matter was unsettled, forced him to accept and act on the judgement and beg for the return of such stock as had not already been eaten at a feast.

Both Ikpungkara and Okundom enjoyed ritual recognition and acceptance by the priests council, for they were among the groups which included the Ward Leaders, the diviners, and certain women's associations, that came successively in procession to the Village Head's compound for the first public rites at the Odjokobi spirit shrine at the seasonal festivals. There, like those of the other groups, their members received the blessing of the spirit by being smeared across the breast by the priest with chalk paste prepared at the altar.

On the other hand, neither Okundom nor Ikpungkara regarded themselves as mere agents or subordinates of the village priests council. Indeed, some of their members strongly repudiated such a suggestion. They said that the Yabot had their own 'messengers' (i.e. junior kinsmen whom they sent to call people they wished to speak with), and, furthermore, that they had their own spirit, which was independent of the fertility spirits of the matriclans and both justified and protected their own actions.

Ikpungkara and Okundom resembled the Yakamben of the wards in demanding the provision of memorial feasts and fees for the admission of successors from kinsmen at the deaths of members.[7] These were means of increasing the collective prestige of these associations and acceptance of their secular authority. In this they differed from the council of village priests, where membership was directly associated with appointment to ritual

[7] For an analysis of the relation between these associations and the kin groups of their members in Yakö mortuary ceremonial see Forde (1962).

office and no question of succession fees or the provision of feasts by the clans arose.

Conclusion

From this outline of the different levels at which various agencies exerted some form of social control in Umor beyond the limits of the local patriclan groups, it will be seen that, with respect to both the ward and to the village as a whole, there were separately developed organizations which claimed independent authority according to the circumstances of the activity or dispute. Supported by the sanction of spirits in their custody, they could require certain actions in the public interest, prohibit other actions, notably violent behaviour, and also demand that alleged offences and disputes within their sphere of authority be brought before them for inquiry and judgement. They claimed, in brief, the right to act as deliberative, executive or judicial authorities; although in many cases their *raison d'être* in the eyes of the Yakö was the performance of rituals which sustained and safeguarded the welfare of part or all of the community. But these bodies did not constitute a segmentary system of kin groups. Their members did not consist exclusively or mainly of the heads of clans. Lineage organization did not extend beyond the patriclan and the matriclan, and authority derived from it was confined within these comparatively small unilineal groups.

In the traditionally dominant governing body of the ward—the Yakamben whom we have called the Leaders—there was succession to membership from certain lineages and patriclan heads were admitted. But there was no formal chain of authority or ritual continuity between the patriclans and the ward. The Ward Leaders were sustained by their own spirits and were not regarded by the Yakö as a conclave of clan elders, nor did they function as such. They viewed their ritual powers, their rights and obligations territorially in terms of the ward and its population. For it they performed an annual rite and a periodic initiation of its boys. They recognized the formation of new age-sets and through their Announcer (Edjukwa) called for the public services of the more junior ones. The Ward Leaders heard and gave judgement in disputes within the ward. But they, themselves, had organized no powers of punishment or coercion with which to enforce their judgements. In cases of flagrant misbehaviour or defiance of a judgement they could only rely on their overlapping membership with the senior grade of an independently organized ward association—the Ebiabu—to secure this. Thus, while they had provided a form of ward government which, so long as it did not interfere with the established rights of patriclans and of other associations, appeared to have been respected, they had, in their mode of recruitment and their stress on spirit powers with respect to initiation and the moral unity of the ward, also the character of a cult group consisting of a closed association of notables. It was perhaps their weakness as an executive body that accounts in part for the rapid decay of their secular powers in recent times. For when members were called for from each of the wards to serve on the District Native Court established in the twenties, only one Ogbolia was put forward and accepted by the Administration as a warrant chief. And within ten years or so, the Native Court had supplanted the Yagbolia and the Yakamben of the wards as the most general means for securing redress for private wrongs.

Within the wider framework of the village community, neither the Yakamben as a body nor its priest head Ogbolia was directly responsible to the village council of priests. That the latter had a different and wider sphere of both ritual and secular authority which should, in the interest of harmony and prosperity, be respected, was generally recognized by the Ward Leaders and Yakö in general. But this implied only a co-operative, albeit in some contexts a deferential, relation between two organizations that were autonomous in their respective spheres. Apart from the Village Head, who had no ward residence, a matriclan priest was at one and the same time a member of the village priests council and of the Leaders of the ward in which his spirit shrine was situated. And other members of the village council were usually also Leaders in their wards.

When we consider the council of village priests it might be argued that its ritual head, who was explicitly recognized as Head of the Village, should be regarded as a chief in the political sense, as one who, supported by his council, exercised centralized authority over the village community. If this were acceptable, the political organization of Umor might still, perhaps without too much forcing of the evidence, be placed within the category of 'centralized, hierarchical, state-like forms of government', which

Fortes and Evans-Pritchard distinguished as the alternative to acephalous systems of segmentary lineage organization. The establishment of a separate and central compound, outside the territory of any of the wards, in which the Village Head resided, where important village rituals began and where the priests council assembled to deliberate on village affairs and give judgement on disputes—all this might give colour to such a view. But it would not only ignore the crucial lack, and indeed disavowal, of secular means of enforcing decisions and judgements. In terms of the combination of features taken as characterizing such a system, we can recognize the priests council as a 'centralized authority' only in the moral and ritual spheres. As a judicial institution these were its only modes of enforcement. Where these were challenged its sole resort was to approve or accept the coercive action of other bodies. Furthermore, it lacked 'administrative machinery' for carrying out any decisions it might reach on public affairs. Here again it had to depend on the concurrence and action of other village or ward associations.

Secondly, the status of the priest of the premier fertility spirit Odjokobi as Head of the Village (Obot Lopon) was that of a *primus inter pares* rather than of a chief enjoying distinctive status who was advised and checked by a body of councillors of lower rank. The priest of Odjokobi was nominated to, and approved and installed by, the council as a whole in the same manner as the other members. The rights of the Village Head with regard to hearing, giving judgement, and in particular collecting fees and fines had been an issue among the Yakö in the past. It was recounted in the thirties that the previous Village Head had sent his messengers on his own account to summon alleged offenders and had heard cases without summoning other members of the Yabot. This was held to be against custom and caused discontent and protest. On the other hand it was recognized that, where a minor private wrong was in question, the Village Head need not summon the whole council, which did not in any case assemble regularly in full session. The practice was for complainants and defendants to inform those Yabot with which they were connected by kinship, residential, or ritual ties and for those concerned to meet in the Village Head's compound for the hearing.

It should also be noted that the Village Head did not receive tribute. Small gifts of food were often brought to the priests council during village ceremonials but there was no general obligation to maintain him. His matriclan and the men of the ward from which he came were said to have an obligation to contribute materials and labour for the repair or rebuilding of the house and compound of the Village Head, and he could no doubt get help from both these sources. A compulsory offering that might be regarded as ritual tribute was the bringing of any leopard that had been killed to the compound of the Village Head. But it was Okpebri, not the Village Head, who took charge of carcasses and it was the Okengka cult association which conducted the rituals and admitted the leopard killer to its membership.

The mortuary ritual of the Village Head, while usually more protracted than that of other priests, did not differ essentially in procedure or ideology. Accounts of the burial of human heads and of cannibalism associated with it, which were discreetly placed in the past, were probably not distinctive, for the 'head hunting' associations that were formerly active were said to have obtained victims for the mortuary rituals of other priests.

We must conclude, therefore, that despite their considerable moral as well as ritual authority and the very general acceptance of their judgements on public issues and private disputes, the council of village priests in Umor and, so far as they are known, those of the other Yakö communities, cannot be regarded as the apex of a pyramidal form of centrally administered government. Individually the powers and the authority of the priests of the Yakö fertility and other spirits find closer analogues in those of the custodians of Earth shrines among the Southern Ibo, or again among the Lowiili, Tallensi, and other peoples of Northern Ghana.

The tradition of compact settlement and the double system of descent among the Yakö has resulted in a pattern of large communities composed of closely neighbouring territorial patriclans, and of dispersed matriclans in each of which membership is scattered over the whole community. With a considerable growth of population these conditions appear to have fostered a closer association of the matriclan priests who embodied positive values of peaceful co-operation. Their formal organization for the conduct of public rituals on behalf of the community would have further enhanced their moral authority. The priests of other cults were incorporated into this body, which accordingly acquired an essentially associational character as a self-regulating corporation that co-ordinated both the complex series of ritual activities significant for the village as a whole and the exercise of ritual sanctions by the priests of these various cults.

In the large and dense aggregation of population a number of other punitive spirit cults were adopted and lined in some cases to material coercion for the protection and regulation of individual and kin-group rights within the framework of both major territorial divisions or wards and of the settlement as a whole. The absence of secular powers of enforcement in the case of both the Ward Leaders and the village priests facilitated the emergence and exercise of such powers through independent associations, notably Ebiabu within the wards and Okundom and Ikpungkara in the village at large.

Thus indigenous government in Umor was effected through the loosely co-ordinated deliberations, judicial decisions, and executive acts of self-perpetuating spirit cult associations, the ritual powers and moral authority of which were in some cases buttressed by physical coercion of recalcitrants. These associations were operative at two general levels of organization—the ward and the village. But neither within nor between these two levels was there an explicit hierarchy of authority. Respect for generally acknowledged rules of public conduct, the maintenance of order, the settlement of disputes, and the compensation of wrongs ultimately depended on the measure of authority, common understanding, and coincident interests among the associations. And this was in part at least fostered by the considerable overlapping of their memberships both within and between these two levels of organization.

7 THE TRADITIONAL AUTHORITY
SYSTEM OF THE NAVAJOS

Mary Shepardson

Mary Shepardson obtained her A.B. and M.A. from Stanford University and her Ph.D. from the University of California at Berkeley (in anthropology, 1960), and has been Research Associate at the University of Chicago since 1961. She has published many papers on the Navajo.

T HE TRADITIONAL authority system of the Navajos before the Conquest differed in important respects from the authority system that was established on the Reservation. In the first place, the Conquest eliminated an important group, the raiding party with its power role of "war chief." Second, before the Conquest, members of the tribe acknowledged no external, superordinate authority; afterwards, they were forced to. The United States Government conferred authority on headmen or chiefs who were appointed by the Navajo agents to serve as contact officials with members of the tribe. The purer form of traditional authority must be reconstructed from historical documents and the reminiscences of aged informants.

The basic assumption of this study is that any society which subsists over time must have some systematic allocation of power and authority to make final decisions and control disruptive behavior. Some person or persons must possess legitimate authority to make decisions for which he or they, are accountable, decisions or commands that certain individuals or groups feel obligated to obey. It is this ingredient of mutual obligation, rights, and duties that differentiates a relationship of legitimate authority

FROM M. Shepardson, "Navajo Ways in Government," *American Anthropologist* 65, No. 3, Part 2 (1963), 118–45, by permission of the author and of the editor, *American Anthropologist*.

from a market or exchange relationship, as Zelditch points out (1955:311).

Weber bases his analysis of authority on the concept of the orientation of coordinated action to an order which must be carried out and enforced by a responsible agency (1947:56). "Imperative coordination" (Parsons' translation of *Herrschaft*) is the probability that certain specific commands from a given source will be obeyed by a given group of persons. There may be a variety of motives for obedience to commands, such as custom, affectual ties, material interest, and ideal motives, but a criterion of every true relation of imperative coordination is a certain minimum of voluntary submission. The voluntary submission results from a belief in the legitimacy of the command, and thus one needs to know the kind of legitimacy that is claimed, the kind of administrative staff that guarantees it, the mode of exercising authority, and the type of obedience. Of these, the most important for classification of an authority system is the kind of legitimacy claimed for it.

Weber suggests three pure types of authority, according to the basis for the claim to legitimacy: rational-legal, traditional, and charismatic. A "rational-legal authority" rests on the belief in the legality of normative rules and the right of those elevated to authority under such rules to issue commands. A "traditional authority" rests on an established belief in the sanctity of traditions and the legitimacy of those exercising authority under them. "Charismatic authority" rests on devotion to the specific and exceptional sanctity, heroism, or exemplary character of the individual person, and of the normative patterns of order revealed or ordained by him (Weber, M. 1947:324–29).

Navajo Authority

We have seen that the Navajo tribe, as it existed before the Conquest, had no centralized authority. It never convened as a group, but it was distinctly bounded by the limits of acceptance of a common culture, that is, a system of shared customs, beliefs, and values that was considered binding on the society. A common language delimited the tribe. Sections of the tribe controlled and defended a common territory. A network of kinship and affinal relations, widely dispersed as the result of clan exogamy, and a common ceremonial system served to integrate the society and give a sense of distinctiveness to the *Diné* or *People*. Navajos neither raided nor made war upon each other, but they intermittently raided and made war upon all other nearby groups, Indian and white. The tribe represented the ultimate bounds of legitimacy or sovereignty, since no non-Navajo person or group was recognized to have the right to exert control over the members of the tribe.

The Navajo authority system may be classified as "traditional." Weber elaborates on the definition cited above:

> The person or persons exercising authority are designated according to traditionally transmitted rules. The object of obedience is the personal authority of the individual which he enjoys by virtue of his traditional status. . . . The person exercising authority is not a "superior" but a personal "chief". . . . His commands are legitimized in one of two ways: (a) partly in terms of traditions which themselves directly determine the content of the command and the objects and extent of the authority. In so far as this is true, to overstep the traditional limitations would endanger his traditional status by undermining acceptance of his legitimacy, (b) in part, it is a matter of the chief's free personal decision, in that tradition leaves a certain sphere open for this . . . [since] the obligations of obedience on the basis of personal loyalty are essentially unlimited [Parsons corrects this in a note to "unspecified" rather than "unlimited"]. So far as his action follows principles at all, these are principles of substantive ethical common sense, of justice, or of utilitarian expediency . . . not formal principles. The exercise of authority is normally oriented to the question of what the chief . . . will normally permit, in view of the traditional obedience of the subjects and what will, or will not, arouse their resistance (1947:341, 342).

The Navajo authority system is "traditional," but when we try to fit it into Weber's pure category we feel a certain uneasiness. Zelditch has expressed this in his analysis of the Ramah Navajo and has settled for admitting the existence of "elements of traditional authority" (1955:303). One of the difficulties is that Weber's type is based on the concept of an authoritarian society in which the designation of the chief is by ascribed status, a society in which he exercises coercive control and enjoys a large area of freedom for personal whims and acts of personal dominance. This does not fit the Navajo case. Even the further refinements of "gerontocracy" and "patriarchalism" cannot contain the Navajo system.

The most primitive types of traditional authority are the cases where a personal administrative staff of the chief is absent. . . . The term "gerontocracy" is applied to a situation where so far as imperative control is exercised in the group at all it is in the hands of the "elders" . . . most familiar with the sacred traditions of the group. This is common in groups which are not primarily of an economic or kinship character. "Patriarchalism" is the situation where, within a group, which is usually organized on both an economic and a kinship basis, as a household, authority is exercised by a particular individual who is designated by a definite rule of inheritance. . . . The decisive characteristic of both is the conception . . . that this authority, though its exercise is a private prerogative of the person or persons involved, is in fact preeminently an authority on behalf of the group as a whole. It must, therefore, be exercised in the interests of the members and is thus not freely appropriated by the incumbent. . . . He is hence still to a large extent dependent on the willingness of the group to enforce it. Those subject to authority are hence still members of the group and not "subjects." But their membership exists by tradition and not by virtue of legislation or a deliberate act of adherence. Obedience is owed to the person of the chief, not to any established rule. But it is owed to the chief only by virtue of his traditional status. He is thus on his part strictly bound by tradition (Weber, M. 1947:346).

Navajo authority was ultimately validated by the myths and by an appeal to Old Navajo ways. Transgression of taboos and deviance from the accepted ways, it was believed, resulted in disharmony and illness. Navajo authority was personal, personally defined in particular situations; a Navajo owed loyalty to persons rather than to the community or the tribe as an abstract idea (Zelditch 1955:304). Thus there is a difference from Weber's pure type, in that none of the Navajo authority roles was designated by ascription. They were not hereditary; they were always in some manner "elective." Even the authority patterns of the kin roles were flexible, since alternative residence patterns and the nearly equal status of men and women in major family and community decisions made it possible for Navajo adults, at least, to choose the authorities to whom they wished to submit. Specialists such as war leaders, hunt leaders, and curing-ceremony leaders, who had achieved skill in learning the necessary rituals, were selected for particular occasions. Their following was always voluntary. The *natani,* or peace leader, was not allowed areas of uncontrolled personal whim and dominance; his role was traditionally defined as nonauthoritarian and noncoercive, his power was to be exercised in the interests of the group. It was based on the respect in which he was held as a person. Any attempt on his part to overstep his authority would destroy the basis of its legitimacy—that is, the respect and confidence without which he could not command obedience.

Early white observers described the Navajo authority system as "anarchy" (Letherman 1855:288). Authority, however, was never completely diffuse, nor was it appropriated at random. The locus of authority was in the various functional groups, the biological family, the extended family, the outfit, the local group, the raiding party, the hunting party, and the ceremonial gathering. In so far as the authority for decision-making and control in these groups was ultimate, that is, was subject to no higher authority, it was political. The highest authority lay in the agreement achieved within the group after matters had been "talked over." Only then did the *natani* act as the authority figure for the group. Only on raids, at the hunt, or at a ceremony was absolute authority accorded to the ritual leader, and then only for a specific purpose. It is possible to characterize his authority as partly charismatic since it depended to some extent on personal skill. But it depended even more on the efficacy of the traditional ritual and in no wise represented the "revolutionary" force of Weber's type charismatic authority.

The basis then for legitimacy, the validation of "imperative coordination" in pre-Conquest Navajo society, lay in the fact that the actions of the members of the society were oriented to a normative order, to accepted values and beliefs, and to the correctness of certain sanctions for inducing conformity. Navajos believed in a harmonious universe; they believed that illness and disaster resulted from upsetting the balance and that ritual means could restore harmony. There was agreement on certain patterns of cooperation within groups, structured with great flexibility around kinship and affinal ties, for economic subsistence, co-residence, sexual satisfaction, and the raising of children. There was agreement on general property concepts, use rights in land, the correctness of dividing personal property at death, and on the value of acquiring property, of hard work, of reciprocity, of generosity. Decisions should be unanimous if possible, should be "talked over" with all interested adults, and should be executed voluntarily. All positions should be open to the "good man" or the "good woman," although customarily the public roles were played by men, older men who had attained wisdom. Disputes should be settled through compromise and arbitration. Force should be used only against witches and aliens. Conformity should be secured through respect, praise, cooperation. Deviance should be punished through disrespect, ridicule, and withdrawal of cooperation. In the extreme case of witchcraft, punishment should be death, administered either as self-help by the injured parties or by community agreement.

In brief, the Navajo authority system was traditional; obedience was voluntary; power was exercised by particular persons in particular situations; and there was no supreme leader, no hierarchical chain of command, no monopoly of force.

The Role System

As we saw in Chapter I, the role system is a synonym for social structure, the ordering of the personnel of a society into related positions or roles which are defined in terms of reciprocal expectations, rights, and duties (Siegel 1954). The concept "role" was defined as a set of expectations applied to the incumbent of a position in a system of social relationships (Gross, Mason, McEachern 1958:60). *Role* is the point at which individual behavior becomes social conduct; the point at which the conflicts are sharpest and the motivation for social change appears.

The focus of this study is on those positions in Navajo society which carry institutionalized authority, those roles in which the actors have the right to expect obedience to their commands. The role may be studied in terms of the individuals or groups over whom the authority may be exercised; in terms of the function of the authority and its duration; in terms of the method of recruiting the role player, and his motivations for conforming with expected role behavior; and in terms of the conflicts within a role, between roles played by the same person, and among role definers.

Reichard, whose material was gathered from aged informants, draws a rather formal picture of Navajo tribal leadership in the pre-Conquest period. She says:

> The political organization was vested in twelve war and twelve peace chiefs who formed a council . . . the appointment of the war chiefs was a special honor bestowed for prowess in warfare;

. . . the peace chiefs were selected on the basis of eloquence and perhaps of good judgment and uprightness . . . women could be chiefs as well as men (1928:111).

Most anthropologists disagree now with her theory that there was a centralized political organization with a stated number of chiefs. Hill says that the Navajo tribe never functioned as a unit in concerted action and that Navajos were never brought under the leadership of a single individual or group for a common purpose. He does, however, believe that there was a distinct separation of war and peace authority (1954:14, 15).

The historical record indicates this separation of powers. Fray Alonso de Benavides, writing in 1634, describes his meeting with a Navajo at Santa Clara Pueblo:

> One of their famous chieftains, a very belligerent individual was here at that time recruiting a large army in order to fall upon and massacre all the Christians. He was a cousin of the leading cacique who governed them (1945:87).

This chief was so impressed by Benavides that he agreed to make peace, although he regretted that peace should be offered at this time "when he had made such elaborate preparations for exterminating them all at one stroke, but since peace was such a fine thing he could not help accepting it." Later Benavides' emissary addressed the Navajos, speaking of "so many captains among you" (Benavides 1945:85–88).

It appears from this that there were a number of leaders and that there was a distinction between a governing "cacique" and the war chiefs. In Benavides' account a war chief makes peace, although according to Hill's informants this could only be done by a peace chief (1936:19). Spanish reports mention a number of "chiefs" who were made "generals" in the Spanish Army and given subsidies to keep them quiet (Van Valkenburgh 1945:69). Many Navajos signed peace treaties over the years with both Spaniards and Americans, but whether the majority of such men were war chiefs or peace chiefs we do not know. In some cases, however, as with Narbona, Zarcillas Largas, Ganado Mucho, and Antonio el Pintado, we know that they were peace chiefs.

Reichard indicates that the role of war chief was a status position bestowed as an honor (1928:111), but Hill says that it was achieved by knowing the ritual of War Ways. As we have noted, volunteers for the war party were recruited for the particular occasion:

The formation of a war party was in the hands of a shaman-leader, who knew the songs, prayers and observances of one of the several Ways of going to war. In payment for his ritual service such a man received a larger share of the plunder. . . . Such an individual who had confidence in the power of his ritual to defeat the enemy, would go among his able-bodied friends and relatives . . . and ask for volunteers to accompany him to war. For a raid, four to ten men were needed; for a reprisal thirty to two hundred. . . . The man who organized the party was in complete command of all its members. . . . If a boy or man desired to become a war leader, he sought out a shaman-leader of the Way which he desired to learn and asked for instruction (Hill 1936:7, 8).

Kluckhohn and Leighton are of the opinion that Navajo warfare should not be exaggerated since it consisted of raids for sheep and horses for the most part, and never approached the cultural importance to Navajos of the war complex among the Plains Indians (1948:5).

The role of hunt leader required a knowledge of ritual Hunt Ways. The expedition was under his absolute control and his authority was validated by a success which must have depended upon practical skill as well as ritual knowledge. Anyone could learn the hunting ritual who wished to. Usually the learner paid his teacher, unless he was a relative. The leader was recompensed by receiving the largest share of the kill (Hill 1938:97, 100).

There were two kinds of curing practitioners, the Diviner, whose skill was charismatic in that it depended upon a "gift," and the Singer, who had learned a Chant and whose authority was based on ritual skill. Diviners were diagnosticians who through "star-gazing" or "hand-trembling" could discover the cause and cure of an illness. The services of both Diviner and Singer were solicited by the patient and his family, and they were remunerated (Wyman 1936:236).

Anyone who wished could become a Singer provided he learned the Chant or Chants. He was expected to pay for instruction unless he was taught by a relative. During a ceremony the ritual leader exercised absolute authority and was held responsible for the outcome. Some Sings attracted participants from other communities, and as many as a thousand people might gather for one of the more important ceremonies. A Singer's influence would extend beyond the ceremonial occasion only if he was endowed with the personal qualities that inspired respect, the qualities associated with a *natani*.

The peace chief or headman or *natani* role more nearly approximated the role of a modern political leader. His authority appears to have extended beyond his family or outfit and to have been of longer duration than that of the war chief. At one time there may even have been bands with single leaders such as Canyoncito under Sandoval. Patterns, areas of authority, and the number of peace chiefs were flexible. Most of the historical reports indicate several chiefs with limited authority in each region.

The role of *natani* ideally required wisdom, exemplary character, oratorical ability, personal magnetism, and proven skill in both practical and religious aspects of the culture. The *natani* was usually a practitioner of Blessing Way. The office was not remunerative and it was not hereditary. Kluckhohn points out, however, that there is a perceptible tendency for leadership to continue in the same family line, and he gives the example of Ramah, where the position of headman went from the father, Many Beads, to his son, to his son-in-law, to the son's daughter's son, and to another grandson. In 1955 still another grandson of Many Beads was elected Chapter President (Personal communication 1960).

The headman was chosen after a canvass of the area, men and women having an equal voice in the selection, which ideally was unanimous (Hill 1954:16). The Franciscan Fathers report a ceremony of induction (1910:422), and Wyman and Kluckhohn describe Chief Blessing Way as the ceremonial "which was, and perhaps still is, used when a chief or headman is installed. It is said to enable a man 'to make powerful speeches'" (1938:19). The chief's success depended upon his own personal qualities and his ability to secure cooperation and retain respect. He was expected to address both local meetings and meetings in other communities, to deliver talks on ethical problems, to advise people to work hard and live in peace. The *natani* acted as local economic director, planning the community work for planting, cultivation, and harvesting. He arbitrated, on request, disputes over damages, trespass, and land claims, and acted as mediator in quarrels. He was expected to dispense hospitality to visitors and to serve as diplomatic representative to other communities (Hill 1954:18).

Much the same qualities, except perhaps for the oratorical

ability and the knowledge of Blessing Way, are the attributes
that define the roles of father of a family, head of an extended
family, and leader of an outfit, which we have examined in the
chapter on social structure.

Before we analyze the authority roles we have just discussed,
another interesting problem deserves attention. Although there
were *natanis,* rich stock-holders, ceremonial leaders, and war
chiefs, all positions which carried prestige in the society, such
leaders seem to have made no attempt to form associations or to
interact more frequently among themselves as status groups. For
example, interaction was more frequent within the kin groups
than it was between rich men from various groups. Ceremonial
leaders did not gather together as such nor did they seek to put
up barriers against entry to the "profession." No positions in
Navajo society were drawn exclusively or even predominantly
from any one status group. There were slaves in early Navajo
society, and later there were peons, but no systematic study has
been made of them and it is possible that they were not present
in large enough numbers to affect the structure of the society profoundly. Reports from early American contact, such as that of
Calhoun in 1849, describe a "war party" and a "peace party"
among Navajos, but it is more likely that there were differences
of opinion within each community than that there was any wider
grouping such as a "party" of those who agreed on the issues of
peace or war.

One outside view of Navajo authority roles before the Conquest is of interest. An Army surgeon named Letherman writes
in 1855:

> They have no hereditary chief—none by election. . . . Everyone
> who has a few horses and sheep is a "headman", and must have his
> word in the councils. Even those who by superior cunning have
> obtained some influence are extremely careful lest their conduct
> should not prove acceptable to their criticising inferiors. The "jun-
> tas," or councils are generally composed of the richest men, each
> one a self-constituted member, but their decisions are of little
> moment unless they meet the approbation of the mass of the peo-
> ple; and for this reason these councils are exceedingly careful not to
> run counter to the wishes of the poorer but more numerous class,
> being well aware of the difficulty, if not the impossibility, of en-
> forcing any act that would not command their approval (1855:
> 288).

To summarize: all the authority roles in Navajo society were achieved, except for the minor role of hand-trembler, which had a special charismatic quality. The sphere of competence was traditionally specified. Even the kinship roles, which were to some extent ascribed by birth, sex, age, and marriage, had their achievement component, since no kinship or affinal position automatically conferred a fixed amount of authority on the incumbent. Easy divorce, the wide ramification of kin and affinal ties, the flexibility of residence patterns, and the negative valuation of coercion among relatives made it necessary for a Navajo to achieve genuine authority in a family group by means of special attributes and performances within the framework of the common normative order.

This leaves us the problem of role conflicts, that is, conflict within a role, conflict between roles played by the same person, and conflict among role definers. All roles that were fully institutionalized in traditional Navajo society were oriented to the accepted normative order. There is no evidence, before the Conquest, that Navajos ever challenged their system of beliefs and values. This was not an authoritarian belief system, according to Ladd, but rather a series of prescriptions of what one ought to do or ought not to do in order to be healthy and happy (1957:265). To act competently within this system, however, was not always easy, and a series of values clashed within each institutionalized role. The emphasis on harmony and generosity and the value of ceremonial participation contradicted in certain situations the emphasis on the value of acquiring goods, and of practical activities in agriculture and herding. The value placed on acquiring wealth conflicted with the belief in equal status, with the result that the rich man ran the risk of being accused of witchcraft. Likewise, the ceremonial practitioner who was obligated to perform his ritual ran the risk of being suspected of using his knowledge for bad ends. The *natani* was caught between the need to secure consensus of opinion and the need for decisive action.

Conflicts in roles arising from conflicts among role definers were in some cases inherent in the structure. For instance, in a matrilineal society men owed obligations to their families of origin and also to their families of procreation. As interests became differentiated into pastoralists and agriculturists, raiders and farmers/herders, conflicts arose as to which interests the *natani* should speak for. In cases of arbitration or mediation, the *natani* was caught between his family obligations, if relatives were involved, and his commitment to render justice. Further role conflicts affected both *natani* and war chief, that is, whether he was accountable to a small group of followers, to a locality, or to a broader section of the tribe.

The conflict within the role system was chiefly between war and peace leaders. The right of raiders was generally recognized in Navajo society and their activity was considered "an important practical pursuit" (Kluckhohn and Leighton 1948:5). The war leader was supposed to obtain the consent of the *natani* before instituting a raid, but he rarely did so (Hill 1936). Reprisals frequently victimized groups who had not been involved in a raid, and this, certainly, must have caused friction among role players.

Although there were no strong corporate groups demanding conflicting loyalties of the same person as in some highly structured African societies, conflicts did exist within roles and between roles. Perhaps the lack of a clear hierarchy among roles contributed to the conflicts.

The analysis of role conflicts will assume even more importance when we discuss the four interacting authority systems of the present day. Anthropologists have frequently tended to overemphasize the harmony, because of homogeneity, of the simple societies, and often they have attributed observable conflicts to the culture contact situation. No human society has yet achieved Utopia; certainly traditional Navajo society, with its raiding and enslaving and the retaliation that this provoked, did not find the perfect plan.

8 COMPETITIVE LEADERSHIP IN TROBRIAND POLITICAL ORGANIZATION

H. A. Powell

H. A. Powell is Lecturer in Anthropology at the University of Newcastle upon Tyne, England.

TROBRIAND POLITICAL ORGANIZATION is in a real sense conterminous with the processes by which individual leaders arise, create, and for a time maintain followings, and ultimately lose their power so that the areas they have dominated resolve once more into their component local groups, which then remain autonomous until the emergence of a new area leader.

Perhaps the best way shortly to describe indigenous Trobriand political organization is as a variant of the systems of competitive individual leadership by 'Big Men' common in adjacent parts of Melanesia, which is modified in the Trobriands, at least in Northern Kiriwina Island, by the system of rank. This restricts eligibility to compete for political leadership in any given locality to the members of the highest ranking matrilineal descent group or sub-clan (*dala*) associated with it, and at the same time tends to ensure that amongst them one man is always singled out as at least the potential leader of the locality. Upon him the population's economic and political relationships tend to focus so that it becomes organized as his following, and tends

FROM the *Journal of the Royal Anthropological Institute* 90, No. 1 (1960), 118–45, by permission of the author and of the Council of the Royal Anthropological Institute, London. The paper has been slightly shortened here, and a table showing population figures for Trobriand villages and one map have been omitted.

This paper is based on research carried out when the author was a Horniman student in Northern Kiriwina Island from May 1950 to May 1951. Dr. Powell wishes to record his debt to the Horniman Fund and its Trustees, and to the Australian National University for a supplementary grant.

to co-operate as a unit in competition with similarly led and
organized populations of other localities. Trobriand political activity thus consists in a continuing process of creation, expansion,
and contraction of followings and areas of influence by men
qualified to compete for leadership. The followings and areas of
influence thus established are however conterminous with the
careers of the leaders who create and maintain them. They do
not crystallize into or become stabilized as permanent major
chiefdoms or administrative hierarchies, but disintegrate when
their creators lose support or die, so that their successors must
in effect start again the whole process of building up followings
for themselves. But as we shall see the attribute of rank confers
on those who possess it certain advantages which provide them
with the nucleus of a following as well as with the right to aspire
to expand it at least to the extent commensurate with their rank.

I   DEMOGRAPHY

A. *General*

Population Information from Annual Reports and Censuses
and from native sources indicates that since about 1900 at least
the native population of Kiriwina Island has remained fairly
stable at about 7,000 inhabitants, divided among roughly eighty
major named villages, giving an overall average of some eighty–
ninety inhabitants per village. Triangulation of United States
Army Air Force aerial survey maps of about 1947 gives a total
area of approximately seventy square miles, or 45,000 acres,
for the Island. The overall density is thus about one hundred
persons per square mile, but as the scatter of villages on the
maps indicates, varying fertility of the land tends to concentrate
the population in the cultivable areas which probably bear a
population of 130 or more per square mile, while approximately
17,250 acres are uncultivated for various reasons and have no
village sites.

Communication There are no serious physical obstacles to
travel throughout the Island, and the regional diversification of
resources and techniques described by Malinowski (1935:12–23)
promotes contacts between even distant localities. Economically
at least the total population may be regarded as a single group
larger than most equivalent groups in neighbouring areas of

Melanesia. However this relatively high population density and frequency of interaction does not appear even in pre-European times to have been accompanied by any serious shortage of or competition for land.

Pressure on Land   The Trobriand economy was still in 1950–51 based on the patterns of subsistence production described by Malinowski (esp. 1935, *passim*). My field data indicate that the average household numbers about 3.25 members, and requires rather less than an acre of garden land annually for all purposes. On this basis the total annual requirement of the whole population works out at about 2,200 acres, whereas about twice this amount is available after allowing for losses of cultivable land to village sites, etc., and assuming that the plots require on average at least seven years to recover after two seasons' use. There is some evidence that the population may have been larger in olden times, while the introduction of metal tools may, by increasing the efficiency of cultivation, have reduced the annual land requirement per household to some extent. Even so my data suggest that the land as at present cultivated could support an appreciably larger population without undue strain on its fertility, under normal circumstances.

Food Supply   A surplus of land does not however ensure in itself that food will always be plentiful, and the traditions of famine reported by Malinowski (esp. 1935:160–63) are supported by Government records. These show that in 1900–1 the whole Massim area and south-east New Guinea were seriously affected by drought, while food shortages occurred in the Trobriands serious enough to require at least local relief by the Administration at intervals of four to six years up to the mid-nineteen-thirties, when separate records of Trobriand affairs were no longer published. This incidence of local food shortages, the result usually of irregular rainfall, supports Malinowski's appreciation of the importance and social utility of the role of local leaders in providing reserves against such natural hazards. Island-wide famines such as that of 1900–1 tended completely to disrupt the existing social order, and afterwards the various districts and component villages would, without help from European sources, tend to be forced to compete with each other for the means to restore their prosperity.

Isolation   One factor which in other parts of the world seems

to act as a catalyst in promoting the establishment of overall
centralized political organization, namely external competition for
land, seems to have been absent in the history of the Tro-
brianders. Their Islands are of course relatively isolated from
the territories of neighbouring peoples, who in any case appear
to have been less coherently organized politically than the Tro-
brianders under indigenous conditions.

It might be expected against this background that political
organization in the Trobriands might take the form of loose and
impermanent associations between basically autonomous local
groups, motivated to co-operate with each other by spatial proximity and diversification of resources, but at the same time to
compete by other factors such as the underlying uncertainty of
food supplies which tend to create tensions between 'haves'
and 'have nots'. At the same time in the absence of pressure
on land as such and of external threats to the Islanders' control
of it there would be little advantage, and perhaps some disadvantage, to the individual local populations in subordinating
the element of competition in their relationships with each other
to that of co-operation by accepting a permanent overall political
control. These expectations would be found to accord quite well
with the nature of the political organization of at least Northern
Kiriwina Island, where the factors outlined above are most effective.

B. *The Autonomous Local Group*

In principle and in many respects in practice the autonomous
local group was, under indigenous conditions, and remains to-day,
the individual village, the typical physical characteristics of which
have been well described by Malinowski (1922:49–62; 1935:
3–12). The villages are small; Omarakana, the largest, has a
population of only ninety-two, while Kasanai has a population
of forty-three, with an average of sixty-five residents per village.
Other villages are smaller still, and not many are larger than
Omarakana, which is about average size in terms of the figures
given in the last section for the whole Island. The social composition of the villages varies, some, e.g. Tilakaiwa and Wakailua,
being of a 'simple' type in which the village site and its adjacent
garden and other lands are traditionally owned and controlled
by a single matrilineal sub-clan (*dala,* see Malinowski 1935:

345–46). Others, e.g. Omarakana, Kasanai and Yolawotu, are of various 'complex' types, in which two or more sub-clans share rights of ownership and exploitation of a single village site and associated lands in a number of different ways. These differences matter less for present purposes than the fact that, whatever they may be, the village population always constitutes a single unit politically. There is always in any village one sub-clan at least whose members are recognized as its 'owners' (Malinowski 1935:chap. 12, sect. 1), other residents deriving rights from them as affines or clan kin; and where there is more than one such owning sub-clan, one of them is always recognized as senior in status. The recognized leader of this sub-clan is also the recognized leader, or headman as Malinowski called him, of the village population. A village cluster may be (v. map) defined for present purposes as an aggregate of villages the populations of which tend to regard themselves for many purposes and to operate as a single unit in relation to the populations of other like clusters. The villages of a cluster tend to some extent to be marked off from other neighbouring villages, and their populations thrown together, by a degree of spatial isolation, but probably more effectively by a sense of solidarity derived from tradition and common interests. This solidarity is manifested in and reinforced by co-operation between the populations of the component villages in economic and other activities, including various forms of competition with the populations of other clusters, such as formal warfare or, nowadays, games such as cricket and football (cf. Powell 1952).

The sub-clans, like the villages, are small in terms of population. The total population of the Omarakana cluster (as recorded in 1950–51) is 325, in which are represented all four of the Trobriand clans (*kumila*) and thirty-nine sub-clans, giving an average of less than ten members per sub-clan. Further members of all these sub-clans live in other clusters also, but these figures represent about 80 per cent of the members of the sub-clans with rights of ownership in the villages of the Omarakana cluster, and about the same proportion of the membership of the other sub-clans represented in the Omarakana cluster similarly live in the clusters in which their sub-clans have rights of ownership. The largest of the sub-clans owning the villages of the Omarakana cluster is the Lobwaita of Tilakaiwa village,

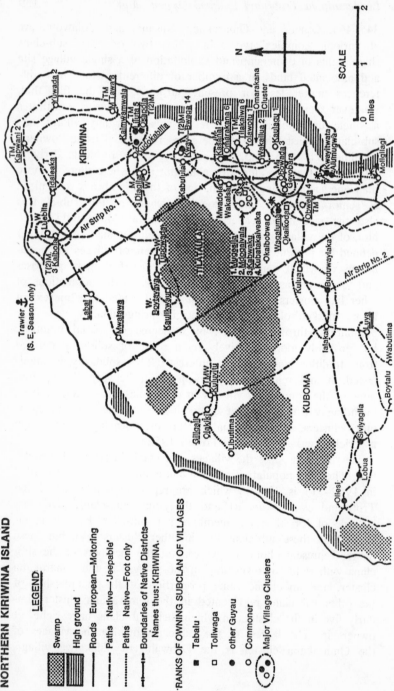

NORTHERN KIRIWINA ISLAND

LEGEND

Swamp

High ground

Roads   European—Motoring

Paths   Native—'Jeepable'

Paths   Native—Foot only

Boundaries of Native Districts—
Names thus: KIRIWINA.

RANKS OF OWNING SUBCLAN OF VILLAGES

■ Tabalu

□ Toliwaga

● other Guyau

○ Commoner

◉ Major Village Clusters

⚓ Trawler
(S. E. Season only)

SCALE

miles   0   1   2

N

KIRIWINA

Uwada 2

TM Kapwani 2

Idaleaka 1

T

W Liebila

T(2)M 3 Kaibola

M Tawa 3

W Kaimwanwala

TM Luta 5

Osapola

Kudokabilla

M Dlaglla
W 3

T(2)M
Bwaga 14

TM Kasanai 2

M Kwaywata

T(2)ME

Omarakana 6

TM Kabulula

Mwadola
Wakals

T(2)M 20

1. Mugeilla
2. Mdonaiwala
3. Kabwaku
4. Kubatakaiveaka

Wagaluma

Okaikoda

Okaibobwao

Thakaiwa 6

Yolawotu T

Wakailua 2

Kaulagu 1

Omarakana Cluster

Obowada 3

Geyobra

Kwayitwata
Alumugwa

Motigiagi

Opwella 4
TM

Kuiua

Buduwaylaka

Air Strip No. 2

Labai 1

W Boytalu
Kaulikwau'

Tubowada

Mwatawa

Iaiekai

Luya

TILAYUYA

TMW
Kuiyuiu

Libutima

Olakiki

Gilligilli

KUBOMA

Siviagila

Lobua

Oliesi

Boytalu   Wabutma

Air Strip No. 1

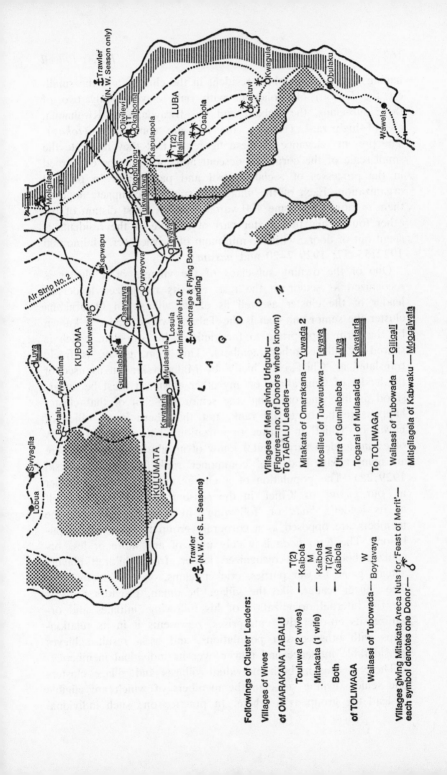

Followings of Cluster Leaders:

Villages of Wives

of OMARAKANA TABALU

Touluwa (2 wives)	—	T(2) Kaibola
Mitakata (1 wife)	—	M Kaibola
Both	—	T(2)M Kaibola

of TOLIWAGA

Wallassi of Tubowada	—	W Boytavaya

Villages giving Mitakata Areca Nuts for 'Feast of Merit' —
each symbol denotes one Donor —

Villages of Men giving Urigubu —
(Figures=no. of Donors where known)
To TABALU Leaders —

Mitakata of Omarakana	—	Yuwada 2
Mosilieu of Tukwaukwa	—	Teyava
Utura of Gumilababa	—	Luya
Togarai of Mulasaida	—	Kavataria

To TOLIWAGA

Wallassi of Tubowada	—	Giligall
Mitigilagela of Kabwaku	—	Mdogalyala

LUBA

KUBOMA

IKULUMATA

L A G O O N

Trawler (N. W. Season only)

Trawler (N.W. or S.E. Seasons)

Anchorage & Flying Boat Landing

Air Strip No. 2

Administrative H.Q.

Losuia

having fifty-three members resident in the cluster, and the small-est the Gawari of Yolawotu with only eleven. Only two of these sub-clans, the Tabalu and the Bwaydaga or Kwainama, are of high rank (*guyau*), the rest are commoners (*tokay*). The present relevance of these figures is that they illustrate the small scale of the corporate descent and local groups concerned in the processes of social control and particularly in political organization. Each of the villages is spatially compact, none of them is more than some 400 yards from the most distant of the other four, while the greater part of the life of the residents is spent out of doors, with the minimum of privacy (cf. Malinowski 1922:55–57; 1929:7–20 and *passim*).

One of the owning sub-clans of the villages of a cluster is recognized as senior to the rest, and its recognized leader as leader of the cluster as well as of its village. In Omarakana cluster the senior sub-clan is the Tabalu, whose leader is known by the term appropriate to the rank of his sub-clan, which is shared by all its other members. This term, *guyau*, is freely translated as 'Chief' or 'Chiefly' by Malinowski; but as used of the leader of Omarakana or any other cluster it must be under-stood as implying only that the senior sub-clan of that cluster happens to be of *guyau* rank, not that there is an office of *guyau* or 'Chief' in cluster organization. The relative seniority of *guyau* leaders varies, but I know of no cluster, although there are many village leaders of 'commoner' rank (*tokay*, Malinowski 1929:28). The population of a cluster may refer to its leader as 'our *guyau*' or 'Chief' in the sense indicated, and to itself as its leader's *boda* or 'following', in contexts in which the members are opposed as a corporate group to other like popu-lations. The term *boda* is widely used of any more or less or-ganized body with a recognized leader, from children playing a team game to war parties, cricket teams, or political factions. The cluster leader, like the village headman, provides a focus for the internal organization of his following, initiates and or-ganizes its co-operative enterprises, represents it in its relation-ships with other cluster populations, and as a result achieves considerable influence and power over its individual members.

There is thus in both individual villages and village clusters one senior owning sub-clan the members of which are eligible to lead the group as a whole. In practice one such individual always achieves, or has thrust upon him, leadership of a sub-clan and its village; but a cluster may at times, e.g. after the death of one recognized leader, remain leaderless, unless and until one of those eligible succeeds in establishing his ascendancy over, or eliminating, his possible competitors. At such times the cluster tends to lose its organized unity as a political group, but not its social identity, which is promoted and reflected in other ways as well as political. Indeed the emergence of a recognized leader, though necessary if the cluster population is to co-operate as an organized political group, may be regarded as the result rather than the cause of the wider social unity of the cluster. This unity is particularly well evidenced in the marriage relationships of the component village populations, as reflected in the distribution of marriage gifts (*urigubu,* Malinowski 1935: chap. 6).

In 1950 the male household heads of the Omarakana village cluster (v. map), in which Malinowski did much of his field-work, received over 75 per cent of their *urigubu* gifts from donors living in the cluster, while over 80 per cent of the presentations they made were to recipients in the cluster, the remainder in each case being from donors or to recipients outside the cluster. In the same village 56 per cent of all the gifts received and 55 per cent of those given were between residents. In contrast the recognized leader of the cluster, Mitakata, the leader of its highest ranking sub-clan (the Tabalu of Omarakana village), made only three presentations, all to men living in his own village, but received gifts in respect of his twelve marriages from seventy-six individual donors, fifty-seven (75 per cent) of whom lived in villages other than those of the Omarakana cluster. These figures reflect at the same time the importance of the cluster leader in the external relationships of the cluster as a political unit, and the inter-relation of the populations of the villages of the cluster by intermarriage, which persists whether at any given time the cluster has a recognized leader or not. On the other hand the high frequency of intra-village presentations reflects the fundamental autonomy and independence of the component villages within the framework of cluster unity. This autonomy is reflected also in the fact that individual villages always have recognized leaders, while clusters may not.

II THE SYSTEM OF LEADERSHIP

A. *The Achievement of Leadership*

   1. Village Leaders The process of becoming the recognized
leader whether of village or cluster is initially the same; a man
must become leader of a sub-clan and its village before he can
become cluster leader, by competitive selection within the group
qualified by membership of the senior owning sub-clan of the
village to lead its population. The process of selecting the next
leader begins almost as soon as his predecessor achieves recognized leadership, and is particularly apparent in the operation
of two mechanisms of the kinship and marriage systems, namely
urigubu and *pokala*. The former is of course the system of
marriage presentations; the latter is a system of presentations
between senior and junior members of the same sub-clan or clan.

   Pokala (cf. Malinowski 1935:345 and footnote) Junior
members of a sub-clan are expected to render gifts and services
to their seniors, who in return are expected to confer assistance
and material benefits on the juniors. Thus a young man desiring
exclusive use of, e.g., some coconut palms or a plot of land, may
select an 'elder brother' (*tuwa*), 'mother's brother' (*kada*), or
'mother's mother's brother' (*tabu*), whom he knows to have such
property at his disposal, and upon whom he has some personal
claim, e.g. as his 'own' *kada,* i.e. the mother's brother who actually gardened for the young man's father and family of orientation, and thus assumed personal responsibility for him. According
to the nature of the desired return, the young man will render
gifts and services of a greater or a lesser extent, ranging from
small gifts of fish or firewood made as opportunity occurs, to
undertaking to help his senior with his gardening commitments
or the like, and caring for him in illness (notably by guarding
him against sorcery). When he feels he has done enough the
young man will make a formal request in public for the desired
return, and if the senior feels he merits it, it will be made. Any
property allocated to him in this way, especially land, out of the
corporate holding of his sub-clan he can use himself if he wishes;
but its primary value lies in the fact that it is material evidence
of the esteem in which he is held by his elders, and makes it
possible for his juniors to *pokala* him in turn.

The *pokala* has other significances also; it is for instance the primary means of securing from one's seniors a personal inheritance in sub-clan property, and of ensuring that someone, e.g. a particular 'sister's son' (*kada*), will by inheriting such property assume the responsibility of conducting the mortuary rituals for his 'mother's brother' (*kada*), (cf. Malinowski 1929: chap. 6, sects. 2–4). For present purposes however the *pokala* is important as one means by which an ambitious young man can attract attention and build up his prestige among his contemporaries with the aim of being selected as the next leader or 'headman' (*tolivalu*) of his sub-clan and its village. If no ambitious young man emerges in this way, the senior men of a sub-clan will in time single out the likeliest successor to the current headman and require of him the same kinds of services and assistance that an ambitious junior would render voluntarily. Not every young man wishes to be selected, perhaps the majority being content to render the acceptable minimum of gifts and services to their seniors; for the leadership of an average commoner sub-clan and its village tends to be more onerous than rewarding, involving as it does the assumption of increasingly heavy *urigubu* responsibilities without any commensurate increase in the marriage gifts received by the commoner village leader.

Urigubu As Malinowski has indicated, the term *urigubu* refers not only to the annual marriage gift of garden produce but also and perhaps primarily to the whole range of rights and obligations between affines in general, and in particular to the obligations to render gifts and services to the husbands of the women of a sub-clan which rest upon its men; i.e. the obligations between 'brothers-in-law' (*lubou*). Malinowski stressed the dyadic aspect of marriage relationships generally and of the *urigubu* presentations, which are best understood as material tokens of wider obligations, in particular. In fact the *urigubu* responsibilities of a sub-clan are in principle as well as in practice corporate, as are its rights in land, magic, etc., as is clearly apparent in the arrangements for gardening for men of importance, or where there is disparity between the number of men of a sub-clan able to assume formal *urigubu* responsibilities and that of husbands of the women of their sub-clan. In such cases the responsibilities are allocated by the senior men acting in the interests of the sub-clan as a whole, their decisions being expressed by the recognized leader. In assuming or being allocated responsibility for gardening for his sub-clan's senior and most important affines a young man is being prepared for the responsibilities of leadership, as well as acquiring importance in the affairs of his sub-clan.

In 1950–51 the recognized successor to the headman of the Lobwaita owning sub-clan of Tilakaiwa village in the Omarakana cluster was Daibuna, the classificatory sister's son of the headman. Daibuna was a serious-minded and sometimes officious man in his middle thirties, whose efforts in *pokala* had been rewarded by the allocation to him of six plots of land (*baleko,* Malinowski 1935:90) as against the average holding of three to four plots. His achievements as a gardener began before he was himself married, when he undertook to garden for his father on behalf of his mothers' brothers. Later he gardened for one of his classificatory sisters (*luta*), and for the sub-clan leader Monumadoga, as an act of *pokala,* in order to enable him to devote more of his time and resources to gardening for the cluster leader Mitakata. By 1950 Daibuna had been as it were 'promoted' to gardening for Mitakata himself, as the husband of Daibuna's classificatory sister Kadumiyu. At this time there were in addition to Daibuna three other 'brothers' gardening for Mitakata, as well as Monumadoga and Touladoga, the village garden magician, who were Daibuna's and his 'sister's' classificatory mother's brothers. Thus Daibuna was singled out, by acts of *pokala* and by assuming directly a major share in his sub-clan's corporate *urigubu* responsibilities, as the likeliest choice for the next sub-clan and village leader.

Delegation of Responsibility Daibuna's position was made more explicit by his taking over from Monumadoga responsibilities which would have been the latter's had he been in better health. Thus Daibuna initiated and organized the building of a canoe for his sub-clan in connexion with the Kula sailing to Kitava in 1951, led his sub-clan's and village's contribution to a major 'feast of merit' (*paka*) held by Mitakata in 1950, and took the lead in organizing collective activities connected with gardening, such as the fencing of the new season's garden site. This process of delegation of responsibilities to the chosen successor occurs fairly regularly when sub-clan and village leaders are affected by advancing age or ill-health, in order according to informants to maintain effective leadership in the affairs of the groups concerned, especially in their economic and political relations as organized through the *urigubu* marriage relationships with other corporate group leaders, particularly of course the cluster leader.

In practice at least primogeniture seems to be of little significance in determining succession, except at the early stages of selection of a successor, when seniority in age may confer advantages in terms of greater experience and knowledge. As a leader grows older however the likelihood increases that the succession will pass to a member of the second rather than the first descending generation, again in order to maintain continuity in the corporate group's affairs by postponing the likelihood of a further change in leadership. Thus the Tabalu leader of Omarakana cluster To'uluwa (Taolu in Seligman 1910) succeeded his much older classificatory elder brother (*tuwa*) Numakala or Enamakala, and was succeeded by his classificatory sister's daughter's son (*tabu*) Mitakata, the present Tabalu leader. The present leader of the Lobwaita sub-clan of Tilakaiwa village is not the senior man of his sub-clan by birth, having two mothers' brothers and one elder brother alive, and Daibuna his recognized heir is again not the eldest man of his generation of the sub-clan. The sub-clan leader is in effect selected on the basis of his achievements in comparison with those of others eligible by sub-clan membership, age and so on, and the more ambitious or dominating personalities tend in effect to compete with each other for selection. But the intensity of competition tends to vary with the rank of the sub-clan and its importance in local affairs.

2. Cluster Leaders. Pokala, the assumption of *urigubu* responsibilities and the other mechanisms operating in the selection of leaders of ordinary sub-clans and villages operate also where the sub-clan is of high rank and importance in a cluster, but these attributes both intensify competition and modify the forms it takes. The leader of an ordinary commoner sub-clan has little personal advantage from his position; he cannot become a polygynist or accumulate wealth or influence significantly greater than that of other senior members of his sub-clan and village. On the other hand he has to assume responsibilities such as gardening for his sub-clan's senior affines, entertaining important visitors, initiating corporate activities in gardening and so on, and generally trying to keep his village's affairs running smoothly with no real formal authority, since he cannot issue orders, only try to persuade people to accept his recommendations, as we shall see. Where the sub-clan is of high rank and leads a cluster, however, the personal advantages and power accruing to its leader are considerable, and in olden times would-be leaders are believed regularly to have sought to eliminate rivals by fighting and by sorcery or poisoning.

(a) *Rank and Leadership* Rank in the Trobriands is perhaps the more readily misinterpreted because as a system it is not clearly formulated by the islanders themselves (cf. Seligman 1910:693–700). For present purposes rank may be defined as an attribute which characterizes the members of certain Trobriand sub-clans (*dala*) as the proper leaders in the localities with which they are associated. Malinowski has described the privileges and the traditional and mythical bases of rank (1929: 24–31; 1935:33–40), while as he said ignoring some of the complications in the interests of clarity in other directions (1929: 25–26). What ultimately distinguishes sub-clans of rank from others is that they are credited with the possession of peculiar powers which make their members, especially their leaders, dangerous men, and therefore entitled to receive the marks of respect and other privileges, including the accumulation of wealth by polygamy, which in turn enable them to increase the fear in which they are held by the employment of sorcerers (cf. Malinowski 1929:113). Thus the Tabalu sub-clan of Omarakana possess the To'urikuna magic of weather and prosperity by which they are believed to be able to bring famine or plenty on the whole Island (Malinowski 1935:83). To other high-ranking sub-clans are credited other kinds of powers; the Toliwaga sub-clan of Tilataula district, for instance, are believed to possess very potent war magic and skill as fighters, which underlie both their pre-eminence in that district and their traditional role and importance as the military rivals, though the inferiors in rank, of the Tabalu; for the Tabalu magic is considered in the long run more dangerous and more far-reaching than that of the Toliwaga (Malinowski 1922:66–67; 1935:328).

There is thus a major distinction between sub-clans which possess such special powers and those which do not. The former are the 'chiefly' (*guyau*) sub-clans, the latter the 'commoners' (*tokay*); and these are the only major rank categories. Within the *guyau* category however the sub-clans tend to be graded in an order of precedence which reflects ultimately the degree of fear in which their leaders are held, which varies according to the nature of the power attributed to them but also with their nearness to or distance from the populations of different localities. Only the Tabalu sub-clan is everywhere regarded as pre-eminent; otherwise although the classing of a sub-clan as *guyau* or *tokay* is normally unequivocal and uniform, the residents in the various clusters tend to regard their local *guyau* sub-clans as of higher rank than others. These considerations may explain the criticisms of Malinowski's account put forward by the Trobriander Lepani Watson or Gumigawa, as reported by Groves (1956).

This element of relativity in the ranking of *guyau* sub-clans reflects the fact that they are not elements in a single hierarchical system of delegated political authority. Thus the cadet branches of the Tabalu sub-clan deny that the Omarakana Tabalu *guyau* have any authority over them as such (cf. Seligman 1910:694), while my informants like Malinowski's (cf. 1929:110–12; 1935: I 192) asserted that he had no power in the Omarakana cluster as *guyau*, but only as the 'sister's husband' (*lubou*) of the leaders of the other owning sub-clans, in which capacity he was entitled to *urigubu* gifts and services from them. The rank is fully shared by all members of a *guyau* sub-clan (Malinowski 1929: 24 f), but its corporate powers and property are controlled only by its leader, to whom are given wives.

(*b*) *Rank and Succession* Succession to the leadership of a commoner sub-clan concerns primarily the residents in its village and its members living elsewhere. Succession to the leadership of a leading *guyau* sub-clan is the immediate political concern not only of the members of the sub-clan and residents in its village, but also of the rest of the village populations and leaders in the *guyau* sub-clan's cluster, and of the leaders and populations of other villages and clusters over whom the new *guyau* leader may seek to extend his power by claiming wives and *urigubu*. The process of selecting or achieving recognition as the heir of an important *guyau* leader is conditioned by this, for besides obtaining recognition by his predecessor and sub-clan kin, the aspirant leader must gain the support of the other leaders and residents in the cluster and, in the case of so important a sub-clan as the Omarakana Tabalu, of other cluster leaders from whom its leader is regarded as entitled to demand *urigubu*. One of the best ways for the would-be leader to strengthen his claims is by obtaining a wife from one at least of the sub-clans of his predecessor's most important affines.

The traditional rivalry between the sons and the heirs of important *guyau* leaders arises in this connexion, rather than as an element in the father-son-sister's son complex of kinship relations as such, which does not normally involve any significant conflict between a man's duties and rights towards his sister's children on the one hand and his duties and rights towards his own children on the other; these are opposed but complementary parts of the whole. Nor is there usually any apparent conflict between the father's personal attachment to a son and his formal kinship obligations; if he cannot confer on the son benefits of the kind he should pass on to his heir, there are others which he can appropriately bestow on his son. In any case the benefits of a material or any other kind which the ordinary commoner can bestow on either his son or his heir are very limited (Malinowski 1927, *passim*). The potential successors of important cluster leaders are however the potential seekers of *urigubu* tribute from their predecessors' sons. Should a *guyau*'s would-be heir succeed in obtaining a wife from the sub-clan of his predecessor's most important affines during the latter's lifetime, his sons as the future leaders of their sub-clans will be the 'wife's brothers' of the future *guyau* and will have to provide him with *urigubu* gifts and services.

This was the position in the quarrel between Mitakata, the future successor of To'uluwa, and Namwana Guyau, described so graphically by Malinowski (1929:10–13, 113–14), who however interpreted it primarily in terms of conflict between a father's love for his son and his formal kinship obligations towards his sister's son and heir. My informants, including Namwana Guyau's younger brothers Yobukwau (the present leader of their sub-clan) and Kalogusa, discussed the same events as incidents in the rivalry between the Tabalu sub-clan of Omarakana and the Kwainama sub-clan of Osapola. Namwana Guyau was the son of To'uluwa's first wife from the Kwainama sub-clan, which, as the nearest in rank to the Tabalu in Northern Kiriwina, is the sub-clan of greatest importance as a tributary affine of the Tabalu *guyau*. Namwana Guyau was the likeliest successor to his mother's brother Kwoyavila as Kwainama *guyau* leader, and by marrying Orayayse, Namwana Guyau's 'sister', Mitakata had placed himself in the position of being able to demand *urigubu* from the future Kwainama leader and his brothers, and to take over To'uluwa's role as the affinal 'overlord' of the Kwainama in the event of To'uluwa's death. There is no doubt that the two young men disliked each other personally, but this was a contributory factor rather than the cause of the rivalry between them as chiefly 'brothers-in-law' (*lubou*).

Bagido'u and the other members of the Tabalu sub-clan were impelled to intervene, and To'uluwa was unable to prevent their doing so, because in effect the action of Namwana Guyau in having Mitakata charged and imprisoned for adultery with his wife was an attack on the future Tabalu by the future Kwainama *guyau,* which tended to diminish the prestige of the former and enhance that of the latter, and therefore had to be countered by the formal expulsion (*yoba*) of the Kwainama heir from the Tabalu village. It is this aspect of the events which explains their resulting in what Malinowski called 'a deep rift in the whole social life of Kiriwina' (1929:13). The Kwainama have made subsequent attempts to enhance their prestige at the expense of the Tabalu. Yobukwau and Kalogusa have indeed gone so far as to cite European practice and claim that they as his sons should have succeeded To'uluwa, and at least once have sought recognition for this claim by decorating their houses in the style appropriate to the Tabalu, only to be forced to retract by Mitakata and his kinsmen, supported by the Administration.

Similar attacks on the Tabalu would of course in olden times have led to warfare, in which the sons and other followers of the leader would have taken sides. There was and still is a continuous manoeuvring for advantage in local leadership between the leading sub-clans of the various village clusters, so that each such sub-clan tend to endorse as its future leader the man who could enlist the support of the most important rival sub-clans, especially by obtaining a wife from one or more of them (cf. To'uluwa's position when he succeeded Numakala, Seligman 1910:713; Malinowski 1929:113–14). To achieve this the successful heir must overcome any opposition from rivals supported by other factions within the existing leader's following, and enmity between contending heirs and their supporters sometimes leads to the disintegration of the following of an ageing leader. In any case the death of a leader ends his marriages and the relationships established by them between him and his followers. If a successor has been recognized before his death, and has married women from some of the sub-clans of his predecessor's affines, his marriages replace those of his predecessor as political arrangements, while he may be given wives by other sub-clans if his position is strong enough. He may in some cases 'inherit', or perhaps more accurately marry in his turn, any of his predecessor's wives who are still young (Malinowski 1929:114). Otherwise the sudden death of an important cluster leader before a definite successor has emerged might result in a period of uncertainty and sometimes of interfactional fighting before another man of the sub-clan could establish his position firmly enough to demand wives from his predecessor's tributary allies by marriage.

The first public assertion and recognition of the new leader's position seems usually to consist in his organizing and conducting the mortuary rites for his predecessor, whose marriages are ceremonially terminated by these rites (Malinowski 1929:31–34, 130–39, and esp. 292). Informants said that in the case of so important a cluster leader as the Omarakana Tabalu every effort would be made to ensure that a successor was agreed upon as soon as possible after the accession of any given leader. Even so, the recognized future leader tended to try to eliminate possible rivals, especially by sorcery and poison. Both Mitakata and his predecessor To'uluwa were said to have done this; indeed it was in this connexion that To'uluwa first acquired the reputation for sorcery which ultimately led to his imprisonment by the Resident Magistrate (Seligman 1910:665; Malinowski 1929:25; Austen 1945:19, 21). It seems that at the time of his succession To'uluwa had indeed been predeceased by a number of contemporary and younger men of his sub-clan, while in Mitakata's case only one other young man, Uluwaiagu, was alive who might have succeeded To'uluwa (Austen 1945:21). But although there were some who favoured him, it was Mitakata who married a girl of the Kwainama sub-clan and was recognized as the new Tabalu *guyau*, and soon after the completion of the mortuary rituals for To'uluwa, Uluwaiagu became ill and died, some say by poison.

B. *The Exercise of Leadership*

1. Village Leaders I have avoided the terms headman and chief because their use might suggest, as it tends to do in Malinowski's accounts, that the relationship between the Trobriand leaders and their followers is of the general type of, e.g., Polynesian chieftaincy. The indigenous Trobriand village or village cluster leader is not fundamentally a lower or higher official in a constituted administrative hierarchy, nor is his relationship with his followers that of an appointed executive of official policy, except nowadays in so far as the indigenous system of leadership has been integrated into the administrative system imposed by Europeans. That the Trobriand political system appears in some respects to resemble such an administrative hierarchy results from the ability of some individuals to achieve and exercise relatively great, indeed sometimes virtually dictatorial, power. That they can do so is of course one effect of the leadership system; but the power they exercise under this system attaches to them personally, rather than as temporary occupants of permanent offices in which the power is vested. The position of village leaders approximates more closely to occupancy of such an office than does that of a cluster leader, in as much as villages are always politically organized and have recognized leaders while at any given time a cluster may have no recognized leader, and at such a time will hardly constitute a politically organized group. Nevertheless the role of the village leader is not clearly defined, varying with the strength of personality of the individual and being shared to different degrees by other senior members as well.

The Leader's Roles In effect, the village leader's position is that of a combined chairman, spokesman, and representative in external affairs of the corporate village population, whose adult, i.e. primarily married, male members discuss and settle all matters of public interest in more or less formal meetings (*kayaku*; the term denotes any kind of deliberative meeting, not only the 'gardening council' as Malinowski (1935, *passim*) sometimes implies). The leader takes part in these discussions and formulates the decisions or conclusions reached, which are always unanimous. He has no casting vote or final authority in discussion by virtue of his position as such, but his opinions like those of other senior men tend to carry the more weight the stronger his personality and prestige. Particular issues may by common consent be referred to him for decision or action if he is felt to be especially qualified to deal with them, but may equally be referred to other experts in particular fields; e.g. matters of gardening policy may be referred to the garden magician (*towosi*).

The leader may initiate any necessary action on decisions he has formulated, and can employ certain sanctions to this end, though again the duty and right to do so are not exclusively his. Every effort is normally made to achieve unanimous agreement by compromise on all issues of public interest. If on any particular issue the finding of a unanimous solution proves impossible within the village population and others concerned, e.g. the non-resident members of its owning sub-clan, an arbitrator may be sought. This is usually the cluster leader, whose status, not as *guyau* or 'chief' as such, but as the common 'brother-in-law' (*lubou*) or senior clan kinsman (*tuwa* or *kada*) of the leaders and senior men of the component villages, gives him the right to intervene in any affair of his affines or clan kin which may affect his rights in *urigubu* or *pokala* tribute. This status is of course shared by the other kin and affines of the residents of any village, but their potentialities as arbitrators vary directly with their local importance and prestige, and are likely to be much less than those of the cluster leader.

The Leader's Sanctions Since the recognized leader of a village is in effect the representative and spokesman of its corporate population and the leading executive of its policies, refusals to accept his leadership amount to public delicts and arouse the same patterns of reaction as any other offence against law and order. They are subject to the same very effective pressures of public opinion, and to any additional sanctions that the village leader and others as men of influence can exert in the public interest. The most usual of these are discussed from various points of view by Malinowski, and may be listed as follows.

The reciprocal rights and duties of kin and neighbours which embody their mutual interdependence lend great force to public opinion, as Malinowski emphasized (1926:Parts i and ix). This in turn underlies the effectiveness of shame (*agumwasila*) and shaming techniques (*yakala, kakayuwa*; Malinowski 1929:index s.v. Shame, and 408). Severe shaming may result in the formal expulsion (*yoba*; Malinowski 1926:103–4) of a non-member of the owning sub-clan from its village, or the suicide (Malinowski 1926:94–99) of a member of the owning sub-clan, either sequel relieving the sub-clan and village of undesirable members or residents without the need to employ physical force, which would further disrupt kin and local group solidarity. Sorcery (Malinowski 1926:esp. 85–94) is a legitimate sanction when employed by village leaders or senior men in the public interest, but too great a reliance on it opens the leader to the suspicion of inadequacy in the other techniques of leadership and of its employment to his own personal advantage, with consequent loss of support among his followers.

An important and effective sanction not explicitly dealt with by Malinowski is what may be termed deprivation of benefits of kin or local group membership. One of the responsibilities of the recognized sub-clan and village leader is to act as trustee for all the land, trees, magic and other forms of sub-clan property which is not held by individual members. It is in the leader's power to allocate rights of usufruct of such property to members of the sub-clan or residents in the village in response to formal requests by *pokala*; and conversely he can withhold from those who do not accept his leadership any material advantages thus sought. Other senior men with personal holdings of land or other property can exercise the same sanction over their juniors, and the leader depends on their support for the efficacy of this sanction in his hands; for if they do not approve of his action in refusing they can themselves confer the advantages sought. The non-material as well as the material advantages of sub-clan or village membership can be withheld or conferred in this way. Thus a villager may be refused the support of other residents if he refuses to follow the advice of the leaders in a particular project or dispute, or a woman may be refused *urigubu* in respect of a proposed marriage which is not approved by her sub-clan's leader and other senior men.

Physical force is not normally employed as an organized sanction at any rate within the village, nor can it be exerted by a commoner village leader, whose role is relatively ill-defined and whose position differs ultimately from that of the other senior men of his village only in degree, and in practice is often of little more than titular significance. He can employ no effective sanctions to reinforce his position other than those he exercises on behalf and with the support of the corporate village population. As has been indicated the main forces which sustain organized village leadership, in so far as this is necessary in the corporate life of the small groups concerned, are those which operate also in other aspects of social control; namely the pressures upon the individual to conform to the corporate interests and policies of his fellows. These pressures are derived from his close and immediate interdependence with his kin and affines, and these two categories include all his fellow villagers and many others besides.

Notwithstanding this, the Trobriander, as Malinowski emphasized particularly in *Crime and Custom,* is no less inclined than most other people to try to secure personal advantages in illegitimate ways if he thinks he can do so with impunity. But owing to the pattern of living in his small local groups he probably has less opportunity to do so successfully than have residents in large-scale social groups. At the same time there is, as so often in other similar societies, a strong element of relativity in Trobriand concepts of morality, which may afford some outlet for those who find the standards of conformity imposed by intra-village life irksome. Thus theft from a kinsman or neighbour is reprehensible; theft from a stranger may be praiseworthy, provided it brings no retribution on the groups to which the thief belongs (cf. Malinowski 1926:118). But neither the ordinary commoner leader nor any other resident of a village is entitled or able, in the current political idiom, to 'go it alone', whether by breaking other norms of behaviour or by seeking to enforce his will upon his fellow villagers. Given high rank, however, the leader of a village cluster may be able to exercise virtually autocratic powers, at least for some time.

2. Cluster Leaders As we have seen, a recognized cluster leader must first be recognized as leader of his sub-clan and village. As such his position in his village is initially the same in principle as that of a commoner village leader; but the degree of personal power he may achieve as cluster leader may enable him to exercise at times almost dictatorial control over his fellow-villagers. It may be repeated here that this power is not the direct correlate of his rank as such, which is shared by the other members of his sub-clan. They do not however share his personal power, which derives rather from the *urigubu* and *pokala* tribute and the influence he has as their recipient from the other leaders of villages in his cluster and, if he is sufficiently important, from the leaders of other clusters. The respect accorded to men of high rank has already been related ultimately to the special magical and other powers which they as leaders of their sub-clans are believed to control. Thus the Tabalu *guyau* leader of Omarakana is more feared than any other *guyau* leader because of his control of the *to'urikuna* weather magic, but a new leader of the Omarakana Tabalu does not automatically receive wives and tribute from the other cluster leaders of Kiriwina because of this. If he did, there would in practice be a more or less permanent paramount indigenous political leadership for at least the greater part of Kiriwina Island.

In fact the new leader of a *guyau* sub-clan can expect the more or less automatic acceptance of his leadership by the other village leaders and their followers in the cluster. Their allegiance takes the form of their giving him either women of their sub-clans as wives and hence *urigubu* tribute, or recognition as their senior clan kinsman and hence *pokala* tribute, if their sub-clans and that of the cluster leader are of the same clan. Clan kinship and *pokala* tribute are however often felt to be insufficiently definitive as mechanisms of political allegiance, and may be reinforced or replaced by the creation of fictitious affinal relationships. Thus the two Mailasi-owning sub-clans of Yolawotu village are of the same clan as the Tabalu, but for tributary purposes their leaders were counted as kinsmen of Mitakata's senior wife, whose clan was Lukwasisiga, so that they rendered him *urigubu* rather than *pokala*, though he could not have married a woman of either sub-clan without a breach of clan exogamy. Kinship, especially affinal, relationships are manipulated in many ways as political mechanisms, including the substitution of a 'male wife' (*tokwava*) when no nubile female is available to establish a tributary affinal relationship between a *guyau* leader and a *tokay* descent and local group; but whatever the form of the marriage employed, its effect is to place the wife-giving group in the position of tributary affines to the individual to whom the wife is given. This follows automatically on the accession of a new cluster leader only within his own village cluster. He may, as we have seen, already have acquired wives from one or more leaders of other clusters in the process of becoming leader of his own, and to this extent have acquired the nucleus of a following outside his cluster. This is most likely in the case of the most important cluster leaders, such as the Tabalu or Toliwaga; others, such as the Kwainama of Liluta cluster, may neither be entitled nor aspire to seek wives from outside their own clusters.

As the most important *guyau* leader in Northern Kiriwina, the Omarakana Tabalu begins his political career with a nuclear following within his village cluster and perhaps a few additional tributary affines outside it, but he must assert and justify his claims to further wives and tribute from other cluster leaders. Before he can do so he must make a display of the power which he has already achieved, in wealth and in the number of his supporters. He may do this on the occasion of the mortuary rituals for his predecessor, at which as successor he must make as lavish as possible a provision of wealth for ceremonial distribution (*sagali*) to the formal mourners, including of course the brothers of the widows of the dead leader and others (cf. Malinowski 1929:chap. 6, sects. 2–4). Or the new leader may declare a festival of some sort, e.g. of dancing, or nowadays of cricket (*usigola* or *kayasa kiliketi*; cf. Malinowski 1929:213–15, 292–93; Powell 1952). As Malinowski described them, such festivals may be organized by others than political leaders for many reasons, including simple *joie de vivre*; but when staged by political leaders to increase their power and prestige they are usually termed *paka,* and may be regarded as examples of 'Feasts of Merit'.

Having used or created such an occasion for the display of his existing power, wealth and generosity, as manifested in the number of his adherents and the extent of their and his own contributions to the *sagali,* the new Tabalu leader will be ready to demand wives from others. He will approach on a more or less friendly basis leaders of sub-clans who are traditionally supporters of the leader of his own and any others from whom his predecessors may have obtained wives. From yet others, especially the traditional rivals of his own sub-clan's leaders, he may formally demand wives on threat of war, sending messengers with a spear which they stab into the ground of the village while publicly proclaiming their *guyau*'s demand on its leader. He would adopt the friendly approach to most of the leaders of village clusters in Kiriwina district, many of whom

would voluntarily offer him wives if satisfied with his demonstration of success as a leader. He would be most likely to adopt
the second procedure in demanding a wife from the Toliwaga
leaders of Tilataula, but he could attempt this only if his position in Kiriwina district were firmly established. Not all Tabalu
leaders of Omarakana cluster, and it seems none of the other
Tabalu cluster leaders, could attain such strength in the course
of their careers, though to be able to make and enforce this demand seems to have been a traditional aim of the Tabalu *guyau*
of Omarakana. For if successful in this, he would be in a
position to extend the area of his power by similar methods into
Luba, Kuboma, and beyond.

As his external following grew so would the strength of his
control over his followers, especially within the Omarakana
cluster itself. Lesser *guyau* leaders who could not normally extend their powers much beyond their respective clusters could
exercise less control over their cluster following, but nevertheless,
inasmuch as all cluster leaders of *guyau* rank tend to acquire a
plurality of wives and some degree of wealth from outside the
cluster, their power within their clusters tends to be greater if
only in degree than the power of commoner village leaders in
their villages; while important cluster leaders with significant
extra-cluster followings tend to acquire means of enforcing their
leadership within the cluster which are not possessed by minor
cluster leaders.

(*a*) *Intra-Cluster Leadership* Thus the degree and to some
extent the kind of power wielded within the cluster by its recognized leader varies according to the extent of his power outside
it, and in this respect the two aspects of the cluster leader's
power are interdependent. On the other hand the internal position of a cluster leader rests ultimately on the voluntary support
of its population and village leaders, whose prosperity and prestige tend to be linked directly to those of their *guyau*; but the
position of an important cluster leader in relation to his extra-
cluster following tends to rest ultimately on the threat of force,
and his power and prestige are gained at the expense of other
cluster leaders who recognize him as their affinal or clan 'overlord'.

Minor Guyau Leaders However, the majority of cluster leaders can not aspire to acquire significant extra-cluster followings,
but only to preserve their independence of other more powerful

(i.e. higher-ranking in the sense already discussed) cluster leaders, or more usually to obtain as much advantage for themselves as they can by associating themselves as tributary allies with one or the other such leader. As measured in terms of the wealth and services they command, the power of such minor cluster leaders tends to be less significantly greater than that of ordinary village leaders than is the power of major cluster leaders greater than that of the lesser. Thus in 1950 the minor *guyau* leader of Kwaybwaga village cluster had only three wives and a proportionate command of wealth to differentiate his position from that of the other village leaders in his cluster, while Mitakata the leader of Omarakana cluster, despite the effects of fifty years of Mission teaching and Government control, still had thirteen wives. In olden times the Kwaybwaga cluster leader might have had three times as many wives, but the Tabalu *guyau* of Omarakana cluster could have acquired forty or more wives during a successful political career. Again, whereas nearly all, or all, of the Kwaybwaga cluster leader's wives came from kin and local groups within his cluster, all but two of Mitakata's wives, and at least as high a proportion of the wives of his predecessors, came from outside the cluster he led.

The minor cluster leader might have in his following men who rivalled him in the number of their wives, for important men of his own or other *guyau* sub-clans might be polygamists, as might also renowned sorcerers (Malinowski 1929:110); but no such personage could hope to rival the wealth of such a cluster leader as the Omarakana Tabalu. Again the minor cluster leader is usually the tributary affine of a major cluster leader, which tends to affect his power by affording his followers the chance of looking beyond him for leadership, as it were, to the major cluster leader. The latter, on the other hand, would normally owe *urigubu* to no one senior in rank to himself, though he would do so to one or two husbands of women of his sub-clan, as does Mitakata. Thus the lesser *guyau* cluster leader has a position in the cluster which is superior to that of other village leaders and senior men in his following less in terms of the kind of powers he can exercise than in the degree to which he can command powers of the same general kind as can they; but this difference tends to be less than that between his power and that of a major *guyau* cluster leader to whom he in turn makes tributary allegiance.

The minor *guyau* cluster leader then can exercise the same kinds of sanctions over his following as can the commoner village leader over his (cf. section IIB 1), and he does so in much the same way, that is, by persuasion rather than by coercion, and as the most important common affine or clan kinsman of the village leaders, as the village leader is the most important common sub-clan, clan, or affinal kinsman of his followers within his village. If the cluster leader can exercise his rights in terms of these relationships successfully, he focuses the economic, political, and other aspects of the activities of the cluster population upon himself, so that it becomes a single organized unit. In order to promote his own power and safeguard his own interests the cluster leader must in the long run promote also the solidarity and common interests of the component corporate groups of its population; and probably his greatest single difficulty in achieving both these results is the rivalry between and mutual suspicion of the leaders and members of these kin and local groups.

There is as we saw in Section IIB a tradition of solidarity within the village cluster which is promoted by the distribution of members of the owning sub-clans of its villages, by their intermarriage and their interaction with each other as kin, and as neighbours and friends also. But this is the solidarity of autonomous allies or associates, not of dependent segments of a major autonomous unit, and the various owning sub-clans are always jealous of their individual rights in land and other property, and of their prestige. Each kin-group as affines or clan kin of the cluster leader tends to suspect that the other kin-groups may derive more advantage from the association than themselves, and to regard the rest as competitors for his support. He tends to play them off against each other, though he must see to it that he does not appear to favour always the same group rather than the others, either by making excessive demands on one or giving excessive advantage to the rest. In the long run he must try to distribute both the demands he makes in terms of *urigubu* or *pokala* tribute and the reciprocal services he confers equitably. If he does not, sooner or later real or imagined grievances will result in the emergence of opposition from one quarter or another.

A skilful cluster leader will rarely take any action in respect of his relationship with the leader of one kin or local group without consulting or informing his other 'brothers-in-law' or clan 'younger brothers'; and on any matter which may affect the interests of all he will call a deliberative assembly (*kayaku*) which may be attended not only by the village leaders but by all adult males of the cluster in the same way that a village *kayaku* is attended by all the men of the village. Other village leaders may also initiate such an assembly by informing the cluster leader that they intend to hold one, just as the other senior men of a village may initiate a village assembly; and again as in the village meeting, such a cluster assembly may deal with any matter of social control or cluster organization that concerns either the cluster population as a whole, or two or more of its component village or sub-clan populations. Thus in effect each village under its leader deals with its own internal affairs; while the external relationships of the villages with each other, if difficulties arise, tend to become the concern of the cluster leader as the senior kinsman of the village leaders primarily concerned, and, through their relationships with the cluster leader, of the other village leaders as well. But this state of affairs comes about only if the cluster population is effectively led.

The previous discussion of social control in the village and its leader's role therein (section IIB 1) applies broadly to the processes and mechanisms of social control and leadership in the cluster also, with the qualifications that the pressures to co-operation in seeking and carrying out policy decisions tend to be weaker at the level of the cluster because of the basic autonomy of its component kin and local groups, and that the cluster leader's role as the promoter of compromise and unanimity tends to be correspondingly more difficult than is that of the village leader in village affairs. On the other hand the cluster leader tends to have more wealth, power, and prestige to give force to his advice and opinions than has the village leader, though as emphasized previously the degree to which his power exceeds that of the village leaders in his following varies directly with his importance in relation to other cluster leaders.

Major Guyau Leaders As was indicated in Section IIA 2*a*,
each minor leader of a cluster tends to be regarded in his own
cluster as more important than and in this sense senior in rank
to other minor *guyau,* while other major *guyau* tend to be regarded as being of the same or higher rank than the local
cluster leader, since the major *guyau* such as the Tabalu or
Toliwaga tends to obtain tributary allegiance from the minor
guyau cluster leaders in his vicinity at least. The more such
minor *guyau* become his tributary allies and the wider the area
over which they are scattered, the greater and more absolute
tends to be the power of the major *guyau* within his own cluster,
until in the case of the Omarakana Tabalu cluster leader at
least it becomes almost autocratic, while he commands ways of
enforcing his wishes on his intra-cluster followers which are not
available to lesser cluster leaders. For in addition to becoming
wealthy to an extent which makes him in effect independent of
the support of other leading men in his cluster, the Tabalu leader
in particular tends to acquire during his career a band of personal followers or retainers who depend exclusively upon him
for their position in his village and cluster, and whom he can
employ as a sort of executive force and 'strong arm squad'.
The nucleus of this body consists in resident male representatives
of the kin and local groups outside the *guyau*'s own cluster
from which he receives tribute, and especially his 'sons', own or
classificatory. This situation would develop in full only when
the Omarakana cluster leader had built up his following to include the Toliwaga leader of Tilataula, which he could normally
do only under threat of war. Since this has been prevented for
the past fifty years by European administration, the positions
of To'uluwa and Mitakata have been in this respect little more
than ghosts of those attributed to their predecessors. But there
remained in Malinowski's time and still in 1950 some evidence
to support the stories still current of the great power and glory
of former Tabalu *guyau.*

Thus Malinowski made reference for example to the 'strangers'
who lived in Omarakana by right of hereditary service to the
Tabalu *guyau* (1929:9), and the part of the village occupied
by such men was still distinguishable in 1950. Again he refers
to 'hereditary henchmen' whose duty it was to kill people who
offended the *guyau* (1927:65; 1929:376–77), and the last

representative of these, Mosiviyagila of the Siviyagila sub-clan, Lukuba clan, was still alive in Omarakana, though of course shorn of his functions, in 1950. These 'hereditary henchmen' were apparently members of the various leading sub-clans in the village clusters which traditionally allied themselves with a successful Omarakana Tabalu leader, and in return claimed particular privileges, such as bearing the *guyau*'s shield in battle, as well as that of residence in the *guyau*'s village. The branch of the Kwainama sub-clan of Liluta which is now settled as an owning sub-clan in Omarakana seems to have acquired its rights in this way.

Such supporters had privileged positions in the Omarakana cluster but were individually dependent for their enjoyment on the *guyau*'s personal favour, as were his sons. He could therefore rely on their carrying out his wishes even when these were opposed by other residents in the cluster, and could employ them as a sort of executive body in social control in general and in the maintenance of his leadership in particular, as in virtue of his wealth he could employ sorcerers; but there was always the possibility that physical force or sorcery might be employed by the leader in his own rather than in the public interest. He might and sometimes did become too dependent on the support of his personal adherents, who might then abuse their privileged positions, as Namwana Guyau abused the trust of To'uluwa. It is to this possibility in particular that can be related the traditional latent hostility between a *guyau*'s sons and his heirs, which is less an element in the kinship system to be explained in terms of conflicts between paternal love and matrilineal duty, as Malinowski saw it (1926:100–11), than an element in the political system which affects the relation between the sons and the heirs of leading cluster *guyau*, but not of other men where the political significance of the relationship is absent.

In the case of the cluster leader of Omarakana however the presence of the body of personally dependent 'henchmen', including his 'sons', in his village enabled him to exert a degree and a kind of power within his cluster, for good or ill, which is not at the disposal of less important cluster leaders. But the less dependent his extra-cluster importance made him of the support of the majority of the other residents within his cluster, the more dependent he tended to become upon the leaders of other village clusters than his own.

(*b*) *Extra-Cluster Leadership* The role of the cluster leader in the internal political organization of the cluster population may be summarized as the limitation of competition and the promotion of co-operation between the independent corporate groups more or less voluntarily united by their acceptance of his leadership. A similar role accrues to the *guyau* leader who succeeds in building up a significant following outside his own cluster, but whereas within the cluster the emergence of a recognized leader may, it has been suggested, be understood as a consequence rather than the cause of solidarity between the autonomous component groups, the reverse tends to be true of the relationships between the various clusters which recognize the leadership of a major *guyau*.

In the absence of a recognized leader within a cluster there remains a degree of solidarity derived from tradition, kinship links, and other connexions between the component corporate groups. A reflection of this is the fact that certain forms of competitive activity are regarded as inappropriate to the relationship between kin or local groups within the same cluster whether it has an effective leader or not. Formal warfare, for example, as against impromptu brawling which tends to result in the intervention of the senior men of the villages concerned and of the cluster leader if his interests are affected, apparently never occurs between component villages of the same cluster, nor does the formal 'garden challenge' (*buritilaulo*; Malinowski 1935: 181–87). In the absence of a common 'tributary overlord', however, the relationship between two clusters tends traditionally to be one of rivalry and competition for prestige and power, in the pursuit of which both war and *buritilaulo* challenge are normal and appropriate (Malinowski 1920; Powell 1952). The closer any two clusters are to each other in space the more interests their populations tend to share, while their awareness of each other as competitors is acute also, so that the 'garden challenge' tends to occur most frequently between clusters which are close neighbours, as an alternative to, or sometimes as a first stage in, formal warfare. Three *buritilaulo* occurred in 1950–1, between the Diaghila and Liluta clusters, between the Kabwaku and Kabulula (Kwaybwaga) clusters, and between the Tukwa'ukwa and Okopukopu sections of the following of the Tabalu leader of Tukwa'ukwa cluster (v. map). No formal warfare is known to have occurred of course since the turn of the century, but all three of these challenges resulted in brawling.

A major *guyau* leader, if he is successfully to build up his extra-cluster following, must in his own interests seek to restrain the competitive element in the relationship between its component independent clusters. Thus Mitakata of Omarakana intervened in the quarrel between the Diaghila and Liluta clusters in his indigenous capacity as their common *guyau,* i.e. tributary overlord, as well as in that of Government-recognized senior 'chief'. In neither capacity, it must be added, was his intervention particularly effective; but, as my informants in Omarakana asserted, his messengers would in olden times have been backed by the threat of force, for he would have sent a party of his personal supporters from Omarakana to avenge the implied insult if his intervention were disregarded.

The right of the cluster leader to intervene in the affairs and relationships of his tributary allies or followers outside his cluster is derived, as is his right so to intervene in inter- and intra-village affairs within his own cluster, from his status as the common senior affinal or clan kinsman of those concerned; but whereas his interventions in these capacities within his own cluster are the more effective for the interests, other than their common association with him, shared by its component villages, no such factor favours his interventions in the interrelations of the clusters in his following, in which the competitive element tends to dominate the co-operative. The successful major *guyau* leader must create out of an aggregate of such competing clusters a more or less effectively co-operating following, and he does so in effect by focusing on their relationships with himself the element of competition which otherwise would determine the form of their interaction with each other.

That is, once associated with each other as the Omarakana *guyau*'s tributary allies, his adherents outside his own cluster tend to cease competing with each other directly in formal warfare, *buritilaulo,* dance or other festivals, and so on organized in their own rights by the various minor cluster leaders. Instead, competition between them takes the form of the pursuit of advantages in influence over and benefits from the common overlord at the expense of traditional rivals. Thus, instead of displaying their wealth in festivals organized by themselves, the various minor cluster leaders tend to do so in terms of the lavishness of the *urigubu* tribute presented annually to their overlord, or of the generosity of their contributions to the *paka* 'Feasts of Merit' at which from time to time he displays his wealth and power to the detriment of that of his major *guyau* rivals. Thus in 1950 the Toliwaga leader of Kabwaku cluster organized a major cricket festival, and in reply Mitakata of Omarakana organized a great *paka* of competitive dancing at the following harvest, to restore the balance of prestige in his own favour.

It was in the struggle to extract advantage from the relationship with the Omarakana Tabalu that in olden times his tributary followers sent to live in Omarakana village representatives who could safeguard and try to advance their own sub-clan and cluster leaders' interests on the spot, as it were, and who became members of the body of personal supporters of the *guyau* already referred to. The *guyau*'s grown-up sons, who as we have seen were the likely heirs of the leaders of their respective sub-clans, were in many ways ideally situated to represent their respective clusters in this way, and of course in so doing to incur the suspicion if not the hostility of their father's heirs as well as of each other. Their common opposition to the *guyau*'s sub-clan kin however tended to restrain their suspicion of each other, at least so far as their relationships within their village of residence were concerned. One of the activities of these resident representatives of the *guyau*'s tributary affines seems to have been to inform their principals of political developments which might make it expedient for them to visit Omarakana, and there seems to have developed a sort of *de facto* 'council' of the *guyau*'s following which met either on his or on its members' initiative and considered all matters of interest to the clusters represented. As in dealing with his intra-cluster following, the *guyau* would normally consult all those affected by any proposed course of action before taking any decisions.

For his part the *guyau* in turn sought to play off the various factions within his following against each other by utilizing traditional rivalries between the cluster leaders and so on, so that one receives the impression that a successful Omarakana Tabalu

guyau of olden times would not have been out of his depth in
technique at least in modern world politics. But it seems that
he rarely achieved the kind of autocratic power over his extra-
cluster following that its importance conferred on him in his
dealings with the population of his own village cluster. He could
retain his following in the long run only by majority support,
and if he failed to keep a significant majority of his extra-cluster
followers content with his leadership, those who were disaffected
could find a rallying point for their opposition in the Omarakana
guyau's traditional military rivals, the Toliwaga leaders of Tilataula.

C. *Northern Kiriwinan Politics*

It is, I believe, a safe conjecture that the political history of
Northern Kiriwina Island was in at least recent pre-European
times one of attempts by the Omarakana Tabalu *guyau* leaders
to extend their power as widely as possible in face of the opposition of the Tilataula Toliwaga leaders. The latter do not
seem to have been rivals of the Tabalu for absolute power,
since they seem to have been regarded as entitled only to oppose the expansion of the power of the Tabalu rather than to
expand their own to the same extent. The most recent of the
Kiriwinan wars as described by Seligman (1910:664–68) illustrates this. In 1885 the then Omarakana Tabalu leader Numakala or Enamakala made war on the Toliwaga of Kabwaku,
apparently because the latter refused Numakala's demand for
a wife. Numakala and his followers won and laid waste most of
the villages of Tilataula. By 1899 Numakala had lost much of
his popularity in Kiriwina, and some of his disaffected allies,
including it seems the clusters of Diaghila and Kaibola which
(if they did not join the attack at least were not destroyed in
the subsequent defeat), joined the Tilataula villages and made
war on him. Most of the villages of his allies were destroyed, and
he and his associates were driven into exile near Tukwa'ukwa.
No attempt was made in either war by the winners to prevent
the resurgence of the defeated leaders by taking over their villages or the like. Rather, after To'uluwa, Numakala's successor,
had formally made peace with Moliasi of Kabwaku in 1900, he
was helped by the latter's followers to rebuild his village and
resume his rightful place. To'uluwa subsequently proceeded to

rebuild his following with no little success, despite the opposition of early Mission and Government personnel, as the map shows.

As Seligman says, these events seem to be typical of warfare between the followings of the rival Tabalu and Toliwaga. This suggests that the aim of formal war, as against the raiding which accompanied famines (cf. Malinowski 1935:161–64), was not to obtain a decisive conclusion to the competitive relationship between the two leaders and their followings, but rather to restore the balance of power when the Tabalu *guyau* of Omarakana became so powerful as to threaten to end it; and moreover to restore it in such a way that further competition between those local groups associated with him and those associated with the Toliwaga of Tilataula was not only possible but inevitable. In other words formal warfare was one of the normal forms of competitive political interaction between the followings of autonomous leaders. It could not normally occur between the component clusters of a major *guyau*'s following however; and one criterion of membership of such a following is still whether two clusters are on 'fighting terms' or not.

There were times, it seems, when the Omarakana Tabalu leaders were able to exact wives and tribute from distant areas of Kiriwina, by dominating more or less temporarily the Toliwaga of Tilataula, or perhaps by agreement with them. In 1942 the Trobriand among other islands were evacuated by Europeans because of the threat of Japanese invasion. During the disturbances which followed (cf. Austen 1945:58) the indigenous political situation reasserted itself to the extent that Mitakata of Omarakana made an agreement with Wailassi the Toliwaga leader of Tubowada whereby the former undertook not to take military advantage of the absence of the latter from his district when he decided to plunder European property and native villages on the lagoon, which had prospered by pearl fishing and other trade during the inter-war years to the envy of the inland villages. In return Wailassi agreed to act as Mitakata's emissary and demand wives and tribute on his behalf from the villages of Kulumata, Kuboma, and Luba, which he as Toliwaga could not legitimately demand for himself. Mitakata informed me that had European control not been re-established before Wailassi's efforts on his behalf came to fruition he would have received *urigubu* tribute from a number of lagoon villages and *pokala* tribute from the cadet Tabalu leaders in those districts. He explained that he made this arrangement with the Toliwaga because he expected the Europeans to return soon; in that event the Toliwaga, not Mitakata, would have been responsible for the raids, while otherwise Mitakata would have the advantage of acquiring tributary allies rather than plunder as the result of his policy. When Administrative control was re-established, Wailassi and many of his followers were in fact gaoled for varying periods, to the gratification of Mitakata.

As we have already seen, the other Tabalu leaders in Kuboma, Kulumata and Luba appear never to have sought to extend their followings as did the Omarakana Tabalu leaders. Examination of Map 2 will show that their followings were in 1950 much smaller than those of the two most recent Omarakana *guyau,* and despite the claims of Togarai of Mulasaida and Mosilieu of Tukwa'ukwa there is no real evidence that their relative power was significantly greater in the past. It seems that while in other native districts the general pattern occurred of associations of villages in clusters with recognized leaders, only in Kiriwina was there the tendency for major alliances of clusters to grow under the leadership of the Tabalu of Omarakana. It seems unlikely that the presence of the cadet branches of the Tabalu sub-clan in the various other districts except Tilataula was the result of a deliberate policy of expansion from Omarakana as the Tabalu centre; indeed the insistence of the other Tabalu leaders on their independence of the Omarakana *guyau* argues against such a view. On the other hand the absence of any cadet branch of the Tabalu in Tilataula district suggests that the Omarakana leaders might not lightly accept the existence in that district, perhaps as tributary overlords of the Toliwaga, of a branch of their own sub-clan which, being their equals in rank, might become also their rivals in power. The positions and followings in 1951 of the other Tabalu leaders approximate more or less in size to that which the Omarakana *guyau* might have had when he had become leader but before he began the systematic expansion of his following, and according to informants this would represent the normal limit of expansion of the other Tabalu leaders. Elsewhere in the Islands the system of leadership, and with it the operational significance of rank, polygamy, and *urigubu* as elements in it, may differ from the northern Kiriwinan pattern (cf. Seligman 1910:chap. 51; Malinowski 1922:67–69, 195–96).

III   CONCLUSION

The purpose of this paper has been to describe indigenous Kiriwinan political organization in terms of the dynamics of competitive leadership and of course its concomitant dynamics of 'followership'. These give rise to a continually changing pattern of areas of co-operation among the small-scale autonomous local populations of the Kiriwinan villages.

The normal internal state of the individual village and that of its relationships with the villages associated with it in its cluster is co-operation. This is one result of the focusing of the relationships of the associated populations on particular localized descent groups. The intra-village and cluster co-operation occurs with the minimum of functionally specialized political institutions, arising from the interdependence of the members of the numerically small corporate groups as a function of the institutions of kinship and marriage together with that of rank.

Rank in this sense is a social attribute of certain localized descent groups which focuses on their members the kinship and affinal relationships of the rest of the local population. These relationships provide the necessary definition and continuity in their general social interaction, while their focusing on the subclans of rank introduces the degree of overall organization and leadership necessary to ensure the co-operation of the associated corporate descent and local groups. This implies that the degree of co-operation thus achieved is necessary for the social viability of the autonomous corporate groups, and that the institutions of kinship and marriage and of rank together provide mechanisms necessary and adequate to ensure it.

The cluster aggregate represents the normal limit of permanent relationships of co-operation of its component villages, and beyond this limit their relationships take the form of more or less organized competition with other like cluster aggregates. But at least one of the clusters tends to extend its area of co-operation to include other clusters. This expansion tends however to reach a recurrent critical point, at which the social mechanisms that bring it about cause it to disintegrate into its component permanent clusters, so that the process of expansion begins again. Thus whereas the areas of co-operation established by the association of villages in clusters seem to be stable, those resulting from the expansion of such intra-cluster areas of co-operation are unstable.

These observations suggest that the autonomous localized descent groups and the local groups organized round them are socially more viable when organized into co-operating clusters, and that these in turn are more viable when in organized competition with each other. This implies that under indigenous Trobriand cultural conditions the village clusters represent the optimal extent of areas of permanent co-operation among local populations, and that the optimum relationship between such clusters is one of more or less permanent competition, by which the groups within the clusters are the more strongly impelled to co-operate. Warfare and other forms of institutionalized competition between clusters are thus structurally the means of ensuring intra-cluster co-operation rather than of establishing permanent areas of co-operation wider than the village clusters, and the structural role of the competing leaders, whatever their conscious aims, is the promotion rather than the elimination of this inter-cluster competition.

The discussion has emphasized the village cluster rather than its component descent and local groups as the optimum political unit of permanent co-operation. That this optimum unit is no smaller appears to be the result of the operation of many factors, including those of demography discussed in Section IA. But of all the factors which may determine that this unit is no larger, one at least seems to be the nature of the mechanisms of political organization and leadership in Northern Kiriwina Island.

9 PRESENT-DAY POLITICS
IN THE NEW GUINEA HIGHLANDS

Marie Reay

Marie Reay is Senior Fellow in Anthropology and Sociology at the
Australian National University, Canberra. She is the author of *The
Kuma: Freedom and Conformity in the New Guinea Highlands*
(1959) and several papers, and edited *Aborigines Now* (1964).

THE DEFINITION of politics which underlies this analysis of a
changing political system (or system of power relations) differs substantially from one which is currently fashionable among
social anthropologists. I am defining "politics" as the patterning
of public affairs in terms of power relations. This is a much more
broad and inclusive definition than that of M. G. Smith (1956).
Smith's distinction between "administration" and "politics" and
his reduction of "politics" to "competition in terms of power
and influence" (1956:48) represent a certain advance in anthropological theory respecting politics. Earlier theory, which culminated in the volume *African Political System* (Fortes 1940), had
distinguished between two types of political systems, "states"
and "stateless societies." A state is distinguished from a stateless
society by the presence of some central authority and a distinct
administrative machinery, whereas the tasks of administration
in stateless societies, such as those originally found in Papua-
New Guinea, fall upon the more generalized institutions of social

FROM "New Guinea: The Central Highlands," *American Anthropologist*
66, No. 4, Part 2 (1964), 240–56, by permission of the author and of
the editor, *American Anthropologist*.

A draft of this paper was read in a Symposium on political development
in Australia's Near North at the ANZAAS Congress in Canberra in January
1964. Field work was carried out under the auspices of the Australian
National University.

life, notably those concerned with kinship. Typically, the clan or the lineage acts as a political unit and has political functions. The descriptions of political systems in the African volume divide into descriptions of administrative systems (in those societies which the editors, Fortes and Evans-Pritchard, designate as "states") and descriptions of social structure in its political aspects (in respect of the stateless societies). Smith (1956) saw that a distinction had to be drawn, in more precise terms than the overall distinction between states and stateless societies, if anthropological theory and its contributions to our understanding of political behavior were to proceed. He saw that a system of administration was not the same thing as a political system. But this does not mean, as Smith thought, that the distinction to be drawn was between administration and politics; rather, it means that administration must be distinguished from other kinds of power relations that are relevant to the management of public affairs.

The earlier theory had been based on the premise that political organization referred ultimately to the maintenance of social order and that the net effect of political activity in a given society was social equilibrium. Gluckman (1954; 1955) placed what I think was undue emphasis on the element of conflict in political relations, but contrived to make his ideas continuous with those of Radcliffe-Brown (1940) and others by postulating that social harmony or equilibrium depends upon a balanced opposition in social institutions and behavior. The swing towards competition and conflict from the earlier emphasis on social order came full circle when Smith (1956) divorced administration (which he seems to regard as mere procedure, the implementing of decision) from politics (which he identifies with competition, conflict, and opposition). I would prefer to leave open to empirical inquiry the question as to whether the emphasis in a particular political system is on equilibrium or opposition, and to do this I would include the processes of administration in my definition of overall political organization or behavior. Political scientists concern themselves with such matters as elections, public administration, and so forth: all things that come within the province of the political institutions of Western societies. An anthropologist who is concerned with present-day politics in New Guinea, where specialized political institutions of Western type are being introduced to stateless societies, requires a conceptual framework which can take account of Western political institutions and of the indigenous social structure in its political aspects.

Political behavior is not always competitive; it is often adjustive. The successive adjustments of policy to the interests and traditions of persons and agencies at every level of an administrative hierarchy can substantially alter it. Adjustments to authority occur when administrations have to feed back to the policy makers information that can reassure them that policy is being carried out with some measure of success. Thus Annual Reports to the United Nations can give what may be falsely rosy impressions of the progress in native education by assigning prominence to facts which support the idea of progress; by quoting with merited pride the rates at which the numbers of schools and of pupils enrolled are increasing, without reconciling these with locally born native children's observable lack of continuous academic education in some places; and by the implicit assumption that any education is better than none.

I shall try to analyze here the changing political system of the Kuma, a people I know from spending fifteen months with them in 1953–55 and a further four months with them in 1963. I propose to analyze this changing system by describing three phases in their political development—firstly, the system that pertained when the first patrols entered the Wahgi Valley; secondly, the system that resulted from European efforts at control; and, finally, the patterning of present-day politics in terms of the interplay between the influence of these two earlier phases and political institutions of Western type which have been introduced in recent years. This report is a preliminary analysis of a continuing study, not a final statement of research results.

I

The Kuma, who are increasingly becoming known as "the Minj people" (Ming Agamp), number about twelve thousand. They are a regional division of a wider cultural grouping centered in the "Middle Wahgi" area in the Minj Subdistrict of the Western Highlands, occupying the part of the Wahgi Valley that lies south of the Wahgi River and is centered on the European township or government station of Minj.

These people have a segmentary lineage system of classical

type, although to call their groups "lineages" would give a misleading impression of their interest in genealogical reckoning,
which they play down for reasons of expediency while emphasizing unequivocally the principle of unilineal descent (Reay
1959a:25–52). They are divided into patrilineal clans which
typically include both subclans and smaller lineage-like groups
which I call somewhat infelicitously "sub-sub clans." A few of the
larger clans are divided into two main segments, each of which
includes a number of subclans with their constituent sub-subclans.
The structure of the clans was ever changing: some groups expanding and dividing, and others declining and dying out; some
splitting through internal dissension, with one part migrating to
settle with a different group; others fleeing from their territory in
warfare, with various segments finding refuge with different clans.

The agnatic clan was the territorial unit and formed the only
real political community. I mean by this that clansmen and their
wives and children form the widest public within which some
kind of law and order was traditionally essayed, and that the
units that went to war with each other were always clans, no
matter what allies they persuaded to help them in particular
clashes with their enemies. In all kinds of relations with outsiders,
a man acts not simply as an individual but as a representative of
his clan. Warfare was frequent, and internal trouble within the
clan was not unusual. The Kuma never undertook warfare with
the aim of annexing more territory: there has always been plenty
of land for a people practising shifting agriculture and raising
pigs to satisfy their appetites and obligations. They fought mostly
over women, who have traditionally been objects of exchange between clans, and the most frequent trouble within the clan itself
was over pigs. Marriage was the primary mode of establishing
friendly relations between clans, and each clan divided the external world into clans which were traditional enemies, friendly
inter-marrying clans, and other clans who were at once potential
enemies and potential affines.

I have referred elsewhere (1959a:206) to "anarchic conflict"
between clans, for traditionally each strove to outdo all others
in attaining the values they all sought, the chief of these being
reputation for strength both in numbers and in warfare. When
clansmen were not at war, they maintained the value of warfare
by innumerable methods. All were confident that those clansmen

who had a reputation as sorcerers continued to practise their art between wars, and the Kuma (unlike some other peoples of Papua-New Guinea) directed their sorcery exclusively towards enemy clans. Any death by illness or accident which occurred in such a clan boosted their reputation and increased confidence in their powers, though it did not in itself precipitate a further clash with the enemy. Even the belief in witchcraft, which the Kuma regard as the basest evil because a witch in this society proves traitor to his clan, reinforced the value they put on warfare. Here only a member of the same community as the victim could be accused of being a witch, but being a witch in Kuma belief involved giving sorcery materials to an enemy clan, so the death was still attributable to enemy sorcery. This emphasis on the value of warfare pervaded traditional Kuma life and did not die when the administration banned actual fighting. Even in ceremonies such as the Wubalt food presentation (Reay 1959a: 86–89), which have a peaceful aim-content, the men act out the techniques of warriors on the battlefield, which they express in symbolic ritual conflict with their enemies (Reay 1959b).

The Kuma, however, did not wish to war with every other clan, for such a group, being exogamous, can never be completely self-contained and self-sustaining. It depends upon other clans to provide wives for its members. The simplest way for them to be sure of obtaining wives is to bribe other groups by offering their sisters in exchange, but every exchange of women sets in train a whole series of special relationships between groups. Agricultural and grazing land is plentiful, but at certain stages in the preparations for a Pig Ceremonial, clansmen may need more grazing land than they have access to. They can acquire rights to fatten their pigs on land belonging to friendly clans particularly if they can offer reciprocal rights to stands of pandanus nuts, which do not grow on the low land in the valley basin which is ideal for grazing. Such dependencies which developed between various clans acted as structural checks on warfare.

Even with these checks, the world outside the clan was characterized by much danger and disorder. But, contrary to the tenor of some recent publications (Berndt 1962; Brown 1963), New Guinea Highlands societies—as typified by the clan-communities found in many parts of the Eastern, Western, and Southern Highlands—were not truly anarchic. The subtle pat-

terning of the political aspects of Highlands social structure, with
loyalties interwoven with balanced oppositions, and with structural checks which made the most destructive goals impossible to
attain, ensured that native life was far from chaotic before the
introduction of the Pax Australiana. In 1953–55 it was easy to
exaggerate the contrast between strictly traditional behavior and
behavior which the recent introduction of European control had
managed to modify. The Kuma themselves were immensely impressed by the government's insistence on pacification and enjoyed telling that they had formerly been "like wild pigs"—fighting indiscriminately, killing in random anger, wantonly stealing,
and snatching any women who captured their fancy. The real
pattern was much less extreme but emerged only when I elicited
the details of actual cases of disputes, offences, and so on that
had occurred during the lifetime of my informants and checked
the details against independent versions of the same events.

The maintenance of some kind of order within the clan, and
the ability of a clan's members to reach consensus about going
to war, depended upon the operation of a traditional system of
leadership and authority. The crucial characteristic of this authority system was its reliance on a balance between unformal-
ized personal influence and descent group solidarity.

Each sub-subclan, the smallest recognized group based on an
assumption of patrilineal descent, had a leader who managed its
affairs and represented it in dealings with other like groups. His
was not a formally constituted office, but he was the authorized
locus of power for the group. This role was not named and had
no formal trappings; the incumbent was simply known as "the
first" (*kumna*), and the implication was always that he was the
first among equals. His followers said of him, "People heed
[what he has to say]" (*Agamp pindjip*). The sub-subclan provided the effective work force in Kuma life. It was the unit that
co-operated in carrying out all manner of work a man could not
do unaided. The leader managed this work and arranged for the
allocation of labor in the interests of the group as a whole. When
a member of his group was engaged in a dispute with a member
of some other sub-subclan, the man who was "first" represented
him as advocate, just as his opponent's leader acted as advocate
for him.

The subclan had a leader who was both "first" in his sub-sub-clan and an orator. The Kuma designate his role as *kangɔb ro* (literally "oratory struck"), which I translate freely as Rhetoric Thumper (Reay 1959a:113–30). His function was to represent the subclan and give speeches on behalf of it in its relations with other groups. He also acted as advocate for group members in disputes. Rhetoric is the only highly developed art among the Kuma, and a man who makes accomplished speeches is likely to be sought as a leader in public affairs. The clan itself had no central authority, simply a loose association and balanced opposition of segmentary group leaders.

The men who filled these roles practised a generalized leadership with two facets, management and oratory. Theoretically, their roles were hereditary and the Rhetoric Thumper was the most senior agnatic descendant in a direct line from the founder of the subclan. But in practice a number of other principles qualified that of heredity so that even an hereditary leader had to prove his worth and achieve his authority by his own efforts. Being the eldest son of a former leader and the eldest direct descendant of the subclan ancestor counted little unless he could make the other members of his group heed what he had to say. Often he had a secondary leader to help him. This was generally a man who had more hereditary claim to leadership than himself, and indeed had been groomed for leadership from early childhood but had been passed over through the accident of relative age. On matters affecting the group, the Kuma heed only what a man between the ages of 30 and about 56 has to say. An older man's advice and citing of precedents may be listened to, but he does not normally attempt to direct the affairs of the group. The opinions of younger men who have not yet achieved full manhood are not judged worthy of attention. It has sometimes happened that the authorized leader died or retired when his oldest surviving son was still too young to assume management of the group's activities; this young man has often served as secondary leader and by the time the role is vacant again he may be too old to fill it.

Leadership is highly valued, and many men besides those with an hereditary claim wish to be leaders themselves. Such men of enterprise and initiative can secure a certain following for themselves. They have rarely conflicted seriously with the authorized leaders, and when they have done so they have split off to form groups of their own in which they themselves could be authorized leaders. For, although the Kuma value leadership and personal renown, they value very highly the group itself. A man could achieve personal eminence only as a "strong" (*ŋgi*) man of a "strong" clan. The height of a leader's ambition was to hear people say of him "His name is up on top" (*Kangəm ep minya mim*), and it happened sometimes that the traditional name of his group was dropped in favor of his personal name, although this could not occur in quite the same way once the government officers had recorded the names of the groups in their census books.

In 1954 I knew the only truly great man among the Kuma in recent times, a leader who was known and respected throughout the Wahgi Valley. This was Konangil, Rhetoric Thumper of the most senior subclan of a main segment of Konumbuga, the largest and most formidable of the Kuma clans. In times of peace, he acted as ceremonial leader for his main segment: he organized the prolonged and complex activities associated with the Pig Ceremonial (Koŋgar-Koŋgol), the great festival that takes up to two years to prepare and culminates in a spectacular mass slaughter of most of the clan's pigs; further, he demonstrated his influence beyond his own group by arranging for the other main segment of Konumbuga and two other nearby clans to kill their pigs on the same day. But he was ready to go to war and, under his leadership, the strong and numerous Konumbuga routed their enemies and scattered them far and wide. He was a truly great traditional leader, able to maintain law and order at home and able to achieve eminence for his clan abroad. He was what the Kuma call "a real man, with a name" (*yi wi, kangəm mim*). A few other leaders were also described in this way, but their names faded beside that of Konangil because their records of achievement did not reach as far afield as his.

II

The first European contacts with the Kuma from 1933 onward were intermittent, and the immediate ban on warfare did not take effect till about 1950.[1] The Department of District Services

[1] Both in 1954 and in 1963, about 200 Kuma were guests in the Minj native jail as a result of inter-group fighting. The fighting at both times was disorganized brawling, not organized warfare, which the government had effectively banned.

(now Native Affairs) introduced a system of control which involved the appointment of native officials and the establishment of a Court for Native Affairs. This system of control encouraged the peaceful settlement of disputes by arbitration. The native officials were luluais and tultuls.

Hogbin reports the failure of the luluai-tultul system in Busama, which is situated between Lae and Salamaua in an area Europeans had penetrated before the turn of the century:

> The system probably worked reasonably well so long as the luluai had risen to his position of supremacy by traditional means. If the people already accepted him as a headman any further honour coming from outside was irrelevant: his directions were no more assiduously followed on account of it, nor were his rebukes listened to with greater attention.

> By 1920, however, the last of the headmen had died, and the rungs of the ladder of social advancement had rotted away (Hogbin 1951:151).

The situation was different, however, in the Highlands, where there were still traditional leaders on whom the offices could be appropriately bestowed. It was the practice in the Minj sub-district to appoint a luluai as headman of each significant group—ordinarily as headman for the clan but, in a very large clan, as headman for the main segment. The luluai had to secure native co-operation with the administration's program, chiefly by coercing the labor force of his group into working for one day per week on the roads that were to open up the Highlands. He had to prevent his group from warring with others, and report all disputes involving his group for settlement in the Court for Native Affairs. He was also required to keep order within the group itself. The tultuls were minor officials appointed to help him and each of these was responsible for a particular segment of native society. Typically the clan had one luluai assisted by a number of tultuls representing the constituent subclans.

The Court for Native Affairs heard three types of complaints: disputes involving a wider range of people than the community for which the luluai was responsible; disputes within a clan-community which the luluai had been unable to resolve; and all offences resulting in bodily injury, since the administration viewed physical violence gravely and was trying to halt it. The luluais of any clans involved were required to attend the Court. The magistrates were the Assistant District Officer and his patrol officers. As well as holding court at the Sub-district Office they were itinerant magistrates: whenever a government patrol arrived at a census point, the officer heard any cases the luluai and his clansmen brought before him, and the people of the clan-community were free to listen. In this way the Kuma received much informal training in the conduct of court cases, particularly in the necessity for giving a fair hearing to both sides of a dispute and in the admissibility of different kinds of evidence.

The Kuma and their neighbors have always been a quarrelsome people, and the traditional leaders had to settle disputes within their own segments of the clan and act as advocates for their fellow members in disputes with other units. Group solidarity, which brought all members to the unflinching support of one, seems to have poised the more enterprising or wayward people between confidence that their personal strivings would find unquestioning support within the limits of the group's tolerance and, since they valued the group highly, a sense of responsibility for each other's actions. It was a distinct advantage to belong to a stronger group with a more eloquent leader, and disputes within the community could easily develop into brawls in which people indulged in wrestling, punching, and hair-pulling. Nevertheless, the public hearing of disputes resembled primitive courts and the public discussion of a complaint that someone had committed an offence such as adultery, theft, or witchcraft constituted an informal trial of the accused person. The Kuma relish litigation and, although some of the participants might interrupt proceedings by stormily attacking each other, there was always a recital of the evidence the complainants had collected and a serious discussion of where responsibility for the trouble lay.

The Kuma welcomed eagerly the informal courts which the administration encouraged the luluais and tultuls to hold. These courts were informal in the sense that they had no official recognition in the legislature of the Territory, but local officers of the government encouraged them as an administrative and educative measure. As such, they were extremely successful. The native officials had the Court for Native Affairs to guide them in the administration of justice and particularly in implementing the government's ban on personal violence and inter-clan strife.

The tultuls filled, with slightly more formality but no less flourish, the roles of the traditional Rhetoric Thumpers. The luluai was a new role which was nevertheless continuous with the role of the Rhetoric Thumper who had achieved exceptional eminence. The "real man, with a name" was an obvious choice for luluai. The officers who made the first appointments tried to ascertain which men possessed traditionally authorized power which the government could use to further its aims, and most of the early luluais were men who had made their names as warriors and were persons of substance in their communities. This had the dual effect of consolidating the power (somewhat arbitrary by democratic standards) that these leaders had and also of giving implicit official support for the value already placed on the group. A leader did not have to achieve far-reaching eminence for a named group to be referred to as "his"; he simply had to be the appointed headman of a census unit.

The first man to receive a brass badge of office was Konangil. A new word, "kiap" (any officer of the Department of District Services), had entered the vocabulary of the Kuma. When the kiaps had settled in the eastern end of the Wahgi Valley, representatives of many of the Kuma clans visited them. Some leaders who were more than usually brave went to find out personally what they could about the pale-skinned strangers. Konangil was among them. Others sent men of no account to visit the kiaps and report back to their groups if they ever returned from this risky assignment. In particular they wanted to know how the white men derived their power over people and their power over things. The kiaps issued commands as if they expected obedience, and wherever they went they took native police—black-skinned like the Kuma themselves; immensely powerful, for they could scatter a crowd of jabbering, jostling, and perhaps fighting people by firing into the air their strange new lethal weapons; but always disciplined and docile in the presence of the white man and quick to make sure that the undisciplined and far from docile local natives obeyed his orders. The kiaps' power over things was evident from their inability to travel without a long line of carriers bearing their material possessions, which included trade goods in a seemingly unending supply.

Konangil saw the trade goods and knew that his people had to acquire them. He held a steel hatchet in his hand, judging the lightness and balance that made it easier to use than the traditional stone axe, and testing the keen edge of the blade. He realized that it could free people to spend more time on the ceremonial activities they judged to be necessary to ensure fertility in the clan and its pigs and gardens and which expressed the full meaning and purpose of Kuma life. He contemplated the goldlip and other shells the white men had brought. These were more numerous and of better quality than those that had found their way along the devious trade routes from the coast. The shells were valuable items of ceremonial exchange and personal adornment. A clan that possessed a glut of the finest goldlip would be rich indeed. In fact this dream of Konangil's came true. When his clan was celebrating its Pig Ceremonial at the time of my first visit, I heard his clansmen instruct their friends and relatives to give them Bird of Paradise plumes, not goldlip shell. "We have so much goldlip that it is just like rubbish to us," they said.

Konangil saw the shells as concrete evidence of prosperity. He and his people could acquire enough to use in their own ceremonial exchanges with a surplus to trade for Bird of Paradise plumes and other things they needed. Konangil reasoned that there seemed to be no limit to the white man's wealth, whatever the source of it might be, so he considered very carefully what the white kiaps were demanding in return. The only requirement that involved sacrificing something of importance in Kuma life was the ban on warfare. Konangil's own clan had already achieved remarkable success in warfare, and he was quick to realize that a ban on further wars would consolidate its position. Further, he could see positive advantages which his own group and the rest of the Kuma could derive from living in peace.

Konangil's influence among the Kuma, achieved through traditional leadership and success in warfare, became the greatest single instrument of pacification in the Wahgi Valley. When a cargo cult prophet came to Konangil's territory in 1949 to preach his disturbing visions, the luluai-Rhetoric Thumper banished him promptly. Konangil died in 1955, but his name lives on. There are countless Konangils among the Kuma, all of them named after this man. They in their turn will have namesakes, and (such is the Kuma's tendency to telescope times, events, and persons) I would predict that in time their descendants will credit them with Konangil's unique achievements.

During the height of Konangil's power as luluai, another man was climbing towards a different kind of eminence. Nopnop was not a traditional leader in his subclan, but he too could see ways of turning the advent of the white man to his own advantage. When he was a youth he had visited the kiaps in the eastern part of the valley when he travelled as cook-boy for Konangil and a traditional leader of a neighboring clan. Whilst Konangil and most of the other traditional leaders were content to communicate with the kiaps through the interpreters who invariably accompanied them, Nop realized that being able to speak directly with the white men without an intermediary would give him access to some of the new wealth and perhaps even to the secret of its source. He was one of the first of the Kuma to learn Pidgin, and he soon found employment as a government interpreter. At the time of my first visit, he had bought his way into the traditional system of authority. He had used the money and perquisites he had earned in his work to accumulate bridewealth: enough to get several wives for himself, with a surplus to invest in some of his clansmen's exchanges. By the time I met him, he was a wealthy man. His wealth was an obvious source of power over others, but he did not choose to use this power excepting to support Konangil and the white kiaps. He had further reserves of power derived directly from his work as a government interpreter, for the man who acts as intermediary in court cases becomes a legal consultant for the ordinary native with some complaint to bring before the Court for Native Affairs. He acquires in his own way some kind of "name" which is known beyond the boundaries of his own clan territory. The last time I saw Nop's name at the time of writing, it was on the list of nominations for the House of Assembly in respect of the Minj Open Electorate.

III

When I revisited the Kuma in 1963, a system of local government councils was already in operation. The government had officially replaced the authoritarian rule of the old luluais with an experiment in democratic procedure. Acting upon the failure of the system of native officials in areas where it had been introduced too late, and on the assumption that the general pattern of leadership in New Guinea was that found in a few places by anthropologists and others who were not primarily studying political organization, government departments concerned with the natives decided that "a form of local government was indispensable to restore their self-reliance" (Hogbin 1951: 164). Certainly their dependence on outside authority had increased to the extent that they could not envisage, at least in the Highlands, any alternative form of government to that of native officials with Australian overlordship, so long as the Australians remained in New Guinea. (Many of the Kuma secretly believed in 1953–55 that the white man would eventually desert them, leaving them free to war with each other as before.) One would have thought that this dependence on outside authority could have been discouraged by the government insisting that the natives should elect their own officials democratically, after a program of education in the principles of democracy. In areas where traditional leaders were now installed as native officials, they held their position not only by the sanction of external authority but also by consensus among the members of their community—whether this was reached by coercion, bribery and graft, or other undemocratic means. The planners who decided to abolish the offices of luluai and tultul and replace them by "democratically elected" representatives bearing a different title plainly did not realize that the field officers responsible for implementing the plan would have to coerce the natives into accepting it.

Hearing administration-sponsored reports on the success of the local government council system in New Guinea, I expected to find a system of clan councils integrated into a wider area council. This would have encouraged the harmonious development of Kuma political organization in relationship with the introduced government aims. I envisaged the president and ordinary members of each clan council as being elected more and more democratically rather than being appointed by the government, while still fulfilling the modern equivalents of the functions of the old native officials. But the new system of local government does not recognize political communities which are already established, and the policy of creating new political communities much vaster than the old ones was taken to mean that the old ones should be destroyed. The Kuma as a whole form one such artificially created political community.

The Minj Council, composed of 41 councillors, was proclaimed in October 1961 after the Department of Native Affairs conducted a survey of traditional group structure. It did this through Pidgin-speaking field officers who had little or no anthropological training, drew on one general anthropological account of the Kuma, and did not ask for detailed anthropological data on the group structure of this area which was then available. One way in which anthropology could have helped the administration was in predicting the probable power structure in the new community and the pressure groups this new development was likely to favor unless appropriate precautions were taken.

A clan may have from one to six councillors (kaunsil), according to size, with committee men (komisi) to help them in unspecified ways. Few of the old luluais have been on the Council for the full period since its inception, and many of the members are surprising representatives for any group to have. X, the councillor of one clan I know well, was notorious as a wife-beater in 1953 and at that time he had no other claim to distinction. By 1955 a period in jail for one such offence had prevented X from participating in an important part of the Pig Ceremonial. He was so determined to keep out of jail in future that whenever a dispute occurred he used to stand with his arms ostentatiously folded to demonstrate that his behavior was exemplary from the point of view of the kiaps and the luluai. By 1960 he had impressed certain kiaps with his docility and had been appointed tultul to replace an official who had failed to ensure full participation in the weekly roadwork. (The traditional leader who had held the office at first was dismissed very early for taking part in an inter-clan fight.)

Nopnop is the president of the Minj Local Government Council. His clan, Konumbuga, is the largest as a result of a concatenation of the events and personalities of traditional politics and the consolidation of the early period of indirect rule by luluais. Just as Konangil had hoped, new developments froze the traditional political system at a point where his clan was in a formidable position of dominance. Because it is the largest, it has more councillors than any other single clan. The Konumbuga councillors are thus able to act as a pressure group and are aided in doing so by the proximity of their territory to Minj. This location has enabled them to be the longest established

coffee planters among the Kuma, to derive more money from
other sources than distant people, and to acquire a reputation
among these for success in dealing with the government and
with white people generally. Nearly all the "big councillors"
(Kaunsil ogma:) are Konumbuga, and these few men have
demonstrated their power to override the expressed wishes of
the majority and to prevent some of the other councillors from
acting as ombudsmen as their clansmen want them to do. The
Kuma define a councillor as a black-skinned man who bosses
them (and is self-seeking unless he is personally known to be
otherwise), a stereotype developed through people's experience
of councillors performing their varied roles: as government
spokesmen who are regularly called to Tombil Council House
for meetings with the kiaps; as tax-collectors who determine the
amount of the annual levy and police the payment of others;
as informal magistrates and *ad hoc* legislators on marriage, divorce, and theft; and as unusually affluent members of their
own communities.

The Local Government Ordinance permits the nomination of
council members by the district officer (or his representatives),
and in fact many kaunsils have come to office directly at the
instigation and insistence of the kiaps, often with a token "election" being held to ratify the appointment. When more than
one nomination has come forward, the "election" has been confused by the natives' tendency to vote for all nominees instead
of merely one. Many of the Kuma interpreted the news that
the Council was to replace the luluais as meaning that the old
luluais were not eligible for election. Further, since the kiaps
stressed that the Council was a "new" institution, the Kuma
decided that they should elect "new" men to serve on it. On
the principle that it would be an advantage to have kaunsils
who could communicate directly with the kiaps, they chose the
few men over 30 who spoke Pidgin, irrespective of any other
qualifications or disqualifications they may have had for the
post. X, nominated by the kiaps, has a pitiful smattering of
Pidgin which he picked up on a visit to the coast and has not
improved over the last ten years. His clan has a committee man
(komisi) who has acted for more than ten years as secondary
leader to traditional and government-appointed headmen and
is now the effective organizer of the clan's work force on behalf

of the kaunsil. This komisi continues to act under the direction of the luluai, who is now out of office, and is beginning to supplant the ageing headman as effective leader of the clan-community. X holds informal courts which are lengthy but typically peter out with either a resolution to take them to the Court for Native Affairs or an implicit consensus that other matters are more urgent. The only informal courts I saw effectively resolved in this clan were those the komisi or the luluai or both attended to voice some decisive comment at a crucial stage of the discussion. Inter-clan kaunsils' courts, concerned mostly with marriage and divorce, are also ineffective. The docile X attends Council meetings, but I have never heard him utter a word during these meetings. He has given me two reasons for his silence: he would not dare to express an opinion in the presence of some important men; also he does not feel competent to act as spokesman for his clan. He is trying to gain some competence as spokesman by deliberately practising speech-making. He is well aware that his Pidgin is halting and ungrammatical, and the speech-making he is trying to perfect is traditional oratory in the vernacular, though it is not clear on what occasions he hopes to be able to use it.

The people who vote for the councillors are those who pay local government tax. Despite enormous pressure from the kiaps, the constitution of the Minj Council requires only adult males to pay tax so women have no opportunity to vote in Council elections. This situation was predictable in the light of traditional society in the Highlands and many other parts of New Guinea, and in my opinion the government should not have introduced the principle of free election without imposing universal adult suffrage from the outset.

The tax provides the Council with revenue to carry out works for the benefit of the community. Directly at the suggestion of the kiaps, the Minj Council has been spending its money on fixed allowances for its members, the building of an elaborate Council House (inconveniently sited some miles west of Minj), and construction works on roads and bridges. It has bought two vehicles, one of which provides the European nursing sisters of the Infant Welfare Service with occasional transport. It has plans for establishing new medical aid posts and schools. Not a single item of this program has arisen at the suggestion of any of the councillors themselves. A suggestion of Nop's that a group of relatively wealthy councillors, including himself, should buy a vehicle which would be their joint property has been continuously discouraged, though this could prove to be a useful experiment in cooperative enterprise and the councillors themselves have no means of discovering, without explicit advice, how much money they would have to be prepared to spend or conserve for maintenance.

Despite the expenditure of Council revenue on roads and bridges, clanspeople still have to give one day's labor per week to working on these roads and bridges without pay. They are well aware that there is an education authority with a responsibility for providing schools, since it has already established a school for Europeans and another for natives at Minj. They are well aware that the Health Department has managed to provide a native hospital and a number of aid posts. The department's reliance on Native Affairs officers to arrange Council transport for the sisters in charge of the Infant Welfare Service does not enhance the value of the sisters' important work in native eyes. All in all, the grandiose works program of the Minj Council appears to the Kuma as a strange duplication of powers already held by existing authorities.

In the meantime, kiaps continue to persuade (and, when this fails, coerce) the councillors into raising the tax against the plainly expressed wishes of both the councillors and the ordinary clansmen they represent. They suggest further that people who have no money to pay taxes should take on paid employment for European planters who have to import from other parts of New Guinea. The Kuma do not see themselves as a labor force, and few of them can spare the time from their traditional activities to work for others. They are independent farmers and, though their incomes from coffee are negligible in our terms, many of them are planters in their own right. The Wahgi Valley branch of the Farmers' and Settlers' Association, originally a European club, now has several native members.

In December 1963, newspapers in Papua-New Guinea reported that a native village near Rabaul wanted to "cut loose from the . . . local government system" and "go back to the ways of our grandfathers." (The first of the Tolai local government councils in New Britain was proclaimed as early as 1950.) According to the reports, heavy taxation was directly responsible for these people's explicit rejection of the Western institution of democratic procedure. The Minj Council was proclaimed only two years ago, and it may seem early to be judging its effectiveness. But time is short now in New Guinea, and it is not too early to see that the council system has brought the Kuma total disillusionment with the second phase of political development and their prospects for the future. This disillusionment is expressed most clearly in the successive phases of the Kumas' understanding of the forthcoming elections for the House of Assembly.

IV

The boundaries of the Minj Open Electorate[2] extend far beyond Kuma territories and enclose areas governed by other Councils and by old-style native officials. If the result of the election expresses faithfully the wishes of the Kuma and their immediate neighbors (as expressed in December 1963), a European candidate will be elected with a clear majority. But up to the time I left New Guinea the prospective native voters were unaware of the existence of a much vaster Special Electorate for which candidacy is limited to Europeans. Although they do not know the candidates personally, news that they must select a European representative whom they may have had no opportunity of nominating could well affect their voting in the open election.[3] The slow rate at which native ignorance about the House of Assembly and the elections for it is being dispelled, is not due either to "primitiveness" of the people or inefficiency of Native

[2] The House of Assembly is to have 64 members: 10 appointed by the government and 54 elected by the total voters of Papua-New Guinea. Ten of the elected members have to be Europeans, returned in so-called Special Electorates, which generally embrace a number of Open Electorates. Persons of any race may be returned in the 44 Open Electorates.

[3] The substance of this paper was written in January 1964. Back in New Guinea in February, I found that campaigning by authoritative Europeans on behalf of a Special Electorate candidate and information that it was obligatory to vote for a European as well as for at least one of the earlier known candidates led many natives who wished for European representation to vote for a native candidate in the Open Electorate. They saw this dual representation as an opportunity to get the biracial representation they desired.

Affairs field officers.[4] The elections are at best an *ad hoc* affair, and the administration's emphasis on an elaborate "educative" program for informing the natives about technical procedures for voting has not extended to ensuring that field officers possess information on other aspects of the elections which they can pass on to the natives in time to affect decisions they have to make. Anyone who thinks that the process of administration is not political should ponder the implications of intelligent and well-intentioned officers charged with the duty of informing the natives about the elections long before they themselves had access to the precise details. When the kiaps first told the councillors about the House of Assembly, they described it as a new kind of Council which would have ten members appointed by the government, another ten European members, and 44 native members elected by the people themselves. Kiaps instructed presidents and past presidents of the local government councils to pay their filing fees of £25 each and nominate themselves as candidates for election. They did this eagerly, for they understood that the election was to choose a native to go to Port Moresby and represent his people in personal talks with the Governor General of Australia. The councillors, including the government nominees, did not immediately inform the ordinary clansmen, busy at home with their pigs and gardens and coffee, of this remarkable development.

When three native nominations were already in, a European confused the councillors' conception of the House of Assembly by nominating himself.[5] They now learned that the House of Assembly (not yet known by this term) was a very different

[4] The only technical information concerning the elections which I gave to individual Kuma was information they solicited directly, since I was interested in finding out what knowledge they had derived and were deriving from sources regularly available to them.

[5] Nomination papers and other documents pertaining to the 1964 elections for the House of Assembly use "nominate" as an intransitive verb. A person filling in a nomination paper nominates, in fact, himself. (I am indebted to Mr. Barry Ryan, Assistant District Officer, Minj, for this point.) Thus a retrospective examination of nomination papers after the elections will not distinguish between candidates who have decided to stand for personal reasons (such as political ambition) and those who have nominated themselves in response to other people's urging. The distinction becomes important in respect of European interests and others of whom have decided to stand for election when a significant number of representative natives have approached them to do so.

kind of council from what they had been led to expect. This was the first indication to the Kuma that nearly 100 Europeans might be voting as well as the 30,000-odd potential native voters: the first indication, too, that if the combined natives and Europeans chose, they could select a European representative. Ordinary clansmen first heard of the impending elections about this time as news drifted in leisurely chains through relatives of the councillors in such a way that few natives, apart from a select group of prominent councillors, realized that Europeans were eligible for election. As with other "council" matters, several degrees of knowledge and interest appeared simultaneously within each clan. Two councillors, representing groups which are somewhat remote in easterly and westerly directions from Minj, told me at this time that they and their clansmen would vote for a native living at or near Minj for the new Territory-wide council. Such a candidate, they said, would be well aware of what was going on among the Europeans in the township and administrative center and would be able to gain some enlightenment for the people as a whole.

The Kuma had entered the third phase in the enforced adoption of democratic procedure. They were confused, and even the councillors recognized that they had been major instruments in bringing about this confusion. "We have fouled the thinking of the natives," several of them complained in my hearing, using Pidgin. One added, "We are like babies who have fallen out of our mothers' net bags and tried to walk before we have learned to stand." Both councillors and clansmen welcomed the news that they could choose a European to represent them. Some councillors even suggested that, since the native people had already demonstrated their incompetence to choose councillors who were capable of guiding and leading them, the Europeans alone should vote or at least tell the natives who would be an appropriate European to represent both races. At the time of my departure from New Guinea in December 1963, two of the three native candidates had decided to withdraw their nominations and support a European. When nominations closed early in January 1964, however, their names were still on the list together with those of two European candidates.

Both the European candidates promised to take representative natives with them to House of Assembly meetings if they were elected, and this led the councillors to hope that they might use the techniques of decision-making they had become acquainted with in the Council House to determine how many representatives they needed in Port Moresby. They decided that, instead of the single member provided for, it would be preferable for them to elect four representatives for the one electorate: one European, with a native to support and learn from him, for each of the regions north and south of the Wahgi River. Two years' experience of the kiaps' insistence that they should reach their own decisions (even if kiaps recognized these decisions only when they were consistent with the administration's broad aims) had led them to expect that they would be able to modify the rules of the election. Although kiaps had discouraged initiative among the councillors by rejecting every spontaneous suggestion regarding the expenditure of Council funds, questions concerning the structure and constitution of the Council itself formed a field in which native representatives had been able to prevail against some of the kiaps' recommendations (for example, the suggestions that women should pay tax, vote, be elected to office, and have clubs of their own). The matter of how many representatives the people of the Wahgi Valley and its environs should have in Port Moresby seemed to the councillors to be the same kind of issue as those they had been successful in resolving.

By December 1963, both councillors and clansmen had formulated quite clearly their current political aspirations. These are not the same as the aspirations expressed by the villagers near Rabaul, who want to return to the ways of their grandfathers. The Kuma also want to go back, but what they desire (and hoped in December would eventuate as a result of the 1964 elections) is the abolition of the unsuccessful local government council system and a restoration of the earlier system of indirect rule through native officials. They see the luluai-tultul system as a golden age which is not too remote to re-establish and re-live. I suspect that all over Papua-New Guinea different kinds of native political aspirations are blossoming with the same diversity as the original political institutions showed, in accordance with different regional emphases, both in the indigenous political system and the history of development experienced there. Assuming that this is true, it would seem to be timely to consider some kind of local self-determination which would allow for the integration of diverse systems of local government with an imposed central government which would eventually be a national one.

The government's "educational program," explicitly concerned with familiarizing the natives with a particular technique of voting, has expressly avoided guiding natives in the kinds of issues appropriate for fighting elections and the qualities of character that democratic representatives should have. One can predict with certainty that the elections themselves will increase, not lessen, the confusion and disillusion of the Kuma and their neighbors. Elements of cargo belief, which have been safely dispersed over a number of spheres in recent years, could easily crystallize in a native attempt to restore the golden age for which the people hanker.[6] The Kuma, including their most prominent councillors, are ready to admit the mistakes they have made during the administration's attempts to coerce them into becoming democratic. The administration and the policy makers in Canberra seem to require a generation to pass before they can comfortably admit the errors they also have made, and even then they are likely to find only a partial solution to the problems they themselves have created. Democracy, the rule of the majority, is not the only conceivable choice for a country destined to determine its own future. The rule of consensus, which operated in most of the traditional political systems, would itself be an adequate basis for modern government, provided those traditional means of reaching consensus which prevent the recognition of basic human rights can be effectively abolished.

[6] By February 1964 all three native candidates had agreed upon a modern version of cargo ideology as a common policy, involving the abolition of the local government council system. If one of them is elected it is unlikely that he will ever voice these ideas outside the network of his own kin and local native acquaintances.

10 NYAKYUSA AGE-VILLAGES

Monica Wilson

Monica Wilson is Professor of Social Anthropology, School of African Studies at the University of Cape Town, South Africa. Her chief publications include *Reaction to Conquest* (1936, 1961), *The Analysis of Social Change* (with Godfrey Wilson, 1945), *Good Company* (1951), *Keiskammahoek Rural Survey*, Volume 3: *Social Structure* (1952), *Rituals of Kinship Among the Nyakyusa* (1957), *The Peoples of the Nyasa-Tanganyika Corridor* (1958), *Communal Rituals of the Nyakyusa* (1959), *Divine Kings and the 'Breath of Men'* (1959), *Langa: A Study of Social Groups in an African Township* (with A. Mafeje, 1963), and many papers, especially on the Nyakyusa, Pondo, and Xhosa.

THE NYAKYUSA age-village system is a peculiar one. The local unit consists not of a group of kinsmen, as it does in most parts of the world, but of a group of age-mates with their wives and young children. It therefore has some intrinsic interest and its peculiarity raises many theoretical problems.

The Nyakyusa are a Bantu-speaking people living in the Great Rift Valley at the north end of Lake Nyasa. They are cattle owners and cultivators, with elaborate techniques of green manuring and rotation, and unlike most of their neighbours they practise fixed, not shifting cultivation. Well fed and vigorous, they have been an expanding population in a relatively empty country, and at the present time they, together with the contig-

FROM the *Journal of the Royal Anthropological Institute* 79 (1949):21–25, by permission of the author and the Council of the Royal Anthropological Institute.

The material on which this paper was based was collected by the author and her husband, Godfrey Wilson, between 1934 and 1938. He was then a Fellow of the Rockefeller Foundation and she of the International African Institute. The present tense refers to that period.

uous and culturally similar Ngonde people, and small groups absorbed by them, probably number about a quarter of a million. The census returns are far from exact.

The Nyakyusa long remained isolated from the outside world, for their valley is cut off by high mountains and the stormy waters of the north end of the Lake. They were scarcely touched by the slave trade and Europeans first visited the country in 1878, though the Ngonde, whose country is more accessible, had long traded with the Arabs.

Traditionally, the Nyakyusa were divided up into a number of small independent chiefdoms, numbering anything from about 100 to 3,000 married men. They developed no centralized political authority before the coming of the Europeans. The related Ngonde, on the other hand, had a paramount chief, the Kyungu. The reason for the difference in development between these groups turns on their relations with the outside world. The people of Ngonde were sending ivory to the coast and receiving cloth and guns in exchange long before Europeans came to their country. The priest of the main sacred grove of the country controlled this trade, and through his control developed far-reaching secular power, whereas a similar priest among the Nyakyusa developed no such secular power, for they had no trade with the outside world. The Nyakyusa centre of worship, Lubaga, was much more inaccessible than Mbande, that of the Ngonde. A similar tendency towards centralization as trade with the coast developed can be traced among some of the neighbouring groups also.

The Nyakyusa are patrilineal and patrilocal. Members of agnatic lineages of a depth of three or four generations are bound together by their common interest in the cattle which circulate within and between lineages, and by the supposed mystical interdependence of kin, but the lineage is not a corporate one. Kinsmen do not live together. A village consists of a group of age-mates with their wives and young children, while the men of one lineage are scattered through the chiefdom, and may even be in different chiefdoms. Polygyny is the ideal of every pagan, and is achieved by a substantial proportion of the men over 45. In a conservative part of the country nearly a third of the adult men had more than one wife. This is made possible by a gap of ten years or more in the average marriage age of men and women. Except in some wealthy Christian families, men rarely marry before 25, and commonly not until nearer 30, while the girls are betrothed about eight, and go finally to their husbands when they reach puberty. There is an elaborate puberty-marriage ritual for girls, very similar to that of the Bemba, but no circumcision or initiation of men.

Marriage is prohibited between the descendants of a common grandfather, and much disliked between descendants of a common great-grandfather, but there are no clans, or defined exogamous groups.

The age-village starts when a number of herd-boys, about ten or eleven years old, build together at the edge of their fathers' village. They have been practising building huts for some time, as small boys in other cultures do also, but when they reach the age of ten or eleven they actually go to live in their huts, sleeping and spending their spare time in them, though still going to their mothers' huts for meals. A boy should not and does not eat alone, but a group of friends eat together, visiting the mother of each member of their gang in turn. This system is regarded not only as being congenial to small boys (as with us) but also as moral. For the Nyakyusa eating with age-mates is a corner stone of morality, and a boy who comes home alone often to eat is severely scolded.

Moving out of the parent village to sleep is directly connected by the Nyakyusa with decency. They say that a growing boy should not be aware of the sex activities of his parents, *and therefore* he must not sleep at home, even in a separate hut, but in a different village altogether. As they put it, "the night is full of lewd talk" and that is all right between equals, but not before people of another generation. Their idea of "mixed company" is not male and female, but fathers and sons.

A boys' village starts quite small, with, perhaps, not more than ten or a dozen members, but it grows as young boys from the fathers' village, or from other men's villages in the neighbourhood, become old enough to join it. When the original members are fifteen or sixteen years old the village is usually closed to any further ten-year-olds, who must then start a new village on their own. Conditions vary with the density of population in the neighbourhood and other factors, but generally the age-span within a village is not more than about five years, and a village numbers between 20 and 50 members.

The boys who thus establish a village continue to live together through life. When they marry they bring their wives to the village. As their sons grow up they move out to build villages of their own. Daughters often move out, too, marrying men in other villages, but they may and quite often do marry an age-mate of their father and remain in the village. A village (*ikipanga*) consists of a group of male contemporaries with their dependants, not in a site, and it retains its identity no matter how often it moves.

The men of a village are all of an age and bound together by a common life shared from early youth, but the women in any village are of diverse age and experience. As we have already seen, men usually marry as their first wives girls about ten years younger than themselves, but not all the men of a village marry at the same time, and as they grow older they continue to marry young girls as junior wives. Often the junior wife is a niece—a brother's daughter—of the senior. Moreover, wives are inherited from elder brothers and fathers, so that a man may have some wives older than himself and others who are very much younger.

Once in each generation there is a great ritual at which administrative power and military leadership are handed over by the older generation to the younger. At this ritual there is a new deal in land. The men of the retiring generation move to one side to make room for the expanding villages of the younger generation, but it is not simply a transfer of land from one village of fathers to one of sons; the boundaries within the chiefdom are all redrawn, and the old men move even when there is unoccupied land available for their sons. The only land excluded from the new deal are the very valuable fields made in the craters of extinct volcanoes, and these are inherited, like cattle, within lineages.

At this ritual, which is called *ubusoka,* the "coming out," each village of young men is formally established on its own land, one of its members is appointed as headman, and its relative status in the hierarchy of villages in the chiefdom is demonstrated. At the same time the two senior sons of the retiring chief are recognized as chiefs, and the old chief's country divided between them. The division does not become absolute until the old man's death, but he was expected to die very soon after the "coming out," and if he did not do so from natural causes he was probably strangled. The Nyakyusa theory is that he died from "the chilling breath" of his people who loved his sons rather than him. The fact that old chiefs do not now die off as they used to do is one of the political problems of the country; power tends to remain in the hands of the older generation much longer than before a European administration was established.

Although chiefdoms were thus divided each generation, they did not necessarily become smaller, because the Nyakyusa were expanding, spreading out in a sparsely inhabited land, and also the conquest and absorption of one small chiefdom by another was constantly going on.

The allocation of land and the selection of a headman for each village of young men is made by the retiring chief, and the headmen of the villages of his generation, who are his advisers and against whose advice he dare not act, since they are believed to have a mystical power over him. Village headmen are always commoners. Sons of chiefs and sons of village headmen of the previous generation are not eligible, for, the Nyakyusa say, if a son of a headman were chosen each generation he would become a chief. The headmen are the leaders of the people, the *commons,* and a contrast is constantly being made between chiefs (*abanyafyale*), on the one hand, and commoners (*ama-fumu*) on the other. The village headmen are the *amafumu* par excellence: that is, the "great commoners."

At any one time there are three age-grades: that of the old men who are retired from administration but whose leaders have certain ritual functions to perform; that of the ruling generation which is responsible for defence and administration; and that of the young men and boys who have not yet "come out," but who fight when necessary under the leadership of men of their fathers' generation, though in their own age units.

Within each grade are a varying number of villages each composed of near contemporaries. The ages of the men in each grade vary, of course, with the date of the last "coming out" ritual. Just before such a ritual the old retired men will all be over 65, while the ruling generation includes those between about 35 and 65; just after such a ritual everyone over 35 is retired, and those from about 10 to 35 are in office. The youngest members of a generation taking office have at first very little share in public life, but individuals may gain power later, through inheriting the position of an older brother.

The age grouping is somewhat modified by the system of inheritance, under which a man's heir, who is his next younger full-brother or, under certain circumstances, a half-brother, or his senior son, may take over his homestead and his social personality. An heir, though he be much younger than other men of the village, is treated as one of themselves. Were all heirs to move into the homesteads of their elder brothers and fathers, villages would continue indefinitely, but in fact they do not. Very often the heir chooses to remain in his own village, a member of his own age-set. An heir must move if he succeeds to the office of village headman or priest of the chiefdom, for acceptance of such office is an obligation. It is possible also that movement by inheritance is more common from the junior villages of an age-grade to senior villages of the same grade, than to villages of another grade, but of this I am not certain. Our information on the conditions determining the heir's choice to move or not move is inadequate.

In theory only villages of three generations survive, and we found on analysing all the villages of the chiefdom we knew best that this was very nearly true in practice. Only one village of the great-grandfathers' generation survived, and it had only eleven members.

The village, then, is the land-holding group, its members dividing among themselves the land allocated to their village at the "coming out." The homesteads, each surrounded with bananas, are built compactly in a group, while the main fields are all together on the fringes of the village. Beyond the fields lies the common pasture land. Families each work their own fields and control their own produce, but in cultivating certain crops they must keep in step with their neighbours. Failure to do so is thought to reduce the yield for everyone. Neighbours' cattle are herded together—to herd one's cattle alone is a proud and boastful thing to do—and in any major undertaking such as housebuilding, both neighbours and relatives from other villages cooperate. Traditionally, fellow villagers had certain responsibilities for each other's *torts;* they fought as a group in war and in defence against big game; and they formed and still form a defensive unit against the supposed attacks of witches.

Above all, the village is the group within which the good life, as the Nyakyusa conceive it, is possible. The good life consists in *ukwangala,* that is, enjoyment of the company of one's equals. The good man is one who is urbane and sociable, a fine debater, a witty raconteur, one who entertains, sharing with his fellows whatever good food or drink he may have, for *ukwangala* requires *ifyakwangalela* . . . the wherewithal for the enjoyment of good company, that is, food and beer. Conversation is held to be the school of law, of logic, and of manners; therefore a man must not keep aloof, or live like a hermit apart in the bush, and he must live with contemporaries rather than kinsmen, since easy communication is limited between men of different generations by the respect required of juniors for their seniors. As for *ukwangala* with women, that is impossible. Women are fit for love-making, not for friendship.

Good fellowship in the village is not merely a pious ideal but a virtue with which at least outward conformity is enforced by fear of witchcraft. The man who does not *ukwangala* but is morose and solitary, or brusque in his manner, or who eats alone, grudging his neighbours a share in the food and beer his wives prepare for him, and one who neglects to provide feasts on certain recognized occasions, is likely either to be accused of practising witchcraft, or to think himself the victim of it. Witches, the Nyakyusa say, act primarily from the lust for food; they gnaw men inside to assuage their hunger for meat, and steal the milk of cows. But they do not attack indiscriminately; they select as victims those against whom they have a grudge. Moreover, the village, as a group, is believed to defend itself against witchcraft, but only the virtuous are protected. Evil-doers are said to be left to the witches, or directly punished by their fellows through a power closely akin to the power of witchcraft.

Witchcraft (*ubulosi*), the Nyakyusa think, is something innate and tangible; it consists in pythons—several of them—in the bellies of men, which are discoverable at an autopsy. Certain individuals are born with it and exercise it for their own nefarious ends. Other individuals have a power called *amanga* which is also innate though not visible at an autopsy, and which is used in defence against witchcraft and to punish wrong-doers. Our Nyakyusa friends made no consistent distinction between the nature of the two types of power, but they were quite clear about the differences in use: witchcraft is used illegally and immorally by individuals, while the power of defence is used to protect the village, or falls upon wrong-doers as the chilling "breath of men," and it is exercised by the village as a whole, under the leadership of the headman. Everyone is agreed that sickness results both from witchcraft and from "the breath of men," but the interpretation of a particular case often varies with the viewpoint of the individual. The sufferer will speak angrily of "the witches," while other people tell one that he neglected to kill a cow when his wife died, or he failed to share some beer which came from his in-laws, or swore at his father, and the neighbours were angry. It is the murmuring of neighbours which brings the "chilling breath" that causes paralysis, or recurrent fever, or some other ill. Public opinion in the village is thus believed to be mystically effective. The disapproval of neighbours spells ill-health.

The first question I asked myself when I began to reflect on this peculiar system was "why age-villages?" Why should the Nyakyusa social structure differ so profoundly from that of any other African people of whom we have evidence? We know far too little about the history of Africa and, I think, will always know too little to offer an answer in such terms as I have offered for the development of a centralized chieftainship in Ngonde and not among the Nyakyusa. According to their own traditions, the chiefs of the Nyakyusa came down in a series of migrations from the Livingstone mountains to the East, about ten generations ago. They found in the valley a people who had not yet discovered the use of fire, but who ate their food raw, and by virtue of their great gift to the aborigines, fire, the invaders became chiefs. (It is a myth which is common enough in Africa.) Some say that the invaders also brought the first cattle. The Kinga who still live on the Livingstone mountains also acknowledge kinship with the Nyakyusa and share with them in a common sacrifice to a supposed common ancestor; but culturally the Kinga are totally different from the Nyakyusa. They live in kinship villages, not age-villages, and have no elaborate age-organization, so far as we could discover. The Nyakyusa themselves have no idea whether age-villages came in with the chiefs or were indigenous to the valley, or developed after the conquest. Their myth of origin is not fixed in time, but postulates an invention to meet a social necessity. Once, they say, a certain chief looked upon his son's wife and saw that she was beautiful and said, "she is fit to be a queen (*umwehe*)," and took her; and men thought that very bad and said that henceforth fathers-in-law should never see their daughters-in-law lest they be tempted to commit incest with them, *and so* fathers and sons live in different villages, for if they lived in the same village father-in-law and daughter-in-law would always be seeing one another. In short, the Nyakyusa say that they live in age-villages in order to avoid incest between father-in-law and daughter-in-law.

This myth points us to other questions which we can answer and which, I think, take us further in the understanding of society than any purely chronological answer to my original question, "why age-villages?" I asked myself next: "how does the Nyakyusa system of age-villages really differ from the age organizations of other African people?" and: "what other peculiarities of Nyakyusa society are there which may be connected with age-villages?"

Division of functions between successive generations is, of course, common enough. The great "coming out" ritual of the Nyakyusa, with the transfer of power from one generation to another, is in no way unique, but is typical of many East African peoples, the Nyakyusa form being particularly close to that of the Chaga, who had the same combination of chieftainship and age-organization, and among whom also the functions of defence and administration were undertaken by the same, the ruling generation.

The peculiarity of the Nyakyusa organization consists in the fact that men of an age-set continue to live together in one village after marriage, bringing their wives to the village of the age-set. Warrior villages or barracks exist (or existed) among the Masai, the Zulu, and the Swazi. The cattle posts of the Tswana and Pedi, and the club houses of the Kipisigis and Kikuyu also provided social centres and sleeping quarters for age-sets as yet unmarried, but so far as we know only the Nyakyusa bring their wives to the living quarters of the age-set. Masai, Zulu, Swazi, Tswana, and Pedi all establish their wives in the villages of agnatic kin. (I say as far as we know, for another age-village organization may well turn up elsewhere in Africa. It had not been noticed among the Nyakyusa before my husband went there, though they had been administered under the system of indirect rule for ten years, and a substantial book had been published on the Nyakyusa and Ngonde people.) It is possible also that the Nyakyusa are the only people who forbid a grown son to sleep in his father's homestead at any time. The Zulu, Swazi, Tswana, and Pedi all permit warriors to sleep at home when not on duty in barracks or cattle post.

This life-long territorial segregation of the generations is, as we have seen, connected by the Nyakyusa themselves with decency in sex life. For them morality consists first in the separation of the sexual activities of successive generations, and, secondly, in close friendship and co-operation with equals. The feeling that the sex activities of parents and children should be kept quite separate is, of course, very common—perhaps universal. We can see it in our own society, and it appears in one form or another in most, if not all, the East and Central African groups of which we have knowledge. Adolescent children sleep apart from their parents; avoidance taboos limit familiarity between father and daughter-in-law, and so on. The Nyakyusa peculiarity lies in the extreme to which this separation is pushed.

Why should they go to such extremes? I have no complete answer to this question but one or two points are relevant. First, the Nyakyusa have no male circumcision or initiation, no formal recognition of the sexual maturity of males; therefore, any young man past puberty is a potential mate for a woman of his own age. Where circumcision is customary no male who has not yet been initiated is regarded as adult and a grown woman scorns him as a mate even in extra-marital relations. Therefore, among the Nyakyusa grown sons are potential lovers of their fathers' junior wives, some of whom will be of their own age or younger; whereas among the Chaga and other East African groups who practise circumcision they are not acceptable to women until they have been initiated. Secondly, the marriage age of men is late and that of girls very young, so that there are many bachelors and very few girls available to them. At the same time the polygyny rate is high and most polygynists are middle-aged or elderly, so there are many young wives of polygynists who are bored with their ageing husbands. Thirdly, the Nyakyusa permit the inheritance of a father's widow by his sons, a practice regarded as improper by certain other peoples who practise the levirate. A son is required to treat all his father's wives as mothers while his father and father's full-brothers are alive, and sex relations with a father's wife are treated as a heinous offence, but after the death of the father and his full-brothers these same women become wives of their former sons, with the limitation that a man cannot inherit his own mother or her kinswoman. It is scarcely surprising, therefore, that the seduction of the young wives of an ageing father is a common theme for scandal, and that a father's jealous fears are matched by those of his son.

I argue that there is a connection between the existence of age-villages and the fear of incest between step-son and step-mother on the one hand, and between father-in-law and daughter-in-law on the other, and suggest that certain features of the Nyakyusa social system facilitate incest of the first type, and so increase fear of incest of the second type. Fathers drive their adolescent sons out of their village lest they make love to their mothers, and the sons reciprocate, insisting that when they do marry they should continue to live apart lest their fathers seduce their wives. The incest theme elaborated in one fashion among people organized in clans, and practising clan exogamy, and in another among people practising brother-sister avoidance, finds yet a different expression in age-villages, of which the overt purpose is the separation of sons and mothers, of fathers-in-law and daughters-in-law.

The constant emphasis on the importance of *ukwangala*—good fellowship with contemporaries—is both an expression and a condition of the age-village organization. Kinship bonds are strong; wealth in cattle depends upon co-operation with kinsmen and good health is believed to be dependent on such co-operation also; but the good life, as the Nyakyusa define it, can only be achieved in the age-village which cuts across kinship connections. The fear of witchcraft and "the breath of men" compels generosity and conformity with public opinion in the village and creates a sense of mutual dependence between neighbours. It is my contention that the peculiar form of witch beliefs among the Nyakyusa, with the emphasis on lust for meat as a main incentive to witchcraft, the belief in the defensive power of the village headman and other men in the village, and the fear of "the breath of men," an innate power exercised by a village group to punish a member who has done wrong, is directly related to the age-village organization.

11 "CLIENTSHIP" AMONG THE MANDARI OF THE SOUTHERN SUDAN

Jean Buxton

Jean Buxton is visting Lecturer in African Sociology at the University of Oxford. She is the author of *Chiefs and Strangers* (1963), and several papers, mainly on the Mandari.

THE MANDARI are a small tribe of pastoralists living in the acacia grasslands and broad-leaved woodland of the Southern Sudan. Their northern neighbours are the Nilotic Dinka and Atuot, and to the south and east they are bordered by the Bari-speaking tribes of whom they are the most northerly offshoot. They number about 30,000 and are dispersed in two groups—an inland one living west of the Nile who claim to be the true Mandari, and to whom this article chiefly applies, and two other groups of different stock, calling themselves Sera and Köbora who inhabit a narrow strip of land along both banks of the Nile.

I describe here a form of servile institution which is found among Mandari, and which I have called a system of "clientship". Many features of this institution are unfortunately no longer directly observable; since the setting up of the Sudan Administration clientship, which suggested a form of slavery, has been discouraged. For this reason chiefs and notables are reluctant to admit they have clients living with them; while the latter have come to feel that a stigma attaches to their status and will not admit that they are clients. The obtaining of information is also made difficult by the fact that differences in status have become obscured in recent times. The power of chiefs and the prestige of their religious office has been lessened through the creation of administrative chiefships often given to people who are not of

FROM *Sudan Notes and Records* 37 (1957), 100–10, by permission of the author and the editor of *Sudan Notes and Records*.

true chiefly status. Chiefs are poorer and can no longer support many retainers.

The Mandari have no centralised political system. Their country, before the creation of seven administrative divisions, was composed of a large number of small independent chiefships each occupying a well-defined territory. The important nuclear group in each chiefship was a clan whose members are said to own the land; and the hereditary chief, *mar,* was always from a lineage of this land-owning group, *komonyekokak.*

A number of these widely separated land-owning clans are linked by ties of a common ancestry, tracing their origin to a mythical ancestor who came from the sky, at the time when Mandari say the earth and sky were joined by a rope which was later severed.[1] Clans of this type have the power of performing rites for their land and interceding for rain. Other "land-owners" who do not belong to this group hold their land by right of conquest or primary occupation.

In each chiefship, apart from the land-owners, there is a large non-related population composed of clients, split-off segments from other chiefships, and persons residing with maternal relatives or affines. All outsider lineages are attached to the land-owning nucleus through real or fictitious kinship-links traced to the original host or relative who received the founder client or incomer; when there is no blood tie, however, they intermarry with the land-owners. The land-owning clan itself is exogamous.

It is difficult, and in a sense irrelevant, to try and assess the proportion of clients in relation to land-owners at the present time. Many conditions which made clientship attractive, or a survival factor in the past, no longer apply. Few people attach themselves to chiefs, and those who do usually come from neighbouring tribes. I have found a high percentage of Dinka among individual contemporary clients, which reflects the relatively poorer conditions in the Aliab, where inferior soil and drought alternating with flooding makes failure of crops a frequent occurrence.

Again the number of client lineages which represent the descendants of former clients vary considerably in different chiefships. In some there are only a few such groups, in others there are more client lineages than lineages of land-owners. In most

[1] These clans say their founders all originated from Mandari bora country near Mount Tindalu.

cases, however, the total number of land-owners is greater than the people from outside. In one chiefship where I lived, the land-owning clan had six lineages and eight client lines; of which two were attached to the powerful lineage of the chief. The latter also had one Bor Dinka client who had pledged direct allegiance to him; a client family of a man and wife and two sons of mixed Atuot/Mandari extraction; and an extended family of Mandari clients.

From what Mandari say it would appear that in the past there was a higher proportion of clients, many families of whom are said to have died out during the last century, when slave-raiding dispersed Mandari groups. Famine years and epidemics among herds also made it impossible for chiefs to provide for their retainers.

The word for a client is *timit* (pl. *timisi* or *tumonuk*). A *timit* is a man who because of misfortune or misdeed has lost his kin group or has been expelled from it, and having neither property nor kin seeks to attach himself to a chief or other notable who will act as his protector. The protector to whom the client attaches himself I call the "host". Clientship involves the performance of duties on the part of the client in exchange for protection, which amounts to a merging of the individual into the kin group of the host. In one sense the word "timit" only applies to the individual when he first comes to the host without kin and property. Once he has been received into the family of the host, and has been given a wife who has borne children he has acquired both kin and property. But clientship is also a *status;* the status of an individual who has exchanged his personal liberty and mobility, for the benefit of protection which is legal, political and economic. There are many poor persons who are not *timit,* because they are living as land-owners in their own country and have kinsmen who support them. The status of "client" involves the loss of kin and a coming in from *outside.* Thus in the past if a man's chiefdom was defeated in war and its members dispersed, he might go to a chief elsewhere, and offer himself as a client. His original land-owning status was relinquished with the status of client he assumed with his new allegiance. While a client is therefore a special type of person, the word "timit" may also be used in a general sense to describe people who are mean and behave as if they were without wealth or property. In the same way the word "Mar"—chief—may be used to denote people who are generous and open-handed. This reflects the way Mandari represent these two types of person ideologically.

Clients in Mandari do not, and did not in the past as far as is known, form an ethnic group. In fact, they were notoriously of mixed origin. According to folk-lore, and the stories of the founding of client groups, fugitives from Dinka, Atuot, Moru, Bari, Nyangwara and Aliab, came and attached themselves to early Mandari chiefs and eventually founded small lineages which still exist at the present time all over the Mandari country. The distance traversed by fugitives from other tribes would seem to make them very typical clients, because their kin groups were forgotten and there was no further interaction between them and their own people. They lost not only kin, but tribal membership.

A common cause which led a man to accept client status was defeat in war. Hunger and disease were other factors, and children were sometimes brought to Mandari by parents from neighbouring tribes during famine. The child was paid for in grain, and brought up in the homestead of the purchaser, the parents having no further rights over it.

Fugitives from justice, and persons separating from their kin because of quarrels also became clients. Many client groups say their founder became a client because of the killing of a brother or close agnate; or because of conflicts over the inheritance of rain-making powers and over succession to chiefship. Such factors were also responsible for the dividing up of whole groups of people, as well as for individuals becoming the clients of chiefs. When a powerful group separated off, however, they often in time founded a new chiefship, or became "settlers" in chiefships already *in situ*. They did not become clients because they came in numbers, and with cattle and wives. They were a welcome addition and were usually allotted land, intermarrying with the local land-owning line. The position of a single man, or a man and wife, was less advantageous, because they were entering into the relationship as *individuals,* and it was only by accepting client status that they could make themselves acceptable to a protector. Persistent thieves and persons thought to have the evil eye also became clients; they were in danger of retribution in their own chiefship, and were unwelcome as settlers with relatives elsewhere.

There is a common theme running through the stories of how clients are found or arrive, and become attached. These stories may only be a way of rationalising a relationship and may have no real reference to the specific case, but they are put forward again and again. Each land-owning line has its own variations of how the ancestor clients were found. It generally goes something like this, "Our ancestor found his client wandering in the bush", or "the wife of our ancestor found him sitting on an ant-hill, in a tree, by a pool, and so on, when she was collecting firewood", or again "a child heard a cow lowing in the khor, and found our client with his bull". Then whoever found him either ran back and spread the news and the notable came out to see, or he was taken back at once, and questioned and gave his reasons for wandering about in the bush; he was eventually prevailed upon to settle, or else asked to be allowed to do so.

A prospective client might also intimate that he wished to serve the chief by coming and sitting near the chief's meeting tree—*toket;* when questioned he would say he had "come to the Mar", which was a way of pledging allegiance. He might also take a hoe and go and weed a field. In these examples we see that while a man wishes to become a client he also wishes to be persuaded; it has to appear that he is needed as much as he himself wishes to gain protection. And this is consistent with clientship, which is essentially a free association at the outset. A measure of volition is also necessary on both sides for the relationship to continue; although it will be seen that as the client becomes more completely absorbed into the host's kin group, it becomes increasingly difficult, and finally almost impossible, for him to leave it alive.

When a client first arrives he is without power or the means of providing for himself. Within the host's family he is usually called by his own name, but he may be spoken of as "our man" *ngutu likang,* or "our brother" *laser likang,* or when not present as "our client". It is not courteous to call a client "timit" to his face, as this constitutes a form of insult. He is addressed and referred to in a kinship idiom, as only by linguistic identification can he be incorporated in the community where he has no ties of cognition or affinity.

By outsiders, that is, by non-members of the chiefship, he is spoken of as the "brother" of the host; and in the past important clients who were assistants to chiefs were addressed as Mar or *monybang* "owner of the homestead", as a mark of respect, and also because it is not customary for an outsider to imply differentiation of status within another group. Mandari say that people fought in the past because of insults to clients; "he is our man, it is not for another person to call him timit". An insult to a client is also an indirect way of insulting the host. Thus the offensive songs sung by members of one chiefship against another during dances often name persons who are clients of the chiefship rather than members of the land-owning line. When these songs are sung on social occasions fighting may break out because of the implied insult to the land-owners.

While "brother" is the correct way to address a client within the land-owning line, everyone knows that the client has no blood tie, and whether the people of the host's lineage choose to address him in a courteous fashion depends on many things; his own character, the relative ages of the persons concerned, and the degree of affection in which the client is held. If a master is harsh, or continually abuses a client with reference to his status, the client may seek another patron and then the host loses a retainer.

After his incorporation the client no longer uses the name of his natal lineage, but is grafted on to his host's line. His children continue to bear the name of the host's lineage, but it is characteristic of the client institution that after several generations a client line is divided off from the main land-owning stem and given its own name which is often a nick-name referring to some characteristic by which the clients have come to be known. For instance, the name Mo'kido was given to a group of people called Kulundo, who came from Moru to the Lorogak clan during a famine. Mok means "to hold"; kido "chest", and describes the way they were hugging themselves in hunger. Other names refer to the place or tribe from which the original client was said to come, hence Jokari Jöngö—the name of a client line from Dinka (Jöngö) attached to Jokari. If descendants of a client are few they continue to be merged individually in the direct line of the host. In this case when reciting genealogies Mandari tend to leave them out altogether. This shows that in spite of terminological identification for social purposes hosts do not think of their clients as forming part of their agnatic line.

Duties of the Client

The work of the client differs little in kind from that undertaken by any adult Mandari, and includes the cultivation of the host's fields, the building and repair of dwelling huts, grain stores, and kraals for goats. In these tasks the client works together with the wives and offspring of his host. His work differs in the quantity he is expected to do, and the fact that it is never rewarded with beer, as is usual for work undertaken for non-kin. After a client marries and has a homestead of his own, the obligation to cultivate the fields of the host continues, and assistance is expected from his wife and children.

The client's main duties, however, are peculiar only to persons who have client status, and are those which attach him to the person of his host. He accompanies him wherever he journeys, acts as guard, porter, protector or messenger. One task always performed by a client is the roasting of the kill in the bush during a hunt, and the cooking of the meat of a sacrifice which is attended away from the host's village, when a portion of meat is eaten before the return journey. Male clients do not, in general, cook or prepare food, which involves specialised knowledge belonging only to women. Neither do their regular duties include women's work, such as fetching water or firewood, although they may have to perform these duties, as do poor Mandari, who are not clients, under pressure of circumstances.

The client's attendance on his host calls for watchfulness and devotion. His place is by his master to protect him and attend to his needs. Clients therefore do not usually spend long periods in the cattle camps unless sent there by the host. The client's cattle, when he owns any, are herded with those of his host by youths of the land-owning line, or by a son of the client. During the day the chief's client sits behind his master under the meeting tree where the chief gives judgements; he refills his pipe, fetches charcoal, and hands out tobacco to the elders. Less favoured clients help to prepare and carry food and beer to the meeting tree where it is divided among the elders by the client who is the chief's assistant. This client also listens to conversation, and reports anything which may be of interest to the chief. In pre-government days spying for the host was also important, and clients might pretend to pledge allegiance to a rival chief in order to gain information about the fighting strength of a rival territory. Those discovered acting in this way were killed, and the fear that clients might become informers may have been one of the reasons for the killing of those who tried to change allegiance.

Marriage and Property of the Client

Small communities of clients always encircle the homesteads of chiefs, and these retainers gave protection in the past when raiding and fighting were widespread. As each client acquired a wife he built a homestead and cultivated his own fields while continuing to assist the wives of the host.

The client had a right to the produce of his hut, which he used for the feeding of his family and for the entertainment of neighbours and members of the host's hamlet. If the host wished for assistance with grain or beer he could approach the client and ask his help. On such occasions he always "begs", as the Mandari put it, and never "takes"; in the same way the client will always if possible comply.

Cattle and goats can be owned by clients, but are always few in number. A client family can in time build up a small herd, by the judicious marriage of daughters, when as the biological father of the bride a client receives an animal, while the host who gave the dowry for her mother takes the larger part. When a client line of long standing finds bridewealth independently, the descendants of the original host receive an ox as "kinsmen of the bride" when a daughter of the line marries. Alternatively, clients may receive animals on the marriage of their host's daughters, particularly if they are favoured clients of mature age, and I have seen such payments made.[2]

It is usual for clients to have only one wife, although there is nothing specific to prevent a client having a number. His ability to acquire more than one depends on economic factors, and the status and co-operation of his host. In the past important clients of wealthy chiefs might have several. It is considered desirable for

---

[2] Malundit, a Bor Dinka client, received a cow on the marriage of Diyö, elder daughter of Chief Korondo of Dari, and an ox on the marriage of Banye, the younger daughter.

a client to marry a woman of the same status, although nothing expressly forbids him to marry the daughter of a non-client, if the father was willing to accept a low bridewealth and a son-in-law with no true agnatic kin. Economic and prestige considerations, however, usually prevented such alliances. Poor persons sometimes saw the advantage of marrying a daughter to a client if he was favoured by the chief, because it linked their family hut with a powerful protector. Females of client lines often made non-client marriages, and if beautiful might be married by neighbouring chiefs as junior wives, for considerable bridewealth. Present-day marriages where both persons are of client extraction may be cemented with cattle, but with fewer than those paid by land-owners for their brides, and goats are often accepted in lieu.

In the past the initial marriages of clients pledging allegiance were arranged by the host and elders, who handed over a girl of client status, or a young female captive, whom they had reared, to a client as a reward for good services.

It is permissible for a host to marry daughters of client lines attached to collateral lineages of his own clan, but he will never marry the daughters of his own clients or those of his close agnates. This is important because it prevents the merging of the host's line with lines of its own clients. It is also consistent with the "sentiment" of kinship which exists between host and client, and with the fact that the host gave assistance with bridewealth for the girl's mother, who because of this is the "wife" of the host's lineage, and her child its "daughter". Members of non-related client lines intermarry freely with each other, and with collateral lineages of land-owners. The presence of these outsiders provides unrelated brides near home within a political unit which, in the past, settled disputes by compensation rather than by fighting.

Status is inherited through males; therefore, if a woman marries into a land-owning line her children are land-owners even if she is of client stock. If a free woman marries a client, her children rank as clients. It must be remembered, however, that as the client proves himself with time, his status in relation to the land-owners tends to become more advantageous, and this change is more marked in relation to his descendants. The ability of a client to better his position is largely dependent on whether he can found a large family; it also depends in some

degree on the type of person he is himself. Certain clients who
figure in folk-lore as founding lineages which are powerful at
the present time, were youths from land-owning lines who had
fled their countries because of fighting within the agnatic line.

One such favoured client, for instance, was a fugitive son
of the Mar of Rume, who came with his younger brother to
Böndöri chiefship because their father had caused by accident
the death of their mother. After travelling many days in the bush
with their two dogs, and enduring great hardships, the youths
are said to have arrived in Böndöri country where they hid in
an old ant-hill, from which they watched the people of Böndöri
hoeing their fields. In the evening when the latter hid their
hoes in a bush and left the fields, the boys took them out and
completed the work. They did this for several days, and then
made themselves known to the astonished people. The Mar of
Böndöri invited them to remain, which they did. The younger
son became a mighty hunter and warrior, and the Mar eventually
gave him his beautiful daughter Alak who had been continually
refused to suitors of chiefly birth. When she bore sons, the Mar
of Böndöri regularised the position of father and offspring by
saying that their line was to stand as a half-brother lineage, and
not as sister's sons, to Böndöri. The drum, the symbol of chiefship, was also handed over to the client's children, and the
land-owning line placed under a conditional curse, which would
operate if any member of the land-owning line abused them by
reference to the original status of their forebear. The descendants
of this client are called Nyayo, and when people speak about
the Böndöri land-owning clan to-day, they refer to it as the
Böndöri-Nyayo.

This story shows the original status of a client being raised
to that of land-owner, through marriage with the daughter of
the host. A female link is treated as a male link in favour of
the client's children, and the origin of the begetter is slurred
over. Mandari explain this raising of status as a way of getting
round the difficulty of a chief's daughter and her children taking
on client status through marriage. It is also, I think, indicative
of the way in which the problem of the client's indeterminate
status can be solved—the client is given the daughter of the
chief in order that he may acquire equality. This does not appear to be an isolated case, and other founders of groups which
are politically important to-day are said to have been clients

who came as destitutes from other tribes, married daughters of their hosts, and later came to supersede the land-owners whose lines became weaker and weaker, while those stemming from the clients became more and more powerful.[3]

Clients at the present time are not given the daughters of chiefs, and even in the past the majority of clients who founded lineages never got themselves accepted as land-owners, nor did they become politically dominant. If they multiplied, however, few disabilities attached to them, other than the fact that they could never be land-owners and were enjoined to remain with their hosts. This obligation to remain is in a sense a moral obligation, as the original host gave legal and political protection and bridewealth for the marriage of the ancestor client. The relationship between land-owning line and client line grows into one of mutual interdependence, and continued ability to draw on protection carries with it the obligation to serve the host's people, while the land-owners recognise that people of a client line which is numerically strong cease to be clients in the narrow sense of the word.

The Legal Disabilities of the Client

At the present time it is difficult to observe the kind of situation in which the "legal" disabilities of the client become apparent. With the introduction of chief's courts all individuals in theory have equal legal rights, and a client can bring an action against his host if he wishes. In fact, a client cannot improve his position by acting in this way, but rather runs the risk of losing the patronage of his host. The host-client relationship is not one in which the host will often commit a wrong against the client, because of the censure of public opinion, and the balance of other factors arising out of the relation.

When clients are involved in litigation at the present time, their hosts defend them in the courts, paying fines, or helping them to bring actions. In the past the host avenged wrongs against the client as wrongs against a "kinsman". *Vis-à-vis* other groups the client was merged as a male agnate in the powerful line of the host, and if a client was killed by someone of another group, the host was under the obligation of carrying out blood vengeance.

[3] For example, Mokido superseded Lorogak, and Jabour ousted Wöjur.

It would appear certain, however, that the disabilities of the
client in relation to his host's group were more pronounced in
the past. A client whose master chose to ill-treat him had
virtually no appeal. The ultimate sanction for the good treatment of the client was based on the services he rendered. If
the client was consistently ill-treated the elders might remonstrate
with the host, pointing out the shame attaching to the ill-treat-
ment of a man who had no other protector and who served him
well. Public opinion, backed by the fact that there is a definite
standard of behaviour expected of a chief or notable, was the
surety for the client's wellbeing. Hosts who were mean and cruel
also lost retainers, and those who were generous and benevolent
were known by repute and gained them. Clients were thus protected by the nature of clientship and its relation to the political
machine as a whole. The only redress for the individual client
in the final instance was to flee, and I am told that clients
tried to do this if their lot was unhappy, or if they had committed a serious wrong against the host. Clients and their families
who tried to leave in this way were, if possible, intercepted
and killed, to prevent them offering their services to rival chiefs.
One has the impression from what Mandari say, and from
observation of the behaviour of client and host at the present
time, that the former were generally well treated and held in
affection by their hosts. Both were bound together in close
proximity; but having no blood tie, the relationship did not
contain the tensions which are present between two siblings who
have rights in common over persons and property.

The status of the individual client in relation to the host, is
again different from that of a client lineage in relation to a land-
owning lineage. Clientship is a dynamic relationship during the
life of a man and onwards throughout the lives of his descendants. The client as an individual has a very close association with the host, and therefore in some ways his position is
stronger, while in others it is weaker. Members of a client
lineage have a less intense association with the land-owner to
whom they are attached, and the difference in status between
client and land-owner becomes less marked. The services any
one individual gives are less frequent, as is also the assistance
received. Emphasis is on the privileged position of the land-
owners, rather than on the under-privileged position of the clients.

The ambiguity of client status may be seen clearly in connection with the close association of the evil eye and witchcraft with this type of person. It must be remembered that clients come from the "bush". For this reason their background can never satisfactorily be explained. People who are land-owners know all the links between their people, back to the founder. They can show that their lineage is ritually pure. Clients from outside are different; they may have left their chiefship because of nefarious practices and it is quite logical to suspect them. The way in which bad ritual characteristics are believed to be inherited helps to keep the lines of land-owners clear while making these characteristics a function of client lineages. I do not mean that all client lines are considered bad, but that once the association is made it is easy for it to be perpetuated. This is significant because it places client lines only under a ritual stigma, in contrast with land-owners, to whom beneficial religious powers are exclusive.

Mar-Timit

Further consideration must be given to the relationship which existed between a chief and the client who was chosen to go through the installation ceremonies of chiefship with him, because I believe that the ideology of clientship is most clearly brought out when we consider the position of this special client. He was chosen either because he had been installed with a previous chief or because he was a youth whose personality made him suitable for office. It appears it was usual for such a client to be a young man, and never more than middle-aged, whereas a man was often of advanced years by the time he was installed as chief.[4]

Information about the ceremonies was obtained from a number of chiefs and elders of different territories. None of the present chiefs have been installed, and I only met one client who had been through the ceremonies.

The installation of a chief *gwita na mar* was always accompanied by great festivities, and was attended by visitors from neighbouring chiefships, who according to tradition brought the sacred oil for the anointing; the ceremony itself being performed

---

[4] Succession often passed to the brother of a dead chief, and then back to his son, if the latter was a youth at the time of his father's death.

by the visiting elders and never by the new chief's own people.
The climax of the ceremony was when the new chief was placed
on a cow-hide together with two selected clients, and bathed
in water by the visiting elders, after which calabashes of milk
were poured over his head and body. The female elders accompanying the visitors wiped the milk from his head and face,
and he was anointed with simsim oil brought by the visitors,
while they addressed him saying "Let your body be cool—
may you hold your country well and look after visitors".[5]

During the anointing, the two clients sat by the chief and
the one selected to be his personal assistant was bathed in the
same way. Mandari say "The client is a mar as well, he is
gwita, too". After the anointing the elders took the hands of
the client and joined them with those of the chief addressing
them as follows:—"You are brothers, you must remain together".
Then they instructed the client, "You are Mar also. If the Mar
is away you must look after the people and entertain visitors".

The other client who sat with the Mar, and who is his messenger, was not anointed. Mandari say "He is gwita by mouth
only", meaning he is verbally instructed. Other clients took
no part in the ceremony. The new chief and his personal client
were then secluded for five days in a hut, during which time
they both received new names. On their re-entry into the community an ox was sacrificed for the protection of the chief by
the elders of his line.

A very intense relationship was established between Mar and
client because of the sharing of these ceremonies. At the end
of the isolation the Mar elect had become the Mar, and the
client his officiating shadow-personality. The latter from then
on would be treated with respect and addressed as Mar. He
became the operative aspect of "marship", because once the
Mar had been installed he should never become involved in
argument, use harsh words or rebuke people. The client in his
stead became responsible for giving unpleasant commands, for
keeping order at the meeting tree, and for seeing that people
did not shout or quarrel in the presence of the Mar. If the Mar

[5] Mandari say when a new chief was to be installed, the visitors from a
rival section who came to perform the ceremony were elders, and the chief
client belonging to its Mar. The latter never came himself, but was represented by this client.

was absent the client could sum up for him during a case, or put forward his point of view. Mandari say "He knows what the Mar would say, and says it for him".

By extension of the equivalence which was established between chief and client, and arising from it, we find a special type of intimacy existing between the two. For example, when food was brought to the Mar by the clients who acted as menials (and there was much of it, because every wife cooked food to be taken to the place where the Mar was eating with other elders) the Mar ate first while his client sat behind him. When he had taken a few mouthfuls the client might lean forward and take the food away, at the same time wiping the mouth of the Mar with his hand, and saying, "My brother, why do you spoil your mouth with filth like this?" Then he finished the food himself, handing the next dish to the Mar. He might help himself to this as well and to anything he fancied that the Mar was eating. Mandari joke about this behaviour saying, "The Mar is in the hands of his client, and is hungry. As soon as he tries to eat the food is taken away from him. His wife therefore brings special delicacies to the Mar at night when the client is sleeping." The client might also make free with the chief's tobacco. Behaviour of this kind might be considered a form of joking relationship, which prevented conflict between two personalities which have become to some extent merged. I think it is certainly clear that the client cannot satisfactorily be considered alone; and to understand fully his role we must examine both sides of the partnership and speak of a composite social personality, "Mar-timit". That Mandari see it in this way is, I think, brought out by their constant complaints that there are now no "Mar" because there are no "timit", and vice versa. These two could not be separated in practice and on the ideal level; and when they went they went together. The complementary roles of chief and client have fallen apart as the social personalities of chief and client have changed; the chief is no longer installed; he is no longer "owned by the people, but by the government". In the past the mar-timit relationship reflected two important factors in chiefship, that of ruler and servant of the people which Mandari reiterate when they say "He is our Mar. We put him there so that we can eat [off] him".

Looking at clientship to-day, out of its original context, and when much of the traditional client-host behaviour has been abandoned, it is difficult to see what the institution really represented. In a wider ideological context we can see its importance as an integral part of that given and unchanging social order which is upheld for Mandari by religious myths, and to which they give verbal support when they say "In the past big men were from God, now everyone thinks he is Mar".

I should mention that in the myths about the early Mandari world, ancestor Mar and their clients were still doing things together, and often the client appears to be more sagacious than the Mar, or is instructing people in certain actions rather than the Mar. In one of these stories the sentiment is expressed that the death of the host brings about the death of the "social personality" of the client, and so he is shown as choosing physical death. This client was the assistant of Mar Desa, an early Mandari culture hero; and when the latter died, his client pleaded to be buried in the grave. He asked, "Who will now care for, and feed me, and see that I am not abused, now my Mar is dead? If the Mar is dead, I will die as well." The chief's relatives reasoned with him all day as he lay in the open grave, telling him he should rather live and serve the chief's sons, "Your time will come another day, because all men must die". Eventually they became tired of trying to persuade him and covered him over with earth.

The sky-being, Mar Nykwac Jakda who is looked upon as the "father" of all the Bora clan founders, including Mar Desa mentioned above, was the prototype Mar, who divided up Mandari country. We are not told who his clients were; only that at his descent from the sky he was accompanied by a brother Ruelli and a woman, both of whom returned to the heavens. When he settled on earth he is said to have found "people" living there, and to have married one of their women. The presence to-day near Mount Tindalu, the place of Mar Nykwac Jakda's descent, of small dispersed groups claiming to be of a pre-Bora stock, whose previous way of life was different from that which spread with the Bora, suggests that the first clients may have been found from these people. If we assume that the coming of the Bora ancestor and the gradual domination of the country by his descendants conceptualises the arrival of a powerful group from outside, the client land-owner partnership may have been a way in which the incomers solved the problem of a remnant population already *in situ*. The fact that some of the pre-Bora lines are said to have handed over their religious powers relating to the land to other conquering groups in exchange for cattle is not, however, in itself sufficient evidence for us to assume this to be so, and it might equally well be that the client institution was always common to the Bora, whoever they may have been, and was continued by them when they came to a new homeland. It could also have been a permanent feature of a society which was divided into land-owning lines with religious powers, and into lines of non-land-owners who lacked these powers and played a complementary role.

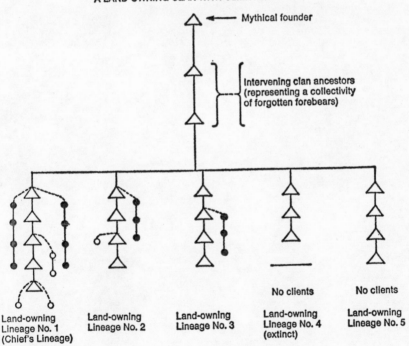

A LAND-OWNING CLAN WITH CLIENT LINEAGES

← Mythical founder

Intervening clan ancestors (representing a collectivity of forgotten forebears)

Land-owning Lineage No. 1 (Chief's Lineage)

Land-owning Lineage No. 2

Land-owning Lineage No. 3

No clients
Land-owning Lineage No. 4 (extinct)

No clients
Land-owning Lineage No. 5

Key:

△ Land-owner
● Client of named lineage
○ Client of unnamed lineage, or individual client
---- Client-host relationship

12 THE MAPUCHE RESERVATION AS A POLITICAL UNIT

L. C. Faron

L. C. Faron is Professor of Anthropology at the State University of New York, Stony Brook. Besides *Mapuche Social Structure,* he is the author of *Hawks of the Sun: Mapuche Morality and Its Ritual Attributes* (1964), and several papers on the Mapuche.

IN THIS CHAPTER I propose only a partial consideration of Mapuche political organization, partial in the sense that the reservation is taken as a political entity vis-à-vis the Chilean government in the context of colonialism and the reservation system. The political issue of greatest importance is the status of Mapuche society. This centers around the "question" of reservation land.[1]

We have seen that chieftainship implies political as distinguished from purely kinship organization and that it hinges on the reservation system per se. In its body of Indian legislation, the Chilean government deals with Mapuche reservations as a totality. However, in actual practice at the local level of administration, the segmentary nature of Mapuche political units compels government agencies to deal with single reservations and individual chiefs in matters pertaining to reservation land. In this sense, each reservation is an autonomous political unit with respect to other reservations.

FROM *Mapuche Social Structure: Institutional Reintegration in a Patrilineal Society of Central Chile* (Urbana: University of Illinois Press, 1961), pp. 102–22, by permission of the author and the University of Illinois Press.

[1] I am arbitrarily excluding a detailed treatment of the ritual attributes of political leadership, as exemplified in the office of priest-chief (*nullatufe*), understandable only through a discussion of religious morality and its ritual expression. Mapuche morality is an important integrative force of sufficiently complex structure to justify its analysis in a separate monograph, and, for the most part, in the subcolonial context in which it thrives.

Reservation status entitles the Mapuche to special consideration in Indian courts and in the Ministry of Lands and Colonization. As Chilean citizens, though, the Mapuche also have a
series of rights and obligations irrespective of reservation status
which brings them under the jurisdiction of national courts, the
authority of which is backed by the Chilean police force, military
organization, and penal institutions. Nevertheless, the question
of land rights (corporate *vs.* severalty status) is central to
Mapuche political organization. It is largely as title holder of
reservation land that the chief enjoys political leadership. It is
membership in a reservation community that conditions the individual's political interests and goals. The eventual disposition
of reservation land continues to be the primary issue around
which Mapuche-Chilean relationships center in the political
sphere of social action. The preamble to the contemporary condition may be stated in historical terms.

For more than 300 years after the Spanish invasion of Chile
the Mapuche maintained considerable autonomy over the region
south of the Bío Bío River. Horacio Lara (1889:241) expressed
himself on this matter in the following words: "La Araucanía
seguía prestandose a la faz del mundo como una sección territorial independiente de nuestra República, con sus costumbres
y su independencia propria. . . ." But toward the end of the
colonial era a series of forts and towns was re-established south
of the Bío Bío—Los Angeles, Nacimiento, Antuco, and Santa
Barbara were founded between 1742 and 1758. South of the
Mapuche stronghold, Osorno, San Pablo, and Río Bueno were
established with the effect of delimiting the southern extension of
Mapuche-held territory. These towns did not serve as jumping-
off points for immediate settler penetration of the Indian zone,
however.

While little is really known about the details of Mapuche
politico-military organization during most of this long era, the
fact that they were able to resist white settlement of their heart-
land suggests an organization that could be called into play
when the occasion demanded. It must not be overlooked, though,
that they had the advantage of sheer weight of numbers, which,
perhaps more than tactical maneuvers and organizational ability,
accounts for their successful resistance. Also, because of a lack

of centralized political authority, the Spaniards and later the Chileans were forced to conquer one small residential aggregate after another, the defeat of one such group not entailing the submission of the rest. In any case, the long-range successes of the Mapuche were always at the expense of the stability of local residential groupings throughout the colonial and early republican periods.

By the 1850's there was increased colonization of the southern part of central Chile. Several towns were also built near and along the Pacific coast south of Concepción. Nueva Imperial was founded in 1852 and Toltén in 1867. South of Villarrica and Valdivia a number of settlements were also established. In this same period the provinces of Arauco and Llanquihue were created. Through immigration from Europe and the northern provinces of Chile white population increased to more than 100,000 by the end of the nineteenth century in this part of Chile. The greatest impetus to colonization came after the War of the Pacific and after the pacification of the Mapuche. McBride described the settlement of Araucanía in these words: "Small blocks of territory, chiefly in the foothills of the Andes and in the deeper forests, still harbored clusters of Indian families who clung to their native speech, apparel, and customs. But white settlement was spreading. New provinces were created: Bío Bío in 1875, Malleco and Cautín in 1887—thus the whole of the Frontera was incorporated into the national domain" (1936:295–96). I might add that large blocks of Mapuche continue to live in the Central Valley on land now cleared of forest. With the establishment of reservations, the Mapuche were effectively brought under the administration of the national government and were influenced by its political and legal systems.

It is my feeling that most if not all the speculative reconstructions of prereservation political organization have to be dismissed, largely because the early chroniclers and even the more sophisticated ethnographers of the late nineteenth century saw Mapuche social and political organization in terms of European models founded on territorial units which seem to have no basis in fact. Cooper (1946), from whom the following excerpts are taken, gives an unbiased appraisal of the historical material on military and political organization:

Some major features of the system . . . are quite clear. There was no peacetime over-all chief, no centralization of authority. . . . Furthermore, such authority as was invested in kinship heads and local "chiefs" was very limited—exclusively or almost exclusively consultative and persuasive, with little or no coercive power. They had no recognized rights to inflict punishment, to claim tribute or personal service, or to demand obedience from their kinsfolk or "subjects." The latter paid no attention to them and did as they pleased if the leaders showed themselves arrogant or domineering [724].

Decisions regarding peacetime affairs and warlike undertakings were usually made in conferences of the responsible men and sub-heads at the house or meeting-ground of the head or "chief" after free expression of views and by common agreement. There was a certain loose hierarchy of honor and status (rather than authority proper) embracing higher and lower heads and "chiefs" —which brings us to the less clear features of the . . . socio-political structure [725].

In the course of time, particularly after the beginning of the 19th century, a certain increase in the executive and judicial power and authority accrued to peacetime headmen . . . and the earlier atomistic peacetime political structure assumed somewhat greater unity, cohesion, and hierarchization. But the basic democratic forms and functions persisted largely intact [726].

In writing of law and legal procedure, Cooper has this to say:

The chief crimes recognized were adultery and wife-stealing, murder, theft, homicidal sorcery, and treason. The offended party and his kin dealt with the offender; in earlier times headmen and other caciques had little or no authority to try cases or to pronounce judgment. Adultery, murder, and sorcery were punishable by death, and sometimes were actually so punished; but more commonly, in cases of adultery and murder, composition was resorted to, with payment of strings of llankas . . . [726].

Today, certain behavior is defined as extralegal by Chilean standards, serious departures from national law being handled by Chilean institutions empowered to enforce law and order. The Mapuche go to law for the settlement of disputes involving certain crimes and torts, but within the reservation community traditional sanctions deal effectively with other antisocial acts of a different nature. Most important among these are the ones which involve sorcery and which the Chilean courts usually refuse to consider seriously. Ostracism, ridicule, and the threat of sorcery continue as sanctions on most if not all reservations and larger communities. In certain instances, therefore, the

Mapuche "take the law into their own hands," applying traditional moral principles in the ordering of social action. But matters involving property and personal rights not capable of being dealt with by traditional means are ultimately resolvable by recourse to the Chilean system of courts and law-enforcement agencies.

Mapuche: "People of the Land"

After the declaration of Chilean independence in 1810, the new national government assumed responsibility for colonizing the Mapuche stronghold south of the Bío Bío River. In general, the republican government's efforts followed the pattern established during the colonial period. On the one hand there was an attempt to protect the Mapuche from the sharp practices of land grabbers, and on the other to provide a means for eventual absorption of the Indians into the national population. Provision was made for the sale of Indian-held land and the relocation of Mapuche on haciendas and in newly founded towns. A great amount of Indian land was alienated through fraudulent practices which ranged from purchase at unrealistically low prices to outright usurpation. The effort to get the Mapuche to settle in Chilean towns, however, failed just as it had throughout the colonial period.

By the middle 1800's the Mapuche became quite restive under the resurgent pressures of white colonization and a heightening of fraudulent acquisition of land. The Chilean government modified its Indian policy at the legislative level in an attempt to facilitate colonization while minimizing the danger of fraudulent expropriation of Mapuche land. In 1866 the government began to map reservation lands which were inalienable except through legal purchase after formal *división*. Again, the government was primarily interested in curtailing speculation in land and in implementing the peaceful colonization of Araucanía. To the latter end, the Mapuche were continually encouraged to abandon their reservations and to work as laborers in small towns or on haciendas. To foster acculturation, the reservation law of 1866 provided that one-eighth of the household heads of a reservation could vote to relinquish reservation status and sell their land. It was written into the law that the Mapuche were not permitted to buy back the land after the dissolution of the reservation. Where *división* took place, the Indians were divested of their land, and large sections of their territory were expropriated by white colonists who had often duped them into voting for *división*. There is no evidence, however, that these Indians became tenant farmers on the haciendas or laborers in the towns, to any appreciable extent. Rather, landless Mapuche moved into virgin territory or took up residence with landed Indians, seeking the protection of the headmen of these groups.

The rebellion of 1868–70 ensued and resulted in further unsettling and shifting of the Mapuche population. Those Indians near centers of white penetration abandoned their lands, retreated to less accessible regions, or joined the vast number of Mapuche who migrated to Argentina. This was still a time of large reservations and much unmapped land which allowed the Mapuche considerable mobility and made them a continual military threat. It was a period of intermittent hostilities—raids (*malones*) among the Mapuche themselves as the displaced groups jostled one another, and raids against the encroaching white farms and towns.

While Chilean armies were occupied with Peru and Bolivia during the War of the Pacific, the Mapuche staged their last general uprising, which ended in their defeat, pacification, and settlement on small reservations. After 1883, their territory was studded with military garrisons and Chilean towns, and crosscut by a network of roads and railroad lines. Unoccupied, that is, unregistered, land was taken over by the government and disposed of in several ways.

Reservation laws have been modified occasionally for the purpose of inducing the Mapuche to abandon their traditional way of life and make available their lands for white colonization. A "one-eighth" clause provided that the chief should obtain three times as much land as ordinary household heads when severalty holdings were allotted, in accordance with a vote of one-eighth of the reservation in favor of *división*. It was perhaps felt that the chief, on this inducement, could muster sufficient votes in favor of *división*. South of Cautín Province *división* and the consequent sale of land took place on a tremendous scale after 1866. But when the Mapuche came to realize their plight there was strong resistance to the law. Reservations were not being dissolved with nearly the rapidity the government had expected. In 1927 it was decreed that application for *división* could be made by a single family head, rather than one-eighth of the household heads. Again, the chief was favored, although the net was broadly cast to catch any individual desiring freehold status. Clarification of this law the following year went a step farther and made it explicit that the government, if the need arose, could divide the reservations *at its own discretion!*

The Mapuche continue to live under the threat of absolute and arbitrary governmental power.[2] There has consequently been a reaction to *división* on the part of the Mapuche, manifest in both the symbolism of cultural nationalism and the action programs of political nationalism, and by the concrete fact that very few reservations have been divided since. In 1931 the law was again modified to the extent that now agreement of one-third of the household heads of a reservation community is needed before application for *división* may be made. The government's intentions and hopes seem not to have changed, however. This is reflected quite graphically by the fact that a census of Mapuche lands is broken down into "reservations divided" and "reservations to be divided," the latter category including all communities now having reservation status.

The reservation policy, involving as it does the entire problem of the disposition of Mapuche lands, is the main area in which Chilean and Indian politico-legal structures overlap. National-level politics and laws have had tremendous influence on reservation political structure and legal concepts. *Admapu* (customary law) has been brought into closer approximation with the Chilean system, and the latter has made concessions to Mapuche juridical and social beliefs and practices.

Before proceeding with a discussion of Mapuche law and political organization, which cannot be divorced from the Chilean politico-juridical system, it might be well to outline briefly the Chilean governmental structure. In the first place, Chile is a republic with a National Congress, composed of a Senate and a House of Deputies, a system of courts, and a military and police organization. The nation is divided into numerous Provinces which

[2] A communication from Professor Alejandro Lipshutz, December 27, 1960, relates that the National Congress has recently passed a law involving the dissolution of the reservations and that the only hope for their preservation depends on the personal intervention of the President of Chile.

are subdivided into Departments, Subdelegations, and Districts, each with its elected or appointed head and administrative body. An *Intendiente* heads each Province, a Governor each Department, a Subdelegate each Subdelegation, and an Inspector each District. Mapuche are Chilean nationals and, upon proof of literacy, attain with maturity the right to vote and to be elected or appointed to any of the nation's political offices. In 1953 there were two Mapuche *Diputados,* several Inspectors, a number of *regidores,* and at least one *alcalde* in Cautín Province. The then Minister of Lands and Colonization was born and spent his early years on a reservation.

Deputies are elected from one or more Departments, depending on population, there being a proportion of one deputy to each 30,000 inhabitants. In the indigenous zone, especially in Cautín Province with its estimated 100,000 or more reservation-dwelling Indians, the Mapuche are able to swing local elections, even where they are not actually in the majority, due to the existence of numerous splinter parties. They are becoming more conscious of regional-national politics and are forming vocal pressure groups, literally Indian parties, through which they express themselves on the national scene.

The Ministry of Lands and Colonization has jurisdiction over Indian affairs. Special courts and judges hear land claims and other cases involving reservations, but violations of civil law are heard in regular Chilean courts open to whites and Indians alike. Specifically, the Indian judges (*Juezes de Indios*) handle *división*. In appearing before the Indian courts (*Juzgados de Indios*) the Mapuche is entitled to legal representation (*abogado procurador*). In all, the government administers an indigenous zone almost the size of the state of Delaware.

Nevertheless, this represents a territory vastly reduced over the course of the last hundred years. Immediately after the rebellion of 1880–82 Mapuche society seems to have been in a state of turmoil. It is estimated that many thousands of Indians migrated across the Andes at this time to escape military reprisal or because they had been routed out of their former settlements at points of white penetration.

Within Araucanía there was also tremendous population movement as groups shifted en masse to the Andean foothills or southward to and across the Toltén River. The greatest pressures were brought to bear on the Mapuche from the north and west. Forested, virgin territory was opened up during this period as much by the Mapuche themselves as by the white colonists. Aside from the general historical accounts there are other data which add to the impression of great population mobility between 1880 and the first two decades of the twentieth century. In the *título* records, for example, it is not uncommon to read that witnesses for the applicant chief knew him and his *familia* for only as little as fifteen or twenty years in some instances, indicating a short occupancy in the area. Mobility is given tacit recognition in the reservation legislation, as well, for it is stated (e.g. *Ley* No. 4,111, June 1931, Art. 27) that an Indian will be considered a legal resident only on the reservation in which he earns his livelihood, regardless of the fact that he might be mentioned in various *títulos*.

In large parts of Araucanía the registration and mapping of reservations was proceeding slowly, and, as towns sprang up and farm colonies developed, the Mapuche continued to withdraw. With the establishment of railroads and roadways throughout the frontier, the Indians were put off their land with little or no compensation. Some reservations were not mapped and registered under a chief until as recently as the second decade of the twentieth century—almost thirty years after the end of hostilities. During this interim, the social and political organization of the reservation Mapuche was undergoing significant change, and a new social stability was achieved under the reservation chief.

Chieftainship

It will be remembered that in time of peace the prereservation Mapuche lived in numerous autonomous groups under the leadership of a kinship elder, the *lonko,* and that the authority of the *lonko* was minimal and subject to rather easy circumvention. In the nineteenth century there seems to have occurred a crystallization of military powers in the hands of *lonkos* who were able to secure a following during time of hostility. But military defeat or even dissension within the group sufficed to negate the *lonko*'s authority, with the result that segments of residential groups tended to fragment off. There was considerable physical mobility and continual population flux which operated to modify the composition of Mapuche society at the local-group level.

To a large extent there was a transfer of military-like authority to the new peacetime office of chief. Ultimately, cessation of hostilities contributed to the waning of the chief's military power, but this development was in fact delayed by the reservation system, which vested the chief with important political status in dealing with Chilean governmental agencies.

There was a carry-over of wartime sentiment manifest in pride of "race," of war exploits, of traditional cultural values, and the demonstration of a great deal of hostility and distrust against whites. Although the Chilean government kept the Mapuche under surveillance through its army and police force, the internal operation of the reservation communities was left in the hands of the Mapuche themselves. It seems that governmental agencies were not large enough or powerful enough at this time to enforce strict conformance to Chilean law throughout the extensive indigenous zone. This left great authority in the hands of the chiefs, who profited from anti-Chilean feelings among their people. The authority of the chiefs has diminished in the area of Mapuche-white relationships for a number of reasons, not least of which are the lessening of feelings of hostility toward the whites and the development of divergent economic interests among the reservation population.

When land became limited and title to it vested in the chief and hedged in by governmental restrictions, the chief controlled the basic wealth of the community. Stressful situations within the community were no longer resolved simply by one segment moving away to establish a household beyond the authority of the local leader. One may move out from the paternal roof and set up a new household within reservation limits, provided there is available land. But one does not leave the reservation, unless it is decided to relinquish land rights and, indeed, give up the Mapuche way of life.

Even in setting up a new household within the reservation, individuals were required to seek permission of the chief, and in a certain measure this is so today. However, since most reservation land is already claimed through usufruct it usually remains for an arrangement to be made within a family group (often a minimal lineage) in regard to whether or not some fields will be made available to one of the members who might want to establish a household of his own. The important thing is the total-group aspect of reservation life. Adjustments may be worked out between or within families on an *ad hoc* basis, but it is the friction between the larger segments of the population, rather than intrafamilial disputes, that is no longer resolvable by emigration.

The extension of the chief's control over a sedentary population is a result of scarce land and the reservation system. The chief receives the support of those individuals most dependent upon him and generally has the allegiance of his entire patrilineage. His authority is sanctioned, on the one hand, by the Chilean government, to the extent that it does not conflict with Chilean law, but on the other hand it is weakened by the government's more recent policy of dealing directly with individual Mapuche rather than through the agency of their chief. This is so especially in matters of crimes and torts, since the development of a larger and more efficient police force in the indigenous zone and a more sophisticated attitude on the part of the Mapuche themselves about going to court.

Chieftainship also is weakened when the original title holder dies. If the successor to leadership is a man who is ritually adept and personally liked he will continue to hold sway over the reservation group, but in the absence of these qualities and if the population is composed of several kingroups, especially if these have increased in membership, his task is difficult. This must be related to the land problem, however, to be understood. Under Chilean law, there is really no legal heir to the *título de merced*. When the original title holder dies, no change is made by registering the land in the name of his heir. Rather, the original holder is still referred to in all matters of reservation business with the governmental agencies, and Mapuche applying for settlement of land disputes or obtaining documentary evidence (most often for the purpose of establishing credit with the government) of residence state that they are of such-and-such a reservation, mentioning the original chief's name, although he might have died fifty or more years ago. The people, therefore, are legally entitled to act in their own behalf, even though in many instances they are not fully aware of their freedom or the intricacies of the law, and are generally bewildered and discouraged from acting in an individual capacity by the impersonality of Chilean legal procrastination.

In the prereservation period, whatever authority a *lonko*
might have exercised was limited, inasmuch as members of his
group could always elect to move out. This was not true in the
case of the post-reservation chiefs, whose local group not only
lacked mobility but increased in size, thereby adding to his
following. In this increase, however, lay the seeds of discord
which have come to sap the chief's power in cases where he
is unable to provide ritual leadership.

Guevara (1929:298) argued that as new households were
established on a reservation, and the number of people inhabiting
the old unilocal household decreased, the *lonko* or chief thereby
lost control over them, and his prestige and authority diminished.
Since Guevara is an accurate observer, it may be assumed that
this tendency was already apparent around the turn of the century. However, it is likely that it occurred only around Chilean
towns where acculturation proceeded more rapidly and land pressure was greater. Guevara was forecasting rather than describing
a common situation. It is true that in the long run neolocal households attain more economic independence. Notions of private
ownership of land have developed and communal agricultural
activities have declined in importance or at least frequency. While
this is the general situation today there is no evidence that such
developments took place on any appreciable scale until population pressure became sufficiently great. These developments were
not concomitant with the establishment of reservations; they characterize a mature situation. In the long range, Guevara was
correct, but to stress this long-range aspect of politico-economic
development alone is to overlook the important intermediate stage
in which chieftainship flourished. It was a shrewd forecast, but
the powers of chieftainship are only recently waning—and largely
in the area of Chilean-Mapuche relationships. Mutual antagonisms between the Chileans and the Mapuche were for a long
time deterrents to the loss of the chief's authority over his reservation group. To a certain extent this may be said to be operative
still in times of crisis.

In parts of Araucanía where there is less pressure on land and
where *división* is not a subject which is hotly contended among
the reservation population, chieftainship is noticeably stronger in

the economic sphere. Communal labor is more frequent and carried out on a larger scale. Communal land is used for grazing and gathering wood and is still under the jurisdiction of the chief. If an individual wishes to clear communal woodland for the purpose of farming it, permission has to be granted. In these matters there is an informal conclave of elders who make the decisions, but the chief is their spokesman and the official arbiter. The individual resident has a recognized right to continue his petition in the hope of swaying the leader's opinions by showing cause.

Significant modifications have taken place in Mapuche social structure since the imposition of a Chilean administrative system. Reservation social structure is qualitatively different from that of prereservation times. Before the period of peaceful reservation living, sociopolitical units fluctuated or changed in size. Since the imposition of reservation restrictions a greater population stability has come about, communities made up of unrelated kingroups have evolved, and reservation leadership has acquired political aspects over and above kinship allegiance.

Stated differently, the characteristic prereservation social unit was a kinship rather than a political group. For the most part it was a small, autonomous domestic unit. In establishing reservations the Chilean government attempted to follow this traditional social alignment. We have seen, however, that reservations were composed of dominant kingroups and one or more remnant groups of nonrelatives. This situation really approximated the Mapuche wartime organization, rather than the normally highly segmentary structure characterized by weak leadership in the hands of a *lonko*. So today's reservations continue to comprise a congeries of small communities which, in the framework of colonial administration, are essentially autonomous political groups with respect to one another.

Although the Chilean government legislates with regard to all reservations as a totality, it deals in most matters under the law with individual reservations, for example when a petition for *división* is made, or with individual persons, such as when credit is sought by the Mapuche farmer, or when the Mapuche enters into a relationship with another individual on a contractual or other legal basis. This holds, too, in the courts where torts and crimes are adjudicated.

But on the supraindividual level, each reservation has a sense of separateness, underscored by dominant kinship alignments, political organization in the hands of a chief and adult males, territorial distinction, economic resources, sponsorship of religious ceremonials, and so forth. Among these homologous units there exists relative over-all stability. Factors of cultural and political nationalism tend to integrate these otherwise independent units with respect to certain national issues, but this is outside the traditional peacetime political structure, and will be discussed later.

On the one hand there is the supreme political authority of the Chilean government. This is mediated at the local level through Indian-affairs officers, courts, and police. On the other hand there is Mapuche customary law enforced by chiefs. The chiefs mediate Chilean law on the reservations. To the extent, however, that the chief's role has been usurped by governmental action, by an effort to break up the reservations and deal individually with the Mapuche as Chilean nationals, chieftainship has been considerably curtailed.

It seems clear that the rise of chieftainship depended on the reservation system. The Chilean government was at first unable to administer the segmented Mapuche communities except through numerous agents at the local level. Relationships between Chileans and Mapuche were through the offices of chiefs and the several governmental officials at the provincial level. When the chiefs could no longer monopolize these relationships, largely owing to the growth of divergent economic interests on the reservations and a developing political awareness on the part of the ordinary Indian, their organizational authority began to slip from them. The government abetted this decline by fulfilling many of the services performed by the chiefs. For example, local government officials are entrusted with policing the reservations, building and maintaining schools, improving agriculture, encouraging industry and commerce, repairing roads and other public works, and many other things that formerly fell to the reservation Mapuche under the direction of their chiefs. The national government intentionally established a mechanism for effectively bypassing the power of chiefs. The intention is symbolized in one respect in the various "percentage" clauses in the land-allotment legislation.

Today, shorn of many former powers, the chief is still a political figure. His leadership is most apparent in times of stress —for example when some national legislative gesture threatens the existence of the reservations or when crops fail and credit is badly needed—when the people look toward him to represent them in reservation matters. Depending on his national political views—essentially on whether or not he stands for *división*— he is aligned with and backed by an Indian pressure group, of which more will be said in a moment. In most cases, he is one of the best informed and politically astute men on the reservation, for which he earns respect and a following. He is plied with political questions and consulted by the household heads. He is expected to act on the wishes of his people, but he is not always expected to do so successfully. When he fails it is recognized more fully that the chief's power is on the decline, but people nevertheless rally around their chief time and again if he continues to stand by their trust in him. There is a strong in-group feeling which bolsters the chief's authority in matters which involve the reservation group with outsiders and which is partly dependent on his ritual leadership.

In summary, then, strong chieftainship developed in a wartime situation and was reinforced under the reservation policy which followed the final pacification of the Mapuche. Mapuche leaders emerged because of their position in a lineage structure and because of their personal qualities, which included being formidable warriors, good tacticians, and knowledgeable individuals. When peace came throughout the Frontera, the chief's role as warrior ended, but he was still the most likely representative of the residential group and the logical successor to leadership. New qualities of leadership were called for, however, in time of peace. The chief had to be able to fight for his people's rights as these were defined by government legislation and the reservation system. It soon became apparent that short of open hostilities—a tactic tried on a small scale repeatedly for several decades after 1884—the chief as such was growing ineffectual as a leader in the larger political sphere. Each time the government proposed and passed new reservation legislation there was an uneasy stirring among the Mapuche, whose chiefs acted only as intermediaries and not as powerful agents on their behalf.

It was seldom the case that chiefs came off to advantage in

their dealings with colonists or the government. Rather than
negotiate advantageously, they tended to remain stubborn and
recalcitrant in their frustration. For a long generation their people
reinforced this recalcitrance, hostility, and withdrawal. Gradually,
as economic and political interests became more individualized,
the people eased away from the purely political and economic
control of their chiefs. The chief could not satisfy the several
families which comprised the reservation group if there was
a divergence in their wants, and the family heads themselves
took over a good measure of the authority formerly vested
in the chief. The government exploited this situation in its policy
of *división*. To some extent the decline in chieftainship correlates
with the development of Mapuche political pressure groups which
express themselves on the regional and national level of Chilean
political organization, and with the increasing participation of the
reservation Indians in Chilean elections.

Mapuche Pressure Groups

There are several Indian pressure groups, often referred to as
"societies," which serve Mapuche interests. The two most important of these are *Corporación Araucana* and *Unión Araucana*.
They support different sides of the controversy over the reservation system. In general, the *Corporación* holds against *división*
while the *Unión* supports it, although there are issues such as
governmental assistance in education, the Mapuche standard of
living, and so forth, which serve to unite the groups.

   Corporación Araucana was established in 1910 under the name
of *Sociedad Caupolicán* and reorganized around 1935 under its
present name. The reorganization was a response to increased
membership after the recent reservation laws which seemed to
threaten the existence of the reservations. The *Corporación* has
an official leadership and a treasury supported by contributions.

   Unión Araucana is a much smaller organization, and is strongly
influenced by the Capuchin missionaries who have headquarters
in Padre Las Casas, a barrio of Temuco. It was founded in the
late 1920's. The *Unión* stands for allotment of reservation lands
into severalty holdings, and some of its official membership are
outspoken in favor of rapid absorption of the Mapuche into
Chilean society. They see more and better education as the
best means of effecting acculturation of the Mapuche. They feel

that there should be effective government prohibition of immediate sale of severalty holdings as protection for the Indians against the whites who may try to cheat them of their newly acquired land. In long-range terms I suspect this is also the stand for the more enlightened members of the *Corporación,* the difference being—and it is quite significant—that they envision a more gradual process. They have a different timetable. The rank-and-file members, however, perhaps do not see too clearly that ultimate division of reservation land and incorporation of the Indian into Chilean society is a goal of their most informed leadership.

Corporación Araucana is interested in maintaining the present reservation system and acquiring government assistance for the betterment of the Indians. The *Corporación* argues from historical evidence that *división* means, under present conditions, a transfer of lands from Mapuche to Chilean, and points to developments in provinces contiguous to Cautín as twentieth-century examples. *Corporación Araucana* emphasizes the gradual intellectual, moral, and material uplifting of the reservation Mapuche. It suggests that when the Mapuche are able to hold their own against white landowners (date unspecified), the time for *división* will have come. The reservation system is not defended on romantic grounds but on those of common sense and expediency. Among the less politically enlightened Mapuche, however, the emphasis seems to be placed on the romantic side of the issue— a preservation of the good old days.

Both groups are vocal in the public press and through elected representatives and appointees at all levels of government. The following quotation, taken from the newspaper *La Nación* of Santiago (printed in *Boletín Indigenista,* Vol. 4, No. 3 [June 1944]:115–17) bears this out:

> Don Ovaldo Vial, Minister of the Department of Tierra y Colonización, received a telegram yesterday from the Araucana Corporation, with headquarters in Temuco, informing him that in a special meeting it was decided to congratulate him for his interest in Indian problems. The telegram went on to state that the aim of the Araucanan Indians was to change their policy and organization, to obtain representation, to reorganize their education, economy and hygiene along progressive lines.
> The telegram also stated that for the past ten years they had been

the victims of inhuman exploitation because of the present juridical
system of the Indian courts. Their present dire poverty was a result
of the authorization of expropriations and illegal sales of their lands.
In view of our impossible situation—due to the present Law governing Indian Courts, we take the liberty of informing you that
we repudiate the present legal system and believe that, since the
problem is economic and social in nature, a reform of this law
should be based upon a recognition of this fact.

In conclusion, the Araucana Corporation requested Sr. Vial to
receive their representative, Don Venancio Cunuepan, who would
report to him on the vital needs of the Indians. In this way they
hoped to enlist the Minister's aid in drawing up a new version of the
present Law which would affect two hundred thousand Indians,
making it possible for them to fulfill their two-fold ambition: work
their fields and increase the wealth of the nation.

It is common to read declarations and arguments in the
Temuco newspapers in which the major factions express themselves. The *Unión Araucana,* in addition, publishes its own official bulletin, *El Araucano,* in which its position is continually
explained and editorial attacks are made against opposition
groups.

I quote in full a short editorial blast from *El Araucano*
(August 1953:4) which I trust will serve to point up its feelings
against the major opposition groups as well as illustrate the sort
of issues abroad in Araucanía:

> Es una gran mentira la especie que anda en el campo y que, al
> parecer, es divulgada por los dirigentes de la Corporación Arau-
> cana, en el sentido que solo los socios de la mencionada Sociedad
> recibiran Créditos en la Caja Agraria de Temuco, a cuenta de los
> fondos que oportunamente se destinaran por el Supremo Gobierno
> para esa finalidad.
>
> Todos los indígenas, si, *todos los indígenas,* sean ellos partidarios
> de la Corporación Araucana o no partidarios de esta Sociedad,
> siempre que reunan las condiciónes que exigiran los respectivos
> Reglamentos de la Sección de la Caja de Crédito Agrario, recibiran
> su aporte. De esto, no dude nadie. Así debe ser y así sera.
>
> Nuestros socios, simpatizantes y todos los mapuches, en general,
> tendran en nuestra secretaria los pormenores para la consecución
> de esos créditos. En breve abriremos una Secretaria Permanente
> para atender a todos los indígenas gratuitamente. Por ahora, está
> encargado el Sr. Esperidion Antilef, en Padre Las Casas, Villa
> Alegre esquina La Paz, la atención de los socios que deseen
> créditos.

This article and the political dissension it suggests among the Mapuche came in the wake of a rumor that the Chilean government was going to make available 30,000,000 pesos (roughly 150,000 dollars in 1953) to be loaned in small amounts to Mapuche farmers. Since it is almost impossible for the Mapuche to establish private credit, this latest news fell "among the Mapuche like a shower in time of drought."

It is not to be imagined that even a large part of the reservation Mapuche are well versed in regional and national politics, although every male has some notion of the issue of *división.* As Titiev has pointed out (1951:57n), the Mapuche tend to be suspicious of politicians, many of whom they regard as interested primarily in feathering their own nests. This holds for Mapuche politicians as well, but the feeling is not quite as strong in regard to their venality and opportunism. Nevertheless, politicians are often referred to as *hombres de negocios,* an expression which suggests that they are interested in their own personal gain and are ready to be bought out.

Reservation Mapuche seem to follow local leadership in aligning themselves with or in opposing the platforms of the Indian pressure groups. The Indian political societies in turn back candidates committed to their particular views. There is then a chain of political influence from local leadership, say a chief or another respected man on a reservation, through one of the Indian societies, to one of the national political parties having a favorable Indian "plank" in its platform.

At election time there is a considerable effort made to get out the vote on the reservation. Local politicians or their backers ride out to the country and hold political rallies. They harangue the Indians, make political promises, and ask for support. Although there is universal suffrage in Chile, few women vote. This is partly because there are fewer women able to pass the literacy test, partly because few women hold identification cards (issued to all adults by the Chilean government), but primarily because political activity is considered a male concern. As more young women receive elementary-school education on the reservations, this picture will undoubtedly change.

Outside pressure is put on the males, however, and a great effort is made to get them to the polls. The various candidates for office arrange for trucks to transport the voters from the reservations to the towns. On election day, which is a national holiday, there are always trucks on the roads and many carts which will take passengers. Incidentally, there is no ban on the sale of alcohol during the voting hours, with the result that the election-day crowds throng the towns and frequent the wine and beer dispensaries looking for excitement and entertainment.

Political propaganda is distributed in the towns and at the rallies in the country. Most of the handbills pass from one individual to another and are widely disseminated on the reservations, where they are explained to the illiterate. Although illiterates cannot vote, they often hold important positions in the reservation community, being elders of the lineage. There is fairly keen interest among the young and middle-aged men. Many of the older people, if they are not too suspicious and cynical about the politicians and their promises, are very cautious in expressing favor for one candidate or another. The older Mapuche show a good deal of interest in learning who a certain Indian candidate is, that is, to whom he is related, where he lives or where he was born, and tend to form their opinion of him on the basis of what they might know about his relatives.

Allegiance to these pressure groups symbolizes a factionalism which crosscuts Mapuche society. In concluding this section, I offer the following example of factionalism at the local, reservation level. It will serve to point up something of the connection between a chief's loss of traditional political power, his new role as a member of one of the Mapuche pressure groups or political societies, and how the question of *división* affects political relationships on the reservation.

A chief in the Roble Huacho region, a younger son of the original title holder of reservation land, inherited his office from his elder brother in 1949, when the latter died. The title had passed to the older brother at the time of the father's death some thirty years before. The brother's sons were considered too young to assume the responsibility of leadership, all being under thirty at the time. These young men acknowledged this in 1949 and said that the transference of title to their uncle was *admapu,* that is, in conformance with customary law. Several factors have operated to change their position today.

At the present time these young men claim that the title to reservation land is no longer of importance to them, that they are interested only in *división*. They point out that the Chilean government does not officially recognize the transfer of chieftain-ship from the original title holder to a succession of heirs. But this is an ex post facto rationalization, also doubtless reflecting awareness of the legal aspects of the reservation system as well.

One of these young men, however, is now an active member of the *Unión Araucana,* an organization in favor of *división*. He has mustered a sufficient number of household heads to vote in favor of *división,* one-third being the minimum required. A plea for *división* was made before the *Juez de Indios* in 1951, at which time the legal machinery went into action with reference to this specific reservation. There has been the inevitable delay in such negotiations, for reasons previously stated.

The chief is opposed to *división,* since he is a large landholder and would stand to lose part of his holdings if the reservation were apportioned into severalties. In his turn, the chief has at-tempted to gain control of the family heads in opposition to *división*. However, he was not able to muster the more than two-thirds needed to invalidate the petition for *división*. Since there has been delay in dividing the reservation land, though, the less politically enlightened members who are in favor of *división* accuse the chief and his supporters of having bribed the *Juez de Indios*. These individuals were originally followers of the present chief, after his assumption of the title. They backed him because they feared the Chilean government and felt more secure under his leadership. Now they have been reoriented politically by the propaganda of the *Unión Araucana,* mediated to them through one of the most respected members of the com-munity and region. With this shift of allegiance, founded on an awareness that they could possibly acquire more land than they had at present, they withdrew their support from the chief, aligning themselves with the opposition faction. The nucleus of this faction was merely a segment of a sublineage to which the chief belonged, and of which, indeed, he is still a respected elder.

The present political split corresponds very closely to a situa-tion of haves and have-nots with respect to reservation holdings. The ones with little land back the *Unión Araucana* in its protest against the maintenance of the reservation system, although not for many of the *Unión*'s idealistic reasons. The chief, as most chiefs, is allied with conservative political elements represented by the *Corporación Araucana*. I do not suggest that these two Indian parties are characterizable solely in terms of their position in regard to the land policy of the government, although this is the aspect of their platforms which is important to the bulk of the reservation Mapuche. The have-nots, those with insufficient land, therefore, tend to align themselves against the larger land-owners and the chief, although they may be equally distrustful of the Chilean government and its elected officials.

In the context of the reservation system and reservation life in general this position with regard to land rights tends to have important repercussions in other spheres of social action. If enough family heads are in opposition to the chief on his stand with regard to *división,* his influence in the economic and political spheres of activity tends to diminish. Otherwise, the chief, while perhaps not as important a figure in the organization of agricultural and other labors as formerly, retains a great deal of prestige as a titular organizer and leader, and has very real importance with respect to religious ceremonialism, the organization of fiestas and games, and other activities having a ritual aspect.

13 THE TRADITIONAL POLITICAL SYSTEM OF THE YORUBA

Peter C. Lloyd

P. C. Lloyd is Reader in West African Studies in the University of Birmingham, England. He is the author of *Yoruba Land Law* and of many papers on the Yoruba.

M ANY TRIBAL SOCIETIES have a form of government in which the descent groups play an important part; but the position of these groups in the more highly developed kingdoms has rarely been adequately stressed. Attention has been drawn to the intricacies of the governmental structure and to the complexity of the ceremonies and ritual surrounding chieftaincy and kingship. In far less detail is it described how the members of the government are chosen to occupy their positions or what is the constitutional relationship between them. It is in the West African coastal kingdoms in particular that the system of descent groups (agnatic, uterine and cognatic) plays a vital role in the relationship between the government and the mass of the people.

In their introduction to *African Political Systems,* Evans-Pritchard and Fortes divided the societies described into two groups (1940:5–15). One group had government—centralized authority, administrative machinery, and judicial institutions—in which power corresponded with wealth and status. The framework of these societies was the administrative system; the societies described were amalgams of different peoples; their rulers controlled an organized force to uphold their authority. Such were the kingdoms of the Southern Bantu. The other set, typified by

FROM *Southwestern Journal of Anthropology* 10 (1954), 366–84, by permission of the author and of the editor, *Southwestern Journal of Anthropology.*

the Nuer and Tallensi, lacked government in the above sense; there were no sharp divisions in rank, status or wealth; the structure of unilinear descent groups or lineages was the framework of the political system. This classification clearly separates the societies in this book, but being largely descriptive rather than analytical it lacks the precision necessary to deal with societies falling between these broad groups, and particularly those of coastal West Africa, such as the Yoruba in their numerous kingdoms each with a slightly different political structure. It is often difficult to define when government begins, for the possession of centralized authority, administrative machinery, and judicial institutions can be ascribed to quite simple structures such as those of the Kabba Yoruba. The differences between the societies described in *African Political Systems* were overstressed since those writers dealing with the centralized kingdoms largely ignored the place of the lineage system in these societies, while those dealing with the simpler societies discussed little else.

Realizing the importance of the lineage system in West African societies, Dr. Paula Brown (1951) classified them according to the presence or absence of lineages, associations (such as age grades and title societies) and the state in the political structure. Four categories emerged: the societies such as the Tallensi whose political structure is based on lineage alone; those such as the Ibo which have lineages and associations; those where lineages, associations, and the state are found together as with the Yoruba and Mende; and finally those where lineages and associations play a negligible part but where the state is supreme, Ashanti, Dahomey, and Nupe being examples.[1]

Her definition of the lineage and its internal organization is conventional. In discussing the role of age grades and sets and title societies such as the Yoruba *ogboni* and Mende *poro* she filled a gap in earlier classificatory systems. But her definition of an association, "an organised and corporate group, membership in which does not follow automatically from birth or adoption into a kin or territorial unit," is applicable to the supreme council of chiefs in her state, as well as many other groups therein. The state is again not defined but described—it has administrative hierarchies, district organization, chiefs and kings with agents

[1] Dr. Brown's work is often marred by the use, unfortunately inevitable, of poor ethnographic data.

and advisers, courts at different levels in the structure, and mythical and ritual support for political supremacy. It is clear from the context that she is thinking of the well-known characteristics of West African kingdoms, but such features, if taken to their simplest level, are not confined to states but to any political unit sufficiently large for leadership not to be confined to one man. The implication is that the state has these features in greater quantity but what the quantitative limits are to be is not mentioned. Thus the two categories used—association and state—overlap, and both are wide and vague in the extreme: they provide a useful opportunity for discussing some features of different societies but they are inadequate as a basis for classification.

The feature neglected in so many of these descriptions of tribal political systems is the constitutional relationship between the various institutions and associations which comprise the system. Thus, in the case of the Yoruba kingdoms, the most important component parts of the political structure are the descent groups, with their own internal structure and organization, the various forms of age grade and set, with or without an associated grade of chiefs in charge of the sets, the title societies in which one may rise from the lowest to the highest level by payment of fees and title-taking, the councils of chiefs whose titles are often vested in individual descent groups, and kingship. In each such institution one must know how a man joins or how a man is chosen to assume a title, and on what conditions he holds the office. One must know the chain of authority in the political system by which the opinions of the people are transmitted to the government and by which the decisions of the legislators are transformed into administrative action and finally executed. One must know how far the decisions of one body are binding on others and wherein lies the ultimate power of assent or veto.

I propose to describe here four types of Yoruba political structure, stressing these features and ignoring most others. This is scarcely novel, being the method used by constitutional lawyers for centuries. The conclusions reached, being from a limited range of societies, will not lead immediately to a new classification of political systems; wider comparison is essential. The method, however, may be of value.

Writers on the Yoruba have often caused confusion by their
unawareness that the various sub-tribes have widely differing
political constitutions. In the absence of good studies of any
one sub-tribe, they have tended to produce a composite system,
comprising elements from different sub-tribes which are not found
together in practice. This is an easy error: the same symbols of
office are used by men whose offices are constitutionally different.
A common set of titles is found in almost all sub-tribes, Oyo
being the principal exception.[2] The term *iwarɛfa* is applied in
Kabba to the chiefs of the *oʃugbo* society. The same cultural
traits appear as the embellishments of widely differing constitutions.

This study is of the traditional political structure, not of its
modern forms.[3] This involves one in reconstruction of institutions now far decayed. Decay has gone farthest in the various
title societies. The age grade system which provided warriors
proved useless to wage the nineteenth century tribal wars. The
title societies were usually ignored by early British administrators
who did not recognize their political importance. Deprived of
a place in the constitution, they became mere social institutions
which most Christians refused to join because of the ritual of
the admission ceremonies, and Muslims outlawed because of the
Koranic injunction against joining secret societies. Conversely,
virility has been maintained in those institutions still exercising
control of government and of land.

The Kabba Yoruba or Owe

The Yoruba of Kabba Province are in the extreme northeast
of Yoruba country. They were composed of several small and
independent sub-tribes, between which there were fewer differences in culture than between the group as a whole and
neighboring sub-tribes. Kabba town is now the Divisional headquarters and is peopled by the Owe sub-tribe whose constitution is outlined here. The population (1952) of the Kabba
District, which is the modern administrative unit embracing the
Owe people, is 15,000; the population of Kabba town is 7,300.

The legends of the Owe people tell that their founder came
from Ile-Ife, the cradle of the Yoruba, though, unlike other

[2] Examples of these common titles are *aro, osa, ɛjɛmu, ɔdɔfin,* etc.
[3] I.e. of the political structure of the mid-nineteenth century.

Yoruba, they do not seem to embellish this statement with explanations of how and why he migrated. This man had three sons who founded the adjacent towns of Kabba, Dolu, and Katu. Kabba is now much larger than the other two towns, having been used by both the Nupe invaders of the nineteenth century and the British as their headquarters. The founder of Kabba had three sons, the descendants of each of whom divided into two groups, so that there were six agnatic descent groups in the town, each of which lived in territorially adjacent compounds and possessed distinctive lineage names. These three towns remained the main settlements of the Owe people, and although some built homesteads and small villages at their farms these had no administrative significance and people remained for political purposes members of their own town and lineage.[4]

At the head of each lineage was the *olori ɛbi* or eldest man. Regular meetings of lineage members are said to have been held, at which matters affecting lineage members and their disputes, the organization of the compound and the control of farm land were discussed. Each extended family—a group of persons descended from a man recently deceased and probably living around one courtyard of a compound—also had its *olori ɛbi*. It was suggested that all these *olori ɛbi* met together at regular intervals, although it was not clear what they discussed and whether their field of jurisdiction differed markedly from that of the title grades. In any case most *olori ɛbi* appear to have been members of one of the three senior grades.

The grades through which a man passed to reach the senior titles began as untitled age grades associated with a youth's economic status. The first grade was known as *olusele*. Boys entered at the age when they began to work on their father's farm. At the annual admission ceremony new entrants accompanied the already initiated to the bush, where the new entrants shared bananas among his seniors. The boys flogged each other with lighted torches of grass and then danced through the town to the senior chief. The second grade was entered when a boy reached puberty (or when he was of marriageable age, opinions now differ). Previously he had worked entirely on his father's farm. Now he was ready to start his own small farm on which

---

[4] I use the term lineage for convenience; it differs slightly from the lineage in other Yoruba towns.

he would work half the week in order to feed himself. Entry into this grade consisted solely of the entrant being accompanied by three or four kinsmen from the grade, and asking his father for a full-sized hoe. It would appear that all young men passed into these two grades on reaching the necessary age.

The first title grade was known as *igɛmɔ*. On reaching this a man no longer worked on his father's farm. The would-be entrant went first to the three members of the senior title grade to notify them of his wish to enter the grade, and to pay a fee. He also named his title, there being no fixed titles. Later, after another fee, the senior chiefs conferred the title and the existing members of the grade laid their *ɔpa* staffs on the ground, made a sacrifice and prayed for the new entrant. Throughout the week the new member feasted the older members of the grade. Membership of this grade conferred the right to use the *ɔpa* staff and also a red cap. The number of *igɛmɔ* titles were unlimited and although it is said that some men never became members, it was believed that most adult men did in fact take titles.

Entry into the next grade—the *orota* grade—was by a similar process, the fees being approximately double those of the *igɛmɔ* grade. Membership gave the titleholder the right to use a special stool (*apopo*), to wear a beaded hat and beads round the neck, to have a much more ceremonious funeral than other men, and to be relieved from farm work. There was a fixed number of *orota* titles and a man could only take one after the death of a previous holder. The traditional ranking order of these titleholders is now uncertain, but it was probably determined by the length of time the title had been held.

The senior grade is that of *ololu* (sometimes known as *iwarɛfa*). Among the Owe there were three titles in this grade, *ɔbaro, ɔbajɛmu,* and *ɔbadɔfin.* The Nupe invaders made the Obaro of the mid-nineteenth century into a district head over all the Owe under their own system of indirect rule. Later the British continued the process, trying at one period to make him Emir of all Kabba Division! From the Owe legends and from examination of the neighboring sub-tribes, whose senior grades were less affected by these changes, the traditional (in this case pre-Nupe) custom appears to have been as follows. The three titles were of equal status; one had to be held in each of the three Owe towns, though not necessarily the same one each time; the titleholders were elected to the position by the members of the *orota* grade, heavy fees being paid by the candidates to the electors. The *ololu* chief could wear coral beads on his wrist and ankles and sit on a leopardskin. His installation consisted of small ceremonies and feasting, though not giving him the same ritual position and authority as those of a Yoruba king.

The government of the Owe was conducted by the *ololu,* who, it is said, could do nothing except on the advice of the *orota,* who in turn were advised by the mass of adult men— the *igɛmɔ.* The *igɛmɔ* held separate meetings from those of the *ololu* and *orota.* Each grade of titleholder had special ritual duties in connection with the town's major deity, Ebora. The functions of government appear to have been but crudely divided between the different groups of titleholders; the *ololu* and *orota* made the decisions, the *igɛmɔ* executed them.

Although wealth appears as the prerequisite of membership of the higher title grades, it must be remembered that Kabba was, and still is, economically backward; slave-owning was rare and the people were more raided than raiders. Opportunities for the accumulation of wealth were limited to hard work and the possession of sons. There does not appear to have been any restriction of title-holding to a small semi-hereditary group.

The Ekiti

The sixteen Ekiti kingdoms are located in the east of Yoruba country. Ado is the largest, with a population (1952) of 62,000 persons. Ado Ekiti, the metropolitan town of this kingdom and now the Divisional headquarters, has a population of 24,000 persons, but the town consists of three adjacent settlements each with its own chief but acknowledging a common ruler, the Ewi. The largest of these settlements, Oke Ewi, the seat of the Ewi with a population of 14,000 people, is described here as an example of the Ekiti type of political structure.

The Ewi traces his descent from a royal prince at Ile Ife, who, it is claimed, left this town and travelled to Benin with the Oba of Benin, only to leave him later and retrace his steps. At Ado he and his followers met some people, but these either submitted peacefully or were conquered and their descen-

dants form one agnatic descent group in Odo Ado, the large
settlement adjacent to Oke Ewi. Today there are fifteen patrilineages in Oke Ewi besides that of the Ewi himself; the elders
of some of these claim that their founders travelled with the
Ewi, those of others cite the towns, usually in Akoko country,
from which their founders came. Oke Ewi is divided into five
quarters, one of which, Irona, is of more recent creation than
the remainder. Each quarter has the compounds of one or two
large lineages together with those of two or three smaller ones.
Compounds of segments of the royal lineage are found in each
quarter.

As in other Yoruba towns, the male members of the lineage
lived in a single, or adjacent, compounds. The lineage head
(*olori ɛbi*) was the oldest male lineage member; he succeeded
to his position without ceremony on the death of the previous
holder. He presided over the lineage meetings held in his own
part of the compound, at which matters affecting the lineage
were discussed. The lineage was a gerontocratic institution: disrespect to an elder was punishable by a fine of palm wine or
kola nuts to be consumed at the meeting. The lineage head had,
however, little more than moral authority over his members.

In Ekiti every man belonged to an age set (*ɛgbɛ*); these had
primarily social functions. They were constituted informally every
two and a half to three years when the boys concerned reached
the age of nine or ten years. Thus brothers (unless twins) could
not be in the same *ɛgbɛ*. Each set received a name from the
Ewi, usually denoting some historic event. It had an acknowledged leader who achieved this position by his personality and
not by formal appointment. At weekly meetings the members
discussed the town's affairs and their personal problems. Moral
pressure was put on those who offended against social codes.
Members of an age set helped each other at farm work and in
performing obligations to a future father-in-law.

The *otu* are a series of grades through which a man passes
from childhood to elderhood. In Oke Ewi they were named
ejiwere for young children, followed by *oriʃu, ipaiye* or *origbo,
ɛgiri* or *eʃe,* and *igbamɔ agbakin* or *ijogun.* At the age of forty-
five years a man became an elder, *agba ilu.* The grades each
had an age span of nine years. It would appear that there were
no admission ceremonies for the first two grades. To subsequent

ones the entrant provided a feast for existing members; more complex ceremonies are not remembered. Passage from one grade to another was an individual affair, but it was not suggested that men ever failed to rise according to their age. The grade marked the economic status of a man from the time he started to work on his father's farm to the time when he was fully independent of his father. It also determined the public work expected from him. Youths in the second grade were strong enough only for weeding; in the third grade they could do road-making; in the fourth and fifth grades a man was available for war. An elder was relieved of public work. Age grade members also cleared shrines and collected food to be used at festivals. In some towns it was explicitly stated that a man might not take a chieftaincy title until he had become an elder. Oke Ewi has a series of titled chiefs known as ɛlɛgbɛ whose duties must have been related to the ɛgbɛ, though exactly how is not clear, since the age grade system is now almost lost and many ɛlɛgbɛ titles vacant. It is said that each lineage and often segments within a lineage had its own ɛlɛgbɛ. The nine senior ɛlɛgbɛ were selected from any lineage by the Ewi and chiefs, although two of the titles were reserved for members of the royal lineage. The duties of the ɛlɛgbɛ were to organize public work in the town, to organize the warriors at war and in defence of the town, to carry out other commands of the senior chiefs, and to voice the opinions of the young men of the town. There was in Ado a further company of young men known as ɛfa whose duties were the policing of the town; men were enrolled from any lineage.

The senior chieftaincy titles of Oke Ewi were divided into three groups, the chiefs of the two senior groups being known as *ihare* and of the junior group as *ijoye*. The first group of *ihare* comprised the *olori marun,* the five senior chiefs. The second group comprised five ɛlɛsi and, ranked below them, the *ijɛgbɛ* chiefs. All these titles were ranked in order of seniority. Four of the members of the *olori marun* were the quarter chiefs of the four older quarters of the town; the fifth resided, by historical accident rather than by design, in one of these quarters. These titles were hereditary in the largest lineages in the town. Many of the ɛlɛsi and *ijɛgbɛ* titles were hereditary in certain lineages, the remainder being bestowed by the Ewi and chiefs on any person who was prominent in the town and also popular within his own lineage, although attempts were continually being made by holders to convert them into hereditary titles. The *ijoye* chiefs were headed by a chief whose title was hereditary in one lineage; the remaining chiefs were elected by the Ewi and chiefs, or sometimes directly by the quarter chiefs. An examination of the distribution of titles in Ekiti towns shows that where the town had a small number of lineages each had one of the senior *ihare* titles; where there were more lineages, the largest obtain these *ihare* titles but the remaining titles were shared equitably among the lineages.

When the title of a chief was hereditary within a lineage, it was usually the right of the lineage members to elect the holder. When the funeral ceremonies were completed, the Ewi sent to the lineage head inviting him to present a candidate. Such a man was elected at a lineage meeting, the predictions of the Ifa oracle being used to sway opinions and give the choice supernatural sanction. The principle that each segment of the lineage should hold the title in turn was often overlooked when one candidate received the support of the majority. The Ewi and chiefs had no right to interfere in the election except to ensure that the proper methods were carried out—a large enough loophole for intrigue. If the lineage members failed to agree upon a candidate, the Ewi and chiefs might appoint one themselves. The Ewi had the right to appoint three of the hereditary chiefs, one from each group, who by tradition had free access to his own apartments in the palace. No *ihare* or *ijoye* chief might lay down one title to take another more senior one, but εlεgbε chiefs might drop their titles to assume *ihare* or *ijoye* titles. When the candidate for the title was presented to the Ewi and chiefs for their formal approval, he would commence making a series of payments to the Ewi and chiefs. The installation ceremonies of all *ihare* chiefs were performed by the Ewi; they included much feasting of the existing chiefs.

The Yoruba king (ɔba) was more than a chief; he was a divine king and the personification of the whole town. A crowned king traced his descent directly from Oduduwa, the creator of the Yoruba. The title of Ewi was hereditary in two segments of the ruling lineage founded by the first Ewi, the founder of Ado. These two segments were founded by the sixteenth Ewi, who is said to have reigned in the late eighteenth century. Members of segments tracing descent from earlier Ewis were not eligible. On the death of the Ewi the most senior *ihare* acted as regent but did not sit in the palace; a woman of the royal lineage sat within the palace to control palace affairs alone. This regent invited the head of the royal lineage to present his candidates. The title rotated strictly from one segment to the other; in Ado the candidate had, in addition, to have been born while his father was on the throne, but this rule was not followed in all towns. The *ihare* chiefs discussed the merits of each man, sounded the opinions of the young men through the ɛlɛgbɛ and consulted the Ifa oracle. The ultimate responsibility for electing a new king rested with the *ihare;* members of the royal lineage could not overrule their choice. The installation of the Ewi, a most complex set of ceremonies, was performed by the chiefs. Whereas a chief promised at his installation to obey his king and accept the advice of his lineage members, the new king promised to rule well, acting on the advice of his chiefs. Ewi and chiefs held office for life; they could be removed only by being asked by those who elected them to take poison and die. This was of very rare occurrence in Ekiti.

Members of the ruling lineage (known as ɔmɔ ɔba) had no rights to any *ihare* or *ijoye* titles; they were eligible for certain ɛlɛgbɛ titles however. Some princes had been sent out of Ado to rule over farm settlements; these took a title from the settlement which became vested in the lineage which they founded in the settlement. These titles gave no status in Oke Ewi itself.

In the Ekiti town, meetings of chiefs and people took place at almost every level of the political structure. Opinions expressed in lineage meetings were conveyed by the lineage head to the chief within the lineage. (In the lineage meeting a titled chief ranked according to his age; his position as a chief conveyed authority in town affairs only and not in purely lineage matters.) The young men expressed their views in the age set and age grade company meetings and these were taken to the chiefs by the ɛlɛgbɛ. Each quarter chief held regular meetings at which all the chiefs of his own quarter attended. Each group of chiefs met separately as well as at a large meeting at which the *ihare* spoke. The Ewi remained in seclusion within the palace, receiving the conclusions of his senior *ihare* arrived at on the outer verandah of his palace, and announcing them as his own decisions. These decisions, with royal authority, were then reported to the εlεgbε and the lineage heads, together with instructions for the action to be taken. The senior *ihare* remained in the palace most of the day, their duties being wholly conciliar.

The authority of the Ewi and his councils of chiefs extended to all affairs and included the administration of the town, the appointment of chiefs, war and tribute, the arranging of the major town festivals, and the judgment in the first instance of major crimes and the appeal of minor cases. There appear to have been no special meetings reserved for discussion of any one of these matters.

The Oyo

Ibadan Province is located across the geographical center of Yoruba country and contains many large towns; here over fifty percent of the population lives in towns whose population exceeds 50,000 inhabitants. This great size is due largely to the wars of the early nineteenth century, when the Oyo Empire began to crumble through internal strife and the Fulani invaders, based on Ilorin and Bida, attacked southward. The Yoruba were safe only in the forested country where the Fulani cavalry could not operate, and the inhabitants of the destroyed towns of the savanna country fled to these towns within the forest. The armies of these towns were themselves continually on slave-raiding expeditions, living off the countryside which also became depopulated, the people of the smaller towns fleeing to the larger towns for protection. The size and rate of this immigration posed new problems for the government of these towns.

Iwo, one of these towns, has (1952) a population of 100,000 inhabitants. These are domiciled within an area of two square miles; an urban density of eighty persons per acre. There are over 500 compounds in the town, belonging to approximately 200 patrilineages. The town is divided into four quarters. In one of these, Isale Oba, are found most of the compounds of the royal lineage; in Gidigbo and Oke Adan are the compounds of most of the older lineages in the town. Molete is a quarter largely peopled by those whose ancestors came to the town in the nineteenth century.

Iwo was founded by a man who was, it is claimed, a son of a woman Oni of Ife; he was driven from Ile-Ife after his mother's death in retaliation for her harshness as a ruler. He settled in several places before reaching the present site and legends say that he had collected a considerable entourage before reaching Iwo. Later immigrants came from towns in the Owu kingdom, from towns now destroyed and almost forgotten but which may have been either Owu or Egba, and, in increasing proportion in the late eighteenth and nineteenth centuries, from Oyo.

The Yoruba lineage was headed by the *bale* (father of the house), its oldest male member. Formal lineage meetings (*ipade*) seem to have been held at irregular intervals, so many lineage members living for much of the year on their farms. Ceremonies and religious festivals provided occasions for the meetings, however. As a result of the large size of many compounds, the Iwo *bale* and several other old men were usually able to remain at home, being fed and maintained by contributions from junior members. These men, sitting together on the verandah of the *bale*'s compound, composed, as it were, a permanent committee of the lineage. The powers and duties of the Iwo *bale* are similar to those of lineage heads elsewhere in Yoruba country.

There are no formal age grades today in Iwo, and little record of their past existence can be found. The modern ɛgbɛ are social clubs with functions similar to those of Ekiti and Ijebu but membership is not automatic; one joins an ɛgbɛ of one's choice, age (within broad limits) and wealth being determining factors. Public work in the town was, however, carried out by the young men, but it was organized through the compounds. Instructions would be given to each *bale* to provide a certain number of young men to work. The chiefs supervised the work. The young men of each compound informally recognized one of their number as a leader, *olori ɔmɔle,* a position held until the man became accepted regularly into the meetings of the lineage elders at about the age of forty-five years. There were no initiations into grades, no regular meetings of members of the same grade, and no chiefs responsible solely for such age grades.

The *Ogboni* society exists today in Iwo, but its membership is very small and no old men could remember that it ever formed a constitutional part of the government of the town, as in Ijebu. The society has been attacked by Muslims and the Oluwos of Iwo have successively been staunch Muslims since the mid-nineteenth century. Within Iwo it was said that men from lineages

founded by Owu migrants "knew most about *ogboni*." (The senior
civil chiefs, Osa and Aro, are such men and their titles are said
to be *ogboni* titles in other sub-tribes, though they are lineage
titles in Ekiti.)

In Iwo the chiefs were divided (as in Ibadan, from which the
structure may have been copied) into two groups, the civil chiefs
and the war chiefs. In each group the chiefs were ranked in
order of seniority of their title. Almost all these titles were
hereditary in a single lineage, the legends stating that it was
bestowed upon the immigrant lineage founder to "compensate him
for his lost rights in his town of origin." Whereas in all towns
it was held that since the title was bestowed by a king he might
also take it away, Iwo is the only town described here where this
does appear to have happened, and informants cite two nineteenth century cases where a title was cancelled when the holder
had rebelled against the Oluwo.

The method of appointment of the chiefs, whose titles were
hereditary within the lineage, did not differ from that of Ekiti
and will not be repeated here.

The title of the Oluwo, of king of Iwo, was hereditary within
the royal lineage. This lineage is not now segmented in the usual
manner. The twelfth Oluwo, Lamuye, came to the throne c. 1830
and reigned until 1906, during which time Iwo became a powerful town and many of the trophies of war, including newly conquered land, were bestowed upon the sons of Lamuye. After his
death five of his sons succeeded to the throne and it was considered that the title would henceforth be held only by the
descendants of Lamuye. In 1952, however, when the title became vacant, the descendants of Lamuye could not agree among
themselves, and the title went to the descendants of the Oluwo
reigning before Lamuye.[5] The appointment of an Oluwo followed the usual procedure for kingship; the senior town chief
would invite the head of the royal lineage to present candidates
when the chiefs in council would then debate these and make
their selection.

The position of the royal lineage in Iwo appears to be unique.
As in other Yoruba towns the members of this lineage were
known as ɔmɔ ɔba; while some of them obtained titles, this

---

[5] It is no longer remembered how the title was inherited before the reign
of Lamuye.

gave them no position in the government of the town, and in Ekiti and Ijebu neither the members of the lineage nor even the close relatives of the king seem to have exercised authority, either informal or constitutional, in their towns. In Iwo there were two sets of royal titles bestowed by the Oluwo. In the first group all the titles belonged to members of the royal lineage. The most senior titles now belong to the sons of Lamuye. Other titles have been given to prominent men of segments descended from the early Oluwo. These titles, held for life and not hereditary, were distributed by the Oluwo on the advice of the senior title-holders in the group. Royal titles of the second group were granted to immigrants who came to the town in the nineteenth century and who put themselves under the protection of the Oluwo, their leader receiving a daughter of the Oluwo as a wife. This group was headed by Oloya whose lineage, it is said in the legends, was founded by the son of the daughter of the first Oluwo. Most of these titles were vested in the lineage of the first holder of the title, and the appointment of new holders was made in a similar manner to that of the hereditary town chiefs.

Only a small number of the lineages in Iwo were able to have hereditary chieftaincy titles vested in them. In the remainder the *bale* was the only official. The *bale* was usually responsible to the chief in charge of his quarter, that is to the senior civil or war chief in Gidigbo or Oke Adan, to Oloya in Molete, and to the Oluwo or the senior royal titleholder in Isale Oba. The remaining chiefs had no official territorial jurisdiction though they may have considered themselves in charge of the compounds neighboring their own. Ties of patronage had, however, often developed between chiefs and individual lineages; these were usually formed in the nineteenth century when refugees put themselves under the protection of individual chiefs in the town. The patron's lineage founder was perhaps from the same town as the refugees; often the patron gave land to them. The Oluwo was the largest patron, giving out land conquered in the early nineteenth century to these newcomers; other members of the royal lineage who were given control of this land also became powerful in this way. Members of these protected lineages paid tribute through their patron and went to war with him, in the same manner as members of his own lineage. Titled chiefs were elected solely by their lineage members; members of related lineages or lineages bound by ties of patronage had no rights to participate in the election. Thus the chiefs of Iwo were elected by a minority of the townspeople.

The government of Iwo rested with the town chiefs; they met daily on the outer verandah of the palace, carrying their decisions to the Oluwo. Inside the palace the Oluwo sat surrounded by the royal chiefs of both groups, also discussing the town affairs. These had no official place in the constitution but because of the close relationship of some with the Oluwo and the large numbers of people represented by them all, their opinions carried much weight so that the Oluwo could often overrule his town chiefs' decisions. With the backing of his personal followers the Oluwo was able to set the town chiefs against each other, so that instead of forming a block united against him they would come individually to him secretly to beg for favors. From the time of Lamuye at least, and possibly as a result of Muslim influence, the Oluwo was not an unknown person hidden in the palace but a man regularly seen by his chiefs and people.

The Ijebu

As a fourth example of a Yoruba political constitution, that of the Ijebu might be cited. In contrast with that of Iwo just described the government of Ijebu Ode, the metropolitan town, is perhaps the most complex in all Yoruba country. The reconstruction of the traditional system is particularly difficult since not only have many of the traditional institutions been given no place in the modern local government, with the result that most titles are vacant, but as a consequence of trading activities the Ijebu have become by far the wealthiest sub-tribe, with the inevitable weakening of traditional social ties.

Ijebu Ode is probably one of the oldest of Yoruba towns. Today it has a population of 26,000, considerably larger than that of any neighboring settlements;[6] it was a capital town surrounded by many smaller satellite towns. Legends say that modern Ijebu Ode was founded by Obanta, the first Awujale or king. It is claimed that he came from Ile-Ife but it seems possible that he came in fact from Benin. Almost all the lineage elders in Ijebu

---

[6] Ago Iwoye and Ijebu Igbo, now large towns, were both formed when small settlements near the Ibadan border were obliged to come together for protection.

Ode claim that their ancestors came either before Obanta or with him; the land was apparently distributed among the indigenous people before he came, and there appear to have been many kings whom Obanta displaced. Since Obanta fifty Awujales have reigned; Obanta probably reigned between the thirteenth and fifteenth centuries. It is claimed that since his reign the kingdom was never destroyed, and contact with neighboring kingdoms seems to have been slight. It is said that in the nineteenth century no stranger could ever sleep in Ijebu Ode and leave it alive.

Ijebu Ode is today divided into twenty-five quarters. Legends are told that the people of a quarter are descended through both males and females from a man who came before or with Obanta. Sometimes two or more such groups of people live within one quarter. Each quarter (*itun*) was headed by an *oloritun;* he was usually the oldest man in the quarter although men who were too senile were sometimes passed over. In some cases the title passed from the oldest man in one part of the quarter to the oldest in another. The *oloritun* held meetings within their own compounds of all adult men in their quarter; their authority and jurisdiction seem to have been very similar to that of lineage heads in other Yoruba towns. Recruitment to the cognatic descent groups of the Ijebu differs from that to the lineages of other Yoruba. A man (or woman) belongs in theory to as many groups as he can trace ancestors. In practice he acknowledges membership of only a few groups—usually those associated with the land on which he lives and farms, and those with which his parents were closely associated. These cognatic descent groups exercise many of the functions of the lineage, including land holding.

Every Ijebu man belonged to an age set; these were constituted at three year intervals when youths reached the age of fifteen to eighteen years. The set was given a name by the Awujale which it retained forever. The members of sets met regularly for social purposes in a manner similar to the εgbε in other Yoruba towns. There were no formally constituted grades as in Ekiti. The members of these age sets were collectively known as the *ipampa*. As in other towns the organization of the young men is difficult to reconstruct. Ijebu Ode was divided into three parts in each of which was a titled chief responsible for the organization of the *ipampa* in his own area. These chiefs today claim that their titles have always been hereditary within one or two lineages and that

the holder is elected by the members of his descent group with
the acquiescence of the *ipampa* members.

The *Ogboni* society, known in Ijebu as *oʃugbo,* was an important institution of government. It is said that in the old days
almost every man joined. Entry was by a series of fees fixed by
the existing members in relation to the wealth of the candidate.
There seems to have been no barrier to entry except that a man
of bad character would have been refused admission. Entry could
be at an early age, for there were grades within the society for
young men; a man could join before his father died but he could
not rise above his father. One grade appears to have been reserved for men whose fathers were dead. One rose through the
grades by paying fees which entitled one to be initiated into the
more secret rituals. The *oʃugbo* were headed by the Oliwo, followed by the six *iwarɛfa* chiefs; Apena was the messenger. Only
Oliwo and Apena were known outside the society; the identity of
the *iwarɛfa* was known only to members. The *iwarɛfa* were
elected by the *oʃugbo* members and the Oliwo was succeeded by
the senior *iwarɛfa.* The Awujale, whose authority was necessary
to found an *oʃugbo* branch, was himself a member of the
oʃugbo, holding the title Olurin, but he rarely took his seat, a
slave deputising for him.

The palace organization of the Awujale was highly complex,
reminiscent more of Benin than of a Yoruba town. Slaves were
organized into nearly twenty groups, each with their specific
functions. Included among these was a title society open to
freeborn Ijebu known as the *ifɔrɛ* society. This society had
several grades—*ɔlɔgben,* junior *ɔlɔwa,* senior *ɔlɔwa,* and *otu*—
and was headed by Olotu Ifore. Any man might join if he
could afford the fees. He indicated his desires to one of the
palace slaves, who informed the Awujale, who gave permission
for the title to be taken. Subsequent ceremonies were performed
in the palace.

Each descent group in Ijebu Ode appears to have had its
own elected titled chief but these were only for performing
group rituals and carried no political office. In fact if such a
chief obtained a political title he had to relinquish his priestly
title. Exceptions to this were the Olisa title which was the senior
title in the town below the Awujale, it being said that Olisa
ruled the town while the Awujale ruled the kingdom. Ranked

below Olisa was Egbo. The founder of Egbo's descent group
is said to have come from a Benin town in the time of the
tenth Awujale and to have held the title from that time. Both
these titles were hereditary within the group.

Other important titles were the senior slave, Ogbeni Odi, and
Ogbeni Oja, a title filled alternately from among the senior
slaves and the *otu* grade of the *iʃɔrɛ* society.

The title of Awujale was hereditary in the male line within
the royal descent group. This group now has four segments,
each tracing its descent to an Awujale who is believed to have
lived in the late eighteenth century. The new Awujale must have
been born to a previous Awujale while he was actually reigning.
On the death of an Awujale the slaves (*odi*) were responsible
for most of the ritual; they also presented the new candidates
to the town chiefs for their final selection.

There were no special titles reserved for members of the
royal descent group and it is uncertain how far they participated
in membership of the title societies. They certainly belonged to
the age sets. Children of an Awujale were often sent to rule
subordinate towns, where they held the title Otunba, it being
thereafter vested in the descent group founded by them.

Government of the town was a combination of all these institutions. The highest authority, before the Awujale, was the
ilamuren society, comprising the Olisa, Egbo, Ogbeni Oja, and
the members of the *iʃɔrɛ* society. All members of this society
had to be members of the *oʃugbo* society, though ineligible for
senior titled posts in it. Similarly a new Olisa, Egbo, or Ogbeni
Oja had to advance through all grades of the *iʃɔrɛ* society to the
rank of *otu*.

To sum up: the *oloritun* had authority within their own
quarters; it is said that they used to meet together although
the functions of such meetings are not clear. Each age set met
separately and then together under their own chief to discuss
matters affecting individual members and the organization of
public work. The *oʃugbo* society met regularly every seventeen
days in their own meeting place: here the affairs of the town were
discussed and cases involving the more serious crimes were
heard, such cases going on appeal to the *ilamuren* society. The
ilamuren society met in the palace. Their decisions were carried

by a slave to the Awujale, secluded within the palace, who gave them his assent.

The villages around Ijebu Ode had a more simple constitution. In many cases the people of a village claimed descent from a single founder and the segments of this descent group formed the quarters of the village. The title of the senior chief in the village (*olori ilu*) together with those of his second, third, fourth and fifth in command (ɛkeji ilu, ɛkɛta ilu, ɛkɛrin ilu, ɛkarun ilu) passed in turn to each segment, each titleholder moving up a post on the death of the *olori ilu*. The villages possessed their own *oʃugbo* societies complete with all grades and an *ipampa* society, often with chiefs elected by the members. These societies were subordinate to those in Ijebu Ode. The villages had no title society such as the *ifɔrɛ* society and no *ilamuren* society. Village heads referred matters to members of the *ilamuren* society in Ijebu Ode.

Summary

The description of the constitutions of the four Yoruba towns has been made with a limited purpose in view—that of outlining the different political institutions and their constitutional powers, their membership and the part played by the lineage. Omitted have been the rituals and ceremonials surrounding kingship and chieftaincy, the part played by religion, details of the methods of administration, and the strains which are produced in the everyday working of the constitutions. Of the four diverse constitutions outlined, that of the Owe is unique in lacking kingship; these people have little knowledge of their own history or of the antiquity of their institutions. The oldest of the constitutions is that of Ijebu Ode in the sense that the town was founded before the arrival of the present dynasty several centuries ago, and that no catastrophic event since then would appear to have happened to overthrow the original constitution. The youngest is the constitution of Iwo, for the town itself was founded probably in the sixteenth or seventeenth centuries and the flood of immigrants in the nineteenth century must have produced many changes in the government of the town.

In each town the descent group was a gerontocratic institution with a large membership, the adult males having a common residence. All matters affecting descent group members only were decided ultimately by the group's head (though appeal to the town government might be made). Since the descent group of members corporately held farm land and town land, and since male members of a patrilineage often plied a common craft, matters discussed at meetings covered an extremely wide range. The authority of the head of the descent group was mainly moral; he was nearly always believed to be very much older than the remaining elders and hence to be able to approach more effectively the ancestors and deities.

Each of the towns had a government responsible for the external relations of the towns including the declaration of war, for the maintenance of law and order, including police work, and the administration of justice, for the control of rituals affecting the whole town, and for a variety of social and economic matters such as fixing the times of harvest or bush burning. In none of the towns did the government consist of a committee of the heads of the descent groups, and these men did not have authority, by virtue of their position, outside the group: always the government consisted of a separate set of institutions standing apart from the group. These institutions have been grouped as associations, lineage chieftaincies, and kingship.

Title grades and societies were most prominent in Kabba, Ekiti, and Ijebu. They might be divided into age set and grade systems, by which young men formally expressed their opinions and were organized for public work, and the title societies. In Iwo there were no such political institutions and public work seems to have been organized through the lineage. Membership of an age set was automatic and hence universal. There seems to have been no suggestion in either Kabba or Ijebu that membership of the title societies—the title grades of the Owe or the *iʃɔrɛ* society or the *oʃugbo* society of Ijebu Ode—became restricted to any small hereditary section of the community; instead it is suggested that most men joined the *igɛmɔ* grade in Kabba or the *oʃugbo* society in Ijebu. In both these the appointments to the highest posts were by election by the members, although wealth to perform the necessary ceremonies was a prerequisite of the successful candidate.

In Ekiti and Iwo government was carried out mainly by chiefs whose titles were vested within certain lineages. Such hereditary titles were filled by election by the lineage members, the king and remaining chiefs having no power to overrule the decision of the lineage members except on technical grounds. In Ekiti it is noticeable that every lineage was represented by at least one chief, usually elected by his lineage but in some instances appointed by the king in council. In Iwo the size of the town alone would have made such a system unworkable; here the lineage heads were responsible to chiefs, the tie being one of patronage.

The institution of kingship was remarkably similar in the three towns possessing it. In each case the title was hereditary within the descent group of the founder or conqueror of the town; in each it was the town chiefs—the lineage chiefs or the heads of the title societies—who had the ultimate control of the election of the king. In Ekiti and Ijebu, where the king was a figure hidden from view and, in theory, exercising little power of his own, the remaining members of the royal descent group occupied little or no constitutional position in the town; they were debarred from holding most titles. Iwo was completely atypical in this respect, the history of the early and mid-nineteenth century probably being responsible. The king became a war leader and, being a Muslim, hastened the decay of many of the traditional rituals; the rewards of battle, and especially land, bestowed upon his closest kinsmen and followers gave them, through patronage, a physical power which more than balanced the constitutional power of the chiefs from the non-royal lineages. This process was accentuated by the long reign of Lamuye and the consequent accession of five of his own sons: the checks to power which in other towns were achieved by rotating the title through a number of lineage segments did not operate.

If we were to group these four types according to the classification adopted by Dr. Brown (1951), the Owe of Kabba would probably fall, with the Ibo, into that group having lineages and associations only, while Iwo, having no associations, could be grouped with Ashanti and Nupe. Ijebu and Ekiti, having descent groups, associations, and state forms, would be in the third group, in which Dr. Brown did in fact place the Yoruba. Yet the features of the state in Ijebu Ode are far more complex than in Iwo. If this classification does not grade the political systems according to complexity, it does grade them according to their probable historical evolution, for the Kabba type is presumably the oldest and that of Iwo has undergone great changes within the last two centuries.

The brief descriptions of the four Yoruba constitutions given here suggests other criteria which may be useful in grouping such kingdoms and which increase our knowledge of them. A similarity between all four political systems is the election of the rulers—the *ololu* of Kabba and the ɔba of the Yoruba kingdoms —by a subordinate group of titled chiefs. The *ololu* and the ɔba were both responsible for the ritual of the town and both were the mouthpieces for official decisions, although the former, lacking the divinity of the latter, probably took a more active part in the government of the town. The election of the king is one of the major features of the constitutions of the Yoruba kingdoms. Second to it is the insignificance, constitutionally, of the members of the royal descent groups; in Ekiti and Ijebu they play little part in the government of the town. Iwo is here the exception, for the royal princes used their economic power to gain a position in which they could often overcome the traditional constitutional rights of the chiefs of the non-royal lineages. While the traditional kings of the Ekiti and Ijebu were divine rulers, personifications of their towns, and governed only by the consent of their councils of chiefs, the king of Iwo was able to become an autocrat.

In comparing the composition of the councils of chiefs in the different towns another grouping arises. Kabba and Ijebu were alike in that these councils were composed of men who had risen through a series of grades in title societies largely through their own wealth.[7] In Ekiti and Iwo the titles of the chiefs who sat on the councils were usually vested in individual lineages and in most cases the members of these lineages had the right to elect the chief. Those so chosen were usually elderly men, and although they had probably displayed their qualities of leadership at an early age, few had held any official position before election to chieftaincy. These two methods by which titled chiefs might be appointed are in striking contrast. They affected directly the prominence of the lineage in the towns: in Ekiti and Iwo it was a more dominant feature of the social system than in Ijebu and Kabba, where age sets and grades and title societies,

[7] This was completely so in Kabba; in Ijebu many titles were gained by other means already described.

of which men of all descent groups were members, took over
some of the functions of the lineage in the former towns. In the
Ekiti towns and in small towns in other areas the titles were
equitably shared so that each lineage had at least one chief; in
such a large town as Iwo itself this was clearly impossible. Thus,
whereas in Ekiti and other small towns every lineage member,
at some time or other, elected his representative to the council
of chiefs, in Iwo such rights of representation were restricted to
a minority.

Other criteria, such as the organization of the staff of the
royal palaces, the organization of the army, and the collection
of tribute, would also be useful in classifying these political
systems, but space has prohibited their description. Those given
above—the appointment of the supreme ruler and the constitutional powers of other members of his descent group and the
composition of the councils of chiefs—enable one to see considerable differences between the constitutions of various Yoruba kingdoms. The same criteria would also illuminate the differences between the kingdoms of other West African societies.

This article, written in late 1953, constituted a preliminary report on
field work carried out in the few previous years. A fuller consideration of
many of the points raised here, together with additional data, has been
published subsequently. In "The Yoruba" in J. L. Gibbs (editor), *Peoples
of Africa,* I have given a general ethnographic account of the Yoruba. In
Yoruba Land Law I have outlined the social and political structure not
only of Ekiti and Ijebu but also Ondo and Egba. The role of the *Oba*
(especially in Ekiti) has been discussed in "Sacred Kingship and Government Among the Yoruba" (Lloyd 1960).

This article does not explore the difference in structure and function between the agnatic descent groups of the northern Yoruba and the cognatic
descent groups of the Ijebu. I have described the former in "The Yoruba
Lineage" (Lloyd 1955) and have compared the two structures in "Agnatic
and Cognatic Descent Among the Yoruba" (forthcoming).

14 NUPE STATE AND COMMUNITY

S. F. Nadel

The late S. F. Nadel was Professor of Anthropology at the Australian National University, Canberra. He was the author of *A Black Byzantium* (1942), *The Nuba: An Anthropological Study of the Hill Tribes of Kordofan* (1947), *The Foundations of Social Anthropology* (1951), *Nupe Religion* (1954), *The Theory of Social Structure* (1957), and many papers.

I. COUNTRY AND PEOPLE. THE PROBLEM

1

IN CENTRAL NIGERIA, between 8°30′ and 10°30′ N. lat., lies Nupe-land. Two rivers form its boundaries, the Niger to the south and west, the Kontagora river to the north. Another river marks its central axis: the Kaduna. The boundary to the east is formed by the gradually rising land, which eventually reaches the hills of Gwari country. It is a low, open, fertile country, covering roughly 7,000 sq. m., inhabited by a population who were known from the ancient days, and all over Nigeria, as an industrious and able people. The census of 1931 gives their number as 326,000, but for various reasons one may safely take it to be considerably higher, probably up to half a million.

Nupe, more exactly *nupeci* (pl. *nupecizhi*), is the name they give to themselves. This name, however, refers, with one exception, only to the tribe as a whole, not to the various subdivisions or sections of the tribe that exist. A man asked about his origin would always give the name of the sub-tribe he belongs to first, and only afterwards add: 'but we are all Nupe'. These

FROM *Africa* 8, No. 3 (1935), 257–303, by permission of the International African Institute. The paper has been very slightly shortened.

sub-tribes are not all of the same category. There are sections that trace their traditions and genealogies back to the most ancient period of their history, which means, for the Nupe, to the days before the advent of their culture-hero Tsoede. Such sections are the Bení, east of the Kaduna, the Ébe, north of the Kontagora river, the Kyedya, in the Niger valley, and also one small and scattered group of people in the sparsely populated area between Kaduna and Niger, who have only the one name 'Nupe' for themselves. Other sub-tribes link up their origin with the coming, and the 'new order', of Tsoede: the Batacízhi, the 'marsh-dwellers', or the Gbéde, inland from Jebba and Mokwa. There exist also one or two sections which, apparently of comparatively recent origin, appear to be the result of some process of colonization or migration. To this group belong the 'Kusopá', or 'keepers of the [kola] plantations', in the centre of Nupe-land, and the 'Zhitáko', or Dibo, in what is to-day Agaie Emirate.

A great deal of migration seems to have taken place among the Nupe, small groups detaching themselves frequently from their own sub-tribe, and moving into the territory of another sub-tribe—hunters in search of game, or farmers seeking better farming-grounds. Besides, also groups of foreign origin have been absorbed by the Nupe, forming to-day a section of their own, almost a Nupe sub-tribe, completely Nupe-ized in language and custom: the Benú, of Bornu extraction, in Kutigi and Enagi; or the Yoruba settlements all over Nupe, which are known by the name of *Konú* (literally 'prisoners of war'). This process of assimilation and absorption is still going on: Nupe language and Nupe forms of social organization are adopted to-day by a section of the Kakanda, a riverain tribe on the southern border, or groups of Gwari, adjoining Nupe-land in the north-east.

What, then, does Nupe mean? What type of unity, what bonds of integration constitute the racial or cultural unit of the Nupe as a tribe?

The sections, or sub-tribes, are above all territorial and cultural units. They speak the same dialect, and are often united by kinship ties and the consciousness of common descent. The territorial factor is indicated in some of their names already (e.g. Zhitáko, 'the [men] down below'; Batacízhi, 'the marsh-dwellers'). And corresponding to this fact of the same or similar environment, they often represent units of economic co-opera-

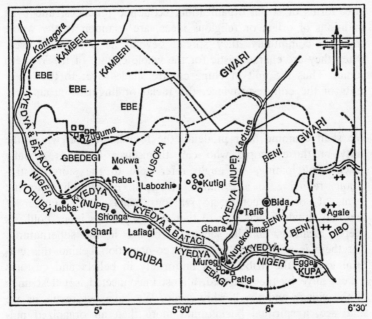

▲ Capitals of the ancient Nupe Kingdom. o°o Benû settlements (Bornu settlers).
- - - - Boundaries of Nupe according to ++ Benî settlements outside of Benî country.
      Barth (1850). ◻◻ Settlements of branches of the original
——— Present boundary of Bida-Emirate.   Nupe dynasty.

tion as well: the Kyedya are the boatmen of the Niger; the Kusopá the kola planters, and the name Batací is now used in Bida more and more for 'fisherman' (or a special type of fisherman) in general.

For the Nupe as a whole, quite apart from migration and inter-tribal movements, the situation is much more complicated. One would naturally look first of all to language as the strongest link. But some of the sub-tribes show a considerable difference in their dialects: the Dibo, and still more the Ébe, differs actually from Nupe proper not less than, e.g., the language of the neighbouring Gwari people. But nevertheless every Nupe, asked about this, would maintain that the Ébe are Nupe—and so say the Ébe themselves—whereas the Gwari are only 'relatives'. The factor of common culture again presents difficulties: certain culture-traits, e.g., religious rituals, are limited to sub-tribes, or even villages. And where, on the other hand, features of Nupe culture, forms of social organization, economic practices, and even traditions of origin or religious ideas, are common to the whole of Nupe community, they spread beyond its borders as well. Often they are characteristic for the whole culture of the Western Sudan. Thus the unit of Nupe culture shades over to the larger units of the culture-province, the racial or linguistic group.

2

We shall examine later in detail the foundations on which the unity of those people who call themselves Nupe is actually based. Anticipating, we might refer here to the store of traditions referring to a common origin; to certain characteristic forms of social structure; to religious beliefs, to a number of seasonal rituals which give to their life's cycle its inner hold, its deeper meaning, and its sacred anchorage in the supernatural. Yet there is no general system of co-operation behind this cultural unit of the 'tribe'. This uniformity in beliefs and customs is kept alive by the scattered, almost unconnected, smallest units of the village and the kinship-group. We have before us, as we shall see, a spiritual background more than an organized uniformity, an idea rather than an actual machinery of co-operation.

Yet such a machinery of large-scale co-operation exists in Nupe; there exists a system organizing comprehensive uniformity which gives to the name 'Nupe' a new, different meaning. It is not coterminous with tribe, nor identical with tribal section, or association of tribal sections. It may cut across the cultural and linguistic units, and may alter the boundaries of economic co-operation. Its mark is political allegiance to the sovereignty of the Nupe kingdom, and residence in the territory of the Nupe State.

Among the Nupe traditions and myths of origin one group of traditions stands out very clearly: the cycle of stories that tell about the adventures and feats of the culture-hero Tsoede, or Edegi.[1] They describe how he came to Nupe from the south, from Idah, how he settled first among the Bení and Kyedya, and how eventually he gained power over the whole country.

[1] According to the (not always identical) genealogies of the Nupe kings which have been preserved in the books of the first Mohammedan historians of Nupe, Tsoede's rule over Nupe was established at about A.D. 1500.

With him he carried powerful symbols both of religious and of worldly rulership, which he distributed among the towns and tribes of Nupe. He united them under his leadership, and gave them law and jurisdiction, binding them to his throne by tributes and taxes and ceremonial oaths of allegiance. He established a dynasty, built a capital, Gbara, and from there expanded the Nupe kingdom to the south and to the north, both in peaceful penetration and colonization, and in wars of conquest.

We have to leave out here the question of the historical facts, possibly embodied in this tradition of Tsoede. To us it is important as an illustration of the new social principle that is superseding, in the tradition, the organization of tribes, villages, or territorial sections. Whether it contains historical truth or not, the tradition is sociologically relevant as a 'mythical charter' (to borrow this term from Professor Malinowski), which anchors the existing political structure of the Nupe state in the awe-inspiring sphere of mythical, or semi-mythical, happenings. Most probably this myth of Tsoede never was universal among the Nupe people. To-day, at any rate, we find it strongly alive only in the territory of Nupe kingdom, and its character of a clearly remembered, paramount tradition fades away as soon as we go beyond its boundaries. Characteristically the distribution of the 'mythical charter' and the boundaries of the kingdom within Nupe-land coincide.

The question of the boundaries of the original Nupe kingdom is not very easy to settle. Conquests, internal and external warfare, and dynastic feuds have often altered the boundaries, and sometimes even led to a split of the whole country.[2] The young Nupe kingdom seems to have been limited to the river valleys of Niger and Kaduna, not stretching very far inland to the east and north. At the time of its greatest power the Nupe kingdom is said to have reached as far as Gbagéde in the north and Onítsa in the south. But still at the time when Barth visited the Sudan, in the middle of last century, Nupe kingdom extended over a wide area, stretching into Kamberi and Gwari country

[2] Dynastic rivalry led to the establishment of two small independent Nupe 'kingdoms', the old *etsu*ship of Zuguma, now under Kontagora, and the more recent Emirate of Patigi, now under Ilorin. In their organization they are strict copies of the ancient Nupe kingdom out of which they both sprang. Other Nupe communities which became independent emirates under the Fulani only are Agaie, and the small districts of Lafiagi and Shonga.

298 S. F. Nadel

to the north, and into Yoruba and Yagba territory to the south.
It left out, however, small groups of Nupe, Ébe, and Dibo, in
the south, north, and east (Barth 1857: II 641). It might appear,
therefore, as if our distinction between the Nupe State and the
pre-state, or non-state, organization of the Nupe were merely a
matter of historical or geographical demarcation: on one side
we have the autonomous Nupe villages or districts which remained outside the boundaries of the State; and on the other
side the communities which have been integrated into the framework of the Nupe State. Yet our distinction between State and
non-state Community goes deeper than this. More than to these
concrete, separate communities, it refers to the different principles
which they express, and to the different social forces behind
them. The tribal unit of people who live in the same territory,
possess the same culture, and speak (more or less) the same
language involves bonds of unity and forces of integration. And
the small co-operative organizations which this culture evolves
—village communities, kinship groups, political units—are again
based on integrative factors and binding forces. But the State,
where it absorbs the cultural uniformity of the tribal area, and
where it unites the small political units under its new super-
structure, does more than merely adopt the former, and continue
and develop the latter. In its organization it ignores to a certain
extent the possibilities of integration embodied in the tribal and
cultural unit; and over and above the village or kinship co-
operation it establishes new, and different, forms of organization.
We may here enumerate the three main principles which characterize State organization: (1) It is non-tribal in character,
i.e.—in modern terminology—it distinguishes between extraction
and (political) nationality. (2) A central authority enforces social co-ordination within the State boundaries. (3) The authority
is entrusted to a privileged ruling class, detached from the bulk
of the population. In the sense of this antagonism we introduced in our title the contrasting dualism State and (non-state)
Community; and in this sense we shall make it the subject of
our investigation.

3

Modern sociology has introduced the distinction between 'Community' on one side and 'Society', with its paradigm the State,

on the other, as a distinction between two categories of integrative forces in society. The integrative forces working within the 'Community' are described as more spontaneous and natural in origin, based on the more direct relations binding together men who are of the same kin, speak the same language, profess the same religion, or live close to each other on the same piece of land. The integrative forces of 'Society', on the other hand, are more artificial, more indirect, and their validity is based on formulated norms and statutes (Toennies 1926). How far this dualism in fact coincides with our State and non-state Community will become clear in the course of our analysis. But for us here, as in the case of Toennies' analysis of the modern society, 'Community' and 'Society' are principles essentially interrelated. The binding forces of 'Community' do not vanish where the 'State' builds up its organization; and the influence of the State machinery does not penetrate the whole social group equally, or to an equal degree. In Nupe-land, as in our modern society, the unit of kin and place, the community of language or religion, holds its own within, and often against, the framework of the State.

This becomes of special methodological importance for our investigation. For it shows that in our study of the non-state Community we are not reconstructing dead forms of society, and not describing fictitious evolutions, but analysing living forces which are working side by side in the native society of to-day. The native, in fact, is well aware of this complex sociological situation. He would speak of himself as a Nupe, or a native of this or that village, and of this or that sub-tribe. But besides all that he would call himself a *'za 'tsu Nupe,* a 'king's man', and in this terminological distinction he summarizes the whole system of different rights and duties, ties and obligations, entailed in his belonging simultaneously to the different social units. And with this we have stated the programme and method of our investigation. It will be an analysis of the forces of social control valid in each of these social units. We shall ascend from the smallest to the largest group, from household and village, over tribal section and tribe, finally to the political system of the State. And for each of these units, our leading question will be: how is co-ordination of social activity controlled and enforced within the group? Or, in other words: what does social

control, and co-ordination of social activity, mean to the individual who happens to be born as a Nupe, of a certain section,
in a certain village, and who happens to be, besides all that, a
citizen of Nupe kingdom, a 'king's man'?

II. FAMILY AND VILLAGE GROUP

1

Let me take you first into a typical Nupe village, a village of
perhaps 1,000 people. The Nupe call it *ezhi,* the name which they
also use for town or city. The first things you notice are the
characteristic, large, walled compounds, side by side and quite
close to one another, but yet markedly separated by walls and
narrow paths. One large roomy entrance-hall, *katámba,* leads
into the compound; and here again you find sub-divisions made
by walls and smaller entrance-halls, and again the round,
thatched huts stand close to one another, densely crowding the
place. Only round the hut of the family head there is more space;
and his square hut will be already distinguished from the other
(round) huts by its different architecture. You actually see the
social organization of the village with your eyes. One *katámba,*
one compound, one large family group. The Nupe will always
count in *katámba* when referring to the size of a village, and
will always talk about *katámba,* or *emi* (compound), when informing you about family relationships.

Outside the village proper, sometimes fairly far off, are a number of smaller settlements which belong, politically, to the village. They are founded by people from the village, farmers who
look for better soil, or hunters who want to live deeper 'in the
bush'. These settlements are called *tungá,* and whether they consist of one compound only or whether they grow to the size of a
small village themselves, they will always remain in close contact
with the mother-village, *ezhi,* and only be its outposts, and
'colonies'.

The large family group, or extended family, which lives in
one compound, consists of the family head (*emitsó,* lit. 'the
owner of the house') with his wives, sons and younger brothers,
their wives and children, his unmarried sisters and daughters,
and his old relatives, male or female, who are unable to keep

house for themselves. The family being patrilocal, the married sisters and daughters live in the house of their husband's family. There might be also former slaves living in the compound, and very often also friends or distant relatives who might have come from far and settled down here for ever.

The unit of the family means more than mere household co-operation. It is an influence that covers almost every activity of its members. The individual enters into social activities in the wider field of the village or the tribe only via the family unit, and in virtue of his membership of the family unit. This is valid for religion: its age-old cults and rituals are performed for, and invoked by, the village community as a whole; and family groups, led, or represented, by the elders, form its priesthood and congregation. It is valid also for the sphere of traditional knowledge, which binds people together in the consciousness of common origin, and the consciousness of racial or cultural uniformity; it is again vested in the family as such, and entrusted to the old men who will, some day, hand this knowledge on to the younger generation. It becomes most prominent in political organization.

The ruling of the village is in the hands of a council of elders, the elders being the family heads. At their head stands the Village Chief, or *zhitsú* ('town-king'), he himself a *nũsa,* an 'old one'. As visible manifestation of their rank the elders are given certain titles, and for every Nupe village, at least originally, the equation is valid: number of compounds, number of council members, number of titles existing. The titles are bestowed on the family head by the chief and the rest of the elders as a recognition of his having been accepted amongst the *nũsazhi.* It means that he is regarded as a man whose faultless character and experience, whose ability in farming or a handicraft, make his opinion valuable for the decision of communal affairs. And it means, from the point of view of the *nũsa* himself, that he has accepted a twofold responsibility: towards the section of the village population of which he is now the head, and towards the community, and its ruling body, of which he has become a member.

This principle of twofold moral responsibility manifests itself clearly in the procedure of succession and inheritance. When a family head dies, the members of the family first of all have to come to a decision about the successor. Then they officially inform the village head about it. He has to confirm their choice, and then he summons the whole family and the other elders, and addresses the new family head in a ceremonial manner, explaining to him the rights and duties of his new position. He would remind him of the good reputation of his predecessor, and enumerate to him, one by one, all the members of the household for whom he is now going to work, whom he must be prepared to feed, to clothe, or to marry off. A ceremonial present from the new family head to the chief confirms this pact. And, on the other hand, the family head is actually held responsible by the village community for the behaviour of the members of his house. His responsibility would not be limited to material compensation for delicts or crimes committed by family members. But his whole career as a member of the council of elders would be wrecked by the fact that he has perhaps a son who is an evil-doer, or a wife or daughter of bad reputation. 'How can a man look after the affairs of the village', say the Nupe, 'who cannot manage his own family?'

2

The ranks, or titles, bestowed on the elders, can be of three types: (1) The titles are hereditary, i.e. a special title or rank will always remain in one *emi,* 'house'. It will be inherited as a rule, provided that there are no grave objections, by the eldest living family member, the deceased man's younger brother or eldest son. (2) No hereditary connexion exists between one title and one 'house'; the titles are governed by strict seniority instead, and they change hands according to vacancy and promotion. When a family-head who held a high rank dies, some other family-head who may claim this vacant title will succeed to the deceased man's rank, and more such promotions may take place, until a vacancy occurs which is suitable for the heir of the deceased family-head, who is now going to take his place among the village elders. We shall see later what qualifications exist for this first appointment to a title. (3) Certain titles which are, in fact, only a subdivision of the first type belong so to speak *ex officio* to the heads of certain families. These are families in which the priesthood of a certain religious cult is vested from time immemorial; or families which practise a certain important profession as family work, such as hunters or blacksmiths. It is interesting to

notice that in some cases these latter titles have disappeared
where the profession has lost its vital importance for the village
community. For example, in one place where Hausa immigrants
now do all the blacksmith work, the title of the *májī tswaci,* 'the
master of the blacksmiths'; has now disappeared from the list of
village ranks.[3]

The chief distinction of the different rank-systems, however,
refers to the position of the village chief. His title might be of
either type, hereditary or obtained by promotion. Yet, if hereditary, it would often not be limited to one family only, but would
change, by means of a system of strict rotation, between two or
four (never more) families. Or again, the inheritance of chieftainship might not be left open till the vacancy actually occurs
(as is the custom in the most ancient Nupe villages), but the
successor might be appointed in advance, and given the official
title of an 'heir apparent'.

It is impossible to try to examine here the possible origin of
these variations. In many cases they seem due to historical factors, and to the different cultural influences which have modelled
the social organization of the Nupe. One sociological correlation,
however, stands out clearly in this institution: where the chieftainship of the village represents a rank of the promotion type,
i.e. is not bound up with one family, there exists always a certain
rank among the elders, which is strictly hereditary, and whose
office it is to take charge of the village during the interregnum,
and to organize the new chief's election. Sacred insignia, ancestral
emblems, would form the supernatural background of this authority. And, whereas the family group of the chief would vary from
election to election, this rank-holder would be a hereditary,
sacred, and permanent 'king-maker'. Where, on the other hand,
the chief's rank belongs to the second, hereditary type, the sacred
insignia and emblems would be the property of his own house.
And often his house would also include the village priest, to

[3] There is no definite limitation to the number of ranks in a village. Yet
everywhere the number four seems a prominent characteristic. We have four
ranks, or twice four ranks, or, under certain conditions, four primary ranks,
separated from the rest. The latter type is frequently correlated to the organization of village-wards, of *efu,* of which again there would be four, each
of them comprising a number of compounds. The four primary ranks would
be placed, as ward-heads, *efutsózhi,* over the ordinary family-heads, *emi-
tsózhi.*

whom certain essential religious ceremonies are entrusted. Chief and priest would be regarded as relatives: they are said to be descendants of the same family, of an elder and younger brother respectively. They would almost form a dual rulership of political head and religious head, of the *zhitsú,* the town-king, and the *zhigí,* the man who 'eats' (in the sacrifice) 'for the town'.

The *zhitsú* is the owner of all land. He gives the land freely to every family head who needs it for himself or for members of his family. It is, besides, the duty and privilege of the *zhitsú* to perform certain annual ceremonies, or officially to cause them to be performed by the *zhigí,* which safeguard the welfare of the village and the fertility of the land. The chief's guardianship over village and land is recognized by a regular gift of first crops, the *dzaká,* consisting of early millet or guinea-corn—the staple crops of Nupe—which every family-head presents to the chief twice a year. This gift is never regarded as compulsory, or as a real tax, and the small return gifts in money, which the chief has to give to the people who bring the first crops to his house, emphasize this character of a voluntary present.

3

The individualistic element implied in the system of appointment or inheritance of the ranks, and of the chief's position as well, should not be underrated. The large family group among which the successor for a deceased family-head is to be found gives an ample choice of men who have reached the necessary age and acquired the necessary experience. In many cases long discussions take place, and it is sometimes difficult to decide which one of the younger brothers, sons, or nephews of the deceased should become the successor to the title. In the village it seldom leads to quarrels. On the contrary, I found in many cases that a man would voluntarily resign in favour of his younger brother or nephew if there were good reasons for it. The degree to which this free competition is made use of varies naturally a good deal. I have seen a man of great ability become chief in a place with strictly hereditary chieftainship without being related to the 'legitimate' ruling family by any stronger ties than friendship, and the village elders approved entirely of this 'individualistic' career.

The exception confirms the rule. The free play of individual competition cements the family-born integration within the village community. Allowing for the necessary margin of individuality, it helps to keep the balance of the system as a whole. In the social structure of the Nupe village community this principle can in fact not be ignored. It is embodied in the economic system, in which the distinction between family work and individual work organizes a corresponding division of labour and income. It is expressed in the certain liberty allowed in choosing a profession. It is naturally also expressed, on a different level, in the amount of liberty one has in choosing one's companions and friends. There is no need to stress the importance of those looser, but not necessarily weaker, forms of social relationship which link individual directly with individual, leaving aside the unit of the family group. Friendship, in Nupe, even crystallizes in a special institution: friends will exchange their children, and keep the foster-child like a child of their own till it grows up and returns to its parents, all with the idea of 'strengthening friendship', as the Nupe say.

The institution in which the factor of individuality is given its deepest recognition, and the institution in which, at the same time, individuality and the ties between individual and individual gain significance for the whole social system, are the age-grade societies. In Nupe they exist both among boys and girls, but we will deal here only with the former. There are three such age-grade societies: the *ena wáwagízhi*, the *ena dzákangízhi*, and the *ena gbarúfuzhi*, i.e. the society of the little ones (10–15 years), of the boys (15–20 years), and of the young men (20–30 years). Each of these societies lasts about four or five years. After that the society is dissolved, and a new society, of the next higher grade, is formed. The initiative lies entirely with the boys themselves, they only inform the father about it, and he helps them with food and beer for the general initial festival. Of each grade there exists only one group at a time. And there is no able-bodied boy in the village who would not be member of one or the other group. Were he to be excluded—and exclusion is the heaviest punishment exercised within these 'societies'—he would be disgraced among young and old. At the head of each group is an older boy, or man, often taken from the highest ranks of the next higher grade, whom the boys, who are going to form a society, approach in the beginning and ask to preside over their group. The head of the highest group, whose title is *Ndákotsú*, will be chosen among adults, namely, among those men who have not yet been given a 'real' title, i.e. a title among the elders. His influence will be considerable: he has practically the whole youth of the village under him; they will come to him for advice or arbitration, they would obey his word and follow his leadership.

The main characteristic of these 'societies' is seniority, and their chief work active co-operation. The order of seniority is copied exactly from the order ruling the adult ranks, and is expressed by exactly the same titles. But the position of the father or the relatives of the boy has no influence whatsoever on the rank which he can hope to obtain. The distribution of titles is carried through by the head of the *ena*. It will, in the lowest age-grade society, naturally not be based on any long experience; general reputation of the boys in the village will be the only criterion. In the senior groups the ability and merit of the members will have become more evident, and a redistribution of titles will take place accordingly. The appointments in the highest age-grade society form the last, and most important, official appreciation. These ranks will stick to the young men, after they leave their age-grade society, almost for their lifetime. Everybody would know them by this title only. From their ranks the new age-groups will choose their leaders. And here individual ability has its chance. Here is the opportunity for all those who, in due course, can hope to be admitted to the 'real' ranks of the *nŭsazhi*. The appointment to *nŭsa*-ranks, in fact, almost always corresponds to the career in the young men's societies.

The activities round which these societies revolve are of two kinds: (1) In Nupe country, as in the whole Hausa area, there exists a typical form of co-operation, in particular for farm work, but also for other kinds of work which demand a large body of people working together, e.g., roofing a large hut, building a wall, &c. Such co-operative work (*égbe* in Nupe, *gayá* in Hausa) is organized entirely by the young men's societies. It is carried through under special ceremonial conditions, with drumming and music, and is connected with a certain prize-competition in farming. The son of the man who needs the help of the *égbe* will bring the matter before his group; the owner of the farm will contribute meals, drinks, and presents for the musicians, and the members of the society do the work, advised and led by the head of their group. (2) There are certain social duties amongst the members of the young men's society which will remain valid even after the expiration of the society. They are definitely duties for life. They refer above all to the important crises of life: marriage, childbirth, and death, and here all the members, or late members, of a society are expected to pay the traditional visits, to help in the traditional ceremonies, and to give the traditionally prescribed gifts. In general, they have never to forget that they are comrades and fellows, who have to respect and to honour one another, and who have to keep up the prestige and solidarity of their fellowship.

III. THE SUB-TRIBE

1

This, then, is the social life of the village: a dense net of intimate, organically grown relations, and a system of integration of deep, general, almost 'natural' appeal. Yet it is a system of integration which at the same time involves forces of seclusion, and separation from outside. Even the knowledge of common descent, or ancestral beliefs, which the village group shares with the wider unit of the sub-tribe, is specialized, and narrowed down to principles of essentially local appeal. When turning, therefore, to the new, larger social unit, the sub-tribe, our analysis will to a certain extent boil down to one question: to what extent will these unifying factors which we saw at work in the village stand, or adjust themselves to, the extension of area and group?

We might start with those looser, elastic forms of relationship from individual to individual. Here it must be noted that, speaking generally, excepting the riverain people, the Nupe is not a great traveller. Young men, though, like to travel and to see the world, but the world often means only the narrow boundary of a district or a political Division. And very few of them would like to settle down permanently in a 'foreign' country. Not even the ties of friendship stretch beyond their own country in the narrowest sense. Within the area of the sub-tribe a comparatively small section of the neighbourhood, a few villages in fact, are the field for this play of personal contact. At the dances, or family festivities, one very rarely finds people from places which are more than seven or eight miles away. The institution of the young men's societies, again, never stretches beyond the bound-

aries of village and *tungá*. Foster-children are hardly ever taken
from places farther away. The same situation is reflected in the
marriage-statistics. In many places marriage between *efu* and
efu, i.e. the different parts of the village, or between *ezhi* and
tungá, mother-village and 'colony', is the only known type. In
other places marriage within the whole area of the sub-tribe is
allowed, in theory; but I very rarely actually found marriage
between villages that were not neighbouring places.

2

Let us, then, turn to religion. Among the religious cults practised
in the territory of the sub-tribe we find in fact both common
cults and also cults which are peculiar to one or two places only.
But common cults or not, it is evident that uniformity in religious
practice does not yet constitute an active religious community. In
most cases the rituals and religious cults are definitely local affairs, practised in, and for, one village. Only in three cases I
found a religious cult the significance of which reached beyond
this narrow area, which in fact embraced the whole sub-tribe:
among the Kyedya, the riverain Nupe; in Tafiẽ, in Bení country;
and in Labozhi, in the country of the Kusopá. In the first example a sacrifice performed in Jebba, at the Ketsá, the famous
'juju-rock' of the Europeans, was to appease the Niger river on
behalf of all the riverain people. In Labozhi the sacrifice, human sacrifice in the old days, was to secure good crops for all
the kola-planters. Among the Bení, finally, the chief of Tafiẽ
performed a similar, representative sacrifice as an annual, ritual
confirmation of the political headship which Tafiẽ held over Bení
country. Behind this 'representative' ritual we recognize the motives of strong common bonds. But the important fact is that
these bonds are not essentially bonds of the sub-tribe as such.
They express more than the vague uniformity of culture or race.
In the case of the Kyedya and Kusopá they imply a common
fear and hope, the common eternal fight against the same element, be it the waters of the Dark River, or the soil from which
the planters draw, by difficult and delicate work, the fruit of the
famous kola-nut tree. In the case of the Bení, the religious leadership only reflects political power, and religious co-operation
stands for political union, a subject to which we shall come presently.

In economic organization a similar situation prevails. Markets are meeting-places of exchange for wide areas. Specialities in the production of certain villages, appreciated and sought in other districts, are apt to enlarge the field of economic, and accordingly also personal, contact. The net of supply and demand extends beyond the area of the single village and its close neighbourhood. But the area of economic communication does not coincide with the area of the sub-tribe. It might be smaller, and it might be larger. Its extent is determined by other laws than the traditional and spiritual ties which characterize the sub-tribe. The market institution in Nupe fixes regular market-days twice a week for the smaller, and once a week for the larger places. And this explains itself. For more people, and people from farther away, come to the markets in large places, therefore they must be given sufficient time for the journey. We find, in fact, also the situation that a sub-tribe as a whole represents one producing area; this is the case, for example, with the kola-nut planters, or the fisher tribes. But then the production depends on export, and export might necessitate markets and trading-places outside the area of the sub-tribe; for the kola planters these markets for their produce are actually often far outside their own territory. Thus we see the economic traffic creating its own provinces, cutting across, or stretching far beyond, the area of the sub-tribe.

3

Finally let us turn to political organization. In the majority of cases there is none. In eight of the ten sub-tribes the unit of the sub-tribe has no political meaning. Only in two cases do we find an original and strong form of political co-operation: in the confederacy of the Bení villages, and in the Kyedya colonization of the river banks. The why and how must, however, remain outside this discussion, although, in one case, we shall venture a short, tentative explanation.

The description of the Bení confederacy will have to be, to a large extent, a reconstruction. Twelve 'towns' existed originally in the territory of the Bení. Some of them have disappeared to-day, but others are still important places and known as the most ancient townships of the country. These twelve towns were more or less equal among themselves as regards population, wealth, and actual power. But they all recognized the authority of lead-

ership of one among them: the village of Tafiẽ. This supremacy
was expressed in the annual gift of crops which each member
of the confederacy paid to Tafiẽ. Besides, whenever general political co-operation became necessary, especially in the case of
war, Tafiẽ took the leadership.[4] The authority of Tafiẽ was never
questioned, and is derived, as so many other authorities of Nupe-
land, from the culture-hero Tsoede. For he is said to have invested in the head of Tafiẽ the sacred office of that special cult
which had to be performed in Tafiẽ on behalf of the whole Benĩ
country.

There is a fundamental difference between the Benĩ and the
Kyedya organization.[5] Whereas the Benĩ represent a large inland tribe, or tribal section, living as farmers and craftsmen in a
densely populated area, the Kyedya are few in number; they are
fisher- and boatmen, and live on the narrow stretch of the river-
banks. Their villages are small, poor-looking settlements, often
hardly more than temporary camps. The building-up of their organization is not lost completely in the mythical past, but was
still developing, so to speak, under our eyes. Even during the last
thirty years we find the Kyedya actively colonizing the banks of
the Niger, and the Kaduna. The Kyedya are, and always have
been, an important factor in Nupe country. They 'rule the water',
as the Nupe say. In their hands is concentrated the large traffic
up and down the river. The enormous trade coming from north
and going south, by way of Nupe, must pass through the Kyedya
territory. Cattle- and, formerly, slave-caravans cross the river
on Kyedya boats. Whenever a Nupe king set out on a war
to the south he was dependent upon their support. And during
the campaign of the Royal Niger Company against the troops
of the Nupe king in Bida, in 1895, the Kyedya, joining the European forces, played a decisive role.

The small area near the confluence of the Niger and the Ka-

[4] This political co-operation was still active in the times of the Fulani
wars. When the Fulani army attacked Bida, then one of the twelve Benĩ
villages, the 'town-king' of Bida sent for help to the chief of Tafiẽ. Tafiẽ
then organized the auxiliary army to which each of the Benĩ villages contributed, and this army eventually relieved Bida.

[5] There are two sections among the Kyedya, the Kyedya Gbéde on the
upper Niger, and the Kyedya Táko, the 'down-stream' Kyedya. We refer
here only to the latter and their political organization. (*Editors' note:* these
are the people referred to in later publications as the Kede; cf., Fortes
and Evans-Pritchard 1940.)

duna which the Kyedya must have inhabited originally, is the very centre of this net of trade and traffic. Tradition makes the mythical Tsoede the originator of their colonization and expansion. He is said to have given to a Kyedya man of Muregi the title of *Kuta,* and with the title, and with insignia of power, the rulership over all the river people. If we try to inquire into the 'real' origins, we must undoubtedly not ignore the possible influence of individual enterprise. In fact, in the early history of the Royal Niger Company we find striking examples of the enterprise and organizing ability of some Kyedya chiefs. And besides, are these Kyedya who 'rule the waters' not born travellers and colonizers and even, on a small scale, conquerors? But behind all that there is the unique economic position which is bound to have led to expansion and territorial development. Economic expansion of this type must go hand in hand with political expansion, it necessitates a system of protection and co-operation which only political control can give. Trade settlements become political outposts. And the mother-village, Muregi, the centre for this twofold expansion, organizing and safeguarding this colonizing enterprise, retains for itself the position of the political centre.

At first sight the Kyedya organization might appear only like an extension of the type of community which the village group evolved, embracing here the whole sub-tribe. There is the factor of common kin, and there is the mythical authority behind the supremacy of the chief. There is the system of religious co-operation, represented in the sacred duty of the *Kuta* to send the sacrificial bull to Jebba, where, as we heard before, the sacrifice on behalf of all the riverain people had to be performed. There is also the factor of complete uniformity of culture, education, and profession. In their villages, living next door to people of a different sub-tribe, they keep to themselves, never intermarry, never really share their neighbour's daily life. Yet in this close and coherent unit there is one element which makes this community differ essentially from the forms of community which we have met so far among the Nupe. There is a definite cleavage within their sub-tribe between the 'dynasty' of village heads and the rest of the villagers. These dynastic ranks are not really part of the village, their qualification is not a naturally-grown reputation and status in the village community; their qualification lies only in the fact that they are members of the dynastic family, and have been delegated to these places. They represent a special body, in a way detached from the rest of the community over which they rule. The automatic income which they receive places them on a different plane altogether. They represent, in short, a different, privileged, social class. This definition should not seem exaggerated. This system of a 'privileged class' exists here certainly on a very small scale only. The factors of common kinship relation, the identification of the dynastic family with the common ancestor, the mythical authority behind everything, all tend to smooth out the cleavage. Yet the cleavage certainly exists. We have before us a state, in fact the Nupe State, *in nuce*.

IV. THE NUPE TRIBE

1

Again, when turning from the smaller to the larger unit, when stepping from the unit of the sub-tribe into the wider field of all that is Nupe at large, our first impression is a gradual fading away of links and ties. The factor of personal contact almost disappears, neither friendship nor sex-relation seems to be able to bridge over the gulf between sub-tribe and sub-tribe. Neither kinship ties nor young men's societies form a uniting link. You can test the looseness in the relationship which exists between the various sub-tribes, by trying to obtain information about another, neighbouring sub-tribe. If you find an honest fellow, he will tell you at once that he is not competent and that you had better go to those people themselves; only there, on the spot, can you get reliable information. If not, then be prepared to hear nice stories, tales, pleasantly told, but inaccurate and often erroneous, the truth which might be contained in them often hardly recognizable in the sensational make-up. Yet there is again that general knowledge which forms the basis for the concept 'we Nupe'. You will hear the Nupe talk about certain customs, e.g. the worshipping of idols or the belief in many gods, comparing themselves with other tribes. 'No', they would say, 'we never do that.' 'Yes, you will find it among the Yoruba or Igbira, but we Nupe have only one sky-god, *Sokó.*' You might even hear them talk about a small Nupe community which, according to tradition, has lived in Lagos from the time when the powerful Nupe empire reached almost down to the sea: 'They are still Nupe', they say, 'they still speak Nupe and, above all, they still practise a Nupe *Kuti*' (ritual).

This, then, seems to be the essence of being a Nupe: to speak the same language and to observe the same rituals. Another instance mentioned in the introduction is that of two alien groups, Gwari and Kakanda, which live outside the political boundaries of Nupe, yet which, in the eyes of the Nupe, have become, or are in the state of becoming, Nupe-ized. I have myself seen such a group of Gwari-Nupe: a generation ago they were still bilingual, to-day only Nupe is spoken. They intermarry freely, and have adopted certain elements of the social structure of the Nupe, e.g. the political ranks and titles, the inheritance of chieftainship in rotation, and the ranks of the young men's societies.

There is one group of strangers, however, which forms a definite exception. We refer to the group of settled Fulani who live within the Nupe community. They have been longer than any other of the assimilated groups in close contact with the Nupe. They have married Nupe women, they have adopted Nupe customs, and even in physical features they are often almost indistinguishable. For many generations they have spoken no other language than Nupe, and even Hausa is not very widely spread amongst them. They regard themselves as Nupe good and proper, and will tell you stories about the ancient Nupe history with the same enthusiasm and pride as when talking about their own ancestors, the first Fulani malams who came to Nupe country. Yet to the Nupe they remain strangers. The Nupe have two names for the Fulani: *bororózhi,* for the nomadic cow Fulani, and *góizhi* for those settled town Fulani who seem to have become full members of the tribe amongst which they abide. But the name marks the distinction, they are and remain *góizhi*. The reason for this distinction cannot lie in the racial or cultural difference. It lies in the sociological fact that these Fulani are at the same time the rulers, and represent a privileged, socially detached class in Nupe country. The sharp cleavage is not a cleavage between race and race, culture and culture. Racial antagonism, which might have disappeared in the framework of a socially homogeneous tribal community, here, in the framework of the State, blending with the antagonism of classes, remained alive, and even strengthened with its sentimental elements the inner tension of society.

2

But how strong is actually the existing uniformity and solidarity within this expanding Nupe culture? Save for the vague obligation of offering hospitality to every Nupe, there is no factor of actual co-operation which would embrace the tribe as a whole. What we find are only those units of an elastic uniformity in language and culture, anticipated already in the introduction. We find the common belief in the supreme sky-god *Sokó,* and three or four common religious cults recognizable under the disguise of different names or varying ceremonial details. The foundations of their social and political system, marriage-rules (but not all of them), the institution of age-grade societies and political ranks, are common to all the Nupe. But as regards details and nomenclature, the rank systems may again vary considerably. Even in the material culture there are certain separate 'culture-areas' on a small scale, drawing their boundaries across the Nupe area. And finally the traditions of origin and descent are definitely threefold. There are the sections of Nupe which maintain that they have come originally from Idah, in the south, the same place from which Tsoede is said to have come; the sections which 'always' lived in the same area; and then there is a very ancient and only vague memory of their having come, together with the ancestors of the Yoruba and Borgu, Yauri and Hausa, from Arabia. But just as this last tradition is common among the peoples mentioned in it, so a great number of culture-facts which are all-Nupe are shared by the tribes to the north, east, and west.

But let us again view the situation from the angle of the individual and his social activities. In everything he does he knows himself to be part and member of the tribe, and different from the people beyond the boundary, however closely related in culture they might be to the Nupe. Yet the rules and regulations for his activities are formulated and sanctioned by the narrow group of the family and the village only. And the breach of what we should call tribal rules of conduct, of that comprehensive imperative: 'No Nupe may do that', is punished or ostracized in the narrowest community only.

We realize already that it is the belief in the existing uniformity, more than actual uniformity, that counts: the subjective knowledge that what one does is done by hundreds and thousands of other individuals, and what one is forbidden to do is forbidden to hundreds and thousands of individuals, more than a universal valid system of enforcing this uniformity. And it is, above all, the idea that this uniformity is essential, that it must necessarily oc· cur, should the social life of the group conform to, and express, the idea of Nupe-dom.

But with this the integrative machinery of the tribal unit ends. And, we can add, that of the State must begin. For it must obviously be on this point that the specific, different principle of organization, embodied in the State, must reveal itself. The State cannot base its organization on an amorphous uniformity, on ideas of unity left to the care of a disconnected, almost occasional, social machinery: local traditions, handed-on knowledge, and varying customs. The forms of uniformity valid for the unit of the State, and the methods which it applies to enforce this uniformity, will be the subject of the next, final chapters.

V. THE STATE.—THE DISTRICTS

1

Villages or townships or districts of Nupe, seen as so many social entities, differ in size and population, in details of political or economic organization, in forms of religious life—differ, in short, in all those living, fluctuating characteristics which make up the individuality of a community. Seen as units within the wider political unit of the State, however, they group themselves under the few strict and rigid categories of political status. The Nupe State distinguishes two types of territorial units: towns (or villages or districts) which stand, as royal domains, directly under the king; and towns which are placed as fiefs under the feudal lords of Nupe.[6] For both types 'state' means essentially the same thing: the superposition of a paramount political system upon the existing local systems. The state assumes the position of a highest magistrate above the existing forms of local magistrates. As such it claims the right to confirm or decline the appointment of the local chief, it imposes its fiscal system over and above the types

---

[6] A third type, of a slightly different order, will be dealt with later; it embraces settlements founded by, and accordingly privately controlled by, members of the feudal nobility.

of taxes or imposts which exist locally, and it finally regards part of the jurisdiction as its prerogative. But the organization of this state control varies with the type of political status. In the case of the royal domain the local representation of the central authority, i.e. of the king, is entrusted to a special delegate, as a rule to one of the king's slave officials. Yet this is only a temporary mission which does not attempt to interfere too much with local affairs. The royal delegate visits his area once or twice a year, chiefly for the collection of taxes, and lives for the rest of the time at the king's court. The position of the local chief is, therefore, not deeply affected. He himself becomes, in fact, to a certain extent a representative of the state authority, in so far as he is authorized to collect taxes on its behalf, and to deal with legal and political matters up to a certain point.

The situation in the fief is quite different. Although the feudal lord himself (*egbá* in Nupe, the Hausa *hakimi*) does not live on his fief, his sons, members of his household, slaves or servants, settle there permanently as his representatives. They act on his behalf, and influence through direct and permanent contact a wide range of the local social life. Yet it is evidently in the interest of the strong state not to allow the relation between the feudal lord and his subjects to become too strong, and too permanent. The fief, therefore, is not hereditary, not linked with persons or families, but with rank and office. Change of rank means change of fief, the higher the rank, the larger the fief, or in certain cases the larger the number of small (territorially disconnected) fiefs. With promotion and transfer the fief-holding nobility is prevented from striking roots too deeply in their land and from building up too much of a private state within the state. But this system must, no doubt, break up all continuity of control, and estrange still more the local community and the super-imposed state authority.

This distinction in political status is not based on any natural boundaries of tribes or areas. Nor can we make historical conditions responsible for it. Both types are definitely pre-Fulani. Yet we have evidence of one or two cases where the direct administration as royal domain changed, in comparatively recent times, i.e. under the first Fulani Emirs, into an administration as feudal fief. On the other hand, the Bení confederacy and the Kyedya political organization remained up to the time of the

British rule royal domains. This seems to point to a twofold origin: the ever-expanding Nupe kingdom, increasingly dependent on the military help of the nobility, had to secure their services more and more by granting them landed property in the form of fiefs. But then, only through this indirect feudal administration could the state hope to reach its entire population, above all those disconnected, inert village communities which never evolved, out of their own, a larger political system, like the Bení and Kyedya, which could be fitted so easily into the framework of the state organization.

2

The state super-structure penetrates the different spheres of local political life in varying degree. In its loosest, most detached form it deals with the political apparatus as such, i.e. with local chieftainship.

The existing system of councils and chieftainship, and their activities, restricted as they are to local affairs, are hardly affected. But the appointment of the chief is subject to the approval of the *Etsu* Nupe. This approval has to be sought by the village elders after they have elected or appointed their chief in their old fashion. The *Etsu*, summoning the new chief to his residence, would present him with a state gown, sandals, and (nowadays) a turban, symbols which indicate that the local chief holds his office now by the 'grace of the king'. When rival parties claimed the chieftainship, it would be for the king to decide—and he might not always be impartial in this. But the king's consent implies a certain permanent responsibility towards the village; the villagers had the right to appeal to the king if they were dissatisfied with their chief. Three times would they appeal to the king, and three times would he have to try to reconcile the local ruler and his subjects. But after this he would officially depose him, take away the symbols of office, and bestow them on another man. There are cases reported where the king, induced by bribes, or perhaps personal preference, refused to comply with the 'will of the people'. There was a very simple remedy for this. The village elders simply ruled without the chief. They could not, and did not, appoint a new chief as long as the other, officially recognized chief was still alive. But the ruling would be done as if there were no chief alive, exactly as during an interregnum, i.e. by that head rank whom we called the 'king-maker'.

The influence of the state reaches deeper in the sphere of law. And here also the distinction as to the political status of the local community becomes more evident. The Nupe distinguished in general two types of legal offences: simpler offences which can be settled by 'repairing' the damage which has been done, civil cases in our modern sense (and characteristically the Nupe speak here not of sentence, or judgement, but of *gyara,* i.e. reparation, or arbitration); and grave delicts, 'criminal' cases, which call for formal judgement and punishment, *sheria.* The first type of legal offence was a matter for the village authority. In the royal domain it was dealt with by the chief and the elders, in the fief it was to be handled by the feudal lord in consultation with village chief and elders. The grave crimes, however, which demand *sheria,* judgement, were always a prerogative of the king, and they are, in fact, also called *leifi nya 'tsu,* 'crimes for the king'. It was through the king's local representatives that these matters were brought before the court. The people from the village would report to 'their' delegates in the town, or the feudal lord would have the news from 'his' village, and they would then inform the supreme court of Nupe, the king and his councillors.

But there were exceptions. Certain districts, it seems, which were ruled as royal domains could maintain full and independent jurisdiction over all cases, including the 'crimes for the king'. In some cases a religious fact, the existence of a powerful ordeal, is the explanation. In another case I could actually trace the comparatively recent origin of this legal franchise: it was granted as a special privilege by *Etsu* Masaba to the Nupe town Sakpe, in exchange for heavy direct taxation.

This then seems to point to an inherent weakness in this system of centralized jurisdiction, and to a certain danger of injustice implied in it. Undoubtedly the very fact that crimes were tried in a place far away from where the crime was actually committed, and by a group of people who had little in common with the community whose vital interests were involved in the legal issue, was apt to create misgivings and discontent. The later development could only help to increase this estrangement. For it meant the introduction of professional Mohammedan jurisdiction at the king's court, in the Mohammedan capital of a still largely pagan country. Yet this was not the only, perhaps not even the main source of injustice. A most dangerous element lay in the system of the delegates being the 'recorders' of crimes and offences. It reveals itself as nothing less than an almost institutionalized competition in bribing the king's delegate or the feudal lord. Not having any deeper attachment to the place which they were supposed to take charge of, these delegates could easily be influenced in favour of the better-paying claimant, and easily prevented from reporting a particular case to the king's court. The legal procedure as regards, for instance, debts or theft was in fact quite simple. Up to the value of 10 shillings, I was told, nothing will happen. 'You give the *egbá* half of it, he will quash the case, and you will still have a profit of 5 shillings.' Of course, my informants added, if it was more than 10 shillings then it might be risky, for such an amount is difficult to conceal, and too many people would know about it.

The strongest influence, however, which the state super-structure exercised over the country was linked with tax-collection. The state taxes collected by the royal delegate or the fief-holder were distinguished from the local taxes paid to the village chief. The latter were, as we have seen, only gifts and regular presents of crops which recognized the chief's legal and religious guardianship. Tax, real tax, was paid to the king only. As far back as memory goes it was paid, partly at least, in currency or money; cowrie-shells first, dollars (*Thaler*) and English money later. In the beginning it was a tax levied on households, and combined with a fixed payment in cash (for each household *gbaotá,* i.e. one dollar, or about 3 shillings) an approximately fixed amount of gifts in kind: food for men and horses of the tax-collector's household, and certain 'presents', such as gowns, mats, and so forth. But later on the amount and type of tax changed considerably. The money tax became more and more elastic and more and more arbitrary; slaves were taken in payment; from a general household tax it became a tax on a sliding scale, corresponding to the (estimated) wealth of the family; new taxes were introduced, death duties, market duties, gate tolls; and finally under *Etsu* Umaru Majigi it reached that stage when 'there was no knowing, and no limit', as the Nupe put it.

This tax, except for the gift of food, was divided according to

a fixed scale. The tax from the royal domains belonged to the
king directly; he could, however, return part of it, up to a third,
to his delegate who collected the tax. The tax from the feudal
lands was divided in three parts: one third belonged to the king,
one third to the feudal lord himself, and the remaining third
was divided among his sons and servants who resided as his
representatives in the district. It was understood that the obligations implied in this system were strictly observed. Yet often
enough a powerful feudal lord would break the agreement, in-
fringe the rights of the king, or another fief-holder, by imposing
illegal taxes on their districts. This might turn out to be a dangerous enterprise. For the king would use his whole power, and
apply the most severe reprisals, against a man who thus undermined the organization of the country.

But the feudal lords had other, simpler means of extorting
tribute from their subjects. They levied what the Nupe call
edugí, small tax, in contrast to the *edukó,* regular or main tax.
That is to say, they paid prolonged 'visits' to their places and
lived there, with their whole household, at the cost of the villagers,
till a certain request for money or slaves was fulfilled. This
situation must obviously injure the interest and the position of
the king. It impoverished his subjects, it diminished their ability
to pay the state tax, and even their ability to procure the
necessary amount of crops and food for town and army. Again,
we have records of such unscrupulous feudal lords, even of
the highest rank, having been recalled and deposed by the king.
Yet in the time of the Fulani conquest, with the weakening
of the king's power and the permanent civil wars, this control
must have broken down. It became impossible at the same time
to control the rebellious Nupe elements, and to check the in-
subordinate Fulani vassals. It appears like an admission of
failure that the Fulani Emirs had to introduce a new system of
taxation, over and above the existing feudal organization, the
so-called *ajele* system. It means essentially a return to the system of direct administration as a royal domain, only adapted
now for the whole country. It was, in fact, the usual system of
the Fulani rulers where they had to deal with a rebellious population in a still unpacified conquered territory. For Nupe it
meant that the whole country—both Nupe proper and conquered
territories—was subdivided into a number of large districts. Into

each district twice a year a special delegate was sent, the *ajele*. He was of the royal family, and his private interests were safe-guarded by a special arrangement: he had to bring home a certain amount of money or slaves, the 'over-output' being his. He stayed in the district for about a month each time, and was accompanied by members of his family, slaves, servants, and followers: he in fact commanded a small army strong enough to protect the king's rights not only against a rebellious popula-tion but also against a too powerful 'loyal' nobility.

3

What, one might well ask, did the tax-paying, law-abiding citizen receive in return for his allegiance to king and nobility? Was extortion, bribery, brutal force, the only aspect under which the state revealed itself to its populace? The people were to receive, theoretically, on the whole one thing: security—protection against external and internal enemies, and general security for carrying out the daily work, holding markets, using the roads, and en-joying the profits of one's work. We have seen what protection and security meant in reality. At their best they meant some-thing very unequal and very unstable. This situation must have led to much tension and change within the system, and to frequent attempts to secure better safeguards for civil rights. The rudest way was, of course, rebellion and revolt. But there were other means as well. The position of the royal domains seems, on the whole, to have been safer than the position of the feudal lands. And we have seen that a village could actually obtain the legal franchise of certain royal domains by sacrificing part of its income. But generally there was no possibility for villages or districts as such to change their political status. Priv-ileges which would base the social rights on safer ground could only be secured by, and for, individuals. Individuals could try to gain the private friendship and protection of a feudal lord, or a powerful man at the king's court. Continuous presents and services, leading to a voluntary allegiance which eventually al-lowed the 'protector' permanent control over one's land, were the obligations on the side of the supplicant. Protection against (just or unjust) claims of other people, assistance in matters which had to do with the central authority, were the promises of the protector for services rendered. It leads to an institution which impresses its stamp on the whole social system of Nupe, and of all the Hausa states in the north: the *bara*-ship (from *bara,* Hausa and Nupe, servant), but we might as well call it by the name by which this very same institution was known in Imperial Rome and in the feudal system of medieval Europe: the Roman *patrocinium,* or *clientage.*

4

So far our discussion of the relationship between state and local community has revealed only negative factors, and a deep, almost unbridgeable gulf between the two. Yet it must seem unlikely that a state organization built up like this, unable to base its claims on any bonds of inner unity, should have persisted for centuries without having been shattered, and broken up, over and over again by unrest and revolts beyond repair. Such a situation did no doubt exist in Nupe, at least at the time of the Fulani conquest. But then the Fulani welded again what seemed broken, and tied bonds again which seemed loosened for ever. How?

This situation involves two sets of problems. The first, more general, we know already. It is the question of the forms of unity upon which the unifying state super-structure is based; and of the social machinery, necessary in every society, which would create, develop, or foster such forms of inner unity for the sake of the external political unit. The second, more special problem is: given such a gulf between central authority and local population, are there any means of bridging the gulf, and means of social approach between the two?

The reply to the first question leads us back to our analysis of the tribe and the tribal section, and the loose forms of unit which they represent. Out of this unit the state grew. And with its development went hand in hand a marked concentration of this uniformity. In the wake of political unification follows necessarily an expansion of economic co-operation—reorganization, and reorientation, in many cases. The larger territorial unit, with its new centre of gravity, the populous capital, brings new forces into play, remoulding or absorbing the various existing economic 'provinces'. These forces must also have influenced linguistic development. They must have helped to assimilate dialectical differences, so that to-day we find, within the large, vague group of 'Nupe-speaking people' a close, and real, language-community, the boundaries of which coincide with the boundaries of Nupe State. The social structure of the State has pressed its stamp on this development, and a new differentiation of dialect has taken place, present to-day in every mind: a differentiation which corresponds to the political distinction of capital and districts, and to the social distinction into classes and social strata. Integration and unification reach also those subtle, less tangible factors of moral unity. The political system which undertakes to sanction and enforce moral order everywhere within its boundaries; which binds the people to its fate, making them share its adventures, its conquests, its victories and defeats—all that gives a new meaning to the concept of Nupedom, almost identical with our concept of nationhood. It creates a new consciousness of unity which is kept alive by every song telling about old times, and every story relating the adventures and feats of the kings of Nupe.[7]

In religion and myth these principles of unity gain their strongest expression. Out of the weak uniformity of beliefs and rituals, out of the disconnected local systems of ancestral cults and traditions, the state has created a new religious solidarity. And in its strong appeal, in its elementary binding forces, it has created at the same time binding forces for itself. The centre of this religious integration is that 'mythical charter' of Nupe kingdom which makes the dynasty of Nupe into descendants of the culture-hero of Nupe, Tsoede. Not even in the sphere of myth are rulers and ruled regarded as of one kin. They remain masters and subjects. But they are united by the principle of supreme religious or magical power, vested in the king, and enacted by him, for the people. Political rulership and sacred guardianship over this ancestral heritage are one and the same thing. Relics of Tsoede, regalia, instruments of ordeal, magical emblems, which exist in every larger village in Nupe kingdom are the

[7] Let us not underrate the element of plan and purpose in this: for these songs and stories are composed by the court musicians and the king's 'bards', and from the court they spread, together with fashions, and other factors of (conscious and unconscious) propaganda, all over the country.

symbols of this sacred, ancient pact. And it is revived in every village by the annual performance of a special ritual devoted to the powerful spirit of the ancestor-king Tsoede.

With the Islamization of the country these factors lost their power. The Fulani rulers could seize by force, as they actually did, the royal insignia from the last Nupe king. They could order the destruction of idols and pagan emblems. They could not transfer the authority of the former mythical charter to their own alien rulership. But they could introduce another, younger, and perhaps more powerful uniting force, Islam—Islam as creed, and Islam as education; mosques, limans, and malams in every village—these are the instruments of propaganda. And in every religious service, in every babbling little malam school, this propaganda is enacted. For teaching Islam means teaching the holy cause which sent the conquerors down to this country. Praying to Allah means praying to the God of the powerful, and sharing with them, if not their power, their beliefs. Whatever the true essence of the Mohammedan faith among the Nupe be, and however sparsely it has spread, so far, Fulani rulership did create, or is creating, another mythical charter. It tries again, with its new means, to mould the religious elements into the intensive unit almost of a state church.

And here we find a reply to our second question. One of the means of social approach between rulers and ruled is the adoption of Mohammedanism. It does not, of course, enable people to become members of the ruling class at once. But it does create in a country still to a large extent pagan an intermediary social stratum, placed nearer the rulers than the rest of the population.[8] In fact no institutionalized means of direct and complete class-assimilation exists for the districts of Nupe. Intermarriage is, and always was, very rare. Personal contact, attachment as followers, or 'clients', to the representatives of the ruling class, only leads to the same type of 'middle-class' status as religious assimilation. But then assimilation is, in fact, not always wanted. Village communities, conservative and inert, may refuse to give themselves over freely to the 'new order'. The scope of social assimilation will reveal itself fully only in the place which is 'all State', in the capital of Nupe.

[8] Meek (1925), stresses this social aspect of Islam in Nigeria.

VI. THE STATE. THE METROPOLIS

1

The sociological problem of the capital implies two different aspects: first, the city as a large settlement, i.e. the problem of urbanization; and second, the city as seat of the central authority, i.e. as political centre. It is not necessary to say that the two aspects are intimately connected. But the systematic distinction as far as it will be possible is essential for the recognition of the different influences and social forces which are at work here.

We can express the social processes which are due to the development from small to large settlement in one sentence. They are processes of untying bonds and of loosening contact; they dissolve homogeneous, naturally grown units, and work towards diversification and stratification. Old Bida, the Bení 'town', must have had a population of about 1,000. But in present-day Bida there live nearly 30,000 people, and at the beginning of this century, when the British took possession of the country, Bida was estimated to have a population of 60,000. Quite apart from the cosmopolitan character of such a place, it must seem impossible that the bonds of contact on which the social life of the village community is based should also shape the social life of the large city. What can a 'large family group', say of 100 people, and what can one family head, mean in a town of so many thousands?

It is easy to demonstrate, by this very change of the social role of the family-head, the far-reaching transformation of the whole social structure. With an increase of population, with the spreading of families and the founding of new compounds and settlements, a new situation must arise. The original simple equation: number of compounds equals number of titles, becomes upset. And in particular where a disproportionate or sudden influx of population takes place, a corresponding increase in the number of ranks would be impossible, and meaningless. The title loses its former meaning as a general social recognition of the status of the family-head, and becomes a hereditary, jealously guarded privilege of a limited number of families. A first class-distinction between people who hold rank and people who have no rank, between 'nobles' and 'commoners', comes into being.

In some larger places (e.g. Patigi, Old Agaie) the principle of the moral responsibility of the family-head for the people living in his compound is still retained, adapted to the new conditions: instead of a compound, *emi,* we have now an aggregation of compounds, the village quarter *efu,* or the town district *shiya;* and the head of the family in which the original elder-rank remains vested still holds, with the rank, the position of an *efutsó,* ward-head. But in Bida this last link, and this last factor of continuity, also disappears. The position of the man whom the people living in one town district would regard as their 'natural' head, and as their representative at the king's court, goes to the member of the titled nobility, residing in the district, who happens to have, at the time, the greatest influence.

Another example is the age-grade societies. The comprehensive organization of one age-group for the whole local community must naturally disappear with the development to a large town. But, in addition, the social purpose which gave life and meaning to the age-group disappears as well. In the town, where farming has lost its dominating position, where professional workmen do the repairs which, in the village, are done by communal work, and, above all, where a completely changed system of ranks and offices deprives the age-group of all influence on the social career, the young men's societies cannot be much else but small, disconnected, voluntary associations of young folk, on the scale perhaps of an entertainment club. Their activity is, in fact, restricted to the arrangement of entertainments, and to the traditional attendance of each other's family feasts. A very large number of such associations are scattered all over the town, with fancy names and fancy titles. Once, at a wedding, my wife and I were ceremonially addressed by a young man who held the imposing title of 'loya' (lawyer), on behalf of a society called 'dina' (dinner). Again the title stays with the member for a lifetime, and again, as in the 'true' young men's societies, the order of ranks valid for the single age-group is supposed to be completely independent of the social status which the member's relations have in 'real' life. The abundance of meaningless titles, ruled by a meaningless, futile order, appears to be a recompense for the disappearance of the 'true' general system of adult titles and political ranks. It is characteristic that a highly educated school malam in Bida, who was asked by an administrative officer to compile notes on Nupe customs, could find no better description for the young men's societies in Bida than this: 'From this day on [the day of the foundation of a group] members of the group will salute each other according to the title received and the salutation prescribed. Nowadays everybody in town has his title, some may even have two or more!'

2

The political organization which Nupe culture evolved in the villages and smaller towns embraces, as we have seen, a number of slightly different systems. It led, in different places, to different solutions of the problem of succession, and distribution of political ranks. The organization of the state could pick out that system only, and could develop that solution only, which was in accordance with its inner tendencies. They can be condensed in three statements: territorial expansion; consolidation of the central authority; and, as special application of the latter, safeguarding of the dynastic interests. A new, much more detailed, and much more rigid social stratification develops. At the head of the social system stands, almost isolated, the *Etsu,* the king of Nupe. The king's kindred, severed from the rest of the titled nobility, form the highest social class, the *ena gitsúzhi,* the 'ones who will become *Etsu'.* A twofold class of office nobility, *sarakízhi,* follows: the *ena ndéji,* or town ranks, and the (completely new) *ena 'kŭ,* the war ranks, or military nobility. Then come the 'masses' of the commoners, the powerless, with no position, and no share in the ruling of their country. They are the *talakawa,* the 'poor ones', titled or wealthy though they may be, as the crafts guilds or the traders. But the wealth of the common trader has hardly procured him any social opening yet; and the old titles of the crafts guilds mean, socially, nothing.[9]

[9] These titles also express an interesting state control which the king exercises over the guilds. For the man who holds the title of the guild-head is at the same time the one to whom all orders from the court are addressed, and who is responsible for their execution. We have here a state tutelage of the professional classes which evidently had the purpose of guaranteeing the constant urgent demand of the large city, the huge court, and the ever active army.

Then there are the slaves. But amongst them a special group, the king's court slaves, or slave officials, constitute a separate influential class, with ranks and titles, often more highly placed than the whole nobility. Between nobility and commoners finally we have again that intermediary class of half-free men, the *bara,* or 'clients'.[10]

The isolated position of the king, his supreme aloofness from the rest of the social system, is based essentially on his position as descendant, or heir, of that sacred founder of Nupe kingdom, Tsoede. Still to-day, in the Mohammedan emirate of Patigi, certain ancient sacred rules and taboos dictate the king's food and clothing, and regulate details of court etiquette. Till the Fulani conquest the kingship was separated from the general social system by the very laws of succession. In sharp contrast to the general practice the royal succession was strict primo-geniture, the king's eldest son, holding the title of *shaba,* was the heir apparent. And, at a certain period at least, the royal succession was still more restricted, and narrowed down to the succession of the eldest son 'born in the purple'.[11] The Fulani then, breaking the line of descent of the Nupe kings, also as-similated the royal succession to the general practice of inheri-tance, i.e. the inheritance by a younger brother, or elder brother's son.

Not till then, therefore, did the literal meaning of *ena gitsúzhi,* the 'ones who will become king', come true. The king becomes a *primus inter pares,* the leader of a powerful royal nobility, which is organized in strict seniority, and an election, though of limited scope, replaces the rigid rule of succession. The three highest ranks of the *gitsú*-nobility, *shába, kpotû,* and *mákû,* have special significance as the ranks next to the king—although not necessarily his heirs. They became linked traditionally with

[10] One word about the titles as such. Some of them are new—non-Nupe, Hausa, Fulani, or even Bornu in origin. But the majority of the titles, and above all, the system as such, is essentially Nupe. It existed in the same form in the pre-Fulani capital Raba, and exists today as a true copy in Patigi and Zuguma, where the descendants of the Raba dynasty rule over their petty emirates.

[11] This type of succession, frequently leading to the necessity of a re-gency for an infant king, weakened the king's position, and eventually (un-der Etsu Maazû and Jimada, about 1800) caused those feuds and civil wars which, in the end, enabled the Fulani to seize the power over a dis-united, fratricidal Nupe dynasty.

the heads of the three branches of the Fulani dynasty in Bida, i.e. with the descendants of the three sons of Malam Dendo, the ancestor of the Nupe-Fulani, who were the first Fulani kings of Nupe. Each of the three royal houses still claims to-day the *etsu*ship over Nupe in turn. But they are rivals rather than allies, and, residing in three different districts of Bida, leaders of separate local factions rather than supporters of a common cause. There is, in fact, a strong attachment between the people living in one town district and 'their' dynasty. It becomes prominent enough in town politics; but built as it is on party rivalry, it can revive none of that relationship of moral responsibility towards the whole community which is expressed in the village system of the *emitsó* and *efutsó*.[12]

3

The distinction between *Etsu* and *gitsú*-nobility as regards the economic position is a distinction of degree only. The king receives the largest share from taxes, fines, and booty taken in war. His possession of more money and more slaves—money with which to trade, and slaves to found new farms and new settlements—leads to ever accumulating wealth and capital, and general power of the royal house. On the other hand, the king has to fulfil certain economic obligations. But they never embrace the whole country, and the whole population. He is expected to give certain traditional presents to the members of the nobility; he has to entertain illustrious guests who may visit the capital; from his share he has to pay the annual tribute to Gwando, the mother town of the Fulani conquerors, thus recognizing to the present day the membership of Nupe in the huge Fulani empires of the north, Gwando and Sokoto. He has also to finance certain public works in the capital, the repair of the town mosque, and the upkeep of the town walls. And he has to keep

---

[12] These three branches of the royal dynasty have clearly a clan character, and form an interesting example of the tenacity of an original clan organization. The clan-structure which dominates the social organization of the nomadic Fulani herdsmen has disappeared almost completely among the settled, town-dwelling conquerors, overshadowed by the new principle of grouping which originated in the Fulani *jihad* (holy war), namely, the religious and military leadership of proselytizing and conquering Fulani emissaries. But in Bida the old principle of social organization reappears, revived perhaps by the indigenous custom of rulership in rotation.

out of his private means his *dogarai,* a permanent police force
(originally the king's private slaves) whose duty it is to guard the
town markets and to act as executive in legal and tax matters. In
all matters of administration the king acts in council with his
nobility, both with the princes of his house and the *sarakízhi.* The
general council, *nkó,* is held regularly in the king's house every
Friday, or whenever need arises. In addition, the *gitsúzhi* and
sarakízhi hold separate councils of their own, supplementary or
preparatory to the general *nkó,* and special officers of liaison
form the link between the two councils—in the person of the
nákordi, one of the highest *gitsú* ranks; and between the *nkó* of
the *sarakízhi* and the king himself—in the person of the *sántali,*
one of the king's court slaves.

The *gitsú*-titles are not limited to family-heads in the sense of
the village system of ranks. In the large group of the king's relations every able-bodied adult can claim a rank. And the number of ranks which a family can accumulate will reflect its position among the nobility, above all, among the ever jealous
kindred, and the favour in which it is held by the king himself.
Yet the *gitsú* ranks had, as it seems, little actual influence in the
nkó, and in the discussion on administrative measures the *sarakízhi* had much more to say, and were—as even the Fulani
would frankly admit—much more competent. The chief activities of the *gitsúzhi* were, first, the administration of villages as
fief-holders, and second, war. But in the war again they would
hold no official position, save for one of the royal princes who
would be made *nda 'kū,* 'father of the war', and given the
(merely nominal) leadership of the army. The rest joined as
more or less independent feudal lords, leading on their private
'armies' of relatives and followers, servants and slaves.

But the *gitsú*-nobility holds one privilege which deeply influences the social situation. They were, and still are, landowners
in the modern sense. Land, appropriated by conquest, extortion,
and confiscation, was of no immediate use to the *gitsú*-nobility.
No farmers, living in the town as war-lords and slave-traders,
they were not interested in agricultural enterprise. But they could
send out slaves or *bara* to found new farm settlements, and to
work there as their 'tenants'. It was a very one-sided tenantship.
The farmers had to return half of their output to their masters;
but the latter were not bound by any strict rules, and could freely

dismiss and change their 'tenants'.[13] This system, based to a large extent on slave labour, broke down after the abolition of slavery. But a second way to make use of their landed property was open to the Fulani, namely, to lease it to Nupe farmers who were anxious to get vacant land, particularly near the town. The lease is not hereditary. After the death of a tenant his heirs have to apply again, and to pay again for it. Although to-day the Fulani landlord has no official authority whatsoever to enforce this contract, the peasants would still be very reluctant to invoke the help of the Native Administration against irregularities or extortions of their landlords.[14]

4

What we said about the economic and social position of the *gitsú* class applies more or less also to the *sarakízhi,* save for the actual owning of land, and the holding of royal fiefs (and this became a privilege of the *gitsú*-nobility only under the Fulani). The *sarakízhi* ranks are again hereditary, i.e. the membership of the civil or military nobility remains the privilege of a number of families. The two classes are mutually exclusive, and are again ruled by strict seniority and promotion. Promotions or new appointments are granted by the king in council with the nobility. The *ena 'kū,* the military class, involves certain special offices in war-time: the *maiyaki* is the general in command, the *uban dawaki* is in charge of the horsemen, the *sokyakó* of the foot soldiers, the *ejikó* of the archers, and so on.[15] And, whereas for *gitsúzhi,* members of the civil nobility, or commoners, the military service is voluntary, it is compulsory for the military caste. Their ranks moreover involve a definite responsibility towards the king as to the carrying out of their particular duties. The ranks of the *ena ndéji,* on the other hand, have originated directly from the old system of town elders. Still to-day they bear

[13] Three such 'private' settlements, excellently organized, exist just outside the town walls of Bida. They are called *ésozhi,* and are the property of the three ruling houses of Nupe.

[14] During my stay in Bida it happened for the first time, and was duly commented on amongst the natives, that a peasant refused to suffer the injustice of one of the Fulani landlords, and applied to the native court for arbitration in a matter of his lease.

[15] For some of these titles the 'modern' Hausa name has replaced the old Nupe title, e.g. the head of the military class is to-day generally called *maiyaki,* instead of the old Nupe *tsadza.*

witness to this origin, e.g. the present *ndéji* is the descendant of the original *ndéji* family at the Nupe court of Raba. But the former connexion with a special office in the town administration has vanished completely. What remains can be described only by the vague and general term of 'councillors'.

The specialized office which thus disappeared from the ranks of the civil nobility reappears in another social group: among the king's court slaves. They are, as we have seen, not only officers in charge of the royal household, but also his trusted servants in state affairs, officially appointed tax-collectors, they form his police force, etc. It is not accidental that these offices were not, or not necessarily, hereditary, nor dependent upon a consent of the *nkó*, but granted by the king directly, and *ad personam*.

A few words must finally be said, once more, about the institution of clientage. Here in the town it becomes a completely different thing. It is connected—one is almost tempted to say: like everything in the town—with a title. And 'protection' means now the opportunity of becoming 'somebody', of being lifted from the ignominy of commoners into the sphere of rank and social importance. The types of service expected from the *bara* vary considerably, from the position of a servant for light work to the rank of a major-domo, or the position of a personal friend and confidant.[16] To-day many of the freed slaves have stayed on, as *bara*, in their master's house. Close personal attachment may lead to a semi-hereditary title-holding. A patron will pay the tax for his *bara*, will educate their children and marry off their sons. For the number and quality of the *bara* attached to a house indicates the social position and political influence of the master. Yet what you would call a 'clever' *bara* would chose his protector, leave him as soon as his influence decreases, and look for another, more influential patron. Social climbers with plenty of money may even work their way up to, or become directly, members of the élite of 'clients', a *bara* of the king. And from here his social career might take a new turn. For the position of a king's *bara* is a good jumping-off place for 'real' titles. In assessment censuses and such like the *bara* will be found de-

---

[16] These highest titles would be *sōfáda* and *mijindadi*. Linguistically the difference between *bara* ranks and 'real' ranks, i.e. ranks granted by king and council, is marked by the additional *-kó* (the suffix meaning great) or *'tsu* (i.e. 'of the king'), e.g. *sōfáda* and *sōfádakó*.

scribed mostly as having 'no occupation', or only leisure-time jobs such as hat-making or embroidery. But what we are apt to deplore as a socially detrimental class of idle hangers-on has yet its proper place in the social system.

5

All the ranks which we have surveyed here, whether they involve definite offices or not, imply one element: sharp class-distinction, and, as such, definite regulations of social behaviour. We have before us a system of social gradation of remarkable thoroughness, and for that matter of remarkable conspicuousness. For the Nupe address each other by titles only, never by names. Special formulae of greeting are linked with the different titles. The position in society is marked by the most obvious signs—everyday speech. Social life appears crystallized in a bureaucracy whose elaborate schematism, and most conspicuous symbolism, reminds one of the system of ranks and titles which existed in Imperial Rome, or at the Byzantine court.

The working of such a close system of social gradation is defined by the degree of social mobility, of inter-class transition, which it implies. The dynastic ranks, to begin with, both Fulani and pre-Fulani, were rigidly secluded from the general scope of social promotion. The military and civil nobility, on the other hand, were, to a certain extent, open to new blood. Out of the twenty-two ranks of the civil and military class in Bida to-day, four of the highest titles belong to men who are of low descent not farther back than in the second or third generation. The element of social promotion implied in the system of clientage we have just mentioned. But this scope of social upward movement does not stop at the boundaries of the capital. In a wider sense the system of social stratification comprises the whole country. And on this enlarged scale the commoners in the town, the *talakawa,* the people of no name and title, rank higher than the people and tribes without—with their petty village titles and offices. The town citizen looks down upon the 'village heathen', as the Nupe often put it, ridiculing their habits and character, their fashions and the way they talk, their lack of education and 'urbanity'. There is, of course, more in this than merely distinction of status. Living in the capital, in pre-European times, meant living in the security both of a strongly protected town and of the

safer system of social supervision directly by the central authority. But it also means the opportunity to benefit by the central,
wealthiest market of the country, it means cultural progress, education, development of arts and crafts. There is no doubt, and
it is expressed in all family statistics both in the town and in the
districts, that this situation resulted in a strong and continuous
movement to the town.

The gravest test which such a social system could undergo
occurs in the changed conditions of the present-day native society. Undoubtedly its whole essence has been deeply affected.
With the disappearance of slave-trade, slave-labour, and wars of
conquest, class-distinctions have been reduced to a large extent
to mere distinctions of status, devoid of their former economic
background. Yet they became only more rigid and more impass-
able. For one of the essential means of social promotion, war,
distinction in military service, has ceased to exist. It is true that
another element is creeping in instead, namely, wealth, money.
Traders who were completely excluded from the higher classes
have now been admitted here and there to the ranks of the nobility. Yet among the four titles of 'new men' mentioned, only
one owes his appointment to money. It is amazing to see how
little the meaning which this rigid, almost sterile system of ranks
has for the people has been affected. I have seen three vacancies
occur among the highest ranks in Nupe; and I have witnessed the
ensuing party feuds, the passionate interplay of interests, the bar-
tering for support and influence, in short, all those signs of a
charged social atmosphere which can be characteristic only of a
system which is still intensely alive.

6

European influence has not uprooted the system, but has perhaps
altered its direction. In creating the new offices of the Native
Administration which are so far given only to the titled nobility,
it introduced a new goal, or perhaps better, it reintroduced a
social goal, of more than merely 'status'-function, into the system
of ranks. Court offices or royal fiefs in former days, and appointments to the Native Administration to-day—however big the difference seems—in a certain way mean the same: an incentive to
social promotion, so essential in Nupe society. But this influence
goes beyond the scope of the existing class-distinctions, it is in

fact strong enough to influence, and to assist, the development of a new social class.

There is no doubt that in Nupe, as most probably in the whole Northern Protectorate, a new social stratum is coming into being. It stands outside the narrow rank-system. It is open to commoners, and, at the same time, shares the status of the titled nobility and their influence on political affairs. It is rooted in Mohammedanism and its traditional reverence for knowledge and learning. What the type of this learning is in reality, we will not examine. Malams, 'learned ones', are its representatives, and parents let their children become malams to open this social future for them. Malams intermarry freely with the highest, even dynastic ranks. The daughters and sisters of the high-born become their wives with a very small, nominal bride-price, for such a marriage means *sadaka,* pious alms, as prescribed by the Koran. The *Etsu* himself puts the 'malam' before his name. Malams hold the highest state offices (which actually tend to become more and more hereditary): the office of the *liman* (Iman), *naibi* (his assistant), and *alkali* (Kadi). But also without holding office or titles malams may become very influential factors at the court. Malams of a lower class are attached to any household of consequence. They are advisers and preachers, teachers of the children and confidants of the adults, in one person. But there is the other element in it, that malams need not work, for they will be given alms and presents by everybody, and they will always find a place to live. A large proportion of them only becomes a privileged, idle 'intelligentsia' between the classes.

This group of 'learned men' does not form, perhaps, a social class in the strict sense. It harbours too many shades and distinctions, and lacks the element of solidarity. Yet there are strong links—above all, the common factor of profession, and of a free, individual career. It is here that modern development is bound to play its part. Under modern conditions education, even the mere knowledge of reading and writing, gained new importance. New offices, administrative and educational, were opened to natives. Many high rank-holders who became officials of the Native Administration needed educated malams as secretaries or assistants. But general education, extending the scope of learning, does something far more important. It helps to build up this new social stratum. Extending knowledge, it extends a strong common

bond which will in the end dissolve the exclusiveness of the narrow class-system; provided, of course—we cannot refrain from
adding—that the education is really general, and is really absorbed by the social classes. The idle, aloof malam 'intelligentsia'
is a warning example.

VII. CONCLUSION

We have just touched upon the far-reaching—too far-reaching
for this article—problem of European administration versus native social structure. But there are two aspects of this problem
we must refer to, intimately connected as they are with the contents of this last chapter, which is to be summary and conclusion.

In our introduction we drew attention to a deep antagonism
between two social principles, State and Community. I believe
that in the course of this article the legitimacy of this dualism has
become evident. We could study it, so to speak, in motion, for
our investigation was essentially the investigation of a social system in transition. We placed in the fore of our analysis the
changes in the system of 'social control'. But what we actually
had to deal with was a real and complete transformation of
values, from the changes in the system of social gradation down
to the standard of everyday life. In an important side-issue we
were led to the problem of rural and urban sociology, to the social
cleavage between the town and the provincial districts. There is
no need to stress the special relevance of this aspect as it affects
the problem of present-day development under European administration. But it is essential to realize that this development will
not be determined only by the political situation as such, by such
factors as distribution of political authority, i.e. by the direct influence of European administration on the native governmental
system. Deeper in their effect, because more obscure and more
subtle in their working, are influences which come from other,
quasi-secondary factors. They appear wherever the apparatus of
our civilization appears. They crystallize in schools, churches,
traffic, markets, canteens, hospitals, in all those powerful instruments of integration and unity which yet so easily turn into weapons of distinction and separation.

And another thing: one can say that from the beginning the
British administration was aware of an inherent antagonism in

the social system of the Nupe and of all Fulani emirates in the north, namely, of the fact that the government system which it found in the country, and which it tried to adopt according to the ideas of Indirect Rule, was a government which had been evolved by an alien ruler caste, and which perhaps did not represent the social system of the indigenous population of the country (Lugard 1905:458). The danger then, for an administration under Indirect Rule was obvious. And certain measures to counteract this antagonistic situation might have suggested themselves. We have tried in our analysis to define and to delimit the exact influence of the Fulani element. We had to realize that it was an influence bound to intensify conflicts and to widen gulfs, but not an influence which was responsible for the creation of the political system as such. State and rulership in Nupe are not an importation from outside, due to the conquest by the alien ruler race. Where conquest played its part, it did so as part and parcel of the political development. And where elements of antagonism and tension arose, they arose, not out of a conspicuous clash of races, but out of essentially sociological processes. What emerged from our analysis was a much more subtle development, and a deeper type of antagonism, namely, the almost eternal antagonism of developed State versus that raw material of the Community which, always and everywhere, must form the nourishing soil from which alone the State can grow.

15 ON INCA POLITICAL STRUCTURE

John V. Murra

John V. Murra is Professor of Anthropology at Yale University. He is the author of *Survey and Excavations in Southern Ecuador* (with Donald Collier, 1943), and many papers.

SOME ASPECTS of Inca political organization have attracted attention for centuries, and their functioning is well understood—roads, for example. The enormous territory incorporated through conquest within the Inca state and the broken terrain required some system to keep the periphery in touch with the center and the coast with the highlands, the potential rebels within striking distance of the garrison, the census official reporting to the Cuzco bureaucracy. The road network provided for all that and more. While we still do not know all the intricacies of the *corvée* labor required to build and service these roads and bridges, we nevertheless have a fair picture of what the network was and how it worked (Rowe 1946:229–33; Von Hagan 1955).

There are other aspects of the political system where more research will be welcome: the administrative machinery set up for both direct and "indirect" or traditional rule of the conquered ethnic groups and confederacies requires a new look at the old evidence; so does the army and the function of the military campaign. The writer has elsewhere reported on a new way of viewing the *mitmaq,* the famous colonists resettled by the Ince state (Murra 1956: ch. 8; 1960:393–407).

FROM V. F. Ray (editor), *Systems of Political Control and Bureaucracy in Human Societies,* Proceedings of the 1958 Annual Spring Meeting of the American Ethnological Society, pp. 30–41, by permission of the author, the American Ethnological Society, and of the University of Washington Press.

Meanwhile, the focus of interest continues to be centered on the special features of the Inca system which have made it probably the most studied of American civilizations. From the first European chroniclers publishing their impressions at Seville within two years of the invasion, the sociopolitical structure erected in the fifteenth century in the central Andes has consistently been viewed as unusual, and by some as utopian: here were *gente de razón,* civilized folk, with cities and temples, irrigation and elites; with warehouses to store the surplus. Nobody was "poor" or starving.

This last feature made the greatest impression. Over the years the notion has grown that Inca society when met by the Europeans was a welfare, some say a "socialist," state where "the government insured the individual against every sort of want and, in return demanded heavy tribute . . ." (Rowe 1946:273).

I do not propose here to review this controversy. "Socialist" or "feudal" or "totalitarian"—there is no value in attempts to classify the Inca in terms of European economic and political history. What we need is a re-examination of the evidence in the light of what anthropology has learned in recent decades, ethnographically, in the field, about preliterate but stratified societies, particularly in the Pacific and Africa. When we come to a state structure of this unusual kind, I suggest we ask some anthropological questions about the community and its relations to the state, about the creation of the necessary state revenues, and about the ideology which, in addition to coercion, made this system endure. I doubt if understanding will come if we begin the study with the role of the king, the "commoners" and "noblemen," the bureaucracy, or the state-encouraged worship of the sun.

It was Heinrich Cunow who in the 1890's was the first to place the Incaic data in an ethnographic framework by directing attention to the *ayllu,* the lineage-based community which had been ignored by previous students. His emphasis is still basic to all Inca research.[1]

It is true that the Inca state did establish some revenue-producing estates and "assign" them to the crown or the church.

[1] See the various works of Heinrich Cunow, "Das Verwandschaftsistem und die Geschlechtsverbaende der Inka," *Das Ausland* 64 (1891); *Soziale Verfassung des Inkareiches* (1896); *Geschichte und Kultur des Inkareiches* (Amsterdam, 1937).

Some of this cultivable area, destined primarily for maize-growing (Murra 1956: ch. 1)[2] was created by state-sponsored improvements of previously uncultivated *kishwa* slopes through irrigation and terracing. Where this was not enough, most notably on the coast, lineage lands owned and worked by the conquered tribes, now a peasantry, were alienated and incorporated into the crown's domain. This was probably facilitated by the fact that state alienation and state control through large-scale irrigation were present on the coast before the Incas (Rowe 1948). Cuzco also imposed onerous agricultural, public works, and military *corvée;* it even removed some people from their families and ethnic jurisdiction to assign them to full-time chores as retainers of the crown (Murra 1956: ch. 8). Even so, in 1500 the state apparently could not afford to interfere with the peasant's ability to feed himself and his kinfolk when in need; he continued to do so in the Andes by growing without irrigation the locally domesticated tuber crops within a system of traditional lineage and ethnic tenures.

In 1500, then, there are two dimensions to Inca agriculture and land tenure. In the nature of the system, both sets of rights, those of the state and the traditional ones of the local community, were real, economically and politically significant forces.

It is our job now to clarify the relationship between these two systems. Although they are separable, one of them, the *ayllu* community, functions within the state's framework of economic, social, and political controls. What were the claims made by the crown on the *ayllu,* and what then did the crown offer in return?

Inca history, as dredged from the memory and the knot records of the *amauta,* credits king Pachakuti the Transformer with "inventing" most of the administrative devices which kept a state functioning in the Andes. It is hard to accept this bureaucrats' culture-hero as a historical figure, yet in the light of Rowe's (Rowe 1945), reconstruction of Inca history, which telescopes the kingdom's expansion to a single century this may be true. If Pachakuti and his son Thupa were actually the first real power-wielders and consolidators in the Andes, it is to be expected that this extremely rapid expansion of a true

[2] For one view of the significance of irrigation in the Andes see Wittfogel (1957) and Palerm (1958).

342   *John V. Murra*

state would require new institutional forms and a new ideology. Most of the innovations consisted of reorganizations and of projections onto a wider screen of old, deep-rooted Andean techniques; the others were of necessity new, there being no precedent for some of the problems now faced by the state (Rowe 1946:260; 1948).[3]

When the crown elaborated a system of labor services, the community reciprocal obligations known and understood by all served as a model. Blas Valera calls it "the law of brotherhood": all the inhabitants of the village helped one another to clear the land, plant, and harvest, all of it "without any pay."[4] Newlyweds were entitled to a house built for them "once agreement was reached on a date."[5] If the task was larger and involved several lineages, each took turns until the task was completed.[6]

One cannot now determine with any precision how large these work parties were, how they were organized, or what equivalences and proportions were traditional. There is little doubt that a detailed formula for reciprocity had been devised, particularly for agricultural tasks. Polo says that "when a job is to be done, they never begin without figuring out and measuring what each share would be . . . each family's part is known as *suyu*. . . . Once this is completed, they set out."[7] Tasks were allotted to households, not to individuals.

The community also assumed responsibility for the aged, the widows and orphans, the sick and the lame. Their condition did not prevent them from claiming or holding on to their traditional allotment of land, but, since they were unable to cultivate it,

[3] Rowe has suggested that the administrative system of the coastal kingdom of Chimor was the "principal model . . . borrowed" by the Incas (1948:34–35, 45–46). If further evidence on this point is discovered, it will strengthen Wittfogel's "hydraulic" hypothesis as applied to the Andes (1957). Kirchhoff has postulated the existence of pre-Incaic "true empires" where "conquest took a much more solid form" than in Meso-America (1949:306). If so, Pachakuti and Thupa could have learned their statecraft elsewhere and need not have developed it from *ayllu*, reciprocity-based models.

[4] In Garcilaso de la Vega, "El Inca," *Primera parte de los comentarios reales* . . . [1604], ed. Angel Rosenblatt (Buenos Aires, 1943), p. 245. See also Juan Polo de Ondegardo, "Informe . . . al Licenciado Briviesca de Muñatones . . . [1561]," *Revista Historica,* tomo 13 (Lima, 1940).

[5] Garcilaso, *op. cit.,* p. 195; Blas Valera in Garcilaso, *op. cit.,* p. 82.

[6] Blas Valera in Garcilaso, *op. cit.,* p. 245.

[7] Polo (1940), *loc. cit.*

it was farmed for them by the community.[8] We are told that a local official, a *llakta kamayoq,* supervised the working of such lands.[9] Sometimes supervisory work was assigned to the crippled or old "if sufficient and able." Poma reports that such men were also in charge of distributing irrigation waters.[10]

The community as a whole cultivated some patches of ground to produce the maize beer needed for ritual libations. These should not be confused with the "estates of the church" (Murra 1956: ch. 2). We are dealing here with community responsibilities to local shrines and deities, but our best chroniclers have confused the two, and we owe our ability to discern them at all to the parish-oriented reports of the idol-burners of the early seventeenth century.[11]

Traditional, local chiefs, known as *kuraka,* also had claim to community support. We learn from an early inquiry in 1557 in Huamanga that local chiefs received "no tribute, no salary."[12] The peasants "worked for their subsistence a certain area of fields, and when needed, the house; and they [also] gave them [the chiefs] in rotation [*ayllu* by *ayllu*], men and women to serve them and bring water and wood." Later writers, all of them lawyers and administrators who dealt daily with *kuraka* in and out of court, confirm independently that the chiefs "received no tribute of any kind save respect and the working of their fields"; they were entitled to "services" and their houses

[8] Juan Polo de Ondegardo, *Relación de los fundamentos acerca del notable dano que resulta de no guardar a los Indios sus fueros* [1571]. Colección de Libros y Documentos Referentes a la Historia del Perú, serie 1, tomo 3 (Lima, 1916), p. 60; Garcilaso, *op. cit.,* p. 227.

[9] Polo (1916), *op. cit.,* p. 131; Garcilaso, *loc. cit.*

[10] Felipe Huamán Poma de Ayla, *Nueva corónica y buen gobierno* [1615]. Institut d'Ethnologie (Paris, 1936), p. 799.

[11] Writing fully seventy years after the European invasion, when the Inca land tenure system and particularly the state church had been completely destroyed, they report that the local gods still benefited from the patches of land surreptitiously reserved for them. Such lands were always worked first, and nobody could sow his own before fulfilling his responsibility to the community shrine. See Francisco de Avila (editor), *De priscorum Huaruchiriensium* . . . [1608]. Bibliothecae Nationalis Matritensis edidit Hippolytus Galante. Consejo Superior de Investigaciones Científicas, Instituto Gonzalo Fernández de Oviedo (Madrid, 1942), folio 84ᵛ; Pablo José de Arriaga, *Extirpación de la idolatría en el Perú* . . . [1621]. Colección de Libros y Documentos Referentes a la Historia del Perú, serie 2, tomo 1 (Lima, 1920), p. 43.

[12] Marcos Jimenez de la Espada (editor), *Relaciones geográficas de Indias,* 4 vols. (Madrid, 1881–97), pp. 1, 99.

were built for them much like any one else's house. Apparently they had rights in *ayllu* lands, like any other household, at least in pre-Inca times. Local headmen worked in the fields themselves; others did so only ceremonially.[13]

As we can see even from this obviously incomplete list of labor services and reciprocal exchanges within the community, the governing idea of the system is time, labor time. Beyond such reciprocity, each household was thought of as self-sufficient, and enough access to the society's capital goods was available to make such self-sufficiency the dominant reality.

As we shift now to the state level, nowhere is there mention of contributions in kind, real tribute, or in any medium of exchange. Labor services were provided by the peasant community to the state in addition to but in much the same way as *ayllu* tasks and obligations to their own *kuraka*. Falcon says, "They were only required to work the lands of the Inca, herd their llamas, weave cloth, erect buildings, mine. . . ."[14] Garcilaso states, "They contributed only their personal work, the main tribute being the working of state and church lands."[15] According to Polo: "All that they gave their kings were personal services. . . . No other obligation but work . . . [to the point where today] they resent it more when they have to give a peck of potatoes than when they work for fifteen days with the community at some task."[16]

[13] For additional detail consult the three lawyer-chroniclers: Francisco Falcon, *Representación hecha en concilio provincial* . . . [ca. 1580]. Colección de Libros y Documentos Referentes a la Historia del Perú, serie 1, tomo 2 (Lima, 1918), pp. 144–45, 152; Hernando de Santillán, *Relación del origen, decendencia, política y gobierno de los Incas* [1563–1564]. Colección de Libros y Documentos Referentes a la Historia del Perú, serie 2, tomo 9 (Lima, 1927), pp. 13, 18, 41; Polo (1916), *op. cit.*, pp. 171, 176. See also Cristobal de Castro and Diego Ortega Morejón, *Relación y declaración del modo que en este valle de Chincha* . . . [1558], ed. Herman Trimborn. Quellen zur Kulturgeschichte des praekolumbischen Amerika. Studien zur Kulturkunde, Vol. 3 (Lima, 1951), pp. 243, 245; Poma, *op. cit.*, pp. 197, 218, 456; Garcilaso, *loc. cit.*; Bernabe Cobo, *Historia del Nuevo Mundo* (1653), ed. Marcos Jiménez de la Espada. Sociedad de bibliófilos andaluces, 4 vols. (Sevilla, 1890–1893), pp. 226–27, 243, 245.
[14] Falcon, *op. cit.*, pp. 144, 154.
[15] Garcilaso, *op. cit.*, pp. 232–33.
[16] Polo (1940), *op. cit.*, pp. 165, 169. In a later report he elaborated: "no one contributed from his own things, nor from what he harvested— only the work of his own person" (1916, *op. cit.*, p. 67) and again "the tributes were paid from whatever the Inca and the Sun had earmarked for themselves and not from one's own, nor from what everyone raised" (*ibid.*, p. 88).

One indication of the care and continuity with which the *corvée*-as-reciprocity principle was observed by the state is the provision of beer and food for the work party. This obligation prevailed at the local level: he whose house was being built would fete the workers, and so did the *kuraka* whose fields were being harvested. Projected to the state level, this means that the *corvée* group did not have to provide its own food, tools, or seed; all this was taken care of by the "generosity" of the state, the church, or other beneficiary of the work.[17]

In the formation of a state and the elaboration of its revenue system, one of the most important early steps is the census of population, lands, animals, and current production. The legendary material recorded by Betanzos ascribes to Pachakuti the development of a census.[18] Cieza was told that such quantitative procedures went back earlier, to Sinchi Roq'a.[19] There is no reason to doubt Cieza. The *khipu,* the knot record used for enumeration, existed before Pachakuti, probably even before the Incas, but it is only with the extension and the elaboration of the state and its bureaucracy that the nationwide census came into its own. Fifteen years after the European invasion, knot records of state supplies were still being kept in some areas, indicating the strength and persistence of this princess of bureaucratic practices.[20] Much of what has been written about Inca administration is in my opinion erroneous because of a confusion between census categories, bureaucratic hopes, and real life. Let us test this by asking: who was liable for the *corvée* which was at the heart of state revenues?

The liability was not individual.[21] The household was the unit to which a quota of work was assigned, and beyond it came the *ayllu* or the village. The *kuraka* and, below him, the head of the household saw to it that the labor services were performed. Thus "no one paid tribute who lacked a wife or land, even if he had a child" because he had no formally

---

[17] Falcon, *op. cit.,* pp. 145, 152; Polo (1916), *op. cit.,* p. 60; Garcilaso, *op. cit.,* p. 233; Cobo, *op. cit.,* p. 245.

[18] Juan de Betanzos, *Suma y narración de los Incas . . .* [1551]. Biblioteca Hispano-Ultramarina, tomo 5 (Madrid; 1880), pp. 75–76.

[19] Pedro Cieza de Leon, *Segunda parte de la crónica del Perú . . .* [1550], ed. A. M. Salas (Buenos Aires, 1943), p. 68.

[20] Polo (1916), *op. cit.,* pp. 77, 136.

[21] Polo (1940), *op. cit.,* pp. 148, 150; (1916) *op. cit.,* p. 145.

constituted and enumerated household to back and help him.[22] "It is only from the marriage day on that men became tax-payers and took part in public works."[23]

Youths began by helping their families in working off house-hold and later community and state obligations. They accompanied the army, helped work the fields, and otherwise under-took what one would think of as adult duties.[24] The difference apparently lies not so much in the kind of work done but in the degree of responsibility of the citizen: until marriage, the young were assigned to their tasks by their fathers, who were the responsible ones since they alone were enumerated. Once their own homes were set up the young became responsible for census and *corvée* purposes. Here we see an example of Inca statecraft: *corvée* and "taxpaying" beyond the community's limits are state requirements; marriage is a traditional *rite de passage;* for state purposes marriage becomes the locally meaningful and, the Inca hoped, palatable symbol of the new status not only in the community, but in the wider state structure. This is the origin of the widely held impression that the state "married" the young or supervised their "formal betrothal." What the state actually did was to transform a personal and community threshold into a census device.

The able-bodied, *corvée*-owing adult is described as a *watun runa,* a big man.[25] As long as he was not sick or crippled, the "big man" led his household in the performance of state obligations.[26] We are told that the occasion was defined as a joyous one, the families going to work singing, in their best clothes.[27] It is obvious that an attempt was made to extend to *corvée* duties the feeling-tone of community reciprocal aid. While at work the peasants were, as we have seen, provided with food and beer by the state, and they bore no responsibility for the quality of the harvest. All they owed was their labor; whatever

[22] Castro and Ortega, *op. cit.,* p. 245.

[23] Cobo, *op. cit.,* p. 182.

[24] Jimenez, *op. cit.,* p. 71; Santillán, *op. cit.,* p. 18; Poma, *op. cit.,* p. 203 (illustration, p. 202).

[25] Baltasar Ramirez, *Description del reyno del Piru* . . . [1591], ed. Herman Trimborn. Quellen zur Kulturgeschichte des praekolumbischen Amerika. Studien zur Kulturkunde, Vol. 3 (Stuttgart, 1936), p. 22; Castro and Ortega, *op. cit.,* pp. 240–45.

[26] Polo (1940), *op. cit.,* p. 181.

[27] *Ibid.,* p. 169; (1916), *op. cit.,* p. 60.

they harvested was stored by the state.[28] The quota assigned to each census unit was known and apparently independent of household size; various sources insist that, if one had a larger dependent kin-group, one was through faster and thus considered "rich" or, as they probably put it, more *watun,* bigger.[29]

Equated with the *watun runa* from a citizen's labor-owing point of view were the occupants of the lower rungs of the *kuraka* hierarchy. Unfortunately the data on this point are all clothed in the decimal terminology of the *khipu* census. Garcilaso and Cobo agree that *kuraka* "in charge of fifty and fewer households" worked in the fields like "taxpaying commoners."[30] This would correspond to a settlement of two hundred to three hundred souls, whose leader is likely to be a local man, tied by endless kinship ties to the local community, and in that sense a working member of it. We are told that those responsible for a "hundred or more" households were allegedly free of *corvée.* Other chroniclers disagree: only *kuraka* in charge of five hundred, some say of a thousand, households were exempt.[31]

Part of this confusion arises, of course, because the bureaucratic, decimal, round-numbers approach cannot be made to correspond to either demographic or power realities.[32] Villages,

[28] For more corroborative detail see Cieza de Leon (1943), *op. cit.,* p. 258; Castro and Ortega, *op. cit.,* p. 244; Polo (1940), *op. cit.,* pp. 137–38, 147–48; (1916), *op. cit.,* pp. 60, 70, 96, 100, 127; Falcon, *op. cit.,* pp. 147, 150–52; Santillán, *op. cit.,* pp. 17–18, 38, 42; Pedro Sarmiento de Gamboa, *Historia Indica* [1572] (Buenos Aires, 1943), pp. 103, 117–18; Jeronimo Roman y Zamora, *Republicas de Indias* [1575]. Colección de Libros Raros y Curiosos que Tratan de America, tomos 13–14 (Madrid, 1897), p. 37; Miguel Cabello Valboa, *Miscelanea antartica* [1586]. Universidad Nacional Mayor de San Marcos, Facultad de Letras, Instituto de Etnologia (Madrid, 1951), p. 299; Jimenez, *op. cit.,* Vol. 1, p. 84; Vol. 2, pp. 18, 58, 71; Martin de Morúa, *Historia del origen y de la genealogia real de los Incas* [1590], ed. Constantino Bayle (Madrid, 1946), pp. 322–23; Garcilaso, *op. cit.,* pp. 232–33.
[29] Falcon, *op. cit.,* p. 152; Polo (1940), *op. cit.,* p. 139; Blas Valera in Garcilaso, *op. cit.,* p. 256; Cobo, *op. cit.,* p. 248.
[30] Garcilaso, *op. cit.,* p. 250; Cobo, *op. cit.,* p. 244.
[31] Polo (1940), *op. cit.,* p. 138; Poma, *op. cit.,* pp. 455, 738, 793.
[32] Some modern students accept the decimal vocabulary as reflecting the facts of Inca administration. See Luis Valcarcel, *Del aillu al Imperio* (Lima, 1925), p. 104; Louis Baudin, *L'empire socialiste des Incas.* Institut d'Ethnologie (Paris, 1928), pp. 124–31; Means (1931:292–95); Rowe (1946:267); Helen Constas, *Bureaucratic Collectivism.* Unpublished M.A. thesis, New School for Social Research (New York, 1949), pp. 22, 32; Wittfogel (1957: 117, 309).

even if resettled by administrative fiat, cannot be made to conform to any neat decimal system. Similarly, one village or valley
leader will work with his kin in the fields while another, in
charge of an ethnic community of the same size, will not, according to local power, kinship, or traditional arrangements.
There is no need to set any numerical dividing line between
kuraka owing *corvée* and those exempt. The fact that it appears
at all in the chroniclers' reports may be due as much to the
insistence of the European interviewer as to the propensity for
neatness of the Inca census-takers. It is unlikely that there ever
existed a decimal administrative system as a substitute for the
ethnic *ayllu,* tribe, or confederacy. I suggest that we have confused a census-takers' vocabulary and shorthand for the real
thing.[33]

An example of this contrast between census hopes and reality
are the prohibitions on geographic mobility frequently mentioned
among the rigidities and "totalitarian" features ascribed to the
regime. Santillán states that severe punishment awaited anyone
who ran away from one "town" to another,[34] while Polo says
that "the contributions and distributions [of tasks] were extremely
easy. . . . It was the obligation of everyone not to leave his
land once he was assigned and counted off."[35] We know that
this did not work. People went off to war and never came back,
they were moved as *mitmaq* or became full-time retainers, rose
in rebellion and hid from the enumerator, neglected working
the state lands, abandoned or absconded with loads, and otherwise "failed to tribute."[36] Still, Polo reports accurately, I think,
the spirit prevailing among the census takers.

Some sectors of the state revenue system functioned without
a special call. They were repetitive, foreseeable activities, similar

[33] For further details on the census see Murra (1956: ch. 5).
[34] Santillán, *op. cit.,* p. 20.
[35] Polo (1916), *op. cit.,* pp. 82–83.
[36] Cieza de Leon (1943), *op. cit.,* p. 69; Castro and Ortega, *op. cit.,*
pp. 240, 244. The attempt to "hide" a number of citizens from the census
for personal profit and power led according to legend to the establishment
of *yana* retainers (Sarmiento de Gamboa, *op. cit.,* pp. 115–16; Cabello
Valboa, *op. cit.,* pp. 346–47). Such peculation by royal administrators and
inspectors must have taken place but is only rarely reported by our chroniclers. Poma reflects more closely the sentiments of the populace when he
reports that many of the inspectors and collectors carried "false rumors
and lies" (*op. cit.,* p. 363).

to reciprocal duties the peasant meets as a member of the village community. The administration of this system required primarily custodian duties: the upper echelons saw to it that the *kuraka* enforced the expenditure of *corvée* time.

When we shift from perennial to occasional duties such as the building of roads and fortresses, the expansion of irrigation and terraces, military service or mining, it is evident that the amount of planning required would be much greater. It would require the balancing and adjustment of rival claims of the various groups of bureaucrats for the services of the same number of able-bodied citizens. The king's interests would also play a role. The administrative and institutional expression assumed by all these forces would be of great interest to us but are unavailable in any detail. The legendary material collected by Betanzos, cited above, is probably the best approximation. Before an extraordinary assignment was made, the people responsible for its execution, probably both royalty and major *kuraka,* were gathered at Cuzco. The meeting was administrative, ceremonial, and redistributive—the king "offered beer and *kuka* leaf"; "the *kuraka* were given a five-day feast." The task was then outlined, discussed, and ratified, and the conferees returned to their satrapies laden with gifts.[37] What jockeying for position preceded the meeting, who the participants in the "council" actually were, what measure of opinion and local interest could freely be expressed—all these remain matters of conjecture at the present stage of Andean studies.

What is demonstrable is that in the Inca system all able-bodied males—heads of households—owed labor services to the state, even if they did not always deliver them. This is what Cobo meant when he said that "all [the kings'] wealth consisted in the multitude of vassals which they possessed."[38]

In such circumstances it is interesting that the state made an ideological effort to phrase these exactions in the terminology of traditional Andean reciprocity. It is hard to say how many Inca citizens they had convinced by 1532, but their effort was at least partially successful: it convinced the European chroniclers and some modern students that the Inca crown controlled the country's whole economic and social life for what were es-

[37] Betanzos, *op. cit.,* pp. 60–62, 80, 107–8; Morúa, *op. cit.,* pp. 332–35.
[38] Cobo, *op. cit.,* p. 289.

sentially welfare purposes. In the process we underrate the continuing self-sufficiency and reciprocity of peasant endeavor, even after the Inca conquest, and we misunderstand the nature and aims of the redistributive functions of the crown. Having usurped for state use the *corvée* services of the peasantry and the whole productive effort of the retainers, as well as having eliminated most trade, the crown had at its disposal vast storehouses only a fraction of whose content went for strictly court use.

The variety of warehouses and their contents have frequently been described with awe.[39] In 1547, fifteen years after the European invasion, Polo was still able to feed close to two thousand men for seven weeks with provisions from the Xauxa warehouses. He estimates that there were more than 15,000 *hanegas* (2,400,000 bushels) of foodstuffs still in storage after years of looting and breakdown.[40] One need not accept the chroniclers' estimates as accurate to realize that here were major surpluses, carefully husbanded for large-scale state operations.[41]

Some of the chroniclers emphasize the primarily military purpose of the revenues and stores; others, devoted to the welfare hypothesis, suggest that the main goal was stockpiling for times of need. The state itself justified the accumulation by referring to its gigantic hospitality budget.

The military purposes are unquestioned and need not detain us here. Evidence is also overwhelming that those on *corvée,* the royal lineages, and the bureaucracy were all fed and supplied from state warehouses. Controversy centers on the welfare aims: Blas Valera and Garcilaso de la Vega have created the impression that one of the major characteristics of the Inca state was the provision of reserves against drought, frost, and

---

[39] Francisco de Xerez, *Verdadera relación de la conquista del Perú* . . . [1534]. Biblioteca de Autores Españoles, tomo 2 (Madrid, 1853), pp. 322, 326; Pedro Cieza de Leon, *Primera parte de la crónica del Perú* . . . [1550]. Biblioteca de Autores Españoles, Historiadores Primitivos de Indias, tomo 2 (Madrid, 1862), pp. 74–75; (1943), *op. cit.,* p. 435; Pedro Pizarro, *Relación del descubrimiento y conquista de los reynos del Perú* [1572]. Colección de Documentos Ineditos para la Historia de España, tomo 5 (Madrid, 1844), p. 271; Poma, *op. cit.,* pp. 335, 1150; Cobo, *op. cit.,* pp. 234, 254, 266.

[40] Polo (1916), *op. cit.,* p. 77; also Agustin de Zarate, *Historia del descubrimiento y conquista de la provincia del Perú* . . . [1555]. Biblioteca de Autores Españoles, tomo 26 (Madrid, 1853), pp. 563, 566.

[41] Cieza de Leon (1862), *op. cit.,* p. 397.

famine. This unusual assumption of responsibility, along with the state's prohibition of geographic mobility and alleged interference in marital affairs, has made it possible for some to talk of the "socialist empire of the Incas"[42] while others feel it was the model for Thomas More's *Utopia*.[43]

Valera and Garcilaso were both born in Peru, soon after the European invasion, to European fathers who never quite acknowledged their Andean wives and children. Both moved a good deal among Europeans—Valera as a Jesuit priest who died in Spain, Garcilaso as a resident of the peninsula from his twentieth year. Each felt that his mother's people were misunderstood and underestimated, and both tried to write works addressed to a European audience in order to redress the picture. Both knew Quechua and a good deal about Andean culture and frequently give us unique and most valuable information, but both must be used with great caution when we come to matters which they thought Europeans would misunderstand. Thus both deny the practice of human sacrifice in many labored, contorted paragraphs when it is widely known both historically and archeologically that such offerings were made at special occasions like a threatening calamity or the king's death. Both elaborate Inca history to make it seem longer and more glorious. Both, finally, exaggerate the degree of paternal benevolence assumed by the Inca state for its citizens while contrasting this myth with the stark exploitative reality in which both grew up and in which Valera ministered for several decades.

Such characterization does not mean that their claim of public responsibility for individual welfare in Inca times is a complete fabrication. When Blas Valera speaks of a "law for the poor" (those who could not work their lands were entitled to eat from a public warehouse), he and Garcilaso do explain that there were really no "poor," only persons incapacitated for one reason or another. Where they err is in attributing to the state what continued to be the responsibility of the *ayllu* community.

The welfare illusion is also reinforced by the misunderstanding of the redistributive role of the crown. It did "grant" endless

[42] Baudin (1928); Louis Baudin, *Les Incas du Pérou* (Paris, 1942); and a host of other commentators.
[43] Rojas in Garcilaso, 1943; Luis Valcarcel, *La ruta cultural del Perú*. Colección Tierra Firme (Mexico, 1945), pp. 44–45; Morgan (1946).

352   *John V. Murra*

"gifts and benefactions."[44] The generosity of the chief and, by
projection, of the crown was culturally mandatory: chroniclers
like Betanzos, Morúa and Poma, Garcilaso, Blas Valera, and
Salcamayhua, whose information came from deep in the Andean
tradition, frequently refer to one or another of the kings as
franco y liberal, open and generous, the culture's image of the
good chief. One of the king's honorific titles was *wakcha koyaq,*
"he who loved [cared for] the weak."[45] King Wayna Qhapaq
"never refused any request whatsoever from women . . . whom
he always addressed by kinship terms."[46]

Royalty and those traditional leaders whose support was
needed in the Inca version of "indirect" rule were granted
kumbi cloth, the most valued ritual and political commodity.[47]
In later years land and human beings were also issued when a
special grant was felt necessary (Murra 1956: ch. 2; ch. 3).
Cabello Valboa was told that the second king, Sinchi Roq'a,
"discovered a style to attract these [conquered] nations . . . the
table was always set and the glasses full for as many as wanted
to come. . . ."[48] Sinchi Roq'a may never have existed as a
historical personage, and the "style he discovered"—institutionalized generosity[49]—is as old as surpluses, but Cabello's report
conveys an expectation which in Inca territory survived the rise
of the state.

Such redistribution has little to do with welfare. Its bulk
was expended and "granted" where it was thought that it would

[44] I first met the notion of the Inca economy as a redistributive one in a
paper by Polanyi (1957).
[45] Betanzos, *op. cit.,* p. 80; Santillán, *op. cit.,* p. 40; Garcilaso, *op. cit.,*
p. 61; Juan de Sta Cruz Pachakuti Yanqui Salcamayhua, *Relación de anti-
guedades deste reyno del Pirú* [ca. 1613]. Colección de Libros y Documentos
Referentes a la Historia del Perú, serie 2, tomo 9 (Lima, 1927), p. 100;
Cobo, *op. cit.,* p. 258.
[46] Garcilaso, *op. cit.,* p. 171.
[47] On political use of cloth, see Murra 1962.
[48] Consider Max Gluckman's generalization: "Tribute goods and labour
were inextricably combined. . . . In primitive economics a man with many
goods could do little with them for himself: there were no luxuries to be
bought, there were no profits on capital, the circle of trade was limited.
Therefore a man with plenty—and this applied above all to chiefs—had
either to destroy his goods, as was done in Northwest America, or to give
them away, as was done in Africa. So that when his people worked for the
Lozi king, or brought him tribute, he gave away much of the property he
acquired thus . . ." (Gluckman 1943).
[49] Cabello Valboa, *op. cit.,* p. 274.

do the most good. In this sense, the Inca state functioned like a market: it absorbed the surplus production of a self-sufficient population and "exchanged" it by feeding those on *corvée,* the royal relatives, and the army, and by attempting to secure their allegiance.

It can be argued that such a system could not endure. Elsewhere I have pointed to the *mitmaq* colonists removed from their ethnic community, to the growing population of weaving *aklla* and the *yana* retainers, to the land grants made by the crown to its favorites (Murra 1956: ch. 9), all of them encroachments that in the long run threaten the self-sufficiency of the peasant community. Even so, in 1532, when the system's development was arrested, the basic self-sufficiency of most Andean villages was still a fact.

Notes

(The date in square brackets following the name of the chronicler refers to the year of first publication or writing. The second, modern date refers to the edition used by the writer in the present article.)

16 CHECKS ON THE ABUSE OF POLITICAL POWER IN SOME AFRICAN STATES: A PRELIMINARY FRAMEWORK FOR ANALYSIS

John Beattie

John Beattie is Senior Lecturer in Social Anthropology at the University of Oxford, England. He is the author of *Bunyoro: An African Kingdom* (1960); *Other Cultures: Aims, Methods and Achievements in Social Anthropology* (1964), *Understanding an African Kingdom: Bunyoro* (1965), and many papers, mostly on Bunyoro.

I

OLDER WRITERS about primitive states in Africa and elsewhere often spoke of chiefs and kings as possessing absolute power. But it is plain from the more thorough ethnography of the past half century or so that in fact the authority of such rulers is generally restricted by a wide range of social institutions. There has as yet been little attempt to classify these, and in this article, on the basis of the published material on a few African states, I attempt a preliminary classification of those social institutions which have the effect of restraining those persons in whom political power is vested from abusing that power. On the basis of such a classification it may be possible to suggest certain broad correlations between types of institutionalized control and kinds of political structure. Apart from any methodological and comparative interest which this enquiry may possess, it may have some practical relevance in that an understanding of indigenous political institutions and of the checks and balances which they embody is essential for the comprehension and control of social change. In what follows I deal only with checks which are social (psychological factors, important though they may be, are disregarded), institutionalized (that is, which are established and recognized features of the

FROM *Sociologus* 9, No. 2 (1959), 97–115, by permission of the author and of the editor, *Sociologus*.

societies they occur in), and indigenous (checks imposed from outside, for example by foreign political or other agencies, are ignored). I do not consider "acephalous" societies: checks on the abuse of power by indigenous political authorities can only be studied where such authorities exist.

In this section, I examine briefly certain key concepts. These are *power, authority, political, abuse* (of political power) and *restraint* (of such abuse).

(a) *Power* Bertrand Russell has remarked that power, "the ability to do something or anything, or to act upon a person or thing,"[1] is the fundamental concept in social science. It is, of course, a fundamental concept in all thought, for under its other name of causation it is how we understand change, the succession of events in time. A cause produces its effect, we suppose, because it has the power to do so, and with our unescapable anthropomorphism we commonly think of this power as a kind of latent ability to alter the existing state of things, such as we are conscious of in our own psychic experience. As Hume showed long ago, power is a purely subjective category; we are conscious of it in ourselves, but as far as the succession of events in the external world is concerned it is no more than a useful though rarely analysed hypothesis, a projection of our own experience, not something observed or induced from observation. So fundamentally power is human power, and human power is the conceived ability to produce intended effects, on oneself, on other human beings, or on things. In a sense a man may be said to have power to produce unintended effects, but this is not what we generally mean by human power, which is essentially directed. A man is thought powerful because he can produce intended results, not unintended ones. So the notion is essentially teleological. Men think of themselves as initiating action, determining not determined, and the conscious initiation of action is only intelligible in terms of a pre-perception of some end to be achieved. So a man has power in so far as he can do what he wants to do, and he has social power where in any human relationship he can make others do as he wants them to do.[2] Social power is thus not a substance or quality

[1] Shorter Oxford English Dictionary, 2d edition, 1936.
[2] Cf. Weber, "power is the probability that one actor within a social relationship will be in a position to carry out his own will despite resistance, regardless of the basis upon which this probability rests" (1947:139).

inherent in individuals *qua* individuals, but rather a special aspect of inter-personal relationships.

(b) *Authority*　Unlike power, authority implies right; an armed raider may have power to relieve a shopkeeper of his day's takings, but he does so without authority. And right is a conceptual as well as a social entity; it must be acknowledged by somebody, and it exists only in that recognition.[3] So political authority is more than the mere ability to exercise power; it implies public acknowledgment. Where it exists in institutionalized form it is created and maintained by the social group in which it occurs, and it implies the acceptance of a common system of values in which are included the institutional norms through which the authority is conceived and expressed (Parsons 1941: 768). Since authority implies acceptance, and since acceptance must have some ground, the concept of legitimacy may properly be regarded as the distinguishing feature of authority, as Weber showed (Weber 1947: ch. 37). Authority implies a claim to legitimacy and this claim must be acknowledged as valid by the persons subject to it. Basically, authority depends on the consensus of the community over which it is exercised. Thus the phrase "absolute authority" is strictly speaking a contradiction, for the very concept is a relative one, and refers not to a quality but to a relation. So social authority is the right, not the ability, to exercise power over others, and authority may exist without power, just as power may exist without authority. Since the exercise of some form of institutionalized social power is a condition of the maintenance of a stable system of ordered social relations, a primary concern of social authority is with the maintenance of social order. Social authority may, then, be defined as the right, vested in a certain person or persons by the consensus of a society, to make decisions, issue orders and apply sanctions in matters affecting other members of the society. Such matters will usually be concerned either directly or indirectly with the maintenance of social order. Any person or corporation of persons so vested may be called an authority.

(c) *Political*　The concept "political" is more complex, at

[3] Cf. MacIver, "an authority does not act in his private capacity, but always in virtue of a right conferred on him for this purpose by society" (1947:83). Cf. also Michels, "whether authority is of personal or institutional origin it is created and maintained by public opinion" (1937:315).

least in social anthropology. It is usually defined as having to do with the state, the state being defined as "the body politic as organized for supreme civil rule and government."[4] Like other social concepts which have grown up in the context of Western history, this definition is too narrow to be useful when applied to some of the kinds of societies which anthropologists study. What we need are criteria for identifying certain kinds of social phenomena, and we know that these occur even when the body politic is not so organized. Heller's definition of the state is more useful; for him it is "a territorial organization which is able to enforce its power as against all other associations and persons within its borders, and thus to regulate and give an integrated expression to the interrelated social activities of its inhabitants" (Heller 1937:301). Radcliffe-Brown adapts this classic formulation; he defines political organization as "the maintenance of social order, within a territorial framework, by the organized exercise of coercive authority through the use, or the possibility of use, of physical force" (Radcliffe-Brown 1940: xiv).[5] Here there are really two criteria; the means which characterise political activity, and the ends to which it is directed. The means are physical force or the threat of it, and for Weber this is definitive of the state, which cannot be defined in terms of its ends since it may assume any task (Weber 1948:78). The sole source of the right to use violence is the state, and others can do so only so far as it permits them. Of course Weber was thinking primarily of modern states, which exercise functions vastly more diverse than those of traditional African states. But, as Weber recognized, any state, if it is to survive, must include among its functions the maintenance of territorial order. So the chief end of political activity must be the regulation and control of the social order in a certain territory. The maintenance of this order must depend on a system of social institutions and the values these imply, so one of the things that political organization does is to maintain a body of interconnected moral and legal norms (Fortes and Evans-Pritchard 1940:20). And it relates to all the members of the territorial group; it is, in Mac-

[4] Shorter Oxford English Dictionary.

[5] Cf. Weber; for him the political group is "an imperatively coordinated [i.e. one subject to authority] corporate group in which order is enforced continuously within a given territorial area by the application and threat of force" (1947:141).

Iver's words, "the organ of the whole community" (MacIver 1947:14).

So a political authority is any person vested with the right to issue orders, administer sanctions, etc., in a certain territory, such activity being generally directed, and regarded as being directed, towards the maintenance of the existing social order, and being as a rule backed by the threat of physical force. Whenever such a person, in virtue of his office, effectively commands the service or the compliance of others he exercises political power, and his authority lies in the recognition of his right to do so. The determination of who is or is not to be regarded as a political authority in any particular situation is bound to be a little arbitrary. I have stressed that political power is not best regarded as an attribute which some individuals have and others have not; it is rather a particular category of relationship, in which an individual may stand in some contexts but not in others. The crucial criteria are the extent to which an individual or category of individuals is recognized as a political authority, and the importance of the political role he or it plays. Difficulty in determining who are and who are not political authorities is most likely to arise in the consideration of segmentary, "acephalous" societies, where there is little or no political specialization and no association which claims the monopoly of physical force. Such societies do not, of course, lack social order or structural continuity, and it is legitimate to speak of them as having political systems (in the sense that internal order and external relations are institutionally controlled), but they do not have political authorities in the sense of that term above defined, and I am not concerned with them in this essay.

(d) *Abuse* The dictionary definition of the verb is "to misuse, to take a bad advantage of, to pervert". Its valuational content is at once plain; abuse is bad. Since judgments as to what constitutes abuse in this sense and what does not must vary with the moral standpoint of the observer and his culture, this meaning of the term will not do for sociological analysis. Sociologically, we cannot mean by the abuse of political power its misdirection to morally reprehensible ends, or the use of it not in the best interest of those governed. Nor can we mean its use for a ruler's own private advantage at the expense of the general good, though no doubt this is what generally happens when political power is abused (Fortes and Evans-Pritchard 1940:17). Like other men, a ruler is bound to be actuated some of the time by his private interests and to use his power to gratify these interests. But whether this constitutes abuse can only be decided by reference either to a subjective moral standard (which cannot provide an acceptable basis for sociological analysis), or to what is expected of the ruler, either by members of the society in which he exercises his authority or by somebody else. Only a criterion of this latter type can provide an adequate sociological meaning for the concept. The abuse of political power can only be studied objectively when it is taken to mean what some person or group of persons think to be abuse of political power. This person or group of persons may represent or compose the whole society, in which case public opinion will be the criterion, or it may stand outside the society (as for example a European official does in certain still dependent African societies). Naturally indigenous checks can only occur in the former case. For the purposes of the present analysis, therefore, abuse of political power may best be defined as the failure by a political authority to use such power in a manner which the community as a whole or its representatives regard as conforming to the duties and responsibilities of the office held. This negative formulation permits the inclusion of omissions as well as acts; political power is no less abused when a ruler fails to act in the manner socially prescribed for him than it is when he does something which he should not do.

(e) *Restraint* The notion of restraint or checking is, superficially at least, a simple one; an action or tendency to action is restrained when something occurs to stop it. It has long been recognised that political power is of "an encroaching nature" and so needs to be controlled, and this implies the exercise of counterbalancing power by persons or groups of persons other than the ruler. Power and authority are normally distributed, even in the most "absolute" states. But it is necessary to distinguish the limitation of power from its restraint. No doubt the fact that political authority is vested in other members of a community besides its political head constitutes a limitation on the latter's power. But in itself this can hardly be said to constitute a restraint or check, unless the other power-holding persons or groups can wield sanctions which restrain the ruler from deviating from the prescribed norms. So although the distribution of political power is important in delimiting the amount and scope of power held by any individual, and in determining the type of political organization, it is not in itself directly relevant to the narrower field of restraint. When I speak of social checks or restraints on the abuse of political power, I refer primarily to institutionalized social relationships between political authorities and other persons or groups of persons in the society, an effect of which is to prevent these authorities from behaving in a manner which the governed community or its representatives regard as not conforming to its conception of the duties and responsibilities of office. I am thus concerned with as aspect of the political structure, but not with the whole of it.

II

In this section I examine the ethnographic literature relating to a few reasonably typical traditional African states (I have selected the Ganda, Swazi, Ashanti and Nupe kingdoms),[6] with the aim of identifying and describing some social institutions which have the effect of preventing or restraining the abuse of political power. At once the social phenomena to which the framework sketched in the preceding section is applicable can be seen to fall into two broad types. First, there are certain enduring structural features of the society the very involvement in which of political authorities precludes certain types of abuse of power. Conformity with these normative institutions, for example with a political constitution, itself prevents the ruler from doing what he should not do. And conformity is obligatory; these norms are built into the social system and have the compelling force of law. We are thinking of such normative institutions when we speak, for example, of the common requirement that a king shall consult a

[6] The choice of these is not wholly arbitrary. They are in widely separate parts of the continent (one in east, one in south and two in west Africa); they all differ from one another in important respects; each exemplifies a generic type of African state; and the traditional political systems of all of them have been intensively (though by no means adequately) studied. It must be stressed again that what are considered here are the *traditional* systems of these states, so far as they can be reconstructed; the present situation in all of them is of course something entirely different (though traditional values sometimes have more contemporary significance than is always recognized).

body of advisers before taking administrative action. Of course this is only a check if the king does consult his councillors and attend to their advice. But as long as he does so, it is proper to speak of the institution as a check upon abuse, whatever the sanctions by which deviation from the norm is penalized. Such factors of restraint may conveniently be called *categorical norms,* for they are built into the political system as standardized, compulsory ways of acting. Though they may be and no doubt usually are subject to social sanctions,[7] they are not themselves sanctions.

The second type of checks on the abuse of political power comprises those which become effective only when an established norm is breached. They need not be any less institutionalized, for the likelihood of their being brought into effect is recognized by everybody, and the recognition of this no doubt makes for restraint on the part of political authorities. This sanctioning aspect of legal and political institutions is familiar to scholars; it has been clearly stated by Llewellyn and Hoebel, who emphasize that law, as well as providing for regulation and prevention, also deals with irregularities when they occur. "It is the case of trouble which makes, breaks, twists or flatly establishes a rule, an institution, an authority" (Llewellyn and Hoebel 1941:29). These authors recognize that the distinction between what I have called categorical norms and factors of this latter type, which we may call *conditional norms* (since they only become effective when some categorical norm is breached), is not absolute; the two categories may shade into each other.[8] But it does provide a useful working basis for the classification of ethnographic data relating to the exercise of political authority, from the point of view of the restraint of its abuse.

It also facilitates the formulation of some analytical problems. I tabulate below some more or less institutionalized checks on the abuse of political power, on the basis of the ethnographic material relating to the four African kingdoms mentioned above.

[7] I use the term "social sanction" in a sense approximating Radcliffe-Brown's: "a sanction is a reaction on the part of a society or of a considerable number of its members to a mode of behaviour which is thereby approved (positive sanctions) or disapproved (negative sanctions)" (1952: 205).

[8] They add a third category, that of actual practice. This, however, appears to be rather the existential aspect of the other two than a separate category (Llewellyn and Hoebel 1941:21).

The Abuse of Political Power in African States 363

It can be seen that these checks fall conveniently into the two categories which I have just distinguished. It is also plain that there are some institutions, such as advisory councils, which contain aspects falling into each of the two categories. Thus it is a categorical norm in many societies that rulers shall consult councils before taking decisions, and this convention, so long as it is adhered to, operates to prevent rulers from acting arbitrarily and so abusing their power. But it is further the case in some societies that if rulers neglect to do this their councils may impose penalties on them, such as fining or deposing, thereby bringing into play conditional as well as categorical norms. This need not always happen, however. Some categorical norms are not institutionally associated with any specific conditional norm, and some conditional norms have no specific reference to any particular categorical norm, but may be brought into play in consequence of a breach of any of a number of these. Even where there is an institutionalized association between norm and sanction the link may not be invariable; often one type of conditional norm may be supplemented or replaced by another. This state of affairs permits of a threefold division of institutionalized checks on the abuse of political power. Type A includes those categorical norms which are not associated with specific social sanctions or conditional norms (this is not of course to say that they are unsanctioned). Type B comprises those social institutions which embody both categorical and conditional norms. And Type C are those conditional norms which are not institutionally linked with breaches of any particular categorical norm. There are examples of all three types of check in the Table. It is important to distinguish them, for questions which may appropriately be asked in regard to one type may not be so in regard to the others. Thus the question in what categories of persons the right to apply sanctions is institutionally vested may be asked in regard to checks of Types B and C, but not of Type A. This question, and the more general problem of how far specific types of check may be associated with specific types of social structure, are briefly considered in the next and final section.

III

If the conditional norms listed under Type B and Type C in the Table are examined, five different categories of enforcing

	Categorical Norms		Conditional Norms	
	Description	To whom applicable and where	Description	To whom applicable and where
		Type A		
1.	Ceremonial admonition and oath-taking on accession to office	All political authorities (Ashanti), king (Ganda), chiefs (Swazi), titled fief-holders (Nupe)		
2.	Judicial organization: (a) system of appeal to higher authority	All political authorities (Ashanti), chiefs (Ganda and Swazi), village chiefs and fief-holders (Nupe)		
	(b) restriction of right to impose death sentence	Chiefs (Swazi and Ashanti), chiefs and delegates of fief-holders (Nupe)		
3.	System of clientship	Fief-holding chiefs (Nupe)		
4.	Prohibition of personal property-holding	King and chiefs (Ashanti)		
5.	System of dispersed royal villages	Chiefs (Swazi)		
6.	Systems of appointment and succession:(a) strictly hereditary	King and chiefs (Swazi)		
	(b) on personal qualification only without regard to heredity	Chiefs (Ganda), non-royal fief-holders and some village chiefs (Nupe)		
	(c) Hereditary principle combined with selection on personal qualities	All political authorities (Ashanti), king (Ganda), king and royal fief-holders (Nupe)		

a A defect of this tabulated presentation is that it provides no indication of the frequency of incidence, or relative importance, of the various checks classified; it is not to be assumed that all are of equal weight in the societies for which they are recorded. Nor may it be assumed that the lists are complete; we are dependent for our information on authors not all of whom were interested in the kinds of questions discussed in this paper, and checks which are recorded for one system may well have occurred unreported in others. The table is, therefore, not to be taken as representing a final analysis; it is no more than a summary of what information is available.

b For reasons of space, detailed page-references are not given for the sixty or more ethnographic references contained in the Table. My sources, however, are as follows. For Buganda, Kagwa 1934, Kulubya 1942, Mair 1933, 1934 and 1936, Mukasa 1934 and 1946, Roscoe 1902 and 1911, and Williams 1940.

For the Swazi, Kuper 1937, 1941 and 1947, Marwick 1940, and Schapera 1937. For Nupe, Nadel 1935 and 1942, and Temple 1922. And for the Ashanti, Busia 1951, Fortes 1948, Rattray 1923, 1927 and 1929, and Smith 1927.

Type B

No.				
7.	Advisory and consultative relations with particular individuals: (a) with mothers	All political authorities (Ashanti), king (Ganda), king and chiefs (Swazi)	Mother may scold and rebuke	King (Swazi, Ashanti, probably Ganda), chiefs (Swazi and Ashanti)
	(b) with agnatic kinsmen	King and chiefs (Swazi)	Agnatic kinsmen may rebuke. They may also rebel with popular support	King (Ganda and Swazi), chiefs (Swazi)
	(c) with specific unrelated officials	King and chiefs (Ganda and Swazi)	Officials may remonstrate with ruler and remind him of his duties	King and chiefs (Ganda and Swazi)
8.	Advisory and consultative relations with councils: (a) composed of unrelated officials	King (Ganda), king and chiefs (Ashanti), king and village chiefs (Nupe)	Council may: (a) reprimand (b) decide judicially against ruler (c) impose fine (d) boycott (e) refuse to collaborate in ritual (f) depose (g) appeal to higher authority to depose	(a) King and chiefs (Swazi) (b) King (Ganda) (c) King (Ashanti), chiefs (Swazi and Ashanti) (d) Village chiefs (Nupe) (e) Village chiefs (Nupe) (f) King and chiefs (Ashanti) (g) Chiefs (Swazi)
	(b) composed of both kin and unrelated members	King and chiefs (Swazi)		Chiefs (Swazi)
9.	Compulsory attendance at king's court or council	Chiefs (Ganda and Swazi)	King and council may fine for non-attendance King may regard non-attendance as revolt, and plunder and depose	Chiefs (Ganda)

Type C

10.	Subjects may move out of area of ruler's authority	Chiefs (Ganda and Swazi)
11.	Subjects or subordinate political authorities may revolt	King and chiefs (Ganda, Swazi, Ashanti), fief-holders (Nupe)
12.	Agnatic relatives may revolt with popular support	King (Ganda and Swazi)
13.	King may punish, despoil or depose	Chiefs (Ganda, Swazi, Nupe)
14.	Subjects may appeal personally to king or queen mother	Chiefs (Swazi, ?Nupe)
15.	Subjects may claim sanctuary at royal homestead	Chiefs (Swazi)
16.	Subjects may withhold customary economic services	Village chiefs (Nupe)
17.	Subjects may resort to assassination or sorcery	King and chiefs (Swazi)

agents can be distinguished. First (in regard to subordinate political authorities) a superior political authority, usually the paramount, may impose a fine (Swazi), depose or degrade in rank (Ganda, Swazi, Nupe), plunder (Ganda), or repress by military force (Ganda, Nupe). Second, in three of the four societies considered—Nupe is the exception—a ruler's mother has an institutionalized right to scold or rebuke him. Third, a ruler's agnatic relatives, acting as individuals, may rebuke him (Swazi), or revolt with popular support (Swazi and Ganda); acting as a council they may, among the Swazi, reprimand him, fine him, or (in the case of a chief) appeal to the king to depose him. Fourth, unrelated subordinate officials, as individuals, may remonstrate with the king (Ganda and Swazi); as a council they may reprimand him (Swazi and Ashanti), refuse to collaborate in ritual and boycott him (Nupe), appeal to a higher official to depose him (Swazi), or themselves depose him (Ashanti). Fifth, subjects may appeal personally to the highest political authority (Swazi, Nupe), seek sanctuary at the royal homestead (Swazi), as an organized commoner body, repudiate an unpopular nomination for chiefship (Ashanti), refuse customary economic services (Nupe), move out of the ruler's area of jurisdiction (Ganda, Swazi and probably elsewhere), revolt (all except Nupe, and possibly there), or resort to assassination or sorcery (Swazi).

An analysis of Type B and Type C checks in the Table thus provides a five-fold classification of social checks on the abuse of political power in terms of the various categories of persons who may give effect to them. No doubt these could be more precisely distinguished, and further categories could be identified by deeper and more extensive research; also, it must be remembered that the authorities I have quoted were not, for the most part, directly concerned with questions of abuse of power and its control. But at least a preliminary classification can be proposed, even if this does no more than to systematize available data and to provide a framework for further investigation. At the next level a new series of problems emerges, concerned in particular with the correlation of the institutions just considered, together with those in Type A, with the various types of political and social organization in which they occur. Obviously no comprehensive analysis on these lines can be undertaken here, even on the basis of the limited material used, but a few comments on certain of the institutions noted, regarded in their social contexts, may indicate some areas of possible future research. First the traditional political systems of the four kingdoms I have considered must be broadly, and very briefly, sketched.

The administration of the traditional Ganda kingdom is hierarchically organized, territorial authority being delegated by the king to successive grades of district chiefs who are appointed by him (Roscoe 1911:232–370; Mair 1934:177). The only hereditary offices are the kingship itself, one or two senior chiefships, and the relatively unimportant clan headships (Roscoe 1911: 133–34). Political authority is validated in the last resort by reference to the innate superiority of the ancient ruling line which was (it is supposed) founded in conquest, and to delegation by the king. In the Swazi state, unlike Buganda, political organization is expressed at all levels in terms of agnatic kinship (Kuper 1947: chs. 5, 8). Political authority attaches *par excellence* to membership of the ruling clan of which the king is the head, and which is dispersed throughout Swazi territory. In Buganda the ruling line preserves its exclusiveness and identity against all other elements (Roscoe 1911:81); in Swaziland it expanded territorially and genealogically so that throughout the whole country administration is closely linked with membership of the royal clan (Kuper 1947:111). The chiefs as well as the king command obedience because of hereditary right and not, at least not primarily, as nominees of a central power. In Ashanti two principles are operative. All political office is based on hereditary qualification combined with popular choice, but relationships of subordination and superordination above village level do not follow a kinship pattern, deriving rather from historical and military circumstance and territorial contiguity (Fortes 1948:194; Rattray 1929:94). In Nupe this dual basis of political organization is even more marked; at village level authority is held by the heads of localized lineages, but superimposed upon and quite distinct from this system is a centralized "feudal" structure, in which authority is ultimately sanctioned by conquest and is vested in a hereditary ruling line (Nadel 1942:34–146). The Swazi state is the only one of the four kingdoms considered in which a lineage pattern pervades the political structure from base of apex. In Ashanti and Nupe representation at the lowest level is kinship-based, being replaced at higher levels in Ashanti by a loose political federation which traditionally interfered little with local autonomy, and in Nupe by a powerful and alien feudal organization. In Buganda the non-hereditary "civil service" hierarchy extends to the lowest level, where it operates in conjunction with a relatively unimportant lineage organization in which a limited degree of political authority resides.

I now indicate, very summarily, a few of the more obvious lines of correlation which the Table points to, taking one or two examples of each of the three Types distinguished. I take first a Type A check; ceremonial admonition and oath-taking. This is particularly thorough-going and emphatic in Ashanti, where it is recorded of all levels of chiefs[9]; it is much less marked in the other kingdoms. Its emphasis in the Ashanti state may reflect the important part which the people play in the selection of their rulers; upon the councillors, as representatives of the people, devolves the task of making unambiguously clear to the chiefs what is expected of them. There seems also to be a correlation with the breadth of choice available to electors; where a man is marked down for political office from childhood, as among the Swazi, there is less need to acquaint him formally with his obligations on his appointment. In fact admonition and oath-taking (and indeed accession ritual generally) play little part in accession to political authority in the Southern Bantu kingdom. In highly centralized "feudal" states these admonitory institutions might be expected to apply, if at all, mainly at the highest levels; for the subordinate chiefs obedience and loyalty to the sovereign rather than adherence to explicit administrative norms are the prime desiderata. Among the Baganda oath-taking plays an important part in the king's accession ritual (Roscoe 1911:198; Mair 1934:181), but it is not recorded of appointment to chiefship. This is consistent, also, with the fact that traditionally the king was chosen from a number of equally eligible princes after the death of the former king. The Nupe data are inadequate to sus-

[9] Busia quotes the following admonition to a divisional chief: ". . . do not go after women. Do not become a drunkard. When we give you advice, listen to it. Do not gamble. We do not want you to disclose the origin of your subjects. We do not want you to abuse us. We do not want you to be miserly; we do not want one who disregards advice; we do not want you to regard us as fools; we do not want autocratic ways; we do not want bullying; we do not like beating . . ." (1951:12).

tain or refute any of these correlations. It is obvious, however, that there are testable hypotheses in this field.

Another Type A institution listed in the Table is clientship. Where neither kinship links (as in Swazi and Ashanti) nor popular selection (as also in Ashanti) provide for political representation and protection, an alternative is attachment as a client to a powerful patron, who affords favour and protection in return for certain services and goods. As might be expected, it is reported from the typically "feudal" Nupe state (Nadel 1942:115–46). It might also be anticipated in Buganda (it occurs in some neighbouring interlacustrine Bantu kingdoms, notably Ankole), for Ganda chiefs are neither popularly elected nor affiliated to politically significant groups of kin. Its relative unimportance here seems to be associated with the high degree of centralization and political stability of the traditional Ganda state, where the great chiefs were not merely fief-holding lords (as in Nupe), but also and pre-eminently members of a formal "civil service," responsible to the king for the good administration of their areas.

A third check of a categorically normative kind is embodied in systems of succession and appointment (No. 6 in the Table). The vast range of possible combinations of the principles of heredity and succession, and in the latter case the different categories of persons in whom rights of selection and of participation in accession ceremonies are vested, cannot be discussed here. But there are some obvious correspondences between the principles of appointment to office adopted in the several societies I have considered, and the structural types of these societies; indeed, the former may sometimes be said to be an essential aspect of the latter. Where political authority is vested in particular descent groups the hereditary principle will necessarily be adopted, though it may be combined with a greater or lesser degree of selection. It is obvious, also, that where, as in so-called conquest states, political authority derives more or less manifestly from a central force (which may itself be hereditary), subordinate political authority will tend to derive from this central power, and not, or not exclusively, on the basis of descent. Where both systems are combined in one state, the appointment of the indigenous hereditary authorities, if they are allowed to survive at all, requires at least to be confirmed by the central power. All this is amply illustrated by the ethnographic material examined above.

In Swaziland the hereditary rule prevails, virtually unqualified by any elective principle, though counterbalanced by a highly developed council system (Kuper 1947: ch. 7). In Ashanti, and in the ruling line of Buganda and among the nobles of Nupe, succession to political office is partly hereditary, partly determined by selection from among a number of candidates equally qualified by birth (Busia 1947:9; Roscoe 1911:188; Nadel 1942: 94). And in the two latter kingdoms, which are the most highly centralized politically, the territorial chiefs (Buganda) and non-royal fief-holders (Nupe) are appointed by the central authority with little or no regard to hereditary claim (Mair 1934:163; Nadel 1942:98).

Of the checks in Type B, which include both categorical and conditional norms, I consider here only those implied in consultative and advisory relationships with agnatic relatives, and with unrelated officials. The power of kinsmen to influence a ruler might be expected to vary with the degree to which political power is institutionally distributed among them. Thus in Swaziland many chiefships are held by the king's agnates, and it is they who have most control over him. His relatives may advise and if necessary rebuke him, and a chief's councillors may reprimand him, fine him, or recommend his deposition (Kuper 1947: 67; Schapera 1937:183). And a powerful brother or father's brother may, with popular support, attempt to depose a weak or oppressive king by rebellion (Schapera 1937:184). This danger, met in Swaziland by giving adequate but subordinate political authority to agnates, was met in Buganda by the opposite expedient of depriving the king's brothers of all political power (at some periods of Ganda history by immolating them) (Roscoe 1911:189). There is no suggestion in the literature of any institutionalized advisory or supervisory relationships between the king and his agnates. Their only recourse was to revolt, and they sometimes did so. Similarly, agnatic (or matrilateral) kin appear to have had little formal influence on rulers in Nupe (or Ashanti). When we turn to the influence and importance of unrelated subordinate officials, a different principle is seen to be operative. Where political relations throughout the system are in general conceived in terms of a single structural principle, whether that of agnatic kinship (Swazi) or that of the military and political federation of ever larger but internally similar units

(Ashanti), the principles of representation valid at the lowest levels are still effective at the higher. Thus the Swazi family head may attend and speak at the national council, just as he may in his own local and family councils (Kuper 1947:63), and the Ashanti lineage heads and the people they represent play an important part in the selection of their rulers, whether village chief, important divisional chief, or the Asantehene himself (Busia 1947:9–10). And they may depose the man they have selected if they think that he has ceased to represent their interests (Busia 1947:21). But where two quite different principles of political organization are uneasily juxtaposed (as in the "conquest states" of Nupe and Buganda), the ruling group's tendency to retain political power in its own hands may leave the subordinated majority with little or no constitutional means of representation. The ruling hierarchy, which may have no roots in the country, or only recent ones, and which is subject to no traditional claims from its inhabitants, admit no, or very inadequate, representation by subject groups. This is certainly the case in Nupe, where the council of state consisted mainly of fief-holding nobles resident more or less permanently at the capital (Nadel 1942:87–114). In Buganda an intermediate position was reached; the county chiefs and their subordinates (who composed the bulk of the royal council) were not appointed by the people, but at least they lived in and were responsible for the administration of their areas, and they had their own local advisers through whom the sentiments of their people were conveyed to them (Mair 1934: 177).

Of checks in Type C, only certain aspects of the influence of "subjects" on the political authorities to whom they are subordinate can be considered here; the part, that is, which what we may call popular opinion may play in political life, outside of the formal institutions so far discussed. It is useful, initially, to distinguish two ways in which popular participation in government may be formally achieved. It may be expressed, first, in the determining of what individuals are to be political authorities, as when the people have some say, either directly or indirectly, in the selection of rulers. And it may, secondly, be expressed through the exercise of control over the ruler after he has been appointed. Though both modes of participation normally coexist they are obviously not the same, and each may occur independently. If the term "democratic" be used, as it sometimes is, only in the former sense, then constitutions like that of the Ashanti are democratic, while states like Swazi are not. But it by no means follows that the will of the people was less adequately represented in traditional Swaziland than it was in traditional Ashanti; Swazi tribesmen possessed, through their elaborate council system, a relatively high degree of political power. That the predominance of one type of check involves the lesser importance of the other might be a hypothesis worth investigating. For, all other things being equal, the more representative rulers are in character of the people's will, electorally expressed, the less, it might be supposed, is the need for sustained and institutionalized popular control over them when they are in office. The Swazi evidence, at least, might seem to provide inferential support for such a hypothesis.

In states like Buganda and Nupe, where the central authority derives not from the matrix of the society itself but from outside it, popular opinion is less manifest, though it may express itself through *ad hoc* institutions like clientship or, in the last resort, by emigration or revolt. The Nupe peasant has no say in the appointment of the fief-holding lords to whom he is subject, nor has his Ganda counterpart any voice in the appointment of the major chiefs. Still less can Nupe commoners or their representatives directly influence the chiefs once they are appointed, and the same is true in the traditional Ganda polity. The introduction by the British administration in recent years of "popular representatives" on chiefs' councils in Uganda was accepted without enthusiasm by the established native authorities. Even in these centralized states, however, the maintenance of a certain level of prosperity and general security, and the acceptance of government by those subject to it, are in the interest of rulers no less than governed. Thus, for example, if a Ganda chief loses his subjects by emigration he may be dismissed by the king (Mair 1934:160), and I have noted above that subjects have other means of making their opinions felt. It is plain, also, that in a state centered on a monarch who is conceived as the primary source of all political power the head of the state may be the vehicle as well as the object of checks on misrule which derive from his subjects. A king may force his powerful chiefs to redress the wrongs of subjects who have complained to him, and by aligning himself on the side of his people he may safeguard himself against his chiefs' excessive power. Thus in case of injustice Nupe peasants, like Swazi commoners, could appeal to the king over the heads of the local rulers (though it can hardly be claimed, at least on the Nupe evidence, that much was to be hoped for from such a course) (Nadel 1942:58, 67). And public opinion is diffused through all levels of the political organization, and is not of course restricted to channels specific to it. Its two-way efficacy as a check on misrule is simply expressed in the accompanying figure. Evidently popular opinion deriving from A (the subjects) may impact either on B (the subordinate chiefs) or on C (the paramount ruler) directly, and it may also be conveyed, backed by the appropriate sanctions, to C through B or to B through C.

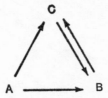

It has been possible here only to indicate a few of the themes, mostly familiar enough in other contexts, which may be suggested by an approach to the study of political systems from the point of view of an analysis of checks on the abuse of power. I have not attempted any sort of exhaustive analysis of a particular political system from this point of view; that would obviously be impossible in the limits of a short article. I have suggested only that an approach to the study of political systems which is centrally concerned with the incidence and types of institutionalized checks on the abuse of political power might justify the re-examination of some already familiar ethnographic material. At the same time, and more importantly, it might make possible the formulation of new hypotheses for testing intensively in new field research, and extensively in the growing mass of cross-cultural material relating to the simpler forms of political organization.

17 STATUS RIVALRY AND CULTURAL EVOLUTION IN POLYNESIA

Irving Goldman

Irving Goldman is Professor of Anthropology at Sarah Lawrence College. He is author of *The Cubeo Indians of the Northwest Amazon* (1963) and of several papers on Polynesia.

INTRODUCTION

CULTURAL EVOLUTION, to rephrase Maitland's classic remark, will be history or nothing. If it is to be history, its proper focus is the culture area, or to be more precise, the comparative study of culture areas. A culture area comprises historically related societies each showing significant variations from a common area pattern. In these variations—their nature, origin, and direction—are revealed the basic processes of cultural development in the area, that is, its cultural evolution. It is from a comparison of culture areas rather than from the comparative study of historically unrelated societies that the more general and more meaningful laws of development may emerge. Boas (1896) was the first to suggest such a comparative procedure as a way to avoid the pitfalls into which the old comparative method had led the nineteenth-century evolutionists.

For a number of reasons, Polynesia is a particularly suitable area for such a comparative study.[1] Since the area was populated

FROM *American Anthropologist* 57, No. 4 (1955), 680–97, by permission of the author and of the editor, *American Anthropologist*.

This paper is part of a study in progress on status in Oceania. The author is grateful to Sarah Lawrence College for a faculty fellowship, and to Margaret Mead for helpful criticism.

[1] A proper evolutionary study of Polynesia should certainly embrace all of Oceania and Micronesia, in particular, where Yanaihara (1946) and Murdock (1948) have already called attention to evolutionary sequences. Because I regard this paper as a trial run of a particular method of analysis

rather late, perhaps within the last 3,000 years (Spoehr 1952), its underlying historical unity is still abundantly clear—even linguistic variations are relatively minor (Elbert 1953). At the same time, Polynesian cultures vary in a continuous series from the "simple" atoll societies of Ontong Java and Pukapuka to the highly organized "feudal" kingdoms of Hawaii. These variations suggest an evolutionary sequence, which is borne out by evidence from tribal historical traditions (presumably reliable for comparatively recent events) and from other sources.

The present paper takes as its starting point the dominant values of Polynesian culture, those involving concern with social status. Polynesian society is founded upon social inequality and, despite an aristocratic doctrine of hereditary rank, permits its members to compete for position, for prestige, and for power. In one way or another, then, the history of every Polynesian society has been affected by status rivalry, and under the proper conditions the effects of this rivalry have been felt in every vital center of the culture. Rivalry raises issues and provokes conflicts that can never be fully resolved. It promotes a sequence of culture changes that take their character and direction in part from the momentum of status rivalry itself and in part from the particular physical and cultural setting of each island. Thus, the differing ecologies of atolls and high islands, variations in population density, varieties of subsistence techniques, levels of economic productivity, systems of property relations, the role of migrations and military conquests, diffusion, and, finally, the specific historical "accidents" that occur in wars, migrations, and contests for power—all influence and are in turn influenced by the dominant motive of status rivalry. Many facets of culture, on the other hand, are only barely touched by status rivalry and lie, therefore, outside the scope of this paper. Data on pertinent physical features are presented in Table 1 and, on diffusion, in the accompanying chart of subculture areas.

---

rather than as an attempted definitive study of Polynesian evolution, I have preferred to simplify the approach as much as possible. For this reason, I have omitted discussion of Fiji, which should ordinarily be linked with Samoa and Tonga, and I have dealt with Samoa only in terms of Manu'a. Western Samoa, more warlike, presents a somewhat different picture. I do not, however, believe that the omissions I have mentioned materially affect the main postulates presented in this paper.

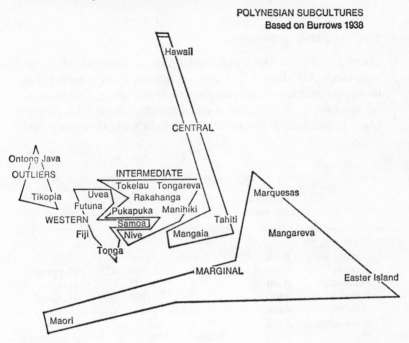

POLYNESIAN SUBCULTURES
Based on Burrows 1938

From the point of view of status rivalry, Polynesian societies can be ranged in approximate order along a scale that expresses variations in the character and intensity of the conflict for position and power. Reading in ascending order, from Ontong Java to Hawaii, this scale divides into three phases which I call "Traditional," "Open," and "Stratified." The Traditional may be considered to represent early stages of Polynesian cultural development, the Open to be illustrative of transitional conditions, and the Stratified, of the culminating phases. Table 1 shows the postulated sequence of cultural development. The societies at the midpoint of each phase are its prototype representatives, and those at the ends are transitional since each phase shades into the next. Retrogressions may have taken place but were incidental to the main lines of development. The process of development, needless to say, was far more complex than the schematic presentation that follows.

THE TRADITIONAL SOCIETIES

Maori represented the Traditional order at the peak of its development. All Maori tribes claimed descent from common first-
immigrant ancestors, and genealogical bonds along with more vital common economic and social interests linked tribe, lineage
(*hapu*), and family (*whanau*) into a tight unit. Hereditary rank

Table 1

POLYNESIAN ECOLOGY AND DEMOGRAPHY

	Physical Character	Sq. Miles	Pop.	Pop./Sq. Mile	Productivity
TRADITIONAL					
Ontong Java	Atoll	n.a.	5,000	. . .	Marginal
Tikopia	Volcanic	3	1,300	433	Marginal
Pukapuka	Atoll	2	1,500	750	Marginal
Tokelau	Atoll	4	1,200	300	Marginal
Manihiki	Atoll	1.5	1,000	285	Marginal
Rakahanga	Atoll	2			
Maori	High	102,000	100,000	9.8	Abundance
Tongareva	Atoll	6	2,000	333	Marginal
Futuna	Volcanic	25	1,000	40	Abundance
Uvea	Volcanic	23	3,000	130	Abundance
Samoa	High	1,200	50,000	41	Abundance
OPEN					
Niue	Atoll	100	5,000	50	Marginal
Easter	High	50	3,000	60	Marginal
Mangaia	Volcanic	27	3,000	111	Abundance
Marquesas	High	400	100,000	250	Marginal
STRATIFIED					
Tonga	High	269	25,000	93	Abundance
Mangareva	Volcanic	6	2,000	333	Marginal
Tahiti	High	593	100,000	168	Abundance
Hawaii	High	6,435	200,000	32	Abundance

Statistics from Freeman (1951) and from the ethnographies. Productivity
is an estimate from the ethnographies. Population figures are not very reliable.

set the pattern for political authority so that the senior male
of one of the senior lineages of the tribe was tribal chief

(*ariki*); the senior male in the senior line in each *hapu* was *hapu* chief; and a senior male was head of his *whanau*. As everywhere in Polynesia, *mana* was an aspect of rank. The Maori related *mana* directly to seniority and protected it by *tapus*. They regarded all males and high-born females as in some degree sacred, attributing the highest sacredness to the *ariki*. By vague genealogical criteria junior lines shaded into commoner status whose lowest branches sometimes served their higher-ranking kin as servants and as menials. Slavery was a temporary condition of war captives. Rank defined authority, economic and other privileges, responsibilities, and etiquette. Conferred by birth, it was demeaned by cowardice, low marriages, capture in war, and by other lapses of dignity. Lost rank was lost *mana*, and for that reason alone, as Best has noted, a Maori vigorously resisted affronts to his rank. When, as rarely happened, chiefs were incompetent, they were replaced.

Maori offered only limited social mobility. Other Traditional societies allowed for more. Manu'a (eastern Samoa) had markedly subverted hereditary rank without quite abandoning it. The *Tui Manu'a*, as high chief, and all subordinate chiefs and talking chiefs held hereditary rank in the Great Fono, but adroit and ambitious men advanced their rank and influence by the judicious use of wealth or assumed leadership outside the formal scheme of the *fono*. In Tongareva, more strongly committed to hereditary rank, wars and conquests often reduced rulers to the status of subjects. There, because of the importance of war, land-wealth and leadership—the ingredients of military success—almost rivaled inherited rank as avenues to power. A similar situation prevailed in Futuna and in Uvea. Futuna, Uvea, and Manu'a, in fact, come close to being Open societies.

Even in such closely knit atoll communities as Manihiki-Rakahanga, lineage rivalries disturbed the orderly succession to chieftainship. Traditions there tell how a dispute between the two wives of an *ariki* over the question of whose son should succeed him was compromised by the creation of a new title, "Land Distributor." The new title-holder then rallied his supporters and eventually two *arikis* divided the rule—unequally.

In several places hereditary rank had barely developed. In Ontong Java a strong man and his followers established the first kingship and, after a series of dynastic wars, one lineage triumphed and set up succession by seniority. Apart from the offices of king and lineage head, rank was of no importance. Rank meant little more in Tikopia and in Pukapuka. Traditions from Pukapuka also suggest that hereditary rank came late and that the first rulers were the old men. Later, four *aliki* contested for supremacy: the winner installed his lineage as the ruling dynasty. But here, too, only the chiefs held rank, the rest of the population being known simply as "the people." In the Tokelaus, age, ability, and material substance were the true measures of status, which was, however, but lightly considered. Only the *matai* ("headman") held office by seniority.

These brief illustrations show the unstable foundations of graded hereditary rank in the Traditional societies. Even those societies, such as the Maori, that had fully incorporated the tradition of graded hereditary rank, broke with it when it conflicted with personal ambition and with differences in ability. These societies retained their traditional character against the Polynesian dictum that fitness supersedes birth only because the tests of fitness were not too severe.

THE OPEN SOCIETIES

Chronic guerrilla warfare posed the most demanding tests of fitness for the aristocracies of the Open societies. As their histories show, the old aristocracies were eventually pushed into the background by warriors and by resourceful political leaders.

Niue had neither aristocracy, priesthood, nor genealogies. The real powers were the warriors (*toa*), who ranked first in the social scale ahead of the *fekafekua,* "servants of the *toa,*" and the *lalo tangata,* "low people," or those who ran away in battle. Niuean traditions, however, describe an initial migration from Samoa and a later invasion from Tonga that brought in a kingship along Tongan lines. In that case, the Niueans may very well have had an aristocracy that later became inconsequential.

On Easter Island a more virile status scale based on wealth and military prowess overshadowed the traditional scheme. The *ariki mau* was a high priest, while the warriors were the temporal rulers. Tribal traditions speak of a common ancestor who was the discoverer and first king of the island. He apportioned the island among his children, each of whom then founded a tribe.

One of the tribes controlled the *ariki* title. In the beginning, Métraux has suggested (1940), the kings were considered to be deities and held absolute power, but in the end the warriors took over, leaving the king only the prestige of his supernatural powers and certain personal privileges.

The Marquesans came closest to maintaining a traditional aristocracy. Yet here, too, achievement scored first. Position and influence went to those who had done most for the tribe. By such criteria the *toa* and the rich stood high. Chieftainship was ordinarily seized by those who had won powerful backing by diplomatic marriages, strategic alliances, and by effective displays of wealth and leadership.

Mangaia illustrates best the transitional character of the Open societies. On that little volcanic island a hereditary aristocracy had been eclipsed by the warriors (*toa*), who commanded the highest prestige, the largest estates, captive vassals, friendly satellites, and because of all these, authority. The hereditary *ariki* held the highest rank, but the effective ruler was the Temporal Lord of Mangaia, chosen from among the greatest warriors. Mangaian traditions tell of efforts to make the Temporal Lordship hereditary. But the conditions that undermined the old aristocracy did not favor its replacement by a new one. The shifting tides of military fortune constantly reshuffled the social order as first one tribe triumphed and then another. At the same time, the urgent requirements of warfare placed a high premium upon fighting skills, upon wealth, and, in general, upon the ability to command followers. The high social mobility perpetuated by these conditions came close to creating a socioeconomic class in place of the older scheme of hereditary rank.

High social mobility was one step toward stratification; the weakening of kinship ties was another. Strong kin ties may be compatible with graded hereditary rank but not with stratification that cuts kinship solidarity at the class line. By the same token, weakened kin ties favor stratification. Traditional kinship governed in Mangaia, but not exclusively. Warfare rearranged descent lines and conditions of residence as men sought safety with their wives' lineage when that lineage was the enemy. Their descendants might then remain with the maternal lineage, return to the paternal fold, or move into still another lineage, depending upon military conditions. By Polynesian standards the lineages became conglomerate, and the traditional patrilocal household became a *mélange* of immediate family kin, distant kin, war captives and others who served as menials in return for protection. Captives had the choice of tribal citizenship or of defiant servitude. Even as servants they shared, along with kinsmen, in some of the privileges of their masters. Warfare added one other strain upon kinship bonds: because of frequent changes of family allegiances, close kin met on the battlefield as enemies. In one such instance, a son killed his own father. Strong warriors heading the largest households as lords and protectors became centers of direct political power. Chiefs bolstered their might by adding to their household a body of trusted warriors.

The Open societies then were definitely exploitative—less so than the Stratified, but far more than the Traditional. In Mangaia, the exploited were mainly the outsiders. Exploitation of outsiders, however, may well set a standard for the exploitation of one's own, as seems to have been the case in the Marquesas and in Niue. There, weak and poor families sought the protection of strong chiefs whom they served as subordinates and to whom they paid tribute for grants of land. These societies have been called emergent "feudal" orders (Handy 1923; Loeb 1926). Because land rights remained open to all tribesmen, the Open societies cannot be regarded as stratified. Even so, some Marquesan chiefs had begun to regard tribal lands as their own (Handy 1923).

Why the Open societies stopped just short of stratification is not quite clear. Perhaps the indecisiveness of their wars prevented the consolidation of power and kept the land systems fluid. Military indecisiveness itself was probably due to rugged terrain, food scarcity, and loose political organization. In Mangaia, to return to that example, bands of enemy warriors might resist indefinitely from the shelter of its many caves. Food shortages and limited economic elasticity *equalized* contending rivals. Even more important may have been their political doctrine of warfare. Because they felt land shortage as their main problem, Mangaian victors *failed to organize* for their own benefit the crop production of defeated tribes but, instead, dispossessed them from fertile taro lands onto unproductive scrub lands. This may have been the least efficient way to strengthen the victor's econ-omy. Moreover, since their goal was to displace an enemy from

his land, there was little basis for a negotiated peace. The en-
feebling wars went on.

Stratification seems to have resulted from the consolidation
of military gains. So long as the Open societies could not
achieve relative political stability, the lines of privilege remained
too fluid to facilitate the formation of classes.

THE STRATIFIED SOCIETIES

Tonga, the least stratified of the Stratified societies, held fully
to the formal structure of graded hereditary rank but changed
its economic content. All Tongans were ranked from the sacred
Tui Tonga at the top to the lowliest commoner at the bottom,
and all social grades were linked by genealogical records that
gave commoners the right to assert their kinship with chiefs.
The *Tui Tonga,* however, held title to all land and awarded
holdings to chiefs according to their rank as well as in proportion to their services to him. The gentry in turn allotted land to
their kin on the same principle. Details of the land system,
unfortunately, are vague. Thomson (1894) and others cited by
Gifford (1929:170) stressed the sovereign rights of the *Tui
Tonga* over land, and Gifford (1929:174) summed up, "A
chief . . . could dispossess his commoners at any time, or transfer them from one part of his land to another, even though
they opposed the move." Apparently, the land system had driven
a wedge between noble and commoner and hence among kinsmen.
In some respects, in fact, the commoners were treated as were
the alien captives in the Open societies (for examples, see Gifford 1929:127).

The orderly arrangement of landholdings by rank was frequently upset by wars, revolts, and political intrigues. To hold
a precarious political balance chiefs rewarded their friends with
land and expropriated their rivals (Martin 1817). In this way,
the highest-ranking titles sometimes lost much of their holdings
and the lower ranks of gentry came to command the largest
estates. Hereditary rank continued to rule etiquette, but influence
and power came from landownership.

The traditional history of Tonga describes the gradual usurpation of power from the priest-king *Tui Tonga* and the consequent
increase in authority of secular rulers, the *Tui Kanokupolu.*

As early as the fifteenth century, these traditions say, ambitious lesser chiefs arranged for the assassination of one *Tui Tonga* after another, acts that led to much turmoil and warfare. As a measure of self-defense, the then King Kauulufonua introduced a buffer by naming his son the secular executive with the title *Tui Haa Takalaua* and with supervision of the plantations as one of his main duties. Later (seventeenth century) the *Takalaua* named his son as a land supervisor with the title *Tui Kanokupolu,* and the latter's line eventually became the real powers. The traditions do not deal with changes in the pattern of landholding. However, frequent and prolonged civil wars for succession during which the Tongan islands were divided into many fortified garrisons may very well have paved the way to a "feudalization" of landholdings. The fact that political power finally went to overseers suggests further that control over land had become a major issue in Tonga after the *Tui Tonga*-ship had begun to decline.

The conflict between the claims of hereditary rank and landed wealth raged even more fiercely in Mangareva, the most "open" of the Stratified societies. The theory of a graded hereditary aristocracy with a supreme chief (*aka-ariki*) at its head lay at the heart of the social order. It was a theory, however, honored more in the breach. Dynastic wars inevitably followed the death of a ruler. The victor seized his enemies' lands and gave them to his followers. Hereditary rank never lost its prestige, but the power and influence that wealth conferred were not easily overcome. Mangarevan society became so mobile, in fact, that for a time a line of commoners held the high office of *aka-ariki*.

Increased social mobility and the system of land tenure accented class lines. Eventually, ten aristocratic families came to own all the land, each ruling its territory as a "feudal" domain. Landowners subleased land-shares to kin and supporters, in return for tribute and military services. At the bottom of the social scale the landless "rats" lived as despised and hungry fishermen, and often had to rob graves for food.

Mangarevan traditions are narrations of dynastic wars, fratricidal strife, and interrupted successions, in the course of which power went from the supreme *ariki* to contending powerful chiefs. The strong expropriated the weak, and the vanquished were driven from the land altogether. Mangarevan traditions bear out rather clearly the postulated sequence: Traditional–Open–Stratified.

In Tahiti, hereditary rank was a more stable feature of the social order than in either Mangareva or Tonga. Chiefs (*arii*) and the landed gentry (*raatira*) were graded by seniority and held landed estates proportionate with their rank. They owed tribute and military services to the supreme chief, but their lands were immune from royal seizure. The bulk of the population consisted of the landless *manahune,* so separated socially from the gentry as to be considered by them as an alien group.

Tahitian traditions speak of an earlier more democratic society conquered and reorganized by invaders. Handy (1930) has, therefore, advanced the theory that Tahitian society was a fusion of a simpler indigenous culture with that of a more advanced alien invading culture. Coming presumably from nearby Raiatea in the seventh century, the invaders set themselves up as the rulers, while the *raatira* came into being by intermarriages of followers of the conquerors and the local population. While details of the process are lacking, the suggestion, at least, is that the *raatira* were given land grants in return for military services and that the *manahune* were, accordingly, forcibly expropriated.

Hawaii carried forward all the features of the Stratified societies and, at the same time, resolved the conflict between centralized and decentralized authority by granting to the supreme chief (*moi*) title to all land in his domain. This differed from the rights of the *Tui Tonga* in that each new Hawaiian administration systematically expropriated its opponents, rewarded its supporters, and curtailed the influence of potential rivals by giving them estates smaller than due their rank. By this "spoils system" the Hawaiian rulers frankly acknowledged the equation: land-wealth equals power. The spoils system promoted social mobility among the upper ranks and left the lower ranks least disturbed. As in all the Stratified societies, land relations were "feudal." The gentry held land in return for tribute and services, and the commoners (*makaainana*) were the landless plantation workers who could be—although they rarely were—evicted. An outcaste group, the despised *kauwa,* were totally removed from the land.

Hawaiian traditions describe close relations with Tahiti; in fact, Buck (in Handy 1933) believes that the Hawaiian nobility came from the Society Islands to impose their rule upon the natives, who became the landless commoners. According to the traditions, the power of the *moi* over the gentry was won by slow degrees and by hard measures. In the course of wars and revolts new ruling lines were created, many were deprived of their landholdings, and others received great estates (Fornander 1916). The ultimate centralization of Hawaiian government came under Kamehameha I, who, like his Tahitian contemporary Pomare I, used European help to carry out traditional political objectives.

All in all, the histories of the Stratified societies point to the sequence: Traditional–Open–Stratified.

PARALLEL SEQUENCES IN CLOSELY RELATED ISLANDS

Another interesting line of evidence on Polynesian evolution comes from a comparison of very closely related neighboring cultures. The pattern of variations shown by Polynesia as a whole apparently has been recapitulated in the histories of individual Polynesian societies and is repeated again among neighboring societies. In this connection, the situation in the Marquesas would have been extremely illuminating if detailed cultural comparisons of all the islands had been possible. Handy (1923) has pointed out that Marquesan cultures varied, the southern islands having less definite social stratification, less definite private ownership of land, and chiefs of lesser sacredness than the northern islands. The southern people, he noted, were more assertive and more independent-minded.

The fact that the variations seemingly characteristic of the area as a whole show up in neighboring islands would seem to demonstrate, first, that these differences are the result of internal developments and of migrations by which a parent culture is carried forward (and sometimes backward) in a new environment, and, second, that the conditions promoting evolution were everywhere active in Polynesia.

Among the societies that are most clearly related by tradition as well as by trait similarities are Samoa–Tonga–Niue; Maori–Tahiti–Hawaii; Easter Island–Marquesas–Mangareva. Other combinations can be considered, but these three illustrate the point well enough. The chart of Polynesian subcultures shows that closely related societies may share common traits and still have different social systems. This is because in evolution new characteristics may emerge but the bulk of changes consists of the repatterning of traditional traits.

Samoa–Tonga–Niue: Samoa and Tonga (Fiji has been omitted from what should be a triad, because of its Melanesian affiliations) are clearly sister cultures; Niuean traditions link it to immigrants and invaders from both. Samoa is the Traditional order being undermined by political ambitions; Niue is a Samoan system shattered beyond recognition by warfare; and Tonga is the evolution of the Samoan type into stratification via warfare.

Marquesas, Easter Island, and Mangareva represent variations in "openness." In Easter Island the contest for social position and power led to the exploitation of captives. In the Marquesas, where "tribal democracy" was still strong, some chiefs had begun to usurp land which they had held in custody for the tribe. In Mangareva this process had gone to the point of complete expropriation.

In the *Maori–Tahiti–Hawaii* group, Maori stands as the culmination of the Traditional order, Tahiti is a stratified phase in which the power and position of local chiefs were sustained by their inalienable land rights, while Hawaii was the Polynesian endpoint in centralized power. If we include Mangaia, which claims kinship with Tahiti, the sequence of variations is the more complete.

PARALLEL CULTURAL CHANGES

Fundamental changes in the Polynesian systems of status appear to have produced major modifications in many basic Polynesian institutions and cultural values. Some basic changes in government, land systems, and kinship have already been brought out. The following section summarizes those additional changes that seem to be most closely related to the evolution inspired by status rivalry. The correlations are not necessarily clear-cut. They refer to central tendencies and generally follow the gradations of the societies constituting a type. Thus, the more "open" of the Traditional societies are apt to show many of the characteristics of the Open societies. It was obviously impossible in this article to present detailed cultural comparisons. Finally, it

should be noted that, while the ethnographic data for this section
are reasonably adequate, they are not complete.

Authority

1. *Government changed from a kinship to a territorial basis.*
This very significant finding has already been made by Burrows
(1939). I would restate it as follows. *Traditional:* Although
chiefs ruled over territories in some places, kinship was still the
main source of authority. *Open:* Authority shifted from senior
kinsmen to strong leaders, and, while it served the interests of
a kin-unified group, it was also exercised over captives and other
aliens, thus introducing a territorial principle. *Stratified:* The
territorial principle was consolidated through the fuller incorporation of conquered peoples into the administrative territory. At
the same time, authority and hereditary succession were strengthened to bolster the ruling dynasties.

2. *Government began to rely increasingly upon physical force.*
Traditional: Chiefs rarely used force against their own people.
Futuna may have been one exception. Manu'an chiefs had life-
and-death powers over their subjects but rarely used them. *Open:*
Force was used mainly against aliens. *Stratified:* Force, including
severe and capricious punishment against one's own people, was
common.

3. *Government became more highly organized. Traditional:*
Government was informal and in its most elaborate forms consisted of chiefs and a council of subchiefs and perhaps priestly
advisors. *Open:* Government was equally informal. *Stratified:*
Mangareva, as the most "open," had, accordingly, the most
informal government. The others had developed a court and a
body of specialized officials. The most elaborate was the Hawaiian
court, a product not only of more complex administrative problems but of an interest in broadening the base of government
by adding officials and creating new status positions.

4. *Religion became an official arm of government.* Government and religion were closely linked in all Polynesian societies
and therefore, as governments developed, so did their religious
sanctions. *Traditional:* Priests and chiefs worked together for
community interests, and in some places chief and priest were
the same person. *Open:* Rule was mainly by strong men who
were less closely dependent upon the priesthood for their au-

thority. In Mangaia, for example, priests who sought political advantage for themselves lost their religious immunities. *Stratified:* A highly organized priesthood followed very closely the political aims of the government, serving primarily the interests of the ruling dynasty—although it could also oppose them—and secondarily those of the community as a whole. Priests were political advisors and regulated the *tapu* system. The Tongan priesthood was the least organized.

5. Tapu *became a political instrument. Tapu,* as the ritual counterpart of *mana* and as a religious device for social control, was universal in Polynesia. As political power developed, *tapu* quite logically became its bulwark. *Traditional: Tapu* emphasized the sacredness of the high-born and was used to conserve crops. *Open:* Mangaia and Easter Island had begun to apply *tapu* directly in the interests of their rulers. *Stratified:* While economic *tapus* served community interests as well, they primarily sanctioned the political and economic privileges of chiefs, gentry, and priesthood.

6. Tapus *came to be enforced by physical as well as by religious sanctions.* This is a corollary to point 5. As *tapus* became political, their enforcement also became political. *Traditional: Tapu* violations were self-punishing. *Open:* Mangaia and Easter Island had penal sanctions. *Stratified:* All used penal sanctions.

7. *The attitude toward human life became more callous.* As warfare, along with conflicts for power and economic advantage, became more prominent, rulers took upon themselves god-like powers over human life. This showed itself, for example, in the attitude of the Tongan chief who cut off the left arms of his cooks simply out of caprice (Gifford 1929:127). It was best revealed, however, in the practice of human sacrifices. *Traditional:* Human sacrifices were either nonexistent or, as in Samoa and Maori, infrequent and minor. *Open:* Human sacrifices were important except in Niue, where they did not occur at all. *Stratified:* Human sacrifices were more common, and in Tahiti and Hawaii reached great proportions. Tahitian traditions say that conditions were once so good they made no sacrifices. Then things got bad, and they began to sacrifice pigs. Finally, a king told them, "We must tremble with fear," and he introduced

human sacrifices (Henry 1928:127). Victims were captives, the
humble, and the politically unreliable.

8. *First-fruits ceremonies became a formal taxation device.*
All Polynesian chiefs had first-fruits privileges. In the *Traditional*
and in the *Open* these tributes were ceremonial, and the offerings
were token symbols. In the *Stratified* the ceremonialism of first
fruits continued but collections became formal, obligatory, and
signs of political loyalty. The redistribution of first fruits was
also universal, but in the Stratified societies this often became
little more than a gesture. In Tonga, for example, the lowly
were given spoiled meat considered unsuitable for the gentry
(Martin 1817:132).

Property

9. *Land tenure changed from a tribal to a feudal basis.* (This
point has already been discussed.)

10. *The lower orders came to bear the brunt of food shortages.* All Polynesian societies accepted some measure of responsibility for the community, but they differed in the degree to
which they did so. *Traditional:* Sharing a common food supply
was common. *Open:* The strong took a larger share but accepted
responsibility for their followers. *Stratified:* The commoners were
neglected. In Mangareva they often had no recourse against
inconsiderate landlords. But, as a rule, everywhere in the Stratified
societies they could leave a lord and join the estate of another.

11. *The distribution of wealth became uneven.* In all Polynesian societies the chief was the center of food redistribution.
In the *Traditional* the distribution was roughly equal; in the
Open, Mangaia and the Marquesas had uneven systems favoring
the chiefs or warriors. In the *Stratified,* chiefs and gentry invariably held the largest shares. It is true that each subchief
redistributed a portion of his share among his followers. By
doing so, however, he bolstered his own political position.

12. *Property attitudes became more predatory.* The *Traditional*
valued property for the physical comforts it provided and as
symbols of rank, but chiefs were only mildly acquisitive and
essentially nonpredatory. The *Open* were predatory mainly at
the expense of aliens. They indulged in rivalrous ostentatious
property displays. In the *Stratified,* wealth was both the price
and the reward of power. Thus, land was the object of predatory

attack and land boundaries were carefully marked and zealously defended.

13. *Land became alienable.* *Traditional:* Land was usually vested in a kinship group, and that made it inalienable except in relatively infrequent cases of conquest. *Open:* Conquest and the absorption of captives led to a more fluid tenure system. *Stratified:* Commoners had lost their traditional rights to land, while, except for Tahiti, even the gentry were no longer secure in their tenure.

Kinship

14. *Kinship bonds weakened.* All Polynesian societies maintained the theory of tribal unity through kinship and allowed commoners to trace their kinship to chiefs. Changes that occurred were more in practice than in formal structure. *Traditional:* Kinship unity was very strong, and even among the high ranks intrafamilial conflicts were occasional. *Open:* Except for Niue, which was more like the *Traditional* in this respect, wars and the internal struggle for power realigned kin and provoked intense intrakin conflict. *Stratified:* Kin ties were strongly affected by political considerations. Discord was at its peak in Mangareva. Class lines reduced kin ties to mere formal recognition. In Mangareva a chief killed a commoner relative who had addressed him by a kin term. In Hawaii the dispersal of kin had gone farthest of all (Burrows 1939).

15. *Political and status motives in marriage became more important.* Rank was a factor in marriage in all Polynesian societies. As status and power became more important, marriage continued to be an advantageous avenue for social advancement. Marriage ritual accordingly was most elaborated among the upper ranks in the Stratified societies.

16. *Caste developed only in the Stratified societies.* Tahiti and Hawaii drew hard caste lines. Caste may be regarded as an intensification of the rank consciousness present in almost all Polynesian societies.

Position of Women

17. Tapu *restrictions on women became more severe.* All Polynesian societies regarded women as in some way defiling. In the *Traditional* and *Open* societies, *tapu* restrictions were, on

the whole, minor (except for Uvea and Maori). In the *Stratified* these tended to become more severe, particularly in Hawaii where husband and wife needed separate living quarters.

18. *Women gained more political rights.* High-ranking women received ceremonial recognition in all Polynesian societies, but only in the *Stratified* (and in the Marquesas) could they become *ariki.*

19. *Primogeniture came to override sex in political succession.* This is a corollary to point 18.

Sexual Practices

20. *Sexual orgies became more prominent.* All Polynesian societies permitted considerable premarital sexual freedom at the same time that they required premarital chastity of high-born women. In Tahiti and Hawaii, orgiastic sexual rites increased postmarital sexual license.

Infanticide

21. Infanticide occurred sporadically in Polynesia but, where it did, it showed interesting variations. In Pukapuka infanticide was in response to population pressure, in Tahiti it was to maintain caste lines, and in Hawaii it was to avoid the nuisance of child-rearing (Malo).

Mourning

22. *Violence in mourning began to turn outward.* Almost all Polynesian mourners showed grief by beating or gashing themselves. However, only in the *Stratified* societies did mourners for a chief or a king turn their violent expressions of grief against other people as well. Tongans, for example, fought bloody sham battles, while Hawaiian and Tahitian mourners killed or maimed anyone unfortunate enough to get in their way.

Warfare

23. *Warfare became more prominent and more serious. Traditional:* warfare was of minor importance except for Maori, Tongareva, Futuna, and Uvea. It was virtually state policy in all the *Open* and *Stratified,* where the motives were usually predatory and where the chiefs and the outstanding warriors were the main beneficiaries of military success.

24. *Combat became more cruel.* The Polynesians were not gentle warriors. However, the *Open* and *Stratified* encouraged, even by Polynesian standards, unusual acts of ferocity against enemies.

Priesthood

25. *The priesthood became more elaborately organized.* Except for Maori, priests were shamans or priest-chiefs, or else the professional priesthood was very simply organized in the *Traditional*. The *Open* (except for Niue which had no priests at all) and the *Stratified* had the most elaborate priesthoods. These reached their peak in Tahiti and in Hawaii.

26. *The priesthood became more political* (see point 4).

27. *Ceremonialism increased* (see point 26).

28. *Ritual became confined to rulers and to the upper ranks.* In part this was a logical development of the doctrine of *mana* that intended to ritualize the life of the high-born, and in part it reflected increasing stratification. In the *Stratified* societies it was leading to the secularization of the lives of the commoners.

Deities

29. *The gods became more vengeful and awesome.* The distribution of the major Polynesian deities such as *Tane, Lono, Tu,* and *Tangaroa* covered most of the islands, but the attributes of the pantheon varied significantly. In the *Traditional* the deities were apt to be either beneficent, neutral, or, at worst, mischievous. In the *Open* and *Stratified* the gods were more threatening and inspired terror by their demands for human offerings.

30. *The gods became more diversified.* This followed no absolute course. However, the *Traditional* (except for Maori) relied upon fewer deities, for the most part ancestor gods, while the *Stratified* had the greatest variety of gods and cults. The situation in the *Open* societies was mixed. Niue, Mangaia, and Easter Island were more like the *Traditional,* and the Marquesas approached the *Stratified*.

Afterlife

31. *Status entered more into the conception of the afterlife.* The *Traditional* attributed no rank distinctions to the afterlife, the *Open* recognized a better afterlife for brave warriors, and the

Stratified were the most status-conscious of all. Tongans did not even acknowledge that commoners had souls (Martin 1817: II 136).

32. *The conception of the afterlife became more unpleasant.* The *Traditional* regarded the afterlife either as more pleasant or as no less pleasant than life on earth. The *Open* and *Stratified* clearly differentiated between good and bad other-worlds and raised the prospects of a most unpleasant afterlife.

Sorcery

33. *Sorcery became more threatening.* All Polynesian societies knew sorcery. In the *Traditional,* only Maori used sorcery actively and even then mainly against other tribes. In the *Open,* sorcery was common only in Mangaia. In the *Stratified,* sorcery was common and very threatening in all.

34. *Supernatural causes of illness became more varied.* Social delinquency or religious neglect brought about supernatural punishment in all Polynesian societies. In the *Stratified,* however, the unprovoked hostility of the gods as well as human hostility in the form of sorcery added considerably to the recognized causes of illness. Chiefs were common victims of envy-inspired sorcery.

Omens

35. *Concern with omens increased.* The *Traditional* recognized some omens, the *Open* many more, and the *Stratified* were the most preoccupied with omens of impending trouble. Hawaiians, whose lives may have been the least secure, were particularly troubled about omens in building and occupying houses.

CONCLUSION

The far-reaching cultural changes correlating with the three postulated types of Polynesian society follow such a consistent course that they lend strong support to the evolutionary hypothesis that has been presented here. They show that Polynesian cultural evolution was not merely a growth in complexity—a vague concept at best—but a development of stronger political controls, more exploitative relationships, more violence, more conflict, and greater general insecurity. The material reveals how step by step the benign casual ethos of cultures such as Pukapuka and Manu'a, for example, is transformed into the fiercer and more violent outlooks of Mangarevans, Tahitians, and Hawaiians. The Hawaiians went so far as to introduce a professional outlook and a passion for betting into the traditional Polynesian devotion to sports. At the same time, we observe the growth of skills in architecture, agriculture, political administration, and in the arts of poetry and balladry. Status rivalry produced conflict and the social and psychological consequences of strife; but it also played a prominent part in promoting craft specialization, the essential precursor of technical progress.

In another positive sense the Polynesians did not accept meekly the increased pressure of arbitrary authority. They checked cruel rulers by revolts and palace *coups* and, if these measures were not appropriate, they plotted private revenges or joined with more humane overlords. It is most striking that all the Stratified societies found it necessary to teach chiefs to be ". . . humble, kind, sympathetic, open-hearted," as Kepelino said of Hawaii (Beckwith 1932:140). Tahitian kings were warned:

> Let not the decrees of death be too frequent, for your own bones will follow the road to death. It will be like the tearing down of your own home by the warrior when the night of darkness is enveloping you, the night that hides sin. Watch your people. Arouse not that which will pain them. You may not be able to find the cure [Handy 1930:41].

In these illustrative injunctions to rulers we see the emergence into explicit form of an ethical code that runs contrary to the spirit of the moment in the Stratified societies. (Malo, who was a member of the Hawaiian court, brings this out very clearly [1951:72 ff].) This, too, we may regard as a significant evolutionary development.

Finally, and in a more general vein, the Polynesian material shows that major cultural changes resulted not so much from the introduction of new elements but rather from a rearrangement and an intensification of traditional widespread Polynesian practices. Thus, new emergents such as "feudal" land tenure, to take but one example, had their roots in the practice of family land supervisors. Yet, once the system of land tenure had shifted to gentry-controlled holdings, the repercussions upon Polynesian society were fundamental indeed.

18 THE CIVIL-RELIGIOUS HIERARCHY IN MESOAMERICAN COMMUNITIES: PRE-SPANISH BACKGROUND AND COLONIAL DEVELOPMENT

Pedro Carrasco

Pedro Carrasco is Professor of Anthropology at the University of California, Los Angeles. He is the author of *Tarascan Folk Religion* (1952), *Land and Polity in Tibet* (1959), and of several papers.

O NE OF THE basic features of the traditional Indian peasant communities of Mesoamerica is the civil-religious hierarchy that combines most of the civil and ceremonial offices of the town's organization in a single scale of yearly offices. I will call it the ladder system. All men of the community have to enter into it and all have a chance to climb up to the highest steps and reach the status of elder. This system is closely connected with all the major aspects of the community's social structure. It has been well defined and here I will mention only a few salient traits (Tax 1937:442–44; Cámara 1952).

It can be characterized as a type of democracy in which all offices are open to all men and in which the operation of the ladder eventually results in everyone sharing in turn the responsibilities of office. The number of positions is always larger in the lower steps of the ladder; errand boys for ceremonial or civil officials and policemen are usually grouped in gangs from different sections or wards of the town who take turns in performing their duties. The higher offices are those of town councilmen (*regidores*) and judges or mayors (*alcaldes*) in the civil government, and several ceremonial stewardships (*mayordomías*) in the cult organization. When a town is subdivided into wards, most often each ward participates equally in the higher levels of the hierarchy; there are parallel offices of the same rank, one for

FROM *American Anthropologist* 63 (1961), 483–97, by permission of the author and of the editor, *American Anthropologist*.

each ward, or a single position rotates year after year among the different wards.

Generally a man alternates between civil and religious positions and, after filling an office, takes a period of rest during which he does not actively participate in the town's civil or ceremonial organization until the time comes again for him to occupy a higher office. As a citizen of the community he has the obligation to serve, and social pressure to that effect is always strong, while the individual will also be driven to apply for offices in order to raise his social status. In the ceremonial organization, office-holding can also be the outcome of a religious vow by which an individual tries to obtain supernatural help through participation in or sponsorship of a public ceremony.

Participation in the lower ranks of the ladder simply involves the performance of menial tasks such as sweeping, carrying messages, or policing the town. Higher offices carry higher responsibilities in the political and ceremonial organizations and usually demand a number of expenditures in the form of sponsorship of festivals and the banqueting connected with the transmission of office. These celebrations are, in effect, feasts of merit in which the consumption of an individual's wealth results in his enhanced social status, and a number of reciprocal exchanges of goods and services center around the organization of festivals. Thus the operation of the ladder also implies that all share in turn the financing of the town's government and ceremonials (Carrasco 1957:19–20).

A number of differences are found within this general pattern. One type of difference relates to the extent to which all men actually share in the highest steps of the ladder. As Tax (1937:443) has pointed out, differences exist between the small towns, in which all men reach the top levels of the ladder, and the large towns, in which only a small proportion of men reach the higher offices. In the first case the ladder is, as we have pointed out, a system for sharing by rotation in the political and ceremonial organization. Individual status differences connected with an individual's place in the ladder tend to coincide with age and in the long run all individuals go through the same steps. In some instances recently reported among the Chinantec and Mixe there is, along with the ladder, a system of age grades, each one forming a well defined group with separate functions in the political and ceremonial life. From the men in the proper grade officials are selected to fill certain positions in the ladder, and completion of one's term in a certain office is followed by entrance into a higher grade. Members of the different grades sit together on separate benches in the town hall or at ceremonial functions (Weitlaner and Castro 1954:160 ff; Weitlaner and Hoogshagen 1960).

In the second case, that is, in the large towns, there are relatively few positions in the higher steps of the ladder in relation to the large population and only the wealthiest achieve the highest ranks, so that there is a certain degree of class differentiation.

Another kind of difference within the general pattern is related to the economic aspects of office-holding. There are three ways of meeting the needs of administration and ceremonials. First, by the use of communal property; second, by taking collections from all villagers—in these two cases the official acts as manager or collector—and third, by the individual contribution of the official, who becomes then the sponsor of the office he holds (Carrasco 1952:28–29, 34). This third procedure is the most important one in modern times, and I have considered it the main one in defining the ladder system in broad terms.

In any case, the group of highest prestige, and in the more conservative communities the ultimate governing body of the town, consists of the men who have gone through the required offices and sponsorships of the ladder. These are usually referred to as *principales* (principals), *pasados* (ex-officers), or, since this grade is reached at an advanced age, *ancianos* (elders). Elders are considered to have done their share for the town and are exempt from communal labor services.

The purpose of this paper is to discuss the pre-Spanish background of this ladder system, and to outline its later development as a consequence of the Spanish conquest. The positions in the modern civil-religious hierarchy are part both of the municipal system of town government introduced in the early Colonial period and of the local organization of the folk Catholic cult. Yearly terms of office were also part of the Spanish regulations and there are many other similarities between the modern Indian village organization and the Spanish municipal system (Font

1952). Consequently it could be assumed that the modern civil-religious hierarchy was basically of Spanish origin. Without denying the undoubtable Spanish contribution to its development, it is the point of this paper to stress its pre-Spanish antecedents and to show how they shaped the introduction of the Spanish municipal organization under the conditions of Colonial rule. Indeed, the social structure of ancient Mexico can be understood only by giving proper weight to the institutions that constitute such antecedents. They combine features of both equalitarian and stratified character, either of which have sometimes been overly emphasized to produce a distorted picture of ancient Mexican society.

Let us examine the features of the pre-Spanish political, ceremonial, and economic organization that are similar to the modern civil-religious ladder system. We are concerned with the existence of a ladder of ranked statuses, the possibility for a wide group of individuals to climb up this ladder, the connection of the ladder with social stratification, and the economic implications of the system. I will use data from the Aztec, with only a few references to other areas of Central Mexico, but similar situations existed in all areas of Mesoamerica about which data are available.

Although an important trait of Aztec society was the hereditary distinction between commoners (*maceualtin*) and noblemen (*pipiltin*), there was a good deal of social mobility. Fr. Diego Durán (1951:II 124–25), one of the best reporters on Aztec society, clearly describes the drive for social advancement and the acquisition of titles and reports three different avenues by which individuals could achieve higher status: warfare, priesthood, and trade.

Both military and priestly advancement were part of the organization of the two types of men's houses. The Youth's Houses (*telpochcalli*), of which there were many, one in each ward, were primarily devoted to the training and the utilization of the commoner young men in warfare and public works. The *calmecac* (Row of Houses) were priestly residences connected with the most important temples of the city to which went the children of the nobility and apparently some commoners vowed by their parents to the priesthood. The calmecac were primarily religious, but warfare and certain crafts were also part of the training and the activities of their members[1] (Sahagún 1938:I 288–98, II 217–25; Pomar 1941:27; Motolinia 1903:254–55).

Young boys, whether of commoner or noble status, entered the men's houses at the lowest steps of a ladder of military or priestly grades. Each grade was signified by differences in haircuts, clothes, and ornaments. Members of each grade, or combinations of grades, assembled at separate halls in the ruler's palace or the temples; they participated as groups with separate functions in the complex ceremonial life, and from each grade were selected determined categories of office-holders.

Young commoner boys entered the Youth's Houses of their wards before puberty and as young boys (*telpochtontli*) were given menial activities such as sweeping or collecting firewood. Upon reaching puberty, the youths (*telpochtli*) were taken to the battlefield first as helpers of experienced warriors but soon to start fighting on their own. From then on success in the battlefield determined the social status of the young man. Those who were able to capture prisoners became Captors (*yaqui tlamani*), different recognition being given according to the tribal origin and number of captives. From among the most successful captors were selected the leaders of youths (*teachcauan*) and the heads of the Youth's Houses (*telpochtlato*). All these assembled in the ruler's palace at the so-called Song's House (*cuicacalli*) where they were available to receive orders to gather their men when needed in public works (Sahagún 1938:I 291–93; II 310, 331–34).

The capture of a prisoner not only contributed to the social advancement of the warrior but involved him in social and ceremonial affairs. The prisoner was sacrificed at one of the great festivals, the captor had to fast and keep vigil in preparation for the event, and he received his prisoner's body with which to

---

[1] The relationship of the *telpochcalli* and the *calmecac* to each other, and to class and ward divisions, needs a detailed study. It is clear that there were a large number of *telpochcalli*, generally speaking one in each ward, although no list of them is available. The names of the *calmecac* are given by Sahagún (1938:I 220–27); some of them still have the names of the original wards of the Aztecs but it is not clear what was the relationship to the wards of the time of the conquest. According to Durán (1951:II 108–9), it was possible to move from the *telpochcalli* to the *calmecac*.

prepare a banquet for his relatives and friends (Sahagún 1938:
I 123–30).

The young men left the Youth's House in their twenties in
order to marry. They were then entered in the ward's tax rolls
and most of them must have in fact withdrawn from the race to
climb up the military hierarchy. In addition to warfare, possibilities for improving status existed within the ward organization,
where there were a number of group leaders for the collection
of tribute and organization of labor drafts, and there were also
the local cults of the various wards and craft groups. The ward
chiefs (*tepixque, calpixque, tequitlatoque* or *calpuleque*) were
usually succeeded by a son or near relative, but qualification for
the office and advanced age were also required. Upon reaching
52 years of age, a man became free from tribute and labor
services and was held in great esteem. The elders of the ward
(*calpulhueuetque*) were an important group in all ceremonial
functions of the ward and were consulted by the ward chief in
all important matters (Zurita 1941:86–90, 111; Durán 1951:I
498, II 223; Torquemada 1943:II 329, 545; Sahagún 1951:58,
106, 124 and passim; Gómez de Orozco 1945:63).

Noblemen had their own assembly hall at the palace, the
House of Nobles (*pilcalli*), where met the close relatives of the
ruler and high officials. The boys of the nobility who entered
the calmecac could also devote themselves to a military career
(Sahagún 1938:I 144, II 309; Durán 1951:II 162; Zurita 1941:
91, 145).

The most successful warriors, these who had captured four
prisoners of the bravest enemy cities, acquired the category of
tequiua (he who has [done] a job). In the palace they assembled at the Eagle's House (*quauhcalli* or *tequiuacacalli*)
where they formed part of the war councils, and they qualified
for high military and governmental offices. Most of the tequiua
were of noble birth. They had been sent as boys to the temple
connected with the warlike cult of the Sun and this religious
connection was kept after their marriage. Brave commoners could
also be raised to the rank of tequiua, but noblemen received
different insignia and ornaments and qualified for higher positions than men of commoner origin (Durán 1951:II 124, 155–59,
162–65, Pomar 1941:34, 38).

From the tequiua were selected a number of officials who

formed the highest councils of government.[2] The military commanders (*tlacatecalt* and *tlacochcalcatl*) formed the ruler's war council; some were of noble and some of commoner status. At the palace they assembled with the tequiua at the Eagle's House. Men of these titles were also placed in charge of subject towns, and the titles had usually been held by a new ruler before assuming his office (Sahagún 1938:I 291; II 107, 138, 310, 329; Codex Mendoza 1938:III 17–18; Monzón 1949:75).

Others from among the tequiua were given special individual titles that placed them in the category of lord's councillors (*tecutlatoque*). They formed the highest courts (the *teccalco* and the *tlacxitlan*) and the ruler could assign them special tasks as the need arose. Most of these positions were filled by noblemen; some reports state that commoners rarely reached them, while others state that—at least in Tetzcoco—men of noble and commoner origin shared some positions (Sahagún 1938:II 317, 330; Zurita 1941:85–86; Pomar 1941:29–30; Tezozomoc 1878:361, passim).

Others among the tequiua became the ruler's executors (*achcacauhtin*) who also had a special assembly hall at the palace (the *achcauhcalli*); these were offices held by men of commoner origin (Sahagún 1938:I 166, 291, 293, II 310).

Information about the terms of office is weak but what there is indicates that political positions were generally held for indefinite periods, for life, or until the holder was advanced to a higher rank; sometimes demotion to untitled commoner status was possible (Zurita 1941:86; Sahagún 1938:II 308; Durán 1951:I 436).

Special groups were the *otomi* and *quachic* (shorn one) warriors, tequiua who made special vows not to step back in the

[2] The most difficult problem in the study of ancient Mexican polity is the proper characterization of this group. Kinship relations, rules of succession, length of tenure, political functions of each title, and possible connection with wards or dependent cities have to be studied. The data of Tetzcoco are somewhat better on some of these questions (Ixtlilzochitl 1952:II 167 ff; Zurita 1941:100–4; Pomar 1941:29–30). The several accounts about the achievement of the rank of *tecuhtli* are also relevant here. Most of them refer to Tlaxcala, Huexotzinco, and Cholula, but the general features also apply to the Valley of Mexico. It seems to be basically a requirement of a period of temple service and large distribution of goods before the assumption of the title (cf. Durán 1951:II 110, 125 mentioned below).

battlefield, had distinctive insignia, and formed an elite corps in the army. They were considered great killers but too wild and not fit for the affairs of government (Sahagún 1938:II 137; Durán 1951:I 169–70, II 163).

A further military grade were the Old Eagles (*quauhueuetque*) or old warriors who performed special tasks as some sort of field commanders and officiated in the funerals of those who died in battle (Durán 1951:I 289, 293, 315; Tezozomoc 1878: 428).

The priestly organization was highly complex and presents a number of problems that would demand lengthy discussion. The main grades of the hierarchy were the following: first that of the young boys who served as Little Priests (*tlamacazton*), mainly occupied in menial tasks in the temples. As youths they became Young Priests (*tlamacazque*). From these the most devout were advanced to the grade of Fire Giver (*tlenamacac*), and from these the two high priests or Feather Snakes (*quequetzalcoa*) were selected. According to one report, advancement in the priestly hierarchy among the Young Priests took place every five years. Some of the young priests went to the battlefield as we have mentioned; others devoted themselves to purely religious activity (Sahagún 1938:I 144, 299; Torquemada 1943:II 185).

The priestly hierarchy was especially complex because of the existence of separate temples devoted to the various deities, each one with different cults and with priests having special titles. The main list of priests that we have in addition to what has been outlined is basically a list of the keepers of each god or temple, most of them seemingly stewards in charge of gathering the things required for the cult of a particular god (Sahagún 1938:I 237–41). These were probably positions of similar rank, but it is not entirely clear how they relate to the ladder given above. They seem to belong in a further rank of old priests. Old age is mentioned as characteristic of the priests named *quaquacuiltin,* which is the title of some of the stewards. Like the Old Eagles among the warriors, this was probably the priestly rank of the elders. In some cases a god's attendants are referred to as his old men (*iueueyouan*) and the ward elders (*calpulhueuetque*) also had ceremonial functions on certain occasions (Sahagún 1938:I 30; 1951:44, 47, 58, 106, 119, 183).

Not all ceremonial functions implied the existence of full time priests. Certain ceremonial activities were in the charge of government officials, warriors, or other householders who resided in the temple for only limited periods of time, in some cases different groups taking turns so that some were always in residence (Sahagún 1938:I 144, 229; Gómez de Orozco 1945:39, 61). A number of other specialized roles in the various cults or great public ceremonies were played by individuals who acted simply as the result of a vow, often in order to be cured of a disease connected with the god being worshipped (Sahagún 1938:I 32, 40, 48–51, 177).

Some old priests retired from their religious life and were then given high titles and positions in government. To judge from their titles, they became part of the group of councillors of the ruler mentioned above (Durán 1951:II 110, 125).

An interesting case is that of the priestly ladder leading to the offices of the two high rulers in the city of Cholula. They were selected from among a number of priests devoted to the cult of Quetzalcoatl; these priests were noblemen from only one ward of the city, that of Tianquiznauac. When they entered the priesthood they turned over all or most of their wealth to the temple and vowed their lives to it, but they could get married and visit their wives overnight. The various grades of this priesthood were signified by different cloaks. New priests received a black cloak which they wore for four years. At the end of this period they received a black cloak with a red fringe which they wore for another four years. They they received a cloak ornamented in black and red which they also wore for a four year period. After this they received black cloaks to wear for the rest of their lives, except the eldest ones who dressed in red and were candidates to succeed to the two ruling officers upon the death of the latter (Rojas 1927: 160–61).

The third road to social advancement was trade. Merchants came from certain wards in the city, and the young men were organized into gangs with their leaders, as were all other commoners, and left on trading expeditions at the service of older traders. When their trips involved them in warfare, as often happened, they could receive titles equal to those of the warriors. Otherwise the trader who accumulated wealth used it in buying slaves for sacrifice; the victim thus offered was the equivalent of the prisoner offered by the captor, and the trader then received the title of Bather, more precisely "He who has purified some-

one for sacrifice" (*tlaltique, tealtianime*). The traders had their
own internal organization and courts; their leaders were the *poch-
teca tlatoque* (trader chiefs) who formed a council for their internal government and the regulation of the marketplace, and
the merchant elders (*pocheteca ueuetque*) were honored guests
of all the social functions of the traders (Sahagún 1959:passim;
Durán 1951:II 125; Zurita 1941:142–43).

Although data are less detailed concerning them, other professional groups also had achievable ranks of their own. Thus the
hunters could reach the titles of Hunting Tequiua (*amizte-
quiuaque*) and Hunting Chiefs (*amiztlatoque*), and in some craft
groups there were ceremonial offerings of slaves to their patron
gods which, as among the traders, probably enhanced the status
of the offerer (Durán 1951:II 130, 297–98; Sahagún 1938:I
46–47, 190; 1959:80, 87).

As we have seen, the possibilities for advancement along the
military and priestly ladders existed within hereditary classes.
Class differences are also related to the economic implications
of the ladder. Men of noble birth inherited not only rank but
also landed estates, and office-holders were rewarded with the
revenue of estates attached to their offices. Commoners who
reached high ranks received with their titles lands that in some
cases were held only for life, in others could be transmitted by
inheritance, the heir joining the ranks of the nobility. In addition
to these individualized sources of income, all the attendants of
the palace, including all the officials, were fed from the ruler's
kitchen and often received presents, mainly clothes and ornaments, from the ruler, whose great storehouses were filled with
the tribute of all subject peoples. Descriptions of wide distributions of goods are a recurrent feature in the accounts of monthly
festivals and military celebrations. Since the ruler, his officials,
the nobility, the temples and men's houses were provided with
lands and tribute, all these individuals and institutions were then
the focal points for the management of public property and the
accumulation and distribution of goods, primarily among the top
levels of society, although something trickled down to commoner
producers (Zurita 1941:85–86, 144–45; Durán 1951:II 161, 164;
Torquemada 1943:II 546; Sahagún 1951:passim; 1954:39; Tezozomoc 1878:passim).

In addition, there is also the system of individual sponsorship of a public function, implying the previous accumulation of goods required for the performance of that function and followed by the achievement of a higher social rank. This is the case of the merchants and craftsmen, or of the one-year-fasters (*mocexiuh-çauhque*) devoted to the cult of Uitzilopochtli. The consumption of wealth required for some of these sponsorships could imply serious economic hardships even to the point of pledging oneself or losing land (Sahagún 1938:I 264–65; Motolinia 1941:35).

The achievement ladder operated within a number of separate social segments. We have seen the three different ladders of warfare, priesthood, and trade. These also existed separately in the different wards, each with its own Youth's House and local temple. Some of these segments were of equal rank and their particular organizations were parallel instances of the same type of organization. But in many cases the achievement ladder was open only to social segments of high inherited status such as the nobility, or people of certain wards, or members of certain lineages. Thus the one-year-fasters of Uitzilopochtli were selected from only six wards in Mexico City (Durán 1951:II 89); in Cholula the ladder leading to the two highest rulers was open only to the noblemen of the ward of Tianquiznauac. In Mexico City the ruler came from a particular lineage (Monzón 1949:75). In cases such as this last one, advancement in the achievement ladder is part of the succession rule. The new ruler does not succeed automatically on the basis of a particular kinship connection. He is elected by the high ranking councillors as that relative of the former ruler—brother, son, or nephew—who has best qualified by advancement along the ladder. Heredity, election, and achievement are thus combined in a complex succession pattern.

The description given applies to Mexico Tenochtitlan, a city of at least 60,000 people (Toussaint et al. 1938:72) that had been extending its power over central and southern Mexico during the century before the Spanish conquest. As a successfully expanding society its upper class had grown to a size greater than that of the average Mesoamerican community and the picture here given can be taken as representative of only the great political centers. Not only did the tribute from large areas flow into the ruler's storehouses, but the nobility and the temples had lands outside the city in what had been foreign territory, especially in the

southern part of the Valley (Durán 1951:I 100, 114, 152; Tezozomoc 1878:253, 271, 286, 305). This and the establishment
of Aztec colonies and rulers in conquered territory provided an
outlet for an expanding upper class. Yet the question can be
raised whether the people of noble birth—especially numerous
because of upper class polygyny—could all follow a successful
career up the military and priestly ladders actually to achieve
positions of economic and political power. The reforms attributed
to Moteuczoma Xocoyotzin are especially significant from this
point of view. This ruler ordered that only persons of noble birth
could be attendants at his palace (Durán 1951:I 416–21; Tezozomoc 1878:578). This should not be interpreted only as a
sharpening of class differences; it also indicates the growth of a
group of noble birth working at the lower levels of the officialdom.
Some of the residents of the palace were artisans working at their
crafts, whose products were consumed by the upper class through
the distributive economy of the palace. Skilled crafts were taught
at the calmecac and were learned by noblemen (Tezozomoc
1949:112; Pomar 1941:38). Palace servants and skilled craftsmen thus formed a middle status group of noble birth but without
political power. Such a group could grow with the development
of a strong political center that produced an ever increasing number of the noble born and at the same time created a demand
for luxury products.

In comparison with Mexico Tenochtitlan, communities of lesser
power, and especially peasant communities, must have had a
type of organization like the one described in reference to the
ward organization, with a thin upper layer and a greater possibility for commoners to achieve commanding positions. Indeed,
while the dominant ethnic groups had a nobility (*pillotl*) and
a ruling lineage (*tlatocatlacamecayotl*), some of them with a
more clear-cut rule of succession than the Aztecs, there were
groups that had no nobility at all and that were ruled by military leaders (*quauhtlato*). The Aztecs themselves in the early
stages of their history belonged in this group (Chimalpahin
1889:27; 1958:46, 56–57, 154).

The importance of hereditary distinctions between noble and
commoner, including substantial differences in land-holding, the
limited number of positions at the higher levels of the hierarchy
in relation to the total population, and the restriction of the

highest positions to the nobility, give to the pre-Spanish ladder system a basically different character from that of the modern Indian. To the extent that high positions were opened to a given segment of society, the achievement ladder was a mechanism for the selection of the ruling group; when hereditary succession was also present advancement along the ladder can also be viewed as a requirement for the validation of hereditary claims. The situation is basically different from that of modern classless communities where the ladder is the mechanism by which every man takes his turn in filling offices.

In spite of these important differences between the pre-Spanish and the modern ladder systems, it is clear that many of the important features of the modern structure were present in the pre-Spanish type. The question now can be raised: how did the pre-Spanish organization change into the present one? We have a case of great similarity and continuity in certain aspects of the social structure, together with a radical change in the cultural forms that followed the suppression of warfare, the introduction of the Spanish system of town government, the eradication of the native religion, and the conversion to Christianity. At the risk of overgeneralizing I will present as a working hypothesis a simplified model of the process of change during the Colonial period and the 19th century.

I submit that the Spanish form of town government and the Catholic sodalities were reshaped and channelled into the main lines of the native political and ceremonial structure. The study of the Colonial Indian already provides us with some data as to the way in which this process took place.

We find first of all a direct continuation into Colonial times of the lower levels of the native organization which were maintained by the Spaniards for the collection of tribute and organization of public works (Durán 1951:I 323, II 166, 223; Torquemada 1943:II 545; Gibson 1952:118–20). Even today we find lesser officials with the title of *tequitlato* and *topil* that are clearly the perpetuation of their ancient namesakes. In the new religious organization the missionaries concentrated their efforts upon the young, whom they gathered together for instruction and used in menial jobs in the church in the same way as was done by the native priesthood (Durán 1951:II 113).

At the middle and high levels of the hierarchy, the introduction of the Spanish system of town government resulted in what I will call dual government, i.e., the old ruling group continued in power at the same time that the officials of the newly introduced system were duly elected, and both groups of officials jointly formed the governing body of the town. I am thinking here of a situation similar to that existing today in the Chiapas highlands where the municipal officials, whose existence is required by the present-day law of the State, rule together with and subordinate to a more complex body of officials forming the traditional government which in turn is clearly a blend of pre-Spanish and Colonial elements (Aguirre Beltrán 1953:122–40; Pozas 1959:133–53). Administrative records, which comprise the bulk of historical sources, will of course provide better data about the legal official organization than about the traditional customary titles or positions. Since the new offices were elective, nothing prevented the continuation of the old methods of achieving office. A number of local differences in the system of electing officials have been reported that depart from the Spanish usage and must be attributed to Indian practice. In many towns the old requirement of noble status for high office continued in effect during the Colonial period; and although the new offices had yearly terms and re-election for the next two years was forbidden, the evidence is clear that the same group of men repeatedly held all the high offices of the new administration, alternating from one to another. Some of the old positions became identified with the new ones. The old *tlatoani,* for instance, for some time was the *gobernador* of the Spanish system, and probably the functions of the old *tecutlatoque* and *achcacauhtin* were identified with the new *alcaldes* and *regidores* (Zavala and Miranda 1954:80–82; Chávez Orozco 1943:10; Gibson 1952:112).

The old system of achieving prestige through ceremonial sponsorship also continued. While the offering of sacrificial victims as a way of acquiring status was eradicated, the related practice of feast-giving and sponsorship of religious functions is reported in early Colonial times by missionaries who saw in it a continuation of the pre-Spanish customs. The well attested identification of native gods and Catholic saints, and consequently of their respective rituals, must also have resulted in the transference of the social prestige value of ritual sponsorship and feast-giving from the old to the new ceremonials. The achievement of the status of *principal* by men of commoner origin who had occupied high office is also attested from the Colonial period (Durán 1951:125–26, 266; Sahagún 1938:III 299–301; Zavala and Miranda 1954:61).

Once this system of dual government was established, the conditions existed for the gradual blending and transformation of the Indian and Spanish elements into a more closely integrated structure. The most important change throughout Colonial times and the 19th century was the elimination of the nobility as a separate group with inherited rank, private landholdings, and exclusive rights to office, with the consequent opening of the entire hierarchy to the whole town. The process started early in Colonial times, first of all because the Spanish conquest destroyed all the large political units, cutting them down to their constituent chieftaincies and depressing them all to the peasant level of organization, with the consequent loss in numbers and importance of the native nobility, especially in the old political centers. Equally important were the efforts of the commoners to eliminate the restrictions against them and to wrestle the control of town government away from the nobility. This process started in the 16th century, but the final disappearance of the native nobility, however, did not take place until the 19th century when Independence abolished the legal privileges of the Indian caciques (Chávez Orozco 1943:14–15; Gibson 1960).

A second change was the decline of communal property used in financing public functions. In early times the tribute surplus and the public lands or cattle of the towns and of religious brotherhoods provided a substantial amount of the wealth consumed by the ceremonial organization. The loss of these public holdings increased the importance of the individual sponsorship of public functions. This is how the term mayordomo, originally steward or manager of a communal holding, has become the general term for the individual who sponsors with his own wealth a religious festival.

These two features, equal opportunity for all to reach high office and the assumption by the office-holder of the economic burdens of office, are what we have defined as key elements of the modern ladder system.

In the Spanish Colonial system the Indian communities, or

Indian republics as they were called, were basically similar to the native reserves of other colonial areas: land was held in common for the exclusive use of the community members and the community was collectively responsible for the payment of tribute and the supply of labor. These were key features in the development of the village (or *municipio*) as the basic social and cultural unit that Tax has compared to tribes (1937:433–44), and they also account for the development of the ladder system along the lines described that imply sharing governmental and ceremonial expenses among the villagers. This is part of an equal distribution among all members of the burden imposed on the community by the State.[3] The ladder system also has a survival value in that it holds the community together by checking the internal economic and social differentiation that tends to disrupt the community, while outside economic and social conditions do not allow its total assimilation into the greater society. After the lapse of the tribute system, it is this survival value that has kept the Indian communities going, although receding more and more into marginal areas. The successful introduction of the Spanish form of village organization in Mesoamerica rests upon the fact that it could adapt itself to the existing Indian social structure, as I have tried to show. It also proved most suitable to the transformation of the native societies into a peasantry of autonomous, equalitarian, and democratic communities.

It has often been said that Mesoamerica, because of the wealth of archeological, historical, and modern data, is an ideal ground for the study of culture change throughout a long time sequence. The fact is, however, that the study of pre-Spanish, Colonial, and modern Indians has usually been carried out by different specialists concentrating on quite different subjects and with few problems in common. I have tried to identify a major feature of the social organization of the Meosamerican Indian at all periods and to outline the main course of its development. While much more work in all the aspects, historical periods,

---

[3] This distribution among its members of the burden imposed by the State upon the peasant community was held by M. Weber (1950:19–24) as responsible for the development of a communistic type of peasant organization. Eric Wolf's (1957) discussion of Mesoamerican and Javanese peasantries is the best comparative study of this type of process.

and regions related to our topic is still necessary, some broad implications of our findings may now be advanced.

We have been discussing a process that involves both continuity in certain aspects of social organization and radical change in others. Change or continuity will receive different emphasis according to whether we consider the structure, the form, or the function of a social institution. We have emphasized the continuity of the structural principles related to the operation of the ladder, since this is the thread that connects the pre-Spanish with the modern forms of political and ceremonial organization. But the introduction of the Catholic cult and Spanish forms of town government meant a radical change in the cultural form of the particular offices or activities through which the structure is concretized. In the peasant segments of pre-Spanish society with little or no internal stratification this must have been the major transformation. In the stratified political centers, however, the total social structure within which the ladder system operated was radically transformed as Indian societies became part of the colonial or national society and were reduced to the peasant level of organization. Together with this a fundamental change took place in the function of the ladder system in relation to the total social structure. The ladder changed from being a mechanism for the selection of personnel or the validation of inherited claims to high office within a stratified independent society to a mechanism for the sharing of responsibilities among members of an unstratified segment, a peasant community within a wider society.

All these changes were part of what is usually defined as a case of acculturation. It cannot be well studied, however, in terms of cultural traits travelling back and forth between cultures in contact, with the social structure that brings people in contact relegated to the background. More fruitful than the usual concept of acculturation as culture contact is the concept of the plural society formed when formerly independent societies with their separate cultural traditions merge into a wider social system. The analysis of the contact situation as a wider social structure becomes then the primary task of an acculturation study. The changes in the internal social structure and culture of a formerly independent society will then be determined by the place it comes to occupy in the new wider society. The importance of

social structure in acculturation was early emphasized (in 1940)
by Radcliffe-Brown (1952:201–2), but as Spicer (1958:433)
has recently pointed out it has often been neglected (cf. also
Smith 1957). In our case the transformation of the politico-
ceremonial hierarchy is a direct function of the peasantization
of the Mesoamerican Indian—the fact that formerly independent
stratified societies became unstratified peasant communities within
a wider social system.

19 POLITICAL CHANGE IN THE KONDMALS

F. G. Bailey

F. G. Bailey is Professor of Social Anthropology at the University of Sussex, England. He is the author of *Caste and the Economic Frontier* (1957), *Tribe, Caste and Nation* (1960), *Politics and Social Change: Orissa in 1959* (1963), and many papers.

Introduction

THE KONDMALS is a sub-division of Phulbani District, which lies in the hills of western Orissa, to the south of the Mahanadi River. At the present time within the whole field of political activity in the Kondmals at least three distinct structures can be perceived. One of these 'belongs' to the Konds, an aboriginal tribe: a second is the caste system: and the third is the system provided by the bureaucratic administration. I am concerned mostly with these three structures, but I take notice also of a fourth, the representative democracy, although I have less material about this than about the other three structures. In this article I discuss the notion of several structures within a single field, and I ask how far it contributes to our understanding of political change.

In the latter part of this eassy I shall describe some of the political changes which have been taking place in the Kondmals, but I shall do so only in outline. All the evidence which led me to make general statements about political activity—in particular case material—will not be included, and I intend to publish it later in another place. Here I discuss the theoretical outline in which the evidence is organized, and I suggest that it may be useful in describing change in other parts of India and elsewhere.

FROM *Eastern Anthropologist* 11, No. 2 (1957), 88–106, by permission of the author and of the editor, *Eastern Anthropologist*.

But I would make it clear at the outset that this outline was developed in relation to the particular material provided by the political history of the Kondmals, and I emphatically do not claim a general validity of it.

The Dynamic Analysis of Structure

Statements about social change are usually presented, explicitly or implicitly, in structural terms. Professor Redfield (1955:11) writes: 'These events . . . lead to a union of people from different castes in what we recognize as classes—people conscious of common cause in the struggle to improve life chances.' Dr. Leach (1954:5) writes: 'If, for example it can be shown that in a particular locality, over a period of time, a political system composed of equalitarian lineage segments is replaced by a ranked hierarchy of feudal type, we can speak of a change in the formal social structure.' Professor Barnes (1954:172) writes: 'The Ngoni Sovereign State has become more and more like a rural district council in a backward area. . . .' In these three examples there are presented three pairs of structures, if I may put it that way, and it is said that in each of them the first structure is giving way, or could give way, or has given way to the second structure. When later I outline the changes that have taken place in political activity in the Kondmals, I write in just the same way, for it is impossible to describe change, or indeed movement of any kind, without putting up at least two fixed points which serve to indicate the direction of movement. A change, in other words, must be plotted by fixed points if it is to be intelligible. One of the purposes of this article is to examine the 'fixed points' and to see how they can be fitted into an analysis of change.

Words like 'fixed,' 'static,' 'timeless,' and especially 'equilibrium' have become bricks which are thrown at structural analysis. It is said that while the analysis is static or timeless, the society which is analyzed is not. But in fact, when a structural analysis is made, the presentation of a static chart of social relationships is only a first stage, and it is followed by deeper analysis which takes account of time and what loosely may be called movement. I shall discuss this 'dynamic' analysis further, since an understanding of it is indispensable to a study of social change.

The basic material of such an analysis is regularized or institutionalized behaviour between *individuals*. These are generalized as statements about relationships between *persons*. The level of structural understanding is reached when generalizations are made about the systematic interconnection of these relationships. We generalize, for instance, about the connection between a political system and a ritual system, or a kinship system and an economic system, and we say that one could not exist in the form that it does without the other. These statements may be made about 'ideal' behaviour, or about 'typical' behaviour: more colloquially, about the 'ought' or about the 'usually do.'

Social relationships are between persons, but in them there is a third element: their content, which is the thing or person about which the two persons are interacting—for instance, about land. Land is itself a variable: it may change by natural accident or in other ways so that the relationship in existence before the change becomes impractical after the change, and an adjustment of some kind becomes necessary. In presenting a static chart of relationships it is assumed that the content of the relationship is held steady and does not vary. There are many other simple examples of this kind of assumption. For instance, in many statements about persons we hold steady the fact that the individuals who in general statements become persons, are born, grow up, grow senile, and eventually die: the *person,* in other words, is ageless and timeless.

No one who has made a structural analysis of any society has been content, to my knowledge, to leave the matter at that point. They do not simply state the norm: the major part of their analysis is taken up with a demonstration of how the structure 'copes with' variations in what I have called the third element. Institutions of succession and inheritance are obvious examples. Another class of institutions within this category are those which deal with deviations and which help to maintain the norm. At this stage the analysis has ceased to be static: it has become dynamic and it deals with movement—not only with 'structural form' (Radcliffe-Brown 1952:192) but also with 'social circulation' (Wilson and Wilson 1945:58).

The structural form can be conceived of, in this way, as a kind of centre-line, across which is drawn a pattern of oscillation to represent the deviations from the norm, and the return to normality. The fact that there is such a return is the reason for the use of the word 'equilibrium.' In some sense an analysis of this kind involves time, but in another sense the analysis is time-less, in that time is not progressive, so much as cyclical. There is an oscillating pattern of norm, followed by deviation, followed by corrective mechanism, followed in its turn by the norm again.

The oscillations or deviations are caused ultimately by what I have called the 'third element' or, to use a more convenient term, by 'outside' factors. The accepted norm, for instance, in the relationship of persons concerning land, may be upset by the fact that there is too little land to go round, or, conversely, be-cause a particular population dies out and their vacant land is taken by others. This is, of course, only one example, and the reader may think of many more. Some of these appear as con-flicts in the behaviour enjoined on the same individual in so far as he is several persons. If a man is both a father and a mother's brother, and is in both roles enjoined to be generous, he may find that in fact he has not sufficient wealth to fulfil both these obligations. Conflicts of this kind often appear to be 'built in' to the structure. A familiar example in India is the conflict of loyalties involved in being both a husband and the member of a joint family (Dube 1955:152). A dynamic structural analysis, once past the preliminary stage of structural form, is concerned with showing that although there are deviations from the norm, such behaviour is deviant (that is, abnormal) and usually is controlled and brought back to the standards of normality by some kind of counter-action. The writer must demonstrate either that deviance and conflict are only apparent, or that, when they do in fact cause a break in the normal relations, there are ways of sealing off the conflict and preventing it from causing anarchy, or of glossing it over so that an ordered social life can continue. In the two examples I have given the corrective mechanism might in India be the *panchayat*—either caste or village— which meets to hear complaints and endeavours to close the breach between the parties. The aim, in short, of a structural analysis is to show that in spite of the potential disruption of social relations which is offered by conflict and deviation, a balance is in the end achieved. There is, in Professor Gluckman's terms, a repetitive equilibrium.

Conflicts of this kind are to be distinguished by the fact that they are resolved or glossed over without any change taking place in the structural form. But in analyzing political activity in the Kondmals I found many conflicts which were not of this kind. There is a potential conflict between the role of husband and the role of joint-family member, but this conflict is solved or contained by other institutions for instance by caste *panchayats*. But in another type of institutional conflict—for which the best term is *contradiction*—there are no other institutions which deal with the conflict except by modifying the structural form. The Konds have a rule that anyone who owns land in a particular village must reside there and take on various social obligations which I will describe later. The Administration, on the other hand, rules that proprietary right is obtained by purchase or inheritance or in various other ways and maintained by the payment of land taxes. Their rule does not take into account obligations to the local community. But in this case there is no third institution which is neutral between these two rules, as the *panchayat* is neutral between the parental family and the joint family, if I may put it that way. If the conflict over land rights is taken to a higher court, this court is in fact part of the Administration, and their judgement can only be to insist on their own rule. An appeal to a Government court is not an appeal to a neutral body, but to a sanction regularly maintaining one rule *at the expense of the other*. In other words, *conflict* takes place between institutions within one structure: when the conflicting institutions belong to different structures then this situation is *contradiction*.

In the third part of this article I go on to describe the political structure of the Konds, in so far as it concerned control over land, and I made a dynamic analysis, showing how variations in the land-population ratio could be adjusted without a change in the structural form. These variations gave rise to conflicts, but not to contradictions.

The Kond Structure

The Kond communities with which I am concerned live in the Kondmals. In their dealings with one another, before the coming of the Administration (and ignoring, for the moment, the presence of alien Oriya colonists in their midst) the Konds were divided into localized agnatic clans. Each clan had its own territory, and residence in that territory involved assuming the obligations of an agnatic kinsman towards the rest of the people living there. Speaking more strictly these units are *composite* clans. They are made up of lineages which frankly acknowledge that they are of different descent, but which treat one another as agnatic brothers and take on the rights and obligations which are thought to inhere in this type of kinship link. It is for this reason that I continue to call them 'clans,' although there is not even the fiction of a common genealogical descent between all the lineages of any of the clans known to me.

The relationships between the different clans in the eastern Kondmals, the area which I know best, are institutionalized either in friendliness or hostility. Those clans who are friends are linked by agnation or fictions of agnation (blood-brotherhood or adoption) and they do not inter-marry. Conversely the enemy are also the people to whom one's sisters go in marriage and from amongst whom one finds brides. This does not, of course, mean that there were never fights within clans or between clans in alliance. There were: this is one of the causes which set the system in motion. But it does mean that it was right to fight people from 'in-law' territory, and wrong to fight people who lived on one's own territory and who were agnates, or who lived on territories agnatically related.

The boundaries of each clan-territory were fixed and known, and clan-solidarity was re-inforced by various ritual means connected with the Earth deity as the protector of the clan-territory. This, in its turn, was connected with agnation, since breaches of the rule of exogamy brought about a situation of mystical danger and jeopardized both human and natural fertility. I have not the space to describe the ritual activities of the clan here.

One of the factors making possible the existence of a structural form of this kind is an appropriate ratio between population and land in each clan-territory. In outlining the structural form of the society so far I have assumed that this was always appropriate. But it is clear in fact that this was not always the case, and that sometimes the population of one territory grew too large to be supported on the land available, and in other territories the population shrank beneath the number which could exploit the territory they owned, and which could protect it from outsiders, who belonged to hostile clans. It is necessary, therefore, to go beyond a 'structural form' analysis, and to discuss the means by which surplus population could be moved from one clan-territory to another, without giving rise to new *types* of social relationships (although, of course, it did, as will be seen shortly, give rise to actual social relations which had not existed before) and without altering the structural form of the total society. I now outline some of these processes, although I, by no means, exhaust the possibilities.

I describe three types of re-adjustment. In the first the clan with a surplus population attacked their neighbours and took their land. In the second the surplus population (or if the movement arose out of internal disputes, the seceding faction) moved off and occupied virgin land, forming a new clan-territory, on the model of the one which they had just left. In the third adjustment sections of the population in a crowded clan-territory moved away and allied themselves to other clans which had or could conquer extra land to support the larger population. I could document all three processes.

In the second process the new clan was internally—with the passage of time—of the same structural form as the clan of which it was an offshoot. Externally it fitted into the total structure by retaining agnatic ties with the parent clan. There could be no marriages beween these clans, and it would be wrong for them to fight against one another. The return to equilibrium in the total structure is here easily comprehended.

In the first process—that of conquering new territory—the fate of those who were defeated is the crucial point in the maintenance of structural form. Conquest can lead to permanent subordination and institutionalized dependence. But there is no room for this kind of relationship in the structural form of the Kond clans. There seem to have been two possibilities. Firstly, the conquered population were exterminated, being either killed or driven out. Secondly, they could remain on their old territory and form a new lineage in the composite clan of their conquerors. Both these processes seem to have taken place.

The third alternative—that of the migration of a section of the population of one clan and its union with another clan—is similar in its essentials to the one just discussed. The migrating

segment became a part of the composite clan which owned the
territory on which the newcomers were settling.

In the second and third processes I have described the *internal* adjustment which preserved the structural form of clans.
But the crucial point is their *external* relationship, especially
when sections migrated and joined a clan which was the 'in-law'
and, therefore, the enemy of the parent clan. There is clear
evidence that in this case the agnatic links which the migrating
section retained with its parent were not allowed to have political
significance, at least not in the long run. The migrating segment
still could not marry into its true parent clan, nor could it marry
into the composite clan which it joined. As far as exogamy was
concerned the migrating section now had double ties. But the
political obligations which were expressed in terms of agnation
lay entirely with the clan which the migrants joined, and on
whose territory they were living. I have no doubt that for a
generation or two there was some modification in the pattern of
institutionalized hostility between a migrant section and the parent clan which it had left, but this was not allowed to blur the
political boundaries. In spite of these cross-linkages of agnatic
kinship, the main political cleavage remained between territorial
groups which expressed their unity in terms of agnatic kinship.

I have here presented the structural form of the Kond political system in outline, and I have described one of the
processes (one among many) which must be taken into account
in a dynamic analysis. An 'outside' factor—the land-population
ratio—may make it impossible to preserve existing relationships.
These are changed, but through various institutions—in the
cases considered through various fictitious forms of agnation—
the original form of the society is preserved and equilibrium is
reached once again. In the structure so far presented there are
conflicts, which can be solved without changing the structural
form, but there are no contradictions.

The Oriya Structure

I have presented the Kond political structure, as if Konds were
the only people present in the Kondmals, and as if they had
political relationships with no one else. But in fact this is not
the case today, and it appears not to have been the case (if we
can trust the annals of the neighbouring Oriya State of Boad)

for at least one thousand years. I deal in this section with the political organization of the Oriyas who lived in the Kond hills. Here I describe the Oriya system, as I did the Kond system, in abstraction from other systems of political relationships. In a following section I shall consider Kond-Oriya relations. Again I would add that this is an outline description. I have in part described this system elsewhere (Bailey 1957), and I intend to give a fuller account in another publication.

The Oriyas founded a number of fortified villages in the Kond hills and each village controlled a limited area around its own settlement. The population of these villages was divided into castes, the main categories being a dominant caste of WAR-RIORS[1] in control of the village, a category of village servants (BARBER, HERDSMAN, BRAHMIN, and so forth), and thirdly, a category of agricultural labourers, the majority of whom were PAN untouchables. The WARRIORS controlled the land, farmed it with the help of their untouchable retainers, and were the main body of fighting men who protected the village both from the Konds and from other Oriya settlements.

The main political cleavage in this society was *not* between castes in a village, but between villages as corporate groups led by the WARRIORS. Oriya villages seem to have been hostile to one another, and although they occasionally combined under the leadership of the Boad King, for the most part the maximal unit of political activity was the village.

The appropriate ratio in numbers of masters to servants was kept in balance by migration. The migrants assumed in their new location the same *kind* of relationships which they had in their old location. In the dominant caste there is some evidence for the accretion of migrant groups through fictitious agnation to the dominant caste of the villages which they joined, but also they seem frequently to have founded new settlements by driving the Konds from the better cultivating sites.

Konds and Oriyas

It is possible to build up a fairly coherent outline of the interaction of Konds and Oriyas before the coming of the Adminis-

[1] The names of most castes are put into English and written in capital letters.

tration, although with the distance in time and the absence of documents there is a lack of corroborative detail and many questions remain unanswered. Secondly, the generalizations I make cover a period of at least a thousand years and may well be inaccurate, because we have in that period practically no evidence of development and change in political relationships.

It is first of all clear that the Konds were attached to the King of Boad State and to the Oriya chiefs in the Kondmals by the loosest of 'feudal' ties. They have been termed the 'subordinate allies' of the ruling groups among the Oriyas. There are traditions among the Konds of having taken part in military expeditions led by the Boad King and in smaller battles under the leadership of the Oriya chiefs resident in the Kond hills. Furthermore many Kond families in the eastern Kondmals bear as their lineage names titles of service under the Boad King. Those whose names indicate kingly service claim that their ancestors served the King of Boad. Those who bear other names say that such people are bastard lineages sprung from the union of a Kond woman and an Oriya of that name.

However the control exercised by Oriya leaders, whether the Boad King or the chief of a fortified village in the Kondmals, was slight. It was maintained by finesse, and by charismatic qualities, and the Oriyas never had sufficient force at their command to undertake a systematic conquest of the Kond country. A further and important reason for the relative strength of the 'subordinate ally' was the segmentary nature of Oriya society in the Kond hills and of the feudal kingdoms from which they came. In all these kingdoms there seem to have been periodical rebellions: the king had very little control over the chiefs in the Kond hills and they did not look to him for support: finally, as I have already said, in the Kond hills the Oriya villages were maximal units of political activity. So far from combining with one another in a concerted effort to bring the Konds to heel, they fought against one another and enlisted the support of the Konds in this fight. In these circumstances it seems to have been easy for Kond groups to play off one Oriya chief against another, and to transfer their allegiance from a chief who had offended them to his enemy. There is documentary evidence of an event of this kind just before the British came to the Kond hills.

I have now enlarged my description of the field of political activity in the Kond hills. There are first the Kond institutions and the Kond political society in which the main cleavage lay between localized composite clans, using the idiom of agnation. Secondly, there are Oriya settlements, internally organized on the basis of caste, and externally forming an egalitarian segmentary system like that of the Konds, the key category being the dominant WARRIOR group. In both these cases it is possible to describe a structure proper—that is to say, to postulate connections between whole fields of regularities, between, say, the political system and the ritual system—between, for example, the political structure and caste rituals in an Oriya village, or between kinship and politics and ritual in the Kond system. But beyond these two there is a third field of political activity between Konds and Oriyas of the kind I have outlined in the first part of this section, and here I do not think it is possible to find a structural form of the same kind as in the two constituent fields. Rather this situation is to be described as two structures in contradiction with one another.

For many centuries there seems to have been a stalemate. The Konds were not strong enough to exterminate the Oriya colonies. The dominant group among the Oriyas, in their turn, were not strong enough or sufficiently united to undertake a systematic conquest of the Konds. The contradiction between their political systems remained potential rather than actual and only came to the surface when the British arrived and gave to the Oriyas sufficient power to begin to impose their system upon the Konds.

Pacification and Political Change

I have outlined elsewhere the story of the Meriah wars and the coming of the British to the Kond hills (Bailey 1957). These events took place between 1832 and 1850. In 1855 a regular civilian administration was established. The resources of the administrators were very slight and they were forced to govern through existing institutions. The existing Kond clan territories, which had already fairly clearly demarcated boundaries and were named, were taken over and used as units for administration. The Tahsildar, who himself was an Oriya, governed through Oriya-speaking men. Some of these, in the eastern plateau of the

Kondmals, were Konds. Elsewhere they were the Oriya chieftains whose role I discussed in the last section. The reasons for this policy were firstly the obvious one that the Tahsildar and his staff knew Oriya but did not know the Kond language: secondly, they liked to have a key person to whom they could delegate responsibility. Thirdly, from their experience elsewhere they were used to dealing with headmen and with villages, and were entirely unfamiliar with the egalitarian segmentary type of political organization of the Konds, which I described in the first part of this article. They were also, of course, relatively familiar with a caste organization. In short, the first effect of the coming of the Administration was to put power into the hands of the Oriyas, and to upset the balance which—from the evidence available —we concluded had existed for a thousand or more years in the Kond hills between Kond and Oriya.

In a previous section I described the processes by which within the Kond system a balance was maintained between land and population, and how there could be re-adjustments in this without upsetting the structural form of Kond society. This adjustment was effected by the rule that those who came to a territory must take on ties of fictitious agnation with the owners of that territory. There were certain changes effected in this process by the presence of the Administration. Firstly, it was no longer possible for a clan to expand its territory by conquest, since warfare was put down. Secondly, the presence of the Administration resulted in an ending of the process of external recruitment and the taking on of ties of fictitious agnation, at the level of the clans. I shall discuss this in greater detail.

There are today in every clan-territory which I examined two categories of villages: those which live on their 'own earth' and those which live on 'bought earth.' Those who live on 'bought earth' acknowledge that they are living within the boundaries of a clan to which they do not belong and they marry with these people and have no fiction of agnation whatsoever with them. Those who live on their 'own earth,' in spite of the composite nature of the clan, consider themselves to be one clan. That is to say, they acknowledge that they came from another place, but by living on the same territory they have come to act as brothers. In every case those who lived on 'bought earth' had come to their present location after the time that the Administration came to the area: those who had taken on the rights and obligations of agnates had come to their present location in the distant past before the Administration arrived in the area.

Before the coming of the Administration a man's rights to land were protected by his membership of the clan which owned the territory on which he lived. The other members of the clan protected him and their joint territory against outsiders, and he was expected to play his part in making the clan an effective political unit. After the Administration came to the area a right to land was no longer validated by membership of a clan and land could no longer be protected or gained by warlike action. The source of power lay with the Administration and it was they who protected property. In other words, the status now relevant to the holding and protecting of property was no longer membership of a composite clan, but—putting it a little ambitiously for that time —citizenship of India.

For many years this citizenship was mediated—and to some extent it still is—through the Oriya or Kond *sirdar* who was in charge of the clan-territory. Access to the Government and an exercise of the rights which the Government guaranteed could best be got by a dependent relationship on the *sirdar*. Consequently the contradiction can be phrased as between the Kond political system and the Oriya system of lord and retainer, although, of course, the factor operative is the presence of the Administration.

Before the coming of the Administration re-adjustments of population to land did not alter the structural form of Kond society. After the Administration arrived, although a certain stability was achieved by the ending of warfare, differential population growth continued to upset the land population ratio. Indeed, the 'land-grabbers' who followed in the wake of the Administration contributed to instability by taking land from Konds. In other words, movement between territories of surplus or displaced population continued. But now the re-adjustment began to alter the structural form of Kond society. Migrants to a new territory no longer found it necessary or advantageous to join the clans on whose territory they settled. They bought the land and then secured their status by getting the backing of the *sirdar* and through him of the Government. The old clans continued in existence, and have done so up to the present day, but they are now maintained by internal recruitment alone. Some have dwindled away until they now consist only of a few families. Others still occupy the bulk of the territory which bears their name. But every migration, every re-adjustment of population to land, represented a 'running down of stocks' in the old Kond political structure, and an increase in the number of people who did not belong to any territorial clan, but who, as political persons, belonged to a group made up of a chief and his dependents. As a result of this the *political* activities of the clan have dwindled almost to nothing.

Konds and the Caste System

By fixing the boundaries between the clan territories and by putting an end to warfare, the Administration weakened the tribal political system. Before the coming of the Administration a Kond group could play off one Oriya chief against another and transfer their allegiance when it suited them to do so. Afterwards this was no longer possible, for a change of this kind would have to be ratified by Administrative recognition of new boundaries, and, so far as I know, this did not happen. Further, as I have explained in the last section, every migration decreased the number of persons who belonged to a territorial clan and increased the number of those whose citizenship was achieved by a relationship with the Government mediated through the Oriya chief.

In addition to this there were various economic processes at work tending to bring individual Konds into relationships of dependence, typical of the caste system and not differing in any essential from the relationships which the men of low caste held at that time towards the dominant WARRIORS. By establishing secure conditions and by making residence and travel safe within the Kond hills for outsiders, the Administration made it possible for a large number of Oriyas of the mercantile class to come into the Kond hills and to set up various kinds of business there. From then on the aboriginals began to lose land to mercantile outsiders. This is a familiar process and I have myself described it at length elsewhere (Bailey 1957).

Those Konds who lost their land either through mercantile processes or through manipulation of the rules of the Administration by the Oriyas who were advantageously placed, had to find some other means of making a living. Some of these migrated, as individual families or in small groups, to the marginal areas in the remoter valleys and there brought new land under cultivation. At some periods it was possible for them to migrate as labourers to the Tea Gardens of Assam. A very few of them found jobs with the Administration or in the world of commerce. But many of them, sooner or later, drifted into the larger Oriya villages and made their living either as plough servants or as casual labourers under the patronage of an Oriya, who was sometimes a WARRIOR and sometimes a member of the recently arrived mercantile castes, prominent among whom were the DISTILLERS (Bailey 1957:186–210). These persons were, in most respects, in the same position economically as, for instance, the untouchable labourers and other dependent castes. The Konds who stayed in their own villages, whether these villages were still part of a territorial clan, or whether they were immigrants and dependents upon a *sirdar,* owned land and had direct access to its produce through their own labour. But those who came to Oriya villages achieved their share in the produce of the land by a dependent relationship as individuals upon their WARRIOR or DISTILLER masters. Konds in their own villages were still members of corporate groups—in some cases a village and a clan and in some cases only a village—with at least vestigial political functions. The Konds who came to Oriya villages were not full citizens in any corporate political groups. They were individuals dependent on upper caste masters, just as were untouchables and other dependent castes, and as such they were 'second-class' citizens.

However, even taking together the original Oriya colonists and those who had come in the wake of the Administration, the total number of Oriyas was small in relation to the total number of Konds. This was due to several factors, prominent among which was the evil reputation of the climate of the Kondmals. Again, the Administration looked with disfavour upon the alienation of Kond land, and took various measures to prevent it. These measures were not entirely successful, but they did prevent any considerable elimination of the Konds as landowners and as 'first-class' citizens. These developments I consider in the following section:

The developments outlined in this and last section can be seen as a contest between the Konds and the Oriyas, and, metaphorically, as a contest between their respective political structures. Up to now I have described the process by which Konds were brought to behave in the Oriya model and were to some degree integrated into the Oriya system. The Konds, as persons in a tribal structure, have never had any effective answer to this. But within the framework of the Administration, which has moved from ambivalence to dislike of the caste system, the Konds began to hold their own. Most recently, in the period of parliamentary democracy, they are beginning to hold the upper hand.

The Administration, the Economy, and Kond 'Nationalism'

The use which the Administration made of the resident Oriya population, particularly the chiefs, and the implicit support which they seemed to give both to these men and to the immigrant mercantile castes, must have intensified the cleavage between Kond and Oriya. Initially at least, it must have seemed to the Konds that the Administration was all on the side of the Oriyas.

The way in which the economy has developed has done nothing to bridge this cleavage or to blur the sharp division between the two peoples. As I have described, for a long time the Konds were the exploited and the Oriyas were the exploiters. As the trading economy has developed further the Konds and the Oriyas have also become something like two separate and opposed classes, not overtly divided by exploitation, as in the process of 'land-grabbing,' but on the lines of specialization. The Konds have become the producers of a cash-crop, turmeric. The Oriyas are the middlemen who buy the turmeric and transfer it to the larger wholesalers. In this field the Oriyas have a stereotype of the Konds as a hard-working but foolish person, good enough to go through the toil of growing turmeric, but not clever enough to handle its marketing. The Kond stereotype of the typical Oriya is the reverse of this: a cunning trader, evading the labour of growing turmeric, but profiting in trade from his wits and lack of scruple. This, of course, is not an uncommon attitude among both producers and consumers towards middlemen and it contains the hint of exploitation. But at this stage I would rather emphasize the aspect of specialization, and the division of the two people into opposed economic classes, each class having at least a potential economic interest against the other—potential in that it can result in common action and a common programme within each group designed to further its own ends at the expense of the other.

This cleavage has been encouraged, perhaps inadvertently, by Government policy. The British Administrators, who followed the first Tahsildar, disliked the mercantile Oriyas, had a milder dislike for the anciently-settled Oriyas, and tended to favour the 'simple' Konds. The same was true of Missionaries who made more converts among the Adibasis and Untouchables than among the Hindu population. Various measures were put into operation to protect the Konds and to prevent the Oriyas from profiting from a rigid administration. The area has always been administered as an Agency and relatively great discretion was put into the hands of the Magistrate. Drink shops were closed and the profits of the DISTILLER castes came to an end to the benefit of the Konds. Restrictions were put upon the transfer of land between Kond and non-Kond. Kond lands were not subject to the ordinary land-tax, but Konds paid a 'voluntary' tax at a low rate, assessed on the ownership of ploughs, and the sum raised was doubled out of Government funds and used for building schools and roads in the Kondmals.

The Oriyas found ways and means of evading the restrictions on the transfer of land, but undoubtedly the intervention of the Administration has prevented the complete pauperization of the Konds. It has also served to give the Konds a wider sense of their own unity, and of their opposition to the Oriyas, transcending the division between the clans, and making the local cleavages between Oriya chiefs and the Kond clans into a wider cleavage between the Oriya community and the Kond community.

Since Independence this process has been quickened and the policy of giving protection and privilege to the Adibasis has been extended beyond a narrow and negative field. Konds are given preferential status in education and in employment by the Administration. They have not as yet profited to any great extent from these opportunities but at least they are firmly aware of their status as Adibasis, and very conscious of the privileges which it carries. The Oriyas who live in the Kond hills now see themselves as the victims of Government policy and feel that the dice has come to be heavily loaded against them. They say jokingly that they would like to be classed as Adibasis, or more realistically, that the privileges extended to Konds should be given to all the cultivating classes in the Kond hills.

Sanskritization

Both in India generally and in the Kondmals the policy of the Administration has wavered between the two extremes of protection (pejoratively called the 'Tribal Zoo'), and allowing unrestricted assimilation. At the present day the intention is to guide assimilation until the Aboriginals are able to hold their own with the more sophisticated populations of the plains. This conflict of opinion appeared from the first moment the British set foot in the Kond hills, and its history, broadly speaking, is a movement away from protection and conservation, as ends in themselves, towards eventual assimilation, even though the means of achieving this may mean a temporary intensification of protective measures. The policy, in other words, has come to be protective, but not conservative. I have not mentioned this conflict of policy in previous sections, because whatever the end in view, and whatever the means employed, the effect was usually to make the Konds aware of the fact that they were different from the Oriyas and opposed to them.

It is at first sight a paradox that while the Konds are pleased to insist that they are Adibasis—for obvious reasons—and while they maintain a traditional hatred of Oriyas (although, of course, there are frequent friendly relations between individuals), they are, nevertheless progressively discarding their own customs and assuming what they consider Oriya customs. There is, of course, a variation between individuals, but even the most 'Oriya-ized' Kond—in the eastern Kondmals at least—is respected by other Konds for his behaviour, and it is not thought illogical to combine outspoken dislike of Oriyas, and outspoken defence of Kond value and custom, with implicit acceptance of Oriya values. The Konds, in other words, are being Sanskritized.

'Sanskritization' is an unpopular word [even with its author (Srinivas 1956:495)], but it is a convenient label for a recognizable process, and I think that time spent in justifying a different verbal monstrosity (Brahmanization, Sanskarization, etc.) would be time wasted. It is the process, and not the name attached to it, which is of interest. Here I have no intention of making an extended analysis of the process, and I intend only to account for the apparent paradox in Kond behaviour. When they are vehemently in favour of their own culture (at least in words) and while they have everything to gain from emphasizing their difference from Oriyas, nevertheless, progressive Konds take on the manners and customs of a Hindu gentleman, and are not spurned by their fellow-Konds for doing so.

'Sanskritic' culture is the culture of the nation and is an India-wide hallmark of respectability, particularly of political respectability. During the independence movement it was one of the symbols of anti-British feeling, and since Independence it has served to give a homespun covering to the predominantly British and western institutions through which the country is governed. I would risk a wide generalization that the politician who depends on popular support is suspect if he is too westernized, and if he is too uncouth he becomes the butt of his fellows. It is, for this reason, I think, that the Konds become more and more willing to take on the model of Hindu behaviour which they get from contacts with Oriyas. As they become more and more integrated into State politics they begin to accept standards of behaviour which are respectable in the State capital. This applies particularly to those few Konds who are active in State politics. But among the Konds, at least of the eastern Kondmals, there is a general awareness derived partly from their own sophisticated people and partly from local Oriyas who loudly ridicule Kond custom, that although it may be a concrete advantage to be designated 'Adibasi,' it is not a source of prestige.[2]

I would not claim that this is a general explanation of Sanskritization and the motives of those who practise it. Clearly all instances of Sanskritization are not connected only with the modern parliamentary system. Nor would I claim that this is a full account of Kond motives in adopting Oriya customs. For many these customs are respected as ends in themselves and accepted as mystical values. But whatever the motive, it is sufficient for my argument that Sanskritic behaviour furthers the aims of the Konds in the modern political system, and that some Konds know this.

[2] Professor D. N. Majumdar informs me that in metropolitan Orissa, 'Kond' is an epithet equivalent to 'bumpkin' or even 'Boeotian.'

Conclusions

It became clear quite early in my field-work in the Kondmals that I would not be able to fit all the complex political activity into the framework of one social structure. There were evident and glaring contradictions. For instance, the ritual attitudes, which the WARRIORS and most of the Untouchables in the Oriya village of Bisipara agreed were appropriate, were in complete contradiction to their political relationship. In a structural analysis the various elements—political, ritual, economic, and so forth—have in the end to be consistent with one another and may not tend towards mutual destruction. But the ritual behaviour of the Untouchables could not be fitted with their political status into one coherent structure. The relationship between these two ways of behaving, whatever else it was, was not one of those 'elements of persistence and continuity' (Firth 1955:2).

A field of social behaviour of this kind could not be analyzed without taking into account social change—not, at least, if any degree of completeness were to be achieved. To make an analysis as of 'one structure' would have meant discarding much of the primary data. Even a cursory glance at the history of the Kond hills—the Meriah Wars and the modern cataclysm of Independence—points at change.

It is not difficult to give a common-sense description of the changes and their direction. A tribal society became intermingled with people whose lives were ordered by the caste system, and both these, in their turn, have become involved in a 'modern' political system (using that term as a convenient short reference to the bureaucratic administration and the parliamentary democracy). But even at this level qualifications need to be made. Although the direction of change is from tribe to caste into a modern system, the Konds are not moving through all these stages. Their excursion into the caste system has been brief, since before they became completely involved that system was itself modified and changed by the Administration, and it now seems that the Konds will never become a dependent caste divided between small chieftaincies. They, with other Adibasis, are becoming a pressure group in State politics.

A more detailed description of this change is made by describing the three structures—tribe, caste, and the modern system, which may, with a touch of grandiloquence, be called the nation. For each of these structures we postulate several interconnected systems, as the Kond kinship system is connected with political control over land, and so forth. I have done this in some detail for the tribal system. For reasons of space I have given a very brief outline of the caste structure, and I have said little of the 'nation' as a structure, because I do not know enough about it.

The abstraction and isolation of a structure of this kind serves two purposes. Firstly, it enables the course of change to be 'plotted,' as the direction of movement is plotted on a map. Secondly, it is a heuristic device for identifying contradictions, between what at first sight are assumed to be interconnected parts of one structure. It highlights the points of contradiction and diagnoses the processes through which change comes about. I would cite again the example of the Oriyas of dominant caste and the Untouchable Oriyas, whose ritual relationship contradicts their political relationship.

The ultimate aim in describing social change is two-fold: first, to plot the course of change: second, to describe the process through which individuals discard a relationship which belongs to one structure and take on a relationship which belongs to a different structure. I have considered in this article mainly relationships through which a man achieves control over land, and, to a lesser extent, relationships through which he achieves other economic ends. In the tribal structure the main political cleavages ran between the Kond clans, and the political 'arena' was filled with clans in competition with one another. After this, for some Konds it became more effective to give their allegiance to a chieftain, and they became divided from one another by the cleavages between these chieftaincies. There was also in this situation a cleavage between the chief and those Kond clans in his neighbourhood, who denied him allegiance or gave him only partial allegiance. Later, with the advent of the Administration and a mercantile economy, there were two developments: firstly, the cleavage between Kond clans ceased to have political significance: secondly, the local cleavages between Kond and Oriya became generalized in the framework of the Administration and State politics, as a cleavage between Konds undifferentiated by clan and Oriyas undifferentiated by chieftaincy. In short, in order to understand what has happened and is happening a progressively wider arena of competition must be envisaged.

The conflicts which exist within a structure seem to be a crucial guide to one of the processes of social change. Examining the structure as an abstraction, we see that there are various institutions which serve to contain or to gloss over these conflicts, and to conserve the structural form. But in a situation of change, these conflicts project people out of one structure into another, if I may reify in order to be brief. Conflicts which resulted in migration since the third or fourth decade of the nineteenth century have in effect eroded the territorial clans and have built up the 'chieftaincies.' Economic conflict between Konds and Oriyas brought about the intervention of the Administration, and this intervention has caused both parties to attempt to further their ends not only within local arenas but also to claim their rights as citizens in the wider arena of State politics. This process tends to erode loyalties both to the clan and to the chief.

But looking for conflict and contradiction is not the only guide to understanding social change.[3] In this article conflict has been my main guide, but there are others which would have to be employed in a more extensive analysis. It would be important to identify the roles which facilitate movement from one structure to another: examples at the present day are the sophisticated Konds who now operate on the margins of State politics; the agents of the political parties who work among the Konds; and the many people whose job it is to guide the Konds towards assimilation with the rest of the population of Orissa.

One line of investigation which is opening up in India and elsewhere is implicit throughout this article. It is an effort to widen the field of research and extend the horizons, both in time and space. I have tried to push my investigations outwards from the village to the region, and to consider not only the present but also the past and the future. To visualize activity within a general field and to see several structures impinging on one another within this field, may help in certain situations (but not, I repeat, in all) to describe social change, and to identify the process and roles through which it takes place. It may also make it possible,

[3] I gladly acknowledge the stimulus of conversation on this topic with Professor Max Gluckman, and of his book *Custom and Conflict in Africa* (1955).

while yet using the traditional anthropological techniques developed in small-group research, to achieve some understanding not only of one small group, but also of the region, or country, or even civilization of which it forms a part.

20 TRANSFORMATION OF SOCIAL, POLITICAL AND CULTURAL ORDERS IN MODERNIZATION

S. N. Eisenstadt

S. N. Eisenstadt is Professor of Sociology at the Hebrew University, Jerusalem, Israel. He is the author of *The Absorption of Immigrants* (1954), *From Generation to Generation: Age Groups and Social Structure* (1956), *Essays on Sociological Aspects of Political and Economic Development* (1961), *Modernization: Growth and Diversity* (1963), *The Political Systems of Empires* (1963), *Essays on Comparative Institutions* (1965), and many papers.

THE INSTITUTIONALIZATION of change, or the development and crystallization of new institutional settings requires the internal transformation of the societies or groups within which it occurs. The capacity for such internal transformation is manifest in structural frameworks or cultural symbols that enable some groups to mobilize new forces and resources without necessarily destroying the existing structure (Eisenstadt 1964c). In modernizing societies, internal transformation is especially critical because modernization requires not only a relatively stable new structure but one capable of adapting to continuously changing conditions and problems.[1]

Modernization, of course, does not imply a "smooth" process

FROM the *American Sociological Review* 30, No. 5 (1965), 659–73, by permission of the author and of the American Sociological Association.

This paper was the 1964 MacIver Award Lecture, delivered at the Presidential Session of the Eastern Sociological Society, April 1965, in New York City. A preliminary version of the first part of the lecture was given at the University of New Delhi in January 1965. The research reported in the paper was sponsored partly by the Air Force Office of Scientific Research through the European Office of Aerospace Research (OAR), U. S. Air Force.

[1] On the concept of modernization see Eisenstadt (1963a) and Halpern (1964).

of "balanced" or "equilibrated" growth. It has always been a revolutionary process of undermining and changing the existing institutional structure. But the possibility of successful institutionalization of an innovating or revolutionary process is never inherent in the revolutionary act itself. It depends on other conditions, primarily the society's capacity for internal transformation.

A society can be forced to modernize under the impact of external forces, and indeed 19th- and 20th-century modernization has meant, to a very large extent, the impingement of Western European institutions on new countries in the Americas, in Eastern and Southern Europe, and in Asia and Africa. Some of these societies have never—or not yet—gone beyond adaptation to these external impingements. Lacking a high degree of internal adaptability, many become stagnant after having started on the road to modernity, or their modern frameworks have tended to break down.[2] Moreover, different societies necessarily develop different institutional patterns, so that the spread of modernization has entailed a great deal of structural diversity.

Modernization, however, is associated with some definite structural characteristics. Among these the most important are a high level of structural differentiation, and of so-called "social mobilization," and a relatively large-scale, unified and centralized institutional framework. Beyond this basic core, the aforementioned structural diversity may develop. These structural characteristics are not to be regarded as simple indices of successful modernization, and their development does not necessarily assure successful modernization. Rather they are necessary but not sufficient conditions for the development and continuity of a modern institutional structure sufficiently capable of dealing with continuously changing problems to assure sustained growth (Eisenstadt 1964a).

Among these conditions, of special importance is the establishment of viable, flexible and yet effective symbolic and organizational centers, responsive to the continuous problems of modernization and able to regulate them. At the same time, a more flexible orientation with new goals and a commitment to the new centers and their needs must be developed among the more active social groups. Here some aspects of the pre-modern structure of

[2] The concept and conditions of such breakdowns are analyzed in Eisenstadt (1964b).

modernizing societies are especially important. With the exception of the African and to some extent the Latin American ones, most pre-industrial societies began modernizing, or were pushed into it, with a relatively complex, differentiated institutional structure. Within the great historical and Imperial civilizations for example, centralized and differentiated structures and organizations already existed, together with *relatively* autonomous basic institutional spheres—political, religious or ideological, and social organization and stratification (Eisenstadt 1962; 1963b).[3]

The centralized frameworks and the relatively autonomous institutional spheres were crucial to the transformative capacities of these societies, for they facilitated the initial modernization and helped make the new modern centers and frameworks work efficiently. Different constellations of these characteristics, however, greatly influence transformative capacity in general, as well as the particular institutional form that modernization may take in a given case.

In the following analysis I shall point out some of the constellations that facilitate—or impede—modernization, focusing on three aspects of the relations among the various institutional spheres in pre-modern societies. The first of these aspects is the relation between the dominant value-system and political institutions; the second is the place of the political system in the stratification system; and the third is the degree of internal cohesion and social autonomy in the major social groups and strata within these societies. I shall attempt to test the fruitfulness of this approach first by analyzing the major Asian societies—China, Japan and India—coming only later to a brief analysis of modern European societies.

China[4]

China has had a long tradition of centralization, and a degree of social, political, and cultural continuity probably unparalleled in the history of mankind. Under the Imperial system Chinese society could absorb many changes brought about by conquests, changes of dynasties and rebellions, yet this great civilization was

[3] On the importance of the concept of center see Shils (1965:199–213).
[4] See Balazs (1964) especially chapters 1 and 2, and Eisenstadt (1963b) which includes additional bibliography on all the societies analyzed here (except Japan).

relatively unable to modernize itself from within, either through reformation of the Imperial system or through the initial revolution that developed against it. True, many reform movements did develop within the Chinese Imperial system, ranging from relatively "conservative," "traditional" attempts to preserve the Confucian ethic and its cultural primacy, to the more radical movements attempting to transform dominant value orientations and to establish a system independent of Confucian orientations and symbols. But as Levenson (1964) and others (Wright 1957; Teng and Fairbank 1965) have shown, these reforms were not very successful either in changing the ideology and institutions of the Imperial system or in creating new, viable frameworks.

Similarly, the first modern revolution against the Imperial system did not establish a viable, modern political system. Many external factors no doubt contributed to this failure, but it is still worthwhile to analyze the influence of some internal factors.

The first such factor is the nature of the legitimation of the Imperial system—the relation between Imperial political institutions and the major cultural centers, ideology and symbols. Here we find, among the great historic Imperial civilizations, the closest interweaving, almost identity, of cultural with political centers. Although in principle many universalistic ethical elements in the dominant Confucian ideology transcended any given territory or community, in actuality this ideology was very closely tied to the specific political framework of the Chinese Empire. The Empire was legitimized by the Confucian symbols but the Confucian symbols and Confucian ethical orientation found their "natural" place and framework, their major "referrent," within the Empire (Eisenstadt 1962; Balazs 1964).

This, of course, was also related to the fact that no church or cultural organization in China existed independently of the state. The Confucian élite was a relatively cohesive group, sharing a cultural background which was enhanced by the examination system and by adherence to Confucian rituals and classics. But its organization was almost identical with that of the state bureaucracy, and except for some schools and academies it had no organization of its own. Moreover, political activity within the Imperial-bureaucratic framework was a basic referrent of the Confucian ethical orientation, which was strongly particularistic and confined to the existing cultural-political setting (Balazs 1964).

The relation between Chinese political and cultural orders is parallel to that between the political system and social stratification. The most interesting point here is that the total societal system of stratification was entirely focused on the political center. The Imperial center, with its strong Confucian orientation and legitimation, was the sole distributor of prestige and honor. Various social groups or strata did not develop autonomous, independent, status orientations, except on the purely local level; the major, almost the only wider orientations were bound to this monolithic political-religious center. Of crucial importance here is the structure of the major stratum linking the Imperial center to the broader society—the literati. This stratum was a source of recruitment to the bureaucracy and also maintained close relations with the gentry. Their double status orientation enabled the literati to fulfil certain crucial integrative functions in the Imperial system (Balazs 1964). Their special position enabled them to influence the political activities of the rulers and of the leading strata of the population. But they exerted this influence by unholding the ideal of a hierarchical social-political-cultural order binding on the rulers and these strata. The very existence of the literati as an élite group was contingent on the persistence of the ideal of a unified Empire.

These characteristics of the literati were among the most important stabilizing mechanisms in the Imperial system, helping it to regulate and absorb changes throughout its long history. But these same characteristics have also severely inhibited development of a reformative or transformative capacity in China's culturally and politically most articulate groups.

Capacity for reform or transformation in the broader groups of Chinese society is also affected by their strong "familism"—the basis of their internal cohesion and self-identity. Familism has often been designated as one cause of China's relatively unsuccessful modernization. But as Levy has shown in his later analysis, it is not the familism as such that was important but rather the nature of the family's internal cohesion and its links with other institutional spheres.[5] The family was a relatively autonomous, self-enclosed group, with but few broader criteria or orien-

---

[5] For the first analysis of Chinese familism from the point of view of modernization see Levy (1952). Levy (1955) has further elaborated and to some extent modified the point of view expressed there.

tations. Beyond the commitment to the bureaucracy of those who attained positions within it, the primary duty of individuals was to increase family strength and resources, not to represent the family's worth according to external goals and commitments.

In combination, these various aspects of Chinese social structure go far toward explaining the weakness of the initial stages of China's modernization. The identity between the cultural and the political orders and the specific characteristics of the literati tended to maintain the dominance of a stagnative neo-traditionalism that continuously reinforced the non-transformative orientations in Chinese culture.

Under the first impact of modernization, Chinese intellectuals and bureaucrats faced certain problems stemming from the fact that their basic cultural symbols were embedded in the existing political structure. Any political revolution or reformation necessarily entailed rejecting or destroying the cultural order. Similarly, the strong ideological emphasis on upholding the social-political status quo inhibited the emergence of new symbols to legitimize new social institutions relatively independently of the preceding order (Teng and Fairbank 1963; Levenson 1964). Hence there developed little capacity for viable, flexible institution building, especially in the legal, legislative or administrative fields. Many such institutions were formally initiated, but they lacked both "pre-contractual" bases of legitimation and the broader societal conditions and resources for effective functioning.[6]

But this weakness of initial reform and revolutionary movements in Imperial and post-Imperial China was only partly due to the ideological identity between the cultural and the political orders. No less important were the relations between political institutions and the system of social stratification. In the social sphere as in the ideological or cultural sphere, there were few points of internal strength, cohesion and self-identity on which new institutional frameworks could be founded or which could support institutional changes.

This weakness was reinforced by the limited reformative capacities of the family. When the Empire crumbled and processes of change swept over it, disorganizing and dislocating the tradi-

---

[6] For the institutional development of modern pre-Communist China see Beckman (1962), especially chapters 23 and 24, and Tung (1964). For some of the problems of legal reform see Michael (1962).

tional structure, and especially the major links to the center—the literati and the bureaucracy—family groups were largely dissociated from the center, but they lacked the strength to create new autonomous links. These family groups tended also to develop neo-traditional orientations, but because they were "closed" groups they could not regulate such demands effectively. In the more modern setting, they became highly politicized, making demands on the new, and for them not fully legitimate center, which sapped the resources available for internal redistribution and thus undermined the new institutional frameworks.

Islam

Throughout its history Islam has emphasized the identity between the religious and political communities, seeking to fuse these two institutional spheres in a manner almost unique in the history of the great universalistic religions (Cahen 1955a). This identity between political and religious communities represents a very important similarity between the Chinese and Islamic societies, though its religious or ideological bases are very different.

The Islamic states, especially the early Caliphates, developed out of a conquest in which a new universal religion was created and borne by conquering tribes. This identity between tribe and religion became weaker in later stages when the more centralized-bureaucratic empires (the Abbasides and Fatimides) developed and ethnically heterogeneous elements were welded together through a common religion and a new political framework, but political and the religious communities were united throughout the history of Islamic states (Lewis 1960; Gibb 1962). Moreover, political issues (e.g., succession, and the scope of the political community) initially constituted the main theological problems of Islam (Rosenthal 1962).

This political-religious unity had specific ideological and structural consequences. Within the Caliphate there developed, on the one hand, a very strong universalistic-missionary orientation and a strong emphasis on the state as the framework of the religious community but subordinate to it. On the other hand, religious functionaries and groups did not develop an overall, independent, and cohesive organization. This combination limited political participation mostly to court cliques and the bureaucracy, but it also gave rise to extreme sectarian movements, some seeking to destroy the existing regime and establish a new, religiously pure and true one, others politically passive. Thus, strong reform movements based on universalistic and transcendental orientations did develop under Islam.[7] But it is very significant that these movements were successful only so far as they were not politically oriented and did not have to establish new central political institutions within the framework of Islamic tradition.

Islam reform movements were more successful in colonial situations, as in Indonesia or in Malaysia, where there were active minorities or where their political objective was to attain independence, and in cultural, educational and economic activities, than they were in the independent Muslim states where they had to try to establish a new Islamic polity. Islamic reform movements in India in the early 20th century, for instance, evinced a relatively strong emphasis on educational and cultural innovation. Subsequently, these movements were transformed into more populist, political ones during the immediate pre-partition period and especially in Pakistan after independence (van der Kroef 1958; 1962; Nieuwenhuize 1958; Prins 1959; Geertz 1965).

Close identity between the political and the religious communities inhibited Islamic reform movements in ways somewhat similar to, but not identical with those in China. In the Islamic states as in China the identity between cultural and political institutions severely limited possibilities for the innovations necessary to develop viable modern legislative and juridical institutions (Rahman 1958; Malik 1963; Dumont 1964b); nor did traditional Islamic prescriptions for appropriate political behavior facilitate legal innovations.[8]

Attempts to build modern nation-states on an Islamic base faced tremendous obstacles. The Islamic tradition was challenged by various new secular-national symbols challenged the Islamic traditions, and efforts to legitimize national identities in terms of Islamic tradition intensified conflicts among various units (Safran 1961; Binder 1964). The history of the attempt to establish an Islamic polity in Pakistan, for example, and similar experiences

---

[7] The first overall exposition of modernization in Islam is probably that of Gibb (1947). For further elaboration see Mahdi (1959), and Hodgson (1962).

[8] On the problems of legal reform and modern Islam see Anderson (1959), Schacht (1963:172–201), and Coulson (1964).

in various Middle Eastern countries, illustrate some of these difficulties (Binder 1958; 1961). Among the older Muslim states, only Tunisia—through a variety of circumstances I cannot go into here—seems to have succeeded, to some extent at least, in overcoming them (Ardant 1961; Moore 1962; Micaud et al. 1964). In Turkey—at the very core of the older Ottoman Empire—new institution building was attempted only through the complete negation of the Islamic tradition at the central political and symbolic level (Lewis 1961).

With regard to the relations between political institutions and social stratification, Islamic patterns are less similar to the Chinese. The system of stratification in many Islamic societies was not focused to the same extent on the state, though in some extreme cases, as in the core of the Ottoman Empire, similar tendencies did develop. But on the whole, various social and cultural groups—e.g., the religious groups, the ulemas—evinced a higher degree of organizational and social autonomy. True, these same groups often became centers of reaction and traditionalism, but their autonomy did create possibilities for intellectual ferment and social change.

Moreover, in many Islamic societies a tradition of local, especially urban, community autonomy existed, even if it was only latent. Although the martial Ottoman rule weakened this tradition, on the whole, it persisted at the peripheries of the Empire, enhancing receptivity to modern intellectual and organizational trends and facilitating the concomitant development of various professional, entrepreneurial, administrative and intellectual groups (Cahen 1955b). But the inability of these groups to develop new, more effective links with the center, or to develop adequate self-regulative mechanisms, gave rise here also to a relatively high degree of politicization. Nevertheless, the major potential for reform and modernization must be sought within these groups.

Japan

The Japanese case is at a different pole of comparison with the Chinese one: here the importance of structural differences exceeds that of ideological or value orientations.

On the purely ideological level one may, at first sight, perceive a strong similarity between the Japanese and Chinese experiences. Indeed, an even more closed, particularistic orientation and collective identity existed in Japan. The identity between cultural and political orders was even closer, and universalistic elements or orientations beyond the existing political and national framework weaker (Bellah 1956; 1962; Earl 1964), so that emphasis on the Confucian ethic (though mixed with Buddhist and Shinto elements) created an even stronger identification with the particular polity than in China.

But paradoxically enough these elements did not greatly impede the internal transformation and modernization of Japanese society, although they influenced the directions and limits of modernization. On the value-orientation level, as well as on that of the structural location of the central symbols of the society, several points of flexibility developed. First the structure of the center in the Tokugawa period differed in several crucial and important aspects from the Chinese or any other centralized Imperial system. The Japanese centralization took place under a special form of feudalism, and although the various autonomous feudal traditions were weakened or frozen they did not entirely lose their vitality (Craig 1961; Jansen 1961). Even more important, the arrangement of Tokugawa political institutions was such that the center was less monolithic than the strong ideological identity between cultural and the political orders might suggest.

The dissociation between the symbolic center, represented by the politically ineffective Emperor, and the politically effective center of the Shogunate obviated several of the potential consequences of a close identity between the polity and the cultural order (Dore 1964). In some ways this organizational duality was equivalent to a dissociation—on the substantive level—between the cultural and the political orders. This has facilitated a political revolution anchored in the ancient Imperial political symbolism and created an almost uniquely successful initial modernization based on neo-traditional orientations and symbols.[9] (Some of the traditional Kingdoms like Morocco, Buganda, or Ethiopia, may also attempt to modernize in this way, though they are handicapped by the absence of a similar dissociation between the traditional symbols and the effective political centers. But Professor

[9] See on this, among others, Jansen (1965), Bellah (1962; 1965), and Passin (1965).

Inkeles has drawn my attention to the fact that a development very similar to the Japanese one has lately been taking place in Nepal.)

The revival of the older symbolic center greatly facilitated and supported the overthrow, by an oligarchic revolution, of the political center of the Shogunate. This continuity of the Imperial tradition was not purely "decorative," but constituted the major focus of the new value orientations and the new national identity, and it greatly helped to mobilize the loyalties of the broader strata (Dore 1965). Such a transformation could not have been so easily attained in China or the Islamic states, where overthrow of the political center would undermine the cultural order, and the mobilization of older traditional loyalties would diminish possibilities for developing a modern, effective political center.

Several aspects of Japanese religion enhanced the transformation. First, the syncretic nature of Japanese religion, and the relative lack of rigid orthodoxy, facilitated the absorption of new contents. Second, strong transcendental orientations, evinced in different ways in some Buddhist and Confucian circles, became more pronounced in the late Tokugawa period, which facilitated the development of independent standards under which various groups or individuals formulated legitimate collective goals (Bellah 1956; Dore 1964). The combination of religious syncretism with this transcendental emphasis facilitated both the redefinition of collective goals according to the more modern orientation of the Meiji oligarchs and the mobilization of wider loyalties in their implementation.

Other aspects of Japanese feudalism were also of great importance in the relatively successful initial modernization of the society. The hierarchically interlocked groups comprising the feudal system of stratification were strongly committed to collective obligations (Norman 1940; Levy 1955; Craig 1961). In their criteria of status and self-identity these groups evinced a relatively high degree of autonomy, but unlike the Chinese groups, these were not closed. Their identity, and the mutual obligations it entailed, were not entirely dependent on the political center. Nor were there homogeneous high-status political-cultural groups like the literati to monopolize the central political and élite positions. The major strata were much more dispersed and heterogeneous: there were clusters of feudal landlords, merchant and intellectual groups, each with some autonomy. Moreover these groups were structurally linked to each other and to the center. All of these characteristics facilitated either self-transformation or a high degree of adaptability to any changes initiated by the center.

This structural aspect of the status system was reinforced by the transcendental elements of the religious orientation, permitting the transfer of loyalties from the old feudal-Shogunate-centered hierarchy to the new center (Dore 1964; 1965).

Certain aspects of Japanese family structure were also important here (Levy 1955). Although the family was a basic focus of solidarity and loyalty in Japan as in China, its place depended to a large extent on its ability to further collective interests. Hence family units could develop semi-autonomous mechanisms to regulate their own activities and problems, minimizing initial demands on the center and conferring upon it the loyalties and resources of family groups (Levy 1955).

Because the older political and feudal regimes contained these seeds of autonomy and self-transformation, Japanese modernization proceeded rapidly. Industrialization, promulgated from the center, mobilized broad groups and strata. A new system of stratification emerged, as the Meiji oligarchs, themselves stemming from secondary aristocratic groups, abolished not only the political power of the older aristocracy but also its status symbols and economic (agrarian) bases. The Meiji monopolized the symbolic and political center, but they often used renovated traditional Imperial symbols to legitimize a much greater status flexibility. Although the status symbols and hierarchy they developed were close to the political center and to the oligarchs in power, emphasizing bureaucratic positions, the monolithic political forms that developed in China did not appear. In rural as well as urban sectors of Japanese society, the Meiji created more flexible, relatively autonomous new criteria for status, making it possible for new groups to crystallize their status (Vogel 1963).

Some of the more specific structural characteristics of Japanese modernization can also be related to specific points of flexibility in the Tokugawa period. Among these the most important was the combination of universalistic and particularistic criteria regulating and channelling social mobility and mobilization. In the educational system, and on the "entry" to occupational statuses, universalistic criteria were applied, especially in the various periods or stages of examinations. But beyond this entrance stage, on almost all levels of the social and occupational structure, various particularistic units, such as school cliques, company and bureaucratic cliques and groups, small labor groups, etc., tended to crystallize. Within these units many traditional forms and attitudes persisted, and little mobility occurred between them. At the same time, however, the extent of overlapping between different particularistic units was relatively small, with few ecological crystallizations of such overlapping, so that particularistic developments did not impede and may even have facilitated status flexibility and recrystallization in certain social groups (Vogel 1963).

This flexibility enabled Japan to deal with many of the problems of modernization, though not with all of them. She could not avoid various breakdowns, the most important of which took place in the late 1920's and early 1930's.[10] During that period various new élites—the more modern and independent middle classes, professional, and intellectual groups, as well as some workers' organizations—attempted to enlarge the scope of their political participation. Failing to absorb these new elements, the modern system broke down and this gave rise to the militarist regimes of the thirties. This development was mostly due to the rulers' attempt to stifle new demands, and to control these new groups and their demands through bureaucratic and military factions under the aegis of Imperial symbols. The initial incorporation of new demands in the early Meiji period was also done through such factions, but because the system was not fully institutionalized it could not cope with the growing dissociation among the modern business and intellectual élites and working-class leaders on the one hand, and the more traditional and oligarchic élites on the other.

Here several weaknesses in the process of Japanese modernization stand out. The first was in the nature of the symbolic transformation of the center. The new, organizationally flexible center established by the Meiji oligarchs embodied no internal transformation of values. The new national identity was couched

[10] Some of the basic data on this period in Japanese history are collected in Morris (1963). For analyses of the Japanese situation in that period see Parsons (1959:275–98), Maruyama (1963), Dore (1965), and Passin (1965).

mostly in terms of particularistic loyalty to the Emperor as Son of Heaven rather than in terms of his representation of any wider (transcendental) or universalistic values. While this Imperial symbolism was flexible enough to absorb many new political orientations, the basic legitimation of the new political community and its activities did not transcend particularistic collective symbols. Hence value orientations through which various new social forces could be legitimated and impinge on the center in autonomous terms, and through which support for various autonomous regulative mechanisms and frameworks could be provided, did not develop (Bellah 1962; 1965; Passin 1963; Maruyama 1965).

Similarly, although the central groups possessed a relatively high degree of status flexibility at a relatively early stage of modernization, this flexibility was not bolstered by an autonomous basis for legitimation and self-perception. The heavy neo-traditionalism of the center did not foster the development of autonomous value orientations and hence limited the ability of various social groups to develop institutional frameworks for mediating among the interests of various groups and evolving a broad base of consensus (Parsons 1959; Dore 1964; 1965).

Only under the impact of external forces (i.e., military defeat) did Japanese modernization make a new start. This new phase is also, as yet, overshadowed by problems from the past, especially the absence of an internal value transformation at the time of Japan's initial modernization.

India

India is probably the only complex and highly differentiated historical civilization that has maintained its cultural integrity without being tied to any particular political framework (Renou, Fillozet, et al. 1947; 1953; Spear 1961; Sinha 1963). This is true not only of the last centuries under Muslim and later English rule but even before that. In India there were small and large states and Imperial centers, but no single state with which the cultural tradition was identified. Classical Indian religious thought did, of course, refer to political issues, and to the behavior of princes and the duties and rights of subjects.[11] But to a much

---

[11] This aspect of Indian political thought is elaborated from different points of view in Varma (1954), Dumont (1962:46–76; 1964a), and Drekmeier (1962). The best known classical text is the Arthashastra (Kautilya 1960). Some additional texts can be found in Bary et al. (1958: 236–58).

higher degree than in many other historical imperial civilizations, politics were conceived in secular terms. The basic religious and cultural orientations, the specific cultural identity of Indian civilization, were not necessarily associated with any particular political or imperial framework; whatever partial identity of such kind might have existed during the period before Muslim domination has been greatly diminished since then. The strength and survival of Indian civilization under alien rule is rooted in the very fact that it was not identified with any political framework.

This basic characteristic of Indian civilization had a very important influence on the initial modernization processes, which began under the aegis of the British and continued during the nationalist movement. Because the cultural and political orders were more or less dissociated, modernization was relatively free of specific traditional-cultural orientations toward the political sphere. The modern center was first established in terms of western symbols and was to some extent detached from the great Indian cultural tradition (Spear 1961). In the Gandhian phase, the political aspirations of the Indian national movement were to some extent couched in traditional symbols or at least were legitimized by some interpretation of such symbols, but this did not create (as it did in Islam) too specific or intensive demands on the institutional structure (Gandhi 1961; Nehru 1961; Rai 1961; Wolfert 1962).

This dissociation was itself at least partially legitimized in terms of traditional ideological orientations. Some of the symbols or values of the new center, expressed mostly in terms of such Western values as political and social justice, could be legitimized in older, classical Indian political terms. This was reinforced by reformist tendencies among the upper strata of Hindu society after 1850, for, significantly enough, the new political-ideological center was to a large extent developed and borne by people coming from the strata—especially the Brahmanic groups—who were the bearers of the historical tradition in its non-political aspects and emphases.[12]

The second relevant aspect of Indian society has to do with the place of the political system in the system of stratification and the internal cohesion of broader social groups and strata.

[12] See the first chapter of the forthcoming work by Krishna. On the reforming potential of Hinduism see Elder (1959) and Singer (1958).

In their identity and in their relation to the political order, these groups evinced a very high degree of autonomy. Parallel to the relative independence of cultural traditions from the political center, castes, villages, and the various networks of communication were highly autonomous, self-regulating in terms of their own cultural and social identity, with but limited access to the political center or centers (Singer 1959; Kothari 1964; Weiner 1965).

For the process of modernization, this autonomy meant that the new political center could develop without intensive demands immediately impinging on it. The broader strata had their own mechanisms for coping with some of the problems of modernization, without becoming disorganized or making excessive demands on the political center. By comparison, the situation in many new states is that broader groups depend on the center so heavily that it cannot crystallize. That this did not happen in India has greatly facilitated the development, first under British influence and then in the nationalist movement through the Congress, of a central, stable institutional structure which maintained order, established a modern framework, and is gradually expanding to incorporate broader groups.

Consequently, a concrete structural feature of modernization has been the continuous recrystallization of traditional frameworks, and especially of the various networks of caste relations. The configuration of castes has been transformed; caste groups have assumed new tasks and adapted readily to new economic and political frameworks.[13] Patterns of traditional caste-mobility persist: i.e., existing subcaste groups assume some new economic, political or ritual tasks more or less within the range set by traditional culture, or they attempt to obtain a better standing within the old, traditional ritual order. But side by side with this pattern a new one has developed, in which the older caste groups gave way to new broader, more differentiated and more flexible networks of caste associations, organized around modern economic, professional and political activities in a great variety of new organizational forms. Often though not always, these new associations crosscut the existing political, social and

[13] The best known analysis of these developments is Srinivas (1962), especially chapters 1, 2, and 4.

economic hierarchies of status (Neteille, forthcoming; Kothari and Hara, in press).

But in these developments there were points of weakness. Although the center was institutionally and organizationally strong and flexible, it did not develop common symbols in which elements of the new culture could be combined with the older traditions so as to create a relatively strong collective identity and commitments to it. This also reduced its ability to provide new symbols that would serve not only as foci of rebellion against the colonial rulers but also as flexible guidelines for institution building (Kothari 1964; Weiner 1965). This weakness became especially critical when the center extended, through universal suffrage, the scope of its activities and consequently its dependence on broader groups. Then the lack of association between the cultural traditional and political framework, which was a point of strength in the beginning, became a point of weakness. The center must create new, binding symbols of collective identity to overcome the more "parochial"—mostly linguistic—symbols of the different regions and states and develop some feeling of political community. This is especially important because these parochial symbols tend to become more crystallized and better articulated as peripheral segments of the society are modernized. The explosive quality of the linguistic question in India today is a manifestation of this problem (Harrison 1960; Friedrich 1962).

A second problem has to do with the extent to which the permissiveness of the broad Indian cultural tradition and its reforming tendencies not only facilitates new institutional frameworks, under external influence, and the continuous adaptation of the traditional groups, but also develops innovative forces, and common integrative frameworks to support continuous institution building. Here the question is whether caste and other traditional groups will develop new, more flexible frameworks, crosscutting different status hierarchies, and new values, orientations, and activities within them, or whether they will mainly reinforce the neo-traditional divisive symbols and groupings.[14]

The internal transformation of the great Asian societies, then, has been greatly facilitated by autonomy of social, cultural and

[14] On these different possibilities see Rudolph (1960), Neteille (1965), and Srinivas (1962).

political institutions. Cultural autonomy has made possible the development of new symbols supporting and legitimizing central institution building, while autonomy in the sphere of social organization has facilitated the crystallization of viable new organizational nuclei without disrupting the pre-existing order, thus enabling the new order to rely, at least to some extent, on the forces of the old one. The relatively strong internal cohesion of broader strata and of family groups, with some status autonomy and openness toward the center, has helped to develop positive orientations to the new centers and willingness to provide the necessary support and resources.

The precise institutional contours of emerging modern systems, as we have seen, depend on the concrete structural location of autonomous institutional spheres.

Conversely, so far as such autonomy is absent, and the social, cultural, and political orders are closely identified with one another, the development of viable modern structures has been greatly impeded. And where family and other groups are closed, they are likely to undermine the new institutional centers by making intensive and unregulated demands on them or by withholding resources. As the Chinese and Islamic examples show, the weak points in emerging new structures depend to some extent on the structural location of the mutually identified institutional spheres.

Protestantism and Modernization in the West

I have confined the preceding analysis to great Asian civilizations that were drawn into modernization from the "base" of a relatively centralized and differentiated Imperial system. In this they differ greatly from African and Latin American societies, which modernized either from relatively undifferentiated social structures without strong centers and a great cultural tradition or which, like most Latin American countries, were mainly peripheral to such centers. But it would be beyond the scope of this paper to examine the extent to which my analysis may be applied to these cases.

Even with regard to these more differentiated and centralized Asian societies, however, structural flexibility was not in itself—as the Indian and Japanese cases indicate—enough to assure the development and continuity of modern institutional frameworks. Flexibility, or the autonomy of different institutional orders, created the conditions under which more active groups and élites could attempt to institute new principles of cultural direction and social integration. But the mere existence of structural flexibility neither assured that such groups would appear nor indicated the type of integrative orientation they would develop.

Indeed, it is the extent to which such groups do develop that has been—especially in China, India, and some Islamic societies—perhaps the major problem facing these societies during their modernization. The root of the problem in these societies was that modernization was a matter of encounter with foreign forces, an encounter beset with the difficulties and ambivalences of colonial or semi-colonial relations. Modernization therefore required that the new élites create a national identity from the encounter with these foreign and often alien forces. The internal capacities of these societies for reformation or transformation may have been crucial to their adaptation to these external forces and to their success in building new institutional structures to cope with these problems. But the very nature of the modernization process in these societies was such that the sources and directions of the cultural transformation, and the potential creativity of different élite groups, were not necessarily given by the same factors that initiated their modern structural transformation.

The earliest modernization—that of Western Europe since the 18th century—permits a fuller analysis of the relative importance of structural flexibility and active cultural transformation in modernization, for here both processes were, from the very beginning, initiated mainly from within. In European—especially Western Christian European—culture the tradition of autonomous cultural, political, and social orders is strong, and here the first and most continuous impetus to modernization did indeed develop. But even in Western and Central European countries, the course of modernization was neither entirely continuous nor everywhere the same.

What requires explanation is the fact that background more or less common to all Western and Central European societies gave rise to different modern institutional frameworks, with greatly varying capacities to sustain change.

One approach to this question is to reexamine Weber's famous Protestant Ethic thesis and some recent criticisms of it. At first glance, it may seem that Weber was dealing not with the structural and cultural variables I have discussed, but mainly with the religious roots of orientations to new types of economic activity. But several recent discussions of Weber's thesis indicate that some of its broader implications may be relevant to the present discussion. Of special interest from this point of view are the comments of Luethy (1964), and Trevor-Roper (1965).

Luethy, and to some extent Trevor-Roper, deny Weber's thesis in the economic field proper, claiming that economic development in Europe was independent of the specific direct impact of Protestantism. They show, for instance, as others have before them, that the first impact of Protestantism on economic life was a restrictive one, as Calvin's Geneva demonstrates. For Luethy, however, the major impact of Protestantism on European history was in the political field. This impact was effected, according to him, through direct reference to the Bible in search of new bases to legitimate authority as well as through the new structural impetus to pluralistic politics which developed through the Counter-Reformation of the Wars of Religion.[15]

Both Luethy and Trevor-Roper admit—indeed, stress—that England and the Netherlands especially, and to some extent the Scandinavian countries, were more successful after the Counter-Reformation in developing viable modern institutions than were most of the Catholic countries. To this they attribute the ultimate, but not the initial success and continuity of modernization in Protestant countries.

Without going into the detailed merits of these criticisms of Weber's thesis,[16] it might be worthwhile to point out that in principle the criticism Luethy directs against Weber could easily be directed against his own thesis. For instance, one could show that the original political impulse of either Lutheranism or Calvinism was not in a "liberal" or democratic direction but rather in a more "totalistic" one.

But apart from such details, both Weber's and Luethy's analy-

[15] In this he is close to Walzer who stresses the Puritans' revolutionary ideology (1963).

[16] Cf. some of the older controversies around the Weber thesis in Green (1959) and Burrell (1964).

ses deal not with the direct economic or political "results" of certain religious beliefs or the activities of religious groups, but rather—as Troeltsch (1958) has already seen[17]—with their more indirect impact. Initially the Reformation was not a "modernizing" movement; it aimed to establish a purer "medieval" socio-political religious order. Protestantism produced an impetus toward modernity only after this initial socio-religious impulse failed. Hence theories that attempt to evaluate this influence or impact of Protestantism necessarily deal with the transformed social orientations of Protestant religious groups after they had failed to establish their initial militant, totalistic aims restricting autonomous activities in both the economic and the political field. From a comparative point of view, the special importance of Protestantism is that the basic Protestant value orientations and social organization contained within themselves the seeds of such transformation. The exact way in which this transformation worked out in the institutional framework of any given society, however, depended not only on the internal predispositions of the Protestant groups but also on some aspects of the preceding social structure and on the *initial* interaction between this structure and the original religious groups.

Here a question not considered by Luethy and Trevor-Roper is very pertinent: the extent to which the Protestant Reformation influenced the development of the social and political flexibility to which they attach so much importance. The Protestant Reformation did indeed have an enormous impact not only on the motivational orientations of its adherents but also, through the social and status orientations of various Protestant groups, on the central political sphere. This impact was not necessarily intended by the rulers who adopted Protestantism, yet it did facilitate the further development of a more flexible and dynamic social system. In the first Protestant societies—England, Scandinavia, the Netherlands, and later in the United States—perhaps even before the full development of a new motivational orientation, the central symbolic and political sphere, and the basic relations between the political and social spheres, were transformed through the incorporation of Protestant values and symbols. This not only reinforced the existing autonomy of these spheres but

[17] One of the most recent critical analyses of Weber which does not take this into account is Elton (1963:321 ff).

created new bases of political obligations and more flexible political institutions.[18]

Protestantism had a similar impact on the internal cohesion and autonomy of the more active social groups in these societies. Most of the Protestant groups developed a combination of two types of status orientation. First was their "openness" toward the wider social structure, rooted in the "this-worldly" orientations which were not limited to the economic sphere, but were gradually extended to demands for wider political participation and new, broader political frameworks and criteria. Second, their status orientations were characterized by a certain autonomy and self-sufficiency. Unlike countries or sectors with a more autocratic or aristocratic tradition, they were, from the point of view of the crystallization of their status symbols, virtually independent of the existing (i.e., monarchical or ecclesiastical) centers of political power.

But such orientations did not develop to the same extent among all Protestant groups in all countries. The full development and institutionalization of such orientations depended to no small degree on the flexibility or "openness" of the existing political and cultural centers, and that of broader groups and strata and their initial reaction to religious innovations. So far as this reaction was restrictive, the transformative potentialities of these orientations could not bear full fruit.

The various interactions between different transformative potentialities and existing structural flexibility could give rise to paradoxically similar—or divergent—results. The influence of the allegedly conservative Lutheranism, for example, took a variety of forms. In the German principalities Lutheranism was indeed very restrictive, because the existing political framework was not an appropriate setting for the development of a national identity and community or for the development of more autonomous and flexible status orientations in the broader strata (Adam 1938; Ritter 1938; 1950; Drummond 1951; McNeill 1954). Here, "traditional" or autocratic rulers of the small principalities adopted the new religious orientations, and in this context the more conservative among these orientations became predominant, often restricting further institutional development.

---

[18] For some of the very numerous analyses bearing on this see Gelder (1943), George (1961), and Little (1963).

Social, Political and Cultural Orders in Modernization   461

But in the Scandinavian countries these religious orientations were integrated into new, wider national communities and developed on the bases of the prior autonomy of the Estates. While they certainly did not impede the development of an absolutist state in Sweden they did help to make possible the subsequent development of these states in a more pluralistic direction (Holmquist 1922; Ritter 1950; Schrey 1951; Schweiger 1962).

Similarly paradoxical results, also demonstrating the importance of restrictive prior situations, are evident in the institutionalization of Calvinism. Of special interest here is the Prussian case, where the institutionalization of these orientations by the absolutist, autocratic Hohenzollerns did not facilitate the development of a flexible and pluralistic political framework, though it did support development of more activist collective political goals (Kayser 1961).

Thus, so far as the initial impact of the religious changes reinforced the seeds of autonomy, which were to a high degree present in all Western and Central European societies, it created the basis of a new political order, not only on the structural-institutional level, but also on the level of central values and symbols which both legitimized these institutions and prompted their further development. Under such conditions, potentially activist religious orientations could take various institutional directions—e.g., economic, or political as in Scotland, or scientific —and become institutionalized, thus reinforcing the continuous development of these societies. But so far as some of these conditions were lacking, these religious orientations were institutionalized in partial, relatively constrictive or discontinuous ways reducing their transformative potential.

The different Catholic countries, on the other hand, demonstrate the limitations of purely structural autonomy. The first impetus of many modern developments—economic, scientific, cultural or political—occurred in Catholic countries too. But the continuity of these developments was greatly impeded by the initial response to many of their more far-reaching consequences and especially to their convergence with Protestantism, which minimized, at least initially, the possibility of continuous development of modern institutions.

The case of Spain (Castro 1954)—in a way the first modern

state—illustrates this pattern most clearly, but it is perhaps even more prominent in the case of France, where the potentially pluralistic impact of various modern trends, including Protestantism, was inhibited by the formation of the French state during the Counter-Reformation. This provided the background for continuous rifts in the central political symbols—between traditional and modern (revolutionary), aristocratic and republican, religious and secular orientations—rifts that persisted till the end of the Third Republic (Luethy 1955).

Only through the juxtaposition of the structural aspects with processes of élite formation and creativity can the transformative potential of any pre-modern society be fully evaluated. The Asian societies with which this discussion began require still further analysis, for which this paper may, perhaps, serve as a starting point.

BIBLIOGRAPHY

Adam, Alfred
  1938 "Die nationale Kirche bei Luther," *Archiv für Geschichte der Reformation* 35, 30–62.
Aguirre Beltrán, Gonzalo
  1953 *Formas de gobierno indígena.* Mexico: Imprenta Universitaria.
Anderson, James N. D.
  1959 *Islamic Law in the Modern World.* New York and London: Stevens.
Ardant, Gabriel
  1961 *La Tunisie d'aujourdhui et de demain.* Paris: Calmann-Lévy.
Austen, L.
  1945 "Cultural Changes in Kiriwina," *Oceania* 16, 15–60.
Bailey, F. G.
  1957 *Caste and the Economic Frontier.* Manchester: Manchester University Press.
Barnes, John A.
  1954 *Politics in a Changing Society.* Cape Town: Oxford University Press.
Balazs, Etienne
  1964 *Chinese Civilization and Bureaucracy.* New Haven: Yale University Press.
Barth, Henry
  1857 *Travels in Central Africa.* Vol. 2. New York: Harper & Brothers.
Bary, William T. de, Stephen N. Hay, Rayal Weiler, and Andrew Yarrow
  1958 *Sources of Indian Tradition.* New York: Columbia University Press.
Beckman, George M.
  1962 *The Modernization of China and Japan.* New York: Harper.
Beckwith, Martha
  1932 *Kepelino's Traditions of Hawaii.* Bernice P. Bishop Museum Bulletin 95.

Bellah, Robert N.

1956 *Tokugawa Religion.* Glencoe, Ill.: Free Press.

1962 "Values and Social Change in Modern Japan," *Asian Cultural Studies* 3, 13–56.

1965 "Epilogue," in *Religion and Progress in Modern Asia,* Robert N. Bellah, ed. New York: Free Press.

Benavides, Fray Alonso de

1945 *Revised Memorial of 1634.* Ed. by Frederic Webb Hodge, George P. Hammond, and Agapito Rey. Albuquerque: University of New Mexico Press.

Berndt, Ronald M.

1962 *Excess and Restraint: Social Control among a New Guinea Mountain People.* Chicago: University of Chicago Press.

Binder, Leonard

1958 "Problems of Islamic Political Thought in the Light of Recent Development in Pakistan," *Journal of Politics* 20, 675–85.

1961 *Religion and Politics in Pakistan.* Los Angeles: University of California Press.

1964 *The Ideological Revolution in the Middle East.* New York: John Wiley.

Birket-Smith, Kaj

1924 "The Country of Egedesminde and Its Inhabitants," *Meddelelser om Grønland* 46.

1928 "The Greenlanders of the Present Day," *Greenland* I, 423–90.

1929 *The Caribou Eskimos.* Report of the Fifth Thule Expedition, 1921–24, Vol. 5, Pt. 1. Copenhagen.

1930 *Contributions to Chipewyan Ethnology.* Report of the Fifth Thule Expedition, 1921–24, Vol. 6. Copenhagen.

1959 *The Eskimos.* Tr. from the Danish by W. E. Calvert. London: Methuen.

Bleek, Dorothea

1956 *A Bushman Dictionary.* New Haven: American Oriental Society.

Boas, Franz

1888 *The Central Eskimos.* Bureau of American Ethnology Annual Report 6. Washington, D.C.

1907 *The Eskimos of Baffin Land and Hudson Bay.* American Museum of Natural History Bulletin 15. New York.

1916 *Tsimshian Mythology.* Bureau of American Ethnology Annual Report 31. Washington, D.C.

Bohannan, Laura

1958 "Political Aspects of Tiv Social Organization," in *Tribes Without Rulers,* John Middleton and David Tait, eds. London: Routledge and Kegan Paul, 33–66.

Bohannan, Laura, and Paul Bohannan

1953 *The Tiv of Central Nigeria*. Ethnographic Survey of Africa: Western Africa, Part VIII. London: International African Institute.

Bohannan, Paul

1954a "The Migration and Expansion of the Tiv," *Africa* 24, 2–16.

1954b *Tiv Farm and Settlement*. Colonial Research Studies No. 15. London: Her Majesty's Stationary Office.

1958 "Extra-processual Events in Tiv Political Institutions," *American Anthropologist* 60, 1–12.

Bolinder, Gustaf

1925 *Die Indianer der tropischen Schneegebiete*. Stuttgart: Strecker und Schröder.

Brown, Paula

1951 "Patterns of Authority in West Africa," *Africa* 21, 261–78.

1963 "From Anarchy to Satrapy," *American Anthropologist* 65, 1–15.

Brownlee, Frank

1943 "The Social Organization of the Kung (/Un) Bushmen of the North-western Kalahari," *Africa* 14, No. 3, 124–29.

Burrell, Sidney A. (ed.)

1964 *The Role of Religion in Modern European History*. New York: Macmillan.

Burrows, E. G.

1939 "Breed and Border in Polynesia," *American Anthropologist* 41, 1–21.

Busia, K. A.

1947 *The Position of the Chief in the Modern Political System of Ashanti*. London: Oxford University Press.

Buxton, Jean Carlile

1963 *Chiefs and Strangers: A Study of Political Assimilation Among the Mandari*. Oxford: Clarendon Press.

Cahen, Claude

1955a "The Body Politic," in *Unity and Variety in Muslim Civilization*, E. von Grunebaum, ed. Chicago: University of Chicago Press, 132–63.

1955b "L'histoire économique et sociale de l'Orient Musulman médiéval," *Studia Islamica* 111, 93–116.

Camara, Fernando

1952 "Religious and Political Organization," in *Heritage of Conquest; The Ethnology of Middle America*, Sol Tax, ed. Glencoe, Ill.: Free Press, 142–73.

Carrasco, Pedro

1952 *Tarascan Folk Religion: An Analysis of Economic, Social and*

Religious Interactions. Middle American Research Institute Publication 17. New Orleans: Tulane University.

1957 *Some Aspects of Peasant Society in Middle America and India.* Kroeber Anthropological Society Papers 16.

Castro, Americo
1954 *The Structure of Spanish History.* Princeton: Princeton University Press.

Chavez Orozco, Luis
1943 *Las instituciones democráticas de los indígenas mexicanos en la época colonial.* Mexico: Ediciones del Instituto Indigenista Interamericano.

Chilver, E. M.
1960 " 'Feudalism' in the Interlascustrine Kingdoms," in *East African Chiefs,* A. I. Richards, ed. London: Faber and Faber, Ltd., for the East African Institute of Social Research, 378–93.

Chimalpahin Quauhtlehuanitzin, Domingo Francisco de San Anton Muñon
1889 *Annales de Domingo Francisco de San Anton Muñon Chimalpahin Quauhtlehuanitzin sixième et septième relations (1258–1612) publiées et traduites sur le manuscrit original par Rémi Siméon.* Paris: Maisonneuve et Leclerc.

1958 *Das Memorial breve acerca della fundación de la ciudad de Culhuacan, und weitere ausgewahlte Teile aus den "Diferentes historias originales"* (Manuscrit mexicain No. 74, Paris). Aztekischer Text mit deutscher Übersetzung von Walter Lehman und Gerdt Kutscher. Quellenwerke zur alten Geschichte Amerikas 7. Stuttgart: W. Kohlehammer.

Clark, James Cooper (ed. and tr.)
1938 *Codex Mendoza,* the Mexican manuscript known as the Collection of Mendoza and preserved in the Bodleian Library, Oxford. 3 vols. London.

Cohen, Ronald
1962 *An Anthropological Survey of Communities of the Mackenzie-Slave Lake Region of Canada.* Ottawa: Department of Northern Affairs.

1966a *The Kanuri of Bornu.* New York: Holt, Rinehart and Winston.

1966b *The Dynamics of Feudalism in Bornu.* Boston University Publications in African History, Vol. 2. Boston.

Cooper, John
1946 *The Araucanians.* Handbook of South American Indians, Bureau of American Ethnology Bulletin 143, Vol. 2, 687–760.

Coulborn, Ruston
1956 *Feudalism in History.* Princeton: Princeton University Press.

Coulson, N. J.
  1964 *A History of Islamic Law.* Edinburgh: Edinburgh University Press.
Craig, Albert M.
  1961 *Chossu in the Meiji Restoration.* Cambridge: Harvard University Press.
Denig, Edwin Thompson
  1930 *Indian Tribes of the Upper Missouri.* Bureau of American Ethnology Annual Report 46. Washington, D.C.
Dore, Ronald P.
  1964 *Education in Tokugawa Japan.* Berkeley: University of California Press.
  1965 "The Legacy of Tokugawa Education," in *Changing Japanese Attitudes Toward Modernization,* Marius B. Jansen, ed. Princeton: Princeton University Press, 99–132.
Dorsey, George A., and J. Murie
  1940 *Notes on Skidi Pawnee Society.* Field Museum of Natural History Anthropological Series No. 27. Chicago.
Dorsey, J. O.
  1884 *Omaha Sociology.* Bureau of American Ethnology Annual Report 13. Washington, D.C.
Drekmeier, Charles
  1962 *Kingship and Community in Early India.* Stanford: Stanford University Press.
Drummond, Alfred L.
  1951 *German Protestantism since Luther.* London: Epworth Press.
Dube, S. C.
  1955 *Indian Village.* London: Routledge and Kegan Paul.
Dumont, Louis
  1962 "The Conception of Kingship in Ancient India," *Contributions to Indian Sociology* 6, 46–76.
  1964a *La civilisation indienne et nous.* Paris: Librairie Armand Colin.
  1964b "Nationalism and Communism," *Contributions to Indian Sociology* 7, 30–70.
Durán, Diego
  1951 *Historia de las Indias de Nueva España.* 2 vols. Mexico: Editora Nacional.
Durkheim, Emile
  1912 *Les formes élémentaires de la vie religieuse.* Paris: F. Alcan.
  1938 *The Rules of Sociological Method.* Tr. by Sarah A. Solovay and John H. Mueller, ed. by George E. G. Catlin. Chicago: University of Chicago Press.

Easton, David
  1959 "Political Anthropology," in *Biennial Review of Anthropology,*
  Bernard Siegel, ed. Stanford: Stanford University Press, 210–62.
Earl, David M.
  1964 *Emperor and Nation in Japan—Political Themes of the
  Tokugawa Period.* Seattle: University of Washington Press.
Eboué, Félix
  1942 *Native Policy in French Equatorial Africa.* Translation of a
  memorandum by M. Eboué, Governor-General, French Equatorial
  Africa, November 1941. Lagos.
Eisenstadt, Shmuel N.
  1956 *From Generation to Generation: Age Groups and Social Structure.* Glencoe, Ill.: Free Press.
  1962 "Religious Organizations and Political Process in Centralized
  Empires," *Journal of Asian Studies* 21, 271–94.
  1963a *Modernization, Growth and Diversity.* Bloomington, Ind.:
  Indiana University Press.
  1963b *The Political Systems of Empires.* New York: Free Press of
  Glencoe.
  1964a "Modernization and Conditions of Sustained Growth," *World
  Politics* 16, 576–94.
  1964b "Breakdowns of Modernization," *Economic Development
  and Cultural Change* 12, 345–67.
  1964c "Institutionalization and Change," *American Sociological Review* 29, 235–48.
Ekblaw, W. E.
  1928 "Material Responses of the Polar Eskimo to Their Far Arctic
  Environment," *Annals of the Association of American Geogra-
  phers* 18, No. 1.
Elbert, Samuel H.
  1953 "Internal Relationships of Polynesian Languages and Dialects,"
  Southwestern Journal of Anthropology 9, 147–73.
Elder, Joseph W.
  1959 *Industrialism in Hindu Society: A Case Study in Social Change.*
  Unpublished Ph.D. thesis, Harvard University.
Elton, Geoffrey R.
  1963 *Reformation Europe.* London: Collins.
Ember, Melvin
  1962 "Political Authority and the Structure of Kinship in Aboriginal
  Samoa," *American Anthropologist* 64, 964–71.
Evans-Pritchard, E. E.
  1940a "The Nuer of the Southern Sudan," in *African Political Sys-
  tems,* Meyer Fortes and E. E. Evans-Pritchard, eds. London: Ox-

ford University Press for the International African Institute, 272–96.

1940b *The Nuer*. Oxford: Clarendon Press.

1940c *The Political System of the Anuak of the Anglo-Egyptian Sudan*. London: P. Lund, Humphries & Co., Ltd., for the London School of Economics and Political Science.

1940d "The Political Structure of Nandi-speaking Peoples of Kenya," *Africa* 13, No. 3, 250–67.

1948 *The Divine Kingship of the Shilluk of the Nilotic Sudan*. Cambridge: Cambridge University Press.

1949 *The Sanusi of Cyrenaica*. Oxford: Clarendon Press.

1951 *Kinship and Marriage Among the Nuer*. Oxford: Clarendon Press.

Fenton, William N.

1940 *Problems Arising from the Historic North-eastern Position of the Iroquois*. Smithsonian Miscellaneous Collection 100. Washington, D.C.

Firth, Raymond

1936, 1957 *We, the Tikopia*. New York: American Book Co., 1936; George Allen and Unwin, 1957 (2d ed.).

1955 "Some Principles of Social Organization," *Journal of the Royal Anthropological Institute* 85, 1–18.

1957 "A Note on Descent Groups in Polynesia," *Man* 57, January 1957, 4–7

Flannery, Regina

1939 *An Analysis of Coastal Algonquin Culture*. Catholic University of America Anthropological Series, No. 7. Washington, D.C.

Font, José María

1952 "Municipio medieval, municipio moderno, municipio indiano," in *Diccionario de Historia de España*, Vol. 2. Madrid: Revista de Occidente, 593–602.

Forde, Daryll

1931 *Ethnography of the Yuma Indians*. University of California Publications in American Archaeology and Ethnology 28. Berkeley, Calif.

1938 "Fission and Accretion in the Patrilineal Clans of a Semi-Bantu Community in Southern Nigeria," *Journal of the Royal Anthropological Institute* 68, 311–38.

1939 "Government in Umor," *Africa* 12, 129–61.

1947, 1959 "The Anthropological Approach in Social Science," *The Advancement of Science* 4, No. 15 (1947), 213–24. Reprinted in *Readings in Anthropology*, Vol. 2, Morton H. Fried, ed. New York: Crowell, 1959, 59–78.

1949 "Integrative Aspects of the Yakö First Fruits Ritual," *Journal of the Royal Anthropological Institute* 79, 1–10.
1950 "Ward Organization Among the Yakö," *Africa* 20, 267–89.
1958 *The Context of Belief.* Liverpool: Liverpool University Press.
1962 "Death and Succession: An Analysis of Yakö Mortuary Ceremonial," in *Essays on the Ritual of Social Relations,* Max Gluckman, ed. Manchester: Manchester University Press, 89–123.

Fornander, Abraham
1916 *Fornander Collection of Hawaiian Antiquities and Folklore.* Memoirs of Bernice P. Bishop Museum 4.

Fortes, Meyer
1940 "The Political System of the Tallensi of the Northern Territories of the Gold Coast," in *African Political Systems,* Meyer Fortes and E. E. Evans-Pritchard, eds. London: Oxford University Press, 239–71.
1948 "The Ashanti Social Survey: A Preliminary Report," *Rhodes-Livingstone Journal* 6, 1–36.
1953, 1960 "The Structure of Unilineal Descent Groups," *American Anthropologist* 55 (1953), 17–41. Reprinted in *Cultures and Societies of Africa,* Simon Ottenberg and Phoebe Ottenberg, eds. New York: Random House, 1960, 163–89.

Fortes, M., and E. E. Evans-Pritchard (eds.)
1940 *African Political Systems.* London: Oxford University Press.

Franciscan Fathers
1910 *An Ethnologic Dictionary of the Navaho Language.* St. Michaels, Arizona.

Freeman, J. Derek
1960 "The Iban of Western Borneo," in *Social Structure in Southeast Asia,* George P. Murdock, ed., Viking Fund Publications in Anthropology, No. 29.
1961 "On the Concept of the Kindred," *Journal of the Royal Anthropological Institute* 91, 192–220.
1964 "Some Observations on Kinship and Political Authority in Samoa," *American Anthropologist* 66, 553–68.

Freeman, Otis W.
1951 *Geography of the Pacific.* New York: John Wiley and Sons.

Fried, Morton H.
1957 "The Classification of Corporate Unilineal Descent Systems," *Journal of the Royal Anthropological Institute* 87, 1–29.

Friedrich, Paul
1962 "Language and Politics in India," *Daedalus* 91, 543–59.

Gandhi, Mohandras Karamchand
1961 "Face to Face with Ahimsa," in *The Nationalist Movement:*

Indian Political Thought from Ranade to Bhave, D. M. Brown, ed. Berkeley: University of California Press, 108–28.

Gayton, A. H.
1939 *Yokuts-Mono Chiefs and Shamans.* University of California Publications in American Archaeology and Ethnology 24. Berkeley, Calif.

Geertz, Clifford
1965 "Modernization in a Muslim Society: The Indonesian Case," in *Religion and Progress in Modern Asia,* Robert N. Bellah, ed. New York: Free Press, 93–108.

Gelder, Enno van
1943 *Revolutionaire reformatie.* Amsterdam: Van Kayse.

George, Charles H., and Katherine George
1961 *The Protestant Mind of the English Reformation.* Princeton: Princeton University Press.

Gibb, Hamilton A. R.
1947 *Modern Trends in Islam.* Chicago: University of Chicago Press.
1962 "The Evolution of Government in Early Islam," in *Studies on the Civilization of Islam.* Boston: Beacon Press.

Gibson, Charles
1952 *Tlaxcala in the Sixteenth Century.* New Haven: Yale University Press.
1960 "The Aztec Aristocracy in Colonial Mexico," *Comparative Studies in Society and History* 2, 169–96.

Gifford, E. W.
1929 *Tongan Society.* Bernice P. Bishop Museum Bulletin 61.

Gilbert, William Harlen
1943 *The Eastern Cherokees.* Bureau of American Ethnology Bulletin 133. Washington, D.C.

Gillin, John
1936 *The Barama River Caribs of British Guiana.* Papers of the Peabody Museum of American Archaeology and Ethnology 14, No. 2. Cambridge: Harvard University.

Gluckman, Max
1943 *Essays on Lozi Land and Royal Property.* Rhodes-Livingstone Papers, No. 10. Lusaka, Northern Rhodesia.
1950 "Kinship and Marriage among the Lozi of Northern Rhodesia and the Zulu of Natal," in *African Systems of Kinship and Marriage,* A. A. Radcliffe-Brown and Daryll Forde, eds. London: Oxford University Press for the International African Institute, 166–206.

1954 *Rituals of Rebellion in South-east Africa* The Frazier Lecture 1952. Manchester: Manchester University Press.

1955 *Custom and Conflict in Africa.* Oxford: Blackwell.

1958 *Analysis of a Social Situation in Modern Zululand.* Manchester: Manchester University Press.

1965 *Politics, Law and Religion in Tribal Society.* Chicago: Aldine Publishing Co.

Gómez de Orozco, Federico (ed.)

1945 "Costumbres, fiestas, enterramientos y diversas formas de proceder de los Indios de Nueva España," *Tlalocan* 2, 37–63.

Goodwin, Grenville

1942 *The Social Organization of the Western Apache.* Chicago: University of Chicago Press.

Green, Robert W.

1959 *Protestantism and Capitalism: The Weber Thesis and its Critics.* Boston: D. C. Heath.

Gross, Neal, Ward S. Mason, and Alexander W. McEachern

1958 *Explorations in Role Analysis.* New York: John Wiley and Sons.

Groves, Murray

1956 "Trobriand Island Clans and Chiefs," *Man* 56, November 1956, 164.

Guevara, Tomas

1929 *Historia de Chili: Chili prehispano.* 2 vols. Santiago: Cacells and Co.

Gusinde, Martin

1937 *Die feuerland Indianer.* Vol. II: *Die Yamana; vom Leben und Denken der Wassernomaden am Kap Hoorn.* Modling bei Wien: Verlag Anthropos.

1946 *Urmenschen in feuerland.* Berlin: P. Zsolnay.

Hagen, V. W. von

1955 *Highway of the Sun.* New York: Duell, Sloan and Pearce; Boston: Little, Brown and Co.

Hall, Charles Francis

1864 *Arctic Research Expedition and Life Among the Esquimaux.* New York: Harper and Brothers.

Halpern, Manfred

1964 "Toward Further Modernization of the Study of New Nations," *World Politics* 17, 157–81.

Handy, E. S. C.

1923 *The Native Cultures in the Marquesas.* Bernice P. Bishop Museum Bulletin 9.

1930 *History and Culture in the Society Islands.* Bernice P. Bishop Museum Bulletin 79.

Handy, E. S. C., and others
1933 *Ancient Hawaiian Civilization.* Honolulu: Kamehameha Schools.

Hansen, Johannes (Hanserak)
1914 "List of the Inhabitants of the East Coast of Greenland," *Meddelelser om Grønland* 39.

Harris, Rosemary
1962 "The Influence of Ecological Factors and External Relations on the Mbembe Tribes of South-east Nigeria," *Africa* 32, No. 1, 38–52.

Harrison, Selig
1960 *India: The Most Dangerous Decades.* Princeton: Princeton University Press.

Hart, Charles W. M., and Arnold R. Pilling
1960 *The Tiwi of North Australia.* New York: Holt, Rinehart and Winston.

Hawkes, Ernest W.
1913 *The "Inviting-in" Feast of the Alaskan Eskimo.* Ottawa: Government Printing Bureau.
1916 *The Labrador Eskimo.* Geological Survey of Canada, Memoir 91, Anthropological Series No. 14. Ottawa.

Hayes, Isaac I.
1867 *The Open Polar Sea. A Narrative of the Voyage Towards the North Pole in the Schooner* United States, *1860–1861.* New York: Hurd and Houghton.

Healy, M. A.
1887 *Report of the Cruise of the Revenue Marine Steamer* Corwin *in the Arctic Ocean in the Year 1885.*

Heller, Hermann
1937 "Political Power," in *Encyclopedia of the Social Sciences,* Vol. 12. New York: Macmillan Co., 300–5.

Henry, Teuira
1928 *Ancient Tahiti.* Bernice P. Bishop Museum Bulletin 48.

Hewitt, J. N. B.
1907 "Iroquois," *Handbook of American Indians North of Mexico.* Bureau of American Ethnology Bulletin 30, No. 1. Washington, D.C.

Hill, W. W.
1936 *Navaho Warfare.* New Haven: Yale University Publications in Anthropology, No. 5.
1938 *The Agricultural and Hunting Methods of the Navaho Indians.* New Haven: Yale University Publications in Anthropology, No. 18.

1954 "Some Aspects of Navaho Political Structure," in *Navaho Customs,* Reprint Series No. 6. Flagstaff: Museum of Northern Arizona.

Hodgson, Marshall G. S.

1962 "Modernity and the Islamic Heritage," *Islamic Studies* 1.

Hoebel, E. Adamson

1936 "Associations and the State in the Plains," *American Anthropologist* 38, 433–38.

1940 *The Political Organization and Law-ways of the Comanche Indians.* Memoirs of the American Anthropological Association, No. 54.

Hogbin, I.

1951 *Transformation Scene: The Changing Culture of a New Guinea Village.* London: Routledge and Kegan Paul.

Holm, G.

1914 "Ethnological Sketch of the Angmagssalik Eskimos," *Meddelelser om Grønland* 39.

Holmquist, Hajalmar

1922 *Kirche und Staat im evangelischen Schweden, Festgabe für Karl Müller.* Tübingen: J. C. B. Mohr.

Huntingford, G. W. B.

1953 *The Nandi of Kenya.* London: Routledge and Kegan Paul.

Ixtlilxochitl, Fernando de Alva

1952 *Obras históricas.* 2 vols. Mexico: Editora Nacional.

Jackson, Sheldon

1886 *Report on Education in Alaska.* United States Bureau of Education.

Jansen, Marius B.

1961 *Sakamoto Rymona and the Meiji Restoration.* Princeton: Princeton University Press.

1965 "Changing Japanese Attitude Toward Modernization," in *Changing Japanese Attitudes Toward Modernization,* Marius B. Jansen, ed. Princeton: Princeton University Press, 43–98.

Jenness, Diamond

1922 *Life of the Copper Eskimos.* Report of the Canadian Arctic Expedition, 1913–1918, 12.

1928 *The People of the Twilight.* New York: Macmillan Co.

1938 *The Sarcee Indians of Alberta.* Nature Museum of Canada Bulletin 90, Anthropological Series 23. Ottawa.

Jones, William

1906 *Central Algonkian.* Archaeological Report 1905. Toronto, 136–46.

1939 *Ethnography of the Fox Indians.* Ed. by Margaret Welphey

Fisher. Bureau of American Ethnology Bulletin 125. Washington, D.C.

Kaberry, Phyllis
1959 "Review of Social Stratification in Polynesia by M. Sahlins," *Sociologus* 9, 181–83.

Kagwa, Sir A.
1934 *The Customs of the Baganda.* New York: Columbia University Press.

Kane, Elisha Kent
1856 *Arctic Explorations in the Years 1853, 1854, 1855.* Philadelphia: Childs and Peterson.

Kaplan, David
1960 "The Law of Cultural Dominance," in *Evolution and Culture,* M. Sahlins and E. R. Service, eds. Ann Arbor: University of Michigan Press, 69–92.

Karsten, Rafael
1923 *Blood Revenge, War, and Victory Feasts Among the Jibaro Indians of Eastern Equador.* Bureau of American Ethnology Bulletin 79. Washington, D.C.

Kautilya
1960 *Arthashastra.* Tr. by Rudrapatna Shamasastry. 5th ed. Mysore: Mysore Printing and Publishing House.

Kayser, Christine R.
1961 *Calvinism and German Political Life.* Unpublished Ph.D. thesis, Radcliffe College.

Kirchoff, Paul
1949 *The Social and Political Organization of the Andean Peoples.* Handbook of South American Indians, Bureau of American Ethnology Bulletin 143, Vol. 5, 293–311.

Kluckhohn, Clyde, and Dorothea Leighton
1946, 1948 (2d ed.) *The Navaho.* Cambridge: Harvard University Press.

Koch-Grünberg, Theodor
1923 *Vom Roroima zum Orinoco.* Vol. 3. Berlin: D. Reimer.

König, Herbert
1927 "Das Recht der polar Völker," *Anthropos* 22, 689–746.

Kothari, Rajni
1964 "The Congress System in India," *Asian Survey* 4, 1161–74.

Kothari, Rajni, and A. Maru
(in press) *Caste and Secularism in India—A Case Study of a Caste Federation.* New Delhi.

Krause, Fritz
1911 *In den wildnissen Brasiliens.* Leipzig: R. Voigländer.

Krishna, Gopal
(in press) "The Development of the Organization of Indian National Congress, 1918–1932," mimeo.

Kroeber, A. L.
1899 "The Eskimo of Smith Sound," *Bulletin of the American Museum of Natural History* 12.
1908 *Ethnology of the Gros Ventre.* Anthropological Papers of the American Museum of Natural History 1. New York.
1925 *Handbook of the Indians of California.* Bureau of American Ethnology Bulletin 78. Washington, D.C.
1946 *The Chibcha.* Handbook of South American Indians, Bureau of American Ethnology Bulletin 143, Vol. 2.

Kroef, Justus van der
1958 "The Role of Islam in Indonesian Nationalism and Politics," *The Western Political Quarterly* 11, 33–54.
1962 "Recent Trends in Indonesian Islam," *The Muslim World* 52, No. 1, 48–58.

Kulubya, O. S. W.
1942 "Some Aspects of Baganda Customs," *Uganda Journal* 9, No. 2, 49–56.

Kuper, Hilda (Beemer)
1937 "The Development of the Military Organization in Swaziland," *Africa* 10, Nos. 1 and 2, 55–74, 176–205.
1941 "Introduction" to the section on Swazi in *The Bantu Tribes of South Africa,* A. M. Duggan Cronin, ed. Vol. 3, Sect. 4. Cambridge: Cambridge University Press.
1947 *An African Aristocracy.* London: Oxford University Press.

Labouret, Henri
1931 *Les tribus du Rameau Lobi.* Paris: Institut d'Ethnologie.

Ladd, John
1957 *The Structure of a Moral Code.* Cambridge: Harvard University Press.

Lantis, Margaret
1946 "The Social Culture of the Nunivak Eskimo," *Transactions of the American Philosophical Society* N.S. 35, Part 3.

Lara, Horacio
1889 *Cronica de la Araucania.* Vol. 2. Santiago.

Leach, Edmund Ronald
1954 *Political Systems of Highland Burma.* London: G. Bell.

Letherman, Jonathon
1855 *Sketch of the Navajo Tribe of Indians, Territory of New Mexico.* Washington: Smithsonian Report.

Levenson, Joseph
  1964 *Modern China and Its Confucian Past.* New York: Doubleday Anchor Books.
Lévi-Strauss, Claude
  1943 "The Social Use of Kinship Terms Among Brazilian Indians," *American Anthropologist* 45, No. 3, 398–409.
  1944 "The Social and Psychological Aspects of Chieftainship in a Primitive Tribe: The Nambikuara of North-western Mato Grosso," *Transactions of the New York Academy of Sciences,* Series 2, 7, No. 1, 16–32.
Levy, Marion J., Jr.
  1952 *The Family Revolution in Modern China.* Cambridge: Harvard University Press.
  1955 "Contrasting Factors in the Modernization of China and Japan," in *Economic Growth: Brazil, India, Japan,* Simon Kuznets, Wilbert E. Moore, and Joseph J. Spengler, eds. Durham, N.C.: Duke University Press, 496–537.
Lewis, Bernard
  1960 *The Arabs in History.* London: Hutchinson.
  1961 *The Emergence of Modern Turkey.* London: Oxford University Press.
Lewis, I. M.
  1961a *A Pastoral Democracy.* London: Oxford University Press for the International African Institute.
  1961b "Force and Fission in Northern Somali Lineage Structure," *American Anthropologist* 63, 94–112.
Lienhardt, Godfrey
  1958 "The Western Dinka," in *Tribes Without Rulers,* John Middleton and David Tait, eds. London: Routledge and Kegan Paul, 97–135.
Little, David
  1963 *The Logic of Order—An Examination of the Sources of Puritan-Anglican Controversy and of Their Relation to Prevailing Legal Conceptions in the Sixteenth and Seventeenth Centuries.* Unpublished Doctor of Theology thesis, Harvard University.
Llewellyn, K. N., and E. A. Hoebel
  1941 *The Cheyenne Way.* Norman: University of Oklahoma Press.
Lloyd, Peter C.
  1955 "The Yoruba Lineage," *Africa* 25, No. 3, 235–51.
  1960 "Sacred Kingship and Government among the Yoruba," *Africa* 30, No. 3, 221–37.
  1964 *Yoruba Land Law.* London: Oxford University Press.

1965 "The Yoruba of Nigeria," in *Peoples of Africa,* James L. Gibbs, Jr., ed. New York: Holt, Rinehart and Winston, 547–82.
(forthcoming) "Agnatic and Cognatic Descent Among the Yoruba."

Loeb, Edwin M.

1926 *History and Traditions of Niue.* Bernice P. Bishop Museum Bulletin 32.

Lowie, R. H.

1920 *Primitive Society.* New York: Boni and Liveright.

1922 *The Religion of the Crow Indians.* Anthropological Papers of the American Museum of Natural History 25. New York.

1924 *Notes on Shoshonean Ethnology.* Anthropological Papers of the American Museum of Natural History 20. New York.

1927 *Origin of the State.* New York: Harcourt, Brace and Co.

Luethy, Herbert

1955 *France Against Herself.* New York: Frederick A. Praeger.

1964 "Once Again—Calvinism and Capitalism," *Encounter* 22, January 1964, 26–39.

Lugard, F. D.

1905 *A Tropical Dependency.* London: J. Nesbit and Co., Ltd.

MacIver, R. M.

1947 *The Web of Government.* New York: Macmillan Co.

Mahdi, Muhsin

1959 "Modernity and Islam," in *Modern Trends in World Religions,* Joseph M. Kitagawa, ed. La Salle, Ill.: Open Court.

Mair, Lucy

1933 "Baganda Land Tenure," *Africa* 6, No. 2, 187–205.

1934 *An African People in the Twentieth Century.* London: Routledge.

1936 "Chiefship in Modern Africa," *Africa* 9, No. 3, 305–16.

1961 "Clientship in East Africa," *Cahiers d'Études Africaines* 2, 315–25.

1962 *Primitive Government.* Harmondsworth: Penguin.

Malik, Hafez

1963 *Moslem Nationalism in India and Pakistan.* Washington, D.C.: Public Affairs Press.

Malinowski, B.

1920 "War and Weapons Among the Natives of the Trobriand Islands," *Man* 20, 5–22.

1922 *Argonauts of the Western Pacific.* London: G. Routledge and Sons, Ltd.

1926, 1940 (3d ed.) *Crime and Custom in Savage Society.* New York: Harcourt, Brace and Co.

1927 *Sex and Repression in Savage Society.* London and New York: The Humanities Press.

1929 *The Sexual Life of Savages In North-western Melanesia.* New York: Harcourt, Brace and Co.

1935 *Coral Gardens and Their Magic.* London: G. Allen and Unwin, Ltd.

Malo, David

1951 *Hawaiian Antiquities.* Bernice P. Bishop Museum Special Publication No. 2. 2d ed. Honolulu.

Mandelbaum, David G.

1940 *The Plains Cree.* Anthropological Papers of the American Museum of Natural History 37. New York.

Maquet, Jacques

1961a "Une hypothèse pour l'étude des féodalités Africaines," *Cahiers d'Études Africaines* 2, No. 2, 292–314.

1961b *The Premise of Inequality in Ruanda.* London: Oxford University Press for the International African Institute.

Marshall, Lorna

1957 "The Kin Terminology System of the /Kung Bushmen," *Africa* 27, No. 1, 1–25.

1959 "Marriage Among /Kung Bushmen," *Africa* 29, No. 4, 335–65.

Martin, John

1817 *An Account of the Natives of the Tonga Islands of Wm. Mariner.* London: J. Murray.

Maruyama, Masao

1963 *Thought and Behaviour in Japanese Politics.* London: Oxford University Press.

1965 "Patterns of Individuation and the Case of Japan: A Conceptual Scheme," in *Changing Japanese Attitudes Toward Modernization,* Marius B. Jansen, ed. Princeton: Princeton University Press, 489–532.

Marwick, B. A.

1940 *The Swazi.* Cambridge: Cambridge University Press.

Mathiassen, Therkel

1930 *Material Culture of the Iglulik Eskimos.* Report of the Fifth Thule Expedition, 1921–24, Vol. 6, No. 1. Copenhagen.

Mauss, M. and M. H. Beuchat

1904–5 "Essai sur les variations saisonnières des sociétés Eskimos: Étude de morphologie sociale," *L'Année sociologique,* 9me année.

Mayer, Philip

1949 *The Lineage Principle in Gusii Society.* International African Institute Memorandum 24.

480   *Bibliography*

McBride, George
  1936 *Chile: Land and Society.* American Geographical Society Research Series, No. 19. New York.
McNeill, John T.
  1954 *The History and Character of Calvinism.* New York: Oxford University Press.
Means, Philip A.
  1931 *Ancient Civilizations of the Andes.* New York: C. Scribner's Sons.
Meek, Charles Kingsley
  1925 *The Northern Tribes of Nigeria.* London: Oxford University Press.
  1931 *A Sudanese Kingdom.* London: K. Paul, Trench, Trubner and Co.
Métraux, A.
  1928 *La religion des Tupinamba.* Paris: E. Leroux.
  1931 "Les hommes-dieux chez les Chiriguano et dans l'Amérique du Sud," *Revista del Instituto Ethnografico del Universidad Nacional de Tucuman* 2, 61–91.
  1937 "Études d'ethnographie Toba-Pilaga," *Anthropos* 32 (1937), 171–94, 378–401.
  1946a *Ethnology of the Chaco.* Handbook of South American Indians, Bureau of American Ethnology Bulletin 143, Vol. 1.
  1946b *The Botocudo.* Handbook of South American Indians, Bureau of American Ethnology Bulletin 143, Vol. 1.
Micaud, Charles A., Leonard C. Brown, and Clement H. Moore
  1964 *Tunisia: The Politics of Modernization.* New York: Praeger.
Michael, Franz
  1962 "The Role of Law in Traditional, Nationalist and Communist China," *The China Quarterly* 9, 124–48.
Michels, Robert
  1937 "Authority," in *Encyclopedia of the Social Sciences,* Vol. 2. New York: Macmillan Co., 319–21.
Middleton, John
  1954 "Some Social Aspects of Lugbara Myth," *Africa* 24, 189–99.
  1955 "Notes on the Political Organization of the Madi of Uganda," *African Studies* 14, No. 1, 29–36.
  1958 "The Political System of the Lugbara of the Nile-Congo Divide," in *Tribes Without Rulers,* John Middleton and David Tait, eds. London: Routledge and Kegan Paul, 203–30.
Middleton, John, and G. Kershaw
  1965 *The Kikuyu and Kamba of Kenya.* London: International African Institute.

Middleton, John, and David Tait (eds.)
1958 *Tribes Without Rulers*. London: Routledge and Kegan Paul.
Montaigne, Michel de
1958 *The Complete Essays of Montaigne*. Tr. by Donald M. Frame. Stanford, Calif.: Stanford University Press.
Monzón, Arturo
1949 *El calpulli en la organizacion social de los Tenochca*. Mexico: Instituto de Historia.
Mooney, James
1896 *The Ghost Dance Religion and the Sioux Outbreak of 1890*. Bureau of American Ethnology Bulletin 14. Washington, D.C.
Moore, Clement H.
1962 "The Neo-Destour Party of Tunisia: A Structure of Democracy?" *World Politics* 14, 461–82.
Morgan, Arthur
1946 *Nowhere Was Somewhere: How History Makes Utopias and How Utopias Make History*. Chapel Hill: University of North Carolina Press.
Morgan, Louis H.
1877 *Ancient Society*. New York: H. Holt and Co.
Morley, Sylvanus Griswold
1915 *An Introduction to the Study of Maya Hieroglyphs*. Bureau of American Ethnology Bulletin 57. Washington, D.C.
Morris, Ivan (ed.)
1963 *Problems in Asian Civilizations: Japan 1931–1945*. Boston: D. C. Heath.
Motolinia, Toribio de
1903 *Memoriales*. Documentos históricos de Méjico I. Mexico.
1941 *Historia de los indios de la Nueva España*. Mexico: Salvador Chávez Hayhoe.
Mukasa, H.
1934 "Some Notes on the Reign of Mutesa," *Uganda Journal* 1, No. 2, 124–33.
1946 "The Rule of the Kings of Buganda," *Uganda Journal* 10, No. 2, 136–43.
Murdock, George Peter
1948 "Anthropology in Micronesia," *Transactions of the New York Academy of Sciences*, Ser. II, 11, 9–16.
1960 *Social Structure in Southeast Asia*. Viking Fund Publications in Anthropology, No. 29.
Murdoch, John
1892 *The Point Barrow Expedition*. Ethnological Results of the

Point Barrow Expedition. Bureau of American Ethnology Annual Report 9. Washington, D.C.

Murra, John V.

1956 *The Economic Organization of Inca State.* Unpublished Ph.D. thesis, University of Chicago.

1960 "Rite and Crop in the Inca State," in *Essays in Honor of Paul Radin,* Stanley Diamond, ed. New York: Columbia University Press, 393–407.

1962 "Cloth and Its Functions in the Inca State," *American Anthropologist* 64, 710–28.

Nadel, S. F.

1935 "Nupe State and Community," *Africa* 8, No. 3, 257–303.

1942 *A Black Byzantium.* London: Oxford University Press.

Nantes, Martin de

1706 *Relation succinte et sincère de la mission du père Martin de Nantes.* Paris.

Nehru, Jawaharlal

1961 "Satyagrapha," in *The Nationalist Movement: Indian Political Thought from Ranade to Bhave,* D. M. Brown, ed. Berkeley: University of California Press, 129–51.

Nelson, E. W.

1899 *The Eskimos about Bering Strait.* Bureau of American Ethnology Annual Report 18. Washington, D.C.

Neteille, André

(in press) *Closed and Open Social Stratification in India.* New Delhi.

Nieuwenhuize, C. A. O. van

1958 *Aspects of Islam in Post Colonial Indonesia.* The Hague: W. van Hoeve.

Nimuendajú, Curt

1914 "Die Sagen von der Erschaffung und Vernichtung der Welt als Grundlagen der Religion der Apapocuva-Guarani," *Zeitschrift für Ethnologie.*

1939 *The Apinaye.* Catholic University of America Anthropological Series, No. 8. Washington, D.C.

1942 *The Sherente.* Publication of the Frederick Webb Hodge Anniversary Publication Fund 4. Los Angeles.

1943 "A Note on the Social Life of the Northern Kayapo," *American Anthropologist* 45, No. 4, 633–35.

1946a "Social Organization and Beliefs of the Botocudo of Eastern Brazil," *Southwestern Journal of Anthropology* 2, No. 1, 93–115.

1946b *The Eastern Timbira.* University of California Publications in American Archaeology and Ethnology 41. Berkeley.

Nordenskiöld, Eraland
1912 *Indianerleben*. Leipzig.
Norman, Herbert
1940 *Japan's Emergence as a Modern State*. New York: Institute of Pacific Relations.
Oberg, K.
1940 "The Kingdom of Ankole in Uganda," in *African Political Systems*, Meyer Fortes and E. E. Evans-Pritchard, eds. London: Oxford University Press, 121–64.
Olson, Ronald L.
1936 *The Quinault Indians*. University of Washington Publications in Anthropology 6. Seattle.
1940 *The Social Organization of Haida of British Columbia*. Anthropological Record 2. Berkeley.
Osgood, Cornelius
1937 *The Ethnography of the Tanaina*. Yale University Publications in Anthropology, No. 7. New Haven.
Palerm, Angel
1958 "Review of K. A. Wittfogel, 1957," *American Antiquity* 23, 440–44.
Parkman, Francis
1856 *Prairie and Rocky Mountain Life; or, The California and Oregon Trail*. Columbus.
Parsons, Elsie Clews
1939 *Pueblo Indian Religion*. Chicago: Chicago University Press.
Parsons, Talcott
1941 *The Structure of Social Action*. Glencoe, Ill.: Free Press.
1959 "Population and the Social Structure of Japan," in *Essays in Sociological Theory*, Talcott Parsons, ed. Rev. ed. Glencoe, Ill.: Free Press, 275–98.
Passin, Herbert
1963 "Stratigraphy of Protest in Japan," in *The Revolution in World Politics*, Morton Kaplan, ed. New York: John Wiley, 12–113.
1965 "Modernization and the Japanese Intellectual, Some Comparative Observations," in *Changing Japanese Attitudes Toward Modernization*, Marius B. Jansen, ed. Princeton: Princeton University Press, 447–88.
Perstiany, J. G.
1939 *The Social Institutions of the Kipsigis*. London: Routledge.
Peters, E.
1960 "The Proliferation of Segments in the Lineages of the Bedouin in Cyrenaica," *Journal of the Royal Anthropological Institute* 90, Pt. 1, 29–53.

Petroff, Ivan

1884 *Alaska: Its Population, Industries, and Resources.* Tenth Census of the United States, 8.

1900 *Compilation of Narratives of Explorers in Alaska.* Reprint of Petroff's Report in the Tenth Census of the United States, 8.

Petrullo, Vincenzo

1939 *The Yaruros of the Capanaparo River.* Bureau of American Ethnology Bulletin 123. Washington, D.C.

Polanyi, Karl, Conrad M. Arensberg, and Harry W. Pearson

1957 *Trade and Market in the Early Empires.* Glencoe, Ill.: Free Press.

Pomar, Juan Bautista

1941 "Relación de Tetzcoco," in *Relaciones de Texcoco y de la Nuevo España.* Mexico: Salvador Chavez Hayhoe, 1–64.

Pompeu, Sobrinho, Th.

1934 "Os Tapuias do nordeste e a monografia de Elias Herckman," *Revista del Instituto Ceara* 48.

Powell, H. A.

1952 "Cricket in Kiriwina," *The Listener* 48 (1227), 384–85.

Pozas, Ricardo

1959 *Chamula, un pueblo indio de los altos de Chiapas.* Memorias del Instituto Nacional Indigenista, 8. Mexico.

Preuss, Konrad Theodor

1919–20 "Forschungsreise zu den Lagaba-Indianern der Sierra Nevada de Santa Marta in Kolumbien," *Anthropos* 14–15, 314–404, 1040–79.

Prins, A. H. J.

1953 *East African Age-class Systems.* Groningen: J. B. Wolters.

1959 "Some Notes About Islam and Politics in Indonesia," *The World of Islam* 6, 124–26.

Provinse, John H.

1937 "The Underlying Sanctions of Plains Indian Culture," in *Social Anthropology of North American Tribes,* Fred Eggan, ed. Chicago: University of Chicago Press, 341–76.

Radcliffe-Brown, A. R.

1940 "Preface," in *African Political Systems,* Meyer Fortes and E. E. Evans-Pritchard, eds. London: Oxford University Press, xi–xxiii.

1952 *Structure and Function in Primitive Society.* London: Cohen and West.

Radin, Paul

1923 *The Winnebago Tribe.* Bureau of American Ethnology Annual Report 37. Washington, D.C.

Rahman, F.
1958 "Muslim Modernism in the Indo-Pakistan Subcontinent," *Bulletin of the School of Oriental and African Studies* 21, 82–99.
Rai, Lala Lajpat
1961 "The Remedy for Revolution," in *The Nationalistic Movement: Indian Political Thought from Ranade to Bhave*, D. M. Brown, ed. Berkeley: University of California Press, 96–107.
Rasmussen, Knud
1921 *Greenland by the Polar Sea*. London: W. Heinmann.
1927 *Across Arctic America*. New York: G. P. Putnam's Sons.
Rattray, R. S.
1929 *Ashanti Law and Constitution*. Oxford: Clarendon Press.
Ray, Berne F.
1932 *The Sampoil and Nespelem; Salishan Peoples of North-eastern Washington*. University of Washington Publications in Anthropology 5. Washington, D.C.
Reay, Marie
1959a *The Kuma: Freedom and Conformity in the New Guinea Highlands*. Melbourne: University Press for the Australian National University.
1959b "Two Kinds of Ritual Conflict," *Oceania* 29, 290–96.
Redfield, Robert
1955 "Forward," in *Village India*, McKim Marriott, ed. Comparative Studies of Cultures and Civilizations, No. 6; American Anthropological Association Memoir, No. 83, June 1955, vii–xvi.
Reichard, Gladys A.
1928 *Social Life of the Navajo Indians*. Columbia University Contributions to Anthropology, No. 7. New York: Columbia University Press.
Renou, Louis, Jean Filliozet, et al.
1947, 1953 *L'Inde classique*. 2 vols. Paris: Presses Universitaires.
Richardson, Jane
1940 *Law and Status Among the Kiowa Indians*. Monograph of the American Ethnographic Society 1. New York.
Rink, H.
1887 "The Eskimo Tribes: Their Distribution and Characteristics, Especially in Regard to Language; With a Comparative Vocabulary," *Meddelelser om Grønland* 11.
Ritter, Gerhard
1938 "Das 16. Jahrhundert als weltgeschichtliche Epoche," *Archiv für Geschichte der Reformation* 35.
1950 *Die Neugestaltung Europas im 16. Jahrhundert*. Berlin: Druckhaus Tempelhof.

Rojas, Gabriel de
1927 "Descripción de Cholula," *Revista Mexicana de Estudios Históricos* 1, 158–70 (Appendix).

Roscoe, J.
1902 "Further Notes on the Manners and Customs of the Baganda," *Journal of the Anthropological Institute* 32, 25–80.
1911 *The Baganda.* London: Macmillan and Co.

Rosenthal, Erwin I. J.
1962 *Political Thought in Mediaeval Islam.* Cambridge: Cambridge University Press.

Ross, John
1819 *A Voyage of Discovery, Made Under the Orders of the Admiralty in His Majesty's Ships* Isabella *and* Alexander, *for the Purpose of Exploring Baffin's Bay, and Inquiring into the Probability of a Northwest Passage.* London: J. Murray.

Roys, Ralph L.
1933 *The Book of Chilam Balam of Chumayel.* Carnegie Institute of Washington, No. 438. Washington, D.C.

Rowe, John H.
1945 "Absolute Chronology in the Andean Area," *American Antiquity* 10, 265–84.
1946 *Inca Culture at the Time of the Spanish Conquest.* Handbook of South American Indians, Bureau of American Ethnology Bulletin 143, Vol. 2, 183–230.
1948 "The Kingdom of Chimor," *Acta Americana* 6, Nos. 1 and 2.

Rudolph, Lloyd I., and Susanne Hoeber Rudolph
1960 "The Political Role of India's Caste Associations," *Pacific Affairs* 33, 5–22.

Safran, Nadav
1961 *Egypt in Search of Political Community.* Cambridge: Harvard University Press.

Sahagún, Bernardino de
1938 *Historia general de las cosas de Nueva España.* 5 vols. Mexico: Pedro Robredo.
1951 *Florentine Codex.* Book 2: *The Ceremonies.* Ed. and tr. by Arthur J. O. Anderson and Charles E. Dibble. Monographs of the School of American Research 14, Part 3. Santa Fe.
1954 *Florentine Codex.* Book 8: *Kings and Lords.* Ed. and tr. by Arthur J. O. Anderson and Charles E. Dibble. Monographs of the School of American Research 14, Part 9. Santa Fe.
1959 *Florentine Codex.* Book 9: *The Merchants.* Ed. and tr. by Charles E. Dibble and Arthur J. O. Anderson. Monographs of the School of American Research 14, Part 10. Santa Fe.

Sahlins, Marshall D.
 1958 *Social Stratification in Polynesia.* Seattle: University of Washington Press.
 1965 "On the Ideology and Composition of Descent Groups," *Man* 97, July–August 1965, 104–7.
Sahlins, Marshall D., and Elman R. Service (eds.)
 1960 *Evolution and Culture.* Ann Arbor: University of Michigan Press.
Sapir, Edward
 1915 "The Social Organization of the West Coast Tribes," *Transactions of the Royal Society of Canada,* Section II, Ser. III, 9.
Schacht, Joseph
 1963 "Problems of Modern Islamic Legislation," in *The Modern Middle East,* Richard H. Nolte, ed. New York: Atherton Press, 172–201.
Schapera, I.
 1937 *The Bantu-speaking Tribes of South Africa.* London: Routledge and Kegan Paul.
 1956 *Government and Politics in Tribal Societies.* London: Watts.
Schrey, Heinz H.
 1951 "Geistliches und weltliches Regiment in der schwedischen Reformation," *Archiv für Geschichte der Reformation* 42, 146–59.
Schweiger, Georg
 1962 *Die Reformation in den nordischen Landern.* München: Kozel Verlag.
Schweinfurth, Georg
 1873 *The Heart of Africa.* 2 vols. London: S. Low, Marton, Low and Searle.
Seligman, C. G.
 1910 *The Melanesians of British New Guinea.* Cambridge: Cambridge University Press.
Service, Elman R.
 1962 *Primitive Social Organization.* New York: Random House.
Shils, Edward A.
 1965 "Charisma, Order, and Status," *American Sociological Review* 30, 199–213.
Siegel, Bernard J.
 1954 *Class Notes, Comparative Social Systems.* Stanford: Stanford University.
Singer, Milton, et al.
 1958 "India's Cultural Values and Economic Development: A Discussion," *Economic Development and Cultural Change* 7, 1–12.

Singer, Milton (ed.)
  1959 *Traditional India: Structure and Change.* Philadelphia: American Folklore Society.
Sinha, H. N.
  1963 *The Development of Indian Policy.* Bombay: India Publishing House.
Sjoberg, Gideon
  1960 *The Preindustrial City.* Glencoe, Ill.: Free Press.
Skinner, Alanson
  1913 *Social Life and Ceremonial Bundles of the Menominee Indians.* Anthropological Papers of the American Museum of Natural History 13. New York.
Smith, M. G.
  1956 "Segmentary Lineage Systems," *Journal of the Royal Anthropological Institute* 86, 39–80.
  1957 "The African Heritage in the Caribbean," in *Caribbean Studies: A Symposium,* Vera Rubin, ed. Institute of Social and Economic Research, Jamaica, B. W. I., University College of the West Indies, 34–46.
  1960 *Government in Zazzau, 1800–1950.* London: Oxford University Press for the International African Institute.
  1966 "A Structural Approach to Comparative Politics," in *Varieties of Political Theory,* David Easton, ed. Englewood Cliffs, N.J.: Prentice-Hall, 113–28.
Southall, A. W.
  1952 *Lineage Formation Among the Luo.* London: International African Institute.
  1956 *Alur Society.* Cambridge: W. Heffer.
Spear, Percival
  1961 *India: A Modern History.* Ann Arbor: University of Michigan Press.
Spicer, Edward H.
  1958 "Social Structure and Cultural Process in Yaqui Religious Acculturation," *American Anthropologist* 60, 433–41.
Spier, Leslie
  1928 *Havasupai Ethnography.* Anthropological Papers of the American Museum of Natural History 29, Pt. 3. New York.
  1930 *Klamath Ethnography.* University of California Publications in American Archaeology and Ethnology 30. Berkeley.
  1933 *Yuman Tribes of the Gila River.* Chicago: University of Chicago Press.
  1935 *The Prophet Dance of the Northwest and Its Derivatives; The Source of the Ghost Dance.* General Series in Anthropology, No. 1. Menasha, Wisc.

Bibliography

Spoehr, Alexander
1952 "Time Perspective in Micronesia and Polynesia," *Southwestern Journal of Anthropology* 8, 457–65.
Srinivas, M. N.
1956 "A Note on Sanskritization and Westernization," *Far Eastern Quarterly* 15, No. 4, August 1956, 481–96.
1962 *Caste in Modern India.* Bombay: Asia Publishing House.
Stayt, Hugh A.
1931 *The Bavenda.* London: Oxford University Press for the International African Institute.
Steensby, H. P.
1910 "Contributions to the Ethnology and Anthropogeography of the Polar Eskimos," *Meddelelser om Grønland* 34.
Stefansson, V.
1914 *The Stefansson-Anderson Arctic Expedition of the American Museum: Preliminary Ethnological Report.* Anthropological Papers of the American Museum of Natural History 14, Pt. 1. New York.
Stephen, Alexander M.
1936 *Hopi Journal.* Ed. by Elsie Clew Parsons. New York: Columbia University Press.
Steward, Julian H.
1938 *Basin-plateau Aboriginal Sociopolitical Groups.* Bureau of American Ethnology Bulletin 120. Washington, D.C.
1947 "American Culture History in the Light of South America," *Southwestern Journal of Anthropology* 3, No. 2, 85–107.
1955 *Theory of Culture Change.* Urbana: University of Illinois Press.
Story, Robert
1958 *Some Plants Used by the Bushmen in Obtaining Food and Water.* Botanical Survey of South Africa, Memoir No. 30. Pretoria.
Sumner, W. G., A. G. Keller, and M. Davie
1927 *The Science of Society.* Vol. 4. New Haven: Yale University Press.
Swanton, John R.
1911 *Indian Tribes of the Lower Mississippi Valley and Adjacent Coast of the Gulf of Mexico.* Bureau of American Ethnology Bulletin 43. Washington, D.C.
1930 "An Indian Social Experiment and Some of Its Lessons," *Scientific Monthly* 31, 368–76.
1931 *Source Material for the Social and Ceremonial Life of the Choctaw Indians.* Bureau of American Ethnology Bulletin 103. Washington, D.C.

1946 *The Indians of the Southwestern United States.* Bureau of American Ethnology Bulletin 137. Washington, D.C.

Tabeau, Pierre-Antoine
1939 *Narrative of Loisel's Expedition to the Upper Missouri.* Ed. by Anne Heloise Abel. Norman: University of Oklahoma Press.

Tait, David
1958 "The Territorial Pattern and Lineage System of the Konkomba," in *Tribes Without Rulers,* John Middleton and David Tait, eds. London: Routledge and Kegan Paul, Ltd., 167–202.
1960 *The Konkomba of Northern Ghana.* Ed. by Jack Goody. London: Oxford University Press for the International African Institute.

Talbot, P. Amaury
1926 *The Peoples of Southern Nigeria.* London: Oxford University Press.

Tanner, John
1940 *An Indian Captivity (1789–1822)*; *John Tanner's Narrative of His Captivity Among the Ottawa and Ojibwa Indians.* Sutro Branch, California State Library, Occasional Papers, Reprint Service, No. 20. San Francisco.

Tax, Sol
1937 "The Municipios of the Midwestern Highlands of Guatemala," *American Anthropologist* 39, 423–44.

Temple, O.
1922 *Notes on the Tribes, Provinces, Emirates and States of the Northern Province of Nigeria.* Lagos: C. M. S. Bookshop.

Teng, Ssu-Yu, and John K. Fairbank
1963 *China's Response to the West: A Documentary Survey, 1839–1923.* New York: Atheneum.

Tezozomoc, Hernando Alvarado
1878 *Crónica Mexicana.* Mexico: Ireneo Paz.
1949 *Crónica Mexicayotl.* Tr. by Adrián León. Mexico: Imprenta Universitaria.

Thalbitzer, William
1914 "The Ammassilik Eskimo," substantially a translation of "Ethnologisk Skizze of Angamagsalikerne," *Meddelelser om Grønland* 36.

Thomson, Basil
1894 *Diversions of a Prime Minister.* London.

Titiev, Mischa
1944 *Old Oraibi.* Papers of the Peabody Museum in American Archaeology and Ethnology 22, No. 1. Cambridge: Harvard University Press.

1951 *Araucanian Culture in Transition.* Occasional Contributors, Museum of Anthropology, No. 15. Ann Arbor: University of Michigan.

Tonnies, Ferdinand
1926 *Gemeinschaft und Gesellschaft.* Berlin: K. Curtis.

Torquemada, Juan de
1943 *Monarquiá indiana.* 3 vols. Mexico: Salvador Chávez Hayhoe.

Toussaint, Manuel, Federico Gomez de Orozco, and Justino Gernandez
1938 *Planos de la ciudad de Mexico, siglos XVI y XVII; estudio historico, urbanistico y bibliografico.* Mexico: Instituto de Investigaciones Esteticas.

Tozzer, Alfred M.
1941 *Landa's relación de las cosas de Yucaten.* Papers of the Peabody Museum in American Archaeology and Ethnology 18. Cambridge: Harvard University.

Trevor-Roper, Hugh
1965 "Religion: The Reformation and Social Change," *Historical Studies* 4, 18–45.

Troeltsch, Ernst
1958 *Protestantism and Progress.* Boston: Beacon Press.

Tung, William L.
1964 *The Political Institutions of Modern China.* The Hague: Martinus Nijhoff.

Turner, Lucien M.
1887 "On the Indians and Eskimos of the Ungava District, Labrador," *Transactions of the Royal Society of Canada* 5, Sect. 2, 99–119.
1894 *Ethnology of the Ungava District, Hudson Bay Area.* Bureau of American Ethnology Annual Report 11. Washington, D.C.

Vaillant, George C.
1941 *Aztecs of Mexico.* Garden City, N.Y.: Doubleday, Doran and Co., Inc.

Vansina, J.
1962 "A Comparison of African Kingdoms," *Africa* 32, No. 4, 324–35.

VanStone, James W.
1965 *The Changing Culture of the Snowdrift Chipewyan.* National Museum of Canada, Ottawa.

Van Valkenburgh, Richard
1945 "The Government of the Navajos," *Arizona Quarterly* 1, 63–73.

Varma, V. P.
1954 *Studies in Hindu Political Thought and Its Metaphysical Background.* Delhi: Motilal Banarsidass.

Vogel, Ezra
  1963 *Japan's New Middle Classes.* Berkeley: University of California Press.
Walzer, Michael
  1963 "Puritanism as a Revolutionary Ideology," *History and Theory* 4, 59–90.
Weber, Max
  1947 *The Theory of Social and Economic Organization.* Ed. by Talcott Parsons. Glencoe, Ill.: Free Press.
  1948 *From Max Weber: Essays in Sociology.* Tr. and ed. by H. H. Gerth and C. Wright Mills. London: Routledge and Kegan Paul.
  1950 *General Economic History,* Glencoe, Ill.: Free Press.
Weiner, Myron
  1965 *Political Change in South Asia.* Calcutta: Firma K. L. Mukhopadhyay.
Weitlaner, R. J., and Carlo Antonio Castro
  1954 *Papeles de la Chinantla: Mayultianguis y Tlacoatzintepec.* Museo National de Antropologia, Serie Cientifica 3. Mexico.
Weitlaner, R. J., and C. Hoogshagen
  1957 "Grados de edad en Oaxacl," *Revista Mexicana de Estudios Antropológicos* 16, 183–209.
Weyer, E. M.
  1932 *The Eskimos.* New Haven: Yale University Press.
White, Leslie A.
  1959 *The Evolution of Culture.* New York: McGraw-Hill.
Williams, F. E.
  1936 *Papuans of the Trans-Fly.* Oxford: Clarendon Press.
Williams, F. L.
  1940 "The Kabaka of Buganda: Death of His Highness Sir Daudi Chwa II, K.C.M.G., K.B.E., and Accession of Edward Mutesa II," *Uganda Journal* 7, No. 4, 176–87.
Wilson, Godfrey
  1939 *The Constitution of the Ngonde.* Rhodes-Livingstone Papers, No. 3. Manchester.
  1951 "The Nyakyusa of South-western Tanganyika," in *Seven Tribes of British Central Africa,* Elizabeth Colson and Max Gluckman, eds. London: Oxford University Press, 253–91.
Wilson, Godfrey, and Monica Wilson
  1945 *Analysis of Social Change.* Cambridge: Cambridge University Press.
Winter, Edward H.
  1956 *Bwamba: A Structural-functional Analysis of a Patrilineal Society.* Cambridge: W. Heffer for the East African Institute for Social Research.

1958 "The Aboriginal Political Structure of Bwamba," in *Tribes Without Rulers,* John Middleton and David Tait, eds. London: Routledge and Kegan Paul, Ltd., 136–66.

Wissler, Clark

1911 *The Social Life of the Blackfoot Indians.* Anthropological Papers of the American Museum of Natural History 7. New York.

1912 *Societies and Ceremonial Associations in the Oglala Division of the Teton-Dakota.* Anthropological Papers of the American Museum of Natural History 11. New York.

1922 *The American Indian.* New York: D. C. McMurtrie.

Wittfogel, Karl A.

1957 *Oriental Despotism: A Comparative Study of Total Power.* New Haven: Yale University Press.

Wolf, Eric R.

1957 "Closed Corporate Peasant Communities in Mesoamerica and Central Java," *Southwestern Journal of Anthropology* 13, 1–18.

Wolfert, Stanley A.

1962 *Tilak and Gohale in Revolution and Reform in the Making of Modern India.* Berkeley: University of California Press.

Wright, Mary

1957 *The Last Stand of Chinese Conservatism: The T'ung-Chih Restoration, 1862–1874.* Stanford: Stanford University Press.

Wyman, Leland C.

1936 "Navaho Diagnosticians," *American Anthropologist* 38, 236–46.

Wyman, Leland C., and Clyde Kluckhohn

1938 *Navaho Classification of Their Song Ceremonials.* Memoirs of the American Anthropological Association, No. 50.

Yanaihara, T.

1946 *Pacific Islands Under Japanese Mandate.* New York: Oxford University Press.

Zavala, Silvio, and José Miranda

1954 "Instituciones indígenas en la Colonia," in *Métodos y resultados de la política indigenista en Mexico,* Alfonso Caso, et al., eds. Memorias del Instituto Nacional Indigenista 6. Mexico.

Zelditch, Morris, Jr.

1955 *Authority and Solidarity in Three Southwestern Communities.* Unpublished Ph.D. dissertation, Harvard University.

Zurita, Alonso de

1941 "Breve y sumaria relación de los señores y maneras y diferencias que habia de ellos en la Nueva España," in *Relaciones de Texcoco y de la Nueva España.* Mexico: Salvador Chávez Hayhoe, 65–205.

INDEX

Abbasides, 445
Abortion, 133
Absolutism, 78
Abuse, of political power, concept, 356, 359–60
Accountability, concept, xiv
Acculturation, 49, 413–14
Acephalous societies, xi, 356; categories, x–xii; political authority, 359
Achievement, ladder, 407. *See also* Aztecs; Mesoamerica
Action, political, ix–x
Adam, Alfred, 460, 463
Adibasis, 431, 432, 433, 434
Adjudication, ix
Administration, 225; machinery, 269, 270; politics, 194
Admonitory institutions, as check on political power, 368
Adolescents: -parents, sex separation, 226
Adultery, 250
Africa, 62, 64, 70, 217, 270, 271, 352n; chiefs, 71, 72; corporate groups, 154; expansion, 111; game, 21; indigenous institutions, 121, 122; modernization, 440, 441, 456; myths, 224; Negro, 63; politics, 63, 65, 355–73; social structures, 224; states, 361 (*see also* under name); stratified societies, 340; tribes, 63–64, 93
Africaans, 17
African Political Systems, 121, 193–94, 269, 270
Afterlife, Polynesia, 393–94
Agaie, 297n; Emirate, 294
Age-grade societies, 270; Mesoamerica, 398–99; Nupe, 305–7, 326; Yoruba, 271, 272, 273–74, 276–77, 281, 285
Age-mates, 217, 218, 219

Age-set system, xiii, 125
Age-villages, 219–27; reasons for, 226–27
Aggrandizement, 69–70
Aggression: Arab, 118. *See* Warfare
Agnatic descent groups, 269
Agnatic kinship, 420
Agnation, 420, 422, 426
Agriculture, xi, 153; Inca, 341, 342–43; theft, 134
Aguirre Beltrán, Gonzalo, 410, 463
Ahongahungaoq, 3
Aivilik Eskimos, 11
Akan chiefdom, 123
Alaska, Eskimos, 3 and n, 7, 8, 9, 10
Alexander the Great, 84
Algonquins, 70, 86
Aliab, 230, 232
Alur, 90
Amazon, Upper, tribes, 48
American aborigines: absolutism, 78; authority, coercive, 70–87; chiefs, 78, concept, 83, titular, 71–76, 78, 79, 81; civil-military fusion, 74; consolidation, 66; council, 81–83; military leaders, 79; police, 73, 74, 78, 79–81, 82; political organization, 63–87; prophets, 85–86; religious factor, 84–87; separatism and integration, 65–70; "soldiers" (*see* Police), 72; tribes, seasonal disintegration, 83; uprisings, 70
American Ethnological Society, 339n
American Indians. *See* American aborigines
American Revolution, 66
Americas, modernization, 440
Anarchy, 418; Navajo, 147
Ancestral cult, 124
Anderson, James N. D., 446n, 463
Andes(ean), 249, 254, 339, 341; cul-

Bemba, 219

Benavides, Fray Alonso de, 149, 464

Bení, 294, 296, 308, 309, 310, 325; confederacy, 316, 317

Benin, 64, 65

Benue River, 109

Bering Strait, 5, 7, 9, 10; Eskimos, 8

Berndt, Ronald M., 197, 464

Betanzos, Juan de, 345, 349, 352

Beveridge plan, 61

Bida, 280, 327, 331n

Binder, Leonard, 446, 447, 464

Bío Bío, 249, 251; River, 248

Birket-Smith, Kaj, 1–2, 4 and n, 5, 6, 7, 11, 13, 67, 71, 464

Blas Valera, 342, 350–51, 352

Bleek, Dorothea, 36n, 464

Blood feud, 2

Boas, Franz, 7, 12, 72, 375, 464

Bohannan, Laura, 97, 98n, 107, 109, 110, 111, 117, 464

Bohannan, Paul, 97, 98n, 99, 107, 109, 110, 111, 116, 465, *Fig.* 1, 99, 100

Bolinder, Gustaf, 85, 465

Bolivia, 48, 252

Böndöri, 238

Bora, 244–45

Bor Dinka, clients, 236n

Borgu, 314

Bororo, 48

Botocudo, 67, 85

Boys: age grades, 273–74, 276, Nupe, 305–7; age-village, 219–20; Aztec, 401–2, 404; Kung Bushmen, 32

B.P. (British Protectorate), 15, 18, 36

Brahmanization, 432

Brazil, 47, 85; authority, 73, non-chiefly, 79–80; tribes, 48, 74, 75, Botocudo, 67. *See also* Matto Grosso

Brew, Dr. J. O., 22

Bride-wealth, 335; clients, 236 and n, 237; Kung Bushmen, 27–28; Mandari, 239

Bristol Bay, Alaska, 3, 10

British Columbia, 72

British Guiana, 72

British Protectorate. *See* B.P.

Brown, Paula, 122, 197, 270 and n, 290, 465

Brownlee, Frank, 39n, 465

Buddhism, 448, 449

Buganda, 367, 368, 369, 370–72, 448

Bunyoro, 355

Burials, 76, 77; Trobriands, 172; Yakö, 140

Burrows, E. G., 388, 465

Busama, 201

Bush, the, 241, 273, 300

Bushmen, 92; expeditions to, 15. *See also* Kung Bushmen

Busia, K. A., 368n, 370, 371, 465

Buxton, Jean C., 229, 465

Bwamba, 101

Byzantium, 333

Cabello Valboa, 352

Cahen, Claude, 445, 447, 465

California, 64, 67, 84

Caliphates, 445

Calvin, John, 458

Calvinism, 458, 461

Cámara, Fernando, 397, 465

Camps, xi

Canada, 71, 93; barren grounds, 6; Eskimos, 6

Canberra, Australia, 215, 293

Canella, 68, 71, 72

Cannibalism, 140

Canyoncito, 151

Cape Prince of Wales, 3

Cape Wolstenholme, 2

Capuchin missionaries, 262

Cargo ideology, 215 and n

Carib, 48

Caribou Eskimos, 1–2, 5, 6, 7, 11, 66–67

Carrasco, Pedro, 397, 465–66

Carrier Indians, 93–94

Caste: India, 418, 454; Kondmals, 419, 428–32; Oriyas, 424; tribal society, 434

Catholic countries, 458, 461

Catholicism, 409, 410, 413

Causation, 356. *See* Power

Cautín Province, 249, 252, 254, 263

Cayapo, 48

Census, Inca, 345, 346, 348

Central Africa, 226

Central Eskimos, 7

Central Europe, modernization, 457

Centralization, 441; center, concept, 441 and n; China, 441, 449; India, 454–55; Islam, 449; Japan, 448–49, 452; trade relationship, 218

Centralized states, x–xiii. *See also* Centralization

Chaco, 48

Chaga, 225, 226

Charismatic authority, 144, 147

Chávez Orozco, Luis, 410, 411, 466

Cherokee, 68

Cheyenne, 67–68, 77, 79, 81–83, 87; chiefs, 71

Chiapas highlands, 410

Chibcha, 69, 77, 85

Chickasaw, 66, 77

Chiefdoms, 117, 123; characteristics,

Quetzalcoatl cult, 405
Quinault, 67

Rabaul, 214
Race, 308
Radcliffe-Brown, A. R., ix, 64, 90, 194,
  358, 362n, 414, 417, 484
Radin, Paul, 73, 80, 484
Rahman, F., 446, 485
Rai, L. L., 453, 485
Raiatea, 385
Rainy season, 50, 116
Ramah Navajo, 145, 151
Rank: advantages, 156; Aztecs, 400ff.,
  407; dynastic, 311–12; leadership,
  168–69; Nupe, 311–12, 333; Poly-
  nesia, 391; succession, 169–71;
  traditional societies, 380; Trobri-
  ands, 168–72, 190–91; types, 301–3
  and n
Rasmussen, Knud, 2, 3, 5, 9, 11, 485
Rational-legal authority, 144
Rattray, R. S., 367, 485
Ray, V. R., 339n
Ray, Berne F., 67, 72, 485
Reay, Marie, 193, 196, 197, 199, 485
Reciprocity, 59–60; leadership, 59–60,
  84
Recruitment, tribes, xii
Redfield, Robert, 416, 485
Reform, 408; China, 442, 443, 444;
  India, 453; Islam, 446
Reformation, 459
Reichard, Gladys A., 148, 149, 485
Religion, xi, 84–87; family unit, 301;
  Inca, 343; India, 452–53; Islam,
  445; Japan, 449; Nupe, 308, 312,
  314, 324, 335; orientation, 456ff.;
  -political community identity, 445;
  Polynesia, 393; -tribe identity, 445;
  unity, 323
Renou, Louis, 452, 485
Representation, principles of, 371
Representativeness, concept, xiv
Reservation. *See* Mapuche reservation
Restraint, 356, 360–61
Revenge, 40–41
Revolt, 372, 395; American aborigines,
  70
Richardson, Jane, 80, 485
Rink, H., 5, 12, 13, 485
Rio Gi-Parana, 48
Rio Roosevelt, 48
Ritter, Gerhard, 460, 461, 485
Rituals, 268, 287, 288, 289, 290, 313,
  410
Rockefeller Foundation, 217n
Rojas, Gabriel de, 405, 486
Role: concept, defined, 148; conflicts,
  154; Navajos, 148–54; political, ix–
  x, xi; social structure, 148

Rome, Imperial, 322, 333
Rondon, Candido Mariano da Silva,
  49
Roscoe, J., 65, 367, 368, 370, 486
Rosenthal, Erwin I. J., 445, 486
Ross, John, 13, 486
Rousseau, Jean Jacques, 59
Rowe, John H., 70, 76, 339, 340, 341,
  342, 486
Royal Anthropological Institute, 63n;
  Journal, 155n, 217n
Royal descent groups. *See* Descent
  groups
Royal Niger Company, 310, 311
Roys, Ralph L., 69, 77, 486
Rudolph, Lloyd I., 455n, 486
Rulers, xiii–xiv, 291, 407, 460; priv-
  ileged class, 298; representative,
  372; selection, 368, 371. *See also*
  Chiefs; Headman
Russell, Bertrand, 356
Ryan, Barry, 212n

Sacrifices, 308, 311; human, 308, 351,
  389–90, 401, 410
Safran, Nadav, 446, 486
Sahagún, Bernardino de, 401 and n–
  402, 403, 404, 405, 406, 407, 411,
  486
Sahlins, Marshall D., xiii, 89, 92n, 106,
  487
Saint-Pierre, Bernardin de, 47n
Salcamayhua, Juan, 352
Samsa, 376n, 378, 380, 386, 387
Sanction(s), ix, 362, 363; defined,
  362n
Sandoval, Chief, 151
Sanpoil, 67, 73
Sanskritization, 432–37
Santiago, 263
Santillán, Hernando de, 348
Sapir, Edward, 72, 487
Sarah Lawrence College, 375
Scandinavia, 458, 459, 461
Schacht, Joseph, 446n, 487
Schapera, I., 19, 370, 487
Schrey, Heinz H., 461, 487
Schweiger, Georg, 461, 487
Schweinfurth, Georg, 65, 487
Scotland, 161
"Seal people," 2
Secret societies, 272
Security, collective, 60–61
Segment, defined, 101
Segmentary lineage systems, xii, 89–
  119; characteristics, 90, 98, 99,
  111, 117, 118; complementary op-
  position, 99, 104–5; defined, 91;
  development, 91, 107; ecological
  preconditions, 101; function, 108;
  Kuma, 195ff.; lineality, 99–102;

Index   **511**

State University of New York, Stony
Brook, 247
Status, 152, 229–30, 231, 237, 241,
247–48, 375–95, 450; orientation,
460
Stealing, 25, 134
Steensky, H. P., 5, 489
Stefansson, V., 9, 10, 489
Stephen, Alexander M., 79, 489
Steward, Julian H., 67, 72, 76, 77,
78, 489
Story, Robert, 23n–24n, 489
Stratification, 340, 388ff.; China, 443,
444; India, 453–54; Islam, 447;
Japan, 449; political system, re-
lationship, 441; Polynesia, 377,
383–86
Sub-clans, 159, 162, 164, 168ff.; lead-
ers, 164
Subgroups, xi
Subtribes, 95, 272, 293–95, 307–12
Succession, 126, 169–72, 241 and n,
301–2, 327, 328–29, 369–70, 407,
445
Sudan, 63, 113, 114, 297; Administra-
tion, 229; Southern, 229ff.
Sumner, W. G., 7, 489
Supernaturalism, ix, xi, xiv, 84, 129;
equalitarianism, 87
S.W.A. *See* South West Africa
Swanton, John R., 66, 68, 78, 489–90
Swazi, 225, 226, 361 and n, 366ff.
Sweden, 461

Tabeau, Pierre, 72, 490
Taboos, 42, 43, 146
Tahiti, 378, 385, 387
Tahsildar, 425–26, 431
Tait, David, x, xii, 89, 490
Talbot, P. A., 65, 490
Tallensi, 90, 101, 148, 270
Tanner, John, 71, 72, 86, 490
Tax, Sol, 397, 398, 412, 490
Taxes, xiv, 210–11, 315–16, 319–20,
346, 348–49
Tecumseh, 70, 87
Teng, Ssu-Yu, 442, 444, 490
Territories, ix, xiii, 20–21
Teton Dakota, 72
Tetzcoco, 403 and n
Tezozomoc, Hernando A., 403, 404,
406, 408, 490
Thalbitzer, William, 5–6, 490
Thomson, Basil, 383, 490
Thupa, 341, 342n
Tikopia, 90, 378, 380
Timit, 231. *See also* Client(ship)
Titiev, Mischa, 66, 74, 265, 490–91
Titles, 326–27, 334; societies, 270ff.,
284; types, 302

Tiv, 89, 90, 97ff., 107, 108, 110, 116.
See also Tiv-Nuer
Tiv-Nuer, 89–90, 97–110
Tokelau, 378, 380
Toltén, 249, 254
Tonga, 376n, 378, 380, 383–84, 387
Tongareva, 378, 379
Torquemada, Juan de, 402, 404, 406,
409, 491
Totalitarianism, 87. *See also* Incas
Toussaint, Manuel, 407, 491
Tozzer, Alfred M., 69, 77, 491
Trade, 8, 218, 310–11, 400, 405–7
Tradition, 144, 146
Traditional societies, 377, 378–80,
388ff.
Trevor-Roper, Hugh, 458, 459, 491
Tribe(s) xi–xii, xiii, 1–3, 48, 68, 91,
93, 95, 96, 99, 108, 116, 312–15;
characteristics, xii, 94n; chief-
doms, distinction, 97; consolidation (*see* Segmentary lineage
systems); defined, 93, 95; evolution, 93; government, 95, 96,
269–71; leadership, 96–97; membership, 232; pagan, 110; religion,
identity, 445
Tribes Without Rulers, 89, 101, 115n
Tributary states, xiii
Tribute, 77, 177; Aztecs, 402; Incas,
76, 340, 344–46, 352 and n; Indians, 77; kinds, xiv; Kung Bushmen, 23; Mayans, 69; Nupe, 320
Trobriand political organization, 155–
92; demography, 156–63; "garden challenge," 185–86; leadership, 164–72, 173–88, 191; rank
and succession, 169–72; sub-
clans, 168ff.; World War II, 189–
90. *See also* Kiriwana Island
Troeltsch, Ernst, 459, 491
Tsoede, 294, 296 and n–297, 311, 314,
323–24, 328
Tung, William L., 444, 491
Tunisia, 447
Turkey, 447
Turner, Lucien M., 5, 7, 12, 491
Tyrants, purges, 107

Uganda, 64, 372
Uitzilopochtli, cult, 407
Umor, 123, 125, 138–39, 141
Unalik Eskimos, 9–10
Uniformity, belief in, 314–15
Unilineal descent groups, xii, 90, 102
Unión Araucana, 262–63, 264, 267;
El Araucano, 264
United Nations, 195
United States, 65, 66, 67, 70, 143,
459. *See also* American aborigi-
nes